SILVERLIGHT™ 4 PROBLEM – DESIGN – SOLUTION

Silverlight™ 4

PROBLEM – DESIGN – SOLUTION

Nick Lecrenski

Wiley Publishing, Inc.

Silverlight™ 4: Problem – Design – Solution

Published by
Wiley Publishing, Inc.
10475 Crosspoint Boulevard
Indianapolis, IN 46256
www.wiley.com

Published simultaneously in Canada

ISBN: 978-0-470-53404-5

Manufactured in the United States of America

10 9 8 7 6 5 4 3 2 1

Library of Congress Control Number: 2009940875

This book is dedicated to my beautiful wife Kristie, my daughter Tabetha, and our newest addition to the family, baby Cheyenne. Without their collective patience over the last nine months this book would not have been possible.

— Nick Lecrenski

CREDITS

ACQUISITIONS EDITOR
Paul Reese

PROJECT EDITOR
Maureen Spears

TECHNICAL EDITOR
Jonathan Marbutt

PRODUCTION EDITORS
Tim Tate
Amy Weintraub

COPY EDITOR
Nancy Rappaport

EDITORIAL DIRECTOR
Robyn B. Siesky

EDITORIAL MANAGER
Mary Beth Wakefield

ASSOCIATE DIRECTOR OF MARKETING
David Mayhew

PRODUCTION MANAGER
Tim Tate

VICE PRESIDENT AND EXECUTIVE GROUP PUBLISHER
Richard Swadley

VICE PRESIDENT AND EXECUTIVE PUBLISHER
Barry Pruett

ASSOCIATE PUBLISHER
Jim Minatel

PROJECT COORDINATOR, COVER
Lynsey Stanford

COMPOSITOR
Craig Johnson, Happenstance Type-O-Rama

PROOFREADERS
Josh Chase, Word One
Carrie Hunter, Word One
Scott Klemp, Word One

INDEXER
Johnna VanHoose Dinse

COVER DESIGN
Michael E. Trent

COVER IMAGE
© Valueline/Punchstock

ABOUT THE AUTHOR

NICK LECRENSKI is a developer with 10 years of experience in a wide range of Microsoft technologies including Visual C++, C#, VB, VB.NET, SQL Server, .NET Framework, ASP.NET, AJAX, Silverlight and more. He has a BS in Computer Science and has worked in various fields from biometrics to financial services. He is also the founder/lead developer of MyFitnessJournal.com, a fitness training website that currently utilizes Silverlight technology and has thousands of registered users.

ABOUT THE TECHNICAL EDITOR

JONATHAN MARBUTT is Vice President of Development for WayCool Software, Inc. based in Birmingham, AL. He has been working professionally in software development since 1996 and has covered various Microsoft technologies from VB6 to .NET. Over the recent years, Jonathan developed using Silverlight to build Rich Internet Line-of-Business applications for the non-profit sector. Through this development, he's focused on User Experience (UX) by utilizing Microsoft products such as Expression Blend and technologies such as Silverlight. You can contact Jonathan at `http://www.jmtechware.com`.

ACKNOWLEDGMENTS

WRITING A TECHNICAL BOOK LIKE THIS ONE is an eye-opening experience. For years, I have been on the other side as the reader of hundreds of books on topics ranging from video game programming to the latest version of ASP.NET. I've never given much thought about how much work actually goes into the writing and producing one of those aforementioned books. Now, as a first-time writer who has completed his first book, I can safely say I'll never take the hard work that authors and publishers perform for granted again. With that said, I want to take the time to thank everyone who helped to make this book possible. First, I want to thank my wife, who despite being pregnant with a due date scheduled right smack in the middle of writing this book, continued to encourage the work that I was doing and put up with many weekends of marathon writing sessions. Needless to say, my chore list has grown since the book started. Next, I want to thank my daughter Tabetha, who I could only take to one Mets game this year because of my busy schedule. Luckily, the team was terrible so it wasn't much of a sacrifice.

Completing a book like this one involves months of hard work from not just me but also the hard-working team at Wrox Press. I can't even begin to convey just how dedicated and professional the Wrox Press team is when it comes to publishing new books but I will make an attempt by thanking those who were directly involved in the completion and success of Silverlight 4 Problem-Design-Solution.

For starters, I want to thank Maureen Spears who was the Project Editor for this book. As a first time writer, it is imperative to be paired with an editor who has a lot of patience. Luckily, I had Maureen on my side throughout the process. Whether it was a breaking change in a beta release or some other crazy issue threatening to sabotage me from hitting a deadline, Maureen was always the calm voice of reason that would assure me that there was nothing to worry about and these things happen all the time. More often than not, just knowing that I wasn't the only writer to hit these roadblocks was usually enough to get me to the next milestone. In addition to Maureen, I also had a wonderful Copy Editor in Nancy Rappaport, who no doubt had her hands full with this project. Thanks to her diligent work, the chapters make logical sense and are grammatically correct. As a full-time software developer, grammar isn't always the first thing on my mind when I write. Of course, although my full-time focus is on programming, when you write a technical book it is vital to have the content reviewed by another professional software developer to ensure that the author doesn't lose the audience along the way. My Technical Editor, Jonathan Marbutt, was an invaluable resource, ensuring that the chapter code not only compiled but also by reviewing the topics discussed in the accompanying chapter.

Finally, I want to thank the two people from Wrox who made this book possible in the first place. Thanks to Paul Reese, the Acquisitions Editor, who from the very beginning was there to help me convert my idea for a book into a real proposal that would eventually kick off the project. Lastly, I'd like to thank Jim Minatel, the Associate Publisher, who I first contacted with the idea. Thanks again, Paul and Jim, for taking the time to listen to my original idea, for providing me with this great opportunity, and for taking a chance on this first-time writer.

CONTENTS

INTRODUCTION

THROUGH THE YEARS, there have been numerous technologies and programming methodologies invented for the sole purpose of enhancing the end user experience of a website. What started out as static content pages in HTML quickly morphed into dynamic pages powered by technologies like ASP.NET. With these dynamic pages, developers could finally put together actual applications on the Web; soon, with additional enhancements like AJAX, full line-of-business applications were moving from the desktop to the Web. One common problem with these existing technologies, however, was their reliance on browser-specific JavaScript code. All too often, it became commonplace to design a page for one browser, only to have that same code fail miserably when viewed by another browser. Sure, with enough hard work and some strange hacks and tweaks, most of these problems could be resolved. Still, these Web-based applications just never seemed to feel as responsive and slick as their desktop counterparts. This is where a technology such as Silverlight comes into the picture.

Although the first major version of Silverlight did not offer much in the way of application development, it did not take long for Silverlight 2 to provide developers with the means to create Web-based applications in .NET code without worrying about browser specifics. As an added bonus, Silverlight also came with rich user interface functionality, such as smooth animations and video support. As good as Silverlight 2 was at solving some of these initial problems, it still lacked some critical features that developers needed to really bring powerful line-of-business applications to the Web. The next release of Silverlight, or version 3, attempted to address this issue by adding several important new features including Theme support, Charting, Navigation, Offline Functionality, and many more. However, even with this release, a couple of features were still absolutely critical to line-of-business applications, not the least of which was support for printing. Enter Silverlight 4. Now with full printing support, implicit styling, improved support for in-place editing of data with the `DataGrid` control, and an updated and more powerful version of WCF RIA Services, you really have all the necessary tools at your disposal to migrate existing line-of-business applications from the desktop to the Web without losing a step in terms of user interface functionality and responsiveness.

I wrote this book for a couple of reasons. First, these latest enhancements to Silverlight are so powerful and address so many of the initial shortcomings of previous versions that I felt compelled to help drive adoption of this great new technology by showing off some of the latest features and how easy it can be to develop a powerful Rich Internet Application (RIA) using some of these features. Second, I felt that although many books have been written about developing websites in general, not many also address the specific challenges that go into the design and implementation of a site as well as the deployment and business side of things.

In this book I will address both of these desires by first walking you through the creation of a fictional online fitness tracking application called FitnessTrackerPlus. Thanks to the unique format of the Problem-Design-Solution series you will see all facets of development, such as requirements for gathering, designing, implementation, and finally deployment. After seeing how to create the site, I will then turn the discussion towards revenue-generating strategies including integration of Pay-Per-

Click advertising and recurring monthly subscriptions using PayPal. Finally, unlike most books, I won't just be covering the final build process. Instead, you will see, step-by-step, how to deploy the final solution to a real shared hosting site.

Before getting started, however, I want to take this opportunity to thank you, the reader, for selecting this book. I sincerely hope you find this book enjoyable and full of techniques that you will be able to apply to your own Silverlight-based solutions.

WHO THIS BOOK IS FOR

This book is specifically geared toward readers who have been actively developing solutions in ASP.NET and Silverlight 2 or 3. This book is not a primer on either of these two technologies. Instead, you will see how to make use of enhancements to the latest version of Silverlight in order to create a Rich Internet Application. In general, I will not be covering in great detail how to develop in Silverlight or the related ASP.NET technology that is required for all Silverlight-based solutions. There is specific coverage of the new features in Silverlight 4 including WCF RIA Services and the new Silverlight Toolkit. In order to get the most out of this book you should have a good understanding of how to use all of the existing Silverlight controls.

WHAT THIS BOOK COVERS

This book covers many topics related to the new features found in Silverlight 4 and the Silverlight Toolkit. The following is a brief outline of what each chapter will be covering.

- **Chapter 1:** Overview of FitnessTrackerPlus.
- **Chapter 2:** Multi-Tier Architecture, XAML, Silverlight 4 Overview, LINQ to SQL, Entity Framework, SQL Server 2008, WCF RIA Services.
- **Chapter 3:** WCF RIA Services with ASP.NET Membership, Role, and Profile providers.
- **Chapter 4:** Silverlight Toolkit, themes and creating a Dashboard.
- **Chapter 5:** Data Entry with the AutoCompleteBox, DataGrid, DataForm, and additional controls from the Silverlight Toolkit.
- **Chapter 6:** More Data Entry with Cascading ComboBox controls and additional WCF RIA Services work.
- **Chapter 7:** Using the new DomainDataSource control for easy data binding and implementing a basic plug-in system.
- **Chapter 8:** Adding Charts to the Dashboard.
- **Chapter 9:** Creating a public journal page with the navigation framework and integrating HTML with Silverlight.

- **Chapter 10:** Social Networking and creating a MySpace Silverlight application.
- **Chapter 11:** Generating revenue with AdSense and PayPal subscriptions.
- **Chapter 12:** Final build and deployment to a live shared hosting provider—Discount ASP.NET.

WHAT YOU NEED TO USE THIS BOOK

To follow this book as well as to compile and run the FitnessTrackerPlus application, you need the following:

- Windows 7, Windows Vista, Windows XP, Windows Server 2008, or Windows Server 2003.
- Any edition of Visual Studio 2010. In the book, I use Visual Studio 2010 but you can compile all the code and run it under the free Express Edition as well.
- Silverlight 4 Tools SDK.
- Silverlight Toolkit.
- WCF RIA Services Framework SQL Server Express 2008.
- Expression Blend (optional for viewing/editing XAML).

CONVENTIONS

To help you get the most from the text and keep track of what's happening, we've used a number of conventions throughout the book.

> *Boxes like this one hold important, not-to-be forgotten information that is directly relevant to the surrounding text.*

> *Notes, tips, hints, tricks, and asides to the current discussion look like this.*

As for styles in the text:

- New terms and important words are *italicized* when first introduced.
- Keyboard strokes are shown like this: Ctrl+A.

- Filenames, URLs, and code within the text look like so: `persistence.properties`.
- Code is presented in two different ways:

```
We use a monofont type with no highlighting for most code examples.
We use bolded monofont to emphasize code that is of particular importance in
the present context.
```

SOURCE CODE

As you work through the examples in this book, you may choose either to type in all the code manually or to use the source-code files that accompany the book. All of the source code used in this book is available for download at `www.wrox.com`. Once at the site, simply locate the book's title (either by using the Search box or by using one of the title lists) and click the Download Code link on the book's detail page to obtain all the source code for the book.

Code snippets that are downloadable from wrox.com are easily identified with an icon; the filename of the code snippet follows in a code note that appears after the code, much like the one that follows this paragraph. If it is an entire code listing, the filename should appear in the listing title.

code snippet [filename]

Because many books have similar titles, you may find it easiest to search by ISBN; this book's ISBN is 978-0-470-53404-5.

Once you download the code, just decompress it with your favorite compression tool. Alternately, you can go to the main Wrox code download page at `www.wrox.com/dynamic/books/download.aspx` to see the code available for this book and all other Wrox books.

ERRATA

We make every effort to ensure that there are no errors in the text or in the code. However, no one is perfect, and mistakes do occur. If you find an error in one of our books, like a spelling mistake or faulty piece of code, we would be very grateful for your feedback. By sending in errata, you may save another reader hours of frustration, and at the same time you will be helping us provide even higher-quality information.

To find the errata page for this book, go to www.wrox.com and locate the title using the Search box or one of the title lists. Then, on the book details page, click the Errata link. On this page you can view all errata that have been submitted for this book and posted by Wrox editors. A complete book list, including links to each book's errata, is also available at www.wrox.com/misc-pages/booklist.shtml.

If you don't spot "your" error on the Errata page, go to www.wrox.com/contact/techsupport.shtml and complete the form there to send us the error you have found. We'll check the information and, if appropriate, post a message to the book's errata page and fix the problem in subsequent editions of the book.

P2P.WROX.COM

For author and peer discussion, join the P2P forums at p2p.wrox.com. The forums are a Web-based system on which you can post messages relating to Wrox books and related technologies and interact with other readers and technology users. The forums offer a subscription feature to e-mail you topics of interest of your choosing when new posts are made to the forums. Wrox authors, editors, other industry experts, and your fellow readers are present on these forums.

At http://p2p.wrox.com you will find a number of different forums that will help you not only as you read this book, but also as you develop your own applications. To join the forums, just follow these steps:

1. Go to p2p.wrox.com and click the Register link.
2. Read the terms of use and click Agree.
3. Complete the required information to join as well as any optional information you wish to provide, and click Submit.
4. You will receive an e-mail with information describing how to verify your account and complete the joining process.

You can read messages in the forums without joining P2P, but in order to post your own messages, you must join.

Once you join, you can post new messages and respond to messages other users post. You can read messages at any time on the Web. If you would like to have new messages from a particular forum e-mailed to you, click the Subscribe to this Forum icon by the forum name in the forum listing.

For more information about how to use the Wrox P2P, be sure to read the P2P FAQs for answers to questions about how the forum software works, as well as many common questions specific to P2P and Wrox books. To read the FAQs, click the FAQ link on any P2P page.

1

FitnessTrackerPlus

An Overview of the FitnessTrackerPlus Application

In the fall of 2008, Microsoft released an update to its new media-centric browser plug-in Silverlight. This update probably wasn't very exciting to end users who may have had Silverlight installed to watch the 2008 summer Olympics, but to developers who make use of Microsoft web technologies, a monumental change had occurred. Silverlight 2.0 finally included the long-awaited support for C#/VB.NET programming directly in the Silverlight world. No longer were developers forced to utilize the plug-in with a JavaScript-based API only. With the addition of C#/VB.NET support, it seemed like Silverlight may have finally made the necessary jump required in order to support line-of-business-style applications. Although a dramatic improvement from its predecessor, Silverlight 2 still left a lot to be desired in terms of line-of-business controls. Luckily, Microsoft has heard developers loud and clear and made several important enhancements in version 3 that specifically addressed line-of-business needs. Although the Silverlight 3 release meant developers had a powerful toolkit at their disposal for creating rich internet applications, some features were still omitted that were absolutely crucial in transitioning line-of-business applications from the desktop to the web. However, with the latest release of Silverlight version 4, these features have finally made it into the runtime, including a new Printing API, RichTextArea, Clipboard API, mouse wheel support, Implicit theming, and right-click event handling to name a few. Features like printing, right-click menus, and clipboard support offer some of the final pieces of the line-of-business missing from the Silverlight puzzle and may, in fact, make this latest release of Silverlight the most exciting yet for developers.

It is the primary intent of this book to introduce you to some of these great new features as well as show you some advanced techniques that you can apply to the development of your own Silverlight-based line-of-business solutions. In this book I will be following the Wrox Problem-Design-Solution style so that each chapter contains a detailed problem statement followed by a design analysis and solution implementation. I will not be discussing detailed API information for Silverlight and the various controls; however, all of this information is available by downloading the official Silverlight 4 documentation from `http://www.silverlight.net`. This book will be taking you through the creation of a fully functional Silverlight 4 line-of-business application while touching on several important topics such as scalable design, social networking, SEO, revenue generation, rich user interfaces, and others.

In this chapter, you learn the following:

- How to take a great idea and build a design to make it into an even better web application.
- What pages you will need for the application.
- What the new Silverlight 4 features are that you'll use to build your application.
- How you'll actually build the application through membership, personalization, journaling, and social networking. You also learn how to monetize the site, as well as test and deploy it.
- What software you'll need to download and install and what the basic setup instructions are for the site.

It is an exciting time for Silverlight development, and with the plug-in installed on millions of computers and newly announced support in MySpace, now is a great time to learn how to incorporate the technology into your own solutions.

PROBLEM

After a few years of full-time software development, I realized that between sitting in a chair for hours on end, and the not-so-great foods that are consumed during those crunch-time marathon coding sessions, I would probably need to consider some healthy habits to offset what can otherwise be a very sedentary work environment and lifestyle. The first step for me was to join a local gym, and watch what I eat when not on a marathon coding session. After a few weeks of working out I started to wonder, "Am I getting the results I was looking for? Are these foods really good for me? In fact, how can I even measure if I am making any progress while spending all of these hours in the gym?" Perhaps most importantly, the programmer in me decided to ask, "How can I write some software to help me keep track of what I do here?"

Most people would have just gone home, hopped on the Internet, and found some software or a web site that does this very thing. As programmers, however, we can just fire up the IDE and write our own instead. I decided that I wanted to create a new Silverlight-based web application that enables people to keep track of diet, exercise, and measurements. It would also be nice if the site could foster a community of users who share success with others through public facing journals hosted on the site, and integration with social networking sites such as Facebook and MySpace. Because this seemed like it could become a pretty popular site that could generate enough revenue to sustain itself, I also wanted to integrate some revenue streams through some form of pay-per-click advertising and monthly premium memberships for access to enhanced features of the site. At this point, the only thing missing was a name for the site and, of course, the implementation. For the name, I decided on FitnessTrackerPlus. I figured the "Plus" suffix will let users know that they are signing up for a more feature-rich site than traditional ASP.NET sites they may have used in the past. Or at least I will attempt to convince myself of that since I couldn't think of a nice catchy Web 2.0 name like Google or Twitter that works well for a fitness-tracking web site.

DESIGN

In this book, you will be creating a Silverlight 4 web application and will be utilizing the new features included in Silverlight 4 to provide the user with a rich user interface that is more responsive than a traditional ASP.NET web site. While the focus will be on creating an online fitness-tracking system, many of the features and techniques discussed can be applied to other line-of-business applications as well. Like most line-of-business applications, the primary purpose of the site is to allow users to enter data and view reports on that data. You will also be adding a social networking aspect to the site as well. In the end, you should be able to leverage the data entry, charting, site structure, SEO, and social networking components when building your own line-of-business applications in Silverlight.

Determining Requirements for the Site

The first step in the design phase of FitnessTrackerPlus is to get a detailed list of requirements for the site. I briefly touched upon some of the most basic high-level features that will be required by the site, but now it's time to flesh out everything. As with any application, it's best to collect as much detail about requirements as possible before writing a single line of code. Changes will always be easier to make at this stage of the game, as opposed to once you have already started coding a solution. The following sections list the major features that FitnessTrackerPlus will include.

Scalable

The more popular a site becomes, the more important it is that the new traffic can be handled without causing problems for existing users. In order to facilitate this, a multi-tiered architecture should be used. This allows the site to grow as the site's popularity grows, as well as keeps a clean separation between user interface, business logic, and data access code.

Rich User Interface

Users will log on to the site to quickly enter daily exercise, foods, and measurements. A rich user interface that utilizes Silverlight helps to ensure that the amount of time performing data entry tasks is minimized. The less users have to spend entering data, the more time they will have to view reports, measure progress, and to interact with others. The key to making this process simple and painless is to ensure that the pages are not cluttered with large data entry forms. The data entry for foods, exercises, and measurements should be simple enough so that users can quickly figure out what they need to do in order to enter information. It is also common in web sites now to provide multiple themes for users so that they can select a favorite color scheme or site layout. Your site should provide a similar theme selection feature that also remembers theme preference so it can be restored on the next login.

Dashboard

Once users successfully log into the site, they should be presented with a dashboard that shows basic fitness information for the current day. The dashboard should provide a simple non-cluttered look and give the user quick access to current measurements, nutrition, and exercise summaries, and any site announcements that you want users to be aware of. Site announcements can be a good tool to let users know about upcoming site maintenance or new features, as well as any features that are currently being worked on for future releases. Such announcements enable you to avoid bulk e-mails that could possibly end up being interpreted as spam.

Nutrition Log

The goal of the nutrition log is to provide a simple way for users to enter the foods they eat and view basic summaries of the nutrients that they consumed during the course of the day. Because that is the primary goal, any control or feature that does not directly make this process easier should not be added to the screen. All too often, you'll find what you think will be a useful web site that provides a service you're looking for only to sign up and find out that the developers have crammed in as many features as possible with little regard to the effect on the overall user interface. It should not require a training manual for people to use any part of your site, especially the data entry. It will be difficult to show your users how they are progressing if they don't come back to the site daily to enter foods. The only way they will consistently do so is if the process is quick and easy.

In order to help users track the foods they eat, you should provide a database of foods that the user can search. With millions of foods on the market, it is not practical or realistic to include every food in your database, so you'll also need to provide a mechanism for users to create and manage custom foods, complete with custom nutrition facts for the given food. The user doesn't want to browse an entire food database on the site in order to find a specific food, so you need to provide an assisted search method. Most sites now have some sort of auto-suggest functionality in search boxes that helps guide the user to the correct entry in the database. Your site should provide similar functionality by taking the first few characters typed and suggesting foods that match the search criteria in the food database. In most cases, you want your users to type in a few letters of a food, click the matching item, and move on to the next food they ate.

Exercise Log

The exercise log will be very similar in functionality to the nutrition log. Again, the primary goal is to provide the user with a quick and easy way to enter daily exercises and workout information. The database should contain a list of well-known exercises that users can search. You should add auto-suggest functionality to the search box as you did with the food search. In addition, to make exercise entry easier, you should break down exercises into various muscle groups and provide users with the capability to browse exercises based on those muscle groups. Just as you probably can't populate your database with every known food, you most likely will miss some exercises that people perform as well, so users should be able to create and manage their own custom exercises.

Measurements Log

One of the most important aspects of the site will be that users can keep track of their current measurements. You want to allow for data entry of a few standard measurements such as weight, BMI, waist, and legs. As you did with the exercise and nutrition logs, you will provide a way for users to create custom measurements that they would like to keep track of. Although keeping track of numerical measurements can be an effective way to measure fitness progress, it would also be beneficial to give users a visual representation of that progress. In order to satisfy this requirement, the site should have a mechanism to upload images of the user when they are entering measurements.

Public Journal Page

Once your users have taken the time to update their journal, they may want to share their updates with other users as well as friends and family. Getting positive feedback when working toward any goal can provide powerful motivation. Your site should allow users the option to share information with others. You can do this by providing a public-facing version of the journal similar to other social networking sites such as MySpace and Facebook. What you want to avoid is forcing the user to share a long, convoluted URL that friends and family have no chance of remembering; you need the site to give the user a friendly URL in the form of `FitnessTrackerPlus/Journals/username`. When users enter that URL in the browser, it should take them directly to the public-facing journal page that matches the username specified. Because some users may not want to share all the information in their journal, you should give them the option of sharing everything or any combination of foods, exercises, measurements, and journal entries. Users should be able to disable sharing of the data or make their journals private again at any time.

Social Networking Integration

Although you are trying to create primarily a data entry application, it would not be wise to ignore the explosion of social networking sites that have been created in the last few years. Most content-based sites have found ways to integrate with popular sites such as MySpace, Facebook, Twitter, and others. Providing this integration further promotes the sharing of information and the ability to gather feedback about the information being shared. Because it's been established already that you are trying to build a new online community right here at FitnessTrackerPlus, you also want to take advantage of what some of the other major social networking sites currently have to offer for integration. In addition to offering your users with the public journal page, you should also provide them with the option to share their fitness information with others on an existing social networking site like MySpace. Now that MySpace offers official support for Silverlight applications, you should be able to create a MySpace application that allows users to share data right from their own MySpace profile page.

Browser History Support

One of the complaints over the last couple of years about Rich Internet Applications, especially AJAX-based solutions, has been the lack of support for basic browser navigation functions. All too often, users would be engaged in a web application that utilized an AJAX library and they would click the Back button on the browser only to be brought all the way back to the home page or login screen. Your application should fully support browser history and navigation features so that at no time will an accidental click of the mouse redirect the user back to a login screen or some other page on the site that is completely unrelated to what they were working on at the time.

Generate Revenue

One issue to consider when starting a site like this is that if it gains in popularity and you want to use a hosting provider that offers technologies such as SQL Server and ASP.NET, you will have to cover the costs associated with that hosting. When starting out, you can most likely get away with one of the many shared hosting providers available online. As the site grows, you may need to look at a dedicated hosting solution. In either case, it would be best if you didn't have to pay for this out of your own pocket. You will need to come up with a way to create revenue to pay for the costs of running and maintaining this site. You can do this by utilizing a pay-per-click advertising service. In addition to the advertisements, you can look at charging a small monthly fee in order for users to have access to the site.

Feel Like a Desktop Application

The most important reason for choosing Silverlight for this site's user interface layer is that it provides users with a rich experience. The best case scenario is for FitnessTrackerPlus to look and feel like a traditional desktop application, complete with features that users have come to expect from those applications, such as mouse wheel support, right click menu options, fluid user interface transitions, and so on. As you develop FitnessTrackerPlus, you need to ensure that you use these common user interface features, now available in Silverlight, throughout the application to give the users the impression that this is not your typical web site.

Silverlight 4 Features

As part of the design, you should also think about what technology you will be using to implement the solution. For this site, the decision has already been made to utilize the new Silverlight 4 runtime to provide the rich user interface required for the application. The latest version of Silverlight provides some long-awaited features that will really help in the creation of a rich data entry site. For example, the public journal feature would have been much harder to implement with the previous version of Silverlight, but the new Navigation Framework makes this type of thing relatively easy to implement.

Let's take a look at some of the improvements in this latest release of Silverlight that will make programming this site much easier than it would have been with an older version.

Navigation Framework

A major benefit of sticking with the existing ASP.NET technology for creating a web site was that pages could be bookmarked and shared, and users could easily navigate from one page to the next using standard features of the web browser. Applications that were written in older versions of Silverlight could not easily mimic this functionality. Although you could create a rich user interface, it was terribly difficult to do some basic things such as support browser history, and Forward and Back buttons. It was also very difficult to have direct links to pages written in XAML. The new navigation framework takes care of all of those issues by allowing developers to create pages in XAML that have full support for browser navigation features as well as deep linking so it is now easy to share XAML-based page URLs. Also included with the new navigation framework is the capability to map long, complex URLs to simple, easy-to-remember ones. This will become important as you work on the public journal page and allow others on the Web to access those pages using an easy-to-remember URL such as `FitnessTrackerPlus.com/username`. The URL mapping located in the App.xaml file is handled by the new `UriMapper` class shown in the following code:

```
<navigation:UriMapper x:Key="uriMapper">
     <navigation:UriMapping Uri="/{user}"
MappedUri="/Views/PublicJournal.xaml?user={username}" />
</navigation:UriMapper>
```

In this case, the URI will be the default `FitnessTrackerPlus.com/username` where the `{user}` will be replaced with an actual username. The `MappedUri` will be the actual path to the XAML page that contains the public journal. As you can see, the Navigation Framework allows for individual XAML pages to behave like a typical ASP.NET page complete with their own query string. The Navigation Framework will also allow you to simulate some of the ASP.NET master page behavior. Using navigation frames, you will be able to create user controls for each feature you are implementing while sharing a common navigation menu and top banner across all of the pages. The Navigation Framework is a significant enhancement to Silverlight and really takes you a large step closer to being able to create web applications that combine a rich user interface with the standard web functionality available in traditional ASP.NET-based web sites.

New Data Controls

With the new release, some important new data controls have been made available including the `DataForm` and `DataPager`. The `DataGrid` control previously had no support for paging data and it became a pretty large limitation of the control, especially if binding to a potentially large result set. The `DataPager` provides paging capabilities to any data set that implements the `IPagedViewCollection`. Because the `ObjectDataSource` supports this interface, you can set the `DataPager` to work in conjunction with the `DataGrid` and provide an efficient paging mechanism for large result sets. The new `DataForm` provides a very powerful way to display detailed information about a data item in a standard data entry form. The `DataForm` has similar functionality to the `DetailsView` in ASP.NET, and in this application, you will use it to provide a data entry screen not only for custom foods, exercises, and measurements, but also for details about individual nutrition and exercise journal entries that are being displayed in the `DataGrid`.

In addition to the `DataForm` and `DataPager` controls, there have been important enhancements to the `DataGrid` control itself, including optimizations to speed up the overall load time of the control, and a variety of column sizing options to prevent horizontal scroll bars from appearing when users resize various column headers.

Control Toolkit

The Silverlight Control Toolkit has been available since version 2 of the runtime was released but the latest release includes some new controls and promotes some other controls into the Stable band. Controls in the Stable band are considered pretty much ready for prime time and have been thoroughly tested. These controls are updated and modified only during bug fix cycles and typically are safe from breaking changes. Preview band controls are subject to modifications that include breaking changes, so there is some minimal risk to using them in a production application. Experimental band controls are really intended for evaluation only. These experimental controls should not be used in production applications, as in most cases they are not feature complete and it is a pretty safe bet that breaking changes will be made between releases. Table 1-1 lists the controls available in the toolkit as well as the current stability status:

TABLE 1-1: Controls Available in the Control Toolkit

TOOLKIT	AVAILABLE CONTROLS
Stable Quality Band	DockPanel Expander HeaderedContentControl Label NumericUpDown Viewbox WrapPanel
Preview Quality Band	Accordion Charting DomainUpDown ImplicitStyleManager LayoutTransformer Rating TimePicker TimeUpDown Eleven themes
Experimental Quality Band	TransitioningContentControl GlobalCalendar TreeMap Drag & Drop Busy Indicator
Available Themes (All are considered part of the Preview Quality Band)	Bubble Crème Bureau Black Expression Dark Expression Light Rainier Purple Rainier Orange Shiny Blue Shiny Red Twilight Blue Whistler Blue

Developers can get access to the source code over at the CodePlex site using the following URL: `http://silverlight.codeplex.com`. The project has been made open source so you can feel free to make changes to the code and integrate those changes into your own projects. If you are not interested in the source code, you can also download just the raw binaries and add them to your Silverlight project. This toolkit provides some great controls and features that are not available from the Silverlight 4 runtime. You will be using them extensively throughout the FitnessTrackerPlus application. The application will make use of the `Label`, `DockPanel`, `Charting`, `TimePicker`,

`TimeUpDown`, `GlobalCalendar`, `BusyIndicator`, and all of the available themes. In the following chapters, I go into detail about each one of these controls and demonstrate how they really provide a large amount of user interface functionality with a very minimal level of development effort.

WCF RIA Services

These new services are an important addition to Silverlight and help provide n-Tier data support based on the new ADO.NET data services. The services also provide a means to perform data entry validation on the client along with paging, sorting, and querying data. WCF RIA Services will also help with the integration of Silverlight applications with the ASP.NET authentication and role management services. Perhaps one of the biggest benefits to this new feature is providing a way to handle change tracking between tiers, which was not straightforward in earlier Silverlight versions when using ORM technologies such as LINQ to SQL or the Entity Framework.

Dynamic, Implicit, and BasedOn Styling

The new dynamic and implicit styling support in Silverlight 4 provides a way to change the currently applied theme at runtime. When attempting to achieve this functionality in previous versions of Silverlight, developers were forced to worry about applying the theme elements to the entire visual tree of controls manually. Dynamic styling also provides the capability to change the theme more than once, a difficult and error prone process before, which sometimes required rebooting the Silverlight application to apply the new theme changes. `BasedOn` styling from which other style definitions can inherit allows you to create base styles and then styles that inherit the settings from that base style. Now you can create a style with some basic settings and when you need to change only one aspect of that style to use in another control, you don't have to copy the entire original style to include that change.

Finally, implicit styling also gives you the ability to declare a style that applies to all controls of the specified type. This gives you a much easier way to share styles across controls and is very similar to CSS based styling. For example, implicit styling allows you to style all `TextBox` controls with a thick border using code similar to the following:

```
<Style TargetType="TextBox">
     <Setter Property="BorderThickness" Value="5" />
</Style>
```

Additional Features

In addition to the major feature enhancements I have mentioned in the previous sections, the following enhancements have also been added to the Silverlight 4 runtime:

- Webcam/microphone access
- ICommand support
- HTML Hosting in Offline mode
- Elevated trust applications
- Local file access

- COM Interop
- Notification API in Offline mode
- Network authentication
- Cross-domain networking support
- Keyboard access in full screen mode
- Text trimming
- Right-to-left, BiDi and complex script
- Offline DRM
- H.264 protected content
- Support for using the Silverlight plug-in as a drag & drop target
- Managed Extensibility Framework
- Support for Google Chrome web browser

SOLUTION

In the "Solution" section of each chapter, I will take you through the complete implementation details required to build the features highlighted during that chapter. This section of the chapter will typically contain the majority of the code snippets along with brief discussions and explanations about what the code is doing and why it is doing it. For this first chapter I won't be getting into any real code, but instead I'll give you a quick overview of what you can expect to see in Chapters 2 through 12.

Chapter 2

The second chapter is all about architecture and a discussion of the various technology choices that are available to Silverlight developers. The goal, of course, is to make sure that choices are made that will allow you to keep a multi-tiered design and implementation with an emphasis on both scalability and performance. This chapter will be broken down into discussions about both the Physical N-Tier design as well as the Logical N-Tier design. I will briefly cover the following technologies before ultimately deciding which ones will be used for FitnessTrackerPlus, along with the reasons why:

- Silverlight Toolkit
- Silverlight Extensions
- ASMX Web Services
- WCF Web Services
- WCF RIA Services
- ADO.NET

- Entity Framework
- LINQ to SQL
- ADO.NET Data Services
- SQL Server
- Oracle
- MySQL

Chapter 3

In Chapter 3 I will focus on how to integrate the ASP.NET Membership, Profile, and Role services into the FitnessTrackerPlus Silverlight application. You will see how the new WCF RIA Services Framework makes integration with these services simple. After completing this integration process, you will then add user registration and login capabilities to the application. Finally, I will take a look at how you can prepare an alternate view of the FitnessTrackerPlus site for those users who may have not yet downloaded and installed the Silverlight plug-in. This way, you will ensure that users without the plug-in can still access the landing page and find out more information about the site before making a decision about installing Silverlight on their own machine.

Chapter 4

In Chapter 4 I will cover the initial design and implementation of the dashboard page. The dashboard page will be the first page that users see after successfully creating a new account and logging into the site. The dashboard page will also provide users with the ability to dynamically select a theme for the site. In this chapter I will show you how to combine the theme files from the Silverlight Control Toolkit with the new Dynamic and Implicit Styling features of Silverlight in order to provide the users with the ability to dynamically change the current site theme. You will also begin to make use of the ASP.NET Profile provider to make sure that the theme selection is saved in the user's profile so that it can be restored upon the next successful login. Finally, you will also see how to use the new `ChildWindow` control included in Silverlight in order to provide users with site announcements.

Chapter 5

Chapter 5 begins the first of three data entry chapters. In this chapter you will be designing and implementing the food log page where users will be able to enter the foods they eat on a daily basis. I will cover how to provide a user-friendly way to search for foods with the new `AutoCompleteBox` control. You will also see how the new `GlobalCalendar` control in the Silverlight Toolkit can be used to provide users with access to previous food log entries.

Chapter 6

In Chapter 6 you will design and implement the exercise log page. Instead of relying on the `AutoCompleteBox` control, you will be making use of a cascading `DropDownBox` solution in order to provide users with an easy way to select exercises for their log. You will also see how to make use of the new `DomainDataSource` control to provide easier data binding with data that you make available through the WCF RIA Services created in your business logic layer.

Chapter 7

In Chapter 7 you will create the final data entry page of the application. The only page left to work on is the measurement log page. On this page, you will be providing users with the ability to keep track of various fitness measurements. To help assist users with some of the calculations, you will be building a plug-in system that will display a special modal calculator control that can be used to calculate the user's BMI value based on parameters supplied by the user.

Chapter 8

In Chapter 8 I will take another look at the dashboard page in order to complete some of the work done earlier. Part of any meaningful dashboard is to provide the users with some visual feedback related to their data. In this case, you will be adding some basic charting components to the dashboard page. As you will see, the latest version of the Silverlight Toolkit makes adding charts to your Silverlight application a breeze.

Chapter 9

In this chapter you will see how to use the features of the new Navigation Framework in order to provide a public-facing version of the user's fitness journal. After your users perform all of the hard work of dieting and exercising, they may want to share their success stories with family members or other users of the site. Now, just in case they don't yet have their own blog or social networking page, you will be creating one right here on FitnessTrackerPlus that they can use. By using the Navigation Framework, you will be able to give every user their very own unique URL to share with others that will lead to a public journal page that includes the user's food, exercise, and measurement log entries. Finally, in order to provide visitors with a means of leaving feedback to the users, you will also build a commenting system that allows for HTML-based comments. That's right—HTML content embedded in a Silverlight application. The best part is that it's not really as difficult as you may think.

Chapter 10

Chapter 10 will cover how to incorporate social networking into FitnessTrackerPlus. There is no doubt that social networking has become a major component of any successful website, and just because you will be developing in Silverlight does not mean you can't jump on the bandwagon as well. In this chapter I will show you step by step how to create a version of the public journal page in the form of a Silverlight MySpace application. This application will be available to any FitnessTrackerPlus user that has a MySpace page. Thanks to the now official support for Silverlight from MySpace, you will see how easy it is to create a Silverlight application using the new MySpace OpenSocial API and the Silverlight extensions for the API.

Chapter 11

In Chapter 11 you will see some possible techniques that you can use in order to generate revenue for the FitnessTrackerPlus application. Whether you deploy FitnessTrackerPlus to a shared hosting provider or you decide to have your own dedicated servers set up to host the site there will most certainly be a cost associated with it. Of course, generating revenue and making a profit off of the site is never usually a bad thing either. In this chapter I will show you how to integrate Pay-Per-Click advertisements directly into the Silverlight application. In case you decide that you don't want to subject your users to any kind of advertisements but still want to generate some money to offset your hosting costs, I will also show you how to charge recurring monthly fees for access to the site by using the Subscriptions feature of the PayPal developer API.

Chapter 12

In Chapter 12 I will cover how to perform the final build steps for the application as well as show you step by step how to deploy the site to a live shared hosting provider in Discount ASP.NET. You will see how Discount ASP.NET provides several unique tools that make deployment of a Silverlight-based site simple and painless. Some of these tools include utilities to manage IIS, SQL Server and more.

Getting Started

Before you move on to the next chapter on application architecture, I wanted to get you started with the project. Silverlight 4 development can be done with the full version of Visual Studio or the freely available Express edition that can be downloaded at `http://www.microsoft.com/Express`. For this book I will be using Visual Studio 2010 Professional Edition as well as the free SQL Server 2008 Express edition with Advanced Services. When downloading the free edition of SQL Server Express, choose the Advanced Services option which includes the SQL Server Management Studio tool, which you will be using throughout this book to make modifications to the application database.

Once you have your development environment set up, you will need to download several installation packages that are required for Silverlight development. All of the required packages are available for download at `http://silverlight.net`. This web site is considered the main source of Silverlight programming information for developers, and contains very useful starter tutorials as well as webcasts and online forums. Once on the site, you will see the following downloads:

- Silverlight 4 Tools for Visual Studio 2010
- Microsoft Expression Blend 3 Trial
- Silverlight Toolkit
- WCF RIA Services

Downloading the Expression Blend Trial is considered optional and I will be providing raw XAML for any user interface code that is presented in the book. Visual Studio 2010 now includes complete designer support for XAML pages, and the Expression tools provide designers with some advanced tools geared specifically towards website designers. As a developer, I find that the improved tooling in Visual Studio 2010 is more than sufficient for developing XAML pages, and will not cover the Blend tool in this book.

After downloading all of the required software, you should install the Silverlight 4 Tools for Visual Studio 2010 first. The installation process for this part of the toolkit can be quite lengthy, so feel free to brew some coffee while waiting. Once the download is complete, you will want to install the WCF RIA Services; this installation is much faster, so don't go anywhere. Finally, you will install the Silverlight Toolkit, which again is not a lengthy installation process. If you have decided to download Blend, feel free to install that at this time along with the offline help file.

At this point, you should have everything you need to get started, so it's time to fire up Visual Studio and create a new project. The code in this book will be written in C#, so I will be using the C# project templates, but if you prefer VB.NET, feel free to work with that language as it will not be terribly difficult to follow the C# code and convert it to corresponding VB.NET code. With Visual Studio open, you will want to create a new Silverlight project. Specifically, you want to use the new Silverlight Navigation Application template, as shown in Figure 1-1.

When you click OK, you're presented with the dialog shown in Figure 1-2, which includes some additional project options. In this dialog, you are asked to supply a name for the ASP.NET web project that will link with the Silverlight application. You can go ahead and leave the default name of FitnessTrackerPlus.Web. The Web project type option should stay set at ASP.NET Web Application Project, and the Silverlight Version option should stay at 4. Finally, be sure to select the Enable WCF RIA Services option before proceeding.

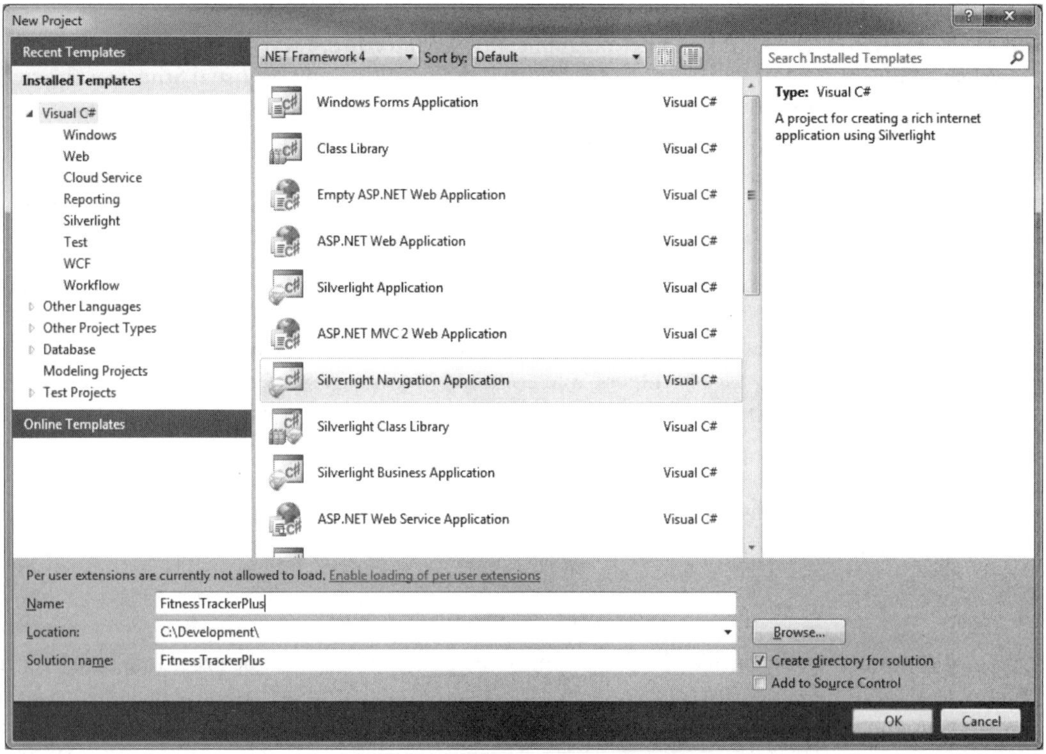

FIGURE 1-1

The Navigation Application project template creates two new projects, one for the ASP.NET web site that will host the Silverlight application called FitnessTrackerPlus.Web, and the Silverlight application project itself named FitnessTrackerPlus. In the Silverlight project, you will notice that a new folder called Views is generated along with App.xaml, and MainPage.xaml. In the Views folder, you will see three new pages called About.xaml, ErrorWin.xaml, and Home.xaml. You will be replacing these with your own pages, but you can see from this sample site that was generated that, unlike previous versions of Silverlight, with help from the Navigation Framework you can finally have real page navigation from XAML pages. At this point you can see the browser button support by compiling and running the application. Figure 1-3 shows the newly generated site running in the browser.

FIGURE 1-2

FIGURE 1-3

You should note how using the browser's Back and Forward buttons enables you to navigate between XAML pages. The URLs generated for these pages support deep linking and will allow users to bookmark and return to the exact XAML page that they were viewing at a later time. The Navigation Framework is probably one of the largest and most important enhancements included in this latest release of Silverlight and will allow you to implement some of the most important features of FitnessTrackerPlus.

Using the Navigation Framework requires very little code to implement. The majority of the work is handled by the framework and all you need to do to utilize it is use the new `System.Windows.Controls.Navigation.Frame` class. In the following code from the MainPage.xaml file, the `Frame` control has its `Source` property set to a relative URL called /Home. The /Home is translated into the full /Views/Home.xaml path by the embedded `uriMapper` object, which is covered later. For now, just know that setting the `Source` property to a valid .xaml file is all it takes to load up the `Frame`.

Available for download on Wrox.com

```
<navigation:Frame x:Name="ContentFrame" Style="{StaticResource ContentFrameStyle}"
     Source="/Home" Navigated="ContentFrame_Navigated"
     NavigationFailed="ContentFrame_NavigationFailed">
     <navigation:Frame.UriMapper>
          <uriMapper:UriMapper>
               <uriMapper:UriMapping Uri="" MappedUri="/Views/Home.xaml"/>
               <uriMapper:UriMapping Uri="/{pageName}"
MappedUri="/Views/{pageName}.xaml"/>
          </uriMapper:UriMapper>
     </navigation:Frame.UriMapper>
</navigation:Frame>
```

Code snippet MainPage.xaml

The actual navigation occurs by setting the `NavigateUri` property of the `HyperlinkButton` controls to the destination page desired. In the following code, the project, Home, and About pages are made accessible by setting the `NavigateUri` property to /Home and /About respectively.

Available for download on Wrox.com

```
<Border x:Name="LinksBorder" Style="{StaticResource LinksBorderStyle}">
     <StackPanel x:Name="LinksStackPanel" Style="{StaticResource LinksStackPanelStyle}">

          <HyperlinkButton x:Name="Link1" Style="{StaticResource LinkStyle}"
NavigateUri="/Home" TargetName="ContentFrame" Content="home"/>

          <Rectangle x:Name="Divider1" Style="{StaticResource DividerStyle}"/>

          <HyperlinkButton x:Name="Link2" Style="{StaticResource LinkStyle}"
NavigateUri="/About" TargetName="ContentFrame" Content="about"/>

     </StackPanel>
</Border>
```

Code snippet MainPage.xaml

As you move further into the FitnessTrackerPlus application, I will go into more detail about the navigation system and all of its benefits, including the new URI mapping feature. Before moving on to the next chapter, you should feel free to launch the default site and see how seamless page transitions are and how you can move forward and backward through the pages using the browser without any additional code, all of it courtesy of the new Silverlight Navigation Framework.

SUMMARY

In this chapter, you have learned some of the history behind the creation of FitnessTrackerPlus, and, more importantly, how you will be leveraging the latest and greatest features of Silverlight 4 to make a rich line-of-business-style application. I briefly outlined the new features that you will be utilizing including the Navigation Framework, Data Controls, Silverlight Toolkit and more. In the Design section I covered the complete list of functional requirements that the site will have to meet, and in the solution section provided you with an overview of what to expect in the coming chapters.

You should also now have all the software required for Silverlight development downloaded and installed, and be familiar with the default navigation project that is created by the project template in Visual Studio. You pretty much have everything in place to really get started on this project. Although this book discusses the creation of an online fitness-tracking site, I strongly believe the techniques used in this site can be applied across a variety of line-of-business web applications. At the end of this book, you will have created a feature-rich Silverlight web application that has a rich data entry system, social networking aspects, and community features, and is even capable of potentially generating revenue from advertising and premium membership subscriptions. It's even possible that after developing and using this application, you might just rethink ordering that large pizza during your next all-night coding session.

2

Prepare to Be Popular

Providing a Scalable Architecture

With the creation of the initial project structure complete in Visual Studio, you can now look at some of the design aspects of the site, specifically how you're going to support N-Tier application development with Silverlight 4. Many new enhancements to Silverlight now make the development of these multi-tier applications much easier than in previous versions. This chapter takes a look at many of these new technologies so that you will be familiar with them and be ready to utilize them as you move forward in the book, implementing new features. These technologies include the new WCF RIA Services platform, LINQ to SQL, Entity Framework and SQL Server Express 2008 with Advanced Services.

In addition to the review of the new Silverlight 4 features, I will also be covering how you can separate your application into multiple layers of functionality to support N-Tier development. Although every site starts out small, you just never know what can happen on the Internet. By supporting this kind of code structure, you can avoid being unprepared for a barrage of new users and instead be fully prepared to handle the eventual millions of users that will be coming to your site as it grows in popularity.

PROBLEM

As you create the FitnessTrackerPlus application, remember that although at first you will most likely be the only site user, at some point, with any luck, you'll have other users. The architecture decisions that you make when building a single-user application are quite different than the ones you must make for a full-blown Internet application that can potentially have millions of concurrent users. There are several distinct problems and challenges that need to be solved when making the site available to other users. For starters, you never really know how many people will find the site useful. Millions of people are online and just as many people are currently going through some form of diet and exercise routine. If a scalable architecture is not designed for FitnessTrackerPlus, even a couple thousand users hitting the site could potentially bring it to its knees. It is essential to ensure that even though you are creating a Silverlight application instead of a traditional ASP.NET site, you are still adhering to the best practices of N-Tier development so that the site can be properly scaled as the number of users grows. The technology that you choose will need to support both logical and physical separation of tiers.

As you work on designing the various tiers of the FitnessTrackerPlus application, you must resist the urge to stop the design process prematurely and jump right into coding. This is especially critical when you work on the user interface design. When designing the user interface it is always best to try and lay out the various screens that will be required for the application. You don't necessarily have to have every little detail thought out, but it is best to take some time now and figure out what screens are needed, and how they should interact with one another. As you have probably discovered in your own development journey, changes to the user interface and application flow can be made rather easily before you start coding. If you try to design these screens on-the-fly as you are coding, you can easily find yourself in a situation where the screen you are developing doesn't interact the way you thought it would with other screens. As you will be responsible for the design, implementation, testing, deployment, and support of this application, you want to be sure to take some of these important design steps early on in the development cycle. Study after study confirms that spending a little bit more time during the design phase reduces not only the number of defects but also the total amount of work required in the coding stage.

Finally, you have to think about what will happen when users hit the home page of the site and do not have the Silverlight plug-in installed. Despite the fact that Silverlight has been downloaded and installed on millions of computers worldwide, you have to assume that eventually someone will arrive at your site who may have no idea what Silverlight is, what it does, or if it is even safe to install. Most users have some familiarity with installing browser plug-ins such as Flash, and probably feel very comfortable with doing that, Silverlight on the other hand they may have some reservations about. You will need to reassure your users that installing Silverlight is not only easy but safe, and you will need to have a mechanism in place that allows users to view your home page even without installing the plug-in.

DESIGN

The "Design" section for this chapter breaks down each of the problems outlined in the previous section. You'll see the various ways of creating a scalable multi-tier Silverlight application as well as coverage of several new enhancements available in Silverlight 4 that make N-Tier Silverlight development much easier than in previous versions. While working through the design of FitnessTrackerPlus, you need to build a solid understanding of some important technologies so you can make informed design decisions. Over the last few years, many different technologies were introduced for both physical and logical tier development. The following list shows the required tiers for both the physical and logical design. The logical tier design also includes a list of some popular Microsoft technologies from which you can choose while you decide on the implementation strategy for FitnessTrackerPlus.

- Physical N-Tier design
  - Presentation Tier
  - Business Logic Tier
  - Data Tier

- Logical N-Tier design
  - Presentation Layer
    - Silverlight Controls
    - Silverlight Toolkit
  - Business Logic Layer
    - ASMX Web Services
    - WCF
    - WCF RIA Services
  - Data Access Layer
    - ADO.NET, Entity Framework
    - LINQ to SQL
    - ADO.NET Data Services
  - Data Storage Layer
    - SQL Server
    - Oracle
    - MySQL
    - DB2

Physical N-Tier Design

The physical architecture usually consists of several distinct hardware layers. This is most commonly referred to as an N-Tier server architecture. An N-Tier architecture will usually consist of, at minimum, data, logic, and presentation tiers — although depending on requirements there could be even more than those three. Each tier is represented by its own hardware. The data tier would consist of a database server whose sole responsibility would be data storage. A server residing in the business logic tier would be responsible for hosting components that perform business logic and data access. Finally, the presentation tier is responsible for the graphical display of the data as well as providing the user with a means to input and manipulate data.

The decision to utilize an N-Tier hardware solution is largely dependent on the volume of traffic you expect your site to attract. At first, you will most likely find that hosting the business logic and database on the same physical tier is sufficient. As your site gains in popularity, however, you will most likely find it extremely beneficial to offload the work of these layers into separate isolated hardware tiers. Many web hosting companies have already done some of this work for you. When deploying your solution, you will most often find that your business logic or ASP.NET/Silverlight application code will reside on one server, while your database tables and data will be stored on a separate physical server. For the most part, you will find that these distinct hardware tiers are set up by hosting providers regardless of whether you are in a shared hosting environment or have your own dedicated server.

Load Balancing

If you are lucky or just really great at marketing, you may even find that you have to move your site out of the hosting provider's servers and into your own dedicated server farm. At this point, you can really start to reap the benefits of having a solid N-Tier hardware design. If you have designed your physical tiers correctly, you should be able to handle the additional load with the help of load balancing. Utilizing a load balancing solution in a server farm can help you manage performance bottlenecks that may occur as the site grows in users. With load balancing, you can potentially add more hardware to the overall solution to help with the additional load and increase performance. Almost all large websites implement some form of a load balancing strategy.

Cloud Computing

Another relatively new consideration you need to be aware of is cloud computing. Although still in the early stages, cloud computing is starting to gain acceptance in several major sites. Currently there are several major players in this space including Amazon, Microsoft, and Google, which offer you the benefits of dedicated hosting providers but with dramatically lower costs. The first player in this arena was Amazon with its S3 storage service, which offered scalable storage that your applications could use with simple web services. Amazon then moved into full-blown site hosting in their cloud with EC2.

Google also offers a similar hosting service with its Google App Engine platform. The newest offering for cloud-based hosting is Microsoft's solution called Azure. Microsoft just recently released details about its new cloud computing solution and hosting packages as well as announcements about competitively priced SQL Server support through this new Azure platform.

> *For more information on how you can benefit from the new Azure platform, check out* Cloud Computing with the Microsoft Azure Services Platform, *Wiley, 2009.*

Logical N-Tier Design

In addition to applying the N-Tier architecture at the physical hardware level, you must also think about separating the work performed at the logical level. The logical level of N-Tier design revolves around the actual implementation code being created. As in a traditional ASP.NET application, you will be best served by separating your Silverlight application implementation into distinct manageable layers of code. By doing this, you will find it much easier to maintain the code over the long run. In addition to ease of maintenance, separating your code into multiple layers ensures that you are adhering to your original scalability requirements.

In order to effectively use an N-Tier hardware architecture, you will need to ensure that your presentation, business logic, and data have been implemented in separate modules that can be hosted in their respective hardware tiers. Although in many cases an N-Tier implementation involves only a presentation, business logic, and database tier, you can sometimes see an additional tier added that is only responsible for data access from the database tier. Typically this layer is hosted on the same physical machine as the business logic layer. A data access layer can provide another layer of separation that helps to ensure your data storage choice can be changed without affecting existing business logic or presentation code. Figure 2-1 shows a typical logical N-Tier design for an ASP.NET/ Silverlight web application along with the technology choices available for each respective tier.

Presentation Layer
- Silverlight 4.0
- Silverlight Toolkit

Business Logic Layer
- ASMX Web Services
- WCF (Windows Communication Foundation) Services
- ADO.NET Data Services
- WCF RIA Services

Data Access Layer
- ADO.NET
- LINQ to SQL
- Entity Framework

Data Storage Layer
- SQL Server
- Oracle
- MySQL
- Access

FIGURE 2-1

Presentation Layer

The presentation layer represents the user interface of FitnessTrackerPlus. This layer of code includes the Silverlight project as well as its parent ASP.NET website project. The site will make use of the standard Silverlight user interface controls as well as some of the new line of business controls that have been added to the latest version of the runtime. You will also need to utilize controls from the Silverlight Toolkit to provide additional functionality, including theme support for your site. Table 2-1 gives you a quick look at some of the Silverlight User Interface controls you will be using to create the user interface of FitnessTrackerPlus.

TABLE 2-1: Silverlight User Interface Controls

SILVERLIGHT 4		SILVERLIGHT TOOLKIT
Border	Image	Accordion
Button	ListBox	AutoCompleteBox
Calendar	PasswordBox	Charting
Canvas	ProgressBar	DockPanel
CheckBox	ScrollViewer	ImplicitStyleManager
ComboBox	Slider	Themes
DataForm	StackPanel	TimePicker
DataGrid	TabControl	TimeUpDown
DataPager	TextBlock	WrapPanel
DatePicker	TextBox	
Grid	ToolTip	
HyperlinkButton		

Silverlight 4 Data Controls

Silverlight 4 has added several new controls that will help present data to the user, and you will be utilizing many of them in the FitnessTrackerPlus application. These controls are as follows:

- `DataGrid`: Provides a table-based presentation of data. Several column types are available in the `DataGrid` including `TextBox`, `CheckBox`, and `Template`. The template type column provides you with the ability to create a custom column type. Styling support includes the ability to customize row backgrounds, show/hide gridlines, show/hide headers, and more. Most important, it provides an easy programming interface for data binding. You will be incorporating many of the `DataGrid` features in both the food and exercise log pages.
- `DataForm`: Creates a rich data entry form based on the custom object associated with the form. The `DataForm` will create all of the necessary labels and controls required to perform data entry on the object using any exposed public properties.
- `DataPager`: When you need to present large amounts of data in the `DataGrid`, the new `DataPager` control will limit the amount of data being displayed at any given time. This control works in conjunction with the `DataGrid` to provide basic paging capabilities.

Presenting Data with the DataGrid

The `DataGrid` is a powerful control in Silverlight. It gives you a very flexible way to present data to the user in a table-like structure with rows and columns. It features rich data binding support and several events that you can hook into during the various stages of data binding. To start using the `DataGrid`, you need to add a reference to `System.Windows.Controls.Data`. After the reference is created, you then need to add the namespace to your XAML, as shown in the following code:

```
<UserControl x:Class="SilverlightControlSamples.MainPage"
    xmlns="http://schemas.microsoft.com/winfx/2006/xaml/presentation"
    xmlns:x="http://schemas.microsoft.com/winfx/2006/xaml"
    xmlns:data="clr-namespace:System.Windows.Controls;
        assembly=System.Windows.Controls.Data">
    <Grid x:Name="LayoutRoot" Background="White" />
</UserControl>
```

Code snippet MainPage.xaml located in the DataGridExample project.

Once you add the required namespace declaration, you can simply add the `DataGrid` to your Silverlight page. The following code shows a `DataGrid` bound to a collection of `Food` objects. The `DataGrid` makes use of both the built-in `DataGridTextColumn` as well as a custom `HyperlinkButton` column defined by using a `DataGridTemplateColumn`:

```
<data:DataGrid x:Name="CustomFoodsGrid" AutoGenerateColumns="False">
    <data:DataGrid.Columns>
        <data:DataGridTextColumn Header="Food ID" Binding="{Binding
Path=ID}" />
        <data:DataGridTemplateColumn Header="Food Name">
            <data:DataGridTemplateColumn.CellTemplate>
```

```
                    <DataTemplate>
                         <HyperlinkButton Content="{Binding Path=Name}"
HorizontalAlignment="Center" VerticalAlignment="Center"
Foreground="#FF0000FF"  />
                    </DataTemplate>
               </data:DataGridTemplateColumn.CellTemplate>
          </data:DataGridTemplateColumn>
     </data:DataGrid.Columns>
</data:DataGrid>
```

Code snippet MainPage.xaml located in the DataGridExample project.

Populating the `DataGrid` control is simple and requires only one line of code. Simply set the `ItemsSource` property to a collection of objects. In the following code, the `CustomFoodsGrid` has its `ItemsSource` property bound to a collection of `Food` objects.

Available for download on Wrox.com

```
public class Food
{
     public int ID { get; set; }
     public string Name { get; set; }

     public Food(int id, string name)
     {
          this.ID = id;
          this.Name = name;
     }
}

public MainPage()
{
     InitializeComponent();

     CustomFoodsGrid.ItemsSource = new List<Food>
     {
          new Food(1, "Bagel With Cream Cheese"),
          new Food(2, "Deli Sandwich"),
          new Food(3, "Cheeseburger"),
          new Food(4, "Root Beer"),
          new Food(5, "Chocolate Ice Cream")

     };
}
```

Code snippet MainPage.xaml.cs located in the DataGridExample project.

Once the data binding takes place, the `DataGrid` then takes care of displaying the food data in a tabular format, complete with a nice default style. Figure 2-2 shows the `DataGrid` displaying the data with the `FoodName` column being represented by the `HyperlinkButton` control that was declared in the custom `DataGridTemplateColumn` declaration.

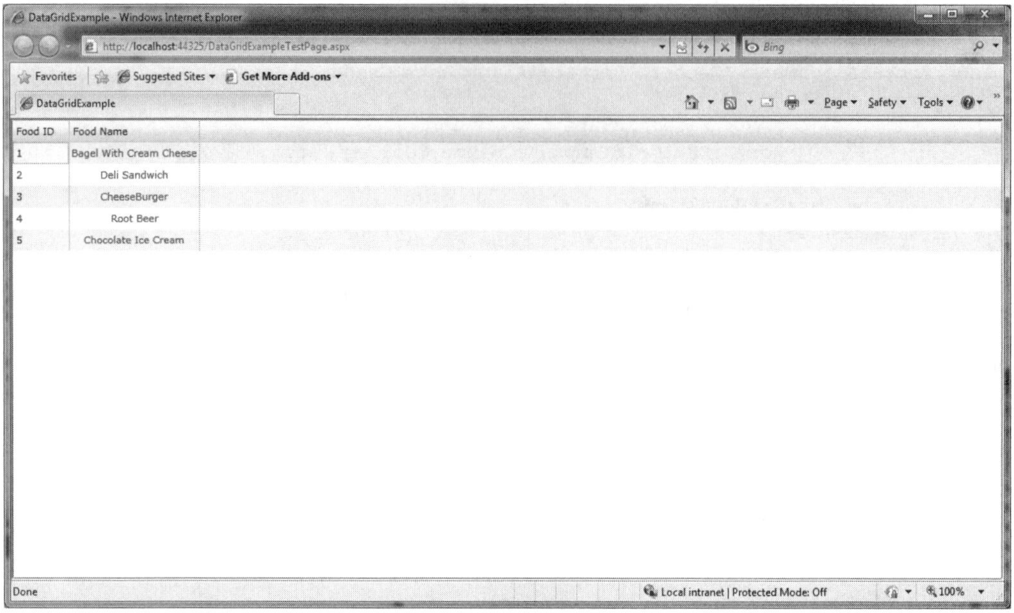

FIGURE 2-2

Rich Data Entry with the DataForm

Now that you have seen how easy it is to display data in the DataGrid, let's take a look at how the new DataForm control provides a great way to present the user with a rich data entry form. As with the DataGrid, you will need to add a new reference to the project in order to use the DataForm. The DataForm is part of the new Silverlight Toolkit, so you will want to add a reference to System.Windows.Controls.Data.DataForm.Toolkit. Once again, don't forget to add the namespace to your XAML before adding the control to the page. Listing 2-1 shows the XAML code required to add a DataForm control to the page.

LISTING 2-1: MainPage.xaml (located in the DataFormExample project)

Available for download on Wrox.com

```
<UserControl x:Class="DataFormExample.MainPage"
     xmlns="http://schemas.microsoft.com/winfx/2006/xaml/presentation"
     xmlns:x="http://schemas.microsoft.com/winfx/2006/xaml"
     xmlns:d="http://schemas.microsoft.com/expression/blend/2008"
     xmlns:mc="http://schemas.openxmlformats.org/markup-compatibility/2006"
     xmlns:data_form="clr-namespace:System.Windows.Controls;
assembly=System.Windows.Controls.Data.DataForm.Toolkit">

     <Grid x:Name="LayoutRoot" Background="White">
          <data_form:DataForm x:Name="CustomFoodDataForm" />
     </Grid>
</UserControl>
```

Working with the `DataForm` is as simple as assigning a business object to the `CurrentItem` property of the `DataForm`. The `DataForm` will do the majority of the work by looking at your business object for any public properties. By default, all public properties are added to the displayed form. Once again, this can be done with as little as one line of code. For example, to create a `DataForm` that allows the user to modify the properties of a particular food, you could simply add the following line of code:

```
CustomFoodDataForm.CurrentItem = new Food(1, "Cheeseburger");
```

If the `Food` class has a `FoodName` property with a public setter method, a `DataForm` like the one shown in Figure 2-3 displays, allowing the user to update the `FoodName`. All this with only one line of code and — most important — no manual creation of a data entry form using `Grid`, `TextBlock`, and `TextBox` controls, as you needed in previous versions of Silverlight.

The default display of the `DataForm` is read-only and, at first, the user cannot make any changes to the data. However, there is a property called `CommandButtonsVisibility` that can be modified in the code behind to have the `DataForm` automatically generate a toolbar with data entry options like Save, Cancel, Edit, etc.

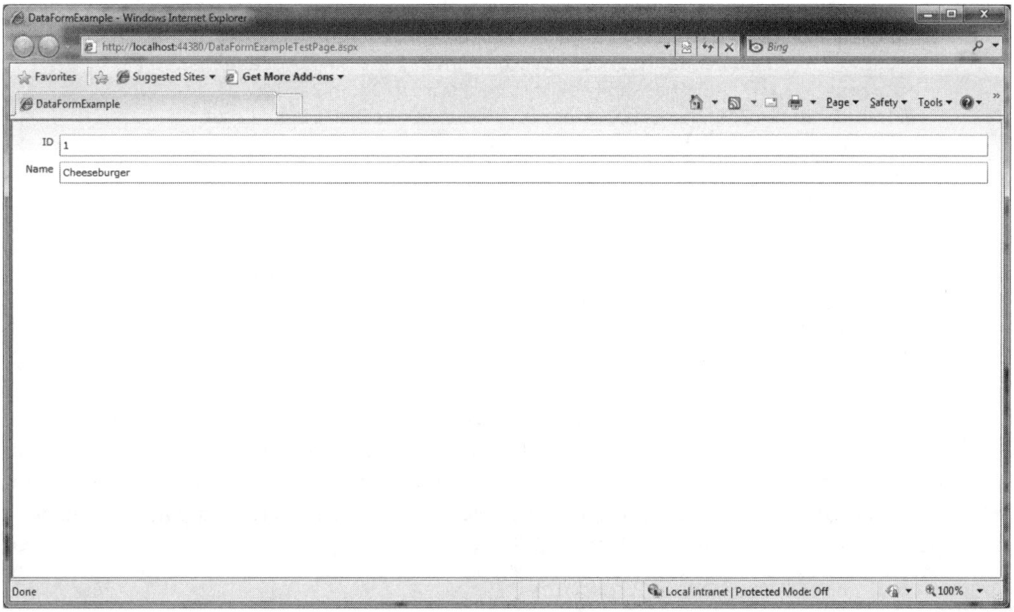

FIGURE 2-3

Although this is a very simple example of how to use the `DataForm`*, I will be providing a much more extensive review of the control in the food, exercise and measurement log chapters. In those chapters, you'll make use of the new* `DataForm` *control to provide users with the capability to not only make changes to entries in those logs, but also create custom foods, exercises, and measurements.*

Providing Paging with the DataPager

Another great addition to Silverlight is the `DataPager` control. This control makes it simple to provide paging of large result sets that are being displayed in a `DataGrid`. Like the `DataForm`, the `DataPager` control resides in the `System.Windows.Controls.Data` assembly. Just make sure to add the reference to the project as well as the namespace to the XAML as you did previously. The property responsible for setting up the paging mechanism is the `Source` property. This property takes a binding expression containing the `Path` and `ElementName` attributes. The `Path` needs to be set to the property of the control that contains the data to be paged, which in most cases will be the `ItemsSource` property of a `DataGrid` control. The `ElementName` attribute is set to the owner of the data source specified in the `Path` attribute earlier. Again, in most cases this will be `DataGrid` control itself. You can also specify the `PageSize` property, which limits the number of displayed rows in the control at any given time. Listing 2-2 builds off of the previous example by adding a `DataPager` declaration to the XAML that hooks up to the `CustomFoodsGrid` declared earlier:

LISTING 2-2: MainPage.xaml (located in the DataPagerExample project)

Available for download on Wrox.com

```
<UserControl x:Class="DataPagerExample.MainPage"
      xmlns="http://schemas.microsoft.com/winfx/2006/xaml/presentation"
      xmlns:x="http://schemas.microsoft.com/winfx/2006/xaml"
      xmlns:d="http://schemas.microsoft.com/expression/blend/2008"
      xmlns:mc="http://schemas.openxmlformats.org/markup-compatibility/2006"
      xmlns:data="clr-
namespace:System.Windows.Controls;assembly=System.Windows.Controls.Data">
      <Grid x:Name="LayoutRoot" Background="White">
            <data:DataGrid x:Name="CustomFoodsGrid" />
            <data:DataPager x:Name="CustomFoodsDataPager" Source="{Binding
ElementName=CustomFoodsGrid, Path=ItemsSource}" PageSize="10" />
      </Grid>
</UserControl>
```

It is important to note that although in the previous example you simply bound a generic `List<Food>` collection to the `DataGrid` to present the data, the `DataPager` requires the data to be stored in an object that implements the new `IPagedCollectionView` interface. If you update the previous example to reflect this change, as well as add enough `Food` objects to the List to create a paging scenario, you will have the following code shown in Listing 2-3:

LISTING 2-3: MainPage.xaml.cs (located in the DataPagerExample project)

Available for download on Wrox.com

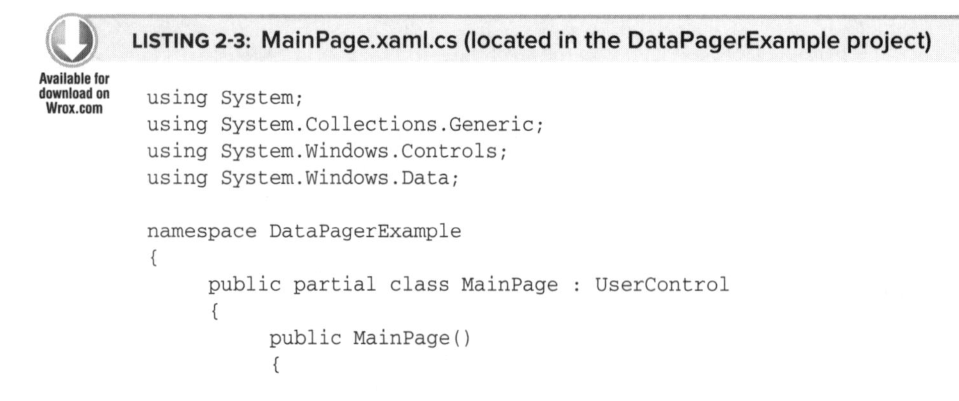

```
using System;
using System.Collections.Generic;
using System.Windows.Controls;
using System.Windows.Data;

namespace DataPagerExample
{
      public partial class MainPage : UserControl
      {
            public MainPage()
            {
```

```
                InitializeComponent();

                List<Food> foods = new List<Food>();

                for (int index = 0; index <= 100; index++)
                    foods.Add(new Food(index, String.Format("Custom Food
{0}", index)));

                CustomFoodsGrid.ItemsSource = new PagedCollectionView(foods);
            }

            public class Food
            {
                public int ID { get; set; }
                public string Name { get; set; }

                public Food(int id, string name)
                {
                    this.ID = id;
                    this.Name = name;
                }
            }
        }
    }
```

As you can see, you simply need to create a large list of `Food` objects and assigning the `List<Food>` to the new `PagedCollectionView`. The `PagedCollectionView` includes a constructor for `IEnumerable` so you can still utilize the generic `List<T>` or any other collection object that implements this interface. Running the example at this point provides you with a `DataGrid` that is now displaying only 10 rows at a time and includes very user-friendly paging controls. Figure 2-4 shows the `DataPager` in action using just the default paging settings and style.

FIGURE 2-4

In this simple example, the paging is taking place on the client so all 100 records are being stored in memory. As you will see in later chapters, when you combine the `DataPager` with the new WCF RIA Services Framework, you will have a very efficient server-side paging mechanism that leaves a small footprint on the client providing the user with a very fluid paging experience.

The `DataPager` is not limited to just the `DataGrid` control either. You could also set up the `Source` property to point to another type of Silverlight control such as a `ListBox` using XAML code similar to the following:

```
<ListBox x:Name="CustomFoodsList" DisplayMemberPath="Name" />
<data_form:DataPager x:Name="CustomFoodsDataPager" Source="{Binding
    ElementName=CustomFoodsList, Path=ItemsSource}"PageSize="10"/>
```

Code snippet MainPage.xaml located in the DataPagerListBoxExample project.

Figure 2-5 demonstrates how the `DataPager` still functions the same as in the previous example even though you are no longer attaching the control to a `DataGrid`.

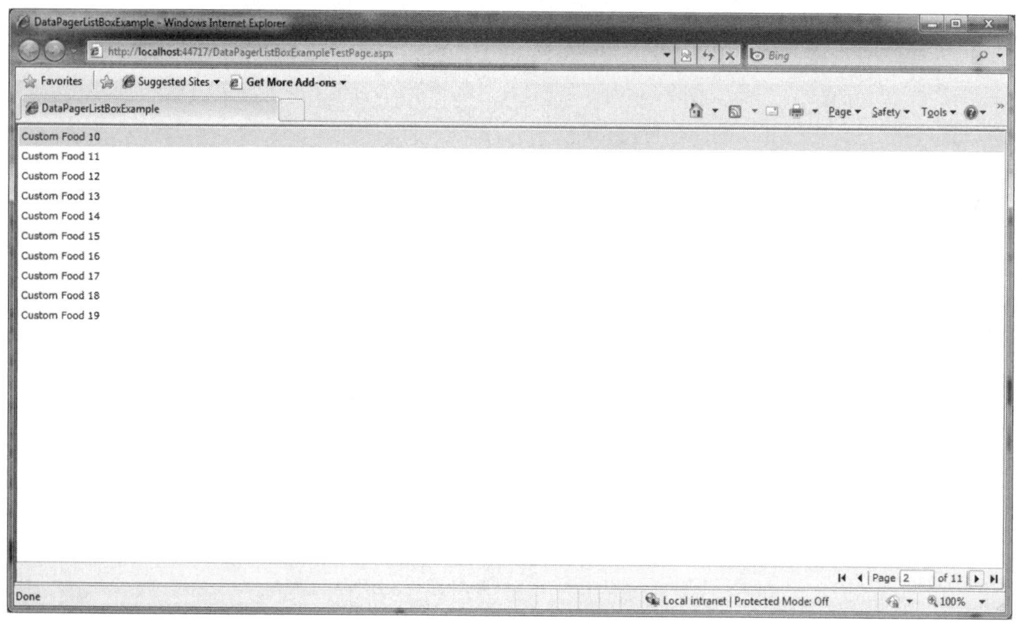

FIGURE 2-5

Element to Element Binding

As you work with Silverlight 4 you may notice that `ElementName` is now a valid attribute in binding expressions of other controls and not just the `DataPager`. The `ElementName` attribute is part of a new feature in Silverlight 4 called Element to Element binding. This allows any Silverlight control to bind to properties of another Silverlight control. This feature can be utilized to provide some interesting possibilities on your site, and it provides the power for the `DataPager` to page data from a variety of source controls. Listing 2-4 shows a simple example of this showing how an `Image` control's size is adjusted by binding to the current value of the slider control. Notice that in Figure 2-6, the image of the book is the default value of the slider or 100; Figure 2-7 shows the image size increases by the value of the slider control as it is adjusted. All of this is done with no work in the code behind. Now this is a pretty trivial example but the feature is clearly very powerful when you combine it with `DataPager` and `DataGrid` controls.

LISTING 2-4: MainPage.xaml (located in the ElementToElementExample project)

Available for download on Wrox.com

```
<UserControl x:Class="ElementToElementExample.MainPage"
     xmlns="http://schemas.microsoft.com/winfx/2006/xaml/presentation"
     xmlns:x="http://schemas.microsoft.com/winfx/2006/xaml"
     xmlns:d="http://schemas.microsoft.com/expression/blend/2008"
     xmlns:mc="http://schemas.openxmlformats.org/markup-compatibility/2006">

     <Grid x:Name="LayoutRoot" Background="White">
          <StackPanel>
               <Image x:Name="WroxImage" Source="Images/Wrox.jpg"
Height="{Binding ElementName=AdjustSize, Path=Value}"
Width="{Binding ElementName=AdjustSize, Path=Value}" />
               <Slider x:Name="AdjustSize" Maximum="1000" Minimum="0"
Value="100" />
          </StackPanel>
     </Grid>
</UserControl>
```

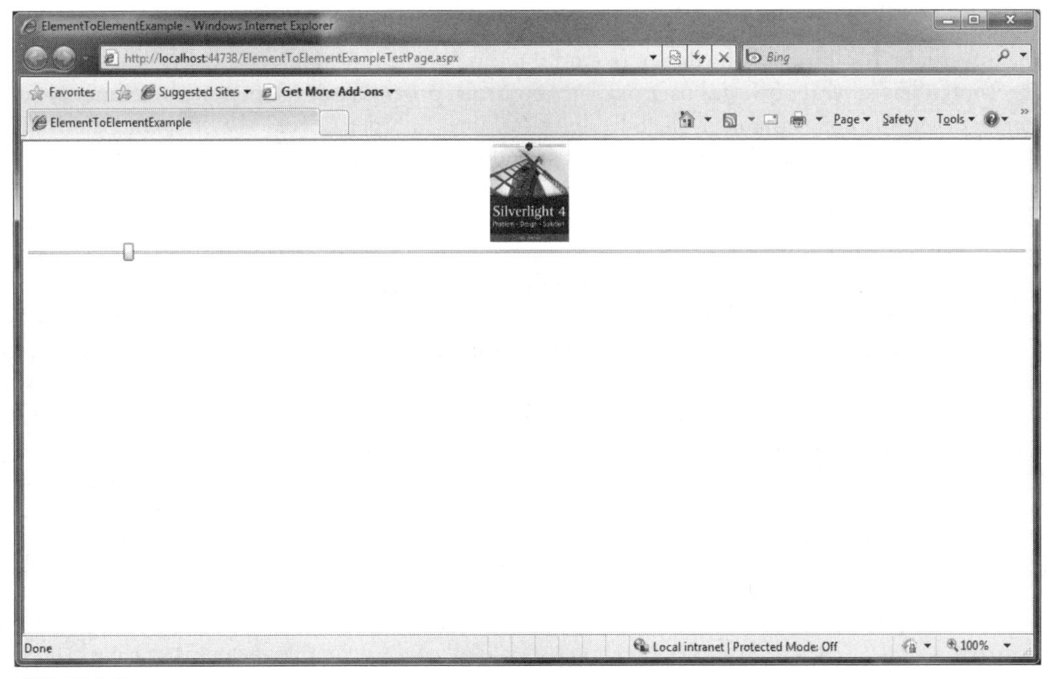

FIGURE 2-6

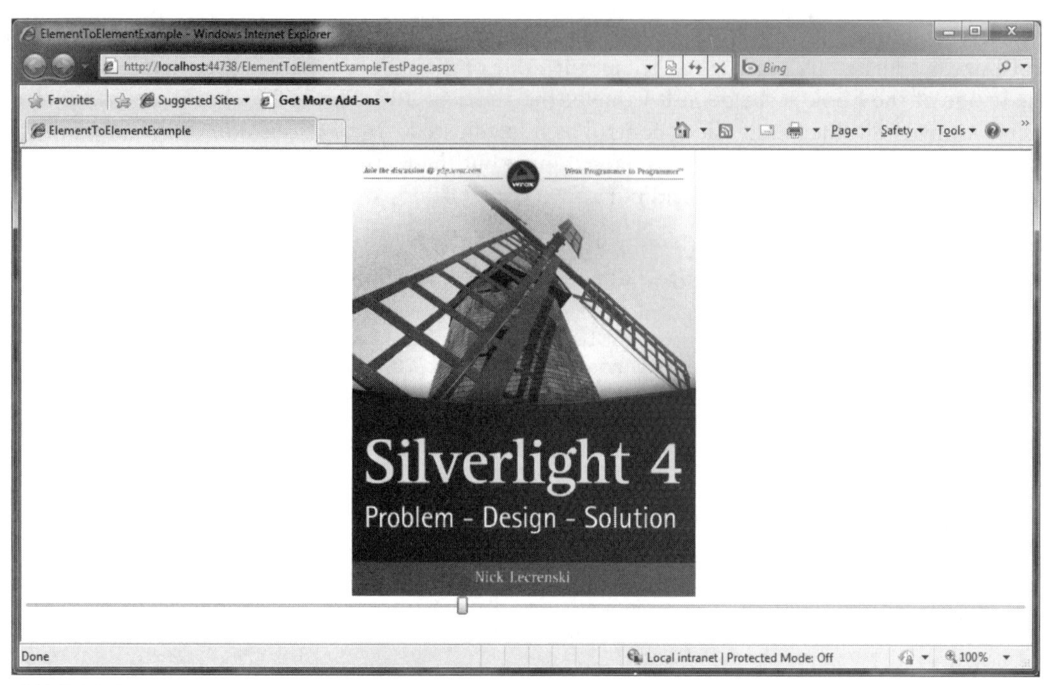

FIGURE 2-7

Silverlight Toolkit

The Silverlight Toolkit made its debut around the time of the initial Silverlight 2 release to web. The Toolkit has several powerful user interface controls, providing developers with additional functionality that was not available in the Silverlight runtime. In order to keep the download size of the Silverlight runtime small, some controls that had been left out were made available through the Toolkit instead. This way, the runtime installation size would not have to grow but developers who wish to utilize the controls can include the libraries in their XAP files. The Toolkit is an open source project that is available at `http://codeplex.com/silverlight`. To strike a balance between providing early versions of controls for feedback and assuring that controls were considered finished, the developers of the Toolkit decided to separate all of the controls into four unique quality bands. These bands are called Mature/SDK, Stable, Preview, and Experimental respectively. By placing the various controls in these bands, developers could make informed decisions about which controls to include in their own mission critical projects. Although it is an open source project it is important to note that the main development team of the Toolkit is composed of Microsoft developers. You can still feel free to contribute to the project and Microsoft has made available both the binary and full source code versions of the Toolkit. As you will see, this Toolkit will become instrumental to the FitnessTrackerPlus application and you will need to become very familiar with a majority of the controls that are included in the Toolkit.

As you develop FitnessTrackerPlus, you will utilize the `AutoCompleteBox`, `DockPanel`, `WrapPanel`, `Accordion`, `Charting`, `TimePicker`, `TimeUpDown`, and all of the available themes that have been generated for the Toolkit. Of course, a host of third-party toolkits is readily available from manufactures such as Infragistics, Telerik, and ComponentArt. Many of these third-party libraries provide similar controls or even more advanced versions of the ones available in the toolkit. When developing your own line-of-business solutions, you may find that a third-party toolkit is a better choice for adding rich Silverlight controls to your user interface. For the FitnessTrackerPlus application, the Silverlight Toolkit provides a benefit that these others simply can't beat — price. The Toolkit is 100 percent free to use and even modify if you wish. It is tough to beat free, and that is why I recommend the use of the Toolkit throughout this book. Now that you have some background on the benefits of the Toolkit, it's time to look at one of its largest features, themes, in a little more detail.

Providing Users with Multiple Themes

When I first started programming, I was very much interested in video game programming. I purchased every single book on creating video games in C++ and DirectX that hit the shelf. I was completely convinced that by reading these and understanding the fundamentals of 3D graphics, I too could create a video game. Unfortunately there is a side of video game programming that I simply neglected to think about during all my excitement, or perhaps chose to ignore because it wasn't that important in line of business applications at the time. The ugly side of video game development was not an impossible-to-understand API, or even matrix multiplication and pixel shading algorithms. Those things I had a chance of actually learning although it might take a considerable amount of time. The aspect of game development that I had underestimated was graphics. I'm not talking about creating the next Halo here; I'm talking about something as simple as Pac-Man. I simply cannot draw video game artwork. At that point, I realized something important that would apply for years to come when creating user interfaces, especially in line of business applications. I am not a designer. I am a developer period. Despite this fact I don't long for the days when gray boring MFC and Visual Basic forms development were the norm and completely acceptable to clients. I actually enjoy the fact that user interfaces have taken a giant step graphically. This is why I was so excited to see the new prebuilt themes that were added to the Silverlight Toolkit. Don't get me wrong — there is no substitution for a professional designer, and you may find that you can create slick user interfaces as easily as any professional designer can. I, however, find the new themes a great way to create a decent-looking user interface without having to recruit the help of a designer, at least not right away.

The requirements for the FitnessTrackerPlus application state that users should be able to select from several available themes. The Toolkit offers 11 themes to choose from so you will be utilizing these as the starting point for styling of the user interface. If you have an artistic ability, you can feel free to alter these or perhaps even add some new themes as you are working on the application. To satisfy the theme requirement, you will be providing users the ability to select from available themes on the fitness dashboard page. This page will be available to the users after a successful logon. You can utilize the new themes in several different ways. The easiest way to add theme support is to wrap existing controls in your XAML with one of the prebuilt theme tags. This can be done by first adding a reference to the main theming DLL found in `Microsoft.Windows.Controls.Theming`. This DLL is required when using any of the themes included in the Toolkit. In addition to this reference, you will need to add references to all of the themes that you wish to make use of. You will be making all of the themes available to your users in FitnessTrackerPlus so you should add references in the project to all of the following themes:

- `Microsoft.Windows.Controls.Theming.BubbleCream`
- `Microsoft.Windows.Controls.Theming.BureauBlack`

- `Microsoft.Windows.Controls.Theming.BureauBlue`
- `Microsoft.Windows.Controls.Theming.ExpressionDark`
- `Microsoft.Windows.Controls.Theming.ExpressionLight`
- `Microsoft.Windows.Controls.Theming.RainierOrange`
- `Microsoft.Windows.Controls.Theming.RainierPurple`
- `Microsoft.Windows.Controls.Theming.ShinyBlue`
- `Microsoft.Windows.Controls.Theming.ShinyRed`
- `Microsoft.Windows.Controls.Theming.TwilightBlue`
- `Microsoft.Windows.Controls.Theming.WhistlerBlue`

With all of the references added, you can see the various themes in action by adding the appropriate namespace definitions and wrapping some of the various Silverlight controls with the various theme tags that are available. Listing 2-5 demonstrates a simple example of the `ShinyRed`, `ShinyBlue`, `BureauBlack`, and `BubbleCream` themes being applied against some basic Silverlight controls such as the `Slider`, `TextBox`, `Calendar`, and `Button`.

LISTING 2-5: MainPage.xaml (located in the BasicThemingExample project)

Available for download on Wrox.com

```
<UserControl x:Class="BasicThemingExample.MainPage"
     xmlns="http://schemas.microsoft.com/winfx/2006/xaml/presentation"
     xmlns:x="http://schemas.microsoft.com/winfx/2006/xaml"
     xmlns:controls="clr-
namespace:System.Windows.Controls;assembly=System.Windows.Controls"
     xmlns:shiny_red="clr-namespace:System.Windows.Controls.Theming;
assembly=System.Windows.Controls.Theming.ShinyRed"
     xmlns:shiny_blue="clr-namespace:System.Windows.Controls.Theming;
assembly=System.Windows.Controls.Theming.ShinyBlue"
     xmlns:bubble_cream="clr-namespace:System.Windows.Controls.Theming;
assembly=System.Windows.Controls.Theming.BubbleCreme"
     xmlns:bureau_black="clr-namespace:System.Windows.Controls.Theming;
assembly=System.Windows.Controls.Theming.BureauBlack">
<Grid x:Name="LayoutRoot">
     <Grid.ColumnDefinitions>
          <ColumnDefinition />
          <ColumnDefinition />
     </Grid.ColumnDefinitions>
     <Grid.RowDefinitions>
          <RowDefinition />
          <RowDefinition />
     </Grid.RowDefinitions>
     <shiny_blue:ShinyBlueTheme Grid.Column="0" Grid.Row="0">
          <StackPanel>
               <StackPanel Orientation="Horizontal">
                    <Button Content="Shiny Blue Button" />
                    <TextBox Margin="10,0,0,0" Width="200" Text="Styled TextBox" />
```

```
                </StackPanel>
                <StackPanel Orientation="Horizontal">
                    <TextBlock Text="Slider" />
                    <Slider Margin="10,0,0,0" Maximum="100" Minimum="0"
Value="0" />
                </StackPanel>
                <controls:Calendar />
            </StackPanel>
        </shiny_blue:ShinyBlueTheme>
        <shiny_red:ShinyRedTheme Grid.Column="1" Grid.Row="0">
            <StackPanel>
                <StackPanel Orientation="Horizontal">
                    <Button Content="Shiny Red Button" />
                    <TextBox Margin="10,0,0,0" Width="200" Text="Styled TextBox" />
                </StackPanel>
                <StackPanel Orientation="Horizontal">
                    <TextBlock Text="Slider" />
                    <Slider Margin="10,0,0,0" Maximum="100" Minimum="0"
Value="0" />
                </StackPanel>
                <controls:Calendar />
            </StackPanel>
        </shiny_red:ShinyRedTheme>
        <bubble_cream:BubbleCremeTheme Grid.Column="0" Grid.Row="1">
            <StackPanel>
                <StackPanel Orientation="Horizontal">
                    <Button Content="Bubble Cream Button" />
                    <TextBox Margin="10,0,0,0" Width="200" Text="Styled TextBox" />
                </StackPanel>
                <StackPanel Orientation="Horizontal">
                    <TextBlock Text="Slider" />
                    <Slider Margin="10,0,0,0" Maximum="100" Minimum="0"
Value="0" />
                </StackPanel>
                <controls:Calendar />
            </StackPanel>
        </bubble_cream:BubbleCremeTheme>
        <bureau_black:BureauBlackTheme Grid.Column="1" Grid.Row="2">
            <StackPanel>
                <StackPanel Orientation="Horizontal">
                    <Button Content="Bureau Black Button" />
                    <TextBox Margin="10,0,0,0" Width="200" Text="Styled TextBox" />
                </StackPanel>
                <StackPanel Orientation="Horizontal">
                    <TextBlock Text="Slider" />
                    <Slider Margin="10,0,0,0" Maximum="100" Minimum="0"
Value="0" />
                </StackPanel>
                <controls:Calendar />
            </StackPanel>
        </bureau_black:BureauBlackTheme>
</Grid>
</UserControl>
```

Running this example will leave you with the screen shown in Figure 2-8.

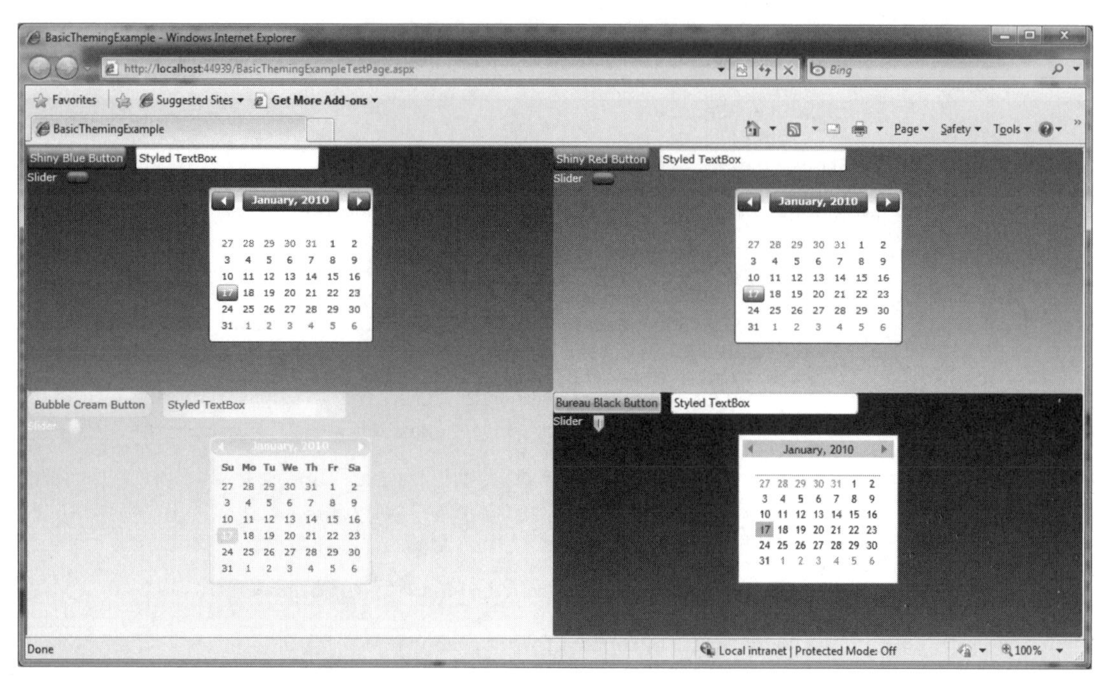

FIGURE 2-8

Although this is one way to utilize the new themes in the Toolkit, it is not terribly useful for the application that you will be building in this book. Your users will need the ability to switch themes at any point they are using the application. The preceding method of theming can be utilized by wrapping all the controls of FitnessTrackerPlus into a selected theme, but there is no way to change the theme because it is declared in XAML only.

Implicit Styling

A new addition to Silverlight 4 is the concept of *Implicit Styling*. This powerful new feature allows you to create a single style and apply it to all controls of a certain type. For example, several `Button` controls were added to a `StackPanel` in the following code along with both an implicit style declaration and an explicit style declaration that will only affect one of the `Button` controls.

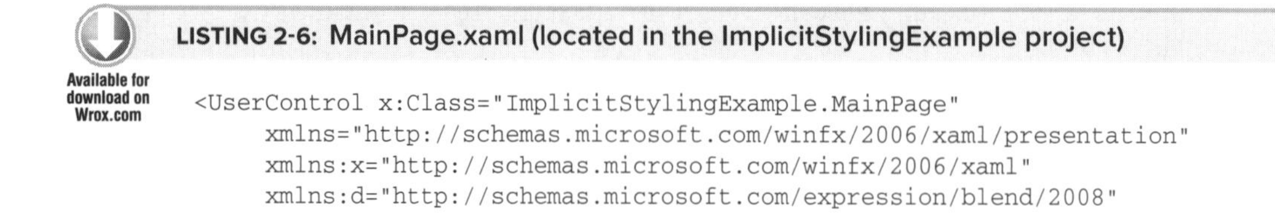

LISTING 2-6: MainPage.xaml (located in the ImplicitStylingExample project)

Available for download on Wrox.com

```
<UserControl x:Class="ImplicitStylingExample.MainPage"
     xmlns="http://schemas.microsoft.com/winfx/2006/xaml/presentation"
     xmlns:x="http://schemas.microsoft.com/winfx/2006/xaml"
     xmlns:d="http://schemas.microsoft.com/expression/blend/2008"
```

```
    xmlns:mc="http://schemas.openxmlformats.org/markup-compatibility/2006">

    <Grid x:Name="LayoutRoot" Background="White">
        <Grid.Resources>
            <Style TargetType="Button">
                <Setter Property="Background" Value="Green"/>
                <Setter Property="Foreground" Value="Blue"/>
                <Setter Property="FontWeight" Value="Bold"/>
                <Setter Property="Width" Value="200" />
                <Setter Property="Height" Value="60" />
                <Setter Property="Margin" Value="10" />
            </Style>
            <Style x:Key="ExplicitButtonStyle" TargetType="Button">
                <Setter Property="Background" Value="Blue"/>
                <Setter Property="Foreground" Value="Red"/>
                <Setter Property="Width" Value="300" />
                <Setter Property="Height" Value="100" />
            </Style>
        </Grid.Resources>
        <StackPanel>
            <Button Content="Implicitly Styled" />
            <Button Content="Implicitly Styled" />
            <Button Content="Implicitly Styled" />
            <Button Content="Explicitly Styled" Style="{StaticResource
ExplicitButtonStyle}" />
        </StackPanel>
    </Grid>
</UserControl>
```

As you can see, a `Style` has been declared without a key defined that targets `Button` Controls. With the new Implicit Styling feature, all `Button` controls that are part of the `Grid` control will automatically inherit this style unless an explicit style declaration is added to the `Button` control. Figure 2-9 shows the first three `Button` controls all have the same `Width`, `Height`, `Margin`, `Background`, and `Foreground` property values whereas the lone Explicitly Styled `Button` control differs.

Dynamic Theme Selection

The new Implicit Styling feature in Silverlight 4 is instrumental in allowing you a quick and easy way to let your users dynamically select an overall theme for the application. Previously, you saw that in order to use the Toolkit themes, you had to wrap all of your application controls with one of the predefined theme tags in XAML. In the latest version of the Toolkit, all of these themes have implicit styles set for all controls; dynamically changing the current theme is as simple as removing the current theme, adding a new instance of the theme the user is selecting and setting the theme's `Content` property to the child controls of your application. Let's take a look at an example that shows this in action.

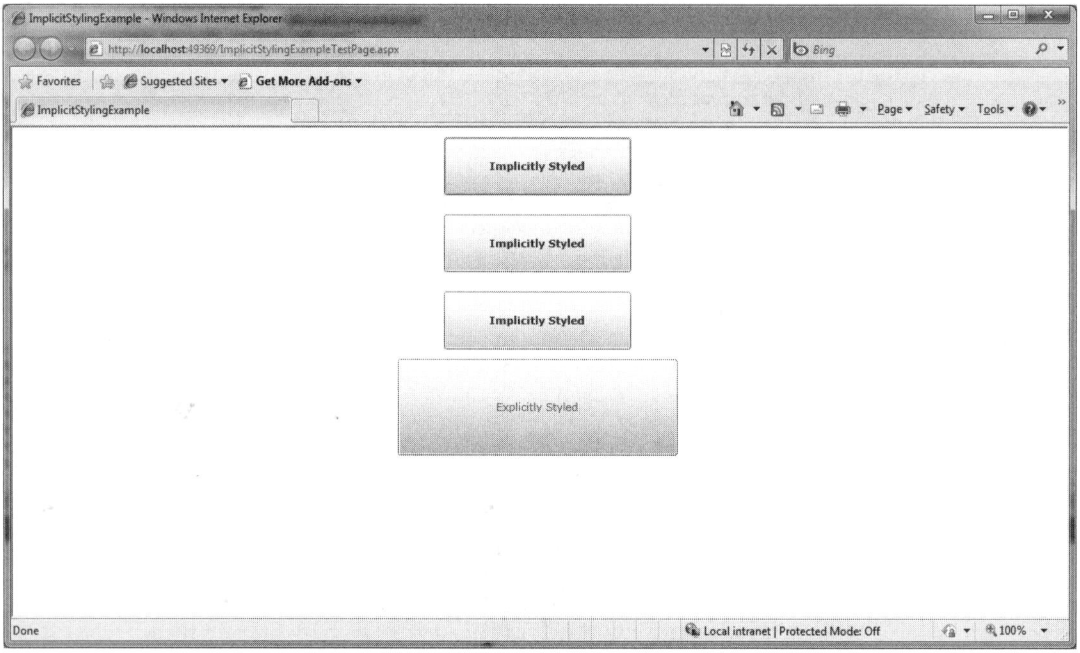

FIGURE 2-9

For starters you should create a new Silverlight Application project and add a new `UserControl` called Controls.xaml. Listing 2-7 shows the XAML code required for this, and as you can see it simply adds several Silverlight controls with no `Style` properties set.

LISTING 2-7: Controls.xaml (located in the DynamicStylingExample project)

Available for download on Wrox.com

```
<UserControl x:Class="DynamicStylingExample.Controls"
     xmlns="http://schemas.microsoft.com/winfx/2006/xaml/presentation"
     xmlns:x="http://schemas.microsoft.com/winfx/2006/xaml"
     xmlns:d="http://schemas.microsoft.com/expression/blend/2008"
     xmlns:mc="http://schemas.openxmlformats.org/markup-compatibility/2006"
     xmlns:data="clr-
namespace:System.Windows.Controls;assembly=System.Windows.Controls.Data"
     xmlns:controls="clr-
namespace:System.Windows.Controls;assembly=System.Windows.Controls">

     <StackPanel x:Name="ControlsRoot">
          <StackPanel Orientation="Horizontal" Margin="0,10">
               <Button Content="Button Control" />
               <TextBox Margin="10,0,0,0" Width="200"
Text="Styled TextBox" />
          </StackPanel>
          <StackPanel Orientation="Horizontal" Margin="0,10">
               <Slider Margin="10,0,0,0" Maximum="100" Minimum="0"
Value="0" />
```

```
            </StackPanel>
            <data:DataGrid x:Name="CustomFoodsGrid" Margin="0,10" />
            <controls:Calendar Margin="0,10" />
        </StackPanel>
    </UserControl>
```

Now in the MainPage.xaml file you simply add a `ComboBox` control that will give the user the ability to select a theme. In addition to this, Listing 2-8 adds an instance of the `Controls` class with no theme set initially.

LISTING 2-8: MainPage.xaml (located in the DynamicStylingExample project)

Available for download on Wrox.com

```
<UserControl x:Class="DynamicStylingExample.MainPage"
    xmlns="http://schemas.microsoft.com/winfx/2006/xaml/presentation"
    xmlns:x="http://schemas.microsoft.com/winfx/2006/xaml"
    xmlns:dynamic="clr-namespace:DynamicStylingExample">
    <Grid x:Name="LayoutRoot">
        <StackPanel x:Name="MainPanel">
            <ComboBox x:Name="ThemeList">
                <ComboBox.ItemTemplate>
                    <DataTemplate>
                        <TextBlock Text="{Binding ThemeName}" />
                    </DataTemplate>
                </ComboBox.ItemTemplate>
            </ComboBox>
            <dynamic:Controls x:Name="Controls" />
        </StackPanel>
    </Grid>
</UserControl>
```

Before writing any code to support the theme switching, you first need to add references to all of the theme DLL files that you want to support. Once this is done, you can start populating the `ComboBox` with a list of available themes. In previous versions of Silverlight you were required to make use of the `ImplicitStyleManager` class to dynamically change the current theme. Since Implicit Styles are supported now by default in Silverlight 4, the `ImplicitStyleManager` class has been removed from the Silverlight Toolkit.

In the code behind, you need to first populate the `ComboBox` with a class that represents the theme to be selected. You should add a `ThemeSelector` class with two properties: a `string` to hold the name of the theme and a `ContentControl` property to hold an instance of the theme object to be used. When created in the code behind, all the theme objects are instantiated as `ContentControl` objects. The following code shows the `ThemeSelector` class that is used.

Available for download on Wrox.com

```
public class ThemeSelector
{
    public string ThemeName { get; set; }
    public ContentControl Theme { get; set; }
}
```

Code snippet MainPage.xaml.cs located in the DynamicStylingExample project

Once you have the class defined, you need to add a new method to populate the `ComboBox` control with all the available themes. In the following code, the `LoadThemeList` method creates a new `List<ThemeSelector>` object and adds new instances of the class using the `System.Windows.Controls.Theming` object for the `Theme` property. This method is called in the constructor of the `MainPage` class so the list is populated and available to the user when the application is run.

Available for download on Wrox.com

```
private void LoadThemeList()
{
     List<ThemeSelector> themes = new List<ThemeSelector>();

     themes.Add(new ThemeSelector { ThemeName = "BubbleCreme",
Theme = new BubbleCremeTheme() });
     themes.Add(new ThemeSelector { ThemeName = "BureauBlack",
Theme = new BureauBlackTheme() });
     themes.Add(new ThemeSelector { ThemeName = "BureauBlue",
Theme = new BureauBlueTheme() });
     themes.Add(new ThemeSelector { ThemeName = "ExpressionDark",
Theme = new ExpressionDarkTheme() });
     themes.Add(new ThemeSelector { ThemeName = "ExpressionLight",
Theme = new ExpressionLightTheme() });
     themes.Add(new ThemeSelector { ThemeName = "RainierOrange",
Theme = new RainierOrangeTheme() });
     themes.Add(new ThemeSelector { ThemeName = "RainierPurple",
Theme = new RainierPurpleTheme() });
     themes.Add(new ThemeSelector { ThemeName = "ShinyBlue",
Theme = new ShinyBlueTheme() });
     themes.Add(new ThemeSelector { ThemeName = "ShinyRed",
Theme = new ShinyRedTheme() });
     themes.Add(new ThemeSelector { ThemeName = "TwilightBlue",
Theme = new TwilightBlueTheme() });
     themes.Add(new ThemeSelector { ThemeName = "WhistlerBlue",
Theme = new WhistlerBlueTheme() });

     ThemeList.ItemsSource = themes;
}
```

Code snippet MainPage.xaml.cs located in the DynamicStylingExample project

With the `ComboBox` populated you now simply need to handle the `SelectionChangedEvent` and switch the currently displayed theme. In the following code, the selected theme is extracted from the `ComboBox` selection. Next, the `Content` property is set to a new instance of the `Controls` object that contains all of the Silverlight controls that need to be themed in this application. Finally, the existing `Controls` object is removed from the visual tree and the new themed version of the `Controls` object is added in its place. This process is repeated every time the user selects a new theme.

Available for download on Wrox.com

```
private void ThemeList_SelectionChanged(object sender,
SelectionChangedEventArgs e)
{
     ContentControl theme = ((sender as ComboBox).SelectedItem as
ThemeSelector).Theme;
     theme.Content = new Controls();

     MainPanel.Children.RemoveAt(1);
```

```
        MainPanel.Children.Add(theme);
    }
```

Code snippet MainPage.xaml.cs located in the DynamicStylingExample project

As you can see, there really isn't much to it other than creating an instance of the desired theme object, setting the `Content` property to all of the controls you need to display, and finally adding that newly themed content back into the visual control tree. Figure 2-10 shows the theme selection options that the user now has.

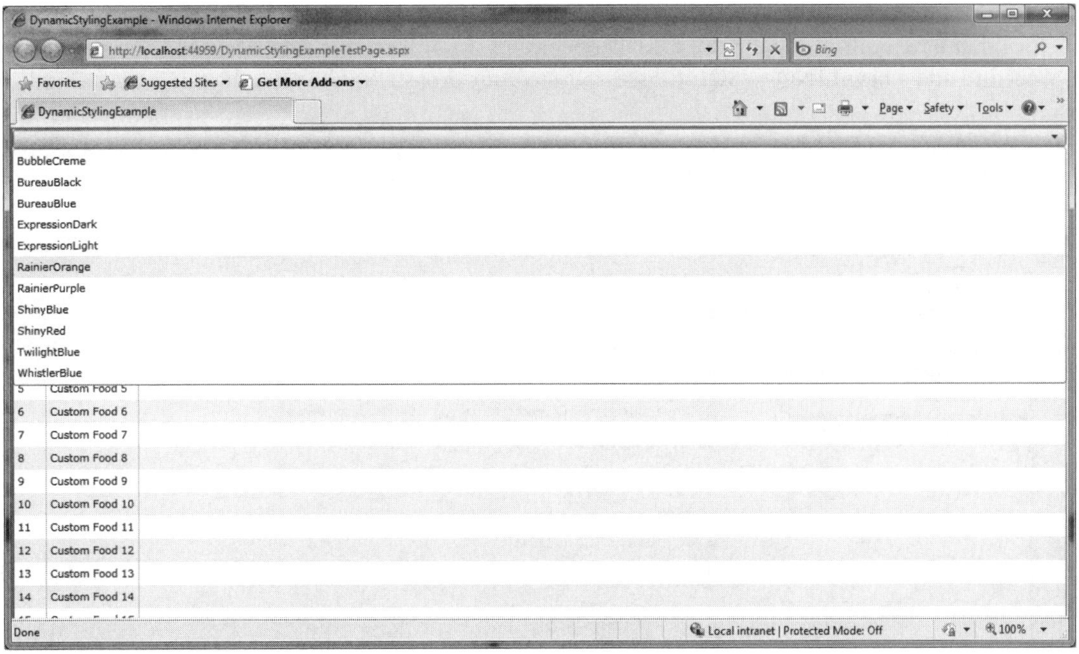

FIGURE 2-10

Data Access Layer

There are several different ways to approach the data access layer when building N-Tier Silverlight applications. Of course, you could use the traditional method of creating custom business objects that interact with a database layer based on ADO.NET. This has been one of the standard methods of data access layer for years now in ASP.NET applications. Providing you utilize WCF- or ASMX-based web services to transport your business objects, you could continue to use an ADO.NET data access layer just fine. A properly designed layer usually lets you change the underlying database easily without making any changes to the business objects. This along with support for multiple database vendors has made ADO.NET a powerful platform for the data access layer. In recent years, there has been a bit of a shift in data access technology away from straight ADO.NET programming and into the world of object relational mapping tools or ORM as a means of data access. Countless ORM tools are available for .NET programming and it would take an entire book to cover even some of them in any depth. I will, however, be covering the basics of two ORM technologies from Microsoft that have been optimized specifically for easy integration into Silverlight and ASP.NET application development.

LINQ to SQL

Microsoft's first foray into the ORM space was LINQ to SQL. This technology provides a simple drag-and-drop interface to create a data access layer. With LINQ to SQL, you can simply open a connection to your database and drag and drop tables onto the design form creating extensible entities that have built-in support for CRUD operations. In order to get started using LINQ to SQL, you need to add a new LINQ to SQL Classes item to your project, as shown in Figure 2-11.

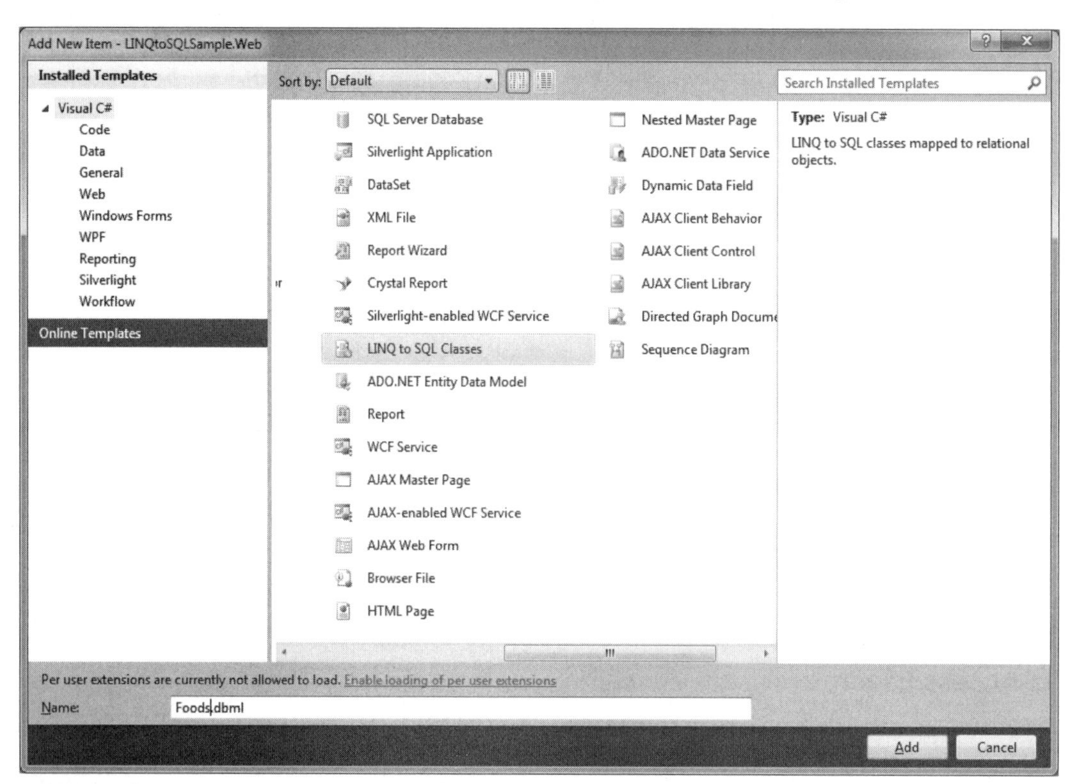

FIGURE 2-11

In this example, a Foods.dbml file is added to the project. If you expand this file you will see a Foods.dbml.layout file and a Foods.designer.cs file. The layout file is the visual form where you drag table definitions. The designer file includes the generated entity classes that are automatically built when you drag a table onto the form. These entity classes are marked as partial so extending them is as simple as creating an additional class file and ensuring that your extension class is marked with the same class name as the entity and the partial declaration precedes it. The power of using a tool like this is that you no longer have to create custom business objects along with ADO.NET plumbing code in order to provide basic CRUD operations for your entities. With the .dbml file open, you should open the FitnessTrackerPlus.mdf file in the App_Data folder of the LINQtoSQLSample project and add the foods table to the form as shown in Figure 2-12.

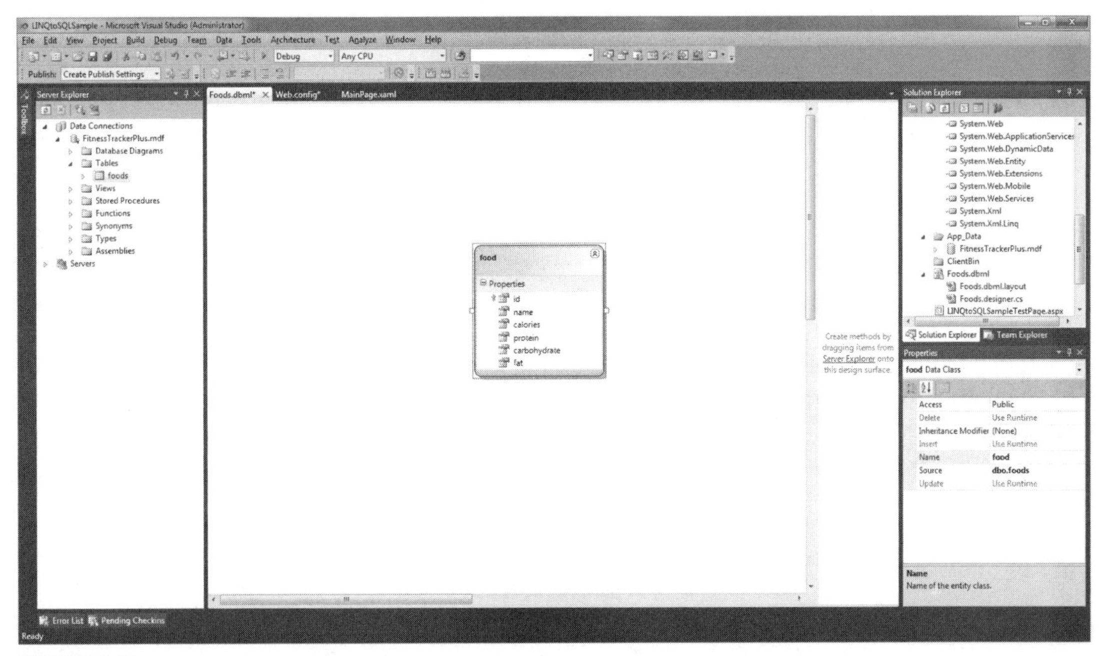

FIGURE 2-12

If you take a look at the Foods.designer.cs file in the ASP.NET project now, you will see that entity classes have been generated for foods table that was dragged onto the form.

If you examine the Foods.designer.cs file you will see that LINQ to SQL has created a partial class that really works well as a complete business object for the food type. Every column in the table is represented by a property, complete with an implementation of `INotifyPropertyChanged`, which will allow controls such as the `DataGrid` to automatically update its current values when these properties are changed for the food object. If the table had any foreign key relationships, they would have been marked with the `Association` attribute. This attribute provides you with the capability to quickly access the full object representing the association without your having to create a separate SQL query. Earlier I discussed how the classes generated by LINQ to SQL are extensible. In addition to the associations, several extensibility methods are generated for you that can easily be overloaded in your own partial class implementations. The following code shows the extensibility methods that are generated for the Foods.designer.cs file.

Available for download on Wrox.com

```
#region Extensibility Method Definitions
    partial void OnLoaded();
    partial void OnValidate(System.Data.Linq.ChangeAction action);
    partial void OnCreated();
    partial void OnidChanging(int value);
    partial void OnidChanged();
    partial void OnnameChanging(string value);
    partial void OnnameChanged();
    partial void OncaloriesChanging(System.Nullable<double> value);
    partial void OncaloriesChanged();
    partial void OnproteinChanging(System.Nullable<double> value);
    partial void OnproteinChanged();
    partial void OncarbohydrateChanging(System.Nullable<double> value);
    partial void OncarbohydrateChanged();
    partial void OnfatChanging(System.Nullable<double> value);
    partial void OnfatChanged();
#endregion
```

Code snippet Foods.designer.cs located in the LINQtoSQLSample project

By overloading the `OnValidate` method, you can easily add custom validation logic to the generated entity. Let's say a user has created a new custom food that needs to be added to the database. You would want to ensure that a food name has been entered on the object. The `OnValidate` method provides a `System.Data.Linq.ChangeAction` enumeration that will tell you what operation is about to be performed on the object. An example of this is illustrated in the following code:

```
partial void OnValidate(ChangeAction action)
{
    If (!ValidateFood(this))
        throw new ApplicationException("Validation failed for custom food");
}
```

In this example, a `ValidateFood` method is called and, if validation fails, an `ApplicationException` is thrown preventing the new food from being persisted to the database.

In order to access these entity classes you need to make use of the generated `DataContext` object. Once you create an instance of this object, you can easily use LINQ queries to access the requested data. The beauty of this is that the `DataContext` takes care of opening and closing the database connection as well as generating all of the necessary T-SQL statements that are required to retrieve the requested data. This is the most significant feature of using one of these newer ORM technologies as your data access layer. Instead of creating complex SQL queries, you can concentrate on requesting data in a much more object-oriented manner. For example, with a relatively simple LINQ query, you can easily retrieve all of the foods in the database that include the word "RICE":

Available for download on Wrox.com

```
public List<food> SearchFoods()
{
    List<food> foods = new List<food>();

    using (FoodsDataContext context = new FoodsDataContext())
    {
        var result = (from f in context.foods
                      where f.name.ToUpper().Contains("RICE")
```

```
                        select f);

            foods = result.ToList<food>();
        }

        return foods;
    }
```

Code snippet FoodService.svc.cs located in the LINQtoSQLSample project

Attempting to do this in a stored procedure or embedded T-SQL would not have been nearly as straightforward, depending on your familiarity with T-SQL syntax. You are, however, most likely familiar with the .NET runtime methods that are available, and being able to make use of `String` methods such as `IndexOf` in order to perform data queries is an extremely powerful function of LINQ.

Updating data in LINQ to SQL is just as easy as querying data. With just a few lines of code, you can save business object changes to the database. All you need to do is update the object properties and call the `SubmitChanges` method of the `DataContext`, as follows:

Available for download on Wrox.com

```
    public void UpdateFoods()
    {
        using (FoodsDataContext context = new FoodsDataContext())
        {
            food firstFood = (from f in context.foods
                              where f.id == 1
                              select f).First<food>();

            firstFood.calories = 100;
            context.SubmitChanges();
        }
    }
```

Code snippet FoodService.svc.cs located in the LINQtoSQLSample project

In a disconnected scenario such as when a Silverlight client calls business logic in web services, the preceding `SubmitChanges` call will not work. The `DataContext` does not automatically handle change tracking in disconnected scenarios. In order to have this working in a Silverlight client, you will need to add a call to the `Attach` method of the `DataContext` before submitting the changes. LINQ to SQL supports optimistic concurrency to perform database updates. There are a couple of options to consider when handling concurrency issues with LINQ to SQL. If you already have a timestamp field in your database tables, LINQ to SQL will use it when handling concurrency issues. In this case, you would pass the value of `True` when calling the `Attach` method and if a conflict occurred, a `ChangeConflictException` would be thrown. An example of this is demonstrated in the following code:

```
    public bool UpdateCustomFood(food customFood)
    {

        bool result = false;

        using (DataLayerDataContext context = new DataLayerDataContect())
        {
```

```
            context.foods.Attach(customFood, true);

            try
            {
                context.SubmitChanges();
                result = true;
            }
            catch (ChangeConflictException e)
            {
                // Handle the change conflict here
            }
            return result;
        }
    }
```

Now if you did not have a timestamp available, you would have a couple of choices. You can either pass in both a copy of the new object along with the original or you can choose to have LINQ to SQL ignore concurrency altogether. Here is the same update method that sends back a copy of the original object along with the updated version:

```
    public bool UpdateCustomFood(Food original, Food updated)
    {

        bool result = false;

        using (DataLayerDataContext context = new DataLayerDataContect())
        {
            context.foods.Attach(original, false);

            original.name = updated.name;
            try
            {
                context.SubmitChanges();
                result = true;
            }
            catch (ChangeConflictException e)
            {
                // Handle the change conflict here
            }
            return result;
        }
    }
```

In this example, the parameter to the `Attach` method is false, which tells LINQ to SQL that you are attaching a copy of the original, unmodified object.

What if you decide that you don't want to worry about concurrency? In the FitnessTrackerPlus application, concurrency really isn't an issue as every operation is on a single per user basis. There are no cases where multiple users will be modifying the same record. In this specific scenario it is probably best to have LINQ to SQL ignore concurrency issues completely. If you look at the properties for the database table columns in the DBML designer you will see a property called `UpdateCheck`. You can select all of the columns in the table and set this value to `Never`. This will tell LINQ to

SQL to ignore all concurrency checks. Although you can get away with this, for FitnessTrackerPlus most line of business applications will have to deal with concurrency issues so in your own solutions you will most likely leave this property alone and either add a timestamp field to your database table or pass in both the original and modified versions of the objects to the `Attach` method of the `DataContext` before calling `SubmitChanges`.

Okay, so this LINQ to SQL thing looks great as a potential data access layer. You may be asking what the catch is. Well the catch is that there is only one provider for LINQ to SQL and that is SQL Server. Although it seemed like a future version of LINQ to SQL was going to be extensible and allow for third-party driver support, this did not happen. Because the extensibility modifications were never made, LINQ to SQL even now supports only working with SQL Server databases. Obviously, this is a large item to consider when designing your application; if you need a data access layer that supports Oracle or MySQL or any other database for that matter, you will not be able to utilize this great tool.

Entity Framework

The Entity Framework is the latest data access layer technology available for .NET programming. There are many important benefits to the Entity Framework, not the least of which is the ability to change the underlying data store to something other than SQL Server. Third-party database support is starting to gain traction and you can find Entity Framework providers for Oracle, DB2, MySQL, and others at the time of this writing. It should also be noted that although the official response from Redmond is that LINQ to SQL will continue to be supported and enhancements to the platform will be made based on customer feedback, Microsoft has planned many of their new .NET 4 technologies around the Entity Framework. Future support for a platform should always be something that you consider before making any investment in a technology platform, especially your data access layer. As you try to understand the Entity Framework features, it's helpful to have a quick comparison of the features that LINQ to SQL offers to determine which is the correct technology choice for your application. Table 2-2 covers some of the main differences between LINQ to SQL and the Entity Framework.

TABLE 2-2: LINQ to SQL versus Entity Framework

FEATURE	LINQ TO SQL	ENTITY FRAMEWORK
Database Support	SQL Server	SQL Server, Oracle, DB2, Sybase, MySQL and any other third-party database through the use of custom provider
Mapping Features	1:1 table to entity mapping	Ability to map entities across multiple tables, providing complete separation from underlying database schema
N:N	No support for N:N relationships, requires intermediate table for support	Support for N:N relationships
Inheritance	Full support	Full support

Getting started with the Entity Framework is very similar to using LINQ to SQL:

1. Create a new Silverlight Application project and from the main ASP.NET web project, add a new item to the project using the ADO.NET Entity Data Model template, as shown in Figure 2-13. The Entity Data Model Wizard appears asking you to choose from the option of generating from a database or creating a new empty model. This example generates from the database.

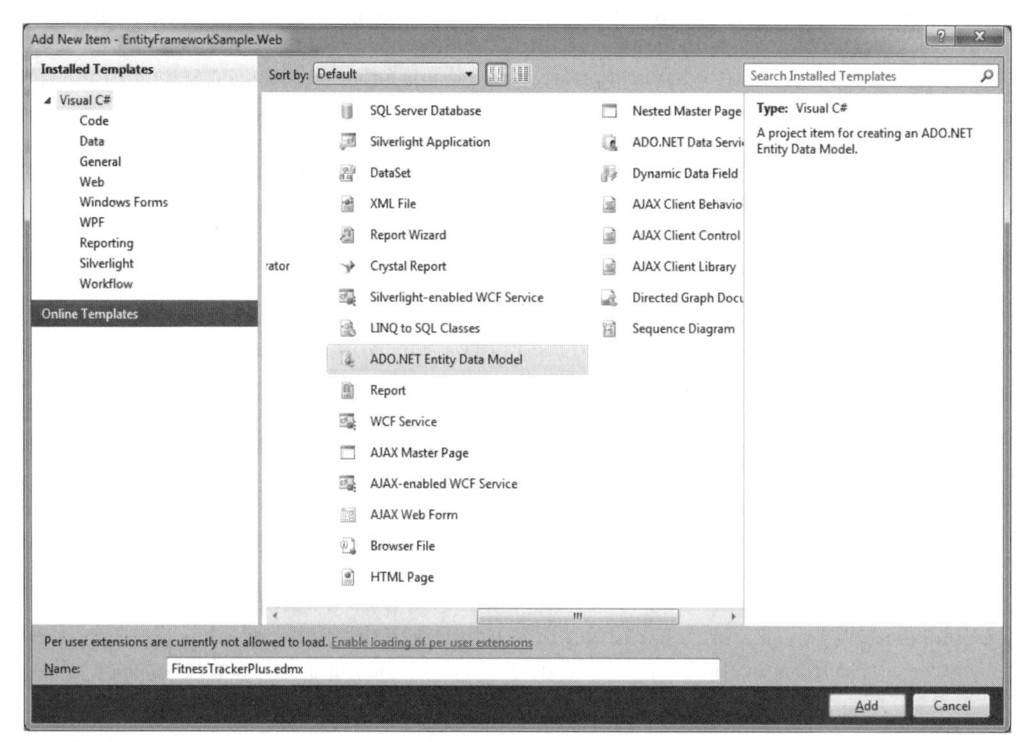

FIGURE 2-13

2. Select database connection information and decide if the connection string should be stored in the web.config file. Figures 2-14 and 2-15 outline both of these steps. In this case, just go ahead and connect to the FitnessTrackerPlus.mdf file located in the App_Data folder of the project. You are presented with the option to choose the database objects that you wish to include in the data model, as shown in Figure 2-16.

FIGURE 2-14

FIGURE 2-15

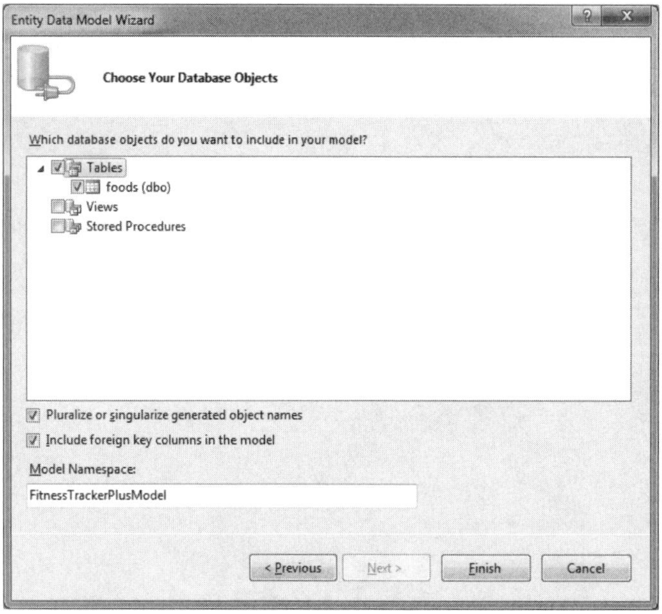

FIGURE 2-16

3. You can expand the table tree item and choose from any of the existing tables in the database. For this example you only have one table called foods, so check that table option.

4. Click Finish. Visual Studio will then create a new FitnessTrackerPlus.edmx file that includes the tables you chose in the previous step. Figure 2-17 shows the designer view with the foods table added.

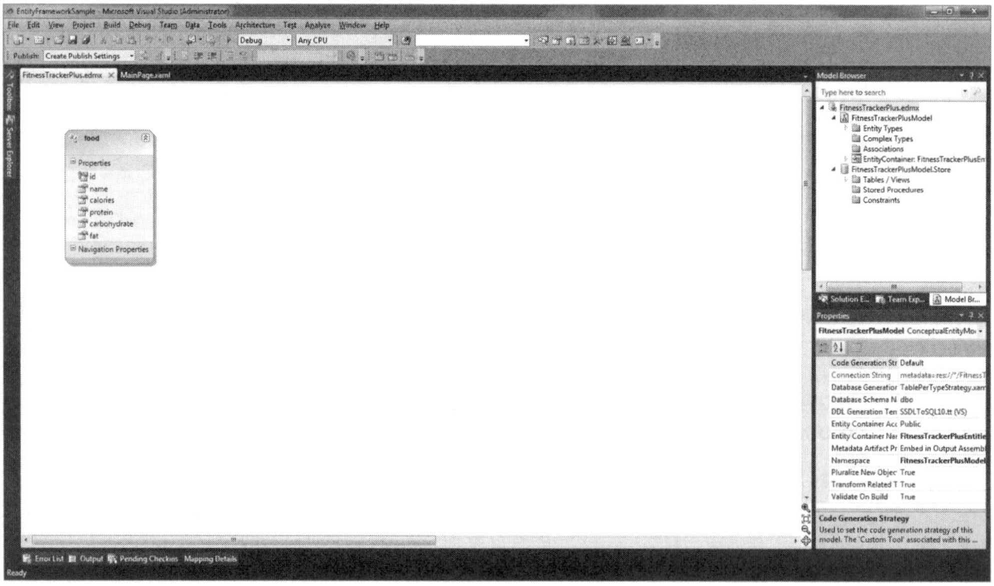

FIGURE 2-17

Performing CRUD-based operations on the entities defined is very similar to using LINQ to SQL. When working in a disconnected environment such as web services with Silverlight, you need to attach entities that are being updated or removed before saving changes. Listing 2-4 shows a very basic WCF web service created with the "Silverlight Enabled WCF Service" template that supports data retrieval, updating, creation, and deletion with the Entity Framework.

LISTING 2-9: FoodService.svc.cs (located in the EntityFrameworkSample project)

Available for download on Wrox.com

```
using System;
using System.Linq;
using System.Runtime.Serialization;
using System.ServiceModel;
using System.ServiceModel.Activation;
using System.Collections.Generic;

namespace EntityFrameworkSample.Web
{
     [ServiceContract(Namespace = "")]
      [AspNetCompatibilityRequirements(RequirementsMode =
AspNetCompatibilityRequirementsMode.Allowed)]
     public class FoodService
     {
          FitnessTrackerPlusEntities model = new
FitnessTrackerPlusEntities();

          [OperationContract]
          public List<food> GetAllFoods()
          {
               return model.foods.ToList();
          }

          [OperationContract]
          public void UpdateFood(food customfood, int calories)
          {
               model.AttachTo("foods", customfood);
               customfood.calories = calories;

               model.SaveChanges();
          }

          [OperationContract]
          public void CreateFood(food customfood)
          {
               model.AddTofoods(customfood);
          }

          [OperationContract]
          public void DeleteFood(food customfood)
          {
               model.AttachTo("foods", customfood);
               model.DeleteObject(customfood);
          }
     }
}
```

The next section will cover some more detailed examples showing elements of the Entity Framework, including the new ADO.NET Data Services. These Data Services act as an additional layer on top of the Entity Framework to provide a full business logic framework on top of WCF web services.

The Entity Framework is an incredibly large framework that works hard to allow you, as the programmer, to perform your data access work against a conceptual model rather than worry about the specifics of the underlying database schema and technology. I cannot begin to cover all of the details of using the Entity Framework in this book and there has been extensive debate online about whether or not the Entity Framework is a better ORM technology than LINQ to SQL. Obviously, if you need to support any database other than SQL Server then the answer is clear. If you are worried only about supporting SQL Server, however, the answer is not so cut and dry. In the "Solution" section of this chapter, I make a technology choice for the FitnessTrackerPlus application and describe my reasoning behind that decision.

> *If you are interested in a very in-depth look at both technologies, consider taking* Professional ADO.NET 3.5 with LINQ and the Entity Framework *by Wrox Press for a read. This book has much more in-depth information on both frameworks, including topics that are out of scope for this particular book.*
>
> *The new exception starts a new stack trace starting from the exact spot where you threw it, making it appear as though this is where the error actually originated*

With the latest enhancements to the Entity Framework, it may seem like Microsoft is pushing hard to make the decision for developers easier, but they have not yet dropped support for LINQ to SQL and have even added complete support for it in their new WCF RIA Services platform, so it does not seem like the debate is going to end anytime soon. For now, you need to review what your database schema looks like and what database platform choice you have made before determining which data access layer or ORM technology you will use in your own projects. Of course, if all else fails, you can always use the traditional ADO.NET objects such as `DataReaders`, stored procedures, and other .NET 2.0 data access concepts.

Business Logic Layer

When designing the business logic layer of the logical tier there are a myriad of technologies at your disposal. You could choose to write your business layer using traditional ASMX web services, WCF web services, ADO.NET Data Services, or even WCF RIA Services, which is the latest addition to the .NET stack of business logic technologies. Regardless of the technology used to create your business layer you will have to make your calls to that layer asynchronously. Silverlight does not support synchronous calls to web services. This introduces some new design challenges that force you to be careful of relying on dependent web service calls. Let's take a look at how you can utilize each of these technologies from a Silverlight application.

ASMX Web Services

If you have written a traditional ASP.NET-based website in the past, then at one point in time you probably had to interact with an ASMX-based web service. In ASP.NET, calls to these web services are synchronous in nature and making use of them is as simple as adding a web reference to the service in your project. Visual Studio makes this relatively painless and creates a proxy class that handles all of the plumbing code required to actually make the web service call. Making use of these services in Silverlight, however, is slightly more complicated than in a traditional ASP.NET code behind page. In a Silverlight project, the web reference has been changed to a service reference, and the calls to the service can no longer be made synchronously. Listing 2-10 demonstrates a simple web service called `ExerciseService` that returns a list of available exercises to the caller. Immediately following this is Listing 2-11, which highlights the `Exercise` business object being used in the web service.

LISTING 2-10: ExerciseService.asmx.cs (located in the ASMXWebServiceCall project)

Available for download on Wrox.com

```
using System;
using System.Collections.Generic;
using System.Linq;
using System.Web;
using System.Web.Services;

namespace ASMXWebServiceCall.Web.Services
{
     /// <summary>
     /// Summary description for ExerciseService
     /// </summary>
     [WebService(Namespace = "http://www.fitnesstrackerplus.com/")]
     [WebServiceBinding(ConformsTo = WsiProfiles.BasicProfile1_1)]
     [System.ComponentModel.ToolboxItem(false)]
     // To allow this Web Service to be called from script, using ASP.NET
AJAX,uncomment the following line.
     // [System.Web.Script.Services.ScriptService]
     public class ExerciseService: System.Web.Services.WebService
     {
          [WebMethod]
          public List<Exercise> GetAllExercises()
          {
               return new List<Exercise>()
               {
                    new Exercise(1,1,"Barbell Bench Press"),
                    new Exercise(2,1,"Treadmill"),
                    new Exercise(3,2,"Jogging 5 Miles"),
                    new Exercise(4,2,"Baseball Practice")
               };
          }
     }
}
```

LISTING 2-11: Exercise.cs (located in the ASMXWebServiceCall project)

Available for download on Wrox.com

```
using System;
using System.Collections.Generic;
using System.Linq;
using System.Web;

namespace ASMXWebServiceCall.Services
{
     public class Exercise
     {
          public int ExerciseID { get; set; }
          public int UserID { get; set; }
          public string ExerciseName { get; set; }

          public Exercise() {};

          public Exercise(int id, int user_id, string name)
          {
               this.ExerciseID = id;
               this.UserID = user_id;
               this.ExerciseName = name;
          }
     }
}
```

After adding a service reference to the preceding web service in your Silverlight project, you will see a reference.cs file, which represents the proxy class that you will be using to call the service. In the case of ASMX web services, the proxy class automatically takes care of creating a version of the web service call that supports asynchronous calling. There is barely any additional work required from you to get this working. The only major difference is that you will need to attach an event handler to the completed event for the method that you are attempting to call. Continuing with the previous example, Listing 2-12 shows the asynchronous call to the `GetAllExercises` method and displays all the exercises returned in a `DataGrid`. Note how the asynchronous form of the method generated for the client is called `GetAllExercisesAsync`.

LISTING 2-12: MainPage.xaml.cs (located in the ASMXWebServiceCall project)

Available for download on Wrox.com

```
using System;
using System.Collections.ObjectModel;
using System.Windows;
using System.Windows.Controls;
using ASMXWebServiceCall.Services;

namespace ASMXWebServiceCall
{
```

```
    public partial class MainPage: UserControl
    {
        public MainPage()
        {
            InitializeComponent();

            ExerciseServiceSoapClient client = new
ExerciseServiceSoapClient();

            // Setup an web service completion event before actually
            // calling the service

            client.GetAllExercisesCompleted += new
EventHandler<GetAllExercisesCompletedEventArgs>(client_
GetAllExercisesCompleted);
            client.GetAllExercisesAsync();
        }

#region Web Service Handlers

        private void client_GetAllExercisesCompleted(object sender,
GetAllExercisesCompletedEventArgs e)
        {
            // GetAllExercisesCompletedEventArgs contains an Error property
            // that can be checked before attempting to use the Result

            // The Result property contains all of the
            // retrieved exercise objects

            if (e.Error == null)
            {
                ObservableCollection<Exercise> exercises = e.Result as
ObservableCollection<Exercise>;
                ExerciseGrid.ItemsSource = exercises;
            }
        }

#endregion
    }
}
```

Note in the event handler that even though the web service is returning a generic `List<Exercise>` object, the Silverlight proxy class has actually returned an `ObservableCollection` in the `Result` property of the `GetAllExercisesCompleted` object, which can be used by controls such as the `DataGrid`. In addition to the reference class generated, you will also see that a new file called `ServiceReferences.ClientConfig` has been added to your project. This file sets up the SOAP endpoint bindings that Silverlight will utilize to make the calls to the web service. Listing 2-13 shows the binding information that has been automatically created for you.

LISTING 2-13: ServiceReferences.ClientConfig (located in the ASMXWebServiceCall project)

Available for download on Wrox.com

```
<configuration>
<system.serviceModel>
     <bindings>
          <basicHttpBinding>
               <binding name="ExerciseServiceSoap" maxBufferSize="2147483647"
maxReceivedMessageSize="2147483647">
                    <security mode="None" />
               </binding>
          </basicHttpBinding>
     </bindings>
     <client>
          <endpoint address="http://localhost:1038/Services/ExerciseService.asmx"
binding="basicHttpBinding" bindingConfiguration="ExerciseServiceSoap"
contract="ExerciseService.ExerciseServiceSoap" name="ExerciseServiceSoap" />
     </client>
</system.serviceModel>
</configuration>
```

WCF Services

In addition to the traditional ASMX SOAP-based web services, Silverlight can also consume WCF services. Consuming a WCF service in a Silverlight application involves many of the same techniques described previously. Once you have installed the Silverlight developer tools, Visual Studio will have made available a new service template that you can use to create WCF services that are ready to be used with Silverlight. The new template is called the "Silverlight-enabled WCF service." What this template does is ensure that the service is created with the `AspNetCompatibilityRequirements` attribute set to `Allowed`. This attribute enables ASP.NET compatibility mode. Without this option enabled the WCF service will not have access to the HTTP pipeline. This means that your service will not have access to the `HTTPContext` object, session state, or any of the other ASP.NET features that are made available to traditional ASMX web services. In most cases, you will want to have access to these objects from your services, especially the session state. This compatibility mode is also required if you want to enable access to the ASP.NET authentication, authorization, or profile services from Silverlight. In the FitnessTrackerPlus application, you will need to have access to all of these items from your services so if you were to choose WCF as your solution for the business logic layer, then this project template is the best way to create those services. Listing 2-14 shows the WCF version of the `ExerciseService` that was created in the previous example:

LISTING 2-14: ExerciseService.svc.cs (located in the WCFServiceCall project)

Available for download on Wrox.com

```
using System;
using System.ServiceModel;
using System.ServiceModel.Activation;
using System.Collections.Generic;

namespace WCFServiceCall.Web.Services
```

```
{
     [ServiceContract(Namespace = "")]
      [AspNetCompatibilityRequirements(RequirementsMode =
AspNetCompatibilityRequirementsMode.Allowed)]
     public class ExerciseService
     {
          [OperationContract]
          public List<Exercise> GetAllExercises()
          {
               // Just return an in-memory data store

               return new List<Exercise>()
               {
                    new Exercise(1,1,"Barbell Bench Press"),
                    new Exercise(2,1,"Treadmill"),
                    new Exercise(3,2,"Jogging 5 Miles"),
                    new Exercise(4,2,"Baseball Practice")
               };
          }
     }
}
```

As you can see, there isn't much different other than a few extra attribute declarations. However, with WCF services you have much more flexibility in the actual data going across the wire than you do with traditional ASMX-based web services. ASMX-based web services rely on SOAP messages being passed between the client and server and in most cases these messages are very verbose. SOAP messages support an XML-based payload, which in and of itself requires additional bandwidth for each service call. WCF offers several different options for output including binary, which dramatically reduces the amount of traffic required for each service call. One important addition to Silverlight 4 was the inclusion of binary WCF support, which means you can now officially create binary WCF services and integrate them with a Silverlight client. WCF services with binary formatted output can be an efficient solution for your business logic layer.

Now WCF services are not entirely without their own set of unique problems. One problem in particular, which can come up during the deployment of a WCF server especially in a shared hosting environment, is errors involving multiple host name support. In cases where you have complete control of the server environment, you can work around this type of issue as you will have full control over the IIS server. In a shared hosting environment, depending on how the hosting provider has configured the IIS server, you could run into the following error when deploying the service:

> "This collection already contains an address with scheme http. There can be at most one address per scheme in this collection."

This error can occur when the shared hosting provider is attempting to support your site being accessed by multiple host names. One example of this is trying to use both FitnessTrackerPlus as well as FitnessTrackerSilverlight as host names that point to the same site. The WCF service can bind only to one of the available host names and without further configuration will give you this error when attempting to access the service. Because you most likely will not have access to the IIS server configuration, you need to devise an alternate solution. There are currently a couple of different ways to handle this problem. One solution involves creating a custom `ServiceHostFactory` and forcing the WCF service to make use of the factory upon its creation. Listing 2-15 shows the WCF service with the additional `ServiceHostFactory` that is required for this implementation.

LISTING 2-15: ExerciseService.svc.cs: (located in the WCFServiceCallAlternateMethod project)

Available for download on Wrox.com

```
using System;
using System.ServiceModel;
using System.ServiceModel.Activation;
using System.Collections.Generic;

namespace WCFServiceCallAlternateMethod.Web.Services
{
     [ServiceContract(Namespace = "")]
      [AspNetCompatibilityRequirements(RequirementsMode =
AspNetCompatibilityRequirementsMode.Allowed)]
     public class ExerciseService
     {
          [OperationContract]
          public List<Exercise> GetAllExercises()
          {
               // Return an in-memory database of exercises

               return new List<Exercise>()
               {
                    new Exercise(1,1,"Barbell Bench Press"),
                    new Exercise(2,1,"Treadmill"),
                    new Exercise(3,2,"Jogging 5 Miles"),
                    new Exercise(4,2,"Baseball Practice")
               };
          }
     }

     public class ExerciseServiceHostFactory: ServiceHostFactory
     {
          protected override ServiceHost CreateServiceHost(Type serviceType,
Uri[] baseAddresses)
          {
               // Multiple Uri values declared, first one is for production,
               // second is for local debugging

               //Uri webServiceAddress = new
Uri("http://FitnessTrackerPlus/services/exerciseservice.svc");
               Uri webServiceAddress = new
Uri("http://localhost:1049/services/exerciseservice.svc");

               ServiceHost webServiceHost = new ServiceHost(serviceType,
webServiceAddress);
               return webServiceHost;
          }
     }
}
```

> *When running the preceding example, be sure to change the port number to the port that is being used by your local development web server or the service will not be found.The new exception starts a new stack trace starting from the exact spot where you threw it, making it appear as though this is where the error actually originated*

In addition to creating the custom `ServiceHostFactory` class, you also need to change the .svc file to use this factory when creating an instance of the service, as shown Listing 2-16.

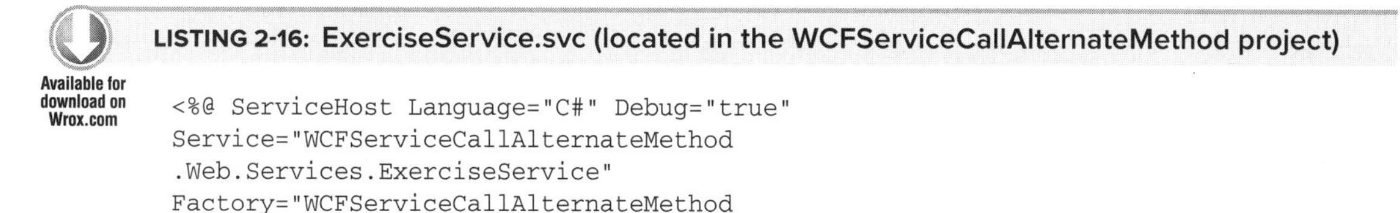

LISTING 2-16: ExerciseService.svc (located in the WCFServiceCallAlternateMethod project)

Available for download on Wrox.com

```
<%@ ServiceHost Language="C#" Debug="true"
Service="WCFServiceCallAlternateMethod
.Web.Services.ExerciseService"
Factory="WCFServiceCallAlternateMethod
.Web.Services.ExerciseServiceHostFactory" %>
```

Once you have successfully built the service, you can add a reference to it from your Silverlight project. You must call the WCF service asynchronously just as was done in the preceding ASMX sample. In the actual creation of the service client object, I have included a parameter to the constructor. When you are implementing your application on a local machine, adding the service reference in the project creates an endpoint in the ServiceReference.ClientConfig file that points to the localhost web server. When you actually deploy the WCF service, that endpoint is no longer valid. Rather than add multiple service references or try to coordinate between the live and local version when you debug, you can simply pass the name of the endpoint that you wish to create in the constructor of the service client.

One simple way to switch between the live and local versions of the service is to pass the binding string into the constructor for the `ExerciseServiceClient`. This alternate constructor takes a string pointing to the binding that should be used in the ServiceReference.ClientConfig file. This technique is demonstrated in the following code where a static `Globals` class holds the two binding string values.

Available for download on Wrox.com

```
ExerciseServiceClient client =
new ExerciseServiceClient(Globals.ExerciseServiceBinding);

client.GetAllExercisesCompleted += new
EventHandler<GetAllExercisesCompletedEventArgs>(client_GetAllExercisesCompleted);
client.GetAllExercisesAsync();]
```

Code snippet MainPage.xaml.cs located in the WCFServiceCallAlternateMethod project

The `Globals` class handles switching between the live and local bindings automatically by making use of a conditional compiler statement. Listing 2-17 shows the `Globals` class.

LISTING 2-17: Globals.cs (located in the WCFServiceCallAlternateMethod project)

Available for download on Wrox.com

```
namespace WCFServiceCallAlternateMethod
{
     public static class Globals
     {
#if DEBUG
          public static readonly string ExerciseServiceBinding =
"ExerciseServiceDebug";
#else
          public static readonly string ExerciseServiceBinding =
"ExerciseServiceLive";
#endif
     }
}
```

The second option you have for resolving the previous multiple host name error is to utilize a new feature of .NET 3.5 called `baseAddressPrefixFilters`. When you add a Silverlight-enabled WCF service to your web project, changes are made to the `<system.serviceModel>` configuration area of the web.config file. In the `serviceHostingEnvironment` section, you can specify which host name you wish to have the WCF service bind to. In the following code, a `baseAddressPrefixFilters` section has been added to the web.config file that forces the service to bind to `http://FitnessTrackerPlus`.

Available for download on Wrox.com

```
<serviceHostingEnvironment aspNetCompatibilityEnabled="true">
     <baseAddressPrefixFilters>
          <add prefix="http://localhost:1121/Services"/>
          <!- <add prefix="http://FitnessTrackerPlus/Services"/> ->
     </baseAddressPrefixFilters>
</serviceHostingEnvironment>
```

Code snippet web.config located in the WCFServiceCallBaseAddressPrefix project

By just simply making use of the `baseAddressPrefixFilter` you can quickly set the appropriate host name for the service depending on if you are running locally or on the production server. This eliminates the need for a custom `ServiceHostFactory` implementation.

ADO.NET Data Services

Yet another possibility for the business logic layer is to make use of the new ADO.NET Data Services framework. This new framework provides an easy way to create REST-based web services to your client layers. These new services provide a wrapper around the existing REST-based functionality in WCF to provide you with a REST-based protocol for accessing your data in the business object layer. You can make use of these services with existing business objects or by wrapping entities created from an ORM technology such as LINQ to SQL or the Entity Framework. In the WCF-based solution outlined previously, it would be necessary to roll your own CRUD operations for each business object in the WCF services. If you wanted to support some additional common line of business features such as data paging, it would require additional custom logic. The ADO.NET Data Services add support for this functionality with minimal coding effort.

To get started with the ADO.NET Data Services in a new project, you will first need to add a web service to your ASP.NET project using the new ADO.NET Data Service template, as shown in Figure 2-18.

In this example, you call the new service FitnessTrackerPlusService. You will now be left with a FitnessTrackerPlus.svc file in the project and if you right-click on the file and select the View Code option, you will be presented with the code in Listing 2-18.

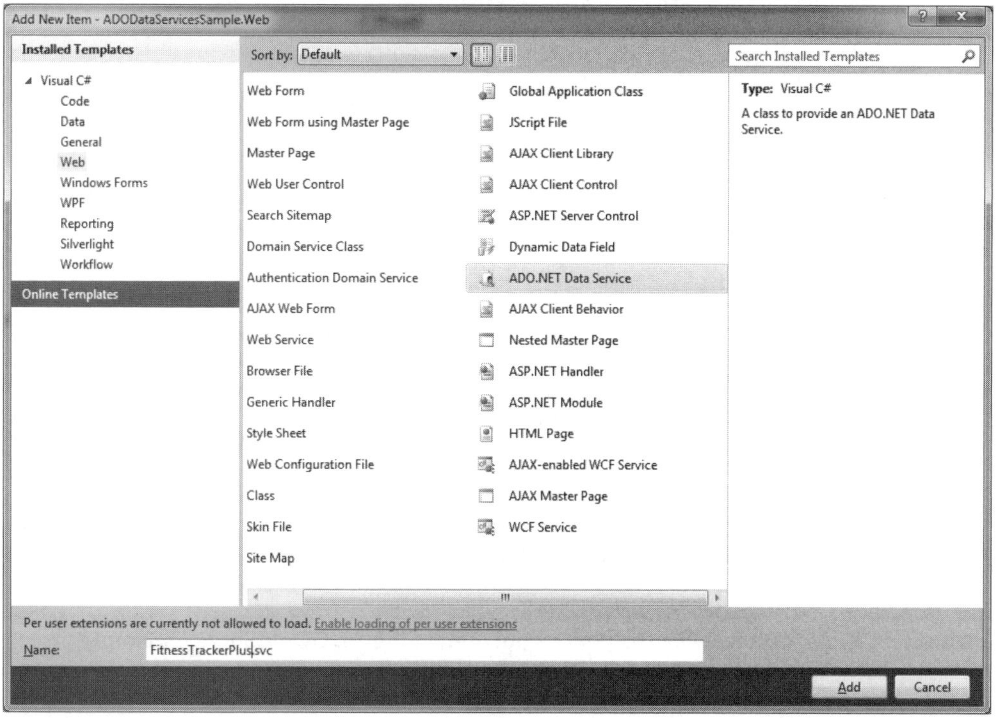

FIGURE 2-18

LISTING 2-18: FitnessTrackerPlus.svc.cs (located in the ADODataServicesSample project)

Available for download on Wrox.com

```
using System;
using System.Collections.Generic;
using System.Data.Services;
using System.Data.Services.Common;
using System.Linq;
using System.ServiceModel.Web;
using System.Web;

namespace ADODataServicesSample.Web
{
    public class FitnessTrackerPlus : DataService< /* TODO: put your data
source class name here */ >
    {
        // This method is called only once to initialize service-wide
        // policies.
        public static void InitializeService(DataServiceConfiguration config)
        {
```

continues

LISTING 2-18 *(continued)*

```
            // TODO: set rules to indicate which entity sets and service
            // operations are visible, updatable, etc.
            // Examples:
            // config.SetEntitySetAccessRule("MyEntityset",
            // EntitySetRights.AllRead);
            // config.SetServiceOperationAccessRule("MyServiceOperation",
            // ServiceOperationRights.All);
            config.DataServiceBehavior.MaxProtocolVersion =
DataServiceProtocolVersion.V2;
        }
    }
}
```

As you can see in Listing 2-18, the first thing you need to do is create a data source class that will be used as the `DataService` type. This class is responsible for actually retrieving and manipulating the data being exposed by the `DataService`. Most of the time, you would be using a LINQ to SQL `DataContext` or perhaps an `ObjectContext` created using the Entity Framework. For this example, let's just use a custom object context called `FitnessTrackerPlusContext`. At a minimum, you must add a couple of public properties to the class that are of the type `IQueryable` in order for ADO.NET Data Services to expose them. Listing 2-19 shows the basic `FitnessTrackerPlusContext` class with `Exercises`, and `Foods` properties that return `IQueryable` types.

LISTING 2-19: FitnessTrackerPlusContext.cs (located in the ADODataServicesSample project)

Available for download on Wrox.com

```
using System.Collections.Generic;
using System.Linq;

namespace ADODataServicesSample.Web
{
    public class FitnessTrackerPlusContext
    {
        private List<Exercise> exercises = new List<Exercise>();
        private List<Food> foods = new List<Food>();

        public FitnessTrackerPlusContext()
        {
            // Create an in-memory database for the Context object

            exercises = new List<Exercise>
            {
                new Exercise(1,1,"Barbell Bench Press"),
                new Exercise(2,1,"Treadmill"),
                new Exercise(3,2,"Jogging 5 Miles"),
                new Exercise(4,2,"Baseball Practice - 2 Hrs")
            };

            foods = new List<Food>
            {
```

```
                    new Food(1, 1,"Banana"),
                    new Food(2, 2,"Chocolate Ice Cream"),
                    new Food(3, 3,"Glazed Donut"),
                    new Food(4, 4,"Coffee w/Cream & Sugar")
                };
            }

            public IQueryable<Exercise> Exercises
            {
                get { return exercises.AsQueryable<Exercise>(); }
            }

            public IQueryable<Food> Foods
            {
                get { return foods.AsQueryable<Food>(); }
            }
        }
    }
```

After creating a `DataContext` class for the service, you then need to take a look at the `InitializeService` method; there you will see some rules that need to be defined. The ADO.NET Data Services require that access rules be defined for each entity being exposed by the context object. Several different options are available for this setting. All settings are applied by using the supplied `IDataServiceConfiguration` object's `SetEntitySetAccessRule` method. This method takes two parameters, the first being the name of the entity set, and the second the permissions or access rules that should be applied to the entity set. The permissions are available using the `EntitySetRights` enumeration. Table 2-3 covers the possible combinations of access rules that can be used.

TABLE 2-3: Entity Access Rights

ACCESS RIGHT	DESCRIPTION
`None`	No rights to access any data
`All`	Permission for full CRUD based access
`AllRead`	Permission for full read access
`AllWrite`	Permission for full write access
`ReadSingle`	Permission to read single data entry
`ReadMultiple`	Permission to read multiple data entries
`WriteAppend`	Permission to create entries
`WriteReplace`	Permission to update entries
`WriteMerge`	Permission to merge entries
`WriteDelete`	Permission to delete existing entries

You can also apply a set of rights to all available entities instead of doing so on a per entity basis. For example, if you want to give read access to both the `Exercises` and `Foods` entities instead of setting the `AllRead` right on each individual entity you could do so with the following line:

```
config.SetEntitySetAccessRule("*",EntitySetRights.AllRead);
```

If you want to give all entity sets read and delete permissions you could opt to even combine permissions in one line using the `or` operator.

```
config.SetEntitySetAccessRule("*",EntitySetRights.AllRead |
EntitySetRights.WriteDelete);
```

Getting back to the example, you want to give full read access to both the `Foods` and `Exercises` properties so the easiest way to go about this is to use the `AllRead` rights setting, which covers reading single and multiple rows. Listing 2-20 shows the updated `DataService` class with the entity rights set and the custom `FitnessTrackerPlusContext` being used.

LISTING 2-20: FitnessTrackerPlus.svc.cs (located in the ADODataServicesSample project)

Available for download on Wrox.com

```
using System.Data.Services;

namespace ADODataServicesSample.Web
{
     public class FitnessTrackerPlus: DataService<FitnessTrackerPlusContext>
     {
          public static void InitializeService(IDataServiceConfiguration
config)
          {
               config.SetEntitySetAccessRule("*", EntitySetRights.All);
          }
     }
}
```

At this point, you can access the service right through the browser and even query the data. The ADO.NET Data Services framework maps specific CRUD style requests to the available HTTP verbs. Table 2-4 shows how each HTTP verb maps to a data service operation.

TABLE 2-4: ADO.NET Data Services HTTP Verbs

OPERATION	VERB
Read	GET
Create	POST
Update	PUT
Delete	DELETE

In the case of the read operation, an HTTP GET is used to retrieve the data. By default the data is sent back in ATOM feed form. For example, if you want to access the Exercises collection, you can navigate from the browser to `http://localhost:1044/FitnessTrackerService.svc/Exercises`, substituting your own port number after `localhost`, of course. This results in all of the created exercises being sent back in an ATOM feed-based form. The data services can also send back the data in JSON form.

> *You must disable RSS feed functionality if you are attempting to view the output in Internet Explorer 8; otherwise, you will see a standard feed form with entries for each of the exercise objects created.*

If you turn off the RSS support, you will see the following XML returned by the data service:

```
<?xml version="1.0" encoding="utf-8" standalone="yes" ?>
<feed xml:base="http://localhost:1044/FitnessTrackerService.svc/"
     xmlns:d="http://schemas.microsoft.com/ado/2007/08/dataservices"
     xmlns:m="http://schemas.microsoft.com/ado/2007/08/dataservices/metadata"
     xmlns="http://www.w3.org/2005/Atom">
     <title type="text">Exercises</title>
     <id>http://localhost:1044/FitnessTrackerService.svc/Exercises</id>
     <updated>2009-05-29T03:59:17Z</updated>
     <link rel="self" title="Exercises" href="Exercises" />
     <entry>
          <id>http://localhost:1044/FitnessTrackerService.svc/Exercises(1)</id>
          <title type="text" />
          <updated>2009-05-29T03:59:17Z</updated>
          <author>
               <name />
          </author>
          <link rel="edit" title="Exercise" href="Exercises(1)" />
          <category term="DataServicesSample.Web.Exercise"
scheme="http://schemas.microsoft.com/ado/2007/08/dataservices/scheme" />
          <content type="application/xml">
               <m:properties>
                    <d:ExerciseID m:type="Edm.Int32">1</d:ExerciseID>
                    <d:UserID m:type="Edm.Int32">1</d:UserID>
                    <d:ExerciseName>Barbell Bench Press</d:ExerciseName>
               </m:properties>
          </content>
     </entry>
     <entry>
          <id>http://localhost:1044/FitnessTrackerService.svc/Exercises(2)</id>
          <title type="text" />
          <updated>2009-05-29T03:59:17Z</updated>
          <author>
               <name />
          </author>
          <link rel="edit" title="Exercise" href="Exercises(2)" />
          <category term="DataServicesSample.Web.Exercise"
scheme="http://schemas.microsoft.com/ado/2007/08/dataservices/scheme" />
```

```
            <content type="application/xml">
                <m:properties>
                    <d:ExerciseID m:type="Edm.Int32">2</d:ExerciseID>
                    <d:UserID m:type="Edm.Int32">1</d:UserID>
                    <d:ExerciseName>Treadmill</d:ExerciseName>
                </m:properties>
            </content>
        </entry>
        <entry>
            <id>http://localhost:1044/FitnessTrackerService.svc/Exercises(3)</id>
            <title type="text" />
            <updated>2009-05-29T03:59:17Z</updated>
            <author>
                <name />
            </author>
            <link rel="edit" title="Exercise" href="Exercises(3)" />
            <category term="DataServicesSample.Web.Exercise"
    scheme="http://schemas.microsoft.com/ado/2007/08/dataservices/scheme" />
            <content type="application/xml">
                <m:properties>
                    <d:ExerciseID m:type="Edm.Int32">3</d:ExerciseID>
                    <d:UserID m:type="Edm.Int32">2</d:UserID>
                    <d:ExerciseName>Jogging 5 Miles</d:ExerciseName>
                </m:properties>
            </content>
        </entry>
        <entry>
            <id>http://localhost:1044/FitnessTrackerService.svc/Exercises(4)</id>
            <title type="text" />
            <updated>2009-05-29T03:59:17Z</updated>
            <author>
                <name />
            </author>
            <link rel="edit" title="Exercise" href="Exercises(4)" />
            <category term="DataServicesSample.Web.Exercise"
    scheme="http://schemas.microsoft.com/ado/2007/08/dataservices/scheme" />
            <content type="application/xml">
                <m:properties>
                    <d:ExerciseID m:type="Edm.Int32">4</d:ExerciseID>
                    <d:UserID m:type="Edm.Int32">2</d:UserID>
                    <d:ExerciseName>Baseball Practice</d:ExerciseName>
                </m:properties>
            </content>
        </entry>
    </feed>
```

Earlier, it was stated that for read operations to be supported by the ADO.NET Data Services, the context object properties that are being exposed must implement the `IQueryable` interface. If you wanted to expand the permission set to include full CRUD capabilities on the `Foods` and `Exercises` objects, the context object would also need to implement the `IUpdateable` interface. Unfortunately, no built-in implementation of this interface is available for custom business objects. In fact, currently only the Entity Framework has a full implementation of this interface that supports update, delete, and create methods from the data services.

> *Creating an implementation of this interface is beyond the scope of this book but there have been some attempts made on sites such as* `http://www.codeplex.com` *that provide full implementations for LINQ to SQL* `DataContext` *classes as well as for potential custom business objects.*

Rather than fight with a ton of custom code to implement `IUpdateable` on the custom context object, let's take a look at what it takes to make use of the ADO.NET Data Services with the Entity Framework, which has full support for all CRUD operations already built into the framework. In this next example, you must first add a new ADO.NET Entity Data Model file to the ASP.NET project called FitnessTrackerPlus. You should include both the foods and exercises tables that are located in the FitnessTrackerPlus.mdf file. Next, you need to add a new ADO.NET Data Service called FitnessTrackerPlus.svc. As in the previous example, you need to specify the `DataContext` class type in the `DataService` template definition. In this case, you simply add the `FitnessTrackerPlusEntities` type that was created with the Entity Framework. As before, you must set the access rights. This time, let's enable the full CRUD operations on the exercises entity but only enable read operations on the foods. Listing 2-21 shows the updated FitnessTrackerPlus service implementation.

LISTING 2-21: FitnessTrackerPlus.svc.cs (located in the ADODataServicesEntitiesSample project)

Available for download on Wrox.com

```
using System.Data.Services;
using DataServicesEntitiesSample.Web.Data;

namespace DataServicesEntitiesSample.Web.Services
{
     public class FitnessTrackerPlus: DataService<FitnessTrackerPlusEntities>
     {
          // This method is called only once to initialize service-wide policies.
          // In this case you are giving read-ony access to the foods table,
          // and full access to the exercises table

          public static void InitializeService(IDataServiceConfiguration config)
          {
               config.SetEntitySetAccessRule("foods",
EntitySetRights.AllRead);
               config.SetEntitySetAccessRule("exercises",
EntitySetRights.All);
               config.DataServiceBehavior.MaxProtocolVersion =
DataServiceProtocolVersion.V2;

          }
     }
}
```

Now that you have the service implementation created and the FitnessTrackerPlus.edmx file configured with the foods and exercises tables, it's time to access the service from a Silverlight client. To start, add a new service reference to the Silverlight project. If you click the Discover button, the wizard should locate the FitnessTrackerPlusService, as shown in Figure 2-19.

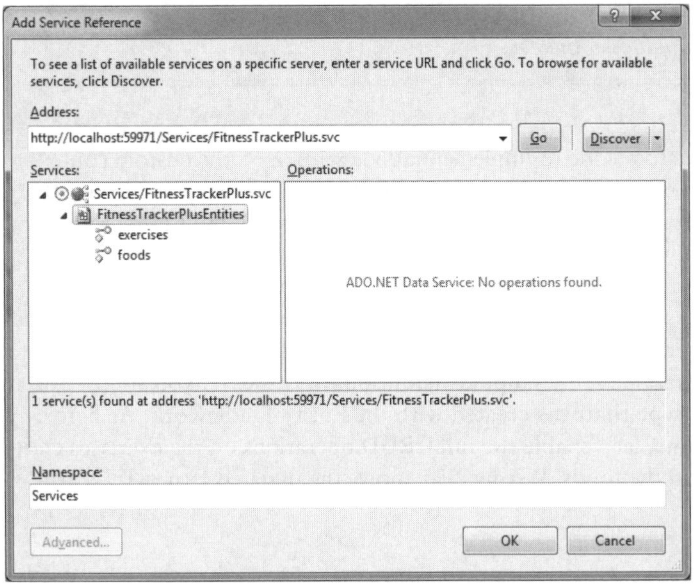

FIGURE 2-19

Once the wizard is complete, you have the necessary proxy class that contains all of the entity definitions as well as the data access methods that were enabled by the calls to the `SetEntitySetAccessRule` method made in the `FitnessTrackerPlusService` earlier. You must also add a reference to the `System.Data.Services.Client` assembly, which provides Silverlight clients with the ability to call the service. As with WCF, all calls to the service from Silverlight must be asynchronous in nature. To retrieve data, you need to create a valid LINQ expression and cast it as a `DataServiceQuery`. The client library takes care of formatting the LINQ query into a valid URI in a format that the service understands. Finally, you need to have a callback method ready to handle parsing the results of the query. Because you need to do this asynchronously, you use the `BeginExecute` and `EndExecute` methods of the `DataServiceQuery object`. This example adds two `DataGrids` to the XAML page and loads them with the first ten available foods and exercises in the database using the `DataServiceQuery` object. Listing 2-22 shows the `DataServiceQuery` operations being performed asynchronously and when completed the results are added to an `ObservableCollection` object that is bound to the appropriate `DataGrid` control.

LISTING 2-22: MainPage.xaml.cs (located in the ADODataServicesEntitiesSample project)

Available for download on Wrox.com

```
using System;
using System.Collections.ObjectModel;
using System.Collections.Generic;
using System.Linq;
using System.Windows;
```

```
using System.Windows.Controls;
using System.Data.Services.Client;
using DataServicesEntitiesSample.Services;

namespace ADODataServicesEntitiesSample
{
     public partial class MainPage: UserControl
     {
          public MainPage()
          {
               InitializeComponent();

               FitnessTrackerPlusEntities entities = new
FitnessTrackerPlusEntities(new
Uri("Services/FitnessTrackerPlus.svc",UriKind.Relative));

               // Create LINQ to Entities queries that will
               // retrieve the first 10 exercises and foods

DataServiceQuery<exercise> exercises = (DataServiceQuery<exercise>)(from e
in entities.exercises select e).Take(10);
               DataServiceQuery<food> foods = (DataServiceQuery<food>)(from
e in entities.foods select e).Take(10);

               // Set up all event handlers

               exercises.BeginExecute(new AsyncCallback(OnExercisesLoaded),
exercises);
               foods.BeginExecute(new AsyncCallback(OnFoodsLoaded), foods);

          }

          private void OnExercisesLoaded(IAsyncResult result)
          {
               DataServiceQuery<exercise> exercisesQuery =
(DataServiceQuery<exercise>)result.AsyncState;
               ObservableCollection<exercise> exerciseList = new
ObservableCollection<exercise>();

               // Complete the query operation and add all exercises returned
               // to the ObservableCollection
               // The result variable being passed into EndExecute will
               // contain all exercises retrieved from the FitnessTrackerPlus
               // service

               var exercises = exercisesQuery.EndExecute(result);

               foreach (exercise exercise in exercises)
                    exerciseList.Add(exercise);

               Exercises.ItemsSource = exerciseList;
          }

          private void OnFoodsLoaded(IAsyncResult result)
          {
```

continues

LISTING 2-22 *(continued)*

```
                DataServiceQuery<food> foodsQuery =
(DataServiceQuery<food>)result.AsyncState;
                List<food> foodList = new List<food>();

                // Complete the query operation and add all foods
                // returned to the ObservableCollection
                // The result variable being passed into EndExecute
                // will contain all foods retrieved
                // from the FitnessTrackerPlus service

                var foods = foodsQuery.EndExecute(result);

                foreach (food food in foods)
                    foodList.Add(food);

                Foods.ItemsSource = foodList;
            }
        }
}
```

WCF RIA Services

Of all the new business logic layer technologies, none of them were designed from the ground up to address some of the unique problems that exist when developing multi-tier Silverlight client applications. Only the new WCF RIA Services framework was designed from the start to address these unique situations. The WCF RIA Services framework is newly available to Silverlight 4 applications and provides a complete business logic layer technology that works with your existing data access layer regardless of whether or not you choose to use LINQ to SQL, Entity Framework, or any other custom data access layer. The WCF RIA Services framework provides built-in functionality for CRUD-based operations on business objects as well as validation support. The extensive validation support is perhaps one of the greatest strengths of the framework in that properties can be easily decorated with validation attributes and those attributes will apply not only on the server side but also on the client side.

Let's take a look at a simple example using an in-memory database of exercise objects that shows how easy it is to expose them to a Silverlight client with validation. You'll use an in-memory database as opposed to a LINQ to SQL or Entity Framework implementation in order to give an overview of the features that are specific to the WCF RIA Services. Unlike the ADO.NET Data Services covered previously, these new services really offer full functionality with all data access layer frameworks and you don't have to worry about losing any features depending on which data access choice you make. I will be covering in much greater detail how to use the WCF RIA Services with the other data access layer technologies as you move through the implementation of FitnessTrackerPlus.

Adding WCF RIA Services Support

When creating a new Silverlight application, you can add support for WCF RIA Services by simply selecting the Enable WCF RIA Services option in the project creation wizard, as shown in Figure 2-20.

FIGURE 2-20

If you already have a Silverlight project created, you can still easily add support for WCF RIA Services by opening up the Silverlight project options window and selecting the ASP.NET project under the WCF RIA Services link, as shown in Figure 2-21.

FIGURE 2-21

To better understand how WCF RIA Services work, let's create a simple example.

1. Add a new LINQ to SQL classes file to the project under a folder named Data. You can call this FitnessTrackerPlus.dbml.
2. Drag the exercises table onto the designer from the FitnessTrackerPlus.mdf file. At this point, you have a data access class that the WCF RIA Services can make use of.
3. To create a new service, you should create a new folder called Services and add a new `DomainService` called `ExerciseService` to the project using the Domain Service Class item template, as shown in Figure 2-22.

FIGURE 2-22

This new template is available after installing the WCF RIA Services framework. After naming the service, you are then presented with a screen allowing you to choose a data source for your service, as shown in Figure 2-23.

4. Select the `FitnessTrackerPlusDataContext` from the list. Once you select the `DataContext`, you are presented with a list of available entities along with options for enabling editing and generated metadata. For this example, you only give the client the ability to query for data. If you want to provide full CRUD support, select the Enable editing option and methods are automatically generated for you to support these additional operations.

5. When you check the "Generate associated classes for metadata" option, you create additional metadata classes for each entity that the WCF RIA Services framework uses to provide its entity validation feature. You will see extensive coverage of the entity validation feature later on in the book so for this example you can leave the option unselected.

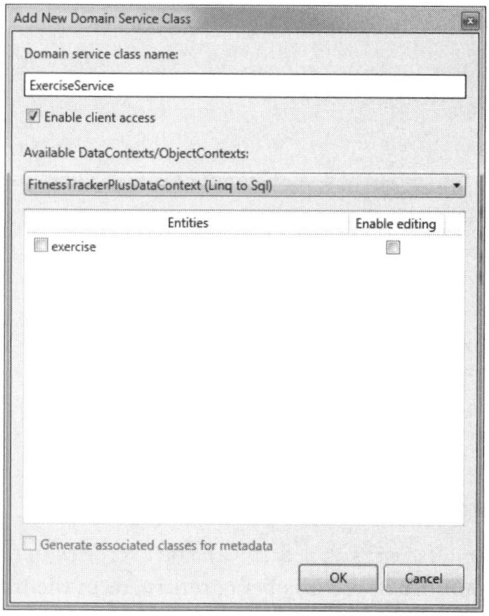

FIGURE 2-23

After making your entity selections, the WCF RIA Service is created and, in this case, will automatically include a data querying method that the client can use to retrieve `exercise` objects from the database. Listing 2-23 shows the `ExerciseService` code generated by the WCF RIA Services Domain Service Wizard. As you can see, by default, you simply have a `GetExercises` method that returns all the exercises from the database.

LISTING 2-23: ExerciseService.cs (located in the WCFRIAServicesSample project)

Available for download on Wrox.com

```
using System;
using System.Collections.Generic;
using System.ComponentModel;
using System.ComponentModel.DataAnnotations;
using System.Data.Linq;
using System.Linq;
using System.Web.DomainServices;
using System.Web.DomainServices.Providers;
using System.Web.Ria;
using System.Web.Ria.Services;
```

continues

LISTING 2-23 *(continued)*

```
using RIAServicesSample.Web.Data;

namespace RIAServicesSample.Web.Services
{
     [EnableClientAccess()]
     public class ExerciseService:
LinqToSqlDomainService<FitnessTrackerPlusDataContext>
     {
          // TODO: Consider
          // 1. Adding parameters to this method and constraining returned
          // results, and/or
          // 2. Adding query methods taking different parameters.

          public IQueryable<exercise> GetExercises()
          {
               return this.DataContext.exercises;
          }
     }
}
```

Limiting the Number of Returned Records

As you can see the default implementation of `GetExercises` returns all the exercises in the database. This isn't very efficient so let's limit the number of records being returned. In the following code, the `GetExercises` method is modified to make use of the `Take` method available in LINQ to SQL to limit the number of records returned to 25.

Available for download on Wrox.com

```
public IEnumerable<exercise> GetExercises()
{
     List<exercise> exercises = (from e in this.DataContext.exercises
                                 select e).Take(25).ToList<exercise>();

     return exercises;
}
```

Code snippet ExerciseService.cs located in the RIAServicesSample project

It is important to note that the generated method `GetExercises` was not named that way by accident. The WCF RIA Services framework follows a very specific naming convention when determining which methods to make available to the client. In WCF and ADO.NET Data Services, any public method would have a corresponding asynchronous client-side method generated by the proxy class.

In WCF RIA Services solutions, that is not the case. Simply designating a method as public will not be sufficient. Instead, WCF RIA Services look for methods that follow a specific naming convention and signature. For example, methods that are meant to query and return data to the client should begin with one of the following prefixes: `Get`, `Fetch`, `Query`, `Retrieve`, and `Select`. Query type methods must also return an `IEnumerable`, `IQueryable`, or a single instance of the entity type. However, you can have any number of parameters in a query method, which can help you to filter the results. Table 2-5 lists the various combinations of naming conventions that you can follow when you add your own CRUD operations, if you wish for them to be exposed by the WCF RIA Services framework.

TABLE 2-5: Naming Conventions for WCF RIA Services Method

DATA METHOD	REQUIRED METHOD PREFIX	REQUIRED METHOD SIGNATURE
Query Data	Get, Fetch, Query, Retrieve, or Select	`IEnumerable<T> GetData()` `IQueryable<T> GetData()`
Create Data	Insert, Add, Create	`void InsertData(T entity)`
Update Data	Update, Change, Modify	`void UpdateData(T entity)`
Delete Data	Delete, Remove	`void DeleteData(T entity)`

If, for some reason, you are unable to follow the WCF RIA Services naming conventions in your own custom methods, you also have the option of adding specific attributes above the method declarations. The WCF RIA Services framework also looks for these attributes when determining which methods to make available to clients. You can use any of the following attributes above your custom methods: `[Query]`, `[Insert]`, `[Update]`, and `[Delete]`. For example, if you have a method that searches for specific foods called `FindExercises`, by default, this method is not exposed to the client. If you were to add the `[Query]` attribute directly above the method declaration then the framework would, in fact, expose it to clients.

Unlike the previous examples for WCF and ADO.NET Data Services, the WCF RIA Services are tightly coupled with the accompanying Silverlight project. This tight integration enables the Silverlight client to access the `ExerciseService` without the additional step of adding a "Service Reference" to the project. Instead of the typical proxy class being generated on the client side, the WCF RIA Services framework provides a `DomainContext` object that corresponds to the `DomainService` created earlier. This client-side class is created in a folder called Generated_Code, which is hidden by default. If you select the Show All Files option on the Silverlight project, you'll see this folder along with a file ending in .g.cs. In this example, the file is called RIAServicesSample.Web.g.cs.

An examination of this file shows that it is very similar to the proxy class files generated when you add WCF or ADO.NET service references to a project. In this file, you will find the various entity classes that are being exposed as well as an `ExerciseContext` class that provides the functionality required to call the `GetExercises` method from the service.

Although accessing the service from the Silverlight client must still be done asynchronously, WCF RIA Services doesn't provide you with an asynchronous version of the `GetExercises` method. Instead, the `DomainContext` object provides `EntityList` objects that represent the entities being exposed, and rely on a `Load` method, which, behind the scenes, asynchronously populates the `EntityList` objects. Listing 2-24 shows how the `ItemsSource` property of a `DataGrid` can be set to the `exercises EntityList` of the `DomainContext` object. Once the `Load` method is completed, the `DataGrid` automatically populates with the results because the `EntityList` implements the `INotifyPropertyChanged` just like an `ObservableCollection`.

LISTING 2-24: MainPage.xaml.cs (located in the RIAServicesSample project)

Available for download on Wrox.com

```
using System.Windows.Controls;
using RIAServicesSample.Web.Data;
using RIAServicesSample.Web.Services;

namespace RIAServicesSample
{
     public partial class MainPage: UserControl
     {
          private ExerciseContext context = new ExerciseContext();

          public MainPage()
          {
               InitializeComponent();

               // Once Load<exercise> completes the exercises entity
               // list will be populated
               // By setting the ItemsSource before the LoadExercises
               // call you can be sure that
               // the DataGrid will populate after the exercises
               // have been loaded

               ExercisesGrid.ItemsSource = context.exercises;
               context.Load<exercise>(context.GetExercisesQuery());
          }
     }
}
```

This is a pretty simple example of how to make use of the WCF RIA Services in a Silverlight client and it barely scratches the surface of what the framework has to offer. There will be much more extensive coverage of the WCF RIA Services features — such as code sharing and validation — in upcoming chapters of the book.

Now there is only one more important area to be concerned with when looking at the logical tier design process. In some ways, it is the most important because it can really alter the decisions you make in every other design tier. That area is the data storage layer, and it does not matter if you are a programmer or database guru; the decision is an important one and most likely will stay with you throughout the life of the project and for years to come.

Data Storage Layer

The final logical tier design decision is the choice of database platform. For most sites, the database will reside on a separate physical machine than the rest of the application logic. The choice of which database to use depends on many factors such as cost, performance, and scalability. For this application, I will focus primarily on the factor that is most important to me, which is cost.

It is extremely difficult to get involved in the age old debate about which database platform is better: Oracle versus SQL Server versus MySQL. At times, it seems like you would have a better chance of seeing Yankee fans happily interacting with Red Sox fans before you would see those in the various Oracle and SQL Server camps agree on anything. The fact is that in the latest releases of both platforms, you will find very powerful database capabilities that will suit your needs quite well. In fact, even the freely available MySQL database engine is starting to gain more traction in enterprise database circles. Now at this point in the book I don't want to start any flame wars between the groups. I'll save that for the solution area of this chapter when I choose the database platform that will be used in this book. Hint: It's not Oracle or MySQL. Anyway, all three have something to offer and although when using LINQ to SQL as your data access layer, you can use only SQL Server, the other data access technologies such as ADO.NET and the Entity Framework interact quite nicely with Oracle, SQL Server, MySQL, and other databases. Let's look at what each of the major platforms has to offer before making a final decision on the data storage layer that you will use for FitnessTrackerPlus.

SQL Server

Microsoft's SQL Server version 2008 is available in several different versions. The least expensive version is SQL Server Express Edition. In fact, it's completely free. This edition comes in three flavors. You can download the Express edition with or without the Advanced Services option. The basic version includes the database engine along with SQL Server Management Studio, which allows you to administer databases from a graphical user interface. The Advanced Services version includes everything from the Basic edition as well as providing full-text indexing and reporting services. In addition to these versions, you can also download the Compact edition of the database, which provides 2MB of storage and full support for T-SQL syntax. This edition is great for embedding with desktop applications that need a standalone database.

Other editions available for SQL Server include the Developer, Web, Workgroup, Standard, and Enterprise versions. Each of these versions has various limitations and size constraints. For example, the free editions are limited to a database size of 4GB and can only make use of 1 CPU. On the other side of the spectrum, the Enterprise edition can make use of the maximum number of CPUs available to the operating system. It also has no restrictions on the overall database size. As you move through the various editions available for SQL Server, the prices range from free to thousands of dollars. Nonetheless as your site grows in size and you find the need to scale the database layer, you will most likely find an edition of SQL Server that fits your needs.

SQL Server is the only database engine that is supported by all available data access technologies in .NET. Support for SQL Server is included in ADO.NET, LINQ to SQL, and the Entity Framework.

There is one caveat, however, and that is SQL Server can be run only on a Microsoft Windows-based platform. If you need to run the database on a non-Microsoft operating system such as Linux, SQL Server is not a viable option.

Oracle

Oracle also provides various editions of its own suite of database technology. Recently Oracle has introduced its own free version of the database engine called Oracle XE edition. Like SQL Server, Oracle has several different editions available based on the needs of your site. Oracle is really the powerhouse of all the database options that you could choose from. It is also, however, the most complex of the bunch. One benefit to Oracle is that it supports multiple platforms so it can be run in a Linux environment as well as Windows. Through the years, Oracle has always been considered the top performer when compared to SQL Server, but SQL Server has undergone so many drastic improvements that the gap has been significantly lowered.

MySQL

MySQL is another database option that is getting more powerful with every release. One of the oldest limitations of MySQL was the lack of stored procedure support. With the latest release, however, stored procedures are fully supported. MySQL is free under the GNU license, as long as the application you are creating that utilizes MySQL also falls under the GNU license. You will not have to pay a licensing fee. If, however, you are developing a closed source product that uses MySQL, you will most likely need to look into purchasing one of the available commercial licenses. As far as speed and reliability go, MySQL has made drastic improvements over the years and can be considered a viable alternative to Oracle and SQL Server. Like Oracle, the MySQL database engine is platform-independent and versions of MySQL can be found for Windows, Linux, and a host of other operating systems.

Access

Everyone at one time or another has had the pleasure of interacting with Access as a database platform. This little database-engine-that-could has been around for many years and has handled the problem of small application-based databases throughout its lifetime. With the introduction of SQL Express, however, the decision to utilize Access as a primary database engine for an application is questionable at best. There is no T-SQL query language available, no stored procedures, and no real support from any of the data access technologies discussed previously other than ADO.NET. Only one major edition of Access is available and it is included in various versions of Microsoft Office. While it can still be a viable candidate as a database for desktop applications, it is a pretty safe bet that you will not be using Access for the FitnessTrackerPlus application or any scalable website that you are implementing in the future.

FitnessTrackerPlus Application Design

Now that you have been introduced to several possible technology choices for the FitnessTrackerPlus application, it's time to take a quick first pass at the overall design of the application itself. Once you have a good feel for what FitnessTrackerPlus will need to accomplish, you can review the available technology and make informed decisions about which frameworks to use in each development tier. In the following sections, you will take a crack at creating an initial design for each of the pages that are required in the FitnessTrackerPlus application. To start things off, let's take a look at what needs to go into the initial landing page.

Landing Page

The first page that users will see when typing `FitnessTrackerPlus.com` is the landing page. In any major website there is perhaps no page more important than this one because it provides, in some cases, your one and only chance to hook potential customers into your application. First impressions are extremely important on the Web, especially if you are creating a site that has many other competitors. If users cannot find the information they are looking for right away or if the landing page just does not seem professionally done, they will leave and no doubt find one of your competitors. Once this happens, it is extremely difficult to get that customer back, which is why you must get this right the first time.

There are several items that you should include on this landing page that most visitors will look for. If they have come here, it is safe to assume that they are looking for an easy-to-use Web-based fitness tracking system, and this page needs to assure visitors that they have come to the right place for this. The following is a list of some basic requirements for the landing page that will ensure you have a professional-looking page for FitnessTrackerPlus:

- A screenshot of the application showing foods, exercises, or measurements being added to a user's fitness journal
- A bulleted list of features and benefits that stand out against the competition and are compelling enough that visitors will want to see more of the site
- Login capabilities for existing users
- A signup link so new users can join
- A footer area with copyright, privacy policy, site information, contact, and terms of service page links
- Site logo across top of screen

Although you want visitors to know precisely what is available here on FitnessTrackerPlus, you don't want the landing page to be too cluttered. Most popular sites now are keeping landing pages simple and highlighting only the most important aspects of the site while providing obvious things such as signup and login capabilities. To get an even better idea of what the landing page should look like, it can sometimes help to sketch out possible ideas. Figure 2-24 shows one possible solution that includes areas for each of the landing page requirements listed.

Earlier in the chapter, while describing the various problems that need to be solved in planning your Silverlight application architecture, I warned about the possibility that users who have never heard of Silverlight will eventually access your site. Despite millions of successful installations and implementations by the 2008 Olympics and even Major League Baseball, for example, you will no doubt see visitors who don't have the plug-in installed on their machines. Not only do you have to prepare some kind of alternate landing page for those users, but you'll also need to convince them that Silverlight is a safe plug-in to install. Most users will already have the Flash plug-in from Adobe installed and will be familiar with why it is required. It is a safe bet that just YouTube alone probably helped facilitate several million installations of the Flash plug-in. In a way, that helps you because users feel pretty safe with Flash, and Silverlight is very similar in concept.

FIGURE 2-24

> *I can't stress enough how important this initial landing page is for this application and any site for that matter. Within seconds, the user should know that FitnessTrackerPlus is a feature-rich, easy-to-use fitness tracking application that, combined with Silverlight technology, provides an experience that can't be found elsewhere.*

Besides making your users feel safe about the plug-in, your landing page needs some text describing what the Silverlight plug-in is as well as easy-to-follow installation instructions. Lucky for us, the developers at Microsoft thought about this in advance and have provided the `PluginNotInstalledTemplate` for the Silverlight control. That seems like a good place to start when designing a solution for this problem.

You want the non-Silverlight version of the page to look as similar as possible to the Silverlight version. As with the Silverlight version of the landing page, you still must display the site's basic features so users know the site's purpose before they go through the process of installing the plug-in. Because all other areas of the site utilize Silverlight functionality, the only other requirements for this template are providing detailed instructions on plug-in installation and descriptive information of the plug-in's purpose, and, again, ensuring that it's safe to install.

Although Silverlight supports most major web browsers, it's beneficial to provide a list of browsers that are currently supported to avoid any user frustration due to an unsupported browser. Since the initial release of Silverlight, developers all too often have ignored the installation experience and relied on the default page that loads when users don't have the browser installed. The default experience is simply a blank page with a button that tells the user to click here to install Silverlight.

Regardless of the application you are building, it is a pretty safe bet that anyone who visits your site expecting a traditional website design and is greeted with this will ignore your site and move on to the competition.

Fitness Dashboard

With the landing page designed, you now need to think about what users will see after they log in to the site. The fitness dashboard page will be the first page seen by users and will give them access to all other areas of the site. From the dashboard the user will need the ability to perform the following functions:

- View current measurements
- View nutrition summary for current day
- View exercise summary for current day
- View any site announcements
- Select a theme to be applied to entire site
- View and update account information such as password and e-mail address

One of the original requirements for the fitness dashboard was the ability to provide announcement information to all of the users of the site without having to resort to bulk e-mail notifications. It would be best if you could do this without forcing the user to leave the dashboard page. What you are looking for here is some type of popup window that contains an announcement for the user. Don't worry about resorting to standard browser popup windows that may be blocked by browser popup blockers. Silverlight 4 now includes an incredibly useful `ChildWindow` control that you can use to display a modal dialog to the user. This would be the preferred way to display the announcements.

Food Log

One of the most important features of the site is providing the ability for users to enter the foods they eat on a daily basis. During the design phase you want to make sure that you come up with the best way to provide this functionality. To ensure that you satisfy this requirement, you can create a couple of user stories that simulate what the user is trying to do while on this page. The following are a couple of potential user stories that reflect what real users may try to do on this page:

- John logs in to FitnessTrackerPlus to enter the foods that he has eaten today. He clicks the Food Log menu link and immediately looks for a search box because he would rather not have to enter all of the nutritional information for the foods. John knows that the site includes an extensive database of foods and he should be able to find a food that matches what he has eaten. He enters the food name into the search box and pages through an extensive list of foods until he finds one that is the best match. After selecting the checkbox presented in the list and then clicking the Add Food button, he sees his food added to a table along with the calories, protein, carbohydrate, and fat values for the given food. It is also nice to see that after all of his foods have been entered a daily total appears that calculates the values of all the basic nutrients that he has consumed.

- Mary has been a user of FitnessTrackerPlus for a few months now and has also been on a diet that commonly requires her to eat the same foods during the course of the week. She notices that instead of searching for matching foods every time she uses her journal she can simply click a list of recently consumed foods and quickly add those to her journal. Now instead of spending minutes searching for the foods she eats, which for the most part are the same every day, she spends only seconds pulling items from the recent foods list into her journal.
- Tom isn't very interested in paging through thousands of search results in order to enter the foods he eats. He notices that the search box offers matching food suggestions as he types and can quickly just click one of the suggestions to add an item to his food log. If he doesn't find a match, he just finishes typing the food and creates a new custom food that lets him enter the nutritional information for the food he is trying to enter. The best part is he has to do this only once and then his custom foods start appearing in the suggestions, which makes it even faster for him to enter foods the next day.

These are pretty basic user stories but they give you an excellent idea of what might be needed on this page.

Exercise Log

The exercise log page will satisfy the requirement of providing the users with the ability to enter the exercises performed on a daily basis. This page will most likely require many of the items that were designed on the food log page. For example, from this page it is reasonable to expect that users will need to:

- Search exercises to find the exercise performed
- Create custom exercises and add them to the journal
- Browse available exercises by muscle group
- View all exercises performed in a table-like format
- Select from recent exercises as well as custom exercises

Because this page requires much of the same basic functionality provided in the food log, you can probably use a screen that looks very similar to the food log in the design.

Measurement Log

In addition to entering foods and exercises, your users will need to keep track of their current measurements. The measurement journal will provide the ability for users to keep track of the following measurements:

- Weight
- Waist
- Legs
- Body Mass Index

In addition to this list of measurements, it is also a requirement to provide the users with the ability to keep and track custom measurements. In addition to this, one of the requirements was providing a feature that lets the users upload an image and to associate it with the measurements being logged. Everyday users should be able to enter current measurements and an image of themselves.

Public Fitness Journal

Now that users have a place to keep track of foods, exercises, and measurements related to their fitness progress, you can turn your attention to providing them with a means to share that information with others. The public fitness journal feature will provide a social networking aspect to the site by giving users a way to share their food, exercise, and measurement logs with other users of the site, as well as other users across the Internet. Users will need to be provided with a URL that will directly access this public journal page. In addition to this important requirement, there are several others that you will need to satisfy on this page, such as:

- Display About Me text for the user
- Display HTML-based comments from visitors who access the page
- Provide a way for visitors to view nutrition, exercise, and measurement logs
- Provide the ability to share uploaded measurement images
- Provide the capability for users to customize what information if any will be made publicly available

Not all users will want to share their information with others so providing a settings screen will give the user a way to turn on/off various aspects of their public journal. This is an important feature of any social networking style site as you will never want to assume that a user wishes for his or her information to be made public. In fact, the default implementation of the public journal will ensure that all journals are private when the user registers with the site. It will be up to each individual user to take the steps required to make their journal public to the rest of the Internet. The public journal is a unique aspect of the site in that when a user is logged into the site they will have access to the settings area of the journal along with access to the other various areas of the site. Users viewing the journal from the direct URL will not see any other menu items or have any access to journal settings. Those visitors will see only the public journal itself along with the site banner and footer areas.

SOLUTION

The solution section of this chapter involves making decisions on which technology you will use for the FitnessTrackerPlus application. I won't go into any implementation steps here as that will be saved for the next chapter where you create the home page, signup, and login. But first, you still have some important decisions to make. You have seen that the architecture is broken up into two major areas: the physical tier and logical tier. In both cases, you will want to concentrate on using technologies that help you create both scalable and maintainable websites. Let's take a look at what you will be using for both areas of the architecture, starting with the physical tier.

Physical Tier

I discussed earlier in the chapter that there are several different methods you can utilize in the physical tier. The most scalable architecture involves separate servers for each major tier. In that case, the user's Internet browser would be responsible for rendering the user interface, a physical application server would handle running the business logic, and finally another physical server would host the actual database where the data is being stored. This allows you to add physical servers to both the business tier and database tier in order to scale the application.

For FitnessTrackerPlus, you will start out with one physical machine for everything. Your web browser will handle the user interface and your machine will also host the business logic and database. As you work toward deploying the application, you will move the business logic and database to separate physical servers. For now, however, during the implementation of the site you will keep everything on your personal machine. Obviously, this won't scale well but right now you are the only user so no worries here.

The only thing left to do is make a decision on the technology you will be using for the physical tier. Because the goal of this book is to help you learn how to build a Silverlight line of business application utilizing Microsoft-based technologies you will be using IIS as the application web server and SQL Server Express for the database. That is not to say you couldn't use another web server with a Silverlight client or even Oracle XE as the database. Silverlight can consume SOAP-based web services just fine so a Tomcat server would work just as well as far as the Silverlight client is concerned. In fact, when you are finished with the book, it could even be a great learning experience to make an attempt at running the site on Tomcat using Oracle XE or MySQL for the database. That just about covers the decisions you need to make for the physical tier. Now you need to take some time and figure out what to use for the logical tier. As you saw previously in the chapter, many technologies are available, all with various pros and cons, so it might take a little bit more time to make a decision about this.

Logical Tier

The logical tier technology decisions now need to be made for the user interface, business logic, and data access layers. I have already explained that my choice for the database layer will be SQL Server Express Edition. This is a free version of the SQL Server database that has all of the required functionality that you will need to create, test, and run the application. Should FitnessTrackerPlus gain in popularity at a rapid pace, it will be no real extra effort to swap the Express Edition for one of the more powerful editions that can handle additional CPUs and larger physical database files.

Making the decision for the user interface is the easiest place to start. The title of this book is *Silverlight 4 Problem-Design-Solution* so it's a pretty safe bet that Silverlight will be your user interface of choice. It may be beneficial at some point in the future to look at what WPF thick clients bring to the table and it could even be a future option to add as a premium feature of the site. For now, however, you will be using Silverlight only during the development of the site.

For the business logic layer, I have covered what seems like an endless supply of choices. Should you use ASMX SOAP-based web services with custom business objects? How about WCF services?

ADO.NET Data Services offer a REST-based platform for accessing business logic so that must be the way to go, right? After all, REST is one of the new buzzwords and many other sites offer REST-based services for consumption. Or maybe the right answer is WCF RIA Services because they were specifically aimed at Silverlight-based clients. In this book, you will be implementing the business logic layer using the new WCF RIA Services platform. This was not an obvious choice, but I felt the WCF RIA Services were the most compelling as they really had Silverlight in mind when RIA was developed. The minimal amount of code required to get the business logic layer up and running alone makes a compelling argument for using WCF RIA Services. In addition to this, I just couldn't ignore how simple it is to get client- and server-side validation through the use of the metadata classes. This is an extremely powerful feature, and if you have ever spent long hours writing validation code, you know that it is not very exciting and typically can be error prone. If you are looking for a fast yet flexible way to create the business logic layer, the WCF RIA Services provide you with exactly that.

Finally as far as the data access layer, I could no longer justify the use of traditional ADO.NET data access for this application. The introduction of ORM technologies has made it significantly easier to access data and for an application such as FitnessTrackerPlus, you would be much better off worrying about user interface and business logic issues than creating plumbing code for database access. Now the choice of which ORM technology to use is much more difficult.

On the one hand, LINQ to SQL is still being supported and, in fact, works quite well with the WCF RIA Services platform that you will be using in the business logic layer. On the other hand it is limited in that it supports only SQL Server. This was perhaps the hardest choice that had to be made for FitnessTrackerPlus. If you have followed the conversations online in various blogs and forums, you will see that there are many developers who feel that the Entity Framework in many ways is bloated and difficult to use in anything but an enterprise scenario or if a database other than SQL Server needs to be supported. Many developers feel that LINQ to SQL just works better and does what developers need it to do without being overly complex. Of course, there is always the worry that while making enhancements to the Entity Framework, at some point Microsoft will just drop support for LINQ to SQL.

Ultimately I made the decision to create the data access layer using LINQ to SQL for a variety of reasons:

- My general experience with LINQ to SQL has matched that of many other developers in that it provides exactly what you are looking for from an ORM technology. Some complex query scenarios that are required for FitnessTrackerPlus just work in LINQ to SQL and for some reason require much more complicated coding solutions when using the Entity Framework.
- One major reason for sticking with LINQ to SQL is the fact that at least currently it runs much faster than the Entity Framework. There have been many benchmarks done online comparing the two technologies and at least in the current implementations LINQ to SQL almost always outperforms the Entity Framework in every test. That is not to say that with the release of .NET 4 improvements to the Entity Framework won't make those performance tests obsolete, but at the time of this writing the Entity Framework simply does not win the performance race.

- Another important consideration for using LINQ to SQL is that you will be using SQL Server exclusively for this book so you do not have to be concerned with third-party database support. In fact, another thing to consider is that there is currently no free Oracle or MySQL provider that fully supports Entity Framework implementations. Where possible, I wanted to keep the cost of developing this site as close to free as possible. Utilizing a free database engine such as Oracle XE or MySQL would be rather pointless if you then had to go out and purchase a third-party driver that supported using the database with the Entity Framework.

SUMMARY

Well this chapter covered a ton of information. You have seen how the physical and logical tier design is an important step to complete before moving on to any implementation phase. For the logical tier design, you have seen a large number of technologies that are at your disposal for the user interface, business logic, data access, and database layers. The powerful new data controls in Silverlight will be utilized to make a rich data entry interface to the FitnessTrackerPlus application. I have also shown you how you can satisfy some of the more difficult requirements by combining the base Silverlight controls with those found in the Silverlight Toolkit. For the business logic layer, there were many different options including ASMX web services, WCF services, ADO.NET Data Services, and the new WCF RIA Services that were specifically geared toward solving some of the N-Tier design issues that can come up with disconnected Silverlight applications. For the data access layer you were shown how the introduction of ORM technology such as LINQ to SQL and the Entity Framework have greatly simplified the amount of work that goes into the creation of a data access layer.

In addition to being introduced to all of these new technologies, solid decisions were made about which of them will be used in the creation of the FitnessTrackerPlus application. During the next group of chapters, you will be making use of Silverlight controls, Silverlight Toolkit controls, WCF RIA Services, LINQ to SQL, and SQL Server Express all to build a solid line of business application that will be able to handle many users and provide quick and painless data entry functionality to your users. With the design out of the way, you can finally move on to the fun and exciting stuff — the code! There is no time like the present so let's get started and create a home page where users can not only find out more about the application but also register with the site and immediately start to reap the benefits of their new membership.

3

Sign Me Up

Using Membership, Authentication, and Profile Services in Silverlight

In the previous chapter, I covered many of the new technologies available for Silverlight development. The solution section offered some choices as to which technologies to use during the development of the FitnessTrackerPlus application. Now you will finally see some of the technologies in action as you begin to implement the actual site. It is always best to leverage as many existing services as possible when creating a new site and ASP.NET has offered several services to facilitate common website tasks such as login, registration, and profile management. Even though you will be developing a Silverlight application, you can still take advantage of the services that are provided by ASP.NET rather than reinventing the wheel. By the end of this chapter, you will have a good working knowledge of how to combine the existing ASP.NET services for Authentication, Membership, and Profile management with the new WCF RIA Services to create a fully working login, and member registration area.

In addition to providing some of these common services to your users, it is also important that this site functions like a traditional website as much as possible. This site should provide integration with the browsers back and forward buttons as well as browser history. In this chapter, you see how the new navigation framework provides you with the tools necessary to ensure that the user experience on this Silverlight site offers the same browser integration available at traditional websites — just with a much richer user interface.

PROBLEM

If you have ever done any work developing a website you no doubt have had to solve some common design problems. For example, how will users access protected pages? How will users register to use the site and how will you let users reset a lost or forgotten password? For the most part, if you were using ASP.NET, you probably made use in one way or another of the

Membership, Authentication, and Profile services. These services provided an easy solution to the common design problems listed, and even included several user interface controls that were tightly integrated with those services. The ASP.NET Membership service consists of a provider-based model that has built-in support for managing users in a SQL Server database. Because the model was provider-based, it isn't terribly difficult to make the modifications required to support other databases, such as Oracle or MySQL as well. The Authentication service provides an easy way to handle login/logout scenarios and the Profile service contains a provider-based model for storing and retrieving individual user properties from a database table. As in the case of the Membership service, the Profile service can be overridden to work against just about any other database provider.

These services have been a great addition to the ASP.NET framework and have saved developers from countless hours of developing proprietary user management code libraries. You, however, are developing a Silverlight application that basically consists only of one ASP.NET page whose sole responsibility is to host the Silverlight plug-in. FitnessTrackerPlus requires all of the same functionality that any other traditional website would have to offer, but developing a completely new mechanism for site authentication and user management would make the development of this site pretty painful. Not to mention these features really aren't related to the business problem that you are trying to solve with the site; so rather than spend a ton of up-front time trying to create these services from scratch, you need to find a way to leverage the existing ASP.NET services.

Once you solve the problem of user management and authentication you will need to move on to making the site feel like a traditional website that provides tight integration with the web browser. You may have been to some Flash-based sites in the past and moved through some data entry screens only to realize that you made a mistake on a previous step, or maybe just needed to review data from a previous page. You see the large flashing warning sign that says "Click this link to go back," but you ignore it anyway because the browser's Back button is practically screaming "CLICK ME INSTEAD."

Sadly, instead of reaching the previous destination page you are greeted with the home page of the site, or worse some cryptic error message page. Oh well — a simple click of the Forward button and you should be back in business. Unfortunately, instead of the page from which you initially started this process, you're again greeted with some other error page. This happens all too often and is the direct result of developers not offering tight integration with the existing web browser controls. It's great to take the time and provide a nice hyperlink that brings the user to the previous page while retaining all the information that the developer needs for the page to work correctly, but the reality is that users know the browser controls. You cannot expect that every user is going to use the custom navigation links that you provide. You do not want the users of FitnessTrackerPlus to go through this same annoyance just because they are interacting with a Silverlight-based site. You will need to ensure that, at any time, if a user clicks the Back or Forward buttons, the site will do exactly what is expected, which is to actually go to the previous or next page of the site.

Finally, the development of the FitnessTrackerPlus home page presents a unique problem. If users hit the home page and do not already have Silverlight installed, by default, they are presented with a generic installation page for the Silverlight plug-in with no explanation as to what Silverlight is or why they see an installation page instead of an online fitness tracking site. As you saw in the previous chapter, the Silverlight plug-in offers a `PluginNotInstalledTemplate` property that you must use to provide visitors with a standard HTML version of the home page that looks similar to what they would have seen if the plug-in had already been installed. There should also be some basic instructions about what Silverlight is and how users can install it.

DESIGN

Now that you have a few different problems outlined that need to be solved, it's time to start thinking about designing solutions to these problems. This chapter, along with the next few, will involve design and implementation of the user interface, database, data access, business logic, and code behind layers. I will be covering each area as its own separate topic based on the feature that is being implemented.

In a perfect world, you might design and implement the data access layer followed by the business logic and wrap things up with the user interface. Everything would link up together perfectly and all of the business objects you designed would work out exactly how the user interface requires them to be. In practice, I have yet to see this actually happen. In most cases, unless you are part of a large development team, this kind of design and implementation just does not take place. If you are part of a small team or if you are the only developer, as is the case with FitnessTrackerPlus, it can become pretty overwhelming to design and implement a layer at a time only to find out that the user interface requires things that you hadn't thought of during the initial design stage.

FitnessTrackerPlus has a pretty extensive list of requirements. I feel that for this application it is best to list the requirements and features that will be needed and then pick a feature and work your way through the various layers required to create that feature. For example, this chapter will require a login and user registration feature. Rather than present you with the entire FitnessTrackerPlus database design followed by the entire data access and business logic layers, I will instead show you the design and implementation of those layers related to only the login and registration features; each individual site feature will have its own separate coverage for each of the logical layers in the order shown that follows:

- User interface
- Database
- Data access
- Business logic
- User interface code behind

The user interface code behind logic that I am referring to covers any control event handlers and business logic required for those event handlers. With that out of the way, let's take a look at some of the requirements that were outlined in the previous chapter and make sure that the design satisfies all of them. The following is a list of the basic requirements that need to be satisfied for this chapter:

- The site requires a user-friendly home page that briefly outlines the benefits of using the site, along with a screenshot of the site in action.
- Users should be able to find a link to the main site registration from the home page.
- Users should have easy access to all supplemental pages of the site such as the privacy policy, terms of service, contact, and about pages.

- All supplemental pages should be implemented in XAML and the user should stay in the Silverlight application at all times. The only traditional ASP.NET page that should be visible to users is the main page that hosts the Silverlight plug-in.
- Users that visit the home page should be able to log in to the site if they have already registered. Login should accept the user's primary e-mail address so that they do not have to remember yet another unique username.
- Users that decide to register for the site should have to provide only a minimal amount of information such as e-mail address and password. Passwords and security answers should be stored in an encrypted format that nobody else can access. This means even site administrators should not have access to this data. Any password or security information should be encrypted using a one-way hash.

> *Although this is not a banking site, and you are not really storing any sensitive information, it is sometimes just easier to tell your users that even you can't access the password. This leaves users with the impression that your site is taking all necessary precautions with data. To some users, even the e-mail address is considered sensitive and the fact that, as a site administrator, you can't view the password can go a long way in establishing a trustful relationship with your users — especially should you decide to add features in the future that do require more sensitive user information.*

- Once logged in, the user should be presented with a dashboard page, which, at this point, is just an empty placeholder page with a logout button
- The dashboard page, and any other pages that require a login, should be locked down and unavailable to anonymous users.
- Users who hit the FitnessTrackerPlus home page and do not have the Silverlight plug-in installed should be presented with an HTML version of the site that provides a link to download the plug-in as well as a description of what the site offers. This alternate view should look as similar to the Silverlight version as possible. The alternate view should not, however, provide access to any areas of the site other than the privacy policy and terms of service, which still need to be enabled should users want to review those policies before making a decision to install the plug-in.

Home Page

The home page for FitnessTrackerPlus will be the first thing that the users encounter when visiting the site. This page has a couple of primary roles, including access to login, user registration, supplemental pages, and an overview of the site features. As promised, I will be splitting up the design discussion of the home page into the logical layers outlined previously.

User Interface

In the previous chapter, I showed you a quick pencil sketch of what the home page should look like. It's time to get a little bit more specific. The latest trend in Web 2.0-style websites is to provide a home page that is not cluttered with slick graphics that can be confusing to the users. This works out great for me as I have no artistic ability anyway — so the simpler the better. This page just needs a logo area, login control, screenshot, feature list, registration link, and links to any supplemental pages. It would be best if you followed the sketch that was created earlier and have the banner and login at the top, the screenshot and feature list in the middle, and finally, the supplemental links in the footer area of the page along with any copyright information.

It seems desirable to include the banner and footer areas throughout the site, and traditional ASP.NET sites could make use of the `MasterPages` feature so that the header and footer areas could be reused throughout the site with no extra work for the developer. Although Silverlight does not have `MasterPages`, it does now provide the new navigation framework that I outlined in the previous chapter. In this case, you will want to add a `Frame` control to the home page with the banner above and footer below. This `Frame` control is responsible for hosting all of the site content. The beauty of using the `Frame` control is that you have full support of the browser's Back, Forward, and History features. When users navigate to the embedded page views, they can simply click the Back button on the browser to return to the previous page with absolutely no additional code being written. This satisfies one of the main requirements of the application, which was to provide a site that has the rich user interface benefits of Silverlight while maintaining traditional ASP.NET page navigation behavior.

Site content needs to reside in controls that derive from the new `Page` class available in the `System.Windows.Controls` namespace. These `Page` controls will all sit under the Views folder that was initially created with the new Navigation project template. The default `Page` control that should display on the `Frame` will be called Home and should consist of the screenshot, feature text, and, of course, a button that provides a large visual link to the user registration page.

The final aspect of the user interface that needs to be ironed out is how to support users that do not have the Silverlight plug-in installed. These users should see an HTML version of the home page that does not include the registration link, or the login control. You should be able to utilize the `PluginNotInstalledTemplate` of the Silverlight control to handle the display of this alternate page. The plug-in will automatically detect if the user currently has Silverlight installed and, if not, it will display any HTML you place in that template.

Database, Data Access

I won't often combine the database and data access in the same section, but in the case of the home page there really isn't any database or data access layer design necessary. At this point, you are only creating pages with static content and basic navigation. There are no related database tables that are essential for the banner, home view, or footer areas.

Business Logic, User Interface Code Behind

For the home page it is safe to combine the business logic and user interface logic into one area as well. Because there will not really be any business entities or data associated with the home page, there won't be much in the way of business logic required either. For the user interface logic you will need something to handle the navigation frame events.

User Registration

The next major feature that needs to be designed is the user registration system. The goal for this design is to create a user-friendly signup page that collects only the minimum amount of data from the visitor that is necessary to use the application. Another goal for this feature is to find a way to make use of the existing ASP.NET Membership, Role, and Profile providers so that you don't have to create registration code from scratch.

User Interface

When thinking about the user interface for the user registration page you want to ensure that you are only collecting information that is needed for visitors to use the site. Through the years I have registered for many different websites and have accumulated countless usernames and passwords. Sometimes I see sites that get the signup page right and ask for minimal information while others require just about every piece of information imaginable. Whenever I encounter a site that wants to know more about me than the IRS, I get a little worried. If I really am interested in using the site, I may just give in and provide the information but I will also be watching my Inbox for a deluge of spam e-mails that mysteriously appear after registering with the site.

Unless you are creating an online banking site or utility site that collects bill payments and you need detailed information about your users, there is just no legitimate reason to collect more data than you actually need for the user to utilize the site. For FitnessTrackerPlus this means requiring an e-mail address, password, and a security question/answer combination that the user can utilize if they need to reset a password. You may be wondering why I chose not to use a username in this case; as your users register at more and more sites it can become increasingly difficult to manage all those usernames and passwords. In many cases, the username that the user is looking for is already taken, which can result in user frustration. Most users have one primary e-mail address. By allowing the use of an e-mail address as opposed to forcing the creation of a unique username for logging in gives the user one less thing to remember in order to use your site. It may take a little bit of additional work during the coding stage, but I really do think your users will benefit greatly by having one less thing to remember.

Database

In ASP.NET-based websites, you have the option of utilizing the standard membership tables created by the aspnet_regsql tool. This tool creates several database tables that you can use to store membership information. If you take a look across the Internet you will see an endless supply of tutorials regarding the design of these tables as well as how to interact with the standard ASP.NET Membership and Profile providers. For the most part, unless you're creating a site from scratch, very rarely do you encounter a real-world scenario where you can actually use these tables and the standard Membership providers that come with ASP.NET. Sometimes you don't even have any control over, or input into, the design of the database tables. Although FitnessTrackerPlus is being created from scratch and would seem to fit the criteria for using the default tables, I have decided against it in favor of a custom database schema. This not only gives the application a little bit more flexibility in the long run but also presents an opportunity to learn how to write custom providers for the

Membership, Profile, and Role services. I don't necessarily want to create more work, but in real-world situations, more often than not, you have to make use of a custom database schema so being familiar with how to create these providers can come in handy, and it really isn't that much extra work.

> *For a more in-depth look at the ASP.NET Membership, Profile, and Role services you should check out* ASP.NET 2.0 Problem – Design – Solution *from Wrox Press. The author, Marco Bellinaso, does a terrific job of explaining the standard ASP.NET database tables as well as the internals of the provider-based model that is available in ASP.NET 2.0 for creating custom Membership, Role, and Profile providers.*

The tables you'll use for FitnessTrackerPlus are somewhat similar to the standard ASP.NET Membership tables with a few exceptions. For example, the user ID field is an integer set up as an identity field. The standard ASP.NET Membership tables utilize a GUID for its implementation of a unique ID. I decided against this for one major reason — cost. As you look into having your site hosted, you may decide to start with a shared hosting solution until your site gains in popularity. Shared hosting sites typically charge for database storage and the cost of that storage is a premium. If you stick with the GUID-style implementation for a unique key, then you will be using an expensive data type for a field that potentially will appear as a foreign key in many other tables throughout the database. You will not want to absorb the cost of this when using a shared hosting provider.

Some will argue that the use of a GUID data type makes data migration easier in the future, but because this site is being created from scratch I don't think that benefit outweighs the potential storage costs associated with the GUID. There are many other fields that are in the standard ASP.NET Membership tables that you will not see in the FitnessTrackerPlus tables. This is by design to save money and space when running the site from a shared hosting provider. It is not uncommon to have only 100MB of database storage from a shared hosting provider; increasing the size of the database can become a costly addition to any hosting plan. This may at first seem like plenty of space, but if your site gains in popularity quickly, you will appreciate optimized tables that use the least amount of required space. Tables 3-1 through 3-6 list information you'll use for setting up user registration in FitnessTrackerPlus.

TABLE 3-1: users

COLUMN NAME	TYPE	DESCRIPTION
id	intr	Unique identity field for users
email_address	varchar(256)	Primary e-mail address for the user
username	varchar(100)	Unique username generated as a combination of e-mail address up to the "@" symbol plus the value of the ID column
password	varchar(256)	SHA1 hash representation of password
locked	bit	Shows if user account is currently locked

continues

TABLE 3-1: users *(continued)*

COLUMN NAME	TYPE	DESCRIPTION
locked_date	datetime	Shows date that account was locked
last_login_date	datetime	Last time user performed a successful login
created_date	datetime	Date user account was created
account_type	int	Type of account created for user
ip_address	varchar(100)	Unique Internet address of user
security_question	int	Security question selected by user
security_answer	varchar(256)	SHA1 hash representation of answer to security question
online	bit	Shows if user is currently logged in to the site
disabled	bit	Used as an alternative to deleting accounts

TABLE 3-2: account_types

COLUMN NAME	TYPE	DESCRIPTION
id	int	Unique identity field for account type
type_name	varchar(100)	Name of account type — currently only FREE and PREMIUM
description	varchar(256)	Description of account type

TABLE 3-3: security_questions

COLUMN NAME	TYPE	DESCRIPTION
id	int	Unique identity field for security question
question	varchar(256)	Question text

TABLE 3-4: roles

COLUMN NAME	TYPE	DESCRIPTION
id	int	Unique identity field for role
name	varchar(256)	Name of role (currently the only roles are Admin and User)
description	varchar(256)	Description of role

TABLE 3-5: users_roles

COLUMN NAME	TYPE	DESCRIPTION
id	int	Unique identity field for user-role relationship
user_id	int	Unique identity of user
role_id	int	Unique identity of role

TABLE 3-6: profile

COLUMN NAME	TYPE	DESCRIPTION
id	int	Unique identity field for profile record
current_theme	varchar(100)	Full name of preferred theme
user_id	int	Unique identity of user

Data Access

The data access layer will consist of LINQ to SQL classes that are generated for the tables outlined in the previous section. Remember that LINQ to SQL class mappings always provide a 1:1 relationship with tables; you should expect there to be classes generated that represent users, roles, security questions, account types, and even a users-roles entity that represents the join table assigning users to various roles.

You will also want to rename the generated LINQ to SQL class mappings because some of the generated classes may conflict with built-in types of the ASP.NET Membership feature. For example, the users table will result in a `user` LINQ to SQL class. Having a `user` class will become confusing as you start to look at the WCF RIA Service's support for authentication, which utilizes a `UserBase` and `UserService` class of its own. To avoid any confusion, you should just capitalize the generated classes and change the users table to `UserInformation`. This way, it will be obvious when you are interacting with one of your custom-generated types versus one built into the runtime.

Business Logic

The new WCF RIA Services provide built-in support for interacting with the ASP.NET Authentication, Membership, and Role mechanisms. By using the WCF RIA Services, you will have an easy mechanism to access these ASP.NET services from a Silverlight client. Because you are not using the standard ASP.NET Membership table mechanism, the business logic will require custom implementations of the Membership, Profile, and Role providers. The custom membership provider will need to implement all the required methods and properties of the `MembershipProvider` interface.

You may also notice that many of the ASP.NET Membership, Profile, and Role interface methods utilize the username as a parameter for retrieving data from the various providers instead of an identity field or your primary key column. Therefore, it is still very much necessary to provide a username column in the database that is unique for every user of the site. In order to facilitate this without forcing the user to create a username during registration, the business logic will need to automatically create a unique username and store it in the database when the user information is created. The easiest way to provide this is to take the first part of the e-mail address up to the "@" symbol and combine it with the unique ID value that is generated from the identity column in the users database table. For example, creating my own account with an e-mail address of `nick@fitnesstrackerplus.com` would result in a username of nick1 being stored in the database if I were the first user to register with the site. Again, the user will not need to remember this username except when providing friends with the unique URL to their public version of the journal. In my case, that URL might end up being something similar to `http://www.FitnessTrackerPlus.com/Journals/nick1`.

The ASP.NET Membership feature provides several ways to create and store passwords in your database. Password storage is configured in the membership section of the web.config file using the `passwordFormat` attribute. This attribute provides the choices in Table 3-7 for password creation and storage.

TABLE 3-7: ASP.NET Membership Password Storage

FORMAT	DESCRIPTION
Clear	Stores the password in clear-text format. This option is for sites that require minimal security. Anyone with access to the user table in the database could potentially view the password of any user including the site administrator in clear text.
Encrypted	Stores the password in encrypted format. Offers higher layer of security than Clear. Passwords can be recovered using a decryption key. In a web farm or load-balancing scenario, the encryption key must be configured the same on all available servers.
Hashed	Creates an SAH-1 hash value of the password text and stores that value in the database. The actual password text is lost and cannot be recovered. It offers the highest layer of security, and passwords can only be reset, not recovered.

Although you will not be collecting any sensitive information in the FitnessTrackerPlus application, it's still better to be safe than sorry. You will be using hashed values for passwords in the database which means that you will not be able to decrypt and recover the original password text. The password recovery system for this site is more along the lines of a password reset feature. Users can have a new random password generated and sent to their e-mail address. Once users receive the e-mail, they can simply log on to the site with the newly generated password and change it to something that is easier to remember in the account settings page. You could argue that the lack of sensitive stored information allows the use of the two-way encryption model, but I still feel it all comes back to trust; if a user contacts you about a missing password and you can say to them that even you as the site administrator cannot access it, he or she will feel that much safer about using the site. It is a small matter of inconvenience to have the user log in with the generated password once and then reset it to something else, but as your site increases in popularity, more often than not, users will appreciate the fact that all their information is safe — especially their login information.

As far as roles go in the site, there will really be only two possible roles for now. All users will belong to the User role when an account is created. In addition, the site administrator will be added to the Admin role, which could be used in the future to handle user administration tasks.

Although you will be creating a custom profile provider, there is really only one property that will be available from the provider at this point, and that is the `CurrentTheme`. The standard mechanism for profile storage in traditional ASP.NET websites is to include all of the profile properties in an XML-based string in the database. I have gone with a slightly different route here by creating a profile table where each profile property is a separate column in the table. By doing this, you can minimize the space required by the profile, eliminating the overhead of additional XML tags.

User Interface Code Behind

The user registration page has one event handler that will need to be implemented and that is for the actual registration button click. In this handler, you will need to validate all the collected information and create a new user account in the database with the supplied values. Any errors that occur during this process should be presented to the user. Although you could redirect the user back to the main home page upon successful registration, I find it more useful to just log the user into the system at that point and move them forward to the dashboard page. No need to force the user to take an additional login step in order to proceed if it can be avoided.

Login Control

Although technically part of the home page, I decided it would be best to discuss the login control as a separate feature. Any time there is a standalone control required during the development of FitnessTrackerPlus, I will try to discuss that control as a feature in of itself. The login control will be located in the banner area of the home page and will provide the necessary functionality for users to log in to the site.

User Interface

Not much is required in the design of the login control's user interface. You will need an area for the user to enter his or her e-mail address as well as a password. If a user enters incorrect login information, the error should be displayed below the control in red so that it stands out as an error. Whenever possible, you should attempt to provide a meaningful error message to the user on a failed login.

Database, Data Access

No additional tables are required for the login control as it will simply make use of the existing tables created for the user registration page. In fact, the only table that the login control actually will require is the users table, which contains the e-mail address and encrypted password. As far as the data access layer, the login control should be able to make use of any classes created for the user registration page.

Business Logic

Because the login control is a completely separate control from the home page, it will need a way to communicate with the parent control. The best way to provide this functionality is through the use of events. The login control should have a public event that the parent control can listen for and act upon when the login is successfully completed. Because the control itself will be handling the presentation of any error messages to the user, it is not really necessary to notify the parent control of any failed login.

User Interface Code Behind

The only required user interface logic for this control is really handling a click event from the submit button that is part of the control. This event will need to take the e-mail address and password supplied by the user and validate it against what is currently stored in the database. The control will need to interact with some kind of Authentication service on the server in order to perform the login.

SOLUTION

The solution section of this chapter covers the creation of the home page, home view, login control, and user registration page. Like the design section, each individual feature will be covered in its own section separated into the user interface, database, data access, business logic, and user interface code behind.

Main Landing Page

At the end of the first chapter, you created a new Silverlight navigation application. The creation of that project resulted in several pages being added that are no longer needed. You can safely delete all of the pages that were included in the project as well as any files that exist under the Views folder. In order to add the main landing page to the project, you will need to add a new `UserControl` to the root of the Silverlight project, and call it MainPage.xaml. Because the old application structure did not use a MainPage.xaml file you also need to update the `Application_Startup` event handler in the App.xaml file so that a new instance of `MainPage` is created and run when the application starts.

User Interface

The landing page itself does not include much in the way of functionality other than a banner area, navigation frame, and footer area. Listing 3-1 shows the complete XAML code for the main landing page of the site.

Available for download on Wrox.com

LISTING 3-1: MainPage.xaml

```
<UserControl x:Class="FitnessTrackerPlus.MainPage"
     xmlns="http://schemas.microsoft.com/winfx/2006/xaml/presentation"
     xmlns:x="http://schemas.microsoft.com/winfx/2006/xaml"
     xmlns:navigation="clr-
namespace:System.Windows.Controls;assembly=System.Windows.Controls.Navigation"
     xmlns:toolkit="clr-
namespace:System.Windows.Controls;assembly=System.Windows.Controls.Toolkit"
     xmlns:controls="clr-
namespace:System.Windows.Controls;assembly=System.Windows.Controls"
     xmlns:fitnesstrackerplus="clr-namespace:FitnessTrackerPlus.Controls">
```

```
    <UserControl.Resources>
        <LinearGradientBrush x:Key="ApplicationBackgroundBrush"
EndPoint="0.5,1" StartPoint="0.5,0">
            <GradientStop Color="#FFFFFFFF"/>
            <GradientStop Color="#FF77A9D4" Offset="1"/>
        </LinearGradientBrush>
        <Style x:Key="BannerAreaStyle" TargetType="toolkit:DockPanel">
            <Setter Property="Height" Value="125" />
            <Setter Property="LastChildFill" Value="False" />
            <Setter Property="VerticalAlignment" Value="Top" />
            <Setter Property="toolkit:DockPanel.Dock" Value="Top" />
        </Style>
        <Style x:Key="LogoBackgroundStyle" TargetType="Border">
            <Setter Property="toolkit:DockPanel.Dock" Value="Left" />
        </Style>
        <Style x:Key="LogoImageStyle" TargetType="Image">
            <Setter Property="Source" Value="/Images/logo.png" />
            <Setter Property="Width" Value="300" />
            <Setter Property="Height" Value="80" />
            <Setter Property="Stretch" Value="Fill" />
            <Setter Property="VerticalAlignment" Value="Top" />
        </Style>
        <Style x:Key="LoginControlStyle"
TargetType="fitnesstrackerplus:Login">
            <Setter Property="toolkit:DockPanel.Dock" Value="Right" />
        </Style>
        <Style x:Key="MainFrameAreaStyle" TargetType="navigation:Frame">
            <Setter Property="Source" Value="Home" />
            <Setter Property="HorizontalContentAlignment"
Value="Stretch" />
            <Setter Property="Margin" Value="0,10" />
        </Style>
        <Style x:Key="FooterAreaStyle" TargetType="StackPanel">
            <Setter Property="HorizontalAlignment" Value="Center" />
            <Setter Property="toolkit:DockPanel.Dock" Value="Bottom" />
        </Style>
        <Style x:Key="FooterLinksAreaStyle" TargetType="StackPanel">
            <Setter Property="Orientation" Value="Horizontal" />
            <Setter Property="HorizontalAlignment" Value="Center" />
        </Style>
        <Style x:Key="FooterTextStyle" TargetType="TextBlock">
            <Setter Property="Foreground" Value="#FFFFFFFF" />
            <Setter Property="FontSize" Value="12" />
        </Style>
        <Style x:Key="FooterLinksStyle" TargetType="HyperlinkButton">
            <Setter Property="Foreground" Value="#FFFFFFFF" />
            <Setter Property="FontSize" Value="12" />
        </Style>
        <Style x:Key="CopyrightTextStyle" TargetType="TextBlock">
            <Setter Property="Text"  Value="FitnessTrackerPlus
Copyright 2009-2010 All Rights Reserved" />
            <Setter Property="Margin" Value="0,10,0,0" />
            <Setter Property="HorizontalAlignment" Value="Center" />
        </Style>
```

continues

LISTING 3-1 *(continued)*

```
    </UserControl.Resources>
    <ScrollViewer x:Name="MainScroll" Background="{StaticResource
ApplicationBackgroundBrush}">
        <toolkit:DockPanel LastChildFill="True">
            <toolkit:DockPanel Style="{StaticResource
BannerAreaStyle}" Height="Auto">
                <Border Style="{StaticResource LogoBackgroundStyle}">
                    <Image Style="{StaticResource LogoImageStyle}" />
                </Border>
                <fitnesstrackerplus:Login x:Name="LoginControl"
Style="{StaticResource LoginControlStyle}" />
            </toolkit:DockPanel>
            <StackPanel Style="{StaticResource FooterAreaStyle}">
                <StackPanel Style="{StaticResource
FooterLinksAreaStyle}">
                    <HyperlinkButton x:Name="HomeLink"
NavigateUri="Home" TargetName="MainSiteFrame" Content="Home"
Style="{StaticResource FooterLinksStyle}" />
                    <TextBlock Text="|" Style="{StaticResource
FooterTextStyle}" />
                    <HyperlinkButton x:Name="SignupLink"
NavigateUri="Signup" TargetName="MainSiteFrame" Content="Signup"
Style="{StaticResource FooterLinksStyle}" />
                    <TextBlock Text="|" Style="{StaticResource
FooterTextStyle}" />
                    <HyperlinkButton x:Name="PrivacyLink"
NavigateUri="Privacy" TargetName="MainSiteFrame" Content="Privacy
Policy" Style="{StaticResource FooterLinksStyle}" />
                    <TextBlock Text="|" Style="{StaticResource
FooterTextStyle}" />
                    <HyperlinkButton x:Name="TermsLink"
NavigateUri="Terms" TargetName="MainSiteFrame" Content="Terms of
Service" Style="{StaticResource FooterLinksStyle}" />
                    <TextBlock Text="|" Style="{StaticResource
FooterTextStyle}" />
                    <HyperlinkButton x:Name="AboutLink"
NavigateUri="About" TargetName="MainSiteFrame" Content="About"
Style="{StaticResource FooterLinksStyle}" />
                    <TextBlock Text="|" Style="{StaticResource
FooterTextStyle}" />
                    <HyperlinkButton x:Name="ContactLink"
NavigateUri="Contact" TargetName="MainSiteFrame" Content="Contact"
Style="{StaticResource FooterLinksStyle}" />
                </StackPanel>
                <TextBlock Style="{StaticResource
CopyrightTextStyle}" />
            </StackPanel>
            <navigation:Frame x:Name="MainSiteFrame"
UriMapper="{StaticResource UriMap}" Style="{StaticResource
MainFrameAreaStyle}" />
        </toolkit:DockPanel>
    </ScrollViewer>
</UserControl>
```

There are a couple of points to note about the preceding code. First, notice how the main container for the page is a `ScrollViewer`. Although you can rely on the browser scrollbar for scrolling large pages in a traditional ASP.NET website, it will not always work when you have large flowing areas of Silverlight content. In the ASPX file that is hosting the control, the Silverlight plug-in has its width and height set to 100 percent. This means that the plug-in will fill in the entire available browser area. This works great until your Silverlight content becomes larger than the available space in the browser window. Because you are using a navigation frame that stretches to fit its internal content, you have no way of knowing in advance how large that content will be.

By placing all the home page controls in a `ScrollViewer`, you can ensure that the users will be able to scroll through any Silverlight content that is too large to fit in the browser window. The only drawback to this is that now you have two scrollbars visible to the user, which doesn't really look that great. This can be solved by disabling the browser's scrollbar with just a few lines of CSS code in the HTML and body tags of the FitnessTrackerPlus.aspx page that hide any overflow. Listing 3-2 shows the updated FitnessTrackerPlus.aspx page

LISTING 3-2: FitnessTrackerPlus.aspx

Available for download on Wrox.com

```
<%@ Page Language="C#" AutoEventWireup="true" %>

<%@ Register Assembly="System.Web.Silverlight"
Namespace="System.Web.UI.SilverlightControls" TagPrefix="asp" %>

<!DOCTYPE html PUBLIC "-//W3C//DTD XHTML 1.0 Transitional//EN"
"http://www.w3.org/TR/xhtml1/DTD/xhtml1-transitional.dtd">

<html xmlns="http://www.w3.org/1999/xhtml"
style="height:100%;overflow:hidden;">
     <head id="Head1" runat="server">
          <title>FitnessTrackerPlus</title>
     </head>
     <body style="height:100%;margin:0;overflow:hidden;">
          <form id="Form1" runat="server" style="height:100%;">
               <div style="height:100%;">
                    <object data="data:application/x-silverlight-2,"
type="application/x-silverlight-2" width="100%" height="100%">
                         <param name="source"
value="ClientBin/FitnessTrackerPlus.xap"/>
                         <param name="minRuntimeVersion"
value="3.0.40624.0" />
                         <param name="autoUpgrade"
value="true" />
                    </object>
                    <iframe id="_sl_historyFrame"
style="visibility:hidden;height:0px;width:0px;border:0px">
                    </iframe>
               </div>
          </form>
     </body>
</html>
```

You now have everything in the `ScrollViewer` control, and if you run the site, you will be able to easily scroll when Silverlight content is larger than the available viewing area. Thanks to one of the most important enhancements to Silverlight 4, you can even scroll easily using the mouse wheel. In previous versions of Silverlight, there was no support for the mouse wheel and users had to resort to dragging the scrollbar with the mouse or clicking the arrow icons on each end of the scrollbar. I don't know about you, but I haven't done this since Netscape Navigator was popular.

Silverlight Not Installed

Now that you have the XAML code for the landing page set up, it's time to get back to another important area of the home page. One of the initial requirements of the site was to provide a version of the home page that users who did not have the Silverlight plug-in installed could access. You want this to resemble the Silverlight version as much as possible. This is accomplished by embedding an HTML DIV tag in the Silverlight object declaration that includes the entire HTML you wish to display to visitors who do not currently have the plug-in installed. In the case of FitnessTrackerPlus, you want to provide HTML that closely resembles what visitors of the site will see if they do have the plug-in. This should include a brief list of site features, a screen shot, links to supplemental pages, and, of course, a link to download the Silverlight plug-in itself. The following code shows an updated version of the Silverlight object declaration that includes the required HTML code:

Available for download on Wrox.com

```
<object data="data:application/x-silverlight-2,"
type="application/x-silverlight-2" width="100%" height="100%">
     <param name="source" value="ClientBin/FitnessTrackerPlus.xap"/>
     <param name="minRuntimeVersion" value=" 4.0.41108.0" />
     <param name="autoUpgrade" value="true" />
     <div class="silverlight_not_installed">
          <div class="banner">
               <div class="banner_left">
                    <asp:Image runat="server" Height="80px"
ImageUrl="~/App_Themes/Main/Images/logo.png" />
               </div>
               <div class="banner_right"></div>
               <div class="clear"></div>
          </div>
          <div class="features">
               <div class="features_left">
                    <asp:Image runat="server"
ImageUrl="~/App_Themes/Main/Images/screenshot.png" Width="400px" Height="300px" />
               </div>
               <div class="features_right">
                    <ul>
                         <li>Keep track of the your foods and exercises daily</li>
                         <li>Monitor common measurements</li>
                         <li>Easily share your journal and results with others</li>
                         <li>Now supporting MySpace</li>
                    </ul>
                    <p>This site requires the use of Microsoft Silverlight
technology.<br /> Silverlight is a free and safe web plugin available from
Microsoft that<br /> assists in the creation of rich internet applications such as
FitnessTrackerPlus<br /> Installation is easy and takes only seconds. Just
click the Silverlight logo below to get started<br />
                    </p>
```

```
                    <a href="http://www.microsoft.com/silverlight">
                        <asp:Image runat="server"
ImageUrl="~/App_Themes/Main/Images/silverlight_logo.png" />
                    </a>
                </div>
                <div class="clear"></div>
            </div>
            <div class="footer">
                <a href="FitnessTrackerPlus.aspx">Home</a> |
                <a href="Privacy.aspx">Privacy Policy</a> |
                <a href="Terms.aspx">Terms of Service</a> |
                <a href="About.aspx">About</a>
            </div>
        </div>
    </object>
```

Code snippet FitnessTrackerPlus.aspx

If you want to test this and actually see what the home page looks like when Silverlight is not installed, you do not need to actually uninstall the plug-in. In Internet Explorer 8, simply click Tools ➪ Manage Add-ons, and disable the Silverlight plug-in and then refresh the page. Figure 3-1 shows the normal Silverlight version of the home page while Figure 3-2 shows the home page that appears for users that do not have the plug-in installed.

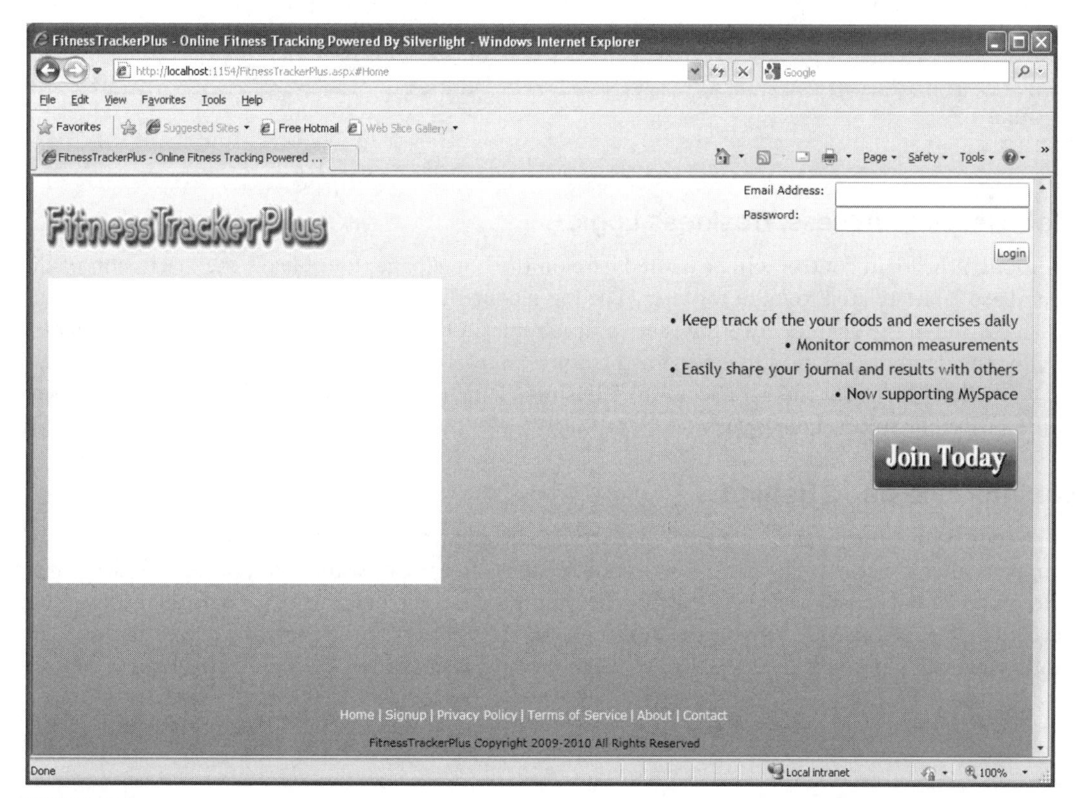

FIGURE 3-1

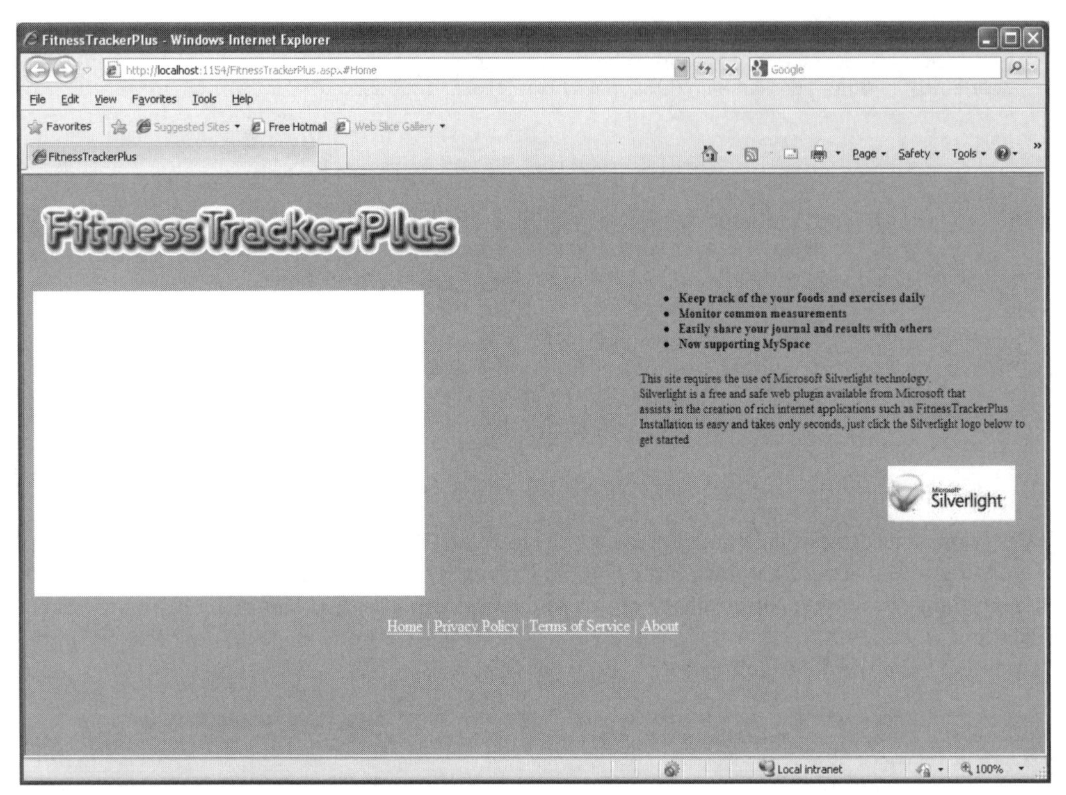

FIGURE 3-2

Database, Data Access, Business Logic

Although the login control will be hosted here on the home page, I will leave the discussion of the database tables related to login for later. The login control is a separate user control and will get its own section in the chapter covering the required tables. Other than the login control, there is not really any database solution to cover for the home page as no other database tables are required. The same will hold true for the data access and business logic layers as there really aren't any business objects specific to this home page.

User Interface Code Behind

The code behind for the main page will need to handle a few things. First you need to take care of what happens after a successful login. You will soon see that after a successful login, the Authentication service provides only some basic profile properties but not the complete `UserInformation` instance. In this event handler, you need to retrieve the `UserInformation` object for the currently logged-in user. The following code shows the `GetUserInformation` method that will be called after the login is complete:

Available for download on Wrox.com

```
private void GetUserInformation()
{
```

```
        // Retrieve the UserInformation class for the logged in user

        UserInformationContext userContext = new UserInformationContext();

        userContext.Load(userContext.GetUserQuery(WebContext.Current.User.Name),
             (GetUserCallback) =>
             {
                  // Store the UserInformation in a global variable so the rest
                  // of the application has access

                  if (!GetUserCallback.HasError)
                  {
                       // Don't navigate from the main page until our global
                       // variables have been setup
                       // every other page requires these to be set before
                       // further processing

                       MainSiteFrame.Navigate(new Uri("Dashboard",
    UriKind.Relative));
                  }

             }, null);
    }
```

Code snippet MainPage.xaml.cs

Another problem that needs to be solved in the code behind of the main page is preventing non-authenticated users from accessing the dashboard page. At this point, visitors who figure out the direct URL to the dashboard page could potentially bypass the login process. Although there is currently no real content on this page, it doesn't change the fact that you will need to prevent this from happening sooner or later. In traditional ASP.NET websites, you were able to make use of the forms authentication setup in the web.config file to prevent anonymous access to various pages. You would usually have something similar to the following code in order to ensure that only authenticated users were able to access a page:

```
<location path="Dashboard.aspx">
     <system.web>
          <authorization>
               <deny users="?" />
          </authorization>
     </system.web>
</location>
```

Currently, Silverlight has no such mechanism in place so you must set up some code manually to take care of this. By handling the `Navigating` event on the main site frame, you can trap requests to the Dashboard page and quickly check the authentication status of the visitor before allowing the navigation to proceed. In the following code, the `Navigating` event is handled and the requested URI is checked to see if the visitor is attempting to access the Dashboard page. The `WebContext` object determines if the visitor is authenticated and, if not, the `Cancel` property available in the

NavigatingCancelEventArgs object is set to true. You can repeat this technique for any other pages that you add to the project later, which should not be available to non-authenticated visitors.

Available for download on Wrox.com

```
private void MainSiteFrame_Navigating(object sender,
NavigatingCancelEventArgs e)
{
    // Protect the following pages from anonymous access

    if (e.Uri.OriginalString.Contains("Dashboard"))
    {
        if (!WebContext.Current.User.IsAuthenticated)
            e.Cancel = true;
        else
            LoginControl.Visibility = Visibility.Collapsed;
    }
    else if (e.Uri.OriginalString.Contains("Home"))
    {
        // When the user logs out of the site they will navigate back to
        // the landing page so enable the login control again

        LoginControl.Visibility = Visibility.Visible;
    }
}
```

Code snippet MainPage.xaml.cs

One last item that needs to be handled here in the code behind for the main page is the signup complete event. Earlier, the design called for users that have completed the signup process to be automatically logged in to the site. The Frame control offers another event called Navigated that is fired once navigation to a page is completed. When a visitor reaches the signup page, this event is fired and it provides an opportunity to hook up an event handler for the signup complete event. The following code shows how the newly registered user is automatically logged in to the site by making use of both events:

Available for download on Wrox.com

```
private void MainSiteFrame_Navigated(object sender, NavigationEventArgs e)
{
    if (e.Uri.OriginalString.Contains("Signup"))
    {
        // If the visitor has navigated to the Signup page you need to hook
        // into the SignupComplete event so that the user can be logged
        // in automatically creating a new account.  An instance of
        // the Signup page is available in the NavigationEventArgs so you
        // can easily hookup a listener for the event.

        FitnessTrackerPlus.Views.Signup signupPage = e.Content as
FitnessTrackerPlus.Views.Signup;

        signupPage.SignupComplete += (s, ev) =>
        {
            WebContext.Current.Authentication.Login(new
LoginParameters(ev.NewUser.email_address, ev.NewUser.password),
(LoginCompleteCallback) =>
            {
```

```
                    GetUserInformation();

                }, null);
            };
        }
    }
```

Code snippet MainPage.xaml.cs

Home View

When the landing page is first loaded, the main navigation frame is set to show the HomeView.xaml page. This page's only role is to display a screenshot of the application as well as a list of features that the site has to offer. Other than that, there isn't much to this control.

User Interface

The user interface for the home view is pretty simple, just a screenshot and a `StackPanel` of feature bullets. At this point, the screenshot is just blank and you won't be able to view a meaningful screen until sometime after the next chapter when you've added a working nutrition log. In addition to the feature list and screenshot, there is a large button that leads users to the registration page. Listing 3-3 shows the complete XAML code required for the home view page:

LISTING 3-3: Home.xaml

Available for download on Wrox.com

```
<navigation:Page x:Class="FitnessTrackerPlus.HomePage"
     xmlns="http://schemas.microsoft.com/winfx/2006/xaml/presentation"
     xmlns:x="http://schemas.microsoft.com/winfx/2006/xaml"
     xmlns:navigation="clr-
namespace:System.Windows.Controls;assembly=System.Windows.Controls.Navigation"
     xmlns:toolkit="clr-namespace:System.Windows.Controls;
assembly=System.Windows.Controls.Toolkit"
     Title="FitnessTrackerPlus-Online Fitness Tracking Powered By Silverlight">
     <navigation:Page.Resources>
          <Style x:Key="FeatureTextStyle" TargetType="TextBlock">
               <Setter Property="FontFamily" Value="Trebuchet MS" />
               <Setter Property="FontSize" Value="16" />
               <Setter Property="Margin" Value="0,0,0,5" />
               <Setter Property="TextAlignment" Value="Right" />
          </Style>
          <Style x:Key="SignupButtonStyle" TargetType="Button">
               <Setter Property="HorizontalAlignment" Value="Right" />
               <Setter Property="Margin" Value="0,20,0,0" />
               <Setter Property="FontSize" Value="20" />
               <Setter Property="Padding" Value="0" />
               <Setter Property="Cursor" Value="Hand" />
          </Style>
          <Style x:Key="SignupButtonImageStyle" TargetType="Image">
               <Setter Property="Source" Value="/Images/signup.png" />
               <Setter Property="Stretch" Value="Fill" />
```

continues

LISTING 3-3 *(continued)*

```
                <Setter Property="Width" Value="150" />
                <Setter Property="Height" Value="60" />
            </Style>
            <Style x:Key="HomePanelStyle" TargetType="toolkit:DockPanel">
                <Setter Property="LastChildFill" Value="True" />
            </Style>
            <Style x:Key="ScreenshotImageStyle" TargetType="Image">
                <Setter Property="Source" Value="/Images/screenshot.png" />
                <Setter Property="toolkit:DockPanel.Dock" Value="Left" />
                <Setter Property="Width" Value="400" />
                <Setter Property="Height" Value="300" />
                <Setter Property="Stretch" Value="Fill" />
                <Setter Property="VerticalAlignment" Value="Top" />
                <Setter Property="Margin" Value="10,0" />
            </Style>
            <Style x:Key="FeaturePanelStyle" TargetType="StackPanel">
                <Setter Property="toolkit:DockPanel.Dock" Value="Right" />
                <Setter Property="Margin" Value="10,30,10,0" />
            </Style>
        </navigation:Page.Resources>
        <toolkit:DockPanel  Style="{StaticResource HomePanelStyle}">
            <Image Style="{StaticResource ScreenshotImageStyle}" />
            <StackPanel Style="{StaticResource FeaturePanelStyle}">
                <TextBlock Text="• Keep track of your foods and
exercises daily" Style="{StaticResource FeatureTextStyle}" />
                <TextBlock Text="• Monitor common measurements"
Style="{StaticResource FeatureTextStyle}" />
                <TextBlock Text="• Easily share your journal and results with
others" Style="{StaticResource FeatureTextStyle}" />
                <TextBlock Text="• Now supporting MySpace"
Style="{StaticResource FeatureTextStyle}" />
                <Button x:Name="SignupButton" Style="{StaticResource
SignupButtonStyle}">
                    <Button.Content>
                        <Image Style="{StaticResource
SignupButtonImageStyle}" />
                    </Button.Content>
                </Button>
            </StackPanel>
        </toolkit:DockPanel>
</navigation:Page>
```

Database, Data Access, Business Logic

Like the home page, the home view control does not interact directly with any business objects or database tables so there is no solution to discuss for the database, data access, and business logic layers.

User Interface Code Behind

The code behind is pretty simple for the home view; all you need is an event handler for the signup button that navigates to the user registration page. Listing 3-4 shows the code behind for the home view page:

LISTING 3-4: Home.xaml.cs

Available for download on Wrox.com

```
using System;
using System.Windows.Controls;

namespace FitnessTrackerPlus
{
     public partial class HomePage: Page
     {
          public HomePage()
          {
               InitializeComponent();

               SignupButton.Click += (s, e) =>
               {
                    this.NavigationService.Navigate(new
Uri("Signup", UriKind.Relative));
               };
          }
     }
}
```

Because you don't have access to the main site frame from this control, you must use the `NavigationService` instance to perform the navigation. All `Page` controls have access to this service and all that happens is that navigation is delegated to the parent frame control. You could try and get an instance of the parent frame and call its `Navigate` method instead, but the navigation framework provides `Page` controls with easy access to this service and it is a much cleaner solution than attempting to hold onto a reference or walk back up the visual control tree.

User Registration

Well, now that you have a working home page and the ability to navigate to supplemental pages, you need to add the capability to register new users. Just because you are developing a Silverlight application does not mean that you have to lose out on the great functionality of the Membership, Profile, Role, and Authentication services provided by ASP.NET. The new WCF RIA Services platform provides tight integration for all of these services and even adds a powerful set of validation settings that can dramatically reduce the amount of code required to create a fully functional user registration system.

User Interface

In the previous chapter, I covered a new Silverlight control that makes it easier than ever to create data entry forms called the `DataForm`. It should be no surprise that for the user registration page the `DataForm` is utilized to automatically create the user interface for you. The `DataForm` requires only that an empty object be set as its `CurrentItem` property and the control takes care of the rest. Listing 3-5 shows the declaration of the `DataForm` along with some custom fields for the e-mail address, password, and security information.

Available for download on Wrox.com

LISTING 3-5: Signup.xaml

```
<navigation:Page x:Class="FitnessTrackerPlus.Views.Signup"
     xmlns="http://schemas.microsoft.com/winfx/2006/xaml/presentation"
     xmlns:x="http://schemas.microsoft.com/winfx/2006/xaml"
     xmlns:navigation="clr-
namespace:System.Windows.Controls;assembly=System.Windows.Controls.Navigation"
     xmlns:fitnesstrackerplus="clr-namespace:FitnessTrackerPlus.Controls"
     xmlns:dataform="clr-
namespace:System.Windows.Controls;
assembly=System.Windows.Controls.Data.DataForm.Toolkit"
     Title="FitnessTrackerPlus—Signup">
     <navigation:Page.Resources>
          <Style x:Key="SignupGridStyle" TargetType="Grid">
               <Setter Property="HorizontalAlignment" Value="Center" />
          </Style>
          <Style x:Key="UserRegistrationFormStyle" TargetType="dataform:DataForm">
               <Setter Property="AutoGenerateFields" Value="False" />
               <Setter Property="AutoEdit" Value="True" />
               <Setter Property="CommandButtonsVisibility" Value="None" />
               <Setter Property="Header" Value="Just fill out the
form below to get started with your own journal." />
          </Style>
          <Style x:Key="RegisterButtonStyle" TargetType="Button">
               <Setter Property="Content" Value="Create My Journal" />
               <Setter Property="HorizontalAlignment" Value="Right" />
               <Setter Property="VerticalAlignment" Value="Top" />
               <Setter Property="Margin" Value="0,20,0,0" />
          </Style>
     </navigation:Page.Resources>
     <Grid Style="{StaticResource SignupGridStyle}">
          <Grid.RowDefinitions>
               <RowDefinition />
               <RowDefinition />
          </Grid.RowDefinitions>
          <dataform:DataForm x:Name="UserRegistration" Style="{StaticResource
UserRegistrationFormStyle}" Grid.Row="0">
               <dataform:DataForm.EditTemplate>
                    <DataTemplate>
                         <StackPanel>
                              <dataform:DataField>
                                   <TextBox Text="{Binding email_address,
Mode=TwoWay}" />
                              </dataform:DataField>
                              <dataform:DataField>
                                   <fitnesstrackerplus:PasswordControl
PasswordText="{Binding password, Mode=TwoWay}"/>
                              </dataform:DataField>
                              <dataform:DataField>
                                   <fitnesstrackerplus:PasswordControl
PasswordText="{Binding confirm_password, Mode=TwoWay}"/>
                              </dataform:DataField>
                              <dataform:DataField>
```

```
                                        <TextBox Text="{Binding security_question,
Mode=TwoWay}" />
                                    </dataform:DataField>
                                    <dataform:DataField>
                                        <TextBox Text="{Binding security_answer,
Mode=TwoWay}" />
                                    </dataform:DataField>
                                </StackPanel>
                            </DataTemplate>
                        </dataform:DataForm.EditTemplate>
                    </dataform:DataForm>
                    <Button x:Name="Register" Grid.Row="1" Style="{StaticResource
RegisterButtonStyle}" />
        </Grid>
</navigation:Page>
```

While looking at this code you should notice that instead of auto generating the form, I decided to show you how to customize the appearance a little bit. By setting the `AutoGenerateFields` property to `False`, you can override how each field will look using simple `DataTemplates`. Two-way binding is used to ensure that the values entered in the various textboxes are automatically saved back to the instance of the `UserInformation` object that the `CurrentItem` is currently set to. There is another reason, however, for creating custom fields in this case, and it relates to the use of the `PasswordBox` control. Because you will be collecting a password during user registration, you would think that you could simply bind that field to a `PasswordBox` and everything would work just fine. Unfortunately, you are not allowed to bind values to the `Password` property of a `PasswordBox` so attempting to use the default `Field` generation won't work for the FitnessTrackerPlus user registration scenario. Instead, a separate user control that contains a `PasswordBox` must be used to perform the binding.

By utilizing the `DataFormTemplateField`, you can add just about any type of control to the `DataForm` and that is exactly what you will do to solve the password binding issue. If you have tried creating a project with the new WCF RIA Services business application template, this is what the auto-generated code will do to solve the issue in its sample application. What you need to do is add a new `UserControl` to the Silverlight project and call it `PasswordControl`. By adding a dependency property of `PasswordText`, you can easily bind to that value in the `DataForm` using the password property of the `UserInformation` object. Listing 3-6 shows the XAML declaration for the `PasswordControl`.

Available for download on Wrox.com

LISTING 3-6: PasswordControl.xaml

```
<UserControl x:Class="FitnessTrackerPlus.Controls.PasswordControl"
             xmlns="http://schemas.microsoft.com/winfx/2006/xaml/presentation"
             xmlns:x="http://schemas.microsoft.com/winfx/2006/xaml" >
    <Grid>
        <PasswordBox x:Name="PasswordValue" />
    </Grid>
</UserControl>
```

Ordinarily, I would hold off on any discussion of the code behind logic, but because the PasswordControl is an integral part of the Signup page user interface, it will be discussed here. In the code behind, you will create the dependency property and ensure that when the control loses focus the internal PasswordBox has its Password property set. Because the DataForm has two-way binding set for the PasswordControl when the LostFocus event is fired, the value of the PasswordText dependency property will be stored back to the DataForm instance. Listing 3-7 shows the code behind logic along with the LostFocus event handler.

LISTING 3-7: PasswordControl.xaml.cs

Available for download on Wrox.com

```
using System.Windows;
using System.Windows.Controls;

namespace FitnessTrackerPlus.Controls
{
      public partial class PasswordControl: UserControl
      {
            public static readonly DependencyProperty PasswordTextProperty =
                  DependencyProperty.Register("PasswordText", typeof(string),
                        typeof(PasswordControl), null);

            public PasswordControl()
            {
                  InitializeComponent();

                  this.LostFocus += (s, e) =>
                  {
                        this.PasswordText = PasswordValue.Password;
                  };
            }

            public string PasswordText
            {
                  get { return base.GetValue(PasswordTextProperty).ToString(); }
                  set { base.SetValue(PasswordTextProperty, value); }
            }
      }
}
```

Database

When utilizing the ASP.NET Membership services, you have the option to utilize the default membership database rather easily. This default database solution provides you with all of the necessary tables for the default providers to work correctly. You could use these as is, but many times you may already have database tables designed to handle user registration that differ from what ASP.NET has to offer. In the database design discussed earlier, you saw how FitnessTrackerPlus is using a completely different set of database tables than what is available with the standard ASP.NET Membership solution.

I went in that direction for a variety of reasons, not the least of which was so that you could see how to handle creating and using custom Role, Membership, and Profile providers rather easily with the WCF RIA Services. The database solution includes the users, user_roles, profiles, and roles tables as well as an additional table that provides various account types that you will be using later on when you need to add premium features to the site. The tables were created by using the table design feature of SQL Server Express Management Studio. Figure 3-3 shows the database diagram for the user registration tables.

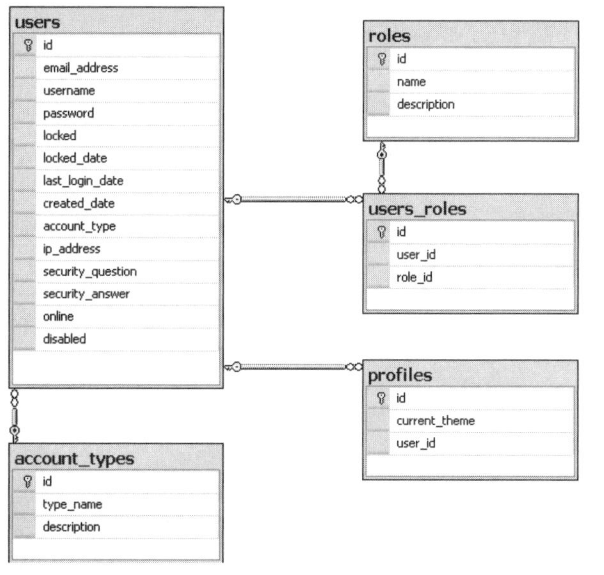

FIGURE 3-3

Data Access

The data access classes are relatively simple to create using LINQ to SQL:

1. Add a new LINQ to SQL classes file to the project and name it Users.dbml.
2. Drag the users, roles, user_roles, profiles, and account_types tables on to the design view.
3. Build the ASP.NET project.

When you build the project, the LINQ to SQL runtime will generate data access classes or entities to represent all the database table objects. The entity classes that are generated reside in the Users.designer.cs file. I won't list the auto-generated code here, but if you take a look at it you will see that entities are generated for each table with properties for all of the columns. As a personal preference and to not confuse the LINQ to SQL `user` entities that are generated with those from the built-in ASP.NET Membership classes, I renamed the user entity to `UserInformation`. I find it easier to use the entities if they adhere to the Pascal case-naming convention. As you will see, all the LINQ to SQL classes generated in this book are renamed to reflect this. Figure 3-4 shows the LINQ to SQL design view for the user registration tables.

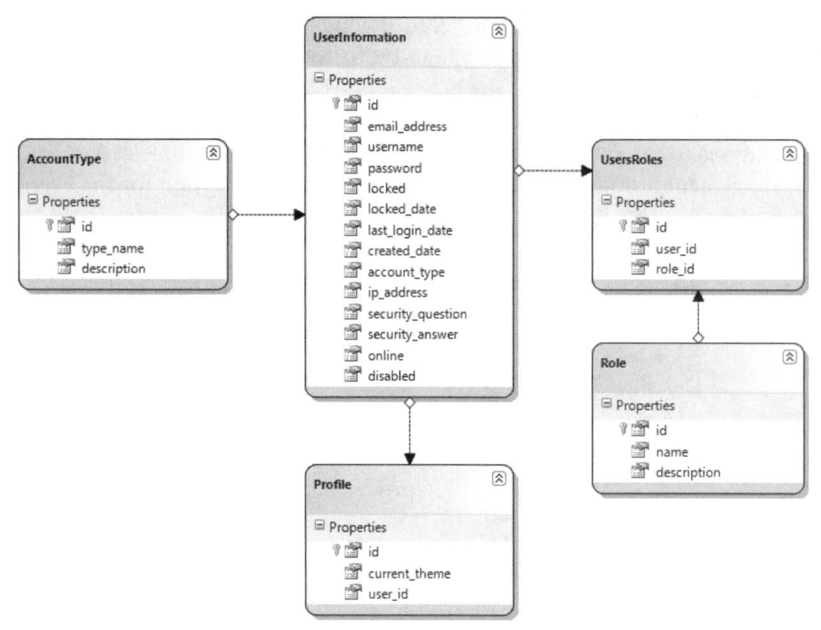

FIGURE 3-4

Business Logic

The business logic for the user registration feature can be broken down into several areas:

1. Create a new `DomainService` called `UserInformationService` that handles CRUD operations against the users table. This service must make use of the `UserInformation` entity class that was generated by LINQ to SQL earlier.
2. Create custom implementations of the Membership, Role, and Profile providers that both the WCF RIA Services `AuthenticationService` class and the new `UserInformationService` you are creating will use.

User Information Service

In the previous chapter you learned how the WCF RIA Services Framework provides a new class called `DomainService` that exposes data to a Silverlight client as well as provides basic web service operations. The first service you'll create for FitnessTrackerPlus is the `UserInformationService`. Typically, when creating `DomainService` classes, you will make use of some of the auto-generated CRUD methods. For this `UserInformationService`, however, you need to do things a little differently. Because this service needs to interact directly with the ASP.NET custom Membership provider it will look a little different than some of the other services you will create throughout the implementation of FitnessTrackerPlus. To get started:

1. Create a new directory called Services in the ASP.NET project. This folder will contain all of the WCF RIA Services created in the project.

2. Right-click that folder and add a new item to the project. Using the new Domain Service Class item template you will create a new service called `UserInformationService`. Be sure to select the `UsersDataContext` from the drop-down list, and check the "Generate associated classes for metadata" option, as shown in Figure 3-5.

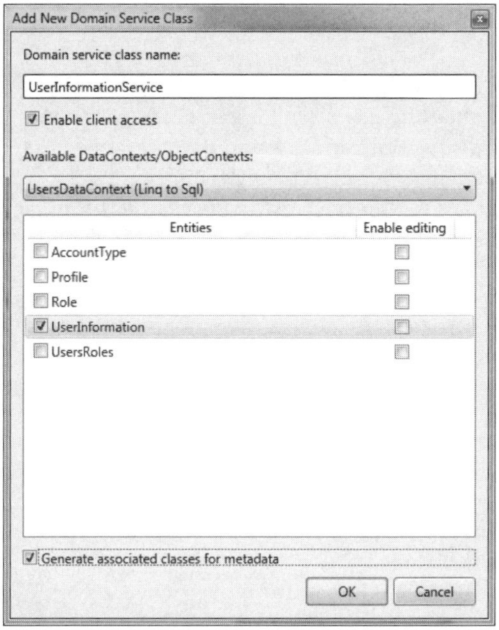

FIGURE 3-5

3. Once the service is created, you'll need to add two new methods:

   - The first method should be called `CreateUser`. Because this method does not follow the naming scheme that WCF RIA Services uses, you need to add the `[Invoke]` attribute just above the method declaration in order for it to be exposed to the Silverlight client. This service method will have the exact same method signature as the `CreateUser` method available in the ASP.NET `MembershipProvider` class. This method is essentially a proxy method that calls into the custom `MembershipProvider` class you will be creating. If any errors occur during the creation of the new user account, you will wrap the error message in a `DomainException` that can be used by the Silverlight client to report the error to the user.
   - The second method required will be used by the Silverlight client after a user has successfully logged in to the site. The method will be called `GetUser` and it will simply make use of the custom `MembershipProvider` class to return an instance of the user's corresponding `UserInformation` class. This instance will contain all the fields available from the users table just in case they are needed by the client. Because this method does follow the naming convention for WCF RIA Services, it is made available to the Silverlight client in the form of a `Query` operation.

As you will see, the WCF RIA Services Authentication service does return a `User` object, but it does not include any data from your custom `users` table. It will only return an object containing things such as the `username`, and `profile` properties. Although these are useful, you may at some point need access to other fields from the users table, which is why this additional `GetUser` operation is created that returns all this additional information. Listing 3-8 shows the updated version of the `UserInformationService` class complete with the `CreateUser` and `GetUser` methods.

> *Take note that because you're implementing a custom* `MembershipProvider` *class, you cannot simply use the static* `Membership.Provider` *instance without first casting to the custom* `FitnessTrackerPlus.Web.Providers.MembershipProvider` *class. If you fail to add this cast, your custom provider method implementations will not be used and instead you will get the default* `MembershipProvider` *behavior.*

LISTING 3-8: UserInformationService.cs

Available for download on Wrox.com

```
using System.Web.Ria;
using System.Web.Security;
using System.Web.DomainServices;
using System.Web.DomainServices.Providers;
using FitnessTrackerPlus.Web.Data;

namespace FitnessTrackerPlus.Web.Services
{
     [EnableClientAccess()]
     public class UserInformationService : LinqToSqlDomainService<UsersDataContext>
     {
          private FitnessTrackerPlus.Web.Providers.MembershipProvider
provider = Membership.Provider as
FitnessTrackerPlus.Web.Providers.MembershipProvider;

          [Invoke]
          public void CreateUser(string username, string password, string
email, string passwordQuestion, string passwordAnswer)
          {
               MembershipCreateStatus status;
               UserInformation createdUser = provider.CreateUser(username,
password, email, passwordQuestion, passwordAnswer, true, null, out status) as
UserInformation;

               if (status != MembershipCreateStatus.Success)
                    throw new DomainException(status.ToString());
          }

          public UserInformation GetUser(string email)
          {
               return provider.GetUser(email, true) as UserInformation;
          }
     }
}
```

User Information Service Metadata

Perhaps one of the most powerful features of the new WCF RIA Services platform is the support for client-side validation through the use of a metadata file. When you generate a new `DomainService` class like the `UserInformation` class, you have the option to automatically generate associated metadata. This optional metadata file allows you to specify attribute-based validation for any public properties of the class. There are several attributes that can be used that allow you to specify various validation aspects such as marking required properties, field lengths, and even regular expressions. Table 3-8 shows all the possible validation attributes you can make use of.

TABLE 3-8: WCF RIA Services Validation Attributes

VALIDATION ATTRIBUTE	DESCRIPTION
`[Required]`	The field must have a value before saving changes to the entity.
`[RegularExpression()]`	Allows you to perform validation of specified property against a regular expression.
`[StringLength]`	Supports setting a minimum and maximum number of characters for a property value.
`[DataType]`	Provides additional type information for property.
`[Range]`	Allows you to specify a valid range value for the property.
`[Custom]`	Provides a mechanism for specifying a custom validation method for the property.

One of the most powerful ways to make use of this new feature is to combine it with the `DataForm` control on the Silverlight client. When you use an entity that has its metadata validation rules specified, the `DataForm` will automatically perform validation against its `CurrentItem` object and display any validation errors. Figure 3-6 shows the user registration `DataForm` with an invalid password length supplied.

As far as adding metadata validation rules to the `UserInformationService`, you need to ensure:

- A valid e-mail address is used.
- The password is at least six characters.
- The security question and answer are less than 256 characters.
- All these fields are required for signup.

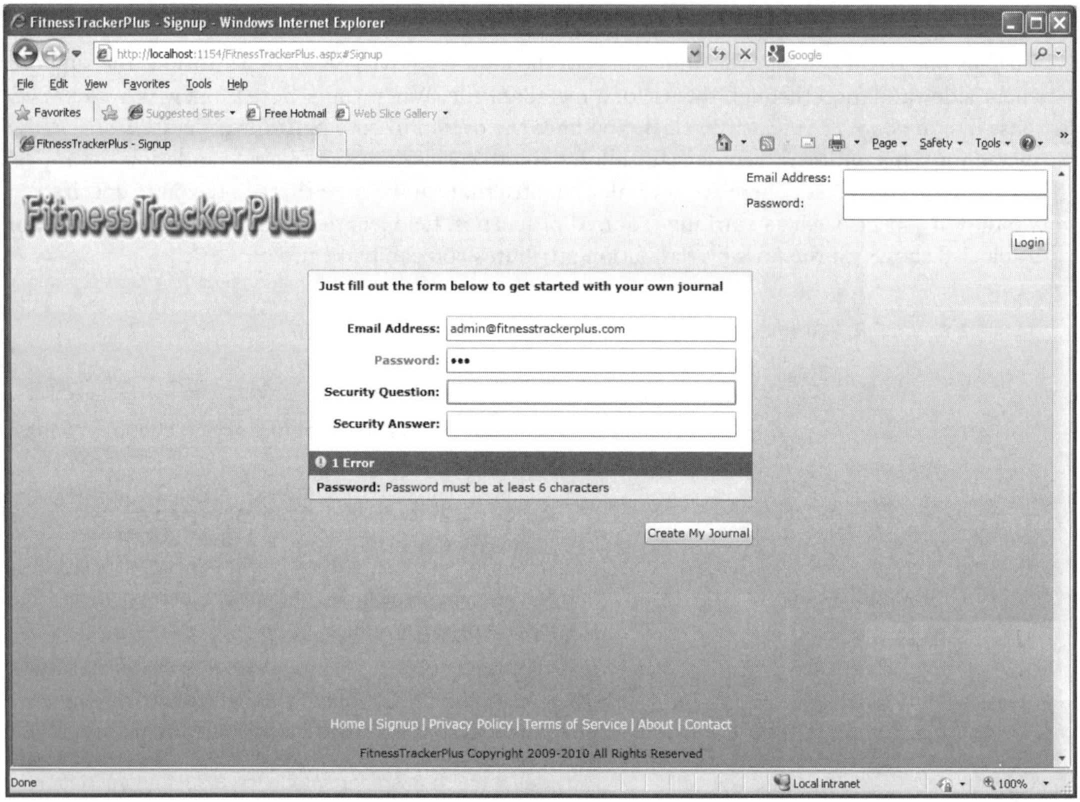

FIGURE 3-6

Listing 3-9 shows the metadata validation rules for the `UserInformationService`.

LISTING 3-9: UserInformationService.metadata.cs

Available for download on Wrox.com

```
using System;
using System.ComponentModel.DataAnnotations;
using System.Web.Security;

#pragma warning disable 649    // disable compiler warnings about unassigned fields

namespace FitnessTrackerPlus.Web.Data
{
    [MetadataTypeAttribute(typeof(UserInformation.UserInformationMetadata))]
    public partial class UserInformation: MembershipUser
    {
        internal sealed class UserInformationMetadata
        {
            private UserInformationMetadata()
            {
            }
```

```
                public int account_type;

                public DateTime created_date;

                public bool disabled;

                [Required]
                [Display(Name = "Email Address:")]
                [RegularExpression(@"^([\w-\.]+)@((\[[0-9]{1,3}\.[0-
9]{1,3}\.[0-9]{1,3}\.)|(([\w-]+\.)+))([a-zA-Z]{2,4}|[0-9]{1,3})(\]?)$",
ErrorMessage = "Invalid email address")]
                public string email_address;

                public int id;

                [RegularExpression(@"\b\d{1,3}\.\d{1,3}\.\d{1,3}\.\d{1,3}\b",
ErrorMessage = "Invalid ip address")]
                public string ip_address;

                public Nullable<DateTime> last_login_date;

                public bool locked;

                public Nullable<DateTime> locked_date;

                public bool online;

                [Required]
                [Display(Name = "Password:")]
                [StringLength(256, MinimumLength = 6, ErrorMessage = "Password
must be at least 6 characters")]
                public string password;

                [Required]
                [Display(Name = "Security Question:")]
                [StringLength(256, ErrorMessage = "Security question may not
exceed 256 characters")]
                public string security_question;

                [Required]
                [Display(Name = "Security Answer:")]
                [StringLength(256, ErrorMessage = "Security answer may not
exceed 256 characters")]
                public string security_answer;

                [StringLength(100)]
                public string username;
            }
        }
}

#pragma warning restore 649    // re-enable compiler warnings about
unassigned fields
```

How does this work? After adding the desired validation attributes in the metadata file, the WCF RIA Services framework ensures that these validation rules are automatically copied to the client-side version of the objects. You may remember from the previous chapter that when you build a project with WCF RIA Services support, the framework generates client-side versions of the server-side business objects and they reside in a ".g.cs" file hidden in the Generated_Code folder in the Silverlight project. If you take a closer examination of the FitnessTrackerPlus.Web.g.cs file that is generated in the FitnessTrackerPlus Silverlight project, you'll see that all the validation attributes you declared in the metadata file have propagated to the client-side version of the objects as well. For example, in the following code, the `email_address` property in the FitnessTrackerPlus.Web.g.cs file includes the same `[Required]`, `[StringLength]`, and `[RegularExpression]` attributes that were declared in the server-side version.

Available for download on Wrox.com

```
[DataMember()]
[Display(Name="Email Address:")]
[RegularExpression("^([\\w-\\.]+)@((\\[[0-9]{1,3}\\.[0-9]{1,3}\\.[0-9]
{1,3}\\.)|(([\\w-]+\\.)+))([a-zA-Z]{2,4" +"}|[0-9]{1,3})(\\]?)$",
ErrorMessage="Invalid email address")]
[Required()]
[StringLength(256)]
public string email_address
{
     get
     {
          return this._email_address;
     }
     set
     {
          if ((this._email_address != value))
          {
               this.ValidateProperty("email_address", value);
               this.Onemail_addressChanging(value);
               this.RaiseDataMemberChanging("email_address");
               this._email_address = value;
               this.RaiseDataMemberChanged("email_address");
               this.Onemail_addressChanged();
          }
     }
}
```

Code snippet FitnessTrackerPlus.Web.g.cs

Notice that in the `set` method of the `email_address` property, the `ValidateProperty` method is called. This is what triggers the WCF RIA Services framework to check for any validation attributes and report any violations of the rules.

One other element of which you need to be aware is the power of combining metadata with the `DataForm` control. If you take a quick look again at the user registration form, which makes use of the `DataForm` control, you'll notice that only `TextBox` controls are being declared for the custom `DataField` templates. Here is the declaration again.

Available for download on Wrox.com

```
<dataform:DataForm x:Name="UserRegistration" Style="{StaticResource
UserRegistrationFormStyle}" Grid.Row="0">
     <dataform:DataForm.EditTemplate>
          <DataTemplate>
               <StackPanel>
                    <dataform:DataField>
                         <TextBox Text="{Binding email_address, Mode=TwoWay}" />
                    </dataform:DataField>
                    <dataform:DataField>
                         <fitnesstrackerplus:PasswordControl PasswordText="{Binding
password, Mode=TwoWay}"/>
                    </dataform:DataField>
                    <dataform:DataField>
                         <TextBox Text="{Binding security_question,
Mode=TwoWay}" />
                    </dataform:DataField>
                    <dataform:DataField>
                         <TextBox Text="{Binding security_answer, Mode=TwoWay}" />
                    </dataform:DataField>
               </StackPanel>
          </DataTemplate>
     </dataform:DataForm.EditTemplate>
</dataform:DataForm>
```

Code snippet Signup.xaml

Now, because the `TextBox` controls are bound to properties of an empty `UserInformation` object, the `DataForm` not only checks the metadata for any validation attributes but also for a `[Display]` attribute. This optional attribute will tell the `DataForm` control what text to place alongside the `TextBox` control itself. This is why you end up with such a polished-looking data entry form, like the one shown in Figure 3-7, without actually declaring any corresponding `TextBlock` or `Label` controls. In this case, the Email Address, Password, Security Question, and Security Answer text is taken from the `[Display]` attribute in the metadata file for each of those properties.

Just fill out the form below to get started with your own journal

Email Address: admin@fitnesstrackerplus.com

Password: ••••••••••••••••

Security Question:

Security Answer:

FIGURE 3-7

As you make your way through the development of FitnessTrackerPlus, you'll see that for almost every entity being exposed by a `DomainService`, you'll also add additional metadata validation rules, and in some cases even custom validation methods.

FitnessTrackerPlus MembershipProvider

To create the custom Membership provider, you first need to add a new class to the Providers folder in the ASP.NET project and call it `MembershipProvider`. All ASP.NET custom Membership providers must inherit from the `System.Web.Security.MembershipProvider` class. Your custom class must override several abstract methods in this class. Although you have to declare these methods in your custom class, you can implement the methods that you don't need by throwing a `NotImplementedException` instead of an actual method declaration. Because you are in complete control over how this custom provider is used, you can get away with only implementing a handful of the required abstract methods that FitnessTrackerPlus specifically uses. These methods include `ValidateUser`, `GetUser`, `GetUserNameByEmail`, `CreateUser`, and `Initialize`.

The `MembershipProvider` base class has several common user registration settings that serve as properties. Some of these settings include things such as minimum password length, password retrieval capabilities, unique e-mail requirements, password format, and more. Typically when you create a custom provider, you override these properties and return the appropriate values for your specific application needs. The following code shows the `MembershipProvider` properties that are overridden for FitnessTrackerPlus:

Available for download on Wrox.com

```
private int minRequiredPasswordLength = 6;
private string applicationName = "FitnessTrackerPlus";

#region Public Properties

public override string ApplicationName
{
     get { return applicationName; }
     set { applicationName = value; }
}

public override int MaxInvalidPasswordAttempts
{
     get { throw new NotImplementedException(); }
}

public override int PasswordAttemptWindow
{
     get { throw new NotImplementedException(); }
}

public override int MinRequiredPasswordLength
{
     get { return minRequiredPasswordLength; }
}

public override bool RequiresQuestionAndAnswer
{
     get { return true; }
}

public override bool RequiresUniqueEmail
{
     get { return true; }
}

public override bool EnablePasswordReset
```

```
{
     get { return true; }
}

public override bool EnablePasswordRetrieval
{
     get { return false; }
}

public override int MinRequiredNonAlphanumericCharacters
{
     get { return 0; }
}

public override MembershipPasswordFormat PasswordFormat
{
     get { return MembershipPasswordFormat.Hashed; }
}

public override string PasswordStrengthRegularExpression
{
     get { throw new NotImplementedException(); }
}

public override string Name
{
     get
     {
          return base.Name;
     }
}

#endregion
```

Code snippet MembershipProvider.cs

The values you return represent the default values that the ASP.NET Membership engine uses during user registration. You can also override these values in the web.config file when you configure ASP.NET to use your custom `MembershipProvider` class. The following code shows the web.config declaration for the FitnessTrackerPlus custom `MembershipProvider` class along with an override for the `minRequiredPasswordLength` property that forces the minimum password length to be eight characters:

Available for download on Wrox.com

```
<membership defaultProvider="FitnessTrackerPlusMembershipProvider">
     <providers>
     <clear />
          <add name="FitnessTrackerPlusMembershipProvider"
type="FitnessTrackerPlus.Web.Providers.MembershipProvider"
minRequiredPasswordLength="6" />
     </providers>
</membership>
```

Code snippet MembershipProvider.cs

The `minRequiredPasswordLength` value specified in the web.config does not automatically propagate to the custom provider. For your custom provider to get this value, you need to implement the `Initialize` method. This method passes a `NameValueCollection` object that you can use to get any override values that were set in web.config. In the following code, the `NameValueCollection` object is checked for an instance of `minRequiredPasswordLength`. If it exists, then the value in the web.config file overrides the internal variable:

Available for download on Wrox.com

```
public override void Initialize(string name,
System.Collections.Specialized.NameValueCollection config)
{
     if (config == null)
          throw new ArgumentNullException("Provider configuration");

     // Initialize base class

     base.Initialize(name, config);

     // Setup default values

     if (config["minRequiredPasswordLength"] != null)
     {
          if (!String.IsNullOrEmpty(
config["minRequiredPasswordLength"].ToString()))
               minRequiredPasswordLength =
Convert.ToInt32(config["minRequiredPasswordLength"]);
     }
}
```

Code snippet MembershipProvider.cs

The next method that you need to implement in this custom provider is the `CreateUser` method. In this method, you must do a few things required by the design. One of the main reasons you are creating a custom `MembershipProvider` class is that you did not want to force users to come up with a unique username. Instead, you wanted to make use of the e-mail address as the primary login key. The default `MembershipProvider` implementation requires the use of a username property for the majority of its methods. By creating the custom provider, you can change these to use the e-mail address instead. You still, however, need a username when you get to the public fitness journal feature as you want the unique URL to be in a format that makes use of a username rather than a complete e-mail address. This being the case, you need to use the algorithm created earlier in the design to ensure that a unique username is also created for each user during signup. This involves combining the first part of the e-mail address with the unique identity field that is available after the record is created in the database. In the following code, you'll see that the `UserInformationService` is utilized to create a new entry in the database for the user. After the user is created, the ID field is then valid and is used to generate a valid username. Next, the user is added to the basic "user" role, which comes into play later on in the book. Finally, a default theme is added to the user's profile:

Available for download on Wrox.com

```
public override MembershipUser CreateUser(string username, string password,
string email, string passwordQuestion, string passwordAnswer, bool isApproved,
object providerUserKey, out MembershipCreateStatus status)
{
```

```
    try
    {
        // Check for valid email address

        if (String.IsNullOrEmpty(email))
            throw new MembershipException(MembershipCreateStatus.InvalidEmail);

        // Check to see if this email address already exists

        if (!String.IsNullOrEmpty(GetUserNameByEmail(email)))
            throw new MembershipException(MembershipCreateStatus.
DuplicateEmail);

        // Check to see if this user already exists

        if (GetUser(email, false) != null)
            throw new MembershipException(MembershipCreateStatus.
DuplicateUserName);

        // Check password length

        if (String.IsNullOrEmpty(password) || password.Length <
minRequiredPasswordLength)
            throw new MembershipException(MembershipCreateStatus.
InvalidPassword);

        // Check security question and answer

        if (String.IsNullOrEmpty(passwordQuestion))
            throw new MembershipException(MembershipCreateStatus.
InvalidQuestion);

        if (String.IsNullOrEmpty(passwordAnswer))
            throw new MembershipException(MembershipCreateStatus.InvalidAnswer);

        // At this point all validation checks have passed so create a
        // new user object
        // and ensure that the password is encrypted using one-way SHA1
        // encryption

        UserInformation newUser = new UserInformation
        {
            email_address = email,
            password =
FormsAuthentication.HashPasswordForStoringInConfigFile(password, "SHA1"),
            locked = false,
            created_date = DateTime.Now,
            account_type = (int)AccountTypes.BASIC,
            security_question = passwordQuestion,
            security_answer =
FormsAuthentication.HashPasswordForStoringInConfigFile(passwordAnswer, "SHA1")
        };

        context.UserInformations.InsertOnSubmit(newUser);
```

```
            context.SubmitChanges();

            // Update the username to reflect the first part of email address and
            // current id
            // This username is only going to be used in the forums and to create a
            // friendly url to a public journal

            newUser.username = String.Format("{0}{1}",
newUser.email_address.Substring(0, newUser.email_address.IndexOf("@")),
newUser.id.ToString());

            context.SubmitChanges();

            // Before leaving we still need to add the user to the site user role

            Roles.AddUserToRole(newUser.email_address, "user");

            // Finally create a profile entry for the new user with a default
            // theme selection

            newUser.Profiles.Add(new Profile { current_theme = "ShinyBlue",
user_id = newUser.id });
            context.SubmitChanges();

            status = MembershipCreateStatus.Success;
            return newUser;
        }
        catch (MembershipException ex)
        {
            status = ex.status;
        }
        catch (Exception)
        {
            status = MembershipCreateStatus.ProviderError;
        }

        return null;
}
```

Code snippet MembershipProvider.cs

One other thing to notice in the previous code is the use of the `HashPasswordForStoringInConfigFile` method. This utility function, available in the `FormsAuthentication` class, provides an easy way to generate the SHA1 one-way encrypted password that the design calls for.

Once you provide the capability to create new users in the `MembershipProvider`, you then need to override the `ValidateUser` method to ensure that the login works correctly with the e-mail address as opposed to the username. In the following code, a LINQ query validates the e-mail address being passed in along with the password. Once again, the `HashPasswordForStoringInConfigFile` helper method compares the plain-text password being passed in with the hashed password that is actually stored in the database.

Available for download on Wrox.com

```
public override bool ValidateUser(string username, string password)
{
     try
     {
          UserInformation currentUser = context.UserInformations.Where(e =>
e.email_address == username &&
e.password == FormsAuthentication.HashPasswordForStoringInConfigFile(password,
"SHA1") && e.disabled == false).SingleOrDefault();

          if (currentUser != null)
               return true;
     }
     catch (Exception)
     {
     }

     return false;
}
```

Code snippet MembershipProvider.cs

One nice thing about making use of the WCF RIA Services `AuthenticationService` is that it internally calls your custom implementation of `ValidateUser` when authenticating users. It does this with no additional work on your part other than letting the ASP.NET engine know about your custom provider in the web.config `Membership` section.

FitnessTrackerPlus RoleProvider

FitnessTrackerPlus will have two roles available to start with: admin and user. Every user that visits the user registration page will be added to the user role. Later on, you may decide to add some kind of administrator page that helps you to manage existing users. In that case, you want to restrict access to such a page as well as any services to the admin role only. The included FitnessTrackerPlus database already has one admin account created and all the default foods, exercises, and measurements are linked to this account. As was the case with the custom Membership provider, the FitnessTrackerPlus `RoleProvider` class must inherit from a base class in the `System.Web.Security` namespace. In this case, it is called, incredibly enough, `RoleProvider`.

Just as you did with the `MembershipProvider`, you need to configure the ASP.NET runtime to make use of your custom role provider by updating the web.config file and pointing it to your custom `RoleProvider` class. The following code shows the necessary additions to the web.config file that point the ASP.NET runtime to the `FitnessTrackerPlus.Web.Providers.RoleProvider` class:

Available for download on Wrox.com

```
<roleManager enabled="true" defaultProvider="FitnessTrackerPlusRoleProvider">
     <providers>
          <clear />
          <add name="FitnessTrackerPlusRoleProvider"
type="FitnessTrackerPlus.Web.Providers.RoleProvider" />
     </providers>
</roleManager>
```

Code snippet web.config

There are several methods and properties that need to be implemented in the custom provider. However, you really want to concentrate on two important methods: `GetRolesForUser` and `AddUsersToRoles`. The first method is called when the `AuthenticationService` performs a valid login and requests any roles that the user belongs to. In the following code, you see that first the `UserInformation` instance is retrieved for the user. Next, the `UsersRoles` association is loaded in the `UserInformation` instance. Once loaded, any roles that the user has been assigned to will be available in the `UsersRoles` property of the `UserInformation` object.

Available for download on Wrox.com

```
public override string[] GetRolesForUser(string username)
{
    List<string> roles = new List<string>();

    try
    {
        UserInformation user = context.UserInformations.Where(e =>
e.email_address == username).SingleOrDefault<UserInformation>();

        if (user != null)
        {
            // The only way to find out what roles have been assigned
            // to the user is to load the UsersRoles association

            user.UsersRoles.Load();

            // Once populated any roles that the user has been assigned
            // to should be available in the UsersRoles property

            foreach (UsersRoles role in user.UsersRoles)
                roles.Add(role.Role.name);
        }
    }
    catch (Exception)
    {
    }

    return roles.ToArray();
}
```

Code snippet RoleProvider.cs

You may remember the `AddUsersToRoles` method from the `CreateUser` implementation in the `MembershipProvider`. If not, all you need to know is that after a new user is created, he or she is added to the "user" role by means of this method. The following code shows how the implementation of this method makes use of the `UserInformationService` in order to insert a new record into the `users_roles` table. This provides the database link between users and roles.

Available for download on Wrox.com

```
public override void AddUsersToRoles(string[] usernames, string[] roleNames)
{
    try
    {
        UserInformation userInformation = null;
```

```
            Role role = null;

            foreach (string username in usernames)
            {
                userInformation = context.UserInformations.Where(e =>
e.email_address == username).SingleOrDefault<UserInformation>();

                if (userInformation != null)
                {
                    foreach (string roleName in roleNames)
                    {
                        role = context.Roles.Where(e => e.name ==
roleName).SingleOrDefault<Role>();

                    if (role != null)
                        context.UsersRoles.InsertOnSubmit(new UsersRoles {
user_id = userInformation.id, role_id = role.id });
                    }
                }
            }

            context.SubmitChanges();
        }
        catch (Exception)
        {
        }
}
```

Code snippet RoleProvider.cs

FitnessTrackerPlus ProfileProvider

The final custom provider that you need to implement is the `ProfileProvider`. The standard implementation of the ASP.NET Profile provider makes use of an XML-based string and adds property values to that string before storing it in the profile table. You will be using a slightly different approach here and instead make use of the profiles table that includes a column for each custom profile property. Each row in the table ties a specific user to all of the property columns. Once again, you need to let the ASP.NET runtime know about your custom `ProfileProvider` class before it will make use of it. The `ProfileProvider` section that is added to the web.config file must also list any of the custom profile properties that will be made available by the runtime. The runtime uses this list to create a collection of `SettingsProperty` objects that you must make use of in your custom provider shortly. The following code shows the updated web.config section related to the custom `ProfileProvider`.

> *So far, you have only one custom profile property, but as you progress through the application, you need to come back to this section of the web.config and make sure it is updated to reflect any new columns in the profiles table.*

Available for download on Wrox.com

```
<profile enabled="true" automaticSaveEnabled="false"
defaultProvider="FitnessTrackerPlusProfileProvider">
     <providers>
          <clear />
          <add name="FitnessTrackerPlusProfileProvider"
type="FitnessTrackerPlus.Web.Providers.ProfileProvider" />
     </providers>
     <properties>
          <add name="CurrentTheme" type="String"
customProviderData="current_theme;varchar;100" />
     </properties>
</profile>
```

Code snippet web.config

FitnessTrackerPlus won't be supporting the concept of inactive profiles, so methods related to those operations won't have any implementation in your custom provider. There are really only a handful of methods that need to be implemented to get the custom Profile provider working, so let's look at the code required.

The first method that you need to implement in the custom provider is the `GetProfile` method. This is called by the WCF RIA Services `AuthenticationService` to retrieve the profile object for the currently logged-in user. You won't need to worry about calling this method in your own code because it occurs behind the scenes as part of that WCF RIA Services integration with the ASP.NET Profile Service I spoke about earlier. Like most of the `MembershipProvider` methods, this one relies on a username being passed, which in your case is actually an e-mail address. You will once again make use of a LINQ query to retrieve the correct profile, but because the profile is associated with the user by means of an identity column, you must add a subquery in the LINQ statement that first grabs the correct ID for the user and then grabs the correct profile object. The following code shows the `GetProfile` method implementation:

Available for download on Wrox.com

```
private Profile GetProfile(string username)
{
     try
     {
          Profile profile = (from p in dataContext.Profiles
                             where p.user_id == (from u in
dataContext.UserInformations
                             where u.email_address == username
                             select u.id).SingleOrDefault<int>()
                             select p).SingleOrDefault();

          return profile;
     }
     catch(Exception)
     {
     }

     return null;
}
```

Code snippet ProfileProvider.cs

Next, you must implement both the `GetPropertyValues` and `SetPropertyValues` methods. For the `GetPropertyValues` method, you are passed a `SettingsPropertyCollection` object that contains a set of `SettingsProperty` objects for each of the custom profile properties that has been specified in the web.config file. You need to create a corresponding `SettingsPropertyValue` object with the `PropertyValue` property set to the appropriate value and add it to a `SettingsPropertyValueCollection` object that is returned when the method is complete. So far, you have only one custom profile property called `CurrentTheme` so the code is relatively simple. Later on, as you add columns to the profiles table, the `foreach` loop in the following code will grow to include those additional profile properties.

Available for download on Wrox.com

```
public override SettingsPropertyValueCollection GetPropertyValues(SettingsContext
context, SettingsPropertyCollection collection)
{
     SettingsPropertyValueCollection valueCollection = new
SettingsPropertyValueCollection();

     try
     {
          Profile profile = GetProfile(context["UserName"] as string);

          // If a profile was found then loop through all profile properties
          // and assign appropriate values

          if (profile != null)
          {
               foreach (SettingsProperty property in collection)
               {
                    SettingsPropertyValue propertyValue = new
SettingsPropertyValue(property);

                    switch (property.Name)
                    {
                         case "CurrentTheme":
                         {
                              propertyValue.PropertyValue = profile.current_theme;
                              break;
                         }
                    }

                    valueCollection.Add(propertyValue);
               }
          }
     }
     catch (Exception)
     {
     }

     return valueCollection;
}
```

Code snippet ProfileProvider.cs

The next method that needs an implementation is the `SetPropertyValues` method. As you may have guessed, this method works similarly to the `GetPropertyValues` but in reverse — you are being passed in a collection of `SettingsPropertyValue` objects, and you need to update the internal private variables to reflect the changes made in these profile properties. As you will see, the WCF RIA Services `AuthenticationService` provides built-in methods for updating and saving changes to the user's profile. Behind the scenes, the `AuthenticationService` calls into your custom `ProfileProvider` class and makes use of the `SetPropertyValues` method in order to do this. The following code shows the implementation for the `SetPropertyValues` method:

Available for download on Wrox.com

```
public override void SetPropertyValues(SettingsContext context,
SettingsPropertyValueCollection collection)
{
     SettingsPropertyValueCollection valueCollection = new
SettingsPropertyValueCollection();

     // Extract the username to retrieve property values for

     string userName = context["UserName"] as string;

     // Get the profile for current user

     FitnessTrackerPlus.Web.Data.Profile dataProfile =
          (from p in dataContext.Profiles
           where p.user_id == (from u in
           dataContext.UserInformations
           where u.email_address == userName
           select u.id).SingleOrDefault<int>()
           select p).SingleOrDefault();

     // If a profile was found then loop through all profile properties and
     // assign appropriate values

     if (dataProfile != null)
     {
          foreach (SettingsPropertyValue propertyValue in collection)
          {
               switch (propertyValue.Name)
               {
                    case "CurrentTheme":
                    {
                         dataProfile.current_theme =
propertyValue.PropertyValue.ToString();
                         break;
                    }
               }
          }

          dataContext.SubmitChanges();
     }
}
```

Code snippet ProfileProvider.cs

User Interface Code Behind

There are a few things that you need to achieve in the user registration code behind. First, you want to initialize the `DataForm` when the page is loaded with an empty `UserInformation` object as well as set up a `Click` handler for the `Register` button. In the following code, the `Loaded` event of the `Signup` page is used for these two tasks.

Available for download on Wrox.com

```
Loaded += (s, e) =>
{
    // DataForm requires an empty instance of the UserInformation object
    // in order to present the required data entry fields

    UserRegistration.CurrentItem = newUser;
    Register.Click += new RoutedEventHandler(Register_Click);
};
```

Code snippet Signup.xaml.cs

Next, when the Register button is clicked, you need to validate the information entered on the screen and create the new user in the database by using the `UserInformation` service created earlier. Because the private `newUser` variable was associated with the `DataForm` and two-way binding was enabled, in the following code, the variable contains all the updated values that were entered on the form. These values are passed into the `CreateUser` method of the `UserInformationService` which, of course, internally makes use of the custom `MembershipProvider` you created to actually store the information in the database.

Available for download on Wrox.com

```
private void Register_Click(object sender, RoutedEventArgs e)
{
    // Use the UserInformation service to create a new user
    // Behind the scenes the custom MembershipProvider's CreateUser method
    // will be called by the service

    if (UserRegistration.ValidateItem() && UserRegistration.CommitEdit())
    {
        context.CreateUser(newUser.email_address, newUser.password,
newUser.email_address, newUser.security_question,
newUser.security_answer, CreateUserCallback, newUser);
    }
}
```

Code snippet Signup.xaml.cs

Finally, if the signup process was successful, you want to fire the custom `SignupComplete` event that the main page uses to automatically log the user into the site and present them with the `Dashboard` page. This is all handled in the `CreateUserCallback` method, as shown in the following code.

Available for download on Wrox.com

```
private void CreateUserCallback(InvokeOperation result)
{
    if (!result.HasError)
    {
        // After successfully creating a new account you want the user to
        // automatically be logged in and redirected to the Dashboard.
```

```
            // By firing this custom SignupComplete event the parent control
            // can perform the login operation when the account has been
            // created.

            if (SignupComplete != null)
                SignupComplete(this, new SignupEventArgs(result.UserState
as UserInformation));
        }
        else
            result.MarkErrorAsHandled();
}
```

Code snippet Signup.xaml.cs

> *When using WCF RIA Services, if an error occurs an* `Exception` *will be thrown unless you specifically call the* `MarkErrorAsHandled` *method.*

Login Control

Silverlight does not currently provide an implementation of a login control as there is in ASP.NET. It is not, however, terribly difficult to create one. The login control will need to make use of the existing ASP.NET Authentication service, which is accessible from the WCF RIA Services. As you will see, it is simple to add support for the Authentication services in Silverlight when using the WCF RIA Services. The login process even automatically makes use of your custom Membership provider behind the scenes.

User Interface

As the "Design" section stated, this login control needs to include a textbox for the e-mail address and a `PasswordBox` for the password entered by the user. As you may have noticed by now, I prefer to keep style information out of the individual control declarations so the styles are all defined in the `UserControl.Resources` section of the XAML file. All user interface controls in FitnessTrackerPlus are implemented that way as it makes applying themes to these controls later on much easier. Listing 3-10 shows the XAML required for the `Login` control.

Available for download on Wrox.com

LISTING 3-10: Login.xaml

```
<UserControl x:Class="FitnessTrackerPlus.Controls.Login"
    xmlns="http://schemas.microsoft.com/winfx/2006/xaml/presentation"
    xmlns:x="http://schemas.microsoft.com/winfx/2006/xaml">
    <UserControl.Resources>
        <Style x:Key="LoginBoxGridStyle" TargetType="Grid">
            <Setter Property="VerticalAlignment" Value="Top" />
        </Style>
        <Style x:Key="LoginTextBoxStyle" TargetType="TextBox">
            <Setter Property="Width" Value="200" />
```

```
            <Setter Property="Margin" Value="10,0,0,0"/>
        </Style>
        <Style x:Key="LoginPasswordBoxStyle" TargetType="PasswordBox">
            <Setter Property="Width" Value="200" />
            <Setter Property="Margin" Value="10,0,0,0"/>
        </Style>
        <Style x:Key="LoginErrorStyle" TargetType="TextBlock">
            <Setter Property="Foreground" Value="#FFFF0000" />
            <Setter Property="Margin" Value="0,5,0,0" />
            <Setter Property="HorizontalAlignment" Value="Center" />
        </Style>
        <Style x:Key="LoginButtonStyle" TargetType="Button">
            <Setter Property="HorizontalAlignment" Value="Right" />
            <Setter Property="Margin" Value="0,10,0,0" />
            <Setter Property="Content" Value="Login" />
        </Style>
    </UserControl.Resources>
    <Border>
        <Grid Style="{StaticResource LoginBoxGridStyle}">
            <Grid.ColumnDefinitions>
                <ColumnDefinition />
                <ColumnDefinition />
            </Grid.ColumnDefinitions>
            <Grid.RowDefinitions>
                <RowDefinition />
                <RowDefinition />
                <RowDefinition />
                <RowDefinition />
            </Grid.RowDefinitions>
            <TextBlock Text="Email Address:" Grid.Row="0"
Grid.Column="0" />
            <TextBox x:Name="EmailAddress" Grid.Row="0"
Grid.Column="1" Style="{StaticResource LoginTextBoxStyle}" />
            <TextBlock Text="Password:" Grid.Row="1" Grid.Column="0" />
            <PasswordBox x:Name="Password" Grid.Row="1" Grid.Column="1"
Style="{StaticResource LoginPasswordBoxStyle}" />
            <Button x:Name="LoginUser" Style="{StaticResource
LoginButtonStyle}" Grid.Column="1" Grid.Row="2" />
            <TextBlock x:Name="LoginError" Style="{StaticResource
LoginErrorStyle}" Grid.Column="0" Grid.ColumnSpan="2" Grid.Row="3" />
        </Grid>
    </Border>
</UserControl>
```

Database, Data Access

The `login` control will be utilizing the same database tables and LINQ to SQL classes that were created for user registration so there won't be any additional work to do in this area of the solution.

Business Logic

Enabling support for ASP.NET Authentication using the WCF RIA Services requires only that you add another `DomainService` class to your project. This service should be called `AuthenticationService` and instead of inheriting from the `DomainService` base class it will need to inherit from the new

AuthenticationBase class. By default, the AuthenticationService is set up to use the UserBase type, which provides access to standard System.Security.Principal properties that are associated with the login operation. You can easily extend this base class to include any custom properties from the profile table that you also want to be available after successful login. Listing 3-11 shows the AuthenticationService implementation. There really isn't much to it other than ensuring that your CurrentTheme profile property is being exposed in the User object. This is really all that you need for the Silverlight client to have access to user Authentication services on the server.

LISTING 3-11: AuthenticationService.cs

Available for download on Wrox.com

```
using System.Web.Ria;
using System.Web.Ria.ApplicationServices;

namespace FitnessTrackerPlus.Web
{
     [EnableClientAccess]
     public class AuthenticationService: AuthenticationBase<User>
     {
     }

     public class User: UserBase
     {
          // Profile properties that should be exposed as part of the
          // User object

          public string CurrentTheme { get; set; }
     }
}
```

One very important thing to watch out for here is not to confuse the User or UserBase class with the UserInformation LINQ to SQL class created earlier. These are two completely different objects and the User object returned after login will not have access to any of the UserInformation properties. At first, this may seem confusing but you have to remember that the logged-in User class is a representation of the System.Security.Principal object which is not the same as your custom UserInformation entity. In theory, you could add all of the UserInformation properties to the User class and override the validation method of the AuthenticationBase class, call into your Membership provider and copy all of the UserInformation properties into new User class properties, but in this case it would be more work than it is worth. You already have the UserInformationService available if you need to expose methods to retrieve specific UserInformation details and you might as well make use of it instead.

User Interface Code Behind

There is one more required step to perform before you can make use of the AuthenticationService that you created on the Silverlight client. Standard DomainService classes will be taken care of by the code generation algorithms of the WCF RIA Services platform. For the UserInformation class, this results in a UserInformationContext class being generated. In order to access the `AuthenticationService` in the Silverlight client, however, you need to add the service as an application-level resource. You can do this by just adding the following XAML to the App.xaml file in the project:

Available for download on Wrox.com

```
<Application.ApplicationLifetimeObjects>
     <app:WebContext>
          <app:WebContext.Authentication>
               <services:FormsAuthentication />
          </app:WebContext.Authentication>
     </app:WebContext>
</Application.ApplicationLifetimeObjects>
```

Code snippet App.xaml

Once you've added the previous code to the App.xaml file, you'll be able to access the service through the `WebContext.Current.Authentication` object.

Getting back to the code behind for the `Login` control, you will first need to handle the `Login` button `Click` event and make use of the `AuthenticationService` you have just created to validate the e-mail address and password that was supplied. In the following code, the `Login` method of the `WebContext.Current.Authentication` object is called and a callback method set up for checking to see if the login was a success.

Available for download on Wrox.com

```
LoginUser.Click += (se, ev) =>
{
     // Use the RIA Authentication service to login the user
     // Behind the scenes the custom MembershipProvider's ValidateUser
     // method will be called to perform the actual login.

     WebContext.Current.Authentication.Login(new LoginParameters(EmailAddress.Text,
Password.Password), LoginCompleteCallback, null);

};
```

Code snippet Login.xaml.cs

For the callback method, you need to check the `LoginSuccess` property of the `LoginOperation` object, and if there are no errors the `Login` control will fire a `LoginComplete` event. Remember, the main page is listening for this event and, when it is fired, will be responsible for navigating to the Dashboard page, which is now available because the user has been authenticated. Now if a failure occurs during the `Login` operation, you need to let the user know by updating the `TextBlock` on the control with an appropriate error message. Here is the code for the `LoginCompleteCallback` method where this all takes place:

Available for download on Wrox.com

```
private void LoginCompleteCallback(LoginOperation result)
{
     if (!result.HasError)
     {
          if (result.LoginSuccess)
          {
               // Let the parent control know that the login was successful
```

```
                if (LoginComplete != null)
                     LoginComplete(this, null);

                // Clearing the error text here prevents the login failed
                // message from being displayed again if the user did fail
                // a login attempt and then eventually succeeded.

                // Without doing this after the user logs out the previous
                // error message would still be visible on the home page

                LoginError.Text = "";
            }
            else
                LoginError.Text = "Login Failed: Please check your email
address and password.";
        }
        else
        {
            LoginError.Text = "Login Failed: Please check your email address
and password.";
            result.MarkErrorAsHandled();
        }
}
```

Code snippet Login.xaml.cs

Running the application at this point will provide you with a working login control and user registration page. This thing is starting to feel a little bit more like a real site now. There is, however, still the issue of what the user sees after a successful login.

Dashboard

The dashboard is the page that the user will interact with upon a successful login to the site. You will see the full design and implementation of this page in the next chapter, but for now you still will need to create it so that you have somewhere to navigate to after a successful login.

User Interface, Database, Data Access, Business Logic

You will be creating the entire user interface for the dashboard in the next chapter so I won't be covering any database, data access, or business logic here. All you need to do for now is ensure that the page exists in the Views folder by adding a new Silverlight navigation page to the Views folder and calling it Dashboard.xaml. The only item currently in the user interface is a single button that performs logout functionality and sends the user back to the main home page.

User Interface Code Behind

Not much is in the code behind right now for the dashboard other than an event handler for the logout button. In this event handler, you call the `Logout` method of the `WCFContext.Current.Authentication` object. Upon completion of this method, navigate back to the main home page. Listing 3-12 shows the current logic behind the dashboard page.

Available for download on Wrox.com

LISTING 3-12: Dashboard.xaml.cs

```
using System;
using System.Windows.Controls;

namespace FitnessTrackerPlus.Views
{
     public partial class Dashboard: Page
     {
          public Dashboard()
          {
               InitializeComponent();

               Logout.Click += (s, e) =>
               {
                    // Use the RIA Authentication service to logout and when
                    // complete redirect the user back to the main home page

                    WebContext.Current.Authentication.LoggedOut += (se, ev) =>
                    {
                         NavigationService.Navigate(new Uri("Home",
UriKind.Relative));
                    };

                    WebContext.Current.Authentication.Logout(false);
               };
          }
     }
}
```

Throughout this book you will notice that a majority of the control event handlers utilize the new lambda expression syntax from .NET. This is strictly a personal preference that I have when coding event handlers that need to interact with web services in Silverlight. All web service calls in Silverlight are asynchronous and require handling some type of completed event. I prefer to keep the calling of the service as well as the completed logic in one control event handler because it consolidates the overall logic of what I am trying to do. You do not have to follow this syntax and creating separate event handlers for completed events is perfectly acceptable. My rule of thumb is that as long as the event handler does not require too many additional levels of nested asynchronous calls I will use lambda expressions to handle it.

Supplemental Pages

I won't be covering the supplemental pages in detail just yet; however, before deploying the site, you'll come back to them and make them functional. For now, you should at least create placeholder controls for each of them so that you have some working links on the main home page. To do this, just create new `Page` controls in the Views folder called Privacy, About, Contact, and Terms.

URI Mapping

There is one last topic to discuss before moving on to additional site functionality, and that is the new URI mapping feature of Silverlight. In the previous chapter I showed you how easy it was to utilize this feature for deep linking or just to hide the full path to the XAML files from the user. You have created several new pages in the application at this point and you may have noticed that the `Navigate` calls never needed to include full paths to XAML files. This was made possible by setting up URI mapping in the App.xaml file. The following code shows the `UriMapper` along with the `UriMapping` entries that are required at this point in the development.

Available for download on Wrox.com

```
<Application.Resources>
     <uri:UriMapper x:Key="UriMap">
          <uri:UriMapping Uri="Home" MappedUri="/Views/Home.xaml" />
          <uri:UriMapping Uri="About" MappedUri="/Views/About.xaml" />
          <uri:UriMapping Uri="Contact" MappedUri="/Views/Contact.xaml" />
          <uri:UriMapping Uri="Privacy" MappedUri="/Views/Privacy.xaml" />
          <uri:UriMapping Uri="Signup" MappedUri="/Views/Signup.xaml" />
          <uri:UriMapping Uri="Terms" MappedUri="/Views/Terms.xaml" />
          <uri:UriMapping Uri="Dashboard" MappedUri="/Views/Dashboard.xaml" />
     </uri:UriMapper>
</Application.Resources>
```

Code snippet App.xaml

That's all there is to it — nothing in the code behind, no other configuration parameters. It requires a very minimal amount of XAML code to get this working, and when I cover the public journal feature you will see that you can even get this feature working with query string parameters just as easily.

SUMMARY

There is a lot of information to digest in this chapter and you have been introduced to many new technologies such as accessing the ASP.NET Membership, Profile, Role, and Authentication services in your Silverlight client. You have seen how easy it is to expose this functionality by utilizing the new WCF RIA Services platform. You should also now be familiar with how easy it is to provide client-side validation and data entry forms using the new `DataForm` control and metadata attribute declarations. Finally, I discussed how easy it is to use the new URI mapping feature of Silverlight to hide the full path to your XAML navigation pages from the user.

At this point, you basically have a working site complete with authentication and user registration capabilities. Although these are great services and are required for any major website, they don't satisfy any real business requirements or provide any added value to the user. Now the fun begins as you create the nutrition log page and make the dashboard do something other than just provide users with the ability to log out of the site. By the end of the next chapter, you will be able to provide a working nutrition log where users can enter the foods they eat daily.

4

Welcome Home

Creating the User's Personal Home Page

Now that you have the ability to register users, it's time to give them a solid landing page for when they log into the site. The last chapter basically left off with a blank page and a logout button just so that you could see how the login/logout functionality worked with the authentication service. Now it's time to put something useful on this page. The home page should provide a dashboard-like look and feel complete with site navigation controls so that other areas of the site are made accessible. In this chapter, you will see how to utilize some of the new controls available in the Silverlight Toolkit to provide an easy navigation menu, as well as give the users the ability to select a preferred theme for the site. Most sites these days allow some kind of customization to be made from the user, and FitnessTrackerPlus will be no different. In the previous chapter, you also saw how to use the new navigation framework to provide page navigation with full browser history integration. Now you will see how to also use the fragment navigation aspect of this framework to ensure that you can continue to provide a master page-like interface that allows you to reuse the banner and footer areas created earlier. Anytime you can avoid duplicating user interface code, you will be one step ahead of the game.

In addition to the site navigation and theme selection, the user home page will provide access to basic account settings such as login information and security questions and answers. You'll also see how to easily provide site announcements from this home page so that you can let users know of things such as site updates or enhancements just in case the e-mail reminder you sent to them ended up in the spam folder. By the end of this chapter, you will have some placeholders for the food, exercise, and measurement summary controls that you will be creating later on in the book.

PROBLEM

Once users log in to any site they expect certain things to be available, not the least of which is some way to navigate to other areas of the site. In a traditional ASP.NET site, several different solutions can be used, ranging from traditional hyperlinks in a list to ASP.NET sitemap and menu controls that are tied to a data source. These sitemaps typically include all of the pages that the user could navigate to while logged into the site. The various ASP.NET controls usually require minimal code to be written and provide quick and easy site navigation. Menu controls typically reside across the top of the page or somewhere on the left side of the page in a list. It is also common to add some JavaScript to provide dynamic menu choices or use CSS techniques to create rollover effects for the various menu items.

Adding Navigation

One thing that you can usually take for granted in a traditional site is that no matter what technology you decide on for site navigation, you always have browser history support and browser control integration for free. It requires no extra code to have your pages added to the browser history or for the correct page to be displayed when the user clicks the Back and Forward buttons on the browser. The exception to this is, of course, AJAX-based solutions. If your site requires AJAX to navigate between various page elements you no doubt have to resort to all sorts of JavaScript tricks or special controls to hook into the browser history and also to react to various browser navigation button clicks.

Applications developed in previous versions of Silverlight had the same challenges as AJAX based solutions in that there is no default integration with the browser history or navigation controls. Luckily, as you have seen in the previous chapters, Silverlight 4 has a new navigation framework that provides this functionality with very little work on your part. You already have a main site home page that includes a banner and footer area. As with ASP.NET master pages, you will want to hold onto the banner and footer area for all other pages that are visible when logged in. Because you'll need some kind of site navigation control on the user home page, the control needs to stay visible as the user navigates through the site pages. At first glance, this seems as easy as adding another navigation frame to the user interface and adding the appropriate page controls for all the necessary site pages. Unfortunately, the navigation framework does not support nested navigation frames integrating with the web browser. This will be the first problem you'll need to tackle in this chapter as you don't want to have to duplicate the site navigation menu controls on every single page you create.

Providing Site Announcements

In addition to site navigation, the user home page should provide access to account settings, theme selection, and site announcements. Because users will be hitting this page after every login, it can be a great place to notify them of any important announcements such as scheduled maintenance, or even planned site enhancements. For the most part, site announcements that involve planned maintenance and down time should typically be communicated to your users via e-mail. In the offhand chance those e-mails reach the spam folder as opposed to the Inbox, you can make use of the announcements control to get your message across.

User-Selectable Themes

Every user has a different idea about how the site should ideally look. Over the last few years it's become common practice to provide several theme choices that a user can apply to all of the controls on the site. It may seem like an unimportant feature, but most users will really appreciate having the ability to tailor the color scheme to something that is more in line with their own individual style. ASP.NET 2.0 has a complete theme and control skinning engine that make it relatively easy for developers to provide multiple themes for a site.

Although Silverlight does not offer the same mechanisms as ASP.NET, through the use of the Silverlight Toolkit, multiple themes are now supported. Even more important, the ability to dynamically switch themes through the use of the implicit styling feature built into the runtime is dramatically improved in Silverlight 4. In previous versions of Silverlight, you essentially had to reboot the user interface in order to change the theme of the application on-the-fly. This would require that you reload the entire visual tree of controls and usually resulted in a sluggish experience for the user. Depending on the size of the site and the number of controls that needed to have styles reapplied, it could take a considerable amount of time for the process to finish. In this chapter, you will see how, thanks to implicit styling and the new themes available in the toolkit, you can switch out the current theme of the site at runtime with just a few lines of code.

Account Settings

In Chapter 3, when users registered for the site, you made sure to collect only the minimum amount of information required to use the site. You will need to give users a way to update this information. A page showing the current user's account settings should include a way to update the e-mail address, password, security question, and security answer. It should also show when the account was created. This page will become even more important as you begin to add premium features to the site in a later chapter.

Adding a Dashboard

One final problem needs to be tackled with this home page and that is answering the question of what should be displayed on this page immediately following the login. Many sites are offering a dashboard-style look and feel for home pages and you can provide the same thing with FitnessTrackerPlus. At a minimum, you should provide a welcome message, the current date, and any site announcements. In addition, this would be a great place to display the food, exercise, and measurement summary controls that were outlined in the first chapter. Although you haven't created the pages required for those features, at this point you can still decide how these will be arranged and roughly how much space each of these summary controls will take up on the user home page. For now, placeholders for these controls will be sufficient until you finish up the work required for those individual controls.

DESIGN

Once again, you have several problems outlined that need to be solved in order to have a fully functional user home page. In general, you need a design that provides a place for site announcements, theme selection, site navigation, account settings and summary controls for food, exercise, and measurements. As in the previous chapter, it will be best to outline detailed versions of the requirements for these features before moving further on in the design process. Here is a breakdown of the requirements that need to be satisfied for this chapter:

- **Site navigation:** Users will need links to food, exercise, and measurement log pages as well as any other additional pages that are going to be created in the future.
- **Navigation framework:** Navigation framework should be used where possible to ensure tight integration with the web browser history and navigation controls.
- **Welcome message:** Today's date and a welcome message should be displayed.
- **Announcement list:** Users should be able to view a list of site announcements as hyperlinks that, when clicked, display a modal child window containing the announcement text.
- **Editable account settings:** Users should be able to view and modify account settings such as e-mail address, password, security question, and security answer.
- **Dashboard controls:** Summary controls for food, exercise, and measurements should appear on the first available view after login.
- **Theme selection:** Users should be able to easily select from several themes, and the current theme should be changed dynamically at runtime immediately following the selection.
- **Theme storage:** The selected theme should be saved to the user's profile and should also be restored upon the next successful login.
- **Logout link:** Users will continue to need a link that performs logout functionality and redirects the user back to the main site home page.

With the requirements set, you can move onto the specific design elements for each feature. As in the previous chapter, I will break down the design and solution for the chapter into the following order: User Interface, Database, Data Access, Business Logic, and finally, User Interface Code Behind.

User Home Page

The user home page, as outlined in the introduction, has two major responsibilities:

- To provide a place for site navigation
- To provide an area where all other pages of the site will be displayed

This will be very similar to the old HTML frame-style design or ASP.NET master pages. You want to keep the existing banner and footer areas visible at all times so the design will have to include those areas. Everything you need to provide has been outlined in the previous requirements, so let's start by looking at the user interface design.

User Interface

ASP.NET provides a great feature called master pages, which makes it simple to reuse areas of a site across multiple pages. For example, if you have a banner and footer area that you want to display across every page of the site, you don't want to have to copy the common code across every ASP.NET page in the site. Instead, you can simply create a new master page to hold the banner and footer content and then add a `ContentPlaceHolder` control to the page, which will be responsible for holding the actual page content. Because there is no feature in Silverlight that corresponds directly with master pages, you will need to look elsewhere in the framework and see if there is anything that the new navigation framework provides that could potentially give you this behavior. You don't want to have to copy the banner and footer XAML code onto every single page, and you are already using a navigation frame on the main site page so it would be best if you can figure out a way to provide a nested navigation frame on the home page that would be responsible for displaying all other pages that are available after login. This would allow you to retain the banner and footer areas that are already being displayed. Of course, because the login control is currently visible in the banner area, you will need to make sure that it is hidden after a successful login and made visible again when the user logs out of the site. Just to make it a little easier to follow, let's take a look at a visual of what the user home page needs to look like. Figure 4-1 shows the basic user interface screen that you're building.

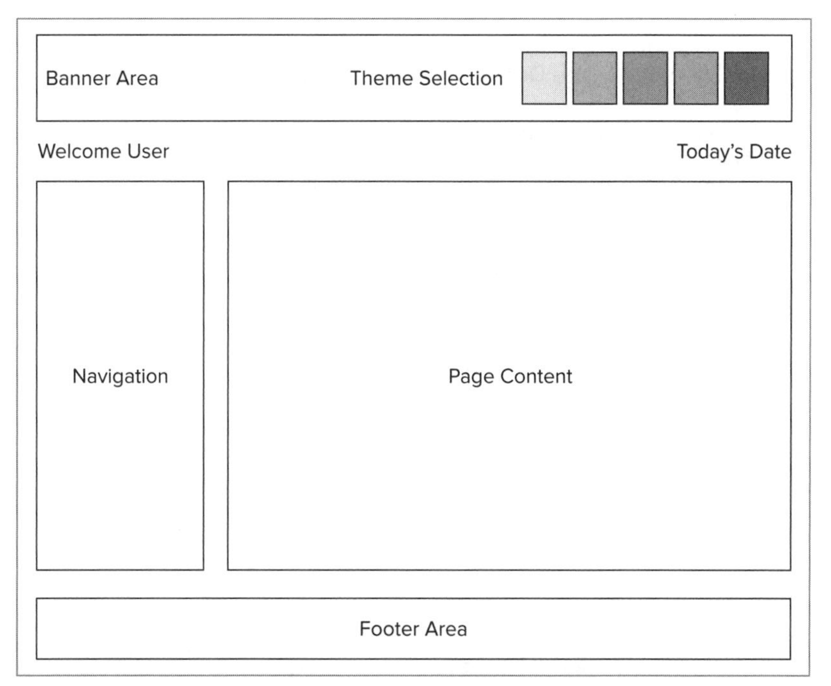

FIGURE 4-1

Although it is a rough sketch of what the screen needs to look like, you can easily see that there is an area for navigation, banner, footer, welcome message, today's date, theme selection, and all other page content.

In the previous chapter, you added a `Frame` control that holds all the main site content. After a successful login, the source of the `Frame` is updated to display the UserHome.xaml page. Because this inner `Page` control will be responsible for displaying the site navigation menu, you need to find a way to add an additional nested `Frame` control to the UserHome.xaml page that will display the content that is available to logged-in users. One drawback to adding more nested `Frame` controls, however, is that you lose the nice browser button integration that currently exists with the outer `Frame` control.

The Silverlight Navigation Framework does not currently support the use of nested `Frame` controls while maintaining tight integration with the browser history and navigation buttons.

So, what exactly does that mean? Well for starters, when you initially added the `Frame` control and set its `Source` property to UserHome.xaml, you should have noticed that the `Title` property of the UserHome.xaml `Page` class was automatically displayed in the browser's title area. You also should have noticed that clicking the browser's Back and Forward buttons cycled through the various pages that were visited with no additional code required. When you add another navigation `Frame` control to the mix, you will effectively lose this capability for all of the nested pages that will reside in that `Frame`. To better understand, take a look at what happens if you introduce a nested navigation `Frame` to the default project created using the new Silverlight Navigation project template. After creating a project with this template, you are left with one main navigation `Frame` with its source property set to Home.xaml, as shown in Listing 4-1.

LISTING 4-1: MainPage.xaml (located in the DefaultNavigationFrame project)

Available for download on Wrox.com

```
<UserControl x:Class="DefaultNavigationFrame.MainPage"
     xmlns="http://schemas.microsoft.com/winfx/2006/xaml/presentation"
     xmlns:x="http://schemas.microsoft.com/winfx/2006/xaml"
     xmlns:navigation="clr-
namespace:System.Windows.Controls;assembly=System.Windows.Controls.Navigation"
     xmlns:uriMapper="clr-
namespace:System.Windows.Navigation;
assembly=System.Windows.Controls.Navigation">
     <Grid x:Name="LayoutRoot" Style="{StaticResource LayoutRootGridStyle}">
          <Border x:Name="ContentBorder" Style="{StaticResource
ContentBorderStyle}">
               <navigation:Frame x:Name="ContentFrame"Style="{StaticResource
ContentFrameStyle}" Source="/Home" Navigated="ContentFrame_Navigated"
NavigationFailed="ContentFrame_NavigationFailed">
                    <navigation:Frame.UriMapper>
                         <uriMapper:UriMapper>
                              <uriMapper:UriMapping Uri=""
MappedUri="/Views/Home.xaml"/>
                              <uriMapper:UriMapping Uri="/{pageName}"
MappedUri="/Views/{pageName}.xaml"/>
                         </uriMapper:UriMapper>
                    </navigation:Frame.UriMapper>
               </navigation:Frame>
          </Border>
          <Grid x:Name="NavigationGrid" Style="{StaticResource
NavigationGridStyle}">
               <Border x:Name="BrandingBorder" Style="{StaticResource
BrandingBorderStyle}">
                    <StackPanel x:Name="BrandingStackPanel"
Style="{StaticResource BrandingStackPanelStyle}">
                         <ContentControl Style="{StaticResource LogoIcon}"/>
                              <TextBlock x:Name="ApplicationNameTextBlock"
Style="{StaticResource ApplicationNameStyle}" Text="Application Name"/>
```

```
                    </StackPanel>
               </Border>
               <Border x:Name="LinksBorder" Style="{StaticResource
LinksBorderStyle}">
                    <StackPanel x:Name="LinksStackPanel"
Style="{StaticResource LinksStackPanelStyle}">
                         <HyperlinkButton x:Name="Link1"
Style="{StaticResource LinkStyle}" NavigateUri="/Home"
TargetName="ContentFrame" Content="home"/>
                         <Rectangle x:Name="Divider1" Style="{StaticResource
DividerStyle}"/>
                         <HyperlinkButton x:Name="Link2"
Style="{StaticResource LinkStyle}" NavigateUri="/About"
TargetName="ContentFrame" Content="about"/>
                    </StackPanel>
               </Border>
          </Grid>
     </Grid>
</UserControl>
```

As you can see, there are two possible links to click, one for viewing the about page, and another for viewing the home page. Running the project at this point will display both the about and home page titles in the browser, as shown in Figures 4-2 and 4-3.

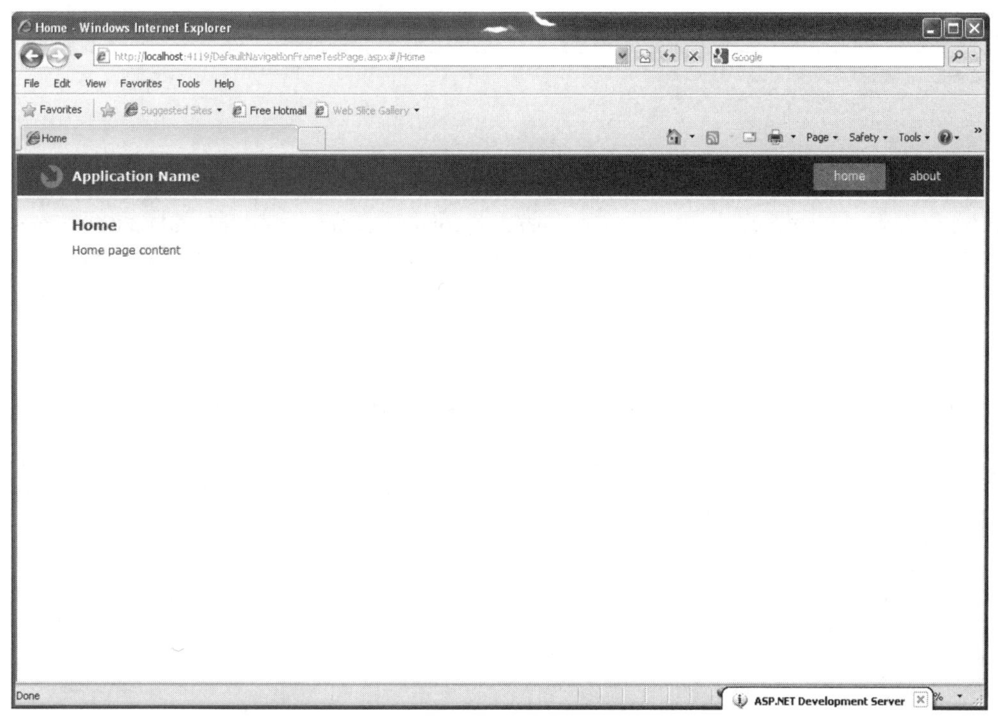

FIGURE 4-2

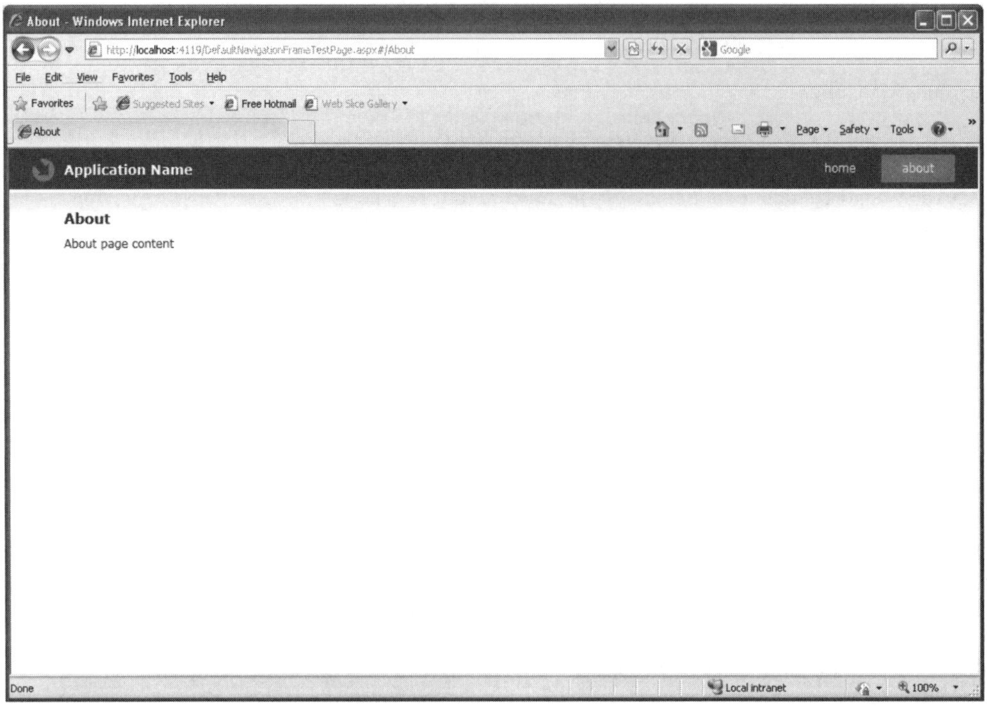

FIGURE 4-3

Clicking the browser's Back and Forward buttons will alternate between both pages updating the title bar accordingly. Now let's see what happens when you add another nested navigation `Frame` to the home page. In order to do this, you will need to create a couple of additional content pages that will display in the nested navigation `Frame`. In the Views directory, create two additional pages called NestedContent.xaml and NestedAdditionalContent.xaml. Listing 4-2 shows the XAML code for the NestedContent.xaml page.

LISTING 4-2: NestedContent.xaml (located in the NestedNavigationFrame project)

Available for download on Wrox.com

```
<navigation:Page x:Class="NestedNavigationFrame.NestedContent"
      xmlns="http://schemas.microsoft.com/winfx/2006/xaml/presentation"
      xmlns:x="http://schemas.microsoft.com/winfx/2006/xaml"
      xmlns:navigation="clr-
namespace:System.Windows.Controls;assembly=System.Windows.Controls.Navigation"
      Title="Nested Content Page">
      <Grid x:Name="LayoutRoot" Background="White">
           <TextBlock Text="Nested Content" Style="{StaticResource
HeaderTextStyle}"/>
      </Grid>
</navigation:Page>
```

The NestedAdditionalContent.xaml page shown in Listing 4-3 is basically the same code but with a different `Page Title` and `Text` property on the `TextBlock` control. In this simple example, you only need to add some text on the pages so that you can easily distinguish between the two pages when navigation occurs. The Home.xaml that is created in the project needs to be modified to include the inner navigation `Frame` and a couple of links to these new pages.

LISTING 4-3: NestedAdditionalContent.xaml (located in the NestedNavigationFrame project)

Available for download on Wrox.com

```
<navigation:Page x:Class="NestedNavigationFrame.Home"
     xmlns="http://schemas.microsoft.com/winfx/2006/xaml/presentation"
     xmlns:x="http://schemas.microsoft.com/winfx/2006/xaml"
     xmlns:navigation="clr-
namespace:System.Windows.Controls;assembly=System.Windows.Controls.Navigation"
Title="Home" Style="{StaticResource PageStyle}">
     <Grid x:Name="LayoutRoot">
          <ScrollViewer x:Name="PageScrollViewer" Style="{StaticResource
PageScrollViewerStyle}">
               <StackPanel x:Name="ContentStackPanel">
                    <TextBlock x:Name="HeaderText" Style="{StaticResource
HeaderTextStyle}" Text="Home"/>
                    <TextBlock x:Name="ContentText" Style="{StaticResource
ContentTextStyle}" Text="Home page content"/>
                    <navigation:Frame x:Name="InnerNavigation"
HorizontalAlignment="Stretch" HorizontalContentAlignment="Stretch" />
                    <HyperlinkButton Content="View Nested Content"
NavigateUri="/Views/NestedContent.xaml" TargetName="InnerNavigation" />
                    <HyperlinkButton Content="View Additional Nested Content"
NavigateUri="/Views/NestedAdditionalContent.xaml" TargetName="InnerNavigation" />
               </StackPanel>
          </ScrollViewer>
     </Grid>
</navigation:Page>
```

When you click the links to perform the navigation on the inner `Frame` control, you will notice that the browser title bar no longer reflects the Title property of the pages being displayed. Figures 4-4 and 4-5 show that regardless of which link is clicked, the browser's title still reflects the original home page title of the main navigation `Frame`.

If you use the browser's Back and Forward buttons, you will also see that they no longer flip between the nested and additional nested content pages. Another drawback is that you no longer have a unique URL being displayed in the browser for each nested page, which effectively breaks any plans you may have had for bookmarking or deep linking to these pages. So now it looks like nested navigation `Frame` controls are going to cause some problems and may not achieve the desired effect of simulating traditional ASP.NET master pages. Is there anything else available in the navigation framework that could potentially help you to work around this limitation? The answer lies in the fragment navigation feature of the navigation framework. This feature allows you to specify a URL for nested pages by simply prefixing them with the `$` character. Going back to the previous example using fragment navigation, you could access the NestedContent.xaml page with the following URL:

```
http://localhost/FragmentNavigation.aspx#/Views/HomePage.xaml$NestedContent.
```

FIGURE 4-4

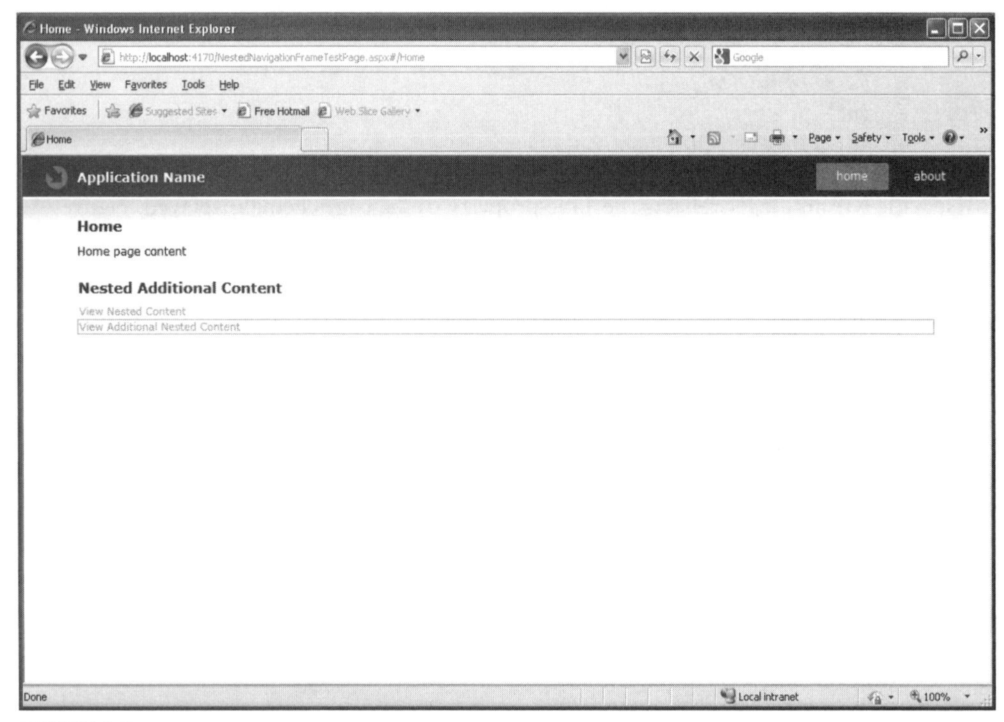

FIGURE 4-5

In order to make use of this feature, you have to first modify the Home.xaml page from the previous sample so that the `Tag` properties of the `HyperlinkButton` controls are set to `#NestedContent` and `#NestedAdditionalContent`. Prefixing the `Tag` values with the `#` character will tell the framework that the URI being created is to be a fragment of the current page being viewed. Next, modify the `HyperlinkButton_Click` event handler, as shown here:

Available for download on Wrox.com

```
private void HyperlinkButton_Click(object sender, RoutedEventArgs e)
{
     string tag = (sender as HyperlinkButton).Tag.ToString();

     NavigationService.Navigate(new Uri(String.Format("/Views/Home.xaml{0}",
tag), UriKind.Relative));
}
```

Code snippet Home.xaml.cs located in the FragmentNavigation project

Note that you are still creating a new URI using the `Tag` property, but now it is being appended to the URI for Home.xaml. Basically, this will tell the navigation framework to navigate to the current page with the specified fragment in the URI. Your work isn't done yet, however, because now you need to hook up to the `FragmentNavigation` event so that you can manually force the nested navigation `Frame` to navigate to the page that was included in the fragment. Here is the event handler for the `FragmentNavigation` event.

Available for download on Wrox.com

```
private void NavigationService_FragmentNavigation(object sender,
FragmentNavigationEventArgs e)
{
     if (e.Fragment == "NestedContent")
          InnerNavigation.Navigate(new Uri("/Views/NestedContent.xaml",
UriKind.Relative));
     else if (e.Fragment == "NestedAdditionalContent")
InnerNavigation.Navigate(new Uri("/Views/NestedAdditionalContent.xaml",
UriKind.Relative));
     else
          InnerNavigation.Content = null;
}
```

Code snippet Home.xaml.cs located in the FragmentNavigation project

Although the `#` character is required when forming the URI, the `$` character is the one that is actually displayed in the URL. At this point, you can navigate between the pages and you will have full browser history support as well as Back and Forward button functionality. Only the title is wrong. Even though you are using the fragment feature and the nested pages have their `Title` property set, the browser will still only use the main navigation frame page title in its display. You can change it but it requires hooking up to the `Navigating` event of the `NavigationService`. When listening to this event, you can find out what fragment is being navigated to and update the title of the page this way.

Available for download on Wrox.com

```
private void NavigationService_Navigating(object sender,
NavigatingCancelEventArgs e)
{
```

```
        if (e.Uri.OriginalString.EndsWith("NestedContent"))
            this.Title = "Nested Content";
        else if (e.Uri.OriginalString.EndsWith("NestedAdditionalContent"))
            this.Title = "Nested Addtional Content";
        else
            this.Title = "HomePage Page";
    }
```

Code snippet Home.xaml.cs located in the FragmentNavigation project

Although this quick sample listens for the `Navigate` event from the home page, you could just as easily listen for it in each nested page and update the title instead. Figures 4-6 and 4-7 show the new nested pages with the updated URLs and page titles.

So after looking at all of the options provided with the navigation framework, it seems you can achieve the desired user interface after all. This will let you keep the banner, footer, and navigation area visible at all times without duplicating any of the XAML for those areas into any of the other site pages.

FIGURE 4-6

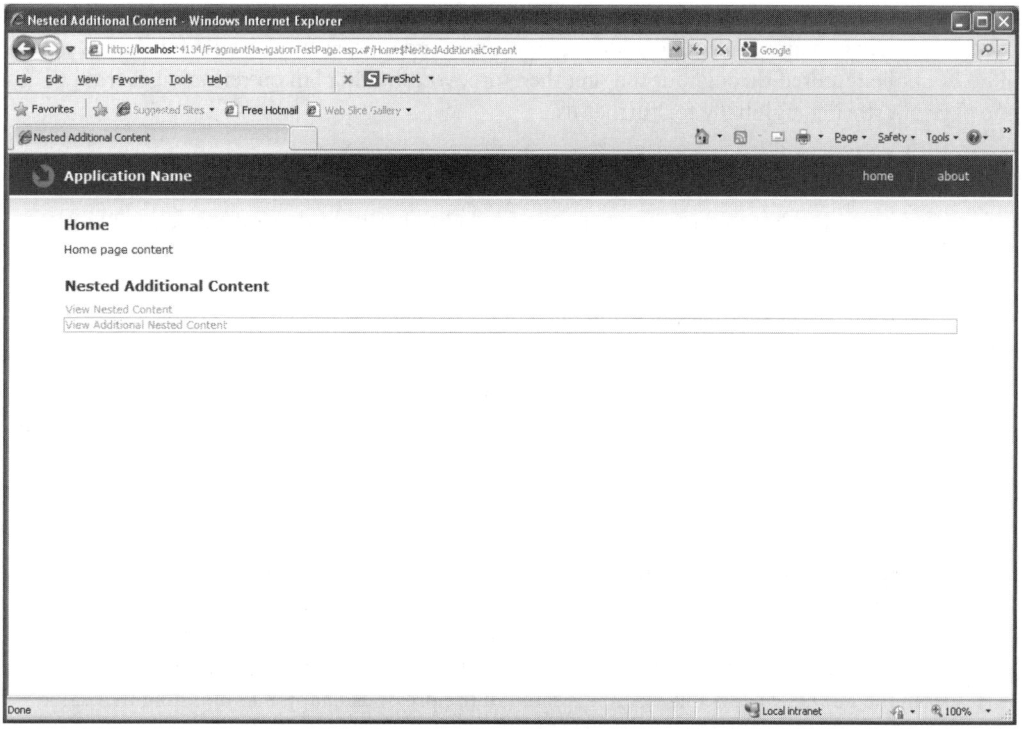

FIGURE 4-7

Database, Data Access

This page should be able to utilize the users table and `UserInformation` LINQ to SQL classes generated in the previous chapter. There should be no other database tables required or LINQ to SQL classes.

Business Logic

The business logic for this page will need to consist of routines that grab the current `UserInformation` object for the logged-in user and store it in some kind of global area. This is necessary for two reasons—the first is to provide a way to grab the `UserName` so you can display a welcome message on this screen, and the second is so that other pages won't have to retrieve the `UserInformation` class over and over again. In ASP.NET, you always have the option of storing information needed by multiple pages in the Session object for the current user. Because everything you are doing is running only on the client, you won't have this collection available to you. By creating some kind of static, globally available class, you have a place to store variables needed by other areas of the site. The `UserInformation` object for the logged-in user contains the e-mail address, username, and unique database ID for that user, which will no doubt be required throughout the site; therefore, you should plan on retrieving it from the user home page but storing it globally for further use.

User Interface Code Behind

There are a few things that the user home page code behind will need to take care of. These are:

- To retrieve the `UserInformation` object for the logged-in user.
- To display a welcome message and current date when the page is first loaded.
- To handle any navigation events fired by the navigation menu control residing on the page. When an event is fired from that control it should contain the page fragment that the nested navigation `Frame` will need to navigate to. It will be up to the user home page to make sure that the event handler is implemented and the nested `Frame` control content is updated when the event is fired.
- To provide users with the ability to switch the currently active site theme. There will be a list of themes available in the banner area and clicking on one of those themes should result in an immediate update of the user interface and all of its controls to reflect that theme. In addition to the theme being changed, you will need to update the user profile to reflect the choice so that it can be restored on the next login. The current user's profile properties should all be available from the `AuthenticationService` created in the previous chapter so updating this value should not be terribly difficult. In fact, the `AuthenticationService` will just delegate the actual profile update request to the custom profile provider class you created in the previous chapter.

Navigation Menu

The navigation menu control will need to provide the user with a list of links to the various pages of the site. This will include links to the food, exercise and measurement logs, public journal, user home, and, of course, logout. If any of these links are clicked, the menu will need to fire an event to the parent to notify it of which link was clicked.

User Interface

The preference for this menu control would be to present a vertical list of page links with an icon on the side of each link representing in some way the page that will be navigated to. For example, the food log link should have an icon representing food followed by the text-based link to the food log page. A control from the Silverlight Toolkit that should fit very well with the user interface for the menu is the new `Accordion` control. This control presents a dynamically expanding list of items to the user and you should be able to override the `Content` property of each `AccordionItem` to create the list of page links required for the control.

Database, Data Access, Business Logic

This control will not need to utilize any of the database tables or LINQ to SQL classes. In fact, there really won't be any need to access any of the business logic services at all because it's primary focus is just firing an event to let the parent know which page link was clicked.

User Interface Code Behind

Because you will be using the new `Accordion` control to implement the menu, the code behind page will need to listen for the `SelectionChanged` event. Once this event is trapped, you will need to create a new custom event to fire to the parent that will include the page fragment to navigate to. Instead of using a complex switch statement on all possible page links, you should just populate the `Tag` property of each `AccordionItem` to reflect the page fragment that you need to include in the event. This will keep the code for the navigation menu relatively simple, and it will be easy to add or remove menu items in the future without having to worry about modifying an existing switch statement or `if else` snippet.

Site Announcements

The Site Annoucements control will be created to present a list of hyperlinks that the user can click to display any site announcements in a modal child window. The control doesn't need to be overly complicated because you are only trying to relay certain important information about the site to the user. A modal child window will present this information to the user without cluttering up the user interface for the home page. The Site Annoucements control should also be visible as soon as the user logs in to the site so it will need to be part of the default view being displayed on the home page.

User Interface

The user interface for this control will be very simple—just a list of hyperlinks that show the announcement headline from the database. If a user clicks on any of the hyperlinks, then the full announcement text will be displayed in a modal child window.

Database, Data Access

The database design for this control consists of one table called announcements. The columns required for this table are shown in Table 4-1.

TABLE 4-1: Announcements

COLUMN NAME	TYPE	DESCRIPTION
id	int	Unique identity field for announcements
title	varchar(500)	Headline of site announcement
content	varchar(max)	Full text of announcement
created_date	datetime	Date announcement was added to database

Once again, you will be using LINQ to SQL to generate the classes required for the site announcements. The generated class will simply be a 1:1 mapping of each column from the announcements table.

Business Logic

A new `DomainService` class will need to be created in order to provide full CRUD capabilities for announcement objects. Although you won't need the "create, delete, or update" functionality yet, you should probably count on including it during the creation of the domain service class. When providing the query method for the service, you should only worry about returning the latest site announcements so that you don't bother the user with out-of-date information. Going back 30 days should be sufficient, and because each announcement has a corresponding `created_date` property, creating this query should be a snap.

User Interface Code Behind

The code behind for the control should be fairly straightforward. You will need event handlers for all of the `HyperlinkButton` controls. In the event handler routine, you will need to load the full text of the selected announcement into a `ChildWindow` control and display that to the user. The `Load` event of the control should handle actually retrieving all of the current announcements from the WCF RIA Service.

Account Settings

The account settings page will be made available through a hyperlink on the navigation control and will provide access to things such as the current user's e-mail address, username, password, security question, security answer, and account creation date.

User Interface

The user interface for this page will require only some `TextBlock` and `TextBox` controls in a `DataForm`. The `DataForm` control provides the easiest way to create a user interface that the user can utilize to modify these values and it also makes it easy to ensure that some values such as the `created_date` and `username` stay read-only. The `DataForm` also gives you the ability to completely customize which fields are visible, and because you will be binding to a `UserInformation` instance with several properties that should not be visible to the user, you will need to ensure that those fields don't appear on the form.

Database, Data Access

The database and data access classes that will be used for this control were already created in the previous chapter. You will really only need to make use of the users table and `UserInformation` classes. No additional tables or LINQ to SQL classes should be necessary.

Business Logic

The business logic required for this control also was created in the previous chapter when you implemented the user registration feature. This control will make use of the `UserInformationService` and, specifically, the update functionality of the service. Even though the `DataForm` will have been customized to hide certain properties, you can still make full use of the validation metadata that was created with the service to validate the form before attempting to update.

User Interface Code Behind

The `DataForm` will be performing the bulk of the work required for this page, but you will still need to load it with the `UserInformation` instance for the current user. That shouldn't be a problem, however, because you already retrieved it when the user home page was loaded and it should still be available in the static global class discussed earlier. After the information is saved to the database, it would probably be a good idea to inform the user that the changes have been saved. A simple `MessageBox` confirming that the changes have been saved should be sufficient and can be displayed in the `DataForm`'s `ItemEditEnded` event handler.

Theme Selection

Although the theme selection feature will not require the use of a separate user control, it is still important to think about how this functionality is going to work from the user home page. Instead of using a `ComboBox` with a list of available themes, I prefer to create a list of colored squares that are each filled with a solid color representing the various themes. When a user clicks the square, that theme will be applied to the site and the selection will be saved to the user's profile in the `CurrentTheme` property. This list of themes should reside in the banner area in the same location as the login control. Because the login control is still visible, you'll need to hide it at login while still displaying the list of themes. Rather than make what will inevitably be a poor attempt at creating a theme from scratch, I recommend that FitnessTrackerPlus make use of the themes included in the Silverlight Toolkit.

I outlined in the second chapter the various themes that are included in the toolkit. The themes are available in both DLL and XAML forms. In most projects, you can just add a reference to the DLL files for each theme that you want to incorporate into your project, but FitnessTrackerPlus will potentially have its own custom controls and backgrounds that will need to be styled according to the theme being selected. By default, you will see that FitnessTrackerPlus uses a blue to white gradient as the main background. If the user switches to the `ShinyRed` theme, this background won't look as good. Therefore, instead of adding references to all of the themes in the DLL form, you will add the raw XAML files instead. By doing this you can easily add any custom styles that are specific to FitnessTrackerPlus without having to add additional DLL projects to the solution. Either way will work, but more likely than not, you'll make frequent changes to these files. So, by working with just the raw XAML, this should make the entire build process much cleaner. You can find the XAML files for each theme in the Program Files\Microsoft SDKs\Silverlight\v4.0\Toolkit\Nov09\Themes\XAML directory.

Fitness Summaries

As it currently stands, the user home page shows a welcome message, today's date, and any site announcements as the default view after logging in. What you want in addition to this is to display daily summaries of foods, exercises, and measurements. You don't yet have a working food, exercise, or measurement log page so there is no point in trying to implement daily summaries yet because you can't log anything. You should, however, think about how these summaries are going to be displayed from the default view. For now, you should think about creating placeholders for these three controls. Figure 4-8 shows what this updated user home page should look like when you ultimately have all three summary controls completed.

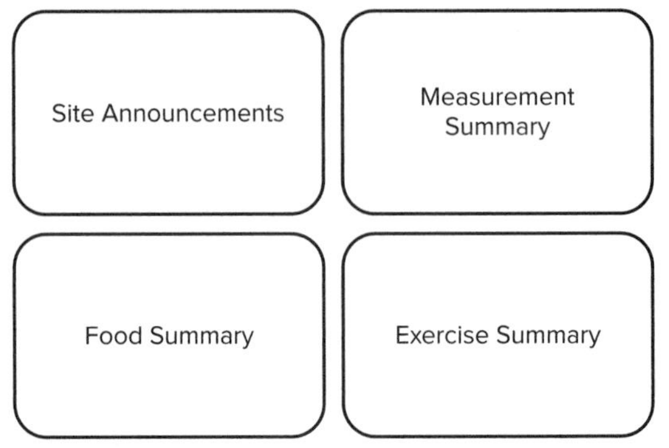

FIGURE 4-8

SOLUTION

Now it's time to take a look at the solution for the features outlined for this chapter. In this section you will learn:

- **Navigation Menu:** How to make use of the new `Accordion` control from the Silverlight Toolkit to make a navigation menu.
- **Dashboard:** Finally, the dashboard will be looked at and you will start to have the beginnings of the daily fitness dashboard. Although you still won't be able to enter foods, exercises, or measurements, you can set up some placeholders for those summary controls.
- **Account settings:** In the previous chapter, you saw how easy it was to register users with the new `DataForm` control combined with the WCF RIA Service validation feature. In this chapter, you will see how you can utilize the validation feature without the `DataForm` in your own custom data entry screen that will provide users with the ability to update existing account settings such as e-mail address, security question/answer, and password.
- **Themes:** How to give your users the option to select a preferred theme for the site using the supplied themes in the Silverlight Control Toolkit.
- **Site announcements:** The requirement to provide site announcements will be satisfied in this section, and through the use of control templates and the `ChildWindow` control it couldn't be any easier.

The most important thing to take away from this solution section is that the improvements made to Silverlight 4 and the Silverlight Toolkit have made all of these things dramatically easier to achieve than in previous versions of the runtime.

Global Variables

Before getting into the various features and controls that make up the solution for this chapter, I wanted to show you an important piece of the FitnessTrackerPlus application that will be used throughout other areas of the book. As discussed earlier in this chapter, there really isn't a client-side alternative to the `Session` object that is available in ASP.NET. Of course, because Silverlight applications are running on the client side only, they have no problem holding the state of various objects. FitnessTrackerPlus has a Globals.cs file that in this case takes the place of the traditional `Session` object from ASP.NET. Now there are about a million and one ways to share variables across multiple pages in a Silverlight application. You could make use of the isolated storage feature, or you could even create your own application level dictionary variable and call it Session.

For this particular application, only a handful of variables need to be made available across the application so a single static class holding static variables will be sufficient. As variables that need to be shared are required, they will be added to this file. The first two are the current `UserInformation` instance, and the currently selected date. You will see why you need to save the selected date versus the current date in the next chapter. Just about every page in FitnessTrackerPlus will need to make use of some property from the current `UserInformation` object. In order to avoid making repeated calls to the `UserInformationService`, you should retrieve the current `UserInformation` object after a successful login and store it in the static `Globals` class. Listing 4-4 shows the code for the `Globals` class.

LISTING 4-4: Globals.cs (located in the FitnessTrackerPlus project)

Available for download on Wrox.com

```
using System;
using FitnessTrackerPlus.Web.Data;
using System.Windows.Controls;

namespace FitnessTrackerPlus
{
     public static class Globals
     {
          public static UserInformation CurrentUser = null;
          public static DateTime SelectedDate = DateTime.Now;
     }
}
```

Navigation Menu

The navigation menu is the gateway to the rest of the site. In traditional ASP.NET websites, it was common to utilize one of the standard menu controls that were available along with a sitemap in order to present the user with a list of available pages. Silverlight does not have any such control or mechanism like a sitemap, but it does provide you with the tools necessary to make rich menu systems with very little code customization. By making use of the new `Accordion` control from the Silverlight Toolkit, you can create a menu that automatically expands and contracts with mouse clicks complete with its own animation.

User Interface

The user interface for the NavigationMenu control consists of an Accordion control along with several AccordionItem controls. The design called for a vertical list of navigation links. Each link is to have an icon followed by some text for the navigation ink. Each item in the Accordion is also to have a sub-menu that consists of HyperlinkButton controls for navigating to sub-pages. The Accordion control has an Items property that allows you to add AccordionItem controls. Each AccordionItem control contains a Header and Content property that can be customized to meet your needs. In this case, you will use the Header to display an Icon and Feature text. You will use the Content property to host any sub-menu items. Listing 4-5 shows the code for the NavigationMenu that includes an AccordionItems collection that will lead the user to the Dashboard, Food Log, Exercise Log, Measurement Log, and Public Journal pages. Listing 4-5 shows the XAML code for the NavigationMenu control.

LISTING 4-5: NavigationMenu.xaml (located in the FitnessTrackerPlus project)

Available for download on Wrox.com

```
<UserControl x:Class="FitnessTrackerPlus.Controls.NavigationMenu"
     xmlns="http://schemas.microsoft.com/winfx/2006/xaml/presentation"
     xmlns:x="http://schemas.microsoft.com/winfx/2006/xaml"
     xmlns:toolkit="clr-namespace:System.Windows.Controls;
assembly=System.Windows.Controls.Layout.Toolkit">
     <UserControl.Resources>
          <Style x:Key="NavigationMenuStyle" TargetType="toolkit:Accordion">
               <Setter Property="ExpandDirection" Value="Down" />
               <Setter Property="Cursor" Value="Hand" />
          </Style>
          <Style x:Key="NavigationMenuItemStyle"
TargetType="toolkit:AccordionItem">
          </Style>
          <Style x:Key="NavigationMenuItemLinkStyle"
TargetType="HyperlinkButton">
               <Setter Property="Margin" Value="20,0,0,10" />
          </Style>
          <Style x:Key="NavigationMenuItemHeaderPanelStyle"
TargetType="StackPanel">
               <Setter Property="Orientation" Value="Horizontal" />
               <Setter Property="Margin" Value="0,0,0,10" />
          </Style>
          <Style x:Key="NavigationMenuItemContentPanelStyle"
TargetType="StackPanel">
               <Setter Property="Margin" Value="0,10,0,0" />
          </Style>
          <Style x:Key="NavigationMenuItemTextStyle" TargetType="TextBlock">
               <Setter Property="Margin" Value="10,0,0,0" />
               <Setter Property="FontWeight" Value="Bold" />
          </Style>
          <Style x:Key="NavigationMenuFoodLogImageStyle" TargetType="Image">
               <Setter Property="Source" Value="/Images/foods.png" />
               <Setter Property="Height" Value="20" />
               <Setter Property="Width" Value="30" />
          </Style>
          <Style x:Key="NavigationMenuExerciseLogImageStyle"
TargetType="Image">
```

```
                <Setter Property="Source" Value="/Images/exercises.png" />
                <Setter Property="Height" Value="20" />
                <Setter Property="Width" Value="30" />
            </Style>
            <Style x:Key="NavigationMenuMeasurementLogImageStyle"
TargetType="Image">
                <Setter Property="Source" Value="/Images/measurements.png" />
                <Setter Property="Height" Value="20" />
                <Setter Property="Width" Value="30" />
            </Style>
            <Style x:Key="NavigationMenuPublicJournalImageStyle"
TargetType="Image">
                <Setter Property="Source" Value="/Images/journal.png" />
                <Setter Property="Height" Value="20" />
                <Setter Property="Width" Value="30" />
            </Style>
            <Style x:Key="NavigationMenuHomeImageStyle" TargetType="Image">
                <Setter Property="Source" Value="/Images/home.png" />
                <Setter Property="Height" Value="20" />
                <Setter Property="Width" Value="30" />
            </Style>
            <Style x:Key="NavigationMenuLogoutImageStyle" TargetType="Image">
                <Setter Property="Source" Value="/Images/logout.png" />
                <Setter Property="Height" Value="20" />
                <Setter Property="Width" Value="30" />
            </Style>
        </UserControl.Resources>
        <toolkit:Accordion x:Name="MenuItems" Style="{StaticResource
NavigationMenuStyle}">
            <toolkit:Accordion.Items>
                <toolkit:AccordionItem Tag="#Dashboard" Style="{StaticResource
NavigationMenuItemStyle}">
                    <toolkit:AccordionItem.Header>
                        <StackPanel Style="{StaticResource
NavigationMenuItemHeaderPanelStyle}">
                            <Image Style="{StaticResource
NavigationMenuHomeImageStyle}" />
                            <TextBlock Text="Home" Style="{StaticResource
NavigationMenuItemTextStyle}" />
                        </StackPanel>
                    </toolkit:AccordionItem.Header>
                    <toolkit:AccordionItem.Content>
                        <StackPanel Style="{StaticResource
NavigationMenuItemContentPanelStyle}">
                            <HyperlinkButton x:Name="DashboardLink"
Content="Dashboard"  Tag="#Dashboard" Style="{StaticResource
NavigationMenuItemLinkStyle}" />
                            <HyperlinkButton x:Name="AccountSettingsLink"
Content="Account Settings"  Tag="#AccountSettings" Style="{StaticResource
NavigationMenuItemLinkStyle}" />
                        </StackPanel>
                    </toolkit:AccordionItem.Content>
                </toolkit:AccordionItem>
                <toolkit:AccordionItem Tag="#FoodLog">
                    <toolkit:AccordionItem.Header>
```

continues

LISTING 4-5 *(continued)*

```
                        <StackPanel Style="{StaticResource
NavigationMenuItemHeaderPanelStyle}">
                            <Image Style="{StaticResource
NavigationMenuFoodLogImageStyle}" />
                            <TextBlock Text="Foods" Style="{StaticResource
NavigationMenuItemTextStyle}" />
                        </StackPanel>
                    </toolkit:AccordionItem.Header>
                    <toolkit:AccordionItem.Content>
                        <StackPanel Style="{StaticResource
NavigationMenuItemContentPanelStyle}">
                            <HyperlinkButton x:Name="FoodLogLink"
Content="Food Log" Tag="#FoodLog" Style="{StaticResource
NavigationMenuItemLinkStyle}" />
                        </StackPanel>
                    </toolkit:AccordionItem.Content>
                </toolkit:AccordionItem>
                <toolkit:AccordionItem Tag="#ExerciseLog">
                    <toolkit:AccordionItem.Header>
                        <StackPanel Style="{StaticResource
NavigationMenuItemHeaderPanelStyle}">
                            <Image Style="{StaticResource
NavigationMenuExerciseLogImageStyle}" />
                            <TextBlock Text="Exercises"
Style="{StaticResource NavigationMenuItemTextStyle}" />
                        </StackPanel>
                    </toolkit:AccordionItem.Header>
                    <toolkit:AccordionItem.Content>
                        <StackPanel Style="{StaticResource
NavigationMenuItemContentPanelStyle}">
                            <HyperlinkButton x:Name="ExerciseLogLink"
Content="Exercise Log" Tag="#ExerciseLog" Style="{StaticResource
NavigationMenuItemLinkStyle}" />
                        </StackPanel>
                    </toolkit:AccordionItem.Content>
                </toolkit:AccordionItem>
                <toolkit:AccordionItem Tag="#MeasurementLog">
                    <toolkit:AccordionItem.Header>
                        <StackPanel Style="{StaticResource
NavigationMenuItemHeaderPanelStyle}">
                            <Image Style="{StaticResource
NavigationMenuMeasurementLogImageStyle}" />
                            <TextBlock Text="Measurements"
Style="{StaticResource NavigationMenuItemTextStyle}" />
                        </StackPanel>
                    </toolkit:AccordionItem.Header>
                    <toolkit:AccordionItem.Content>
                        <StackPanel Style="{StaticResource
NavigationMenuItemContentPanelStyle}">
                            <HyperlinkButton x:Name="MeasurementLogLink"
Content="Measurement Log" Tag="#MeasurementLog" Style="{StaticResource
NavigationMenuItemLinkStyle}" />
                        </StackPanel>
```

```
                    </toolkit:AccordionItem.Content>
               </toolkit:AccordionItem>

               <toolkit:AccordionItem Tag="Logout">
                    <toolkit:AccordionItem.Header>
                         <StackPanel Style="{StaticResource
NavigationMenuItemHeaderPanelStyle}">
                              <Image Style="{StaticResource
NavigationMenuLogoutImageStyle}" />
                              <TextBlock Text="Logout" Style="{StaticResource
NavigationMenuItemTextStyle}" />
                         </StackPanel>
                    </toolkit:AccordionItem.Header>
               </toolkit:AccordionItem>
          </toolkit:Accordion.Items>
     </toolkit:Accordion>
</UserControl>
```

Each `AccordionItem` *has its* `Tag` *property set to a value that will match a* `UriMapping` *entry in the App.xaml file. In the previous chapter, you added entries in the* `UriMapper` *that corresponded to several of the main site pages. Now you just need to add additional entries for all the links defined in the* `NavigationMenu` *control. The following code shows the updated* `UriMapper` *declaration.*

```
<uri:UriMapper x:Key="UriMap">
     <uri:UriMapping Uri="Home"
MappedUri="/Views/Home.xaml" />
     <uri:UriMapping Uri="About"
MappedUri="/Views/About.xaml" />
     <uri:UriMapping Uri="Contact"
MappedUri="/Views/Contact.xaml" />
     <uri:UriMapping Uri="Privacy"
MappedUri="/Views/Privacy.xaml" />
     <uri:UriMapping Uri="Signup"
MappedUri="/Views/Signup.xaml" />
     <uri:UriMapping Uri="Terms"
MappedUri="/Views/Terms.xaml" />
     <uri:UriMapping Uri="UserHome"
MappedUri="/Views/UserHome.xaml" />
     <uri:UriMapping Uri="Dashboard"
MappedUri="/Views/Dashboard/Dashboard.xaml" />
     <uri:UriMapping Uri="AccountSettings"
MappedUri="/Views/Dashboard/AccountSettings.xaml" />
     <uri:UriMapping Uri="FoodLog"
MappedUri="/Views/Food/FoodLog.xaml" />
     <uri:UriMapping Uri="ExerciseLog"
MappedUri="/Views/Exercise/ExerciseLog.xaml" />
     <uri:UriMapping Uri="MeasurementLog"
MappedUri="/Views/Measurement/MeasurementLog.xaml" />
</uri:UriMapper>
```

Code snippet App.xaml located in the FitnessTrackerPlus project

The `Accordion` control itself will fire a `SelectionChanged` event when the user makes a selection. Each sub-menu item consists of a `HyperlinkButton` that will fire its own `Click` event. Sub-menu items have their own `Tag` property set as well, which you will use to force the nested navigation `Frame` to load the appropriate page. That is pretty much all that is required to get the `NavigationMenu` user interface working.

Database, Data Access, Business Logic

As stated in the design, there are no additional database or data access code requirements for the `NavigationMenu` control. There is also no requirement for additional business logic code. All of the functionality for this control is contained in the code behind file.

User Interface Code Behind

The first step required for the code behind of this control is to set up some `Click` event handlers for each of the sub-menu `HyperlinkButton` controls. You should do this in the `Loaded` event for the `Page` to be sure that the controls are available. In the following code, each of the `HyperlinkButton` controls have their `Click` event mapped to a `NavigationLink_Click` event handler method and the main `Accordion` control has a `SelectionChanged` event handler assigned.

Available for download on Wrox.com

```
Loaded += (s, e) =>
{
     MenuItems.SelectionChanged += new
SelectionChangedEventHandler(NavigationMenu_SelectionChanged);

     DashboardLink.Click += new RoutedEventHandler(NavigationLink_Click);
     AccountSettingsLink.Click += new RoutedEventHandler(NavigationLink_Click);
     FoodLogLink.Click += new RoutedEventHandler(NavigationLink_Click);
     ExerciseLogLink.Click += new RoutedEventHandler(NavigationLink_Click);
     MeasurementLogLink.Click += new RoutedEventHandler(NavigationLink_Click);
};
```

Code snippet NavigationMenu.xaml.cs located in the FitnessTrackerPlus project

The next step is to tackle the `Accordion` event handler, which in this case is the `NavigationMenu_SelectionChanged` method. As you can see from the following code, the `Tag` value is extracted from the `AccordionItem` that was clicked and a custom `NavigationMenuItemSelected` event is fired so that the listener of the event can take care of navigating to the correct URI fragment.

Available for download on Wrox.com

```
public class NavigationMenuEventArgs
{
     public string NextAction { get; set; }

     public NavigationMenuEventArgs() { }

     public NavigationMenuEventArgs(string nextAction)
     {
          NextAction = nextAction;
     }
}

public delegate void NavigationMenuEventHandler(object sender,
```

```
NavigationMenuEventArgs e);

public event NavigationMenuEventHandler NavigationMenuItemSelected;

private void FireNavigationEvent(string nextAction)
{
     if (!String.IsNullOrEmpty(nextAction))
          NavigationMenuItemSelected(this,
new NavigationMenuEventArgs(nextAction));
}

private void NavigationMenu_SelectionChanged(object sender,
SelectionChangedEventArgs e)
{
     string nextAction = (MenuItems.SelectedItem as AccordionItem).Tag.ToString();

     if (NavigationMenuItemSelected != null)
          FireNavigationEvent(nextAction);
}
```

Code snippet NavigationMenu.xaml.cs located in the FitnessTrackerPlus project

Handling the sub-menu item `Click` event handler is very similar to the main `Accordion` control's handler. In the following code, the value of the `Tag` property is extracted and passed to the `FireNavigationEvent` method resulting in essentially the same behavior as the `Accordion SelectionChanged` event handler.

Available for download on Wrox.com

```
private void NavigationLink_Click(object sender, RoutedEventArgs e)
{
     string nextAction = (sender as HyperlinkButton).Tag.ToString();
          FireNavigationEvent(nextAction);
}
```

Code snippet NavigationMenu.xaml.cs located in the FitnessTrackerPlus project

It would be nice if this could all be done in one method, but since the `Accordion SelectionChanged` event handler requires a method signature with a `SelectionChangedEventArgs` parameter, and the `HyperlinkButton` uses a standard `RoutedEventArgs` parameter you will need to maintain both handlers.

User Home Page

The home page, as discussed during the design stage, has a couple of primary responsibilities such as providing navigation to the rest of the areas of the site, providing the ability to switch themes, and taking care of welcoming the user to the site. This page is the first page users see after logging in and needs to have a very simple easy to follow interface. Just a navigation menu on the left, welcome message, some themes to select from, and a placeholder for the `Dashboard` control and any other pages that will need to be displayed.

User Interface

The user interface for the home page is actually fairly simple. I already discussed how you can still make use of a nested navigation `Frame` earlier so I won't repeat that lecture. In addition to the nested navigation `Frame`, you will have a separate `NavigationMenu` control. You may have noticed that throughout the user interface code on FitnessTrackerPlus, I have suggested the use of `DockPanel` controls for overall layout. This is a great control that was introduced first in the Silverlight Toolkit, but now is actually part of the Silverlight 4 runtime and can be found in the `System.Windows.Controls` assembly. You could always figure out a way to do similar layouts with `Grid` and `StackPanel` controls, but the `DockPanel` just makes it so much easier to do things such as alignment and filling.

You can see in Listing 4-6 that the `DockPanel` contains the `NavigationMenu` control and the nested navigation `Frame` control. The `LastChildFill` property of the `DockPanel` is set to true, which forces the navigation `Frame` to expand to all the remaining area. The beauty of this is that, when the user enlarges the browser window, the navigation `Frame` automatically expands and the `NavigationMenu` stays the same. You don't have to write any complex code to keep track of the browser window size and resize the navigation `Frame` content accordingly. I still think this is one of the most useful controls in the runtime and doesn't get used enough.

> *The* `InnerNavigation` *control has a default source of* `Dashboard`. *This is done so that the* `Dashboard` *control, which you will see shortly, is always the first item displayed on the user home page. This control will present the welcome message, announcements, food, exercise, and measurement summary controls.*

Available for download on Wrox.com

LISTING 4-6: UserHome.xaml (located in the FitnessTrackerPlus project)

```
<navigation:Page x:Class="FitnessTrackerPlus.Views.UserHome"
     xmlns="http://schemas.microsoft.com/winfx/2006/xaml/presentation"
     xmlns:x="http://schemas.microsoft.com/winfx/2006/xaml"
     xmlns:navigation="clr-
namespace:System.Windows.Controls;assembly=System.Windows.Controls.Navigation"
     xmlns:controls="clr-
namespace:System.Windows.Controls;assembly=System.Windows.Controls"
     xmlns:fitnesstrackerplus="clr-namespace:FitnessTrackerPlus.Controls"
     Title="FitnessTrackerPlus-User Home">
     <navigation:Page.Resources>
          <Style x:Key="MainDockPanelStyle" TargetType="controls:DockPanel">
               <Setter Property="LastChildFill" Value="True" />
          </Style>
          <Style x:Key="NavigationMenuStyle"
TargetType="fitnesstrackerplus:NavigationMenu">
               <Setter Property="controls:DockPanel.Dock" Value="Left" />
          </Style>
          <Style x:Key="InnerFrameStyle" TargetType="navigation:Frame">
               <Setter Property="HorizontalContentAlignment"
Value="Stretch" />
```

```
                <Setter Property="Source" Value="Dashboard" />
            </Style>
        </navigation:Page.Resources>
        <controls:DockPanel Style="{StaticResource MainDockPanelStyle}">
            <fitnesstrackerplus:NavigationMenu x:Name="NavigationMenu"
Style="{StaticResource NavigationMenuStyle}" />
            <navigation:Frame x:Name="InnerNavigation" Style="{StaticResource
InnerFrameStyle}" />
        </controls:DockPanel>
</navigation:Page>
```

Database, Data Access, Business Logic

As explained in the "Design" section, there are no new database tables or LINQ to SQL classes required for the user home page. Because this page is really mostly a placeholder for other content, its primary focus is on providing navigation by listening for events being fired from the `NavigationMenu` control. Consequently, there is no additional business logic required for the user home page.

User Interface Code Behind

With no new business logic or LINQ to SQL classes to worry about, you just need to implement the event handlers for the `NavigationMenu` in the code behind. You already saw that the `NavigationMenu` control works its magic by firing an event containing the URI to navigate to. In Listing 4-7, the user home page just hooks up the event and makes use of the `Navigate` method on the inner navigation `Frame` to ensure that the requested content is displayed.

LISTING 4-7: UserHome.xaml.cs (located in the FitnessTrackerPlus project)

Available for download on Wrox.com

```
using System;
using System.Windows.Controls;
using System.Windows.Navigation;
using FitnessTrackerPlus.Controls;

namespace FitnessTrackerPlus.Views
{
     public partial class UserHome : Page
     {
          public UserHome()
          {
               InitializeComponent();
          }

#region Control Event Handlers

          protected override void OnNavigatedTo(NavigationEventArgs e)
          {
               base.OnNavigatedTo(e);

               NavigationService.FragmentNavigation += new
FragmentNavigationEventHandler(NavigationService_FragmentNavigation);
```

continues

LISTING 4-7 *(continued)*

```
            NavigationMenu.NavigationMenuItemSelected += new
NavigationMenu.NavigationMenuEventHandler(NavigationMenu_
NavigationMenuItemSelected);
        }

        private void NavigationService_FragmentNavigation(object sender,
FragmentNavigationEventArgs e)
        {
            // Extract the fragment URI and navigate to the desired page
            // this should be FoodLog, ExerciseLog, MeasurementLog, etc...

            if (!String.IsNullOrEmpty(e.Fragment))
                InnerNavigation.Navigate(new Uri(e.Fragment,
UriKind.Relative));
        }

        private void NavigationMenu_NavigationMenuItemSelected(object sender,
FitnessTrackerPlus.Controls.NavigationMenuEventArgs e)
        {
            // If the user clicked logout handle it as a special case
            // log the user out of the site and navigate to the main home page

            if (e.NextAction == "Logout")
            {
                WebContext.Current.Authentication.LoggedOut += (se, ev) =>
                {
                    NavigationService.Navigate(new Uri("Home",
UriKind.Relative));
                };

                WebContext.Current.Authentication.Logout(false);
            }
            else
                NavigationService.Navigate(new Uri(e.NextAction,
UriKind.Relative));
        }

#endregion
    }
}
```

In Listing 4-7, you probably noticed a special case in the `NavigationMenuEventArgs` handler. The logout URI is fired from the `NavigationMenu` when the user wishes to log out of the site. There is no real page to load for this, so this special case is handled simply by navigating back to the main site home page. The authentication service will take care of removing the actual authentication token that exists for the session when the `WebContext.Current.Logout` method is called.

Dashboard

You now have the user home page and navigation menu system in place. If you were to run the application and log in, you would be presented with the navigation menu and a blank area to the right of it. The following section covers the Dashboard page, which is the first available view that the navigation `Frame` displays. The `Dashboard` control will be the default view that is displayed after every login. You will need to make use of the `UserInformation` object stored earlier in the `Globals` class in order to present a custom welcome message to the user. Additionally, this Dashboard page will need to contain controls for site announcements as well as food, exercise, and measurement summary controls. You won't have any implementation for the last three mentioned but you will at least have placeholders and a basic UI layout complete.

User Interface

For the user interface, you will need to divide the screen into four equal sections. You need to display site announcements along with food, exercise, and measurement summaries. It would also be nice if as the browser window was expanded each of these four controls equally increased in size along with it. Listing 4-8 shows that you can easily achieve this effect by using the `*` notation on the `Grid` row and column definitions. By assigning a row height of `.5*` and a column width of `.5*`, you will essentially have two rows and two columns with each row taking up 50 percent of available height, and each column taking up 50 percent of available width. The `Grid` definition calls for two rows and two columns, which splits the `Grid` into four equal parts, each of which will contain a summary control or the site announcements.

LISTING 4-8: Dashboard.xaml (located in the FitnessTrackerPlus project)

Available for download on Wrox.com

```
<navigation:Page x:Class="FitnessTrackerPlus.Views.Dashboard.FitnessDashboard"
     xmlns="http://schemas.microsoft.com/winfx/2006/xaml/presentation"
     xmlns:x="http://schemas.microsoft.com/winfx/2006/xaml"
     xmlns:navigation="clr-
namespace:System.Windows.Controls;assembly=System.Windows.Controls.Navigation"
     xmlns:controls="clr-
namespace:System.Windows.Controls;assembly=System.Windows.Controls"
     xmlns:fitnesstrackerplus="clr-namespace:FitnessTrackerPlus.Views.Dashboard"
     Title="FitnessTrackerPlus-Fitness Dashboard">
     <navigation:Page.Resources>
          <Style x:Key="WelcomeAreaDockStyle" TargetType="controls:DockPanel">
               <Setter Property="LastChildFill" Value="False" />
               <Setter Property="Margin" Value="10,0" />
          </Style>
          <Style x:Key="WelcomeTextStyle" TargetType="TextBlock">
               <Setter Property="FontSize" Value="14" />
          </Style>
          <Style x:Key="CurrentDateStyle" BasedOn="{StaticResource
WelcomeTextStyle}" TargetType="TextBlock">
          <Setter Property="Margin" Value="0,0,10,0" />
               <Setter Property="controls:DockPanel.Dock" Value="Right" />
          </Style>
          <Style x:Key="SummaryControlStyle" TargetType="UserControl">
```

continues

LISTING 4-8 *(continued)*

```
                <Setter Property="Margin" Value="10" />
            </Style>
        </navigation:Page.Resources>
        <Grid x:Name="LayoutRoot">
            <Grid.RowDefinitions>
                <RowDefinition Height="20" />
                <RowDefinition Height=".5*" />
                <RowDefinition Height=".5*" />
            </Grid.RowDefinitions>
            <Grid.ColumnDefinitions>
                <ColumnDefinition Width=".5*" />
                <ColumnDefinition Width=".5*" />
            </Grid.ColumnDefinitions>
            <controls:DockPanel Style="{StaticResource WelcomeAreaDockStyle}"
    Grid.Row="0" Grid.Column="0" Grid.ColumnSpan="2">
                <TextBlock x:Name="UserName" Style="{StaticResource
    WelcomeTextStyle}" />
                <TextBlock x:Name="CurrentDate" Style="{StaticResource
    CurrentDateStyle}" />
            </controls:DockPanel>
            <fitnesstrackerplus:Announcements x:Name="Announcements"
    Style="{StaticResource SummaryControlStyle}" Grid.Row="1" Grid.Column="0" />
            <fitnesstrackerplus:MeasurementSummary x:Name="MeasurementSummary"
    Style="{StaticResource SummaryControlStyle}" Grid.Row="1" Grid.Column="1" />
            <fitnesstrackerplus:FoodSummary x:Name="FoodSummary"
    Style="{StaticResource SummaryControlStyle}" Grid.Row="2" Grid.Column="0" />
            <fitnesstrackerplus:ExerciseSummary x:Name="ExerciseSummary"
    Style="{StaticResource SummaryControlStyle}" Grid.Row="2" Grid.Column="1" />
        </Grid>
    </navigation:Page>
```

If you were to run the application, you would notice that all four areas expand in size along with the size of the browser window, an effect that was difficult to achieve in ASP.NET without the heavy use of JavaScript. Figure 4-9 shows the site as it stands, complete with the `NavigationMenu` and `Dashboard`.

Database, Data Access, Business Logic

This may seem like a broken record, but yet again no new database or data access classes are required to get this `Dashboard` control rolling. Don't worry—you will be adding database tables and LINQ to SQL classes soon enough. In many ways, this is a testament to the power of using a framework like LINQ to SQL along with the new WCF RIA Services in that much of the boring middle-tier code that had to be created by hand is now created by the wizard and there really isn't much customization required to get it working in your own solution.

User Interface Code Behind

The `Dashboard` control has a very simple code behind file shown here in Listing 4-9 that basically just loads all of the various summary controls, loads the site announcements, and sets the welcome message to the current user's e-mail address. Finally, the current date is updated and displayed.

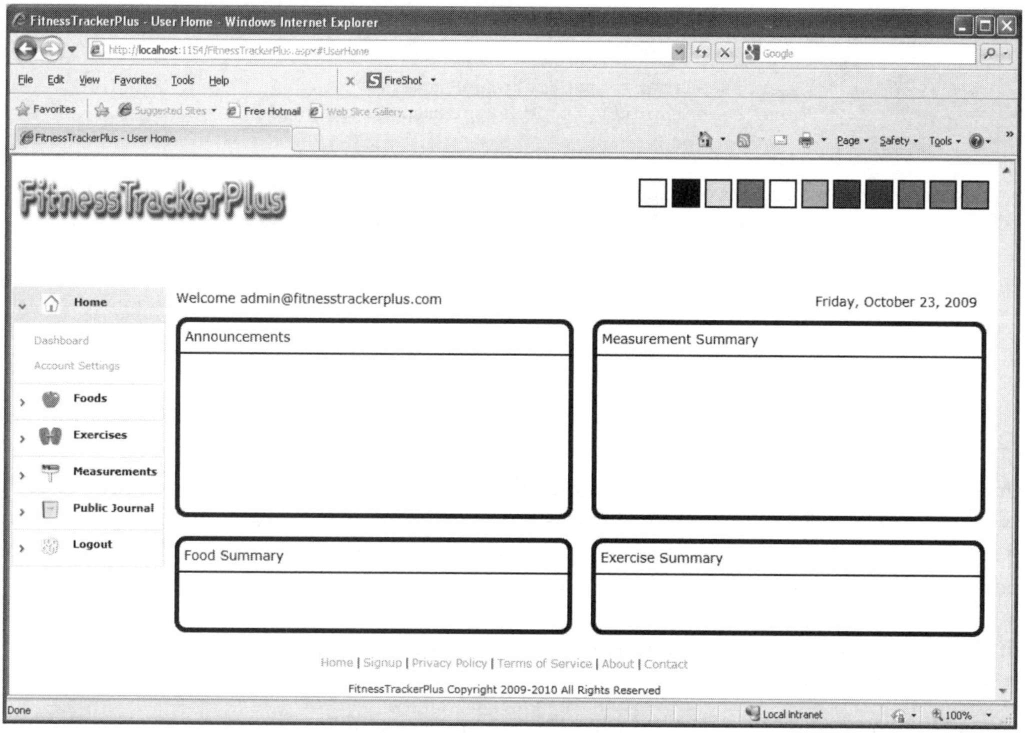

FIGURE 4-9

LISTING 4-9: Dashboard.xaml.cs (located in the FitnessTrackerPlus project)

Available for download on Wrox.com

```
using System;
using System.Windows.Controls;
using System.Windows.Navigation;
using FitnessTrackerPlus.Web.Data;

namespace FitnessTrackerPlus.Views.Dashboard
{
     public partial class FitnessDashboard: Page
     {
          public FitnessDashboard()
          {
               InitializeComponent();
          }

     #region Control Event Handlers

          protected override void OnNavigatedTo(NavigationEventArgs e)
          {
               Announcements.LoadAnnouncements();
               FoodSummary.LoadFoodSummary();
```

continues

LISTING 4-9 *(continued)*

```
                ExerciseSummary.LoadExerciseSummary();
                MeasurementSummary.LoadMeasurementSummary();

                UserName.Text = String.Format("Welcome {0}",
Globals.CurrentUser.email_address);
                CurrentDate.Text = DateTime.Now.ToLongDateString();
            }

#endregion
    }
}
```

Account Settings

Remember how just a short time ago I was bragging that only minimal code was required to get to this point? You probably thought that this was just going to be way too easy. Well, now you'll have the first real challenge of this chapter. The "Design" section required that users have the ability to modify existing account settings such as the e-mail address, password, security question, and security answer. You might think that this would be a perfect place to have just the `DataForm` control that worked so well during the user registration. As the old saying goes—if it looks too good to be true well, in this case it is.

You may have figured that this feature would be as simple as grabbing the `UserInformation` object stored in the `Globals` class and passing it to a `DataForm`. Let the `DataForm` do all of the work and implement an `UpdateUser` method and be done with it. Unfortunately, it isn't so simple; although this would work great for updating the e-mail address and security question, it all falls apart when users update the current password or security answer. Do you have any idea as to why this may not be a great idea? Okay, I will give one quick hint—think about what the values of the password and security answer probably look like in the `UserInformation` object after they are retrieved from the `UserInformationService`. If you guessed that the values of these variables are encrypted, congratulations—you didn't win anything, but at least I know you paid attention in the last chapter. Because the values are encrypted, you can't just bind the `UserInformation` object to a `DataForm` and use the generated form as you did in the user registration screen; for the account settings page, you will need to do a little bit more work up front. The good news is that you can still easily make use of the validation metadata that you created on the `UserInformation` object so client-side validation will still work just as easily. Let's take a look at how all of this is going to work.

User Interface

For the user interface, you now know that you can't just use a `DataForm`, which of course would be the easiest solution. So instead, you will need to manually create a data entry form that provides fields for e-mail address, password, security question, and security answer. Regular `TextBox` controls can be used for the e-mail address and security question, but you should use the `PasswordBox` control for password, confirm password, and security answer fields. Listing 4-10 shows the XAML code for the account settings page.

LISTING 4-10: AccountSettings.xaml (located in the FitnessTrackerPlus project)

Available for download on Wrox.com

```
<navigation:Page x:Class="FitnessTrackerPlus.Views.Dashboard.AccountSettings"
     xmlns="http://schemas.microsoft.com/winfx/2006/xaml/presentation"
     xmlns:x="http://schemas.microsoft.com/winfx/2006/xaml"
     xmlns:navigation="clr-
namespace:System.Windows.Controls;assembly=System.Windows.Controls.Navigation"
     xmlns:controls="clr-
namespace:System.Windows.Controls;assembly=System.Windows.Controls"
     xmlns:data="clr-
namespace:System.Windows.Controls; assembly=System.Windows.Controls.Data.DataForm"
     xmlns:fitnesstrackerplus="clr-namespace:FitnessTrackerPlus.Controls"
     Title="FitnessTrackerPlus-Account Settings">
     <navigation:Page.Resources>
          <Style x:Key="AccountSettingsHeaderStyle" BasedOn="{StaticResource
HeaderTextStyle}" TargetType="TextBlock">
               <Setter Property="Text" Value="Account Settings" />
          </Style>
          <Style x:Key="AccountSettingsBorderStyle" TargetType="Border">
               <Setter Property="BorderBrush" Value="#FF000000" />
               <Setter Property="BorderThickness" Value="5" />
               <Setter Property="CornerRadius" Value="5" />
               <Setter Property="Width" Value="400" />
               <Setter Property="HorizontalAlignment" Value="Center" />
          </Style>
          <Style x:Key="AccountSettingsContainerPanelStyle"
TargetType="StackPanel">
               <Setter Property="HorizontalAlignment" Value="Center" />
          </Style>
          <Style x:Key="AccountSettingsStackPanelStyle" TargetType="StackPanel">
               <Setter Property="Orientation" Value="Horizontal" />
          </Style>
          <Style x:Key="AccountSettingsTextStyle" TargetType="TextBlock">
               <Setter Property="HorizontalAlignment" Value="Right" />
               <Setter Property="Margin" Value="0,10,0,0" />
               <Setter Property="Width" Value="120" />
               <Setter Property="FontWeight" Value="Bold" />
          </Style>
          <Style x:Key="AccountSettingsTextBoxStyle" TargetType="TextBox">
               <Setter Property="HorizontalAlignment" Value="Right" />
               <Setter Property="Margin" Value="10,10,0,0" />
               <Setter Property="Width" Value="200" />
          </Style>
          <Style x:Key="AccountSettingsPasswordBoxStyle" TargetType="PasswordBox">
               <Setter Property="HorizontalAlignment" Value="Right" />
               <Setter Property="Margin" Value="10,10,0,0" />
               <Setter Property="Width" Value="200" />
          </Style>
          <Style x:Key="AccountSettingsButtonStyle" TargetType="Button">
               <Setter Property="HorizontalAlignment" Value="Right" />
               <Setter Property="Margin" Value="0,10" />
          </Style>
     </navigation:Page.Resources>
```

continues

LISTING 4-10 *(continued)*

```
        <StackPanel>
            <TextBlock Style="{StaticResource AccountSettingsHeaderStyle}" />
            <Border Style="{StaticResource AccountSettingsBorderStyle}">
                <StackPanel x:Name="AccountSettingsPanel"
    Style="{StaticResource AccountSettingsContainerPanelStyle}">
                    <StackPanel Style="{StaticResource
    AccountSettingsStackPanelStyle}">
                        <TextBlock Text="Email Address:"
    Style="{StaticResource AccountSettingsTextStyle}" />
                        <TextBox x:Name="Email" Text="{Binding
    email_address}" Style="{StaticResource AccountSettingsTextBoxStyle}" />
                    </StackPanel>
                    <StackPanel Style="{StaticResource
    AccountSettingsStackPanelStyle}">
                        <TextBlock Text="Password:" Style="{StaticResource
    AccountSettingsTextStyle}"  />
                        <PasswordBox x:Name="Password" Style="{StaticResource
    AccountSettingsPasswordBoxStyle}" />
                    </StackPanel>
                    <StackPanel Style="{StaticResource
    AccountSettingsStackPanelStyle}">
                        <TextBlock Text="Confirm Password:"
    Style="{StaticResource AccountSettingsTextStyle}" />
                        <PasswordBox x:Name="ConfirmPassword"
    Style="{StaticResource AccountSettingsPasswordBoxStyle}" />
                    </StackPanel>
                    <StackPanel Style="{StaticResource
    AccountSettingsStackPanelStyle}">
                        <TextBlock Text="Security Question:"
    Style="{StaticResource AccountSettingsTextStyle}"  />
                        <TextBox x:Name="SecurityQuestion" Text="{Binding
    security_question}" Style="{StaticResource AccountSettingsTextBoxStyle}" />
                    </StackPanel>
                    <StackPanel Style="{StaticResource
    AccountSettingsStackPanelStyle}">
                        <TextBlock Text="Security Answer:"
    Style="{StaticResource AccountSettingsTextStyle}" />
                        <PasswordBox x:Name="SecurityAnswer"
    Style="{StaticResource AccountSettingsPasswordBoxStyle}" />
                    </StackPanel>
                    <Button Content="Save Changes" x:Name="SaveChanges"
    Style="{StaticResource AccountSettingsButtonStyle}" />
                </StackPanel>
            </Border>
        </StackPanel>
    </navigation:Page>
```

Even though you won't be using the `DataForm` control, you can still make use of data binding on this page. Note how the e-mail and security question fields are bound to the `email_address` and `security_answer`. By setting the `DataContext` property on the parent control, you will still have two-way binding working on those two fields. You don't want to bind to the password, confirm password, or security answer fields and you will see why shortly. Even though you aren't using the `DataForm` control, you still have a nice data entry form for updating account settings with a minimal amount of code. Figure 4-10 shows the account settings page.

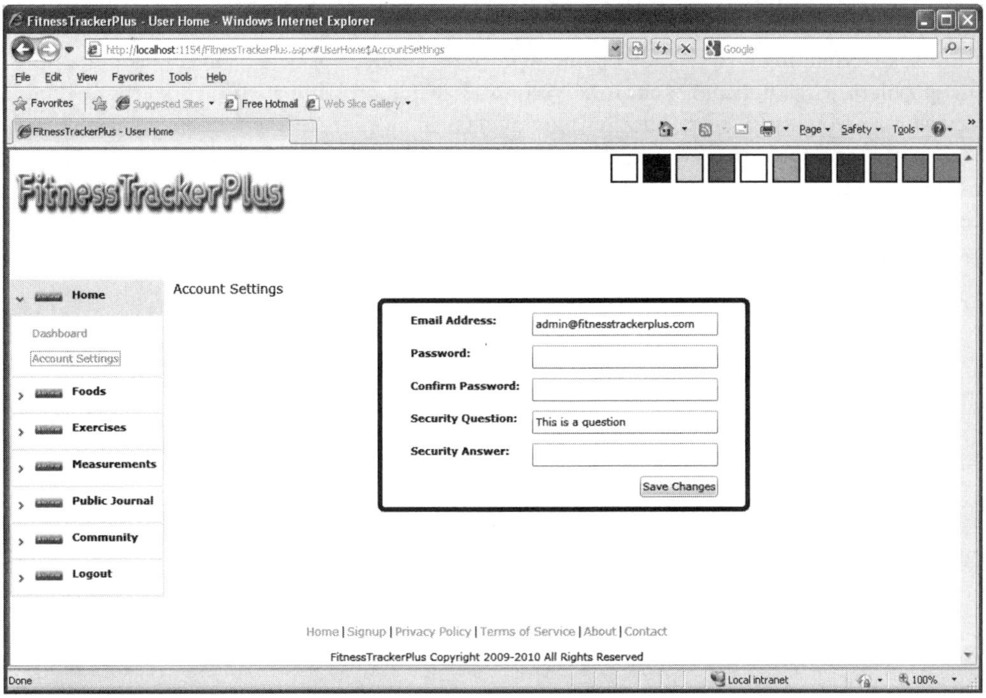

FIGURE 4-10

Database

No new database tables are necessary for the account settings. All of the settings that are being modified reside in the users table defined in the previous chapter, so no further work needed here.

Data Access

In the previous chapter, you created a `UserInformation` LINQ to SQL class file that contained all of the necessary fields from the users table. In the user interface, you saw that an additional `PasswordBox` was used to capture the `confirm_password` property of the `UserInformation` object. A *confirm password field* is used on many sites to ensure that when users make a password change, they have really entered the new password correctly. If the confirm password field does not match the password field, then the update won't occur. Forcing the user to type the password twice like this can help prevent any mistakes while typing the new password. There is nothing worse than changing your password on a site and making a typo. Without a confirm password field to double-check your entry, you could easily end up locked out of your account and be forced to contact the site administrator.

You don't want users of FitnessTrackerPlus to go through all of that hassle so you should provide the confirm password field. A quick look at the users table shows that the `confirm_password` field does not exist anywhere. You could add the field to the database, but again, you don't want to store any information that is really not necessary. The `confirm_password` field is really only used once for client-side validation of the new password. LINQ to SQL generated the `UserInformation` class as a partial class, so extending it to include this new property should not be a problem. You do, however, have one problem with this approach. In Silverlight 2, when creating a "WCFSilverlight Enabled" web service, you can easily create another partial class in a separate UserInformation.cs file. From there, you could add the `confirm_password` property and decorate it with the `DataMember` annotation. This is all that is needed to get WCF to serialize the new property to the Silverlight client. Of course, if you required change notification, you would need to implement the `PropertyChanged` event for the new property. In this implementation, the resulting code might look like the following:

```
public partial class UserInformation
{
     private string confirm_password_value;

     [DataMember]
     public string confirm_password
     {
          get { return confirm_password_value; }
          set
          {
               confirm_password_value = value;

               if (PropertyChanged != null)
                    PropertyChanged(this, new
PropertyChangedEventArgs("confirm_password"));
          }
     }
}3
```

Seems easy enough, right? Well, you aren't using a WCF service in FitnessTrackerPlus. You are using the WCF RIA Services framework, which unfortunately, does not work quite the same way. If you need to add a property that should be serialized to the Silverlight client but is not part of the original database schema you have a couple of choices. The first possibility is to utilize the new shared code feature of the WCF RIA Services framework. In this scenario, you would add a new `UserInformation` partial class to your ASP.NET project and call the file UserInformation.shared.cs. In here, you could add the `confirm_password` property. Any classes, methods, or properties that exist in a shared.cs file will be copied as is into the generated client-side code. Here is what UserInformation.shared.cs would look like.

```
using System.ComponentModel.DataAnnotations;
using System.Web.Ria.Data;
using FitnessTrackerPlus.Web.Data;

namespace FitnessTrackerPlus.Web.Data
{
     public partial class UserInformation
     {
          public string confirm_password { get; set; }
     }
}
```

One major benefit of using the shared code method is that the `confirm_password` field would be available on both the server as well as the client projects. However, you don't really need the `confirm_password` property at all on the server—let's look at the alternate solution.

The alternate solution is to make use of the new computed properties feature of the WCF RIA Services. Any property that you need to add to an existing entity class that does not have a corresponding field in the database and is only needed at the Silverlight client layer can make use of this feature. All you need to do is add the class file to the Silverlight project extending the entity you wish to add the property to. This is very similar to the situation I just described with WCF except now you are extending the entity class on the client. In order to get this working in FitnessTrackerPlus, you first need to create a new directory in the Silverlight project called Computed. This folder will store all entities that are extended for additional computed properties. Next, create a new partial class called `UserInformation` and add the `confirm_password` property, as shown in the code that follows.

Available for download on Wrox.com

```
namespace FitnessTrackerPlus.Web.Data
{
     public partial class UserInformation
     {
          public string confirm_password { get; set; }
     }
}
```

Code snippet UserInformation.cs located in the FitnessTrackerPlus project

That's pretty much all there is to it. Now when you add the `UserInformation` instance to a `DataForm`, you can set up the binding to the `confirm_password` property.

Business Logic

Now that you have the new `confirm_password` computed property, it's time to look at how to validate this property. The only validation rule for this is to ensure that the `confirm_password` matches the `password` property. Because this property resides only on the client, you don't have a corresponding metadata file to add validation attributes to. Not to worry however—the data annotations that you use in metadata files will work just fine in this extended class as well. The following code shows the updated `UserInformation` class with the appropriate validation annotations:

Available for download on Wrox.com

```
using System.ComponentModel.DataAnnotations;

namespace FitnessTrackerPlus.Web.Data
{
     public partial class UserInformation
     {
          [Display(Name = "Confirm Password:")]
          [CustomValidation(typeof(UserInformationValidation),
"ValidateConfirmPassword")]
          public string confirm_password { get; set; }
     }

}
```

Code snippet UserInformation.cs located in the FitnessTrackerPlus project

As you can see in the previous code, rather than relying on one of the standard validation annotations, you are instead making use of a `[CustomValidation]` annotation. Whenever you have a validation rule that doesn't match one of the validation annotations provided by WCF RIA Services, you can always decorate a property with the `[CustomValidation]` annotation specifying the type of validation class and static validation method to be called by the runtime when validation of the entity is performed. In this case, you are telling the framework to look for a class called `UserInformationValidation` and use its `ValidateConfirmPassword` method in order to validate the `confirm_password` property. Because this method is only used in relation to the computed property, you can go ahead and add the code to the existing UserInformation.cs file. Listing 4-11 shows the updated version of the UserInformation.cs file that includes both the computed property and its custom validation class.

LISTING 4-11: UserInformation.cs (located in the FitnessTrackerPlus project)

Available for download on Wrox.com

```
using System.ComponentModel.DataAnnotations;

namespace FitnessTrackerPlus.Web.Data
{
     public partial class UserInformation
     {
            [Display(Name = "Confirm Password:")]
            [CustomValidation(typeof(UserInformationValidation),
"ValidateConfirmPassword")]
           public string confirm_password { get; set; }
     }

     public class UserInformationValidation
     {
           public static ValidationResult ValidateConfirmPassword(string
confirm_password, ValidationContext context)
           {
                 UserInformation current = context.ObjectInstance as
UserInformation;

                 if (current.password != confirm_password)
                       return new ValidationResult("Confirm password and password
fields must be the same");

                 return null;
           }
     }
}
```

When it comes time to perform the actual custom validation logic you can use the supplied `ValidationContext` to gain access to the instance of the entity being validated. From there, you have access to all the properties including the `confirm_password` computed property value. With this information, you can easily compare the `password` and `confirm_password` fields to see if they match. If they don't match, you just return a new `ValidationResult` with an appropriate error message and that message is displayed to the user automatically if you make use of a `DataForm`. Because you are using your own custom data entry form here, you need to take care of displaying the validation error on your own.

User Interface Code Behind

The first item on your agenda for the code behind is to set up an event handler for the `SaveChanges` button. In the following code, the `SaveChanges_Click` event handler method is being assigned in the `Loaded` event for the `Page`.

```
Loaded += (s, e) =>
{
     SaveChanges.Click += new RoutedEventHandler(SaveChanges_Click);
};
```

Code snippet AccountSettings.xaml.cs located in the FitnessTrackerPlus project

Next on the list is making sure that the account settings for the currently logged-in user are bound to the main `StackPanel` control that is hosting all the data entry controls. In the following code, this binding is taking place when the page is navigated to by overriding the `OnNavigatedTo` event.

Available for download on Wrox.com

```
protected override void OnNavigatedTo(NavigationEventArgs e)
{
     AccountSettingsPanel.DataContext = Globals.CurrentUser;
}
```

Code snippet AccountSettings.xaml.cs located in the FitnessTrackerPlus project

The only other work left to do is implement the `SaveChanges_Click` method. In the following code, all the data entry field values are collected and assigned to their respective properties in the `Globals.CurrentUser` object. The validation rules are checked whenever the values of these properties are assigned. If any of these assignments should fail validation, a `ValidationException` is thrown. If everything checks out, the `UpdateUser` method of the `UserInformationService` is called to persist the new account settings to the database.

```
private void SaveChanges_Click(object sender, RoutedEventArgs e)
{
     try
     {
          Globals.CurrentUser.email_address = Email.Text;
          Globals.CurrentUser.security_question = SecurityQuestion.Text;

          if (!String.IsNullOrEmpty(Password.Password))
               Globals.CurrentUser.password = Password.Password;

          if (!String.IsNullOrEmpty(ConfirmPassword.Password))
               Globals.CurrentUser.confirm_password = ConfirmPassword.Password;

          if (!String.IsNullOrEmpty(SecurityAnswer.Password))
               Globals.CurrentUser.security_answer = SecurityAnswer.Password;

          context.UpdateUser(Globals.CurrentUser, (UpdateUserCallback) =>
          {
               Password.Password ="";
```

```
                    ConfirmPassword.Password ="";
                    SecurityAnswer.Password ="";

                    MessageBox.Show("Your account settings have
been successfully updated");

                }, null);
                }
          catch (ValidationException ex)
          {
                MessageBox.Show(ex.ValidationResult.ErrorMessage);
          }
}
```

Code snippet AccountSettings.xaml.cs located in the FitnessTrackerPlus project

Theme Selection

Along with a user friendly home page, most sites these days offer several different themes to choose from. In addition, the user's selection is usually stored so that the preferred theme automatically loads the next time the user logs back into the site. This section covers how theme selection will be implemented in FitnessTrackerPlus. You will be creating a list of available themes and storing the selected theme in the user profile using the `AuthenticationService`.

In previous versions of Silverlight, trying to switch themes dynamically was a chore and performance was lackluster. With the addition of implicit styling support in Silverlight 4, you can easily switch the theme at runtime. To get started adding theme selection to FitnessTrackerPlus, you will need to first add the XAML files to the project. Start by creating a new Themes folder in the Silverlight project and then navigate to the installation location for the Silverlight toolkit themes; this is commonly C:\Program Files\Microsoft SDKs\Silverlight\v4.0\Toolkit\Nov09\Themes. If you continue navigating to the XAML directory, you will be able to add each of the available themes. Remember that you could use the DLL versions of these themes but most likely you will need to add styles for any custom controls that exist in FitnessTrackerPlus, and rather than add several additional DLL projects to the solution it is somewhat easier to just add the XAML files themselves so that you can directly make edits.

Once you have added the required XAML files to the project, you need to make sure that you have set them as resource files, as shown in Figure 4-11.

FIGURE 4-11

User Interface

The user interface for theme selection consists of a `StackPanel` that contains `Border` and `Rectangle` controls that are filled with colors representing each of the available themes. The idea here is that the user will have several theme colors from which to choose; clicking one of the `Rectangle` controls will result in the overall site theme being changed. The `Tag` property is used to store the name of the actual theme file being requested.

Because the design calls for this theme selection to be located in the banner area of the page, you need to add it to the MainPage.xaml file. In fact, the theme selection area basically resides in the same location as the login control. This means that you need to toggle the visibility of both depending on whether the user is logged in to the site or not. Listing 4-12 shows the updated version of MainPage.xaml that includes the necessary controls required for theme selection. Notice how there is a colored `Rectangle` control for each of the themes available in the Silverlight Toolkit:

LISTING 4-12: MainPage.xaml (located in the FitnessTrackerPlus project)

Available for download on Wrox.com

```
<UserControl x:Class="FitnessTrackerPlus.MainPage"
     xmlns="http://schemas.microsoft.com/winfx/2006/xaml/presentation"
     xmlns:x="http://schemas.microsoft.com/winfx/2006/xaml"
     xmlns:navigation="clr-namespace:System.Windows.Controls;
assembly=System.Windows.Controls.Navigation"
     xmlns:toolkit="clr-namespace:System.Windows.Controls;
assembly=System.Windows.Controls.Toolkit"
     xmlns:user_controls="clr-namespace:FitnessTrackerPlus.Controls">
     <UserControl.Resources>
          <Style x:Key="BannerAreaStyle" TargetType="toolkit:DockPanel">
               <Setter Property="Height" Value="125" />
               <Setter Property="LastChildFill" Value="False" />
               <Setter Property="VerticalAlignment" Value="Top"/>
               <Setter Property="toolkit:DockPanel.Dock" Value="Top" />
          </Style>
          <Style x:Key="MainDockPanelStyle" TargetType="toolkit:DockPanel">
               <Setter Property="LastChildFill" Value="True"  />
          </Style>
          <Style x:Key="LogoBackgroundStyle" TargetType="Border">
               <Setter Property="toolkit:DockPanel.Dock" Value="Left"  />
          </Style>
          <Style x:Key="LogoImageStyle" TargetType="Image">
               <Setter Property="Source" Value="/Images/logo.png" />
               <Setter Property="Width" Value="300" />
               <Setter Property="Height" Value="80" />
               <Setter Property="Stretch" Value="Fill" />
               <Setter Property="VerticalAlignment" Value="Top" />
          </Style>
          <Style x:Key="LoginControlStyle" TargetType="user_controls:Login">
               <Setter Property="toolkit:DockPanel.Dock" Value="Right" />
          </Style>
          <Style x:Key="MainFrameAreaStyle" TargetType="navigation:Frame">
               <Setter Property="Source" Value="Home" />
               <Setter Property="UriMapper" Value="{StaticResource UriMap}" />
               <Setter Property="HorizontalContentAlignment"
Value="Stretch" />
               <Setter Property="Margin" Value="0,10" />
          </Style>
          <Style x:Key="FooterAreaStyle" TargetType="StackPanel">
```

continues

LISTING 4-12 *(continued)*

```
                <Setter Property="HorizontalAlignment" Value="Center" />
                <Setter Property="toolkit:DockPanel.Dock" Value="Bottom" />
            </Style>
            <Style x:Key="FooterLinksAreaStyle" TargetType="StackPanel">
                <Setter Property="Orientation" Value="Horizontal" />
                <Setter Property="HorizontalAlignment" Value="Center" />
            </Style>
            <Style x:Key="FooterTextStyle" TargetType="TextBlock">
                <Setter Property="FontSize" Value="12" />
            </Style>
            <Style x:Key="FooterLinksStyle" TargetType="HyperlinkButton">
                <Setter Property="FontSize" Value="12" />
            </Style>
            <Style x:Key="CopyrightTextStyle" TargetType="TextBlock">
                <Setter Property="Text"
    Value="FitnessTrackerPlus Copyright 2009-2010 All Rights Reserved" />
            <Setter Property="Margin" Value="0,10,0,0" />
                <Setter Property="HorizontalAlignment" Value="Center" />
            </Style>
            <Style x:Key="ThemePanelStyle" TargetType="StackPanel">
                <Setter Property="Orientation" Value="Horizontal" />
                <Setter Property="Visibility" Value="Collapsed" />
                <Setter Property="VerticalAlignment" Value="Top" />
                <Setter Property="Margin" Value="0,20,10,0" />
                <Setter Property="toolkit:DockPanel.Dock" Value="Right" />
            </Style>
            <Style x:Key="ThemeBorderStyle" TargetType="Border">
                <Setter Property="BorderBrush" Value="#FF000000" />
                <Setter Property="BorderThickness" Value="2" />
                <Setter Property="Width" Value="30" />
                <Setter Property="Height" Value="30" />
                <Setter Property="Padding" Value="0" />
                <Setter Property="Margin" Value="5,0,0,0" />
            </Style>
            <Style x:Key="ThemeSelectionStyle" TargetType="Rectangle">
                <Setter Property="Width" Value="30" />
                <Setter Property="Height" Value="30" />
                <Setter Property="Cursor" Value="Hand" />
            </Style>
        </UserControl.Resources>
        <ScrollViewer x:Name="MainScroll">
            <toolkit:DockPanel Style="{StaticResource MainDockPanelStyle}">
                <toolkit:DockPanel Style="{StaticResource BannerAreaStyle}">
                    <Border Style="{StaticResource LogoBackgroundStyle}">
                        <Image Style="{StaticResource LogoImageStyle}" />
                    </Border>
                    <user_controls:Login x:Name="LoginControl"
    Style="{StaticResource LoginControlStyle}" />
                    <StackPanel x:Name="ThemePanel" Style="{StaticResource
    ThemePanelStyle}">
                        <Border Style="{StaticResource ThemeBorderStyle}">
                            <Rectangle Fill="MintCream"
```

```
Style="{StaticResource ThemeSelectionStyle}" Tag="BubbleCreme" />
                         </Border>
                         <Border Style="{StaticResource ThemeBorderStyle}">
                              <Rectangle Fill="Black" Style="{StaticResource
ThemeSelectionStyle}" Tag="BureauBlack" />
                         </Border>
                         <Border Style="{StaticResource ThemeBorderStyle}">
                              <Rectangle Fill="Aqua" Style="{StaticResource
ThemeSelectionStyle}" Tag="BureauBlue" />
                         </Border>
                         <Border Style="{StaticResource ThemeBorderStyle}">
                              <Rectangle Fill="SlateGray"
Style="{StaticResource ThemeSelectionStyle}" Tag="ExpressionDark" />
                         </Border>
                         <Border Style="{StaticResource ThemeBorderStyle}">
                              <Rectangle Fill="White" Style="{StaticResource
ThemeSelectionStyle}" Tag="ExpressionLight" />
                         </Border>
                         <Border Style="{StaticResource ThemeBorderStyle}">
                              <Rectangle Fill="Orange" Style="{StaticResource
ThemeSelectionStyle}" Tag="RainierOrange" />
                         </Border>
                         <Border Style="{StaticResource ThemeBorderStyle}">
                              <Rectangle Fill="Purple" Style="{StaticResource
ThemeSelectionStyle}" Tag="RainierPurple" />
                         </Border>
                         <Border Style="{StaticResource ThemeBorderStyle}">
                              <Rectangle Fill="Blue" Style="{StaticResource
ThemeSelectionStyle}" Tag="ShinyBlue" />
                         </Border>
                         <Border Style="{StaticResource ThemeBorderStyle}">
                              <Rectangle Fill="Red" Style="{StaticResource
ThemeSelectionStyle}" Tag="ShinyRed" />
                         </Border>
                         <Border Style="{StaticResource ThemeBorderStyle}">
                              <Rectangle Fill="DodgerBlue"
Style="{StaticResource ThemeSelectionStyle}" Tag="TwilightBlue" />
                         </Border>
                         <Border Style="{StaticResource ThemeBorderStyle}">
                              <Rectangle Fill="CornflowerBlue"
Style="{StaticResource ThemeSelectionStyle}" Tag="WhistlerBlue" />
                         </Border>
                    </StackPanel>
               </toolkit:DockPanel>
               <StackPanel Style="{StaticResource FooterAreaStyle}">
                    <StackPanel Style="{StaticResource FooterLinksAreaStyle}">
                         <HyperlinkButton x:Name="HomeLink" NavigateUri="Home"
TargetName="MainSiteFrame" Content="Home" Style="{StaticResource
FooterLinksStyle}" />
                         <TextBlock Text="|" Style="{StaticResource
FooterTextStyle}" />
                         <HyperlinkButton x:Name="SignupLink"
NavigateUri="Signup" TargetName="MainSiteFrame" Content="Signup"
```

continues

LISTING 4-12 *(continued)*

```
Style="{StaticResource FooterLinksStyle}" />
                         <TextBlock Text="|" Style="{StaticResource
FooterTextStyle}" />
                         <HyperlinkButton x:Name="PrivacyLink"
NavigateUri="Privacy" TargetName="MainSiteFrame" Content="Privacy Policy"
Style="{StaticResource FooterLinksStyle}" />
                         <TextBlock Text="|" Style="{StaticResource
FooterTextStyle}" />
                         <HyperlinkButton x:Name="TermsLink"
NavigateUri="Terms" TargetName="MainSiteFrame" Content="Terms of Service"
Style="{StaticResource FooterLinksStyle}" />
                         <TextBlock Text="|" Style="{StaticResource
FooterTextStyle}" />
                         <HyperlinkButton x:Name="AboutLink"
NavigateUri="About" TargetName="MainSiteFrame" Content="About"
Style="{StaticResource FooterLinksStyle}" />
                         <TextBlock Text="|" Style="{StaticResource
FooterTextStyle}" />
                         <HyperlinkButton x:Name="ContactLink"
NavigateUri="Contact" TargetName="MainSiteFrame" Content="Contact"
Style="{StaticResource FooterLinksStyle}" />
                    </StackPanel>
                    <TextBlock Style="{StaticResource CopyrightTextStyle}" />
               </StackPanel>
               <navigation:Frame x:Name="MainSiteFrame" Style="{StaticResource
MainFrameAreaStyle}" />
          </toolkit:DockPanel>
     </ScrollViewer>
</UserControl>
```

Database, Data Access, Business Logic

No additional database or data access code is required to make theme selection work. For business logic, you will be making use of the `AuthenticationService` in order to modify and save the `CurrentTheme` property of the user profile object. You won't need to write any additional code, however, as everything you need was created in the previous chapter.

User Interface Code Behind

In the code behind you need to take care of switching the currently active theme when the user clicks one of the `Rectangle` controls. Although there is no `Click` event available, you can just as easily do this by adding an event handler to the `MouseLeftButtonUp` event. Because all these `Rectangle` controls will use the same event handler, you can simplify the hookup of these events by iterating through the child controls of the `StackPanel` hosting the `Rectangle` controls. As you iterate through the children, you will gain access to the `Border` control that is the parent for the `Rectangle`. From this point, you simply cast the `Child` property of the `Border` control to a `Rectangle` and assign the event handler to the `MouseLeftButtonUp` event as shown in the following code.

Available for download on Wrox.com

```
foreach (UIElement element in ThemePanel.Children)
     ((element as Border).Child as Rectangle).MouseLeftButtonUp += new
MouseButtonEventHandler(ThemeSelection_MouseLeftButtonUp);
```

Code snippet MainPage.xaml.cs located in the FitnessTrackerPlus project

Now, once you have registered the event listeners for all of the theme selection rectangles, you need to implement the `MouseLeftButtonUp` method. In the following code, you will first extract the theme value that was selected from the `Tag` property of the `Rectangle` control that was clicked. Then you want to save the value in the current user's `Profile` object. Finally, when the asynchronous `SaveUser` call completes you need to actually switch out the current theme. Earlier in Chapter 2, I showed you how to do this with the DLL versions of the Toolkit themes. Although this method works, you would be much better off if you could switch the current theme without removing and adding controls to the visual tree. In the following code, the current theme is switched using the `MergedDictionaries` feature of Silverlight. Because you can easily add and remove items from this collection at any time, you basically clear the collection, build a new `ResourceDictionary` using the raw XAML files for the selected theme, and add that new `ResourceDictionary` object to the `MergedDictionaries` collection. Implicit styling will take care of the rest by ensuring that all the controls in the application are styled according to the XAML in the new `MergedDictionaries` collection you created.

Available for download on Wrox.com

```
private void ThemeSelection_MouseLeftButtonUp(object sender,
MouseButtonEventArgs e)
{
     // Switch the current theme and store in the user profile

     WebContext.Current.User.CurrentTheme = (sender as Rectangle).Tag.ToString();
     WebContext.Current.Authentication.SaveUser(false);

     SetTheme(WebContext.Current.User.CurrentTheme);
}

private void SetTheme(string theme)
{
     this.Resources.MergedDictionaries.Clear();

     ResourceDictionary themeResource = new ResourceDictionary();
     themeResource.Source = new
Uri(String.Format("/FitnessTrackerPlus;component/Themes/
System.Windows.Controls.Theming.{0}.xaml", theme), UriKind.RelativeOrAbsolute);

     this.Resources.MergedDictionaries.Add(themeResource);
}
```

Code snippet MainPage.xaml.cs located in the FitnessTrackerPlus project

Of course, if you already have items in the `MergedDictionaries` collection, you can simply clear the collection. In that case, you must ensure that you only remove the existing theme `ResourceDictionary` object, if one exists.

One last thing that you will need to do is to ensure that the `Background` property of the `ScrollViewer` is set to a color that works well with the theme that was selected. By default, most of the themes do not have the `Background` property set for `ScrollViewer` controls. You should go through each of the theme files and find the `ScrollViewer` style template and add the appropriate `Background` color. The following code shows the `ScrollViewer` style definition from the `BubbleCreme` theme with the `Background` property added.

Available for download on Wrox.com

```
<Style TargetType="ScrollViewer">
    <Setter Property="BorderThickness" Value="1.5,1.5,.75,.75" />
    <Setter Property="Padding" Value="1" />
    <Setter Property="Background" Value="Cornsilk" />
    <Setter Property="BorderBrush">
        <Setter.Value>
            <LinearGradientBrush EndPoint="0.5,1.5" StartPoint="0.5,0">
                <GradientStop Color="{StaticResource DarkColor}" />
                <GradientStop Color="{StaticResource LightColor}" Offset="1" />
            </LinearGradientBrush>
        </Setter.Value>
    </Setter>
    <Setter Property="HorizontalScrollBarVisibility" Value="Auto" />
    <Setter Property="VerticalScrollBarVisibility" Value="Auto" />
    <Setter Property="Template">
    <Setter.Value>
        <ControlTemplate TargetType="ScrollViewer">
        <Border x:Name="Root" BorderBrush="{TemplateBinding BorderBrush}"
BorderThickness="{TemplateBinding BorderThickness}" CornerRadius="4">
            <Grid Background="#FFF9F9E6>
                <Grid.RowDefinitions>
                    <RowDefinition Height="*" />
                    <RowDefinition Height="Auto" />
                </Grid.RowDefinitions>
                <Grid.ColumnDefinitions>
                    <ColumnDefinition Width="*" />
                    <ColumnDefinition Width="Auto" />
                </Grid.ColumnDefinitions>
```

Code snippet System.Windows.Controls.BubbleCreme.xaml located in the FitnessTrackerPlus project

You will need to make the change to the `Background` property in every theme file. It may seem impossible that you're creating a theme engine with this small amount of code, but thanks to the new Implicit Styling support in Silverlight 4 combined with the pre-built themes available in the Silverlight Toolkit supporting dynamic theme selection is easier than ever.

Site Announcements

At this point, you have just about everything you need for a working user home page. Theme selection is working, site navigation is in place, and your users can even update their account settings. The only thing left to work on for this chapter is to add some functionality to that `Dashboard` control to provide your users with important site announcements. The design called for a site announcements control that would provide a list of hyperlinks, which, when clicked, displays the announcement text in a modal `ChildWindow`.

User Interface

For the user interface of the site announcements control you will need to make use of a customized `ListBox` control. Customizing the `ListBox` control involves overriding both the `ItemsPanel` and `ItemContainerStyle`. The `ItemsPanel` will consist of a vertically oriented `StackPanel`. This will be the main container holding all of the `ListBox` items. The `ItemContainerStyle` will consist of a horizontal `StackPanel` that contains a `TextBlock` for the announcement date, and a `HyperlinkButton` that contains the announcement title text. Listing 4-13 shows the XAML code required for the `Announcements` control.

LISTING 4-13: Announcements.xaml (located in the FitnessTrackerPlus project)

Available for download on Wrox.com

```
<UserControl x:Class="FitnessTrackerPlus.Views.Dashboard.Announcements"
     xmlns="http://schemas.microsoft.com/winfx/2006/xaml/presentation"
     xmlns:x="http://schemas.microsoft.com/winfx/2006/xaml"
     xmlns:controls="clr-
namespace:System.Windows.Controls;assembly=System.Windows.Controls"
     xmlns:converters="clr-namespace:FitnessTrackerPlus.Converters">
     <UserControl.Resources>
          <converters:AnnouncementDateConverter
x:Key="AnnouncementDateConverter" />
          <Style x:Key="AnnouncementDateStyle" TargetType="TextBlock">
               <Setter Property="Margin" Value="10,0,0,0" />
          </Style>
          <Style x:Key="AnnouncementLinkStyle" TargetType="HyperlinkButton">
               <Setter Property="VerticalAlignment" Value="Top" />
               <Setter Property="Margin" Value="10,0,0,0" />
          </Style>
          <Style x:Key="AnnouncementListStyle" TargetType="ListBox">
               <Setter Property="BorderThickness" Value="0" />
               <Setter Property="Background" Value="Transparent" />
               <Setter Property="Margin" Value="0,10,0,0" />
               <Setter Property="MinHeight" Value="150" />
               <Setter Property="ScrollViewer.HorizontalScrollBarVisibility"
Value="Hidden" />
          </Style>
          <Style x:Key="AnnouncementHeaderTextStyle" BasedOn="{StaticResource
SummaryHeaderTextStyle}" TargetType="TextBlock">
               <Setter Property="Text" Value="Announcements" />
          </Style>
          <Style x:Key="AnnouncementListItemsPanelStyle" TargetType="StackPanel">
               <Setter Property="Orientation" Value="Vertical" />
          </Style>
          <Style x:Key="AnnouncementListItemPanelStyle" TargetType="StackPanel">
               <Setter Property="Orientation" Value="Horizontal" />
          </Style>
     </UserControl.Resources>
     <Border Style="{StaticResource SummaryBorderStyle}">
          <StackPanel Style="{StaticResource SummaryStackPanelStyle}">
               <Border Style="{StaticResource SummaryHeaderBorderStyle}">
```

continues

LISTING 4-13 *(continued)*

```
                    <TextBlock Style="{StaticResource
AnnouncementHeaderTextStyle}" />
               </Border>
               <ListBox x:Name="AnnouncementsList" Style="{StaticResource
AnnouncementListStyle}">
                    <ListBox.ItemsPanel>
                         <ItemsPanelTemplate>
                              <StackPanel Style="{StaticResource
AnnouncementListItemsPanelStyle}" />
                         </ItemsPanelTemplate>
                    </ListBox.ItemsPanel>
                    <ListBox.ItemContainerStyle>
                         <Style TargetType="ListBoxItem">
                              <Setter Property="Template">
                                   <Setter.Value>
                                        <ControlTemplate TargetType="ListBoxItem">
                                             <StackPanel
Style="{StaticResource AnnouncementListItemPanelStyle}">
                                                  <TextBlock
Style="{StaticResource AnnouncementDateStyle}" Text="{Binding
Path=created_date,
StringFormat='MM-dd-yy'}" />
                                                  <HyperlinkButton
Style="{StaticResource AnnouncementLinkStyle}" Content="{Binding Path=title}"
Click="Announcement_Click" />
                                             </StackPanel>
                                        </ControlTemplate>
                                   </Setter.Value>
                              </Setter>
                         </Style>
                    </ListBox.ItemContainerStyle>
               </ListBox>
          </StackPanel>
     </Border>
</UserControl>
```

Under normal circumstances, I almost always prefer to hook up event handlers in the code behind file. I don't like putting event handler declarations in XAML; I'm firmly in the camp that believes design elements should only reside in XAML files. In the `ItemContainerStyle` for the `ListBox`, however, you are forced to break this rule by hooking up the event handler for the `HyperlinkButton` directly in the XAML file. Another element of the code to note is its use of the new `StringFormat` attribute on the `TextBlock` control. This new attribute was added to Silverlight 4 to replace the cumbersome creation of a special `Converter` class just to format the text that needs to be displayed in a data bound control. For example, in the previous XAML code you wanted to show the short date format for the announcement date. In previous versions of Silverlight this would have required you to create a new class to implement the `IValueConverter` interface just to format the date. Now, you simply make use of the `StringFormat` attribute to accomplish the same thing, but it's much easier.

Database

For the site announcements feature, you will need to create a new database table as outlined in the design. There will be no relationships to other tables in the database, so it is a pretty simple table design. Figure 4-12 shows the database diagram for the announcements table you need to generate.

FIGURE 4-12

Data Access

For data access, you need to add a new LINQ to SQL class file to the project. Next, you must select the announcements table when creating the class and then call the file Announcements.dbml. The only table that you need to drag over is the announcements table. Once again, LINQ to SQL performs the majority of the work. In keeping with the LINQ to SQL naming conventions that you have been following for this project, you also need to rename the class to `Announcement`. Figure 4-13 shows the LINQ to SQL classes design.

FIGURE 4-13

Business Logic

The site announcements feature requires some additional business logic in order to provide the Silverlight client with the ability to retrieve site announcements. For this, you need to add a new domain service to the project and call it `AnnouncementService`. In the service creation wizard, as shown in Figure 4-14, be sure to select `AnnouncementsDataContext`, and select the Enable client access and Generate associated classes for metadata options. You won't be editing announcements in this chapter, but by enabling this option you won't have to worry about going back and adding the functionality later on. For now, you can manually create site announcements by adding entries to the announcements table using SQL Server Express Management Studio.

FIGURE 4-14

Once the wizard creates the `AnnouncementService`, you will need to modify only the `GetAnnouncements` method for now. As you can see in the following code, this method has been modified to return only announcements with a `created_date` within the last 30 days.

Available for download on Wrox.com

```
public IQueryable<Announcement> GetAnnouncements()
{
    // Only return announcements from the last thirty days

    return this.Context.Announcements.Where(e => e.created_date.Date <=
DateTime.Now.Date && e.created_date.Date >= DateTime.Now.Date.Subtract(new
TimeSpan(30, 0, 0, 0)));
}
```

Code snippet AnnouncementService.cs located in the FitnessTrackerPlus project

User Interface Code Behind

The first thing to work on in the code behind file is to load the custom `ListBox` with the announcements. This should be done in the `Loaded` event handler for the `Page` by making use of the `AnnouncementContext` object. Remember that loading data from the `AnnouncementContext` is an asynchronous process so you should set the `Loaded` event handler before actually making the call to load the data, as shown in the following code.

Available for download on Wrox.com

```
Loaded += (s, e) =>
{
     AnnouncementsList.ItemsSource = context.Announcements;
     LoadOperation<Announcement> operation =
context.Load<Announcement>(context.GetAnnouncementsQuery());
};
```

Code snippet Announcements.xaml.cs located in the FitnessTrackerPlus project

Next, you need to handle the display of any announcements. What you want to happen is that when the `HyperlinkButton` containing the announcement title is clicked, a new `ChildWindow` control is created and displayed with its `Content` property set to the `content` property of the announcement object.

The `ChildWindow` control has a `Title` property that can accept any object so you are not just stuck with a generic text property for this. You want the announcement title to stand out so you can create a new bold `TextBlock` and set the `Title` property to use the `TextBlock` when displaying the announcement title. In the following code, the `Announcement` object is extracted from the `DataContext` property of the `HyperlinkButton` that was clicked. Next, a `TextBlock` control is created and formatted to contain the actual `Announcement` content. Finally, the `Content` property of the `ChildWindow` control is set to the `TextBlock` and the `Show` method is called to actually display the modal `ChildWindow`. The `ChildWindow` control contains its own Close icon so you won't need to add any code to take care of closing the window when the user has finished reading the announcement.

```
private void Announcement_Click(object sender, RoutedEventArgs e)
{
     Announcement announcement = ((sender as HyperlinkButton).DataContext) as
Announcement;
     ChildWindow window = new ChildWindow();
     TextBlock announcementText = new TextBlock();

     if (announcement != null)
     {
          announcementText.MaxWidth = 400;
          announcementText.TextWrapping = TextWrapping.Wrap;
          announcementText.Text = announcement.content;
          announcementText.Margin = new Thickness(0, 10, 0, 10);

          TextBlock title = new TextBlock();
          title.FontWeight = FontWeights.Bold;
```

```
            title.Text = "Important Site Announcement";
            window.Title = title;
            window.Content = announcementText;
            window.Show();
        }
    }
```

Fitness Summaries

The final requirement for this chapter was to fill the `Dashboard` control with daily summary controls that would display food, exercise, and measurement summaries. It's a little bit difficult to provide these summaries when you can't even log any foods, exercises, or measurements yet. At this point, you only need to worry about creating placeholders for these controls. You already have a spot for each of these on the Dashboard control. Now you simply need to create the following `UserControls`:

- `FoodSummary`
- `ExerciseSummary`
- `MeasurementSummary`

For organization, you should place them all under the Views/Dashboard path in the Silverlight project. With that complete, you can add instances of these controls in the Dashboard.xaml. In case you missed the declarations earlier in the chapter, here is the code again:

Available for download on Wrox.com

```
<fitnesstrackerplus:Announcements x:Name="Announcements"
     Style="{StaticResource SummaryControlStyle}" Grid.Row="1" Grid.Column="0" />
<fitnesstrackerplus:MeasurementSummary x:Name="MeasurementSummary"
     Style="{StaticResource SummaryControlStyle}" Grid.Row="1" Grid.Column="1" />
<fitnesstrackerplus:FoodSummary x:Name="FoodSummary"
     Style="{StaticResource SummaryControlStyle}" Grid.Row="2" Grid.Column="0" />
<fitnesstrackerplus:ExerciseSummary x:Name="ExerciseSummary"
     Style="{StaticResource SummaryControlStyle}" Grid.Row="2" Grid.Column="1" />
```

Code snippet Dashboard.xaml located in the FitnessTrackerPlus project

That is really all you have to worry about for now with regards to the fitness summary controls.

SUMMARY

Well, that was a lot of information to digest. At this point, you have a fully working user home page complete with site announcements, navigation, account settings, and theme selection. Not too long now and FitnessTrackerPlus will really start to look like a fully functional site. With that, take a quick break, brew some coffee, and get ready for data entry. The next chapter is going to take some time to get through, but by the end you will have a fully operational food log page where you can add, edit, update, and delete food log entries.

5

One More Slice Can't Hurt

Creating the Food Log Page

Now that you have a working user registration and login system, it's time to start thinking about adding some of the main application features. This chapter is the first of three that will cover the various data entry aspects of the application. You'll really begin to see how the new WCF RIA Services Framework greatly enhances the developer experience when writing data entry applications. This chapter focuses on creating the nutrition log page. You will see how easy it is to create rich data entry forms for your users as well as how to take advantage of the powerful data binding functionality built in to the existing Silverlight data controls such as the `DataGrid`.

The fun doesn't stop there, however; you will also see how to make use of new Silverlight Toolkit controls such as the `AutoCompleteBox` and `GlobalCalendar`. The new `GlobalCalendar` control is particularly exciting in that it provides you with a mechanism to customize the style of various calendar days, a feature missing from the standard `Calendar` control. This may not seem very important now but you will soon see how this is a critical piece of the food log page, and it is only made possible by making use of this new enhancement.

PROBLEM

It's been established that the bulk of the work required for this site will be geared around data entry. One of the biggest problems with any site that focuses on data entry is creating an interface that does not frustrate users and is conducive to getting the work done quickly. The data entry process must be painless to users or they will quickly leave the site and find another that is. Users of FitnessTrackerPlus are expected to come to the site on a daily basis to enter foods, exercises, and measurements. It is entirely possible that users will hit the site multiple times per day to perform the data entry, so they need to be able to achieve this quickly and efficiently. In the case of food entry, the site is providing users with an extensive database of existing foods and needs to provide the users with an efficient way to search that database.

It is typical of many sites in this situation to provide a basic search box with pages upon pages of results that closely match the query term. Although this type of search mechanism would be sufficient for most sites, for FitnessTrackerPlus you need something better and more user-friendly. Users may want to add many different foods to their journal each day and requiring them to page through several pages of matching food results is not an efficient use of their time. Remember that it's not the actual data entry that is interesting to the user; it is the ability to view reports, daily totals, and charts that gives the user value in this application. This problem will need some kind of resolution that combines both efficient searching of the database along with the ability to quickly add the matching result to the journal without paging through large result sets.

Despite providing a database of foods for the user to choose from, it is almost impossible to collect nutrition data for every possible food in existence. Because you can't know every possible food that users will want to include in their journal, you will need to provide the options for users to create custom foods. Of course, once these custom entries are created and stored in the database they should also be displayed along with existing database entries when users search for foods in the future.

The data entry process for the food log page will consist of users entering the first few characters of a food into a search box. As the users type, the code will query the database to find any relevant food matches. At some point, the query will return and the users will see a list of possible foods to select from. After the user makes a selection, a new entry will be added to the food log. In order to make the data entry efficient, you won't be requiring users to add additional information, such as serving size consumed. Instead, new food log entries will be created with default serving size information, and users can easily modify the default information after quickly adding all of their foods. Of course, if the users cannot find a sufficient match, then they will always have the option to create a custom food, which will be stored in the database and become available for future queries.

The final problem that you need to work out is how to allow users to access past and future food log entries. By adding the `GlobalCalendar` control to the log page, you should be able to capture any date selection event and reload all of the food log data for the selected date. By doing this, your users will be able to not only modify previous food log entries but also plan ahead and add entries to future days.

DESIGN

For the design section in this chapter, I want to introduce you to another tool that can be helpful in gathering requirements—user stories. I have seen many instances of software being designed in which a list of requirements was drawn up without any attention being paid to how users would actually use the software. User stories are not a new invention—you may have heard of them being called *use cases* as well. This basically entails writing up small paragraphs that outline how a particular user or group of users will utilize a feature of the site. Typically, you pick a feature and write up several scenarios or stories that mimic the various actions that the user will perform. A well thought out story can really give you insight into what actions users might look to perform on the site and even suggest features that you may not have originally planned on but now seem crucial to ensuring the task outline in the story can be achieved.

The food, exercise, and measurement log pages are perhaps the most important pages in the FitnessTrackerPlus application, and the correct design will be crucial to ensuring that the user experience on the site is rewarding. This is not to say that you can't upgrade the site and add features in future releases. In fact, you will always be adding features and enhancements to stay one step ahead of your competition. Nonetheless you want to make sure that you capture enough requirements in this first pass to ensure that the users buy in to what you are offering and that all of the features they would expect to see on these pages are, in fact, available.

User Stories

Writing user stories can really help you to get a better understanding of what users may do while using the features of your site. All too often, you may think you have all of the requirements down only to find out that you left out an important user scenario. You don't necessarily have to beat this thing to death by writing hundreds of user stories but by putting yourself in the shoes of a few users, you most likely will notice things that may have been left out of the initial design. With that said let's take a look at a user story that might cover some of the requirements for the food log.

USER STORY Counting Calories with FitnessTrackerPlus

Jan must finally give in and go on that diet she has been planning, otherwise all of the high school reunion nightmares will come true for sure. She quickly jumps on the FitnessTrackerPlus site that her friend recommended. Although she is extremely skeptical that she will find the site easy and, most important, fast, she decides to register and give it a try.

Once logged into the site, she notices the menu item for the daily food log. She is immediately presented with a simple interface consisting of a search box and a couple of lists for recent and custom foods. Not terribly enthusiastic about the prospects of wading through pages of food listings to find the one that matches she decides to enter the name of the yogurt she ate this morning for breakfast. To her surprise a list of yogurts starts to appear as she types. This seems promising so she continues to type until the best match appears.

This seems way too easy so she clicks the food in the list half expecting to be presented with another list of search results. Instead, the food is quickly added to a table just below the data entry area and the screen is immediately ready for another entry. After adding all of the foods, she realizes that not only are the foods added in an easy-to-read tabular form, but the table has calculated daily totals for the most important nutrients that she wants to keep track of.

Despite all of this working out so great for her, she still thinks there must be a catch. Although every food she has entered seemed to show up in the search result list without forcing her to wade through pages of results, she was sure the latest breakfast cereal she was planning on purchasing would not show up in the list. It just seems impossible that this site could have a database of every single food ever sold. She decides to give it a try and starts to type in the name of the new cereal. To her dismay nothing appears in the search results. Now it seems as though this site is only going to work for her if she eats foods from the database provided on the site.

Before giving up, however, a dejected Jan sees a button for creating a new custom food. She clicks the button and is presented with a modal screen allowing her to enter all of the details of this new cereal.

She quickly grabs the box and enters all of the various nutrition facts from the label. In no time, the custom food is added to the table and even appears to be available the next day when she logs in. FitnessTrackerPlus may be the solution she was looking for after all.

Requirements

After taking the time to write a solid user story for the food log, you should now have a pretty good idea of what is required. Let's take a look at the complete list of requirements extracted from the previous user story:

- Users should be able to utilize an assisted "auto-suggest" style search box when searching through existing foods in the database.
- Users should be able to view lists of foods in a tabular format.
- Users should be able to create, read, update, and delete any food log entries.
- Users should be able to create custom foods if they cannot find an appropriate matching food in the database.
- Users will need the ability to view past, present, and future log entries.

Food Log

The first page you'll add to the site is the daily food log. The primary goal of this page is to give users an easy data entry screen for logging foods. Users of the site may not always have exercises or measurements to track on any given day but, for the most part, they all eat something during the course of the day. For this reason, the food log is, perhaps, the most important of the three log pages. It also happens to be the most difficult to implement for several reasons. The first issue is how to make use of the existing database of foods to assist users in their daily food entry. The food database can contain thousands of different foods. Although many sites simply provide a search box and pages of search results, that type of scenario is a nightmare for your everyday users. This sort of solution might have been perfectly acceptable about five or six years ago, but today, with AJAX technology and, of course, the new version of the Silverlight Toolkit, you can do a much better job.

Another issue you need to work out is how to display the food log entries. Choices range from a simple `ListBox` to even a customized `DataGrid`-based solution. Finally, because it's unreasonable to expect the FitnessTrackerPlus database to have nutrition facts for every food ever created, you need a mechanism to allow users to create custom foods. These custom foods will need to be stored in the database for future use and should also be included in the search results.

User Interface

In order to satisfy the requirements for the food log page, the user interface will need several important components. The design calls for a very simple data entry interface for adding new food log entries. You want to allow users to search for foods from the database, but you don't want them to have to page through a large set of results. The new Silverlight `AutoCompleteBox` control looks like it might be able to provide you with what you are looking for. By making use of this control, you will be able to auto-suggest entries from the default database of foods as the user is typing.

You also need a mechanism for users to create their own custom foods, so a button that displays a modal food creation window will do the trick here. That will get you to the point where you can create new food log entries and custom foods, but where will you actually place the new entries on the screen? Well, because the design calls for a table-like structure for the presentation of log entries, you should be able to make use of the `DataGrid` control.

There is one more thing that you need to consider for the food log page, however—providing users with the ability to view past and future entries. Although Silverlight has a great `Calendar` control built in to the runtime, you know now that it has no provision to change the style of individual calendar days. Instead, you will use the new `GlobalCalendar` control from the Silverlight Toolkit, which provides everything the `Calendar` does but additionally the ability to customize the appearance of individual calendar days, which, as you will see later on in the chapter, is an important feature. Figure 5-1 shows an outline of the controls needed for this page.

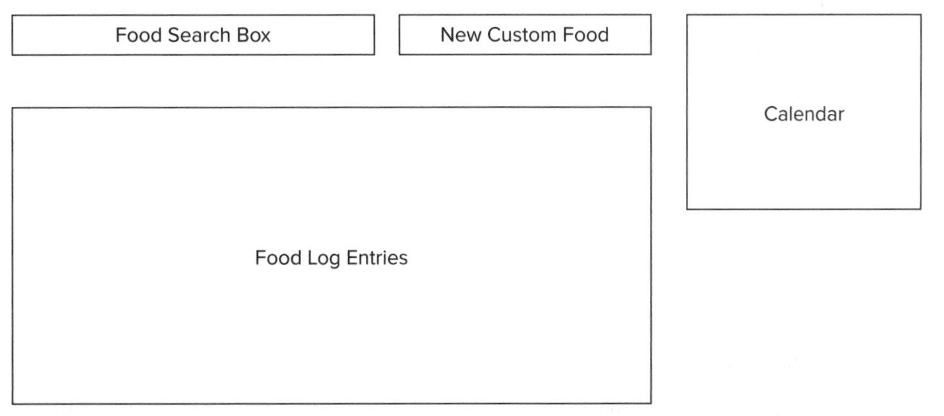

FIGURE 5-1

Another thing that you need to consider with the user interface is that users need some way to update the food log entries after they have been created. This particular interface is streamlined so that users can quickly add their foods without worrying about how many servings they consumed for the given food right away. Basically, the goal is to get users to quickly enter all of the foods and then go back and update serving information. This pattern accomplishes two things:

- It allows users who may not necessarily care about serving information to quickly log their foods and move on.
- It gives the other users who want more control the ability to modify the entries after they have already been added to the `DataGrid`.

Now back to the original question of how you are going to provide users with update and delete capabilities for food log entries. The answer lies in the `DataGrid` itself. There have been many improvements to this control in the latest version of Silverlight, and while you may have had difficulties with things such as in-place row editing in previous editions of Silverlight, you won't have those problems anymore. You'll also see how to make the data entry process more like a desktop application by taking advantage of the new right-click menu support in Silverlight 4. In addition to the in-place editing capabilities of the `DataGrid` control, you will develop a right-click menu that allows the users to delete any selected food log entries.

The final aspect of the user interface you need to consider is how you are going to allow users to add custom foods. The design sketch included a button that users can click in order to create a new custom food. You should plan on displaying a modal `ChildWindow` containing a `DataForm` where users can enter the custom food details. After the user finishes creating the custom food, you should then create a new food log entry using the custom food. Because the custom food is stored in the database, users will see the custom food in the list of results the next time they search for a food using that food name.

Database

The food log page will require several new database tables to be created. You will need a normalized table structure that can hold both foods and food log entries. The first table required will hold all of the food information and nutrition facts. The default database that I have provided contains hundreds of foods already populated in this table but any custom foods that users create will need their own entry in this table. Table 5-1 shows the schema definition for the foods table.

TABLE 5-1: foods

COLUMN NAME	TYPE	DESCRIPTION
id	int	Unique identity field for food.
name	varchar(200)	Name of food.
user_id	int	ID of user associated with food. Default foods will always be associated with admin user or user_id = 1.
serving_size	varchar(200)	Name of serving size for food.
calories	float	Total calories in food.
protein	float	Total protein content in food.
carbohydrate	float	Total carbohydrate content in food.
fat	float	Total fat content in food.

In addition to the foods table you also will need to create the food_logs table. This table is responsible for holding information associated with each entry that is made in the user's food log. Here you will record the date, user, and consumed food along with the number of servings. Table 5-2 shows the schema definition for this table.

TABLE 5-2: food_logs

COLUMN NAME	TYPE	DESCRIPTION
id	int	Unique identity field for food log entry
servings	float	Total number of servings for this entry
entry_date	datetime	Date and time of entry
food_id	int	ID of food associated with this entry
user_id	int	ID of user associated with this entry

Data Access

The data access classes for the food log page will consists of LINQ to SQL classes that have a direct 1:1 mapping between the database tables and the generated classes. You should expect to have one new LINQ to SQL class file containing classes for each of the foods and food_logs tables.

Business Logic

The business logic required for the food log page will consist of a single `DomainService` class with an associated metadata file. This `DomainService` will provide all of the necessary methods to create, update, read, and delete food log entries, and foods. In addition to the default methods that the `DomainService` wizard generates you need methods for the following operations:

- A query method that returns all custom foods for the given user ID.
- A query method that returns all food log entries for given user ID and date.
- A method to create new custom foods.
- A query method to search the food database using specified text and limiting results to a maximum number.

User Interface Code Behind

Although you have a relatively simple user interface design, you won't necessarily have a simple code behind implementation. In fact, over the last few years, one development paradox is that to make the user interface more user-friendly and simple, you often need a more advanced behind-the-scenes implementation.

A few years ago, it may have been acceptable to just throw buttons all over the user interface for every possible action that the user may attempt. Lately, however, with the proliferation of iPhones and other mobile devices, users are seeing a rapidly decreasing number of user interface controls and an increasing number of richer feature sets. For the user, this is a good thing as for far too long interfaces were cluttered and difficult to learn. Luckily, some of the new controls in Silverlight and the Silverlight Toolkit provide you with enough leverage to keep the interface clean and yet still allow your code behind pages to contain complex logic to help ensure that you aren't losing any capabilities. The food log page user interface will consist of an `AutoCompleteBox` control for searching the food database, as well as a `DataGrid` to present the food log entries that have been made. You should expect to have an event handler for the `AutoCompleteBox` that will create a new food log entry when the user makes a selection from the list of search results. The `DataGrid` will also have several events that you will need to implement in order to handle the in-place editing of food log entries.

In addition to in-place editing, you also want to be able to handle the deletion of entries from the `DataGrid`. As described in the user interface design, you won't have the typical delete button per row that you may have seen in some of the `DataGrid` examples on the Web. Instead, each row is going to have a `CheckBox` and there will be a button below the `DataGrid` that users can click to delete all of the selected entries. Alternatively, you will also provide users with a right-click context menu from which they can also delete any selected entries in the `DataGrid`.

Finally, because you are allowing users access to past and future food log entries, you will need to handle the `GlobalCalendarSelectedDateChanged` event and refresh the `DataGrid` with entries belonging to the date that was selected by the user. In order to keep the exercise and measurement log pages in sync with the selection that was made, you should also store this date in the `Globals` class so that if the user switches to the exercise or measurement log page, those pages can load data that is relevant to the date selected. Otherwise, it could become confusing to the user to see data from the selected date on one page and data from the current date on another.

SOLUTION

As stated in the "Design" section of this chapter, you will need to learn how to work with several new Silverlight controls in order to implement the food log page solution. The food log user interface will contain an `AutoCompleteBox`, `DataGrid`, `GlobalCalendar`, and `ProgressBar`. In addition to these new controls, you will also see how to fully make use of WCF RIA Services in a data entry scenario. You have already seen how to make use of this new framework when creating or authenticating users of the site, but the real power comes when you need a full line of CRUD operations supported with minimal amounts of code required. I'm not going to lie—some of these new techniques may feel a little bit strange when compared to traditional web service calls or even calling WCF methods from a Silverlight client, but by the time you are done with this chapter, I'm confident you will be ready to use these new features in your own business applications.

The discussion in the "Solution" section starts with a look at the food log page. As stated, the design calls for a simple user interface containing an `AutoCompleteBox`, `DataGrid`, `Calendar`, and a `Button` for creating new custom foods. While working on the food log implementation you are going to see how to customize a `DataGrid`, use the new `DataForm` control to help users create custom foods, allow delete operations using a right-click menu, and provide users with the ability to manage past and future log entries with the new `GlobalCalendar` control that was introduced in the latest version of the Silverlight Toolkit.

User Interface

The user interface will need to include:

- `AutoCompleteBox`: The `AutoCompleteBox` will be used to assist users in searching for relevant foods to add to their food log. Remember that in order to facilitate a speedy data entry operation, the requirements state to let users enter only food names and make a selection from the `AutoCompleteBox`.
- `GlobalCalendar`: This provides the users with the means to view previous and future food log dates.
- The `DataGrid` controls: These are responsible for not only displaying any food log entries but also for providing the user with the means to make updates to serving information. If users need to change the number of servings they will need to do it after creating the new entry. While in-place editing in the `DataGrid` control may have been challenging in previous versions of Silverlight, it is a breeze now, especially when combined with WCF RIA Services on the backend. Any time the user makes a selection from the control, the data being displayed in the `DataGrid` control should be refreshed. The `DataGrid` also consists of a right-click menu that gives users the ability to delete any selected entries.
- `DataForm`: The user interface will also contain a button that, when clicked, should display a modal `DataForm` where users will be able to enter custom food information and save to the database.

Rather than dump a whole bunch of XAML code on you, I'd like to cover each individual area of the user interface separately. First up is the overall layout of the screen. By now, you should be pretty familiar with how the `DockPanel` control works and, as you may have noticed, you will come to rely on this control to control the layout of most of the pages on the site. In the following code, in addition to one main `DockPanel` control that contains all of the page content, there is also an inner panel that will hold the page header and `ProgressBar` controls.

Available for download on Wrox.com

```
<!--These are located in App.xaml since they are shared across food,
exercise, and measurement log pages -->

<Style x:Key="HeaderDockPanelStyle" TargetType="toolkit:DockPanel">
     <Setter Property="LastChildFill" Value="False" />
     <Setter Property="toolkit:DockPanel.Dock" Value="Top" />
</Style>

<Style x:Key="CalendarPanelStyle" TargetType="StackPanel">
     <Setter Property="Margin" Value="0,10,0,0" />
     <Setter Property="toolkit:DockPanel.Dock" Value="Right" />
</Style>

<Style x:Key="LogPanelStyle" TargetType="StackPanel">
     <Setter Property="Margin" Value="10,5,10,0" />
     <Setter Property="MaxWidth" Value="600" />
```

```
</Style>

<toolkit:DockPanel Style="{StaticResource LogDockPanelStyle}">
     <toolkit:DockPanel Style="{StaticResource
HeaderDockPanelStyle}">
          <!-- Header and Progress Bar go here
Progress bar right aligned>
     </toolkit:DockPanel>
     <StackPanel Style="{StaticResource CalendarPanelStyle}">
          <!-- Global Calendar will go here-->
     </StackPanel>
     <StackPanel Style="{StaticResource LogPanelStyle}">
          <StackPanel Style="{StaticResource
FoodEntryStackPanelStyle}">
               <!-- AutoCompleteBox and Custom Food controls -->
          </StackPanel>
          <!-- DataGrid for food log entries goes here -->
     </StackPanel>
</toolkit:DockPanel>
```

Code snippet FoodLog.xaml

Notice that several styles are shared across multiple log pages and even though they are shown here in the code snippet, the actual styles reside in App.xaml, so that the exercise and measurement log pages can also take advantage of these common styles. After completing the layout of the page, you need to add the header text and `ProgressBar`. The header text will just be the title of the page, which in this case is "Food Log." The `ProgressBar` is a nice addition to the user interface that you can make visible any time there is a potentially length-asynchronous operation taking place. You don't necessarily have to know how long server operations will take so it's not a true progress display that you are trying to show here. All you want to accomplish with the `ProgressBar` is show the user that something is going on in the background. By setting the `IsIndeterminate` property to true, the `ProgressBar` will just show an animation when made visible. Here are the XAML declarations for the header text and `ProgressBar`.

Available for download on Wrox.com

```
<!-- ProgressBarStyle, HeaderTextBaseStyle, and HeaderTextStyle are
all in App.xaml -->

<Style x:Key="ProgressBarStyle" TargetType="ProgressBar">
     <Setter Property="Margin" Value="10,0,10,0" />
     <Setter Property="toolkit:DockPanel.Dock" Value="Right" />
     <Setter Property="IsIndeterminate" Value="True" />
     <Setter Property="Height" Value="20" />
     <Setter Property="Width" Value="300" />
     <Setter Property="Visibility" Value="Collapsed" />
</Style>

<Style x:Key="HeaderTextBaseStyle" TargetType="TextBlock">
     <Setter Property="FontSize" Value="14" />
     <Setter Property="Foreground" Value="#FF000000" />
</Style>

<Style x:Key="HeaderTextStyle" TargetType="TextBlock"
```

```
        BasedOn="{StaticResource HeaderTextBaseStyle}">
        <Setter Property="Margin" Value="10,0,0,0" />
        <Setter Property="toolkit:DockPanel.Dock" Value="Left" />
</Style>

<Style x:Key="FoodLogHeaderStyle" BasedOn="{StaticResource
HeaderTextStyle
        <Setter Property="Text" Value="Today's Food Log" />
</Style>

<TextBlock Style="{StaticResource FoodLogHeaderStyle}" />
<TextBlock x:Name="SelectedDate" Style="{StaticResource
        SelectedDateTextStyle}" />
<ProgressBar x:Name="ProgressBar" Style="{StaticResource
        ProgressBarStyle}" />
```

Code snippet FoodLog.xaml

Next up is the `AutoCompleteBox` control. The `AutoCompleteBox` control has been dramatically improved in the latest version of the Silverlight Toolkit and will provide you with everything you need to assist users during the food search process. For this application, you are concerned with a few properties including `FilterMode`, `MimimumPopulateDelay`, `MimimuPrefixLength`, and `IsTextCompletionEnabled`. In order to get started with the control, you need to add the following namespace in your page namespace list:

Available for download on Wrox.com

```
xmlns:controls_input="clr-
namespace:System.Windows.Controls;
assembly=System.Windows.
Controls.Input"
```

Code snippet FoodLog.xaml

The following is the XAML code for the `AutoCompleteBox` used on the food log page:

Available for download on Wrox.com

```
<Style x:Key="AutoCompleteBoxStyle"
TargetType="controls_input:AutoCompleteBox">
        <Setter Property="FilterMode" Value="Custom" />
        <Setter Property="IsTextCompletionEnabled" Value="False" />
        <Setter Property="Margin" Value="10,0,0,0" />
        <Setter Property="Width" Value="320" />
        <Setter Property="MaxWidth" Value="320" />
        <Setter Property="MinimumPopulateDelay" Value="500" />
        <Setter Property="MinimumPrefixLength" Value="3" />
</Style>

<Style x:Key="FoodSearchingTextStyle" BasedOn="{StaticResource
LogPanelSearchingTextStyle}" TargetType="TextBlock">
        <Setter Property="Text" Value="Searching Foods..." />
</Style>

<TextBlock Text="Search" Style="{StaticResource LogPanelLabelStyle}" />
        <controls_input:AutoCompleteBox x:Name="AutoComplete" Style="{StaticResource
```

```
AutoCompleteBoxStyle}">
          <controls_input:AutoCompleteBox.ItemTemplate>
               <DataTemplate>
                    <StackPanel>
                         <ContentPresenter Content="{Binding name}" />
                    </StackPanel>
               </DataTemplate>
          </controls_input:AutoCompleteBox.ItemTemplate>
     </controls_input:AutoCompleteBox>
<TextBlock x:Name="SearchingText" Style="{StaticResource
FoodSearchingTextStyle}" />
```

Code snippet FoodLog.xaml

Included in the XAML for the `AutoCompleteBox` declaration is a `TextBlock` that acts as a label so users know this is a search box. Also included is another `TextBlock` control that displays a "Searching Foods ... " message as users type in the control. This just adds a little clarity to the interface so that users know that something is actually happening as they type food names in the control. As far as the `AutoCompleteBox` itself, you are setting the `FilterMode`, `IsTextCompletionEnable`, `MinimumPopulateDelay`, and `MinimumPrefixLength` properties to the values shown in Table 5-3.

TABLE 5-3: AutoCompleteBox Properties

PROPERTY	VALUE	PURPOSE
`FilterMode`	`Custom` Possible values include `StartsWith`, `Contains`, `None`, `Custom`	You will be using `String.Contains` logic but instead of returning all possible foods and running the logic on the client, you will perform the filtering on the server so `Custom` is required.
`IsTextCompletionEnabled`	`False`	You want users to make their own selection so set this to false. Otherwise the control will automatically make the closest match by default.
`MinimumPopulateDelay`	3	This value basically ensures that you allow the user at least three seconds to start typing before the actual database query occurs.
`MinimumPrefixLength`	3	This value is used by the control to determine the minimum number of characters that need to be entered before performing a query.

Beside the `AutoCompleteBox` will also be a button for creating custom foods. In the code behind, you'll hook up to the `Click` event to display the custom food creation dialog. The XAML for this button is simple:

Available for download on Wrox.com

```
<Style x:Key="CustomFoodButtonStyle" TargetType="Button">
     <Setter Property="Margin" Value="10,0,0,0" />
     <Setter Property="VerticalAlignment" Value="Center" />
     <Setter Property="FontSize" Value="10" />
     <Setter Property="Content" Value="Custom Food" />
</Style>

<Button x:Name="CustomFood" Style="{StaticResource
CustomFoodButtonStyle}" />
```

Code snippet FoodLog.xaml

The next major control on the page is the `GlobalCalendar`. This control can be utilized by adding the following namespace to the page:

Available for download on Wrox.com

```
xmlns:toolkit="clr-namespace:System.Windows.Controls;
assembly=System.Windows.Controls.Toolkit"
```

Code snippet FoodLog.xaml

As described earlier, enhancements made to this control will finally let you alter the appearance of specific calendar days. This is especially important in the FitnessTrackerPlus application because the `GlobalCalendar` will be used by users to view previous food log entries. In order for users to know which days actually contain food log entries, you need to change the background color of the days containing the entries. This visual clue lets users know which calendar day to select rather than forcing them to remember exactly which days they entered data on. In previous versions of the runtime, it was simply not possible to alter the appearance of specific days, but the new `GlobalCalendar` provides a great mechanism that lets you create a custom `CalendarDayButtonStyleSelector` class along with custom styles that can be applied using the selector. You will see how all of this works in the code behind discussion, but for now, just know that the styles for `ValidLogDateSelector` and `InvalidLogDateSelector` are returned by the `ValidLogDateSelector` class.

Available for download on Wrox.com

```
<!-- Calendar style is shared so it resides in App.xaml -->

<Style x:Key="CalendarStyle" TargetType="toolkit:GlobalCalendar">
     <Setter Property="SelectionMode" Value="SingleDate" />
</Style>

<toolkit:GlobalCalendar x:Name="Calendar" Style="{StaticResource
CalendarStyle}">
     <toolkit:GlobalCalendar.CalendarDayButtonStyleSelector>
          <fitnesstrackerplus_calendar:ValidLogDateSelector>
```

```
                <fitnesstrackerplus_calendar:ValidLogDateSelector.
ValidLogDateStyle>
                    <Style BasedOn="{StaticResource
BasicDayButtonStyle}" TargetType="toolkit_primitives:GlobalCalendarDayButton">
                        <Setter Property="Background"
Value="#FF999999" />
                    </Style>
                </fitnesstrackerplus_calendar:ValidLogDateSelector.
ValidLogDateStyle>
                <fitnesstrackerplus_calendar:ValidLogDateSelector.
InvalidLogDateStyle>
                    <Style BasedOn="{StaticResource
BasicDayButtonStyle}" TargetType="toolkit_primitives:GlobalCalendarDayButton">
                        <Setter Property="Background"
Value="#FFFFFFFF" />
                    </Style>
                </fitnesstrackerplus_calendar:ValidLogDateSelector.
InvalidLogDateStyle>
            </fitnesstrackerplus_calendar:ValidLogDateSelector>
        </toolkit:GlobalCalendar.CalendarDayButtonStyleSelector>
</toolkit:GlobalCalendar>
```

Code snippet FoodLog.xaml

There is something in the preceding code that I want to bring to your attention. Notice how the styles defined in the `ValidLogDateStyle` and `InvalidLogDateStyle` are based on the `BasicDayButtonStyle`. The `BasicDayButtonStyle` is part of the `GlobalCalendar` and requires the following namespace declaration in App.xaml.

Available for download on Wrox.com

```
xmlns:toolkit_primitives="clr-
namespace:System.Windows.Controls.Primitives;
assembly=System.Windows.Controls.Toolkit"
```

Code snippet App.xaml

You also need to include the complete `BasicDayButtonStyle` definition in the App.xaml file in order for the `BasedOn` property to work correctly. I won't list that particular style because it is massive, but if you take a look at App.xaml you will find the complete declaration there. So now that you have a couple of styles designed, how does the `GlobalCalendar` actually make use of them? Well the `GlobalCalendar` is looking for a custom implementation of the `CalendarDayButtonStyleSelector`. In this case, that implementation is the `ValidLogDateSelector` class.

You should create a new folder in the Silverlight project called Utility and add the new class to the project. Now typically this discussion could be held off until the business logic discussion, but I want to show you how this works while the XAML code is still fresh in your mind. After you add the class, the `GlobalCalendar` will call the `SelectStyle` method passing in the current day and the button container object. While in this method you can check the date against a list of valid food log dates to see if there is a match. If the date is contained in the list, you will return the `ValidLogDateStyle`; otherwise, you return the `InvalidLogDateStyle`. Listing 5-1 shows the code for the `ValidLogDateSelector` class:

LISTING 5-1: ValidLogDateSelector.cs

Available for download on Wrox.com

```
using System;
using System.Collections;
using System.Collections.Generic;
using System.Windows;
using System.Windows.Controls;
using System.Windows.Controls.Primitives;
using FitnessTrackerPlus.Web.Services;

namespace FitnessTrackerPlus.Utility
{
     public class ValidLogDateSelector:
CalendarDayButtonStyleSelector
     {
          private static List<DateTime> ValidLogDates = new
List<DateTime>();
          private static FoodContext context = new FoodContext();

          public Style ValidLogDateStyle { get; set; }
          public Style InvalidLogDateStyle { get; set; }

          public ValidLogDateSelector()
          {
               context.GetLogEntryDates(Globals.CurrentUser.id,
                (DatesLoaded) =>
               {
                    if (!DatesLoaded.HasError)
                    {
                         IEnumerator<DateTime> enumerator =
DatesLoaded.Value.GetEnumerator();
                         ValidLogDates.Clear();

                         while (enumerator.MoveNext())
                              ValidLogDates.Add(enumerator.Current.
Date);
                    }

               }, null);
          }

          public override Style SelectStyle(DateTime day,
GlobalCalendarDayButton container)
          {
               if (ValidLogDates.Contains(day.Date))
                    return ValidLogDateStyle;

               return InvalidLogDateStyle;
          }
     }
}
```

As you can see, in the constructor you are getting a list of dates that contain log entries for the currently logged in user. The list needs to be static as the SelectStyle method will be called for every currently displayed date. So if the user switches to a different month you need to perform the lookup logic again. You'll see the business logic for the GetLogEntryDates method soon, but for now just know that it will return a valid list of DateTime objects that contain food log entries.

Finally, after all of that, you are simply left with the DataGrid control. There are a couple of things that you need to think about before just adding a plain old DataGrid to the user interface. Remember you want the users to have full CRUD capabilities on their food log data. This means you have to think about how you want your users to delete entries. Many simple DataGrid definitions just include a delete button per row. I have never really been a big fan of this and prefer having CheckBox controls that can be selected for individual rows and a CheckBox in the header that will select/deselect all entries.

If you have worked with the DataGrid control in the past, you probably already know the dilemmas:

- You can't simply add a CheckBox control to the header of a given DataGrid column. Instead, you need to create a custom header style that includes the said CheckBox control in the template.
- Even though the DataGrid control includes a built-in CheckBox column, you must have it bound to a property in the food log entry in order for it to work correctly. You don't really want to have a separate field just for this. So in order to accomplish the individual row CheckBox you have to rely on a custom column template.

With all of that said, here is the XAML for the DataGrid control, including the custom header style that has the CheckBox control.

Available for download on Wrox.com

```
<Style x:Key="DataGrid" TargetType="data:DataGrid">
     <Setter Property="AutoGenerateColumns" Value="False" />
     <Setter Property="IsReadOnly" Value="False" />
     <Setter Property="Margin" Value="0,10,0,0" />
     <Setter Property="HorizontalScrollBarVisibility" Value="Auto" />
     <Setter Property="CanUserResizeColumns" Value="True" />
     <Setter Property="SelectionMode" Value="Single" />
     <Setter Property="ColumnWidth" Value="SizeToHeader" />
</Style>

<Style x:Key="DataGridColumnHeaderCheckBox"
TargetType="data_primitives:DataGridColumnHeader">
     <Setter Property="Foreground" Value="#FF444444" />
     <Setter Property="HorizontalContentAlignment" Value="Center" />
     <Setter Property="VerticalContentAlignment" Value="Center" />
     <Setter Property="FontSize" Value="10.5" />
     <Setter Property="FontWeight" Value="Bold" />
     <Setter Property="IsTabStop" Value="False" />
     <Setter Property="SeparatorBrush" Value="#FFC9CACA" />
     <Setter Property="Padding" Value="4,4,5,4" />
     <Setter Property="Template">
          <Setter.Value>
               <ControlTemplate
```

```
TargetType="data_primitives:DataGridColumnHeader">
                    <Grid Name="Root">
                         <Grid.RowDefinitions>
                              <RowDefinition Height="*" />
                              <RowDefinition Height="*" />
                              <RowDefinition Height="Auto" />
                         </Grid.RowDefinitions>
                         <Grid.ColumnDefinitions>
                              <ColumnDefinition Width="Auto" />
                              <ColumnDefinition Width="*" />
                              <ColumnDefinition Width="Auto" />
                         </Grid.ColumnDefinitions>
                         <Rectangle x:Name="BackgroundRectangle"
Stretch="Fill" Fill="#FF1F3B53" Grid.ColumnSpan="2" Grid.RowSpan="2"  />
                         <Rectangle x:Name="BackgroundGradient"
Stretch="Fill" Grid.ColumnSpan="2" Grid.RowSpan="2" >
                              <Rectangle.Fill>
                                   <LinearGradientBrush
StartPoint=".7,0" EndPoint=".7,1">
                                        <GradientStop Color="#FFFFFFFF"
Offset="0.015" />
                                        <GradientStop Color="#F9FFFFFF"
Offset="0.375" />
                                        <GradientStop Color="#E5FFFFFF"
Offset="0.6" />
                                        <GradientStop Color="#C6FFFFFF"
Offset="1" />
                                   </LinearGradientBrush>
                              </Rectangle.Fill>
                         </Rectangle>
                         <CheckBox x:Name="CheckAll" Grid.RowSpan="3"
Grid.ColumnSpan="3" Style="{StaticResource DataGridCheckBox}"
Checked="CheckAll_Checked" Unchecked="CheckAll_Checked"  />
                         <Rectangle Name="VerticalSeparator"
Grid.RowSpan="2" Grid.Column="2" Width="1" VerticalAlignment="Stretch"
Fill="{TemplateBinding SeparatorBrush}" Visibility="{TemplateBinding
SeparatorVisibility}"
 />
                    </Grid>
               </ControlTemplate>
          </Setter.Value>
     </Setter>
</Style>

<Style x:Key="DeleteSelectedStyle" TargetType="Button">
     <Setter Property="Content" Value="Delete Selected" />
     <Setter Property="HorizontalAlignment" Value="Right" />
     <Setter Property="Margin" Value="0,10,0,0" />
</Style>

<data:DataGrid x:Name="FoodLogGrid" Style="{StaticResource DataGrid}">
     <data:DataGrid.Columns>
          <data:DataGridTemplateColumn Header="Foods" HeaderStyle="{StaticResource
DataGridColumnHeaderCentered}">
```

```
                <data:DataGridTemplateColumn.CellTemplate>
                    <DataTemplate>
                        <TextBlock Text="{Binding Path=Food.name}"
Style="{StaticResource FoodNameStyle}" />
                    </DataTemplate>
                </data:DataGridTemplateColumn.CellTemplate>
            </data:DataGridTemplateColumn>
            <data:DataGridTemplateColumn Header="Servings"
HeaderStyle="{StaticResource DataGridColumnHeaderCentered}">
                <data:DataGridTemplateColumn.CellTemplate>
                    <DataTemplate>
                        <TextBlock Text="{Binding Path=servings}"
Style="{StaticResource DataGridTextBlockCentered}" />
                    </DataTemplate>
                </data:DataGridTemplateColumn.CellTemplate>
                <data:DataGridTemplateColumn.CellEditingTemplate>
                    <DataTemplate>
                        <TextBox Text="{Binding Path=servings, Mode=TwoWay}" />
                    </DataTemplate>
                </data:DataGridTemplateColumn.CellEditingTemplate>
            </data:DataGridTemplateColumn>
            <data:DataGridTemplateColumn Header="Serving Size"
HeaderStyle="{StaticResource DataGridColumnHeaderCentered}">
                <data:DataGridTemplateColumn.CellTemplate>
                    <DataTemplate>
                        <TextBlock Text="{Binding Path=Food.serving_size}"
Style="{StaticResource DataGridTextBlock}" />
                    </DataTemplate>
                </data:DataGridTemplateColumn.CellTemplate>
            </data:DataGridTemplateColumn>
            <data:DataGridTemplateColumn Header="Cal" HeaderStyle="{StaticResource
DataGridColumnHeaderCentered}">
                <data:DataGridTemplateColumn.CellTemplate>
                    <DataTemplate>
                        <TextBlock Text="{Binding Path=Food.calories}"
Style="{StaticResource DataGridTextBlockCentered}" />
                    </DataTemplate>
                </data:DataGridTemplateColumn.CellTemplate>
            </data:DataGridTemplateColumn>
            <data:DataGridTemplateColumn Header="Fat" HeaderStyle="{StaticResource
DataGridColumnHeaderCentered}">
                <data:DataGridTemplateColumn.CellTemplate>
                    <DataTemplate>
                        <TextBlock Text="{Binding Path=Food.fat}"
Style="{StaticResource DataGridTextBlockCentered}" />
                    </DataTemplate>
                </data:DataGridTemplateColumn.CellTemplate>
            </data:DataGridTemplateColumn>
            <data:DataGridTemplateColumn Header="Carb" HeaderStyle="{StaticResource
DataGridColumnHeaderCentered}">
                <data:DataGridTemplateColumn.CellTemplate>
                    <DataTemplate>
```

```
                        <TextBlock Text="{Binding Path=Food.carbohydrate}"
Style="{StaticResource DataGridTextBlockCentered}" />
                    </DataTemplate>
                </data:DataGridTemplateColumn.CellTemplate>
            </data:DataGridTemplateColumn>
            <data:DataGridTemplateColumn Header="Pro" HeaderStyle="{StaticResource
DataGridColumnHeaderCentered}">
                <data:DataGridTemplateColumn.CellTemplate>
                    <DataTemplate>
                        <TextBlock Text="{Binding Path=Food.protein}"
Style="{StaticResource DataGridTextBlockCentered}" />
                    </DataTemplate>
                </data:DataGridTemplateColumn.CellTemplate>
            </data:DataGridTemplateColumn>
            <data:DataGridTemplateColumn HeaderStyle="{StaticResource
DataGridColumnHeaderCheckBox}">
                <data:DataGridTemplateColumn.CellTemplate>
                    <DataTemplate>
                        <CheckBox x:Name="DeleteEntry" Style="{StaticResource
DataGridCheckBox}" />
                    </DataTemplate>
                </data:DataGridTemplateColumn.CellTemplate>
            </data:DataGridTemplateColumn>
        </data:DataGrid.Columns>
    </data:DataGrid>
```

Code snippet FoodLog.xaml

A couple of additional styles are used throughout the `DataGrid` such as the `DataGridCheckBox` style and `DataGridTextBlockCentered`. All these styles do is ensure that the column data is centered in the container.

With the `DataGrid` declaration complete, it's time to turn your attention over to the right-click context menu that you want to appear whenever the user performs a right mouse click on the `DataGrid` control. To keep this simple, you should just add a new `Canvas` control with a `Border` and a few `TextBlock` controls. Context menus don't need to take up too much space and the only options you want in these menus are those that delete selected entries and cancel the display of the menu. Later on, this may prove to be a good place to add a print entries option as well but for now delete and cancel should be good. The following code shows the XAML for the context menu as well as the accompanying Style declarations.

Available for download on Wrox.com

```
<Style x:Key="RightClickMenuStyle" TargetType="Canvas">
    <Setter Property="Visibility" Value="Collapsed" />
    <Setter Property="Width" Value="150" />
    <Setter Property="Canvas.ZIndex" Value="100" />
</Style>
<Style x:Key="RightClickMenuItemStyle" TargetType="TextBlock">
    <Setter Property="Margin" Value="5" />
    <Setter Property="Cursor" Value="Hand" />
```

```
</Style>
<Style x:Key="RightClickMenuBorderStyle" TargetType="Border">
     <Setter Property="BorderThickness" Value="2" />
     <Setter Property="Margin" Value="5" />
     <Setter Property="HorizontalAlignment" Value="Left" />
     <Setter Property="VerticalAlignment" Value="Top" />
     <Setter Property="Canvas.Top" Value="0" />
     <Setter Property="Canvas.Left" Value="0" />
     <Setter Property="BorderBrush" Value="#FF000000" />
     <Setter Property="Background" Value="#FFFFFFFF" />
</Style>

<Canvas x:Name="RightClickMenu" Style="{StaticResource RightClickMenuStyle}">
     <Border x:Name="RightClickBorder" Style="{StaticResource
RightClickMenuBorderStyle}">
          <StackPanel>
               <TextBlock x:Name="DeleteEntryMenu"
Text="Delete Selected Entries" Style="{StaticResource RightClickMenuItemStyle}" />
               <TextBlock x:Name="CancelEntryMenu"
Text="Cancel" Style="{StaticResource RightClickMenuItemStyle}" />
          </StackPanel>
     </Border>
</Canvas>
```

Code snippet FoodLog.xaml

As you can see there really isn't much to this. Perhaps the most interesting part is that the `Canvas` control has its `Canvas.ZIndex` property set to a high number so that the context menu appears above the `DataGrid` control when it is made visible. In the code behind just before the menu is made visible you will see that the `Canvas` is expanded so that it is the same height and width of the screen and the `Border` control is repositioned in such a way that it appears next to the mouse cursor relative to the `DataGrid` control. Obviously this is a very simple context menu that does the job for this application. However in your own applications you may want to spice it up with some hover brushes and various `TextBlock` styling techniques.

Well, that just about covers the user interface controls that are required. Figure 5-2 shows the user interface in action with some food log entries already created. Figure 5-3 shows the `AutoCompleteBox` working as well. Notice that dates on the `GlobalCalendar` have a different background if there were valid log entries for those dates.

With the user interface implementation complete, you can now move on to the database implementation. The food log page design calls for the creation of several new tables, so let's get started on this.

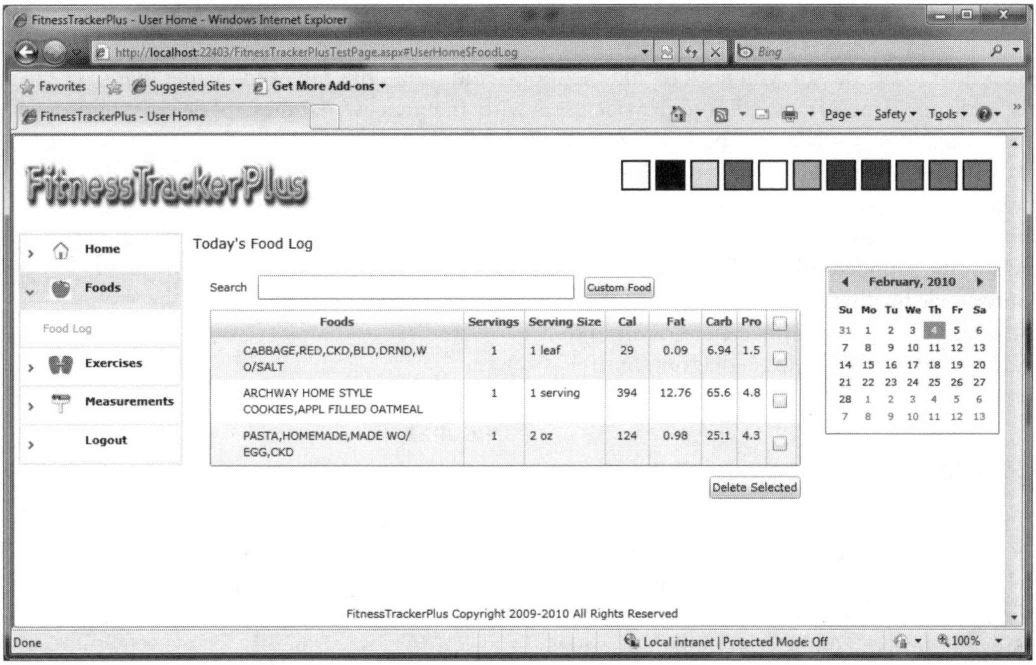

FitnessTrackerPlus - User Home - Windows Internet Explorer

http://localhost:22403/FitnessTrackerPlusTestPage.aspx#UserHome$FoodLog

Bing

Favorites | Suggested Sites ▾ Get More Add-ons ▾

FitnessTrackerPlus - User Home

Page ▾ Safety ▾ Tools ▾

FitnessTrackerPlus

Home

Foods

Food Log

Exercises

Measurements

Logout

Today's Food Log

Search

Custom Food

Foods	Servings	Serving Size	Cal	Fat	Carb	Pro	
CABBAGE,RED,CKD,BLD,DRND,W O/SALT	1	1 leaf	29	0.09	6.94	1.5	
ARCHWAY HOME STYLE COOKIES,APPL FILLED OATMEAL	1	1 serving	394	12.76	65.6	4.8	
PASTA,HOMEMADE,MADE WO/ EGG,CKD	1	2 oz	124	0.98	25.1	4.3	

Delete Selected

February, 2010

Su	Mo	Tu	We	Th	Fr	Sa
31	1	2	3	4	5	6
7	8	9	10	11	12	13
14	15	16	17	18	19	20
21	22	23	24	25	26	27
28	1	2	3	4	5	6
7	8	9	10	11	12	13

FitnessTrackerPlus Copyright 2009-2010 All Rights Reserved

Done

Local intranet | Protected Mode: Off

100%

FIGURE 5-2

FitnessTrackerPlus - User Home - Windows Internet Explorer

http://localhost:1154/FitnessTrackerPlus.aspx#UserHome$FoodLog

Google

File Edit View Favorites Tools Help

Favorites | Suggested Sites ▾ Free Hotmail Web Slice Gallery ▾

FitnessTrackerPlus - User Home

Page ▾ Safety ▾ Tools ▾

FitnessTrackerPlus

Home

Foods

Food Log

Exercises

Measurements

Public Journal

Community

Logout

Today's Food Log

Search grape

Custom Food

Grapefruit, raw, pink and red, all areas

Grapefruit, raw, pink and red, California and Arizona

Grapefruit, raw, pink and red, Florida

Grapefruit, raw, white, all areas

Grapefruit, raw, white, California

Grapefruit, raw, white, Florida

Grapefruit, sections, canned, water pack, solids and liquids

Grapefruit, sections, canned, juice pack, solids and liquids

Grapefruit, sections, canned, light syrup pack, solids and liquids

Grapefruit juice, white, canned, unsweetened

Grapefruit juice, white, canned, sweetened

Grapefruit juice, white, frozen concentrate, unsweetened, undiluted

Grapefruit juice, white, frozen concentrate, unsweetened, diluted with 3 volume water

Grapefruit juice, white, raw

July, 2009

Tu	We	Th	Fr	Sa
30	1	2	3	4
7	8	9	10	11
14	15	16	17	18
21	22	23	24	25
28	29	30	31	1
4	5	6	7	8

FitnessTrackerPlus Copyright 2009-2010 All Rights Reserved

Done

Local intranet

100%

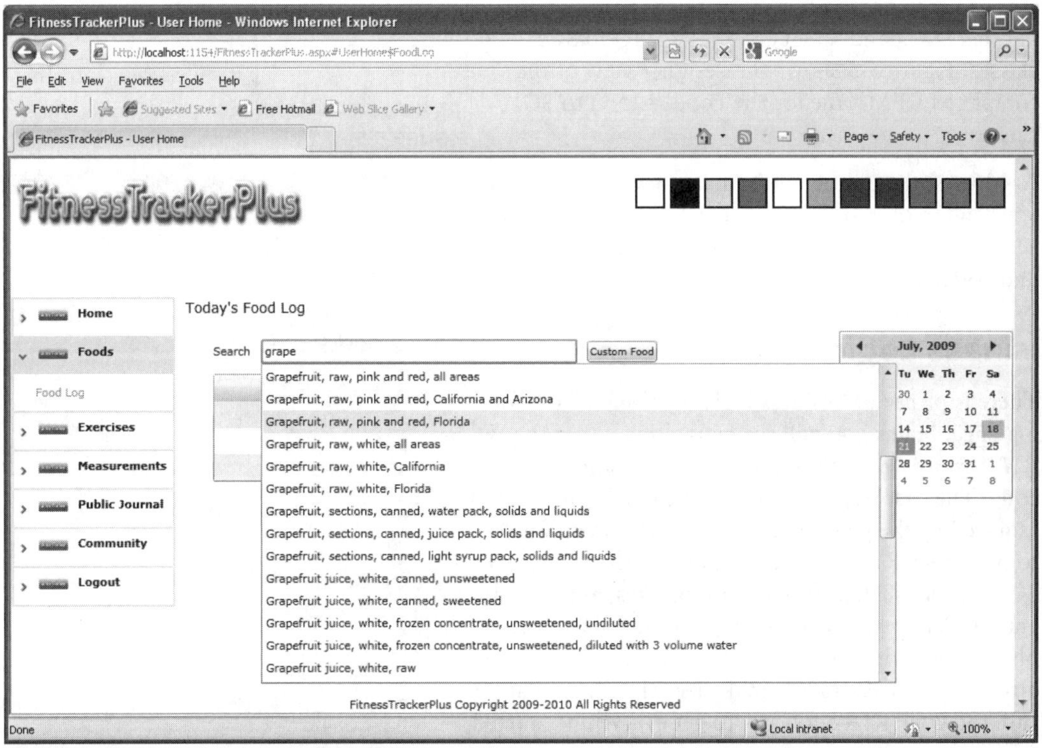

FIGURE 5-3

Database

According to the design, you need to add the foods, and food_logs tables to the database. The design also calls for FitnessTrackerPlus to provide users with an extensive database of default foods to search from. Don't worry—I don't expect you to grab all of the foods in your cupboard and start manually entering the nutrition facts. I took the liberty of supplying some foods and associated nutrition facts in the supplied .MDF file included with the source code for this chapter. You can see the tables along with the defined constraints and relationships in the database diagram in Figure 5-4.

FIGURE 5-4

Data Access

The data access layer for the food log page will require the creation of another LINQ to SQL class file called Foods.dbml. As you did with the other LINQ to SQL classes, you should add this file to the Data folder in the ASP.NET project. After creating the new DBML file, you can go ahead and drag and drop the foods, and food_logs tables onto the designer. Before saving the file, however, you should rename these tables so that the entity creation matches the format you used when creating the `Users` and `Annoucements` LINQ to SQL classes. Figure 5-5 shows the designer view of the completed DBML file for the Foods LINQ to SQL classes.

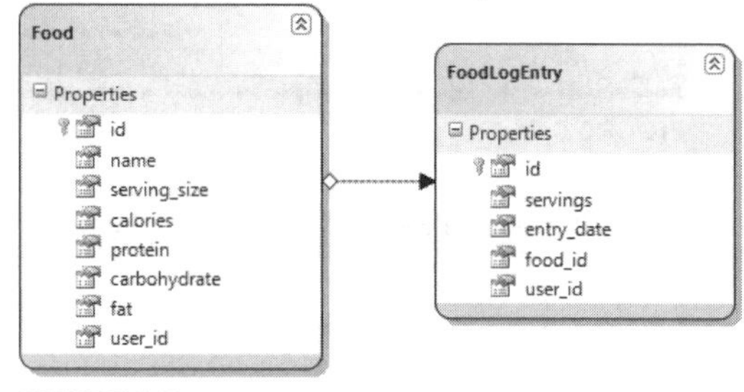

FIGURE 5-5

As always, there is no additional work to perform on your end in order to actually create the various data access classes. All you have to do is save the DBML file and you are ready to go.

Business Logic

There is plenty of business logic required for the food log page, but as you will see by making use of the WCF RIA Services it won't require enormous amounts of code. The first step is to look at the operations that are required by the page. You know that users will need to perform CRUD operations of all of the LINQ to SQL entities such as foods, serving sizes, and food log entries. As in the previous chapters, you should also plan on providing validation for these entities; you already have seen how to make use of the metadata feature for WCF RIA Services. To get everything started,

FIGURE 5-6

you need to add a new `DomainService` to the ASP.NET project in the Services folder. The domain service class name should be `FoodService` and you should check the "Enable client access" option. When choosing the appropriate `DataContext`, you should choose the `FoodsDataContext`. This will display the `Food`, and `FoodLogEntry` entities. You should check the "Enable editing" option for both of them, as shown in Figure 5-6.

Now that the `FoodService` is created, you will see that CRUD operations have already been implemented for all of the selected entities. The first thing that users see when they arrive at the food log page is a display in the `DataGrid` of any food log entries that have been created for the current day. So you should modify the `Query` method for the `FoodLogEntry` entity to look up all food log entries for the given date and user, as shown in the following code:

Available for download on Wrox.com

```
public IQueryable<FoodLogEntry> GetFoodLogEntries(int user_id, DateTime
entry_date, bool load_serving_sizes)
{
     DataLoadOptions options = new DataLoadOptions();

     // Ensure that specific food information is available

     options.LoadWith<FoodLogEntry>(e => e.Food);

     this.DataContext.LoadOptions = options;
     return this.DataContext.FoodLogEntries.Where(e => e.user_id == user_id &&
e.entry_date.Date == entry_date.Date);
}
```

Code snippet FoodService.cs

Because the `name` property of the associated `Food` object must be displayed in the `DataGrid` as well as the `calories`, `fat`, `protein`, and `carbohydrate` values you need to make sure that the LINQ to SQL returns the `Food` property from the query. The line `options.LoadWith<FoodLogEntry>(e => e.Food)` takes care of this problem by telling the `DataContext` object to load the `Food` object associated with each `FoodLogEntry` record. Now, in addition to setting the `DataLoadOptions`, you must also instruct the WCF RIA services to return the associated `Food` entity. This is done by modifying the metadata class for the `FoodLogEntry`. In the `FoodLogEntry` class, you need to add the `[Include]` attribute to the `Food` property as shown here.

Available for download on Wrox.com

```
[MetadataTypeAttribute(typeof(FoodLogEntry.FoodLogEntryMetadata))]
public partial class FoodLogEntry
{
     internal sealed class FoodLogEntryMetadata
     {
          private FoodLogEntryMetadata()
          {
          }

          public DateTime entry_date;

          [Include]
```

```
            public Food Food;

            public int food_id;

            public int id;


            public double servings;



            public int user_id;
        }
    }
```

Code snippet FoodService.metadata.cs

It is important to note that regardless of the `DataLoadOptions` assigned, the WCF RIA Services runtime will return only associated entities that are marked with the `[Include]` attribute. In other words, both steps are required to get this working properly.

After modifying the query method for food log entry retrieval, you need to look at the business logic required for the `AutoCompleteBox`. As users type the first few letters of a food, you want to search the database and return a list of appropriate matches. You will need a custom query method that performs this search. The following `SearchFood` method will query the database for any `Food` object whose `food_name` property `Contains` the search text.

Available for download on Wrox.com

```
[Query]
public IQueryable<Food> SearchFoods(int user_id, int max_results,
string search_text, bool load_serving_sizes)
{
    var foods = (from c in this.DataContext.Foods
                 where c.name.ToLower().Contains(search_text.ToLower()) &&
                (c.user_id == 1 || c.user_id == user_id)
                 select c).Take<Food>(max_results);

    return foods;
}
```

Code snippet FoodService.cs

Because the method does not follow the WCF RIA Services naming convention guidelines for query methods, you need to add the `[Query]` attribute above the method declaration in order for it to be exposed to the client. There are also several parameters to the method that should be explained. You want to search for both default foods and custom foods created by the user so you will need to know the `user_id` of the currently logged in user and make use of that in the LINQ query. You also don't want to return thousands of results, so the `max_results` parameter takes care of limiting the result set.

The final area of custom business logic that you should be aware of is the method used by the `GlobalCalendar` for styling valid log entry dates. The `GetLogEntryDates` method looks for any dates that contain log entries and returns a unique list of those dates to the `GlobalCalendar`. Because you aren't returning any actual entity data, you need to decorate this with the `[Invoke]` attribute to ensure that it is exposed by the WCF RIA services. Here is the code for the `GetLogEntryDates` method:

Available for download on Wrox.com

```
[Invoke]
public List<DateTime> GetLogEntryDates(int user_id)
{
     List<DateTime> dates = new List<DateTime>();

     var entries = from c in this.Context.FoodLogEntries
                   where c.user_id == user_id
                   select c.entry_date;

     foreach (DateTime date in entries)
     {
          if (!dates.Contains(date.Date))
               dates.Add(date);
     }

     return dates;
}
```

Code snippet FoodService.cs

User Interface Code Behind

Now that the business logic is complete, it's time to look at the various event handlers that are required to make the food log page run. To start, let's look at what happens when the page is first loaded. When the user arrives at the food log page they expect to see any food log entries that were created for the currently selected date. This will involve overriding the `OnNavigatedTo` event and loading the entries as shown.

Available for download on Wrox.com

```
protected override void OnNavigatedTo(NavigationEventArgs e)
{
     LoadFoodLog();
}

private void LoadFoodLog()
{
     ProgressBar.Visibility = Visibility.Visible;

     context = new FoodContext();
     FoodLogGrid.ItemsSource = context.FoodLogEntries;

     context.Load<FoodLogEntry>(context.GetFoodLogEntriesQuery(
                                Globals.CurrentUser.id,
                                Globals.SelectedDate, true),
                               (EntriesLoaded) =>
                               {
                                    ProgressBar.Visibility = Visibility.Collapsed;

                               }, null);
}
```

Code snippet FoodLog.xaml.cs

Loading the food log entries from the WCF RIA service requires creating a new instance of the `FoodContext` object and calling its `LoadMethod`. The `FoodLogGrid` only needs to have its `ItemSource` property set to the `FoodLogEntries EntityList`. Once the operation is complete, the `DataGrid` will refresh with the latest results. As you can see, you are displaying the `ProgressBar` before the asynchronous operation is started and hiding it when all of the data is loaded. This will be a common technique used throughout the code behind for all of the data entry pages.

In order for users to start entering foods in the food log, you need to hook up some important event handlers for the `AutoCompleteBox`. You will need handlers for the `ItemFilter`, `Populating`, `DropDownOpened`, `GotFocus`, `SelectionChanged`, and `TextChanged` events, as shown here:

Available for download on Wrox.com

```
AutoComplete.ItemFilter += (se, evt) => { return true; };
AutoComplete.Populating += new
PopulatingEventHandler(AutoComplete_Populating);
AutoComplete.DropDownOpened += (se, ev) => {
SearchingText.Visibility = Visibility.Collapsed; };

AutoComplete.GotFocus += (se, ev) => AutoComplete.Text = "";
AutoComplete.SelectionChanged += (se, ev) =>
{
     if (AutoComplete.SelectedItem != null)
          CreateFoodLogEntry(AutoComplete.SelectedItem as
FitnessTrackerPlus.Web.Data.Food);

     SearchingText.Visibility = Visibility.Collapsed;
};

AutoComplete.TextChanged += (se, ev) =>
{
     if (String.IsNullOrEmpty(AutoComplete.Text))
          SearchingText.Visibility = Visibility.Collapsed;
     else
     {
          SearchingText.Text = "Searching Foods..";
          SearchingText.Visibility = Visibility.Visible;
     }
};


private void AutoComplete_Populating(object sender, PopulatingEventArgs e)
{
     // Search for matching foods and make sure that the ServingSize
     // information is returned

     FoodContext autocompleteContext = new FoodContext();

     AutoComplete.ItemsSource = autocompleteContext.Foods;

autocompleteContext.Load<FitnessTrackerPlus.Web.Data.Food>
(autocompleteContext.SearchFoodsQuery(Globals.CurrentUser.id,
Globals.MaxAutoCompleteResults, AutoComplete.Text, true),
System.Windows.Ria.LoadBehavior.RefreshCurrent,
      (FoodsLoaded) =>
     {
```

```
            if (!FoodsLoaded.HasError)
            {
                AutoComplete.PopulateComplete();

                if (FoodsLoaded.TotalEntityCount == 0)
                    SearchingText.Text = "No foods found";
            }

        }, null);

        e.Cancel = true;
    }
```

Code snippet FoodLog.xaml.cs

The `AutoComplete_Populating` event handler is responsible for calling the `SearchFoods` operation on the server, and it will simply load all returned foods into the `Food EntityList`. When the operation completes, you need to call `PopulateComplete` to let the `AutoCompleteBox` know that you are finished populating the `ItemsSource` with data. If there are no foods returned, you should let the user know using the adjacent `TextBlock`. The adjacent `TextBlock` will remain hidden until the `TextChanged` event is triggered, which occurs as soon as the user starts typing in the control. When the asynchronous loading of the control is complete, the `DropDownOpened` event is triggered causing the `TextBlock` to become hidden again. After the `DropDownOpened` event is fired, the user can now make a food selection from the list of results. After the selection is made, the `SelectionChanged` event is fired and a new food log entry is created using the selected food and default serving information. Here is the code that is responsible for creating the new food log entry:

Available for download on Wrox.com

```
    private void CreateFoodLogEntry(FitnessTrackerPlus.Web.Data.Food food)
    {
        FoodLogEntry entry = new FoodLogEntry();

        ProgressBar.Visibility = Visibility.Visible;

        // Setup new food log entry with selected date, food and current user

        entry.food_id = food.id;
        entry.entry_date = Globals.SelectedDate;
        entry.user_id = Globals.CurrentUser.id;
        entry.servings = 1;
        entry.Food = food;

        context.FoodLogEntries.Add(entry);
        context.SubmitChanges((ChangesSubmitted) => { ProgressBar.Visibility =
    Visibility.Collapsed; }, null);
    }
```

Code snippet FoodLog.xaml.cs

Creating the new entry is as simple as adding a new `FoodLogEntry` object to the `FoodLogEntries EntityList` on the `DomainContext` object and calling `SubmitChanges`. When the operation completes, the new entry will automatically appear in the `DataGrid`. Can't get much easier than that! After the entry is created and the `DropDownBox` is once again collapsed, you will still see the search text sitting in the AutoCompleteBox. Because this may be confusing to the user, you will clear the search text in the GotFocus event.

Now that the AutoCompleteBox functionality is finished, it's time to look at updating the existing entries in the DataGrid. Because the user interface is geared around quickly adding entries to the food log, you aren't really providing users with the option to enter serving information. The idea is that all of the foods are added quickly and then users can go back to the DataGrid and make the appropriate edits to the servings column. This is the only column in the DataGrid that is not Read-Only and has a CellEditingTemplate defined. Luckily, because the servings column is a TextBlock control the DataGrid provides a CellEditingTemplate that contains a TextBox control for updating, so there is no extra work to be done here.

Now you just need to add the code that will actually handle the update operation. When the user double-clicks on a DataGrid row, any non-Read-Only cells will change to their corresponding editing templates. At this point, the user can make changes to the data in the current cell. When the row loses focus, the RowEditEnded event is thrown, so that is where you need to look at saving the changes to the database. By making use of the existing DomainContext you have for the FoodService, you simply have to add the following code to get the changes submitted:

Available for download on Wrox.com

```
private void FoodLogGrid_RowEditEnded(object sender,
DataGridRowEditEndedEventArgs e)
{
    // Submit any food log changes and refresh the DataGrid

    if (context.HasChanges)
    {
        ProgressBar.Visibility = Visibility.Visible;
        context.SubmitChanges((ChangesSubmitted) =>
        {
            ProgressBar.Visibility = Visibility.Collapsed;

        }, null);
    }
}
```

Code snippet FoodLog.xaml.cs

That's all there is to it. First you simply check to see if any changes have been made to the DomainContext by looking at the HasChanges property, then a quick call to SubmitChanges and everything will be saved to the database. You won't even have to write any additional code to get the DataGrid to refresh. All of that is taken care of by the underlying DomainContext and the EntityList of FoodLogEntry objects that the DataGrid is bound to.

DataGrid Enhancements

Before moving on to the custom food creation and GlobalCalendar functionality, I want to make you aware of some enhancements made to the DataGrid for the FitnessTrackerPlus log pages. Sometimes when you complete the data binding operation and you have defined custom column definitions, you may notice that the column sizes don't always seem to line up well and you are often left with additional empty space on the right side of the DataGrid entries, as shown in Figure 5-7.

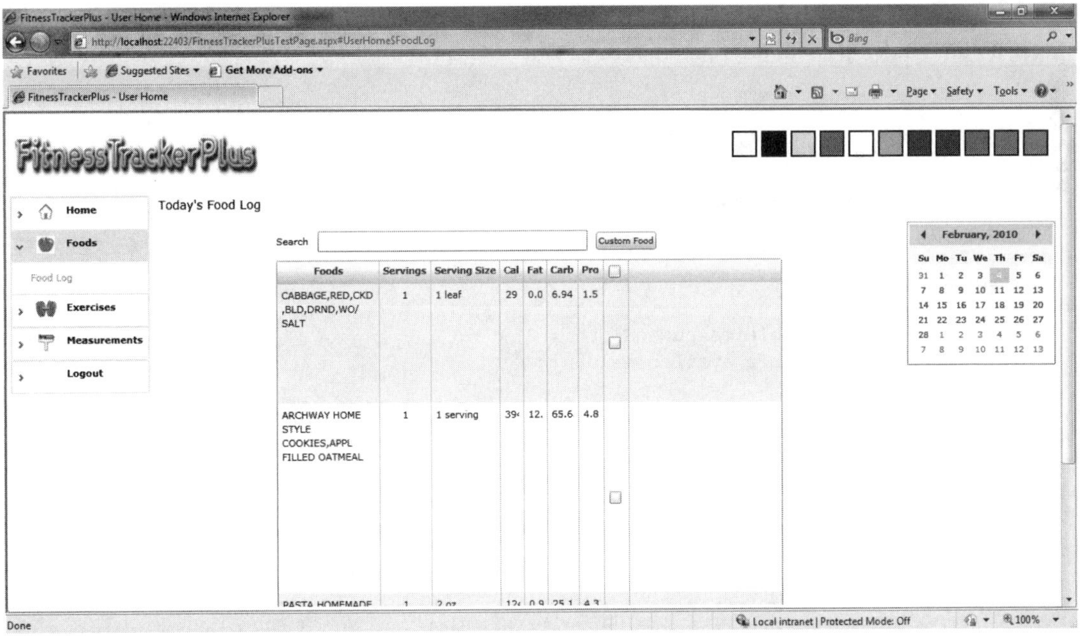

FIGURE 5-7

Perhaps it's nitpicking, but I would prefer that the checkbox column reside all the way to the right of the DataGrid and that the food name column be expanded to fill up the rest of the remaining empty space. Now you can, of course, change the column widths to fixed-width values or even use one of the predefined DataGridLength constants, as shown in Table 5-4.

TABLE 5-4: DataGridLength Values

VALUE	MEANING
`Auto`	DataGrid handles sizing of column width.
`SizeToCells`	Column will be same width as largest cell value.
`SizeToHeader`	Column will be same width as column header value.

Although having these options is great, it won't accomplish the goal of expanding the food name column to use up all available space. What would be ideal here is to be able to define column widths using star sizing like the regular `Grid` control. However, that is currently not an option available in Silverlight so you have to come up with something else. In order to accomplish this, you can add a new static helper class to the utility folder in the Silverlight project called `DataGridHelper`. The following code shows the `ResizeGrid` method that you will use throughout FitnessTrackerPlus to ensure that the CheckBox columns on DataGrid controls are aligned all the way to the right and that the column index passed into the ResizeGrid method is expanded to utilize all the remaining space.

Available for download on Wrox.com

```
using System.Windows.Controls;

namespace FitnessTrackerPlus.Utility
{
     public static class DataGridHelper
     {
          public static void ResizeGrid(int column_index,
DataGrid grid)
          {
               double consumedWidth = 0;
               double availableWidth = 0;

               foreach (DataGridColumn column in grid.Columns)
                    consumedWidth += column.ActualWidth;

               availableWidth = (grid.ActualWidth -
consumedWidth) - 5;

               // Expand the specified column to use up
               // all remaining width
               // Subtract 5 from available width to
               // avoid enabling horizontal scrollbar

               if (availableWidth > 0)
               {
                    grid.Columns[column_index].Width = new
DataGridLength(availableWidth +
grid.Columns[column_index].Width.Value);
                    grid.UpdateLayout();
               }
          }
     }
}
```

Code snippet DataGridHelper

In order to make use of this method you should add an event handler to the LayoutUpdated event on the DataGrid like this:

Available for download on Wrox.com

```
FoodLogGrid.LayoutUpdated += (se, ev) =>
{
     DataGridHelper.ResizeGrid(0, FoodLogGrid);
};
```

Code snippet FoodLog.xaml.cs

Because the food name column is the first column in the DataGrid, you just pass in the index value of zero along with the DataGrid itself. The DataGrid LayoutUpdated event fires whenever a new log entry is created, updated, or deleted from the underlying data source. You also will get the event to fire by resizing the browser window, which ensures that as the DataGrid expands to fill up the available space in the DockPanel control; the column sizes will also be corrected. Figure 5-8 shows the updated DataGrid with the columns correctly sized and arranged by the ResizeGrid method.

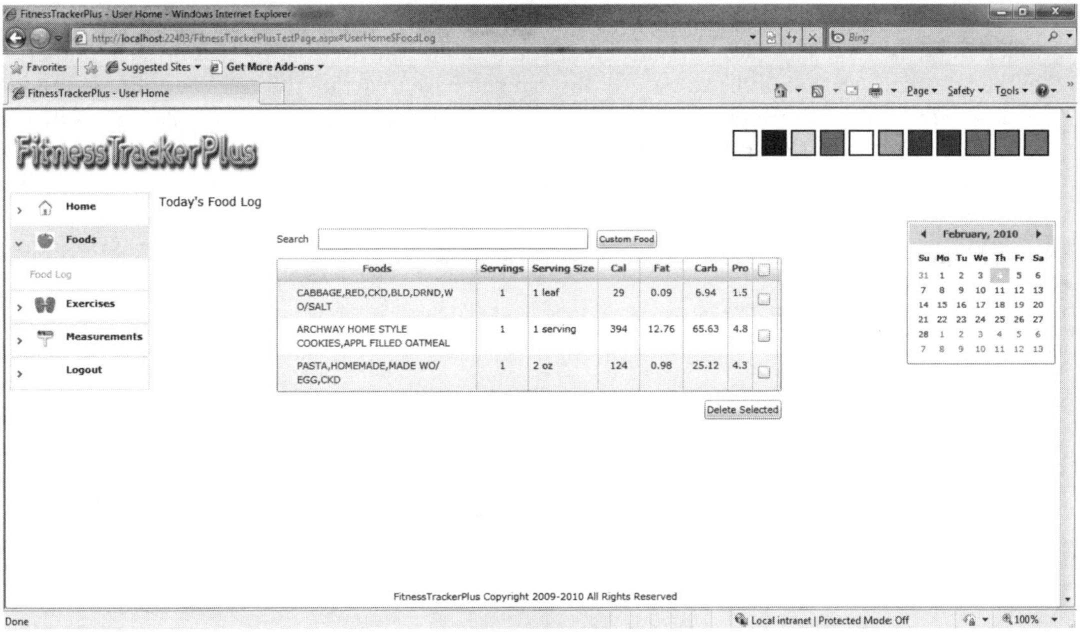

FIGURE 5-8

Adding Code to Select or Deselect All Rows

When designing the DataGrid, you added CheckBox controls to each row, including a CheckBox column for the column header with the intent that clicking the column header CheckBox would select/deselect all of the rows in the DataGrid. You declared a common event handler for both the Checked and Unchecked events in the custom header style. Now it's time to look at the code that will make the Select/Deselect All items functionality actually work. Let's take a look at the following event handler code for the header CheckBox:

Available for download on Wrox.com

```
private void CheckAll_Checked(object sender, RoutedEventArgs e)
{
    foreach (FoodLogEntry entry in context.FoodLogEntries)
    {
        FoodLogGrid.SelectedItem = entry;
        CheckBox selectItem = FoodLogGrid.Columns[FoodLogGrid.Columns.Count -
1].GetCellContent(FoodLogGrid.SelectedItem) as CheckBox;

        if (selectItem != null)
            selectItem.IsChecked = (sender as CheckBox).IsChecked;
    }
}
```

Code snippet FoodLog.xaml.cs

As you can see, the easiest way to achieve this is to loop through all of the `FoodLogEntry` entities that are currently loaded in the `FoodContext` object and make use of the `GetCellContent` call to retrieve the `CheckBox` control for each row in the `DataGrid` and set the `IsChecked` property accordingly. It would be great if there were a `Rows` collection object for the `DataGrid` similar to the one found in the ASP.NET `DataGrid` control that you could iterate over but there is no such property in the Silverlight version of the `DataGrid`. Instead you have to iterate through the collection that is bound to the `ItemsSource` property of the `DataGrid`. You can then access individual rows by using individual items from the `ItemsSource`. In order to delete the selected items from the `DataGrid` you will need to make use of similar code. You will want to handle the item deletion code in the `Click` event of the delete selected items `Button` control. The following is the code for the `Click` event:

Available for download on Wrox.com

```
private void DeleteSelected_Click(object sender, RoutedEventArgs e)
{
    List<FoodLogEntry> entries = new List<FoodLogEntry>();
    ProgressBar.Visibility = Visibility.Visible;

    foreach (FoodLogEntry entry in context.FoodLogEntries)
    {
        FoodLogGrid.SelectedItem = entry;

        CheckBox selectItem = FoodLogGrid.Columns[FoodLogGrid.Columns.Count -
1].GetCellContent(FoodLogGrid.SelectedItem) as CheckBox;

        if (selectItem != null)
            if (selectItem.IsChecked == true)
                entries.Add(entry);
    }

    foreach (FoodLogEntry entry in entries)
        context.FoodLogEntries.Remove(entry);

    context.SubmitChanges((EntriesRemoved) =>
    {
        ProgressBar.Visibility = Visibility.Collapsed;

    }, null);
}
```

Code snippet FoodLog.xaml.cs

The only major difference in this code is that you need to create a temporary list of selected food log entries and delete them from the `FoodContext` outside of the main for each loop. If you attempt to remove the items inside the loop, an exception is thrown because you are essentially modifying the items in the collection while enumerating them—which never turns out well. After removing all of the selected items, a call to `SubmitChanges` takes care of deleting the entries from the database and refreshing the `DataGrid` control to reflect the changes to the collection.

Supporting the Right-Click Context Menu

With the code to delete all selected entries finished you can now turn your attention to displaying and handling the `DataGrid` right-click context menu, which also lets users delete selected entries. In previous versions of Silverlight, when users performed a right mouse click, all they would see is the Silverlight option that showed the About Silverlight windows as shown in Figure 5-9.

FIGURE 5-9

Unfortunately, this makes it impossible to provide users with the traditional context menu behavior to which they've become accustomed in rich, thick client applications. With Silverlight 4, however, this is no longer a limitation and all controls now have corresponding `MouseRightButtonDown` and `MouseRightButtonUp` events.

To get started displaying the context menu from the FoodLog.xaml page, you first need to handle both of the events on the `DataGrid` control. In the constructor just add the following code:

```
FoodLogGrid.MouseRightButtonDown += (se, ev) => { ev.Handled = true; };
FoodLogGrid.MouseRightButtonUp += new
MouseButtonEventHandler(FoodLogGrid_MouseRightButtonUp);
```

Code snippet FoodLog.xaml

In the case of the `MouseRightButtonDown` event handler you need to set `ev.Handled` to `true` and that's all. What this does is tell the Silverlight runtime that you are handling the right mouse click and Silverlight should not display the default context menu. Next, you need to add a handler for the `MouseRightButtonUp` event. In the following code, the `Border` control has its `Margin` property set in relation to the `Canvas` parent control. This is done using the coordinates passed from the `MouseButtonEventArgs` parameter. Once the `Margin` is set the `Visibility` is toggled and the context menu will appear to users.

```
protected void FoodLogGrid_MouseRightButtonUp(object sender,
MouseButtonEventArgs e)
{
     RightClickBorder.Margin = new Thickness(e.GetPosition(RightClickMenu).X,
e.GetPosition(RightClickMenu).Y, 0, 0);
     RightClickMenu.Visibility = Visibility.Visible;
}
```

Code snippet FoodLog.xaml.cs

In case you are wondering how the menu is correctly positioned, well earlier I said that in the constructor, the `Canvas` control that houses the overall context menu was going to be resized to the full height and width of the screen. Once this is done setting the `Margin` property in relation to the parent `Canvas` control will make sure that the `Border` control that contains the right-click menu options is displayed in the correct place. The `Canvas.ZIndex` property being set to a large number ensures that the `DataGrid` information does not bleed through the menu. Figure 5-10 shows the new context menu that appears when the user performs a right-click operation.

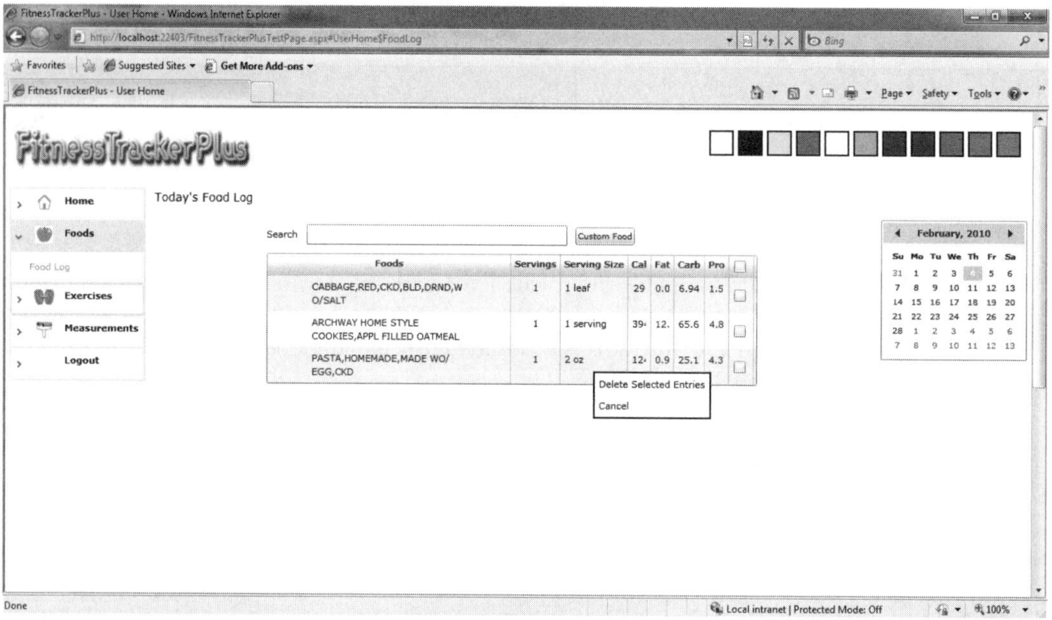

FIGURE 5-10

Now that the right-click menu appears you still need to handle the `MouseLeftButtonDown` event for both the Delete Selected and Cancel options of the menu. In the following code, the `DeleteEntryMenu` event handler just calls the previously implemented `DeleteSelected_Click` event handler in order to perform the delete operation. In addition to this, both the Delete and Cancel handlers ensure that the right-click menu is collapsed before exiting.

```
protected void DeleteEntryMenu_MouseLeftButtonDown(object sender,
MouseButtonEventArgs e)
{
```

```
        DeleteSelected_Click(this, new RoutedEventArgs());
        RightClickMenu.Visibility = Visibility.Collapsed;
}

protected void CancelEntryMenu_MouseLeftButtonDown(object sender,
MouseButtonEventArgs e)
{
        RightClickMenu.Visibility = Visibility.Collapsed;
}
```

Code snippet FoodLog.xaml.cs

Creating the GlobalCalendar Event Handling Logic

One final item that needs to be addressed in the code behind file is the `GlobalCalendar` event handling logic. When the user clicks any given date in the `GlobalCalendar`, you need to handle the `SelectedDatesChanged` event and retrieve all the food log entries for the selected date. Upon retrieving those entries, you then need to refresh the `DataGrid` to reflect the newly selected date. Here is the code for the `SelectedDatesChanged` event that takes care of loading the food log entries for the selected date.

Available for download on Wrox.com

```
Calendar.SelectedDatesChanged += (se, ev) =>
{
        if (Calendar.SelectedDate.HasValue)
        {
                Globals.SelectedDate = Calendar.SelectedDate.Value;
                LoadFoodLog();
        }
};
```

Code snippet FoodLog.xaml.cs

When handling this event, you can't forget to update the `SelectedDate` variable contained in the static `Globals` class. By doing this, you ensure that if the user switches to the exercise or measurement log pages, those pages load data based on the currently selected date rather than the current date—which could potentially be confusing to users expecting to view entries from the date they just selected on the `GlobalCalendar` control.

The following sections cover the control required to allow users to create custom foods and add them to their current food log.

Supporting Custom Foods

Even though you are providing users with a pretty extensive list of default foods to choose from, it is inevitable that they will want to add custom foods to the food log. You already have a `Button` control defined in the XAML code to handle this very scenario and the `Click` event handler will need to display a custom food data entry form in a modal `ChildWindow` that users can make use of for adding the custom food information. You'll want to separate the code for creating the custom foods into a new `UserControl` called `CustomFood`. This new control should be placed in the Views/Food folder in the Silverlight project.

The CustomFood control basically consists of a DataForm with customized DataField declarations that include all of the properties that go into creating a custom food object in the database. Because the purpose of this DataForm is only to handle creating new custom foods, you can safely set the DataForm to be in EditMode right from the start as well as hide any of the command buttons included with the DataForm that are related to navigation of a collection or creating and deleting objects. Listing 5-2 shows the XAML code for the CustomFood control, which shows the DataForm along with the custom DataField declarations:

LISTING 5-2: CustomFood.xaml

Available for download on Wrox.com

```
<UserControl x:Class="FitnessTrackerPlus.Views.Food.CustomFood"
    xmlns="http://schemas.microsoft.com/winfx/2006/xaml/presentation"
    xmlns:x="http://schemas.microsoft.com/winfx/2006/xaml"
    xmlns:data_dataform="clr-
namespace:System.Windows.Controls;
assembly=System.Windows.Controls.Data.DataForm.Toolkit">
    <UserControl.Resources>
        <Style x:Key="CustomFoodFormStyle" TargetType="data_dataform:DataForm">
            <Setter Property="AutoEdit" Value="True" />
            <Setter Property="AutoGenerateFields" Value="False" />
            <Setter Property="Foreground" Value="#FF000000" />
        </Style>
        <Style x:Key="NutritionFactsTextStyle" TargetType="TextBlock">
            <Setter Property="Text" Value="Nutrition Facts" />
            <Setter Property="FontSize" Value="18" />
            <Setter Property="Margin" Value="2,0,0,0" />
        </Style>
        <Style x:Key="RectangleStyle" TargetType="Rectangle">
            <Setter Property="Fill" Value="#FF000000" />
            <Setter Property="Stroke" Value="#FF000000" />
            <Setter Property="Margin" Value="0,5,0,0" />
        </Style>
        <Style x:Key="RectangleThinStyle" BasedOn="{StaticResource
RectangleStyle}" TargetType="Rectangle">
            <Setter Property="Height" Value="2" />
        </Style>
        <Style x:Key="RectangleThickStyle" BasedOn="{StaticResource
RectangleStyle}" TargetType="Rectangle">
            <Setter Property="Height" Value="5" />
        </Style>
        <Style x:Key="TextBoxStyle" TargetType="TextBox">
            <Setter Property="FontSize" Value="10" />
            <Setter Property="TextAlignment" Value="Center" />
        </Style>
        <Style x:Key="LargeTextBoxStyle" BasedOn="{StaticResource TextBoxStyle}"
TargetType="TextBox">
            <Setter Property="Width" Value="200" />
        </Style>
        <Style x:Key="SmallTextBoxStyle" BasedOn="{StaticResource TextBoxStyle}"
TargetType="TextBox">
            <Setter Property="Width" Value="50" />
```

```
                <Setter Property="HorizontalAlignment" Value="Right" />
            </Style>
        </UserControl.Resources>
        <data_dataform:DataForm x:Name="CustomFoodForm" Style="{StaticResource
CustomFoodFormStyle}">
            <data_dataform:DataForm.EditTemplate>
                <DataTemplate>
                    <StackPanel>
                        <TextBlock Style="{StaticResource
NutritionFactsTextStyle}" />
                        <Rectangle Style="{StaticResource RectangleThinStyle}" />
                        <data_dataform:DataField>
                            <TextBox Text="{Binding Path=name, Mode=TwoWay}"
Style="{StaticResource LargeTextBoxStyle}" />
                        </data_dataform:DataField>
                        <data_dataform:DataField>
                            <TextBox Text="{Binding Path=amount, Mode=TwoWay}"
Style="{StaticResource SmallTextBoxStyle}" />
                        </data_dataform:DataField>
                        <data_dataform:DataField>
                            <TextBox Text="{Binding Path=serving_size,
Mode=TwoWay}" Style="{StaticResource LargeTextBoxStyle}" />
                        </data_dataform:DataField>
                        <Rectangle Style="{StaticResource RectangleThickStyle}" />
                        <data_dataform:DataField>
                            <TextBox Text="{Binding Path=calories, Mode=TwoWay}"
Style="{StaticResource SmallTextBoxStyle}" />
                        </data_dataform:DataField>
                        <Rectangle Style="{StaticResource RectangleThickStyle}" />
                        <data_dataform:DataField>
                            <TextBox Text="{Binding Path=total, Mode=TwoWay}"
Style="{StaticResource SmallTextBoxStyle}" />
                        </data_dataform:DataField>
                        <Rectangle Style="{StaticResource RectangleThinStyle}" />
                        <data_dataform:DataField>
                            <TextBox Text="{Binding Path=carbohydrate,
Mode=TwoWay}" Style="{StaticResource SmallTextBoxStyle}" />
                        </data_dataform:DataField>
                        <Rectangle Style="{StaticResource RectangleThinStyle}" />
                        <data_dataform:DataField>
                            <TextBox Text="{Binding Path=protein, Mode=TwoWay}"
Style="{StaticResource SmallTextBoxStyle}" />
                        </data_dataform:DataField>
                        <Rectangle Style="{StaticResource RectangleThickStyle}" />
                    </StackPanel>
                </DataTemplate>
            </data_dataform:DataForm.EditTemplate>
        </data_dataform:DataForm>
</UserControl>
```

In the code behind for the `CustomFood` control, the `DataForm` will take care of validating the user-supplied data using the validation rules that were added to the food metadata file earlier. When the user is finished entering the food and nutrient details, you will need to handle the `EditEnded` event of the `DataForm` with the following code:

Available for download on Wrox.com

```
private void CustomFoodForm_EditEnded(object sender, DataFormEditEndedEventArgs e)
{
    if (e.EditAction == DataFormEditAction.Cancel && CustomFoodCanceled != null)
        CustomFoodCanceled(this, null);
    else
    {
        if (CustomFoodForm.ValidateItem())
        {
            // If validation succeeds then add the food to the database

            foodContext.Foods.Add(CustomFoodForm.CurrentItem as
FitnessTrackerPlus.Web.Data.Food);
            foodContext.SubmitChanges((FoodSubmitted) =>
            {
                if (!FoodSubmitted.HasError && CustomFoodCreated != null)
                {
                    CustomFoodCreated(this, new
CustomFoodCreatedEventArgs(CustomFoodForm.CurrentItem as
FitnessTrackerPlus.Web.Data.Food));
                }

            }, null);
        }
    }
}
```

Code snippet CustomFood.xaml.cs

There isn't really much to this code. You first need to ensure that when the event handler is reached it's not because the user decided to cancel the edit operation. Next, you should perform a call to `ValidateItem` that tells the `DataForm` to perform validation against the custom food object using the validation attributes set in the metadata file. Finally, you should add the new custom food to the `Foods` entity list; a call to `SubmitChanges` ensures that the new `Food` object is stored in the database. Once this operation is complete, however, you should also assume that your users expect that a corresponding food log entry is created in this same operation. After all, the only reason they're creating the custom food is to add a new food log entry. For this reason, you need to create a new custom event that fires from the `CustomFood` class and signifies the custom food creation is complete and the parent control can safely create a new `FoodLogEntry` item using the new custom food information. This is done by firing a `CustomFoodCreated` event to the parent control.

Creating the custom event and associated delegate is simple enough. First you add a public event and delegate signature to the `CustomFood` class like this:

Available for download on Wrox.com

```
public delegate void CustomFoodCreatedEventHandler(object sender,
CustomFoodCreatedEventArgs e);
public event CustomFoodCreatedEventHandler CustomFoodCreated;
```

Code snippet CustomFood.xaml.cs

Then, in the same file but below the `CustomFood` class, you add the following `CustomFoodCreatedEventArgs` class:

Available for download on Wrox.com

```
public class CustomFoodCreatedEventArgs
{
     private FitnessTrackerPlus.Web.Data.Food custom_food = null;

     public CustomFoodCreatedEventArgs() { }
     public CustomFoodCreatedEventArgs(FitnessTrackerPlus.Web.Data.Food
custom_food)
     {
          this.custom_food = custom_food;
     }

     public FitnessTrackerPlus.Web.Data.Food CreatedFood
     {
          get {
                    return custom_food;
                }
     }
}
```

Code snippet CustomFood.xaml.cs

The only item that is relevant to the listeners of this event is the custom food object that was created so you have a public property called `CreatedFood` that listeners can use in order to add a new food log entry using the food. What about if the user cancels the operation? Well, because no custom food will have been created in this case, you can get away with a very simple public event that uses the standard `EventHandler` signature like this:

```
public event EventHandler CustomFoodCanceled;
```

Code snippet CustomFood.xaml.cs

Looking back at the `Click` event handler for the custom food `Button on the main FoodLog page`, you now should be handling the creation of the `CustomFood` dialog as well as creating the new `FoodLogEntry`. The following is the `Click` event handler for the custom food `Button` control:

Available for download on Wrox.com

```
private void CustomFood_Click(object sender, RoutedEventArgs e)
{
     ChildWindow modalWindow = new ChildWindow();
     CustomFood customFood = new CustomFood();

     customFood.CustomFoodCanceled += (s, ev) => { modalWindow.Close(); };
     customFood.CustomFoodCreated += (s, ev) =>
     {
          CreateFoodLogEntry(ev.CreatedFood);
          modalWindow.Close();
     };

     modalWindow.Title = "Add Custom Food";
     modalWindow.Content = customFood;
     modalWindow.Show();
}
```

Code snippet FoodLog.xaml.cs

As you can see, if the custom food is created, you simply create a new `FoodLogEntry` using the `CreatedFood` property of the `CustomFoodCreatedEventArgs` variable. However, if the user cancels the operation, you just close the modal dialog window. Figure 5-11 shows the `CustomFood` control in action.

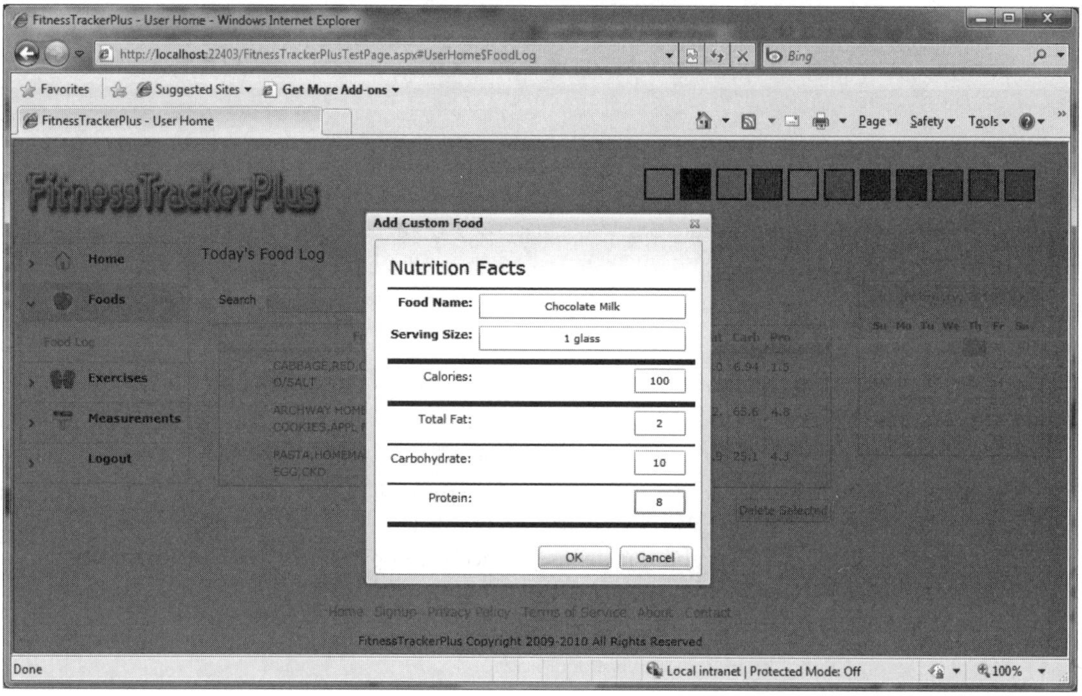

FIGURE 5-11

SUMMARY

You finally have a fully functional piece of the application that solves one of the major requirements of the site. In this chapter, you have seen step by step how to combine the `GlobalCalendar`, `AutoCompleteBox`, `DataForm`, and `DataGrid` controls to create a powerful and rich data entry screen. You have also seen how easy it is to add a middle-tier implementation that combines LINQ to SQL and the WCF RIA Services Framework. I hope that after completing this chapter, you have a really solid understanding of how to leverage all of these techniques in your own Rich Internet Applications built in Silverlight. In addition to all of this, you have also seen some techniques for customizing the out-of-the-box functionality of the `DataGrid` control to further enhance the user interface. At this point in the book, you can even start keeping track of the foods that you eat on a daily basis. You may be unfortunately surprised at just how many calories can get consumed during any given software development session. Don't worry though—after completing the next chapter, you will have a working exercise log page so you will be able to see if you are successfully burning all of those calories by typing thousands of lines of code.

6

Time to Hit the Gym

Creating the Exercise Log

Thanks to the hard work you put in during the previous chapter, users of FitnessTrackerPlus can now keep track of the foods they eat on a daily basis. Now you want to provide them with an easy way to keep track of their exercise routines. Like the food log page you will need to design a user interface that is conducive to logging exercises. This means that the controls used for the food log page may not be the ones best suited for logging exercises. So you will need to design the user interface accordingly.

The information that is logged when creating exercise log entries can vary depending on the type of exercise performed. When logging cardio exercises, users will want to keep track of things such as speed, distance, duration, and so on. However, when logging weight training exercises, users will most likely only care about things such as total repetitions and weight of the exercise performed. For this reason, you will be making use of separate `DataGrid` controls for each exercise type when displaying entries.

You will see how to make use of the new `DomainDataSource` control included in the WCF RIA Services Framework to coordinate operations between each of these `DataGrid` controls as well as filtering the entries being displayed so that cardio exercises appear in one `DataGrid` and weight training exercises appear in another. You will also see how to take advantage of the grouping and sorting features of the `DomainDataSource` controls in order to make sure that weight training exercise log entries are grouped according to their associated muscle group; this makes it easier for users to plan workouts according to the muscle group that they are working.

By the end of this chapter, you will be two-thirds of the way to providing all of the required data entry pages to your users. After this, you'll see how to take advantage of all this data to provide users with powerful charting capabilities that will further help them to succeed in achieving their fitness goals.

PROBLEM

Because no fitness program is complete without both a diet and exercise plan, users of FitnessTrackerPlus will be expecting to keep track of any exercises that they perform on a daily basis. The exercise log page will need to provide users with many of the same things that are provided by the food log page. As required for the food log page, users are expecting a fast, rich user interface for adding exercise log entries. When creating the food log page, you provided users with the ability to select from a fairly extensive list of default foods in order to assist in the data entry process. You should count on providing a similar list of exercises for users on the exercise log page as well. As with the food log page, if users cannot find the exercise they are looking for, you need to provide them with a means to create and store custom exercises that they can add to the exercise log.

The main data entry control for the food log page was the `AutoCompleteBox` control. Users can add new log entries only by searching for a matching food in this control or creating a custom food. For the exercise log page, you need to think about whether or not this control should also be used on this page as the main data entry mechanism. Although you will be providing a comprehensive list of exercises that users can choose from, searching that list may not be the easiest way for users to create new exercise log entries. You may want to see if another control such as the `ComboBox` would be better suited for this scenario. This way, your users could potentially filter exercises by their type such as cardio, weight training, and activities. After selecting an exercise type, another `ComboBox` could be populated dynamically with a list of exercises matching that type. You may have already seen a similar technique used on other websites such as Kelly Blue Book, where you will first select a make, model, and finally a year while attempting to retrieve information about an automobile. This cascading `ComboBox` technique can sometimes be a really quick data entry tool that works well when your total list of items can be filtered and limited to a couple hundred entries as opposed to tens of thousands, as is the case with the food searching mechanism.

An additional problem to be solved is that users will most likely expect to see their exercise log entries grouped according to the type of exercise performed. You will probably want exercises to be separated into three distinct types: cardio, weight training, and other activities. The data collected for these three types of exercises will vary greatly. For example, a user who is entering a cardio exercise such as treadmill running would probably expect to keep track of things such as distance, time, calories burned, and so on. A user who is entering a set of bench press exercises would probably expect to log things such as reps and weight. This will present a challenge not only for the user interface but also for the database table structure. You will have some important design decisions to make when considering the database table structure, such as whether to use one table for all exercise log entries or instead separate exercise log entries into their three distinct types and create individual exercise log entry tables for each of those types.

DESIGN

In the previous chapter, the first thing that was done in the "Design" section was to create a user story that would assist in the creation of the page requirements. Because this can be such a helpful tool user stories will be used to create the requirements list for both this exercise log page as well as the measurements log page in the next chapter. As always, the design will be split out into the major features that encompass the page and will be further broken down into the design discussions for the user interface, database, data access, business logic, and user interface code behind. By now, you should be pretty familiar with the formula being used throughout this book so let's go ahead and get started by creating a user story that simulates what the typical user may do when he or she arrives at the exercise log page.

User Stories

The following are a couple of user stories that should be helpful in creating a list of requirements for the exercise log page. Ideally, both of these stories will be consistent with the behavior of real users that are visiting the site to utilize this feature. As always, you aren't concerned with writing hundreds of these. You just want to try and come up with a scenario that accurately represents what the typical user would expect to see entering exercises into their daily log.

USER STORY New Exercise User

Tom has just started a new exercise regimen at the local gym. This isn't the first time he has done this but he hopes this is the last time. Instead of continuing on with the start/stop cycle of working out that has plagued him in the last few years, he would like to make it part of his daily routine. In order to ensure that he sticks to this regimen on a daily basis, he decides to keep a journal of the exercises he performs each day. If this were 1986, he would run down to the local store and pick up one of those handy spiral bound notebooks and write down every exercise he performs. Lucky for him, the Internet exists and writing all of this information by hand is no longer necessary. He quickly hops on his computer and searches Google for online fitness tracking programs. There on the first page of results he notices FitnessTrackerPlus. After a simple registration process, he clicks on the exercise menu to be presented with his daily exercise log. Now the hard part — how does he actually enter his exercises? Today, he worked on shoulders so he notices a list of muscle groups and selects shoulders. After the selection, all shoulder-related exercises appear in an adjacent list. Now he simply selects the first exercise he performed and instantly the exercise is added to a table below. Well this seems easy enough so he tries another exercise. Unfortunately, the exercise he is looking for does not appear to be available. But he notices a custom exercise button on the same screen. After answering a few questions about the custom exercise, he quickly saves the exercise to his list of custom exercises and the exercise he created is added to the table. The best part is that now his custom exercise is available any time he visits the site. Tom is impressed; the entire process took seconds instead of the minutes it would have taken him to manually write all of the information down in his notebook. The entire process was quick and painless, and it will no doubt become part of his new daily routine.

Requirements

After taking a look at the user story, it's time to come up with the detailed list of requirements for the exercise log page. Of course, in addition to any requirements extracted from the user stories, you also need to make sure that the requirements list covers any of the original problems outlined in the problem section of the chapter.

- Users should be able to view a list of exercises performed in a tabular format.
- Exercises should be grouped in the exercise log based on the type of exercise being added to the log.

- There should be three major types of exercises: Cardio, Weight Training, and Activity.
- All exercises should fall under one of those major categories.
- Weight training exercises should be grouped in the log according to the associated muscle type.
- Users should be able to select exercises by first selecting an exercise type filter, followed by the list of exercises themselves.
- As soon as a selection is made, a new exercise log entry should be created containing the selected exercise.
- Users should be able to create custom exercises when they cannot find an appropriate match in the default list of exercises.
- Users will need the ability to view past, present, and future log entries.
- Users should be able to create, read, update, and delete any log entries.
- Once again, users should have access to a right-click menu in order to delete selected entries.

It shouldn't be much of a surprise that many of the requirements listed match the ones created during the food log design. Users will still need the same basic data entry functions that were designed in the food log and, in fact, you should expect to see similar requirements in the coverage of the measurements log next chapter. Now that the requirements are complete, let's take a look at the most important component of this chapter, which of course is the exercise log page.

Exercise Log

Thanks to the user story created, you now have a complete list of requirements to base the design off of. The design discussion will begin as usual with a look at the proposed user interface for the exercise log page. Remember, above all, that the goal of this page is to provide a quick and painless data entry experience for your users, so you need to make sure to choose the right Silverlight controls for the job.

User Interface

The user interface for the exercise log page will be strikingly similar to the food log page. As in the food log page, newly created entries should appear in a `DataGrid` control. In addition to this, you will also need to provide a way for users to browse for exercises by exercise type and potentially muscle group. The design is calling for a cascading `ComboBox` type of solution similar to the ones found on automobile sites such as Kelly Blue Book or CarMax. These solutions involve `ComboBox` controls where the contents depend on the previously made selection. For example, you will provide a `ComboBox` for choosing one of the available exercise types such as cardio, weight training, or activities. If the user selects cardio or activities, then the next `ComboBox` will be filled with exercises that belong to the selected exercise type. If the user selects weight training, you will need to dynamically display an additional `ComboBox` so that the users can filter the exercise list based on a selected muscle group. In addition to the `ComboBox` controls, you will need to add a `Button` control alongside the `ComboBox` controls that will display a custom exercise creation form. This will be done in case the users cannot find the exercise they wish to log in the default exercise list provided. Once the user finishes entering information related to the custom exercise, a new exercise log entry should be created using the exercise and it should be added to the appropriate `DataGrid` depending on what type of exercise it is.

When designing the food log page, you need only one `DataGrid` to hold food log entries. The exercise log page will require something slightly different. Because there are three distinct exercise types, you will want to group exercises by their associated type. This will require not one but three separate `DataGrid` controls to be used on the page. You will have a separate `DataGrid` for cardio, weight training, and activities.

You might be wondering why you can't just have them all in one `DataGrid` and use the new grouping capabilities of the `DataGrid` control to combine exercises by their type. You could do this but when you think about the columns that will be required for the various exercises, it can start to get complicated. For example cardio log entries will need to store things such as time, distance, level, and so on. Weight training exercises will need to store weight and reps, which of course have no real association with cardio exercises. This type of decision can be a difficult one, but it really boils down to whether or not you want to display all possible columns and have null values be displayed where there is no association. I felt that it could be confusing to the user to have to look at the `DataGrid` and see five or six empty columns for weight training exercises. With that out of the way, let's take a quick look at what design elements are needed in order to get this page working. Figure 6-1 shows the potential user interface for the exercise log page.

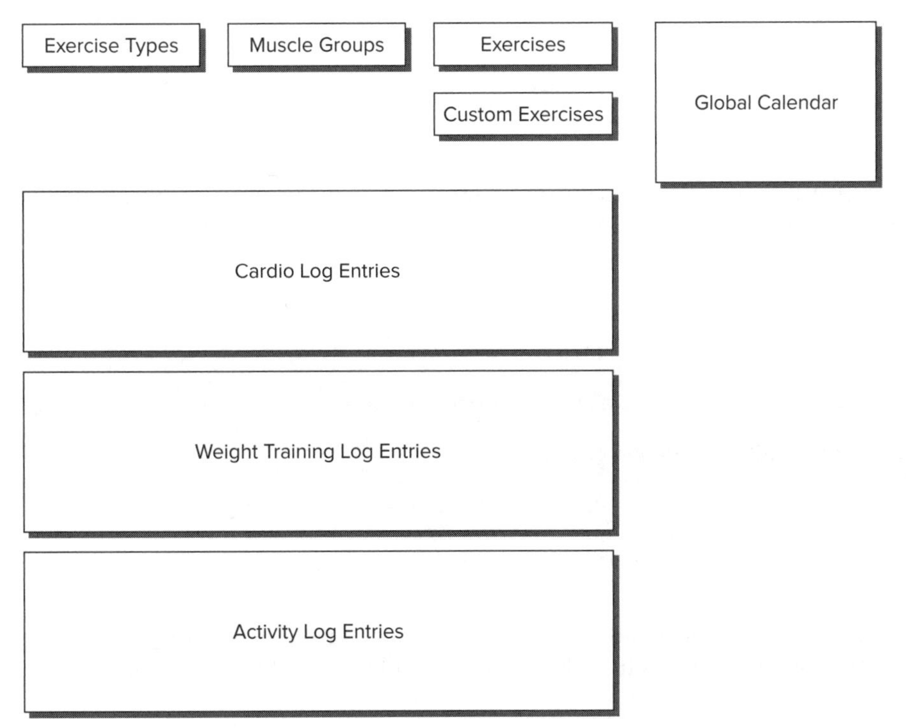

FIGURE 6-1

Database

Several new database tables are required for the exercise log page. You will need tables to hold exercise types, muscle groups, exercises, exercise-to-muscle-group associations, and exercise log entries. Table 6-1 shows the schema for the exercise_types table.

TABLE 6-1: exercise_types

COLUMN NAME	TYPE	DESCRIPTION
id	int	Unique identity field for type
type_name	varchar(50)	Name of exercise type; only three will be available (cardio, weight training, and activity)

The muscle_groups table (Table 6-2) will contain all of the available muscle groups. You won't be allowing users to add to this table so it will contain only the following entries: abs, arms, back, chest, legs, neck, and shoulders.

TABLE 6-2: muscle_groups

COLUMN NAME	TYPE	DESCRIPTION
id	int	Unique identity field for muscle group
group_name	varchar(50)	Name of muscle group (abs, arms, back, chest, legs, neck, shoulders)

Now you will need a place to store the actual exercise information. The exercises table (Table 6-3) will hold all of the default exercises as well as any custom exercises created by the users.

TABLE 6-3: exercises

COLUMN NAME	TYPE	DESCRIPTION
id	int	Unique identity field for exercise
exercise_name	varchar(100)	Name of exercise
exercise_type	int	ID of associated exercise type
user_id	int	ID of associated user

For any weight training exercise, there should be an association to one of the existing muscle groups. The exercises_muscle_groups join table (Table 6-4) will provide this association.

TABLE 6-4: exercises_muscle_groups

COLUMN NAME	TYPE	DESCRIPTION
id	int	Unique identity field for association
muscle_group_id	int	ID of associated muscle group
exercise_id	int	ID of associated weight training exercise

Even though you will be displaying the exercise log entries in three separate `DataGrid` controls, you do not necessarily have to store them in three separate database tables. Regardless of exercise type, all entries will share id, exercise_id, user_id, duration, calories, time, and entry_date columns. Therefore, from a database storage perspective, it doesn't really make much sense to duplicate these columns across multiple tables. Not to mention the added difficulty you would have when writing the business logic as you would have to ensure that entries were added and deleted from the correct tables. Separating the exercise log entries by exercise type makes sense from a user interface perspective, but it doesn't really make sense on the database side. In the following exercise_logs table, you may have NULL column values for reps, and weight when a cardio exercise is entered but that still ultimately will cost less than duplicating the columns that are shared across three separate database tables. The savings in business logic implementation alone is probably worth the use of one table (Table 6-5) for this.

TABLE 6-5: exercise_logs

COLUMN NAME	TYPE	DESCRIPTION
id	int	Unique identity field for entry
exercise_id	int	ID of associated exercise
user_id	int	ID of associated user
duration	datetime	Length of time exercise is performed
calories	int	Calories burned during exercise
distance	float	Distance traveled
incline	float	Incline used, typically found on cardio machines
speed	float	Speed that exercise was performed, used for cardio exercises
reps	smallint	Total number of repetitions performed for weight training exercise
weight	smallint	Total weight used while performing weight training exercise
entry_date	datetime	Date of exercise log entry

Data Access

The data access code will be very similar to the food log page in that you will need to create LINQ to SQL classes for each of the database tables being used in the exercise log page design. Once again, you should be able to achieve this using just one new LINQ to SQL class file containing all of the relevant tables. It really is nice to not have to spend countless hours creating data access classes, now isn't it? Go ahead — you can admit that you no longer miss doing this.

Business Logic

As in the food log page, the business logic needs to consist of a new `DomainService` class called `ExerciseService`. When creating this service you should note that some of the entities added to the LINQ to SQL classes file may not need to have editing enabled. For example, it is unlikely that you will want to allow for editing of muscle groups, exercise types, or the exercise-to-muscle-group relationships. When you create a new `DomainService`, you are always given the option to pick and choose which entities should be enabled for updating. If you don't specifically select the editing checkbox when the wizard is displayed, then the code generator will only add, create, and delete methods to the generated `DomainService`. This prevents you from enabling callers of the service with the ability to modify entities that are Read-Only in nature. After creating the `ExerciseService`, you should ultimately be left with the methods shown in Table 6-6, available to the Silverlight client:

TABLE 6-6: Available Methods

METHOD	DESCRIPTION
`GetExercisesByType`	Should retrieve all exercises for the given exercise type
`GetExercisesByMuscleGroup`	Should retrieve all weight training exercises for the given muscle group
`InsertExercise`	Creates a new custom exercise in the database
`GetExerciseLogEntries`	Retrieves all exercise log entries for the given date and user
`InsertExerciseLogEntry`	Creates a new exercise log entry in the database
`UpdateExerciseLogEntry`	Updates the specified exercise log entry
`DeleteExerciseLogEntry`	Removes the specified exercise log entry from the database
`GetExerciseTypes`	Retrieves a list of valid exercise types
`GetMuscleGroups`	Retrieves a list of valid muscle groups

User Interface Code Behind

In the user interface code behind you will need to accomplish several things. First, you will need to retrieve the list of exercise types so that you can populate the first of the cascading `ComboBox` controls. Once a selection is made from that control, you will need an event handler to either retrieve the exercises for the selected exercise type, or you will need to display the `ComboBox` containing the list of available muscle groups. In theory, because you know in advance exactly which exercise types and muscle groups exist in the database, you could hard code the list in the XAML. I suggest retrieving the data from the database and using data binding anyway because you never know when you may decide to add a new exercise type or muscle group into the application.

After you've provided users with a cascading `ComboBox` setup, they should be able to select an exercise type followed by a specific exercise. You will need an event handler to handle the `ComboBox SelectionChanged` event so that a new exercise log entry will be created and displayed. Speaking of the exercise log entries, you know from the requirements that there need to be multiple `DataGrid` controls on the page to handle the display of the log entries. There should be a `DataGrid` for cardio, weight training, and activities. Ideally you should be able to set the `ItemsSource` property of each `DataGrid` to the same collection of data while adding a filter mechanism so that each `DataGrid` shows only the appropriate exercise type. Of course, this also has some implications for the delete logic. Because you have three separate `DataGrid` controls, you will need to make sure that all three are checked for selected items before applying the delete logic in the Delete button's `Click` event handler. Because you have only one database table for all exercise log entries you will need to set the `ItemsSource` property of each `DataGrid` control to different collections of data.

Supporting custom exercise creation will be very similar to the work you just finished in the previous chapter. You will need to handle the `Click` event of the custom food button and display a modal `ChildWindow` containing the data entry form for custom food creation. You should have fields for the exercise name, type, and if the user selects weight training as the exercise type, muscle group. The muscle group selection should appear only if the user creates a new weight training exercise. Otherwise, it should remain hidden on the `DataForm`.

Just as you planned in the food log page, you will also need to handle the `Calendar` control's `SelectedDateChanged` event and make sure that you display exercise log entries for the selected date while storing the newly selected date in the `Globals` class for other pages to make use of. Any `DataGrid` events related to in-place editing and row deletion will need to be implemented as they were in the food log page as well. One major difference in the delete handler for this page is that you will need to loop through all of the entries in each of the three `DataGrid` controls to build a list of entries to delete.

SOLUTION

Now that you have completed the design of the exercise log page, it's once again time to take a look at the implementation of the required features. This section of the chapter covers creating cascading `ComboBox` controls, handling multiple `DataGrid` controls, and using data binding techniques with the new `DomainDataSource` control from the WCF RIA Services Framework. As always, even though the techniques being demonstrated here are designed for the FitnessTrackerPlus application, you should be able to take what you learn in this section and easily apply it to your own Silverlight-based solutions.

The main feature being implemented in this chapter is the exercise log page. Users will visit this page to enter any exercises performed on a given day. The design of this page calls for the primary data entry tasks to be performed through the use of ComboBox controls. Users will be expected to utilize the ComboBox controls to find a matching exercise. After a selection is made, a new entry is added to the log. As was the case with the food log page, if users cannot find an accurate matching exercise they always have the option of creating a custom exercise and adding that custom exercise to their log. Like the food log page, users will be expected to quickly add all of the exercises performed and then go back to the entries to make updates to any additional information that is related to those exercises. The solution, as always, is broken down into discussions centering on the user interface, database, data access, business logic, and finally the user interface code behind page.

User Interface

The user interface for this page will begin with the same DockPanel container structure that was used when creating the food log page. This structure keeps the data entry controls toward the top of the page with the GlobalCalendar docked at the top right of the page. All the DataGrid controls will reside at the end of the DockPanel declaration and make use of the LastChildFill property on the DockPanel to ensure that the DataGrid area utilizes all of the available screen space. Once again, by making use of the DockPanel along with the LastChildFill property you will ensure that the DataGrid area will stretch to fill all the remaining screen real estate, even if the browser window is resized. The best part is that no complicated JavaScript code is required to get this working.

Control Layout

The following code shows the DockPanel container structure and overall layout of the exercise log page user interface:

Available for download on Wrox.com

```
<Style x:Key="LogDockPanelStyle" TargetType="toolkit:DockPanel">
     <Setter Property="LastChildFill" Value="True" />
</Style>

<toolkit:DockPanel Style="{StaticResource LogDockPanelStyle}">
     <toolkit:DockPanel Style="{StaticResource HeaderDockPanelStyle}">
          <TextBlock Style="{StaticResource ExerciseLogHeaderStyle}" />
          <TextBlock x:Name="SelectedDate" Style="{StaticResource
SelectedDateTextStyle}" />
          <ProgressBar x:Name="ProgressBar" Style="{StaticResource
ProgressBarStyle}" />
     </toolkit:DockPanel>
     <StackPanel Style="{StaticResource CalendarPanelStyle}">
          <toolkit:GlobalCalendar. . .>
     </StackPanel>
     <StackPanel Style="{StaticResource LogPanelStyle}">
     </StackPanel>
</toolkit:DockPanel>
```

Code snippet ExerciseLog.xaml

Because you have already seen the `GlobalCalendar` XAML declaration in the previous chapter, I went ahead and collapsed the declaration in the container. Everything will work the same way for the exercise log page as it did for the food log page regarding the `GlobalCalendar` and the custom styles that are applied to valid log dates.

At this point, you should have the `DockPanel` container set up along with the `GlobalCalendar`, header text, `ProgressBar` control, and a horizontal `StackPanel` that will host the required `ComboBox` controls being used for the data entry. Speaking of the `ComboBox` controls, now would be a great time to add those to the user interface. You will need a total of three controls, one each to host the exercise types, muscle groups, and exercises. As you can see in the following code, the muscle group and exercise `ComboBox` controls are hidden by default. These three `ComboBox` controls will make up the cascading behavior that is required in this chapter.

Available for download on Wrox.com

```
<Style x:Key="ExerciseEntryComboBoxStyle" TargetType="ComboBox">
     <Setter Property="Margin" Value="0,0,10,0" />
     <Setter Property="Height" Value="20" />
</Style>

<Style x:Key="ExerciseEntryHiddenComboBoxStyle" BasedOn="{StaticResource
ExerciseEntryComboBoxStyle}" TargetType="ComboBox">
     <Setter Property="Visibility" Value="Collapsed" />
</Style>

<StackPanel Style="{StaticResource LogPanelStyle}">
     <StackPanel Style="{StaticResource ExerciseEntryStackPanelStyle}">
          <ComboBox x:Name="ExerciseTypes" Style="{StaticResource
ExerciseEntryComboBoxStyle}" DisplayMemberPath="type_name" />
          <ComboBox x:Name="MuscleGroups" Style="{StaticResource
ExerciseEntryHiddenComboBoxStyle}" DisplayMemberPath="group_name" />
          <ComboBox x:Name="Exercises" Style="{StaticResource
ExerciseEntryHiddenComboBoxStyle}" DisplayMemberPath="exercise_name" />
     <Button x:Name="CustomExercise" Style="{StaticResource
CustomExerciseButtonStyle}" />
</StackPanel>
```

Code snippet ExerciseLog.xaml

In the preceding code, the user will need to select an exercise type from the only `ComboBox` that is visible by default. If the user selects weight training then the muscle groups `ComboBox` will be made visible. At this point, the user will need to select from one of the default muscle groups. Once a selection is made, the exercises that match the selected muscle group will be loaded into the third `ComboBox` and that control will be made visible as well. Now if the user happens to select a cardio or activity exercise type, then the muscle groups `ComboBox` will remain hidden and the exercises `ComboBox` will be made visible and loaded with exercises that match the selected exercise type. In either case, once the user makes a selection from the exercise's `ComboBox` control, a new exercise log entry will be created using the selected exercise.

DataGrids for Each Exercise Type

In addition to the ComboBox controls, the design calls for separate DataGrid controls for each of the three possible exercise types. This means that you should have a DataGrid to display exercise log entries for cardio entries, weight training entries, and other activities.

➤ **Cardio grid:** The first DataGrid control added to the page is the cardio grid. The purpose of this DataGrid is to display only the exercise log entries that are associated with cardio exercises. The following XAML code shows the cardio grid declaration added to the exercise log page:

Available for download on Wrox.com

```
<data:DataGrid x:Name="CardioLogGrid" Style="{StaticResource DataGrid}"
     ItemsSource="{Binding Path=Data, ElementName=CardioData}" >
     <data:DataGrid.Columns>
          <data:DataGridTemplateColumn Header="Cardio"
HeaderStyle="{StaticResource DataGridColumnHeaderCentered}">
               <data:DataGridTemplateColumn.CellTemplate>
                    <DataTemplate>
                         <TextBlock Text="{Binding
Path=Exercise.exercise_name}"
Style="{StaticResource DataGridTextBlockCentered}" />
                    </DataTemplate>
               </data:DataGridTemplateColumn.CellTemplate>
          </data:DataGridTemplateColumn>
          <data:DataGridTemplateColumn Header="Duration"
HeaderStyle="{StaticResource DataGridColumnHeaderCentered}">
               <data:DataGridTemplateColumn.CellTemplate>
                    <DataTemplate>
                         <TextBlock Text="{Binding Path=duration,
StringFormat='HH:mm:ss'}" Style="{StaticResource
DataGridTextBlockCentered}" />
                    </DataTemplate>
               </data:DataGridTemplateColumn.CellTemplate>
               <data:DataGridTemplateColumn.CellEditingTemplate>
                    <DataTemplate>
                         <toolkit_input:TimePicker x:Name="Duration"
Value="{Binding Path=duration, Mode=TwoWay}" />
                    </DataTemplate>
               </data:DataGridTemplateColumn.CellEditingTemplate>
          </data:DataGridTemplateColumn>
          <data:DataGridTemplateColumn Header="Calories"
HeaderStyle="{StaticResource DataGridColumnHeaderCentered}">
               <data:DataGridTemplateColumn.CellTemplate>
                    <DataTemplate>
                         <TextBlock Text="{Binding Path=calories}"
Style="{StaticResource DataGridTextBlockCentered}" />
                    </DataTemplate>
               </data:DataGridTemplateColumn.CellTemplate>
               <data:DataGridTemplateColumn.CellEditingTemplate>
                    <DataTemplate>
                         <TextBox Text="{Binding Path=calories,
Mode=TwoWay}" />
                    </DataTemplate>
               </data:DataGridTemplateColumn.CellEditingTemplate>
```

```
            </data:DataGridTemplateColumn>
            <data:DataGridTemplateColumn Header="Distance"
HeaderStyle="{StaticResource DataGridColumnHeaderCentered}">
                <data:DataGridTemplateColumn.CellTemplate>
                    <DataTemplate>
                        <TextBlock Text="{Binding Path=distance}"
Style="{StaticResource DataGridTextBlockCentered}" />
                    </DataTemplate>
                </data:DataGridTemplateColumn.CellTemplate>
                <data:DataGridTemplateColumn.CellEditingTemplate>
                    <DataTemplate>
                        <TextBox Text="{Binding Path=distance,
Mode=TwoWay}" />
                    </DataTemplate>
                </data:DataGridTemplateColumn.CellEditingTemplate>
            </data:DataGridTemplateColumn>
            <data:DataGridTemplateColumn Header="Incline"
HeaderStyle="{StaticResource DataGridColumnHeaderCentered}">
                <data:DataGridTemplateColumn.CellTemplate>
                    <DataTemplate>
                        <TextBlock Text="{Binding Path=incline}"
Style="{StaticResource DataGridTextBlockCentered}" />
                    </DataTemplate>
                </data:DataGridTemplateColumn.CellTemplate>
                <data:DataGridTemplateColumn.CellEditingTemplate>
                    <DataTemplate>
                        <TextBox Text="{Binding Path=incline,
Mode=TwoWay}" />
                    </DataTemplate>
                </data:DataGridTemplateColumn.CellEditingTemplate>
            </data:DataGridTemplateColumn>
            <data:DataGridTemplateColumn HeaderStyle="{StaticResource
DataGridColumnHeaderCheckBox}">
                <data:DataGridTemplateColumn.CellTemplate>
                    <DataTemplate>
                        <CheckBox x:Name="DeleteEntry"
Style="{StaticResource DataGridCheckBox}" />
                    </DataTemplate>
                </data:DataGridTemplateColumn.CellTemplate>
            </data:DataGridTemplateColumn>
        </data:DataGrid.Columns>
    </data:DataGrid>
```

Code snippet ExerciseLog.xaml

- **Weight training grid:** The next `DataGrid` to include in the page is the weight training grid. Only exercise log entries marked as weight training should appear in this grid. As you can see in the following XAML code, the weight training grid needs only a couple of custom column definitions for time, exercise name, reps, and weight:

```
<data:DataGrid x:Name="WeightTrainingLogGrid" Style="{StaticResource
DataGrid}" ItemsSource="{Binding Path=Data,
ElementName=WeightTrainingData}">
```

```
     <data:DataGrid.Columns>
          <data:DataGridTemplateColumn Header="Weight Training"
HeaderStyle="{StaticResource DataGridColumnHeaderCentered}">
               <data:DataGridTemplateColumn.CellTemplate>
                    <DataTemplate>
                         <TextBlock Text="{Binding
Path=Exercise.exercise_name}"
Style="{StaticResource DataGridTextBlockCentered}" />
                    </DataTemplate>
               </data:DataGridTemplateColumn.CellTemplate>
          </data:DataGridTemplateColumn>
          <data:DataGridTemplateColumn Header="Reps"
HeaderStyle="{StaticResource DataGridColumnHeaderCentered}">
               <data:DataGridTemplateColumn.CellTemplate>
                    <DataTemplate>
                         <TextBlock Text="{Binding Path=reps}"
Style="{StaticResource DataGridTextBlock}" />
                    </DataTemplate>
               </data:DataGridTemplateColumn.CellTemplate>
               <data:DataGridTemplateColumn.CellEditingTemplate>
                    <DataTemplate>
                         <TextBox Text="{Binding Path=reps,
Mode=TwoWay}" />
                    </DataTemplate>
               </data:DataGridTemplateColumn.CellEditingTemplate>
          </data:DataGridTemplateColumn>
          <data:DataGridTemplateColumn Header="Weight"
HeaderStyle="{StaticResource DataGridColumnHeaderCentered}">
               <data:DataGridTemplateColumn.CellTemplate>
                    <DataTemplate>
                         <TextBlock Text="{Binding Path=weight}"
Style="{StaticResource DataGridTextBlockCentered}" />
                    </DataTemplate>
               </data:DataGridTemplateColumn.CellTemplate>
               <data:DataGridTemplateColumn.CellEditingTemplate>
                    <DataTemplate>
                         <TextBox Text="{Binding Path=weight,
Mode=TwoWay}" />
                    </DataTemplate>
               </data:DataGridTemplateColumn.CellEditingTemplate>
          </data:DataGridTemplateColumn>
          <data:DataGridTemplateColumn HeaderStyle="{StaticResource
DataGridColumnHeaderCheckBox}">
               <data:DataGridTemplateColumn.CellTemplate>
                    <DataTemplate>
                         <CheckBox x:Name="DeleteEntry"
Style="{StaticResource DataGridCheckBox}" />
                    </DataTemplate>
               </data:DataGridTemplateColumn.CellTemplate>
          </data:DataGridTemplateColumn>
     </data:DataGrid.Columns>
</data:DataGrid>
```

Code snippet ExerciseLog.xaml

➤ **Activities grid:** The final `DataGrid` to add to the page is the activities grid. All exercises that are not marked as cardio or weight training will appear here. This includes any sports, daily activities, group exercise, and so on. The following is the XAML code for this final `DataGrid` control:

```
<data:DataGrid x:Name="ActivityLogGrid" Style="{StaticResource DataGrid}"
ItemsSource="{Binding Path=Data, ElementName=ActivityData}">
     <data:DataGrid.Columns>
          <data:DataGridTemplateColumn Header="Activities"
HeaderStyle="{StaticResource DataGridColumnHeaderCentered}">
               <data:DataGridTemplateColumn.CellTemplate>
                    <DataTemplate>
                         <TextBlock Text="{Binding
Path=Exercise.exercise_name}"
Style="{StaticResource DataGridTextBlockCentered}" />
                    </DataTemplate>
               </data:DataGridTemplateColumn.CellTemplate>
          </data:DataGridTemplateColumn>
          <data:DataGridTemplateColumn Header="Duration"
HeaderStyle="{StaticResource DataGridColumnHeaderCentered}">
               <data:DataGridTemplateColumn.CellTemplate>
                    <DataTemplate>
                         <TextBlock Text="{Binding Path=duration,
Converter={StaticResource DurationConverter}}" Style="{StaticResource
DataGridTextBlockCentered}" />
                    </DataTemplate>
               </data:DataGridTemplateColumn.CellTemplate>
               <data:DataGridTemplateColumn.CellEditingTemplate>
                    <DataTemplate>
                         <toolkit_input:TimePicker x:Name="Duration"
Value="{Binding Path=duration, Mode=TwoWay, Converter={StaticResource
DurationConverter}}" />
                    </DataTemplate>
               </data:DataGridTemplateColumn.CellEditingTemplate>
          </data:DataGridTemplateColumn>
          <data:DataGridTemplateColumn Header="Calories"
HeaderStyle="{StaticResource DataGridColumnHeaderCentered}">
               <data:DataGridTemplateColumn.CellTemplate>
                    <DataTemplate>
                         <TextBlock Text="{Binding Path=calories}"
Style="{StaticResource DataGridTextBlock}" />
                    </DataTemplate>
               </data:DataGridTemplateColumn.CellTemplate>
               <data:DataGridTemplateColumn.CellEditingTemplate>
                    <DataTemplate>
                         <TextBox Text="{Binding Path=calories,
Mode=TwoWay}" />
                    </DataTemplate>
               </data:DataGridTemplateColumn.CellEditingTemplate>
          </data:DataGridTemplateColumn>
          <data:DataGridTemplateColumn HeaderStyle="{StaticResource
DataGridColumnHeaderCheckBox}">
               <data:DataGridTemplateColumn.CellTemplate>
                    <DataTemplate>
```

```
                            <CheckBox x:Name="DeleteEntry"
Style="{StaticResource DataGridCheckBox}" />
                        </DataTemplate>
                    </data:DataGridTemplateColumn.CellTemplate>
                </data:DataGridTemplateColumn>
            </data:DataGrid.Columns>
        </data:DataGrid>
```

Code snippet ExerciseLog.xaml available

Using the DomainDataSource Control

With the DataGrid controls added to the page, you have to make a decision about the data binding implementation being used here. In the previous page, all the data binding logic was taken care of in the code behind using a DomainContext object directly. Although you could potentially implement the data binding here using the DomainContext directly, you would need to add quite a bit of custom code to filter the DataGrid controls appropriately so that they display the appropriate entries based on the type of exercise being logged.

Instead of going down that road, I am going to introduce you to a new control that is included with the WCF RIA Services Framework that makes for a much smoother implementation requiring minimal code in the code behind and providing built-in support for filtering, paging, sorting, and grouping. This new control is the DomainDataSource control, and it is one of the coolest new features of the WCF RIA Services Framework. ASP.NET developers have always had a wide array of data controls that could be used in ASP.NET pages to perform data binding functionality declaratively and with little code in the code behind page required. Most of these controls even provided built-in support for CRUD operations on data objects. With the DomainDataSource control, Silverlight developers finally have a similar solution to the traditional ASP.NET data binding controls. To get started with the DomainDataSource, you first need to add the following namespace declarations at the top of the exercise log page:

Available for download on Wrox.com

```
xmlns:ria_controls="clr-
     namespace:System.Windows.Controls;assembly=System.Windows.Controls.Ria"
xmlns:ria_data="clr-
     namespace:System.Windows.Data;assembly=System.Windows.Controls.Ria"
```

Code snippet ExerciseLog.xaml

You then should add a DomainDataSource control just below each of the DataGrid controls that were defined earlier, leaving you with this XAML code:

Available for download on Wrox.com

```
<data:DataGrid x:Name="CardioLogGrid" .>
<ria_controls:DomainDataSource x:Name="CardioData"
</ria_controls:DomainDataSource>

<data:DataGrid x:Name="WeightTrainingLogGrid" .>
<ria_controls:DomainDataSource x:Name="WeightTrainingData"
</ria_controls:DomainDataSource>
```

```
<data:DataGrid x:Name="ActivityLogGrid" .>
<ria_controls:DomainDataSource x:Name="ActivityData"
</ria_controls:DomainDataSource>
```

Code snippet ExerciseLog.xaml

After adding the `DomainDataSource` controls below each of the `DataGrid` controls, you now need to tell the control how to load the required data. The `DomainDataSource` relies on using an underlying `DomainContext` object that you include in the XAML declaration, as shown in the following code:

```
<ria_controls:DomainDataSource x:Name="CardioData"
     <ria_controls:DomainDataSource.DomainContext>
          <fitnesstrackerplus:ExerciseContext  />
     </ria_controls:DomainDataSource.DomainContext>
</ria_controls:DomainDataSource>

<ria_controls:DomainDataSource x:Name="WeightTrainingData"
     <ria_controls:DomainDataSource.DomainContext>
          <fitnesstrackerplus:ExerciseContext />
     </ria_controls:DomainDataSource.DomainContext>
</ria_controls:DomainDataSource>

<ria_controls:DomainDataSource x:Name="ActivityData"
     <ria_controls:DomainDataSource.DomainContext>
          <fitnesstrackerplus:ExerciseContext />
     </ria_controls:DomainDataSource.DomainContext>
</ria_controls:DomainDataSource>
```

Code snippet ExerciseLog.xaml

Now the `DomainDataSource` will instantiate a new `ExerciseContext` instance when the page is loaded. In addition to the `DomainContext`, you also need to specify the method that will be used to load the `DomainContext`. In this case, you want to assign the `GetExerciseLogEntries` as the `QueryMethod`:

```
<ria_controls:DomainDataSource x:Name="CardioData"
QueryName="GetExerciseLogEntries" AutoLoad="True"
     <ria_controls:DomainDataSource.DomainContext>
          <fitnesstrackerplus:ExerciseContext  />
     </ria_controls:DomainDataSource.DomainContext>
</ria_controls:DomainDataSource>

<ria_controls:DomainDataSource x:Name="WeightTrainingData"
QueryName="GetExerciseLogEntries" AutoLoad="True"
     <ria_controls:DomainDataSource.DomainContext>
          <fitnesstrackerplus:ExerciseContext />
     </ria_controls:DomainDataSource.DomainContext>
</ria_controls:DomainDataSource>

<ria_controls:DomainDataSource x:Name="ActivityData"
QueryName="GetExerciseLogEntries" AutoLoad="True"
     <ria_controls:DomainDataSource.DomainContext>
```

```
            <fitnesstrackerplus:ExerciseContext />
        </ria_controls:DomainDataSource.DomainContext>
    </ria_controls:DomainDataSource>
```

Code snippet ExerciseLog.xaml

By setting `AutoLoad` to true, the `DomainDataSource` will go ahead and perform the query automatically and load the requested entities into the underlying `DomainContext` when the page is loaded. With the `DomainDataSource` declaration complete you then need to modify the `DataGrid` controls to ensure that the `ItemsSource` property is bound to the data loaded by the `DomainDataSource` with the following code:

Available for download on Wrox.com

```
<data:DataGrid x:Name="CardioLogGrid" ItemsSource="{Binding Path=Data,
     ElementName=CardioData}">

<data:DataGrid x:Name="WeightTrainingLogGrid" ItemsSource="{Binding Path=Data,
     ElementName=WeightTrainingData}">

<data:DataGrid x:Name="ActivityLogGrid" ItemsSource="{Binding Path=Data,
     ElementName=ActivityData}">
```

Code snippet ExerciseLog.xaml

If the `GetExerciseLogEntries` method required no additional parameters, your work would be complete and loading the page would result in all three `DataGrid` controls being loaded with data from the `DomainDataSource`. In reality, because the `GetExerciseLogEntries` method actually requires both the ID of the current user and the entry date, the specified query method will fail. That being said, it would appear that there is still some additional work to complete in order to get this working for your solution. Let's start by taking a quick look at how the `DomainContext` is used in each of these `DomainDataSource` controls. Right now, each control has its own `DomainContext` defined. Because all three will effectively be loading data from the same table but filtering according to the requirements, you should be able to share a common `DomainContext` object across all three of the `DomainDataSource` controls. In order to do this, you need to add a new `ExerciseContext` to the `Page.Resources` section at the top of the page.

Available for download on Wrox.com

```
<navigation:Page.Resources>
     <fitnesstrackerplus:ExerciseContext x:Key="ExerciseContext" />
</navigation:Page.Resources>
```

Code snippet ExerciseLog.xaml

Next you need to modify all three `DomainDataSource` controls to point to this `ExerciseContext` instance in the XAML code:

Available for download on Wrox.com

```
<ria_controls:DomainDataSource x:Name="CardioData"
     QueryName="GetExerciseLogEntries" AutoLoad="True"
     DomainContext="{StaticResource ExerciseContext}"
</ria_controls:DomainDataSource>

<ria_controls:DomainDataSource x:Name="WeightTrainingData"
```

```
     QueryName="GetExerciseLogEntries" AutoLoad="True"
     DomainContext="{StaticResource ExerciseContext}"
</ria_controls:DomainDataSource>

<ria_controls:DomainDataSource x:Name="ActivityData"
     QueryName="GetExerciseLogEntries" AutoLoad="True"
     DomainContext="{StaticResource ExerciseContext}"
</ria_controls:DomainDataSource>
```

Code snippet ExerciseLog.xaml

By doing this, you ensure that all three controls will bind to the same `ExerciseContext` instance. Now you just need to configure the required parameters for the specified query method and set up the filtering so that each `DataGrid` displays only the exercise log entries for the specified exercise type. Configuring the `DomainDataSource` control to make use of custom parameters is not terribly difficult. The control can support custom parameters in the form of a `Parameter` or `ControlParameter` declaration. The entry date parameter is changed anytime a user selects a new date from the `GlobalCalendar` control. When a selection is made, you should refresh all of the `DataGrid` data to reflect the date chosen. This is a perfect candidate for a `ControlParameter`. All it takes is to add the `QueryParameters` declaration along with a new `ControlParameter` that assigns the `SelectedDate` property of the `GlobalCalendar` to the `entry_date` parameter of the `GetExerciseLogEntries` method. The `ControlParameter` also includes a `RefreshDataEvent` property that tells the `DomainDataSource` to reload its data when the specified control event is fired; in this case it would be the `SelectedDatesChanged` event on the `GlobalCalendar` control. Here is the XAML code for the `ControlParameter`:

Available for download on Wrox.com

```
<ria_controls:DomainDataSource x:Name="CardioData"
     QueryName="GetExerciseLogEntries" AutoLoad="True"
     DomainContext="{StaticResource ExerciseContext}"
<ria_controls:DomainDataSource.QueryParameters>
     <ria_control:ControlParameter ParameterName="entry_date"
ControlName="Calendar" PropertyName="SelectedDate"
RefreshEventName="SelectedDatesChanged" />
     </ria_controls:DomainDataSource.QueryParameters>
</ria_controls:DomainDataSource>

<ria_controls:DomainDataSource x:Name="WeightTrainingData"
     QueryName="GetExerciseLogEntries" AutoLoad="True"
     DomainContext="{StaticResource ExerciseContext}"
     <ria_control:ControlParameter ParameterName="entry_date"
ControlName="Calendar" PropertyName="SelectedDate"
RefreshEventName="SelectedDatesChanged" />
     </ria_controls:DomainDataSource.QueryParameters>
</ria_controls:DomainDataSource>

<ria_controls:DomainDataSource x:Name="ActivityData"
     QueryName="GetExerciseLogEntries" AutoLoad="True"
     DomainContext="{StaticResource ExerciseContext}"
     <ria_control:ControlParameter ParameterName="entry_date"
```

```
ControlName="Calendar" PropertyName="SelectedDate"
RefreshEventName="SelectedDatesChanged" />
     </ria_controls:DomainDataSource.QueryParameters>
</ria_controls:DomainDataSource>
```

Code snippet ExerciseLog.xaml

Ordinarily I would hold off on discussing code behind logic until the coverage for that section. However, I am making an exception in this case because I want you to completely understand how to get the `DomainDataSource` control working correctly in this particular scenario. Although the `DomainDataSource` control allows you to specify generic `Parameter` objects in the XAML, you can't really do that for the `user_id` parameter here. The `user_id` is available only from the static `Globals` class and because it's static, you won't be able to declare an instance of it in the `UserControl.Resources` section. It's not really a big deal, however, as you can just as easily add the parameter to the `QueryParameters` collection in the code behind, as shown here:

Available for download on Wrox.com

```
public partial class ExerciseLog: Page
{
     private ExerciseContext context = new ExerciseContext();

     public ExerciseLog()
     {
          InitializeComponent();

          Loaded += (s, e) =>
          {
               // Extract a copy of the shared
               // DomainContext from the Page.Resources

               context = this.Resources["ExerciseContext"] as ExerciseContext;

               Parameter user_id = new Parameter();
               user_id.ParameterName = "user_id";
               user_id.Value = Globals.CurrentUser.id;

               // Ensure that the user_id parameter is set for all
               // DomainDataSource controls before the query is executed

               CardioData.QueryParameters.Add(user_id);
               WeightTrainingData.QueryParameters.Add(user_id);
               ActivityData.QueryParameters.Add(user_id);

          };
     }
}
```

Code snippet ExerciseLog.xaml.cs

Once you add the new `Parameter` to the collection in the constructor, the call to `GetExerciseLogEntries` will succeed and all three `DataGrid` controls will be loaded, although at this point they will all contain the same exact data, just different column definitions. This, of course, is where the filtering feature of the `DomainDataSource` control comes in handy. Configuring the filtering feature is as simple as adding `FilterDescriptor` declarations to the `FilterDesecriptorCollection` of the `DomainDataSource` control. In most cases, you simply need to set the `PropertyPath` attribute to the property being filtered, set the `Value` attribute to the value to compare against, and finally set the `Operator` attribute to the one of the various comparison operators that is available. The `FilterDescriptor` supports several comparison operators including `Contains`, `IsEqualTo`, and `IsGreaterThanOrEqualTo`. The following code shows how each of the `DomainDataSource` controls has been configured for filtering on the exercise log page:

```
<ria_controls:DomainDataSource x:Name="CardioData"
     QueryName="GetExerciseLogEntries" AutoLoad="True"
     DomainContext="{StaticResource ExerciseContext}"
<ria_controls:DomainDataSource.QueryParameters>
     <ria_control:ControlParameter ParameterName="entry_date"
ControlName="Calendar" PropertyName="SelectedDate"
RefreshEventName="SelectedDatesChanged" />
     </ria_controls:DomainDataSource.QueryParameters>
     <ria_controls:DomainDataSource.FilterDescriptors>
          <ria_data:FilterDescriptorCollection>
               <ria_data:FilterDescriptor
PropertyPath="Exercise.ExerciseType.type_name" Operator="IsEqualTo"
Value="Cardio" />
          </ria_data:FilterDescriptorCollection>
     </ria_controls:DomainDataSource.FilterDescriptors>
</ria_controls:DomainDataSource>

<ria_controls:DomainDataSource x:Name="WeightTrainingData"
     QueryName="GetExerciseLogEntries" AutoLoad="True"
     DomainContext="{StaticResource ExerciseContext}"
     <ria_control:ControlParameter ParameterName="entry_date"
ControlName="Calendar" PropertyName="SelectedDate"
RefreshEventName="SelectedDatesChanged" />
     </ria_controls:DomainDataSource.QueryParameters>
     <ria_controls:DomainDataSource.FilterDescriptors>
          <ria_data:FilterDescriptorCollection>
               <ria_data:FilterDescriptor
PropertyPath="Exercise.ExerciseType.type_name" Operator="IsEqualTo"
Value="Weight Training" />
          </ria_data:FilterDescriptorCollection>
     </ria_controls:DomainDataSource.FilterDescriptors>
</ria_controls:DomainDataSource>

<ria_controls:DomainDataSource x:Name="ActivityData"
     QueryName="GetExerciseLogEntries" AutoLoad="True"
     DomainContext="{StaticResource ExerciseContext}"
     <ria_control:ControlParameter ParameterName="entry_date"
ControlName="Calendar" PropertyName="SelectedDate"
RefreshEventName="SelectedDatesChanged" />
     </ria_controls:DomainDataSource.QueryParameters>
<ria_controls:DomainDataSource.FilterDescriptors>
          <ria_data:FilterDescriptorCollection>
               <ria_data:FilterDescriptor
PropertyPath="Exercise.ExerciseType.type_name" Operator="IsEqualTo"
```

```
Value="Activity" />
          </ria_data:FilterDescriptorCollection>
     </ria_controls:DomainDataSource.FilterDescriptors>
</ria_controls:DomainDataSource>
```

Code snippet ExerciseLog.xaml

As you can see, each filter is set up to ensure that only the entries for the correct exercise type will appear in the `DataGrid` control. The beauty of this solution is that because you are sharing a `DomainContext` between all three of the controls, you don't have to worry about coordinating update and delete operations once you implement those features.

All the remaining elements of the user interface are basically the same as they were for the food log page. The `DataGrid` controls will still be using the `CheckBox` column so that users can select multiple rows when deleting entries. You will also still have a `CheckBox` control in the header of the delete column that will perform the Select/Deselect All logic as well. As far as the "Delete selected entries" `Button` control, when you get to the code behind everything should work the same way with the exception that instead of looking for selected items in one `DataGrid`, you will need to check all of the `DataGrid` controls before the call to `SubmitChanges` occurs.

Once all of the required controls are added to the user interface, you are left with the data entry screen shown in Figure 6-2.

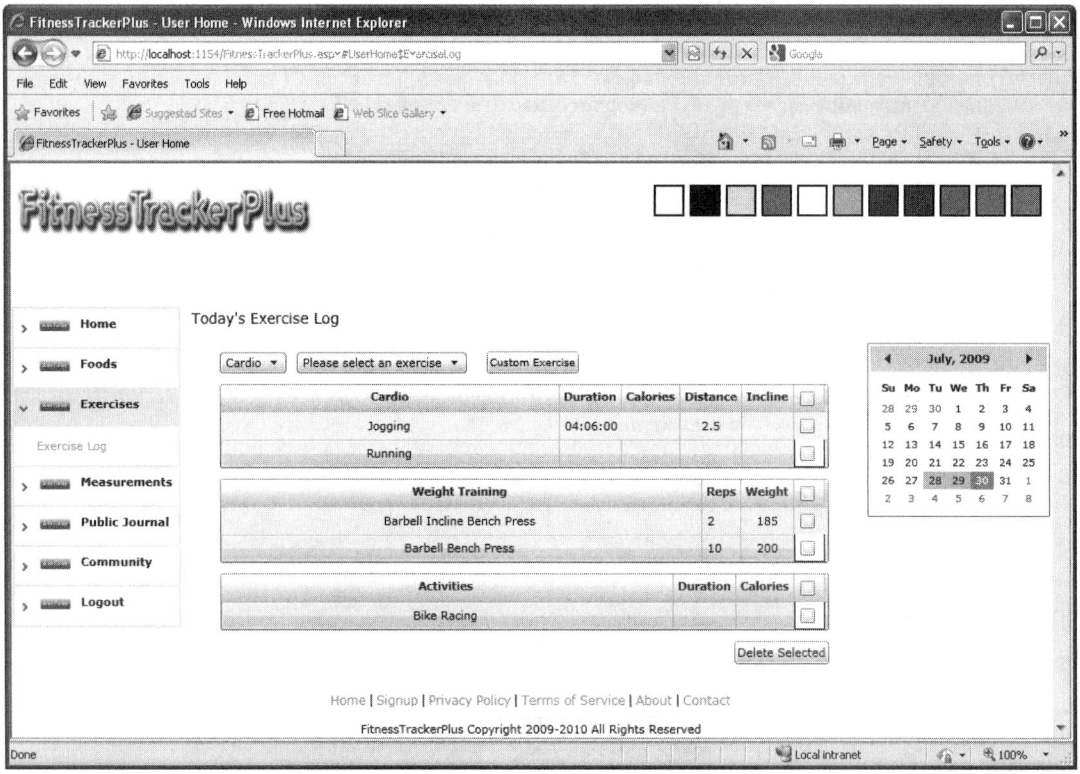

FIGURE 6-2

Database

The database design calls for the creation of the following new tables:

exercise_types, muscle_groups, exercises, exercises_muscle_groups, and finally exercise_logs. The exercise_types table should be pre-populated with the available exercise types, as shown in Table 6-7.

TABLE 6-7: Exercise Types

ID	TYPE_NAME	DESCRIPTION
1	Cardio	Cardio Exercises
2	Weight Training	Weight Training Exercises
3	Activities	Additional Activities

In addition to populating the exercise_types table, you also need to provide a default list of supported muscle groups. You won't be allowing users to add to this list so it should be populated manually and left alone. As you will see in the "Business Logic" section, you won't even expose methods for updating, inserting, or deleting from this or the exercise_types tables. These tables are basically being used to store constant values for exercise types and muscle groups. Table 6-8 shows how the muscle_groups table should be created.

TABLE 6-8: Muscle Groups

ID	GROUP_NAME
1	Neck
2	Shoulders
3	Chest
4	Arms
5	Abs
6	Legs
7	Back

Finally, because users will expect to select from a list of existing exercises, you also need to populate the exercises table. All you have to do is add a couple of hundred exercises to the table and that should be sufficient. Did that get your attention? Don't worry — I have already done that work and included some sample exercises in the exercises table of the supplied MDF file for this chapter. I have also added the appropriate entries in the exercises_muscle_groups table that associates the various weight training exercises with the corresponding muscle group.

After creating the tables, you then need to set up all of the required relationships, as shown in Figure 6-3.

Data Access

Just as you did with the food log page, you will need to add another LINQ to SQL classes file to the project in order to create the required business objects for this page. To get this working, you should add a new LINQ to SQL classes file to the Data folder of the ASP.NET project and call it Exercises.dbml. Once the file is created, you then need to drag all of the newly created exercise tables onto the design surface, as shown in Figure 6-4.

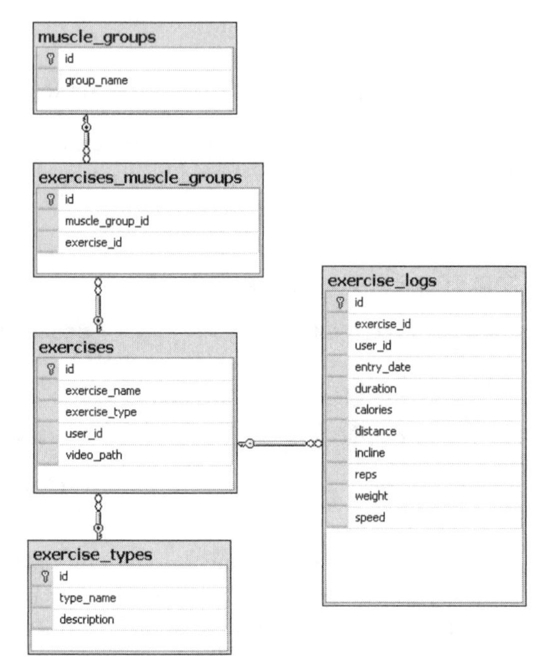

FIGURE 6-3

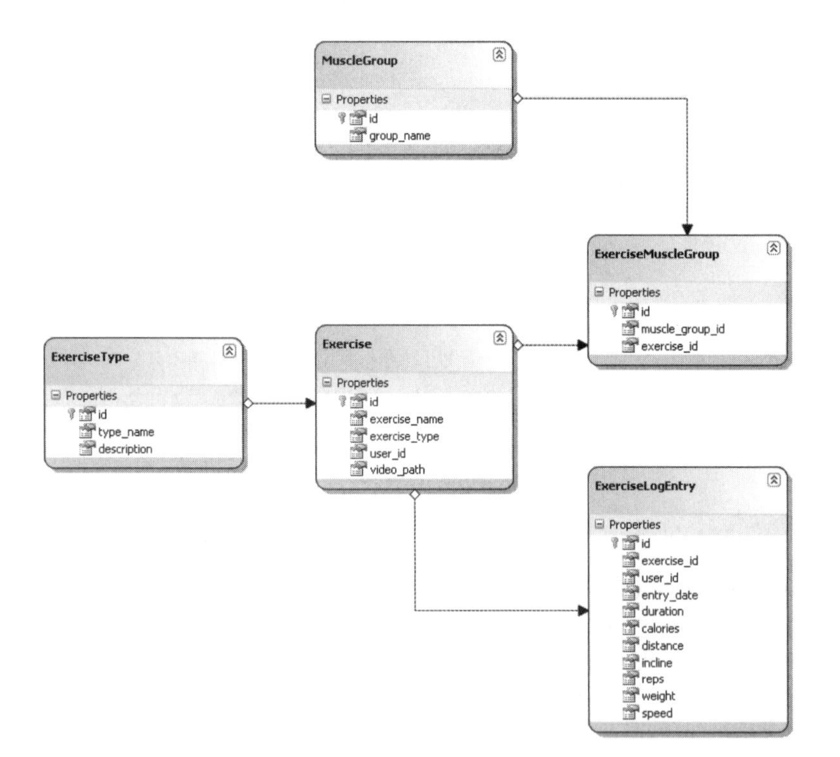

FIGURE 6-4

Finally you should save and rebuild the ASP.NET project in order to generate the required data access entity classes.

Business Logic

The business logic for this page will require the creation of a new `DomainService` called `ExerciseService`. Now typically you have been exposing all of the available entities and providing complete CRUD capabilities for them in the domain services that you have created up to this point. For the exercise service, however, there are some tables that need only read access enabled for the client with other operations disabled. For example, the exercise_types and muscle_groups tables are not expected to change, and users should not be allowed to create, update, or delete from either of these two tables. In order to restrict these operations, you just need to ensure that the "Enable editing" option is not selected for those entities, as shown in Figure 6-5.

FIGURE 6-5

The ExerciseService Class

Let's take a look at some important methods of the `ExerciseService`. When the exercise log page loads, both the `ExerciseTypes` and `MuscleGroups` `ComboBox` controls need to be loaded with a list of default exercise types and muscle groups to select from. The `ExerciseService` provides both a `GetExerciseTypes` and `GetMuscleGroups` method, as shown in the following code, which will be used by clients to populate their respective `ComboBox` controls:

Available for download on Wrox.com

```
public IQueryable<ExerciseType> GetExerciseTypes()
{
     List<ExerciseType> exerciseTypes =
this.DataContext.ExerciseTypes.ToList<ExerciseType>();
     exerciseTypes.Insert(0, new ExerciseType { id = -1,
type_name = "Please select an exercise type" });

     return exerciseTypes.AsQueryable<ExerciseType>();
}

public IQueryable<MuscleGroup> GetMuscleGroups()
{
     List<MuscleGroup> muscleGroups =
this.DataContext.MuscleGroups.ToList<MuscleGroup>();
     muscleGroups.Insert(0, new MuscleGroup { id = -1,
group_name = "Please select a muscle group" });

     return muscleGroups.AsQueryable<MuscleGroup>();
}
```

Code snippet ExerciseService.cs

> *Note how an additional object is inserted into each of the collections before being returned to the client. This object will always have an ID less than zero to distinguish it from real items retrieved from the database. The purpose of this is to present some direction to the user after the* `ComboBox` *controls are populated. It is not always obvious to users what they need to do when presented with a bunch of* `ComboBox` *controls; add to that the fact that after data binding occurs, the* `ComboBox` *behavior is to not automatically provide a default selection, and you may have a good recipe for user interface confusion. I always like making use of this technique because it becomes simple to provide guidance to the user, and after the data binding occurs you simply have to set the* `SelectedIndex` *property to zero and the custom message is displayed.*

Now of course you have to filter this instructional value in any `SelectionChanged` event handler to make sure that you don't actually try to use the value in any code behind logic. Because the list of exercise types and muscle groups is static and should not be altered by users, you did not select the "Enable editing" option when creating the `ExerciseService`. Because of this there are no other methods generated by the wizard for these entities.

Once users make a selection from the `ExerciseType` or `MuscleGroup` `ComboBox` controls they will then need to select an exercise to add to the exercise log. Because you are supporting the creation of custom exercises, you will need to have methods for all CRUD operations on the `Exercise` type. Instead of just retrieving all exercises in the database, however, you need to break this action down into two separate methods. You will need a query method for retrieving exercises by exercise type as well as a method for retrieving exercises by a specified muscle group.

The first method, `GetExercisesByType`, performs a LINQ-based query to retrieve any exercises that are default or custom, and are associated with the specified exercise type. The next method, `GetExercisesByMuscleGroup`, performs another LINQ query to retrieve any exercises matching both the "Weight Training" exercise type from the exercise_types table, as well as the specified muscle group. In order to perform the query, a LINQ-based join statement is needed as you will need to query the `ExercisesMuscleGroups` join table to find exercises associated with the specified muscle group. Here is the code for both of these exercise retrieval methods:

Available for download on Wrox.com

```
public IQueryable<Exercise> GetExercisesByType(int user_id, int exercise_type)
{
     List<Exercise> exercises = (from c in this.DataContext.Exercises
                                 where (c.user_id == 1 || c.user_id == user_id) &&
                                 c.exercise_type == exercise_type
                                 orderby c.exercise_name ascending
                                 select c).ToList<Exercise>();

     exercises.Insert(0, new Exercise
                                {
                                     id = -1,
                                     exercise_name = "Please select an
exercise"
                                });

     return exercises.AsQueryable<Exercise>();
```

```
}

public IQueryable<Exercise> GetExercisesByMuscleGroup(int user_id,
int muscle_group)
{
     List<Exercise> exercises = (from c in this.DataContext.Exercises
                                 join d in this.DataContext.ExerciseMuscleGroups
                                 on c.id equals d.exercise_id
                                 where (c.ExerciseType.type_name ==
                                        "Weight Training" &&
                                       (c.user_id == 1 || c.user_id == user_id) &&
                                        d.muscle_group_id == muscle_group)
                                       orderby c.exercise_name ascending
                                       select c).ToList<Exercise>();

     exercises.Insert(0, new Exercise
                            {
                                 id = -1,
                                 exercise_name = "Please select an
exercise"
                            });

     return exercises.AsQueryable<Exercise>();
}
```

Code snippet ExerciseService.cs

Both of these methods make use of the technique described earlier for adding an additional record to the retrieved collection of entities that will instruct the user to make a selection in the bound `ComboBox` control. Because you are also supporting custom exercises created by users, you will also need to include the following insert, update, and delete methods:

Available for download on Wrox.com

```
public void InsertExercise(Exercise exercise)
{
     this.DataContext.Exercises.InsertOnSubmit(exercise);
}

public void UpdateExercise(Exercise currentExercise)
{
     this.DataContext.Exercises.Attach(currentExercise,
this.ChangeSet.GetOriginal(currentExercise));
}

public void DeleteExercise(Exercise exercise)
{
     this.DataContext.Exercises.Attach(exercise);
     this.DataContext.Exercises.DeleteOnSubmit(exercise);
}

public void InsertExerciseMuscleGroups(ExerciseMuscleGroup exerciseMuscleGroup)
{
     this.DataContext.ExerciseMuscleGroups.InsertOnSubmit(exerciseMuscleGroup);
}
```

Code snippet ExerciseService.cs

The `InsertExerciseMuscleGroups` method is included in this list because if a user creates a new weight training custom exercise you will need an additional record in this table to associate the newly created exercise with the specified muscle group.

Retrieving the Exercise Log Entries

The ExerciseService class will also be responsible for providing the client with CRUD methods for the exercise log entries. In the following code, the default implementations are used for the Insert, Update, and Delete operations.

Available for download on Wrox.com

```
public void InsertExerciseLogEntry(ExerciseLogEntry exerciseLogEntry)
{
     this.DataContext.ExerciseLogEntries.InsertOnSubmit(exerciseLogEntry);
}

public void UpdateExerciseLogEntry(ExerciseLogEntry currentExerciseLogEntry)
{
     this.DataContext.ExerciseLogEntries.Attach(currentExerciseLogEntry,
this.ChangeSet.GetOriginal(currentExerciseLogEntry));
}

public void DeleteExerciseLogEntry(ExerciseLogEntry exerciseLogEntry)
{
     this.DataContext.ExerciseLogEntries.Attach(exerciseLogEntry);
     this.DataContext.ExerciseLogEntries.DeleteOnSubmit(exerciseLogEntry);
}
```

Code snippet ExerciseService.cs

In order to properly filter the exercise log entries into the appropriate `DataGrid` controls, you need to ensure that both the `Exercise` and `ExerciseType` properties are returned in the `ExerciseLogEntry` object. Just as you did in that case, you need to create a custom `DataLoadOptions` instance that specifies the additional entities that need to be returned. The following code shows the `GetExerciseLogEntries` implementation that includes the additional `DataLoadOptions`.

Available for download on Wrox.com

```
public IQueryable<ExerciseLogEntry> GetExerciseLogEntries(DateTime entry_date,
int user_id)
{
     DataLoadOptions options = new DataLoadOptions();

     options.LoadWith<Exercise>(e => e.ExerciseType);
     options.LoadWith<ExerciseLogEntry>(e => e.Exercise);
     this.DataContext.LoadOptions = options;

     return this.DataContext.ExerciseLogEntries.Where(e => e.user_id == user_id &&
e.entry_date.Date == entry_date.Date);
}
```

Code snippet ExerciseService.cs

Don't forget that you also need to add the `[Include]` attribute to both the `Exercise` entity of the `ExerciseLogEntry` class as well as the `ExerciseType` entity of the `Exercise` class, as shown in the following code:

Available for download on Wrox.com

```
[MetadataTypeAttribute(typeof(Exercise.ExerciseMetadata))]
public partial class Exercise
{
    internal sealed class ExerciseMetadata
    {
        // Metadata classes are not meant to be instantiated.
        private ExerciseMetadata()
        {
        }

        [Include]
        public ExerciseType ExerciseType;
    }
}

[MetadataTypeAttribute(typeof(ExerciseLogEntry.ExerciseLogEntryMetadata))]
public partial class ExerciseLogEntry
{
    internal sealed class ExerciseLogEntryMetadata
    {
        // Metadata classes are not meant to be instantiated.
        private ExerciseLogEntryMetadata()
        {
        }

        [Include]
        public Exercise Exercise;

    }
}
```

Code snippet ExerciseService.metadata.cs

The final area of business logic required here is to ensure that the `GlobalCalendar` style can update its calendar days to reflect valid log entry dates. In the previous chapter, you created a custom style selector that was used by the `GlobalCalendar` to style dates that are associated with valid log dates differently from dates with no entries. It won't make much sense to use the same class for the exercise or measurement log pages so each page will require its own `CalendarDayButtonStyleSelector` implementation. This means that the `ExerciseService` will also need a service operation that returns dates that have log entries associated with them. For the exercise log page, you will create a new class called `ValidExerciseLogDateSelector` and place it in the Utility folder of the Silverlight project. It will have its own collection of valid dates just like the `ValidExerciseLogDateSelector` did and will call the `GetLogEntryDates` of the `ExerciseService` shown here:

Available for download on Wrox.com

```
[Invoke]
public List<DateTime> GetLogEntryDates(int user_id)
{
    List<DateTime> dates = new List<DateTime>();

    var entries = from c in this.DataContext.ExerciseLogEntries
```

```
                    where c.user_id == user_id
                    select c.entry_date;

        foreach (DateTime date in entries)
        {
            if (!dates.Contains(date.Date))
                dates.Add(date);
        }

        return dates;
    }
```

Code snippet ExerciseService.cs

User Interface Code Behind

With the business logic complete, it's once again time to turn your attention to the user interface code behind implementation. As usual, the best place to start is to take a look at what happens when the page is first loaded. To start, you need to ensure that the user can create new exercise log entries. Users will start off by selecting an exercise type, followed by an exercise. If the user selects a weight training exercise, then the muscle group's `ComboBox` should be made visible so that the user can filter exercises by the selected muscle group. In order for this to work you need to populate the exercise types and muscle groups by making use of the `GetExerciseTypes` and `GetMuscleGroups` methods of the `ExerciseContext`, as shown in the following code:

Available for download on Wrox.com

```
context = this.Resources["ExerciseContext"] as ExerciseContext;

context.Load<ExerciseType>(context.GetExerciseTypesQuery(),
LoadBehavior.RefreshCurrent, (ExerciseTypesLoaded) =>
    {
        if (!ExerciseTypesLoaded.HasError)
        {
            ExerciseTypes.ItemsSource = ExerciseTypesLoaded.Entities;
            ExerciseTypes.SelectedIndex = 0;
        }

    }, null);

context.Load<MuscleGroup>(context.GetMuscleGroupsQuery(),
LoadBehavior.RefreshCurrent, (MuscleGroupsLoaded) =>
    {
        if (!MuscleGroupsLoaded.HasError)
        {
            MuscleGroups.ItemsSource = MuscleGroupsLoaded.Entities;
            MuscleGroups.SelectedIndex = 0;
        }

    }, null);

Exercises.ItemsSource = context.Exercises;
```

Code snippet ExerciseLog.xaml.cs

Remember that you already have an `ExerciseContext` that you can use sitting in the `Page.Resources` section. You should continue using that instance for any interactions you need to have with the `ExerciseService`.

Implementing the ProgressBar Control

I typically like to show a `ProgressBar` control to users whenever any potentially long running operation is being performed so that users don't sit around wondering what's happening to the user interface. In the food log page you used a `ProgressBar` with the `IsIndeterminate` property set to true. You will use the same type of `ProgressBar` on this page as well. In the food log page, you had to toggle the `Visibility` property of the `ProgressBar` before and after any load operations in order to display the status to the user. On this page, you will use a different technique to display the `ProgressBar`. Instead of toggling the visibility in various calls to the `Load<T>` method, you will instead use the new element-to-element binding supported by Silverlight. The `DomainContext` object has an `IsLoading` property that you can actually bind the `ProgressBar` to. By doing so any time the `DomainContext` is performing a load operation, the `ProgressBar` will automatically be displayed without any additional code on your part. Here is the code to set up the binding between the `Visibility` property of the `ProgressBar` and the `IsLoading` property of the `DomainContext`:

Available for download on Wrox.com

```
Binding binding = new Binding();
binding.Source = context;
binding.Path = new PropertyPath("IsLoading");
binding.Converter = new ProgressBarVisibilityConverter();

ProgressBar.SetBinding(ProgressBar.VisibilityProperty, binding);
```

Code snippet ExerciseLog.xaml.cs

Because the `Visibility` property does not directly translate into a `bool` type property, you need to make use of another `IValueConverter` class to perform the translation. In this case, you add a new class called `ProgressBarVisibilityConverter` to the `Converters` folder in the Silverlight project and add the following code shown in Listing 6-1:

LISTING 6-1: ProgressBarVisibilityConverter.cs

Available for download on Wrox.com

```
using System;
using System.Windows;
using System.Windows.Data;

namespace FitnessTrackerPlus.Converters
{
     public class ProgressBarVisibilityConverter: IValueConverter
     {

#region IValueConverter Members

          public object Convert(object value, Type targetType, object parameter,
System.Globalization.CultureInfo culture)
          {
```

continues

LISTING 6-1 *(continued)*

```
                bool isLoading = (bool)value;

                return (isLoading == true ? Visibility.Visible:
Visibility.Collapsed);
            }

            public object ConvertBack(object value, Type targetType,
object parameter, System.Globalization.CultureInfo culture)
            {
                throw new NotImplementedException();
            }

#endregion
    }
}
```

Creating New Exercise Log Entries

After getting all that squared away, you need to turn your attention to actually creating new exercise log entries. Once the exercise types and muscle groups `ComboBox` controls are populated, you need to write some code to handle the `SelectionChanged` event in order to populate the `Exercises` `ComboBox` with appropriate exercises. In the case of the exercise types `ComboBox` if the weight training type is selected then the muscle groups `ComboBox` needs to be made visible; otherwise, just retrieve the list of exercises for the selected type using the `GetExercisesByType` query, as shown in the following code:

Available for download on Wrox.com

```
ExerciseTypes.SelectionChanged += (se, ev) =>
{
    ExerciseType selectedType = ExerciseTypes.SelectedItem as ExerciseType;

    if (selectedType.id > 0)
    {
        if (selectedType.type_name == "Weight Training")
        {
            MuscleGroups.Visibility = Visibility.Visible;
            Exercises.Visibility = Visibility.Collapsed;
        }
        else
        {
            context.Load<FitnessTrackerPlus.Web.Data.Exercise>(
context.GetExercisesByTypeQuery(Globals.CurrentUser.id, selectedType.id),
LoadBehavior.RefreshCurrent, (ExercisesLoaded) =>
                {
                    if (!ExercisesLoaded.HasError)
                        Exercises.Visibility = Visibility.Visible;

                }, null);

            MuscleGroups.Visibility = Visibility.Collapsed;
```

```
            }
        }
        else
        {
            MuscleGroups.Visibility = Visibility.Collapsed;
            Exercises.Visibility = Visibility.Collapsed;
        }
};
```

Code snippet ExerciseLog.xaml.cs

The same basic technique applies to the muscle groups `ComboBox` with the only difference being that the `GetExercisesByMuscleGroup` query should be used instead:

Available for download on Wrox.com

```
MuscleGroups.SelectionChanged += (se, ev) =>
{
    MuscleGroup selectedGroup = MuscleGroups.SelectedItem as MuscleGroup;

    if (selectedGroup.id > 0)
    {
        context.Load<FitnessTrackerPlus.Web.Data.Exercise>(
context.GetExercisesByMuscleGroupQuery(Globals.CurrentUser.id, selectedGroup.id),
LoadBehavior.RefreshCurrent, (ExercisesLoaded) =>
                {
                    if (!ExercisesLoaded.HasError)
                        Exercises.Visibility = Visibility.Visible;

                }, null);
    }
    else
        Exercises.Visibility = Visibility.Collapsed;
};
```

Code snippet ExerciseLog.xaml.cs

> *Note that in both cases you should set the* `LoadBehavior` *to* `RefreshCurrent`*. This needs to be done to ensure that the list of exercises cleared of existing values before repopulating. If you fail to set this option, the list of exercises will just continue to grow depending on the exercise type or muscle group selection. For example, if a user selects cardio exercises, the* `Exercises ComboBox` *control will be filled with cardio type exercises. Because by default the* `LoadBehavior` *for* `Load` *calls is set to* `KeepCurrent`*, if the user then selected the activities exercise type, the list of activities would be appended to the list of exercises and now the* `Exercises ComboBox` *would display exercises for both exercise types, which is not what you want here.*

You're now at the point where users should be able to select an exercise to add to the log. You need a couple of things to make this happen:

- A method that will actually create the new exercise log entry. The method for creating new exercise log entries is called none other than `CreateExerciseLogEntry` and takes an `Exercise` object as its only parameter.
- A `SelectionChanged` event handler for the `Exercises ComboBox` that will pass the selected exercise to that method.

```
private void CreateExerciseLogEntry(FitnessTrackerPlus.Web.Data.Exercise
exercise)
{
     ExerciseLogEntry entry = new ExerciseLogEntry();

     // Setup new exercise log entry with selected date, exercise
     // and current user

     entry.exercise_id = exercise.id;
     entry.entry_date = Globals.SelectedDate;
     entry.user_id = Globals.CurrentUser.id;

     context.ExerciseLogEntries.Add(entry);
     context.SubmitChanges((ChangesSubmitted) =>
          {
               if (!ChangesSubmitted.HasError)
               {
                    if (exercise.ExerciseType.type_name == "Cardio")
                         CardioData.Load();
                    else if (exercise.ExerciseType.type_name ==
"Weight Training")
                         WeightTrainingData.Load();
                    else
                         ActivityData.Load();
               }

          }, null);
}
```

Code snippet ExerciseLog.xaml.cs

There isn't much to the method other than making sure the `exercise_id`, `entry_date`, and `user_id` parameters are set up correctly. Then you simply add the new entry to the `ExerciseLogEntries EntityList` on the `ExerciseContext`. After the call to `SubmitChanges` is complete, you need to take a peek at the type of exercise that was loaded so that rather than refresh all three `DomainDataSource` objects, you will need to refresh only the one containing the new entry. With this method ready to go, all you need to do is handle the `SelectionChanged` event of the `Exercises ComboBox`, passing in the selected exercise as shown.

```
Exercises.SelectionChanged += (se, ev) =>
{
     FitnessTrackerPlus.Web.Data.Exercise selectedExercise =
```

```
Exercises.SelectedItem as FitnessTrackerPlus.Web.Data.Exercise;

     if( selectedExercise.id > 0 )
          CreateExerciseLogEntry(selectedExercise);
};
```

Code snippet ExerciseLog.xaml.cs

That takes care of creating exercise log entries using one of the default exercises — now what about custom exercises?

Supporting Custom Exercises

In order to provide the ability for users to create custom exercises, you need to add a new `UserControl` called `CustomExercise` to the Exercise folder of the Silverlight project. Once the control is created you need to add a `DataForm` and some customized `DataField` templates. Listing 6-2 shows the XAML for the `CustomExercise` control:

Available for download on Wrox.com

LISTING 6-2: CustomExercise.xaml

```
<UserControl x:Class="FitnessTrackerPlus.Views.Exercise.CustomExercise"
     xmlns="http://schemas.microsoft.com/winfx/2006/xaml/presentation"
     xmlns:x="http://schemas.microsoft.com/winfx/2006/xaml"
     xmlns:data_dataform="clr-namespace:System.Windows.Controls;
assembly=System.Windows.Controls.Data.DataForm.Toolkit">
     <UserControl.Resources>
          <Style x:Key="CustomExerciseFormStyle"
TargetType="data_dataform:DataForm">
               <Setter Property="AutoEdit" Value="True" />
               <Setter Property="AutoGenerateFields" Value="False" />
               <Setter Property="Foreground" Value="#FF000000" />
          </Style>
          <Style x:Key="LargeTextBoxStyle" TargetType="TextBox">
               <Setter Property="FontSize" Value="10" />
               <Setter Property="TextAlignment" Value="Center" />
               <Setter Property="Width" Value="200" />
          </Style>
     </UserControl.Resources>
     <data_dataform:DataForm x:Name="CustomExerciseForm"
Style="{StaticResource CustomExerciseFormStyle}">
          <data_dataform:DataForm.EditTemplate>
               <DataTemplate>
                    <StackPanel>
                         <data_dataform:DataField>
                              <TextBox Text="{Binding Path=exercise_name,
Mode=TwoWay}" Style="{StaticResource LargeTextBoxStyle}" />
                         </data_dataform:DataField>
                         <data_dataform:DataField>
                              <ComboBox x:Name="ExerciseTypes"
DisplayMemberPath="type_name" />
                         </data_dataform:DataField>
```

continues

LISTING 6-2 *(continued)*

```
                        <data_dataform:DataField>
                            <ComboBox x:Name="MuscleGroups"
DisplayMemberPath="group_name" />
                        </data_dataform:DataField>
                    </StackPanel>
                </DataTemplate>
            </data_dataform:DataForm.EditTemplate>
        </data_dataform:DataForm>
</UserControl>
```

When users create new custom exercises, you want to make sure that they associate one of the available exercise types to it. Also, if they are creating a weight training exercise, a muscle group association should be made. In order to ensure that the user not only supplies a name for the exercise but also makes a valid selection for the exercise type, you should add a couple of new validation rules to the metadata file for the `ExerciseService`, as shown in the following code:

Available for download on Wrox.com

```
[MetadataTypeAttribute(typeof(Exercise.ExerciseMetadata))]
public partial class Exercise
{
    internal sealed class ExerciseMetadata
    {
        // Metadata classes are not meant to be instantiated.
        private ExerciseMetadata()
        {
        }

        [Required]
        [Display(Name = "Exercise Name:")]
        public string exercise_name;

        [Required]
        [Range(1,3, ErrorMessage = "You must select an exercise type")]
        public int exercise_type;

        public EntitySet<ExerciseLogEntry> ExerciseLogEntries;

        public EntitySet<ExerciseMuscleGroup> ExerciseMuscleGroups;

        [Include]
        public ExerciseType ExerciseType;

        public int id;

        [Required]
        public int user_id;

    }
}
```

Code snippet ExerciseService.metadata.cs

When the custom exercise control is first loaded, you need to set the `CurrentItem` property of the `DataForm` to a new `Exercise` object. You also should hide any of the command buttons because this form will be used for creating new exercises only.

```
CustomExerciseForm.CommandButtonsVisibility =
DataFormCommandButtonsVisibility.Commit |
DataFormCommandButtonsVisibility.Cancel;
CustomExerciseForm.CurrentItem = new FitnessTrackerPlus.Web.Data.Exercise {
user_id = Globals.CurrentUser.id };
```

Code snippet CustomExercise.xaml.cs

In the `DataForm` declaration you aren't binding the list of exercise types or muscle groups to any property of the `Exercise` object. This is partly because the `Exercise` object does not really have anything that will map to a list of all available exercise types and muscle groups. Still, you need to find a way to populate these lists somehow. In order to get this to work, you need to manually bind these controls to the appropriate collections. However, if you try and access them directly you will notice that they are not available in the IntelliSense window. The trick to accessing these controls or any controls declared in a custom `DataField` template is to hook into the `ContentLoaded` event of the `DataForm` and make use of the `FindNameInContent` method. As long as you make the call to `FindNameInContent` in the `ContentLoaded` event handler you should have no problem grabbing a handle to the instance of these controls. Once you have that, you can use an `ExerciseContext` to actually populate the `ComboBox` controls, as shown in the following code:

Available for download on Wrox.com

```
        private void CustomExerciseForm_ContentLoaded(object sender,
DataFormContentLoadEventArgs e)

private void CustomExerciseForm_ContentLoaded(object sender,
DataFormContentLoadEventArgs e)
{
     ComboBox exerciseTypes =
CustomExerciseForm.FindNameInContent("ExerciseTypes") as ComboBox;
     ComboBox muscleGroups =
CustomExerciseForm.FindNameInContent("MuscleGroups") as ComboBox;

     context.Load<ExerciseType>(context.GetExerciseTypesQuery(),
LoadBehavior.RefreshCurrent, (ExerciseTypesLoaded) =>
          {
               if (!ExerciseTypesLoaded.HasError)
               {
                    exerciseTypes.ItemsSource = ExerciseTypesLoaded.Entities;
                    exerciseTypes.SelectedIndex = 0;
               }

          }, null);

     context.Load<MuscleGroup>(context.GetMuscleGroupsQuery(),
LoadBehavior.RefreshCurrent, (MuscleGroupsLoaded) =>
          {
               if (!MuscleGroupsLoaded.HasError)
               {
                    muscleGroups.ItemsSource = MuscleGroupsLoaded.Entities;
                    muscleGroups.SelectedIndex = 0;
```

```
                }

            }, null);

        exerciseTypes.SelectionChanged += (sev, eve) =>
            {
                ExerciseType selected = exerciseTypes.SelectedItem as
    ExerciseType;

                if (selected != null)
                {
                    if (selected.id > 0)
                    {
                        if (selected.type_name == "Weight Training")
                            muscleGroups.Visibility = Visibility.Visible;
                        else
                            muscleGroups.Visibility = Visibility.Collapsed;
                    }
                    else
                        muscleGroups.Visibility = Visibility.Collapsed;

                    // The exercise_type field is required so you must
                    // set this in order to pass validation

                    if (select.id > 0)

                     (CustomExerciseForm.CurrentItem as
    FitnessTrackerPlus.Web.Data.Exercise).exercise_type =
    selected.id;
                }
            };

        muscleGroups.SelectionChanged += (sev, eve) => { selectedGroup =
    muscleGroups.SelectedItem as MuscleGroup; };
    }
```

Code snippet CustomExercise.xaml.cs

Once the user is finished entering the custom exercise details, you will need to actually create the exercise in the database and, just as you did when providing support for custom foods, you should fire an event to the hosting control so that a new exercise log entry can also be created using the new custom food. Once again, in order to create the new custom food, you should handle the `EditEnded` event of the `DataForm` as shown:

Available for download on Wrox.com

```
public delegate void CustomFoodCreatedEventHandler(object sender,
CustomExerciseCreatedEventArgs e);

public event CustomFoodCreatedEventHandler CustomExerciseCreated;
public event EventHandler CustomExerciseCanceled;

CustomExerciseForm.EditEnded += new
EventHandler<DataFormEditEndedEventArgs>(CustomExerciseForm_EditEnded);

private void CustomExerciseForm_EditEnded(object sender,
```

```
DataFormEditEndedEventArgs e)
{
     if (e.EditAction == DataFormEditAction.Cancel &&
CustomExerciseCanceled != null)
CustomExerciseCanceled(this, null);
     else
     {
          if (CustomExerciseForm.ValidateItem())
          {
               // If validation succeeds then add
               // the exercise to the database

               context.Exercises.Add(CustomExerciseForm.CurrentItem as
FitnessTrackerPlus.Web.Data.Exercise);
               context.SubmitChanges((ExerciseSubmitted) =>
                    {
                         if (!ExerciseSubmitted.HasError)
                         {
                              // If the exercise was a weight training exercise we
                              // need to add an entry to the
                              // exercises_muscle_groups table

                              FitnessTrackerPlus.Web.Data.Exercise customExercise =
CustomExerciseForm.CurrentItem as FitnessTrackerPlus.Web.Data.Exercise;

                              if (customExercise.ExerciseType.type_name ==
"Weight Training")
                              {
                                   ExerciseMuscleGroup exerciseMuscleGroup = new
ExerciseMuscleGroup { muscle_group_id = selectedGroup.id, exercise_id =
customExercise.id };

                                   context.ExerciseMuscleGroups.Add(
exerciseMuscleGroup);
                                   context.SubmitChanges((
ExerciseMuscleGroupSubmitted) =>
                                        {
                                             if (
!ExerciseMuscleGroupSubmitted.HasError)
                                             {
                                                  if (CustomExerciseCreated !=
null)
                                                       CustomExerciseCreated(this,
New CustomExerciseCreatedEventArgs(customExercise));
                                             }

                                        }, null);
                              }
                              else
                              {
                                   if( CustomExerciseCreated != null )
                                        CustomExerciseCreated(this, new
CustomExerciseCreatedEventArgs(customExercise));
                              }
```

```
                        }

                    }, null);
                }
            }
        }

        public class CustomExerciseCreatedEventArgs
        {
            private FitnessTrackerPlus.Web.Data.Exercise custom_exercise = null;

            public CustomExerciseCreatedEventArgs() { }
            public CustomExerciseCreatedEventArgs(FitnessTrackerPlus.Web.Data.Exercise
        custom_exercise)
            {
                this.custom_exercise = custom_exercise;
            }

            public FitnessTrackerPlus.Web.Data.Exercise CreatedExercise
            {
                get
                {
                    return custom_exercise;
                }
            }
        }
```

Code snippet CustomExercise.xaml.cs

In order to use the `CustomExercise` control from the `ExerciseLog` page, you must add an event handler for the `Click` event of the custom exercise button. In this event handler, you just create a new instance of a `CustomExercise` control and display it in a new modal `ChildWindow`.

Available for download on Wrox.com

```
CustomExercise.Click += new RoutedEventHandler(CustomExercise_Click);

private void CustomExercise_Click(object sender, RoutedEventArgs e)
{
    // Show a modal dialog with the create custom exercise form

    ChildWindow modalWindow = new ChildWindow();
    CustomExercise customExercise = new CustomExercise();

    customExercise.CustomExerciseCanceled += (s, ev) => { modalWindow.Close(); };
    customExercise.CustomExerciseCreated += (s, ev) =>
        {
            CreateExerciseLogEntry(ev.CreatedExercise);
            modalWindow.Close();
        };

    customExercise.DataContext = new FitnessTrackerPlus.Web.Data.Exercise();

    modalWindow.Title = "Add Custom Exercise";
    modalWindow.Content = customExercise;
    modalWindow.Show();
}
```

Code snippet ExerciseLog.xaml.cs

Updating and Deleting Exercise Log Entries

With that code complete, users can now create new exercise log entries using one of the default exercises or by creating their own custom exercises. Next up is providing them with the ability to both update and delete these entries. Because users cannot alter the details of a given exercise entry until it is created, you will need to ensure that updating the entry details is simple and painless. For the most part, the `DataGrid` columns have their `CellEditingTemplate` set to a `TextBox` control that users can use to enter numeric values such as calories, distance, reps, weight, and so on. However, there is one column that you should take a better look at. The duration column in the cardio and activity log is intended to be used by users to enter the total time that they performed the exercise. Ideally, there would be some kind of masked textbox control that you can use similar to the one provided in the AjaxControlToolkit for ASP.NET based solutions. Although there is no such control in this release of Silverlight, you do have the option of using the new `TimePicker` control instead. The `TimePicker` control works only with `DateTime` types so although you only really care about hours, minutes, and seconds for the duration column, you will still need to use a full `DateTime` column in the database for the duration field. In order to start using the `TimePicker` control you first need to add the following namespace declaration at the top of the page:

Available for download on Wrox.com

```
xmlns:toolkit_input="clr-
amespace:System.Windows.Controls;assembly=System.Windows.Controls.Input.Toolkit"
```

Code snippet ExerciseLog.xaml.cs

With the namespace declared, you can easily add the `TimePicker` to the `CellEditingTemplate` of the duration column:

Available for download on Wrox.com

```
<data:DataGridTemplateColumn.CellEditingTemplate>
     <DataTemplate>
          <toolkit_input:TimePicker x:Name="Duration"
Value="{Binding Path=duration, Mode=TwoWay}" />
     </DataTemplate>
</data:DataGridTemplateColumn.CellEditingTemplate>
```

Code snippet ExerciseLog.xaml.cs

Because you want the `TimePicker` to display time in a format such as "HH:mm:ss" you will need to do some additional work. The default behavior of the control does not really work for what you are trying to accomplish. Now, because the control is embedded in a `DataTemplate`, you can't just simply access the control and add the required customizations so you will need to hook up the `PreparingCellForEdit` event on the `DataGrid`, which is fired as soon as the `DataTemplate` switches to the `CellEditingTemplate`. In this event handler, you can easily gain access to the `TimePicker` control and make the necessary modifications. The following code shows the `PreparingCellForEdit` event handler and the modifications required to make the `TimePicker` useful for helping users to enter a duration value:

Available for download on Wrox.com

```
private void ExerciseLogGrid_PreparingCellForEdit(object sender,
DataGridPreparingCellForEditEventArgs e)
{
     DataGrid grid = sender as DataGrid;
```

```
        ExerciseLogEntry entry = e.Row.DataContext as ExerciseLogEntry;
        TimePicker duration =
    grid.Columns[e.Column.DisplayIndex].GetCellContent(e.Row) as TimePicker;

        if (duration != null)
        {
            duration.Minimum = new DateTime(DateTime.Now.Year, DateTime.Now.Month,
    DateTime.Now.Day, 0, 0, 0);
            duration.Maximum = new DateTime(DateTime.Now.Year, DateTime.Now.Month,
    DateTime.Now.Day, 23, 59, 59);
            duration.PopupSecondsInterval = 1;
            duration.PopupMinutesInterval = 1;
            duration.Format = new CustomTimeFormat("HH:mm:ss");

            // As entries are created they will default to a duration of null,
            // initialize the TimePicker to 00:00:00

            if (entry.duration == null)
                duration.Value = new DateTime(DateTime.Now.Year, DateTime.Now.Month,
    DateTime.Now.Day, 0, 0, 0);

            // Adjust the column width to fit the TimePicker control

            grid.Columns[e.Column.DisplayIndex].Width =
    new DataGridLength(duration.ActualWidth);
        }
    }
```

Code snippet ExerciseLog.xaml.cs

As you can see, you want users to be able to set values in a 24-hour range so you need to set the `Format` property to the `CustomTimeFormat` "HH:mm:ss". You also want to make sure users can increment the seconds and minutes fields by a step of one, hence the `PopupSecondsInterval` and `PopupMinutesInterval` being set to one. The custom `DateTime` objects used for the `Minimum` and `Maximum` values basically enable users to select any valid 24-hour range for a time. Finally, because the `TimePicker` control will take up more space than the `TextBlock` used to display the `duration` property when the `DataGrid` is not in editing mode, you are increasing the column width to the size of the `TimePicker` control before it is actually displayed. This prevents the user from having to manually resize the column to see the entire `TimePicker` control. Once the user actually makes a selection using the control and the row edit is complete, you still have the problem that the `TimePicker` will display a `DateTime` data type. This means that even though the `TimePicker` allowed the user to select a duration in the "HH:mm:ss" custom format, the `TextBlock` that displays the duration property will show the complete `DateTime` value. Because no actual date is used, the user would be presented with a full `DateTime` string and an invalid date. Of course you don't want the user to see a date at all here, just the custom time format. Luckily this small problem is easily solved using the new `StringFormat` attribute in the data binding string of the `DataGrid` column.

Once the cell editing templates are taken care of, adding the code to actually save the changes to the database is simple. Once again, you are hooking up to the RowEditEnded event for each DataGrid and making a call to SubmitChanges using the ExerciseContext.

Available for download on Wrox.com

```
CardioLogGrid.RowEditEnded += new
EventHandler<DataGridRowEditEndedEventArgs>(ExerciseLogGrid_RowEditEnded);

ActivityLogGrid.RowEditEnded += new
EventHandler<DataGridRowEditEndedEventArgs>(ExerciseLogGrid_RowEditEnded);

WeightTrainingLogGrid.RowEditEnded += new
EventHandler<DataGridRowEditEndedEventArgs>(ExerciseLogGrid_RowEditEnded);

private void ExerciseLogGrid_RowEditEnded(object sender,
DataGridRowEditEndedEventArgs e)
{
     // Submit any exercise log changes and refresh the DataGrid

     if (context.HasChanges)
          context.SubmitChanges();
}
```

Code snippet ExerciseLog.xaml.cs

That takes care of implementing the create, read, and update scenarios for each of the DataGrid controls. The only thing left is to work out the details of the delete operation and the CheckBox select/deselect logic.

Using the VisualTreeHelper

When you were working with the food log page, you only had to worry about one DataGrid control. This made the logic for the CheckBox header column pretty straightforward. You could safely iterate through all of the food log entries loaded by the DomainContext. The fact that each of the DataGrid controls on the exercise log page filters entries based on the associated exercise type means that you can't just iterate through all the loaded exercise log entries in order to determine which CheckBox controls to toggle.

One solution might be to iterate through all of the loaded exercise log entries and create a large switch statement based on the exercise type in order to determine which DataGrid contains the header CheckBox that was clicked. A better method is to find a way to iterate specifically through the ItemsSource collection on the DataGrid that is hosting the column header CheckBox that was actually clicked. Unfortunately, a brief glance at the Parent property of the column header CheckBox control does not show a DataGrid control. So how do you find out what DataGrid is actually hosting the control? The answer lies in using the Silverlight methods available for walking up the visual tree of controls. You can use the VisualTreeHelper.GetParent method, passing the header CheckBox as a parameter, and walk through the tree of parent controls until you eventually reach the DataGrid hosting the control. Rather than make a ton of nested calls to this method, however, you should instead add a new method to the DataGridHelper class you created in the previous chapter and have this method return the parent DataGrid using the supplied CheckBox column header control as shown in the following code.

Available for download on Wrox.com

```
public static DataGrid GetParentGrid(CheckBox checkBox)
{
     Grid innerGrid = VisualTreeHelper.GetParent(checkBox) as Grid;
     DataGridColumnHeader header = VisualTreeHelper.GetParent(innerGrid)
as DataGridColumnHeader;
     DataGridColumnHeadersPresenter presenter = VisualTreeHelper.GetParent(header)
as DataGridColumnHeadersPresenter;
     Grid outerGrid = VisualTreeHelper.GetParent(presenter) as Grid;
     Border innerBorder = VisualTreeHelper.GetParent(outerGrid) as Border;
     Grid borderGrid = VisualTreeHelper.GetParent(innerBorder) as Grid;

     return VisualTreeHelper.GetParent(borderGrid) as DataGrid;
}
```

Code snippet DataGridHelper.cs

Once you have access to the parent DataGrid hosting the CheckBox, Selecting/Deselecting All of the row level CheckBox controls becomes trivial. Now you can just iterate through all of the exercise log entries contained in the ItemsSource property and toggle the CheckBox controls in the last DataGrid column to match the CheckBox header. In the following code, a CheckAll_Checked method is added to the code behind of the ExerciseLog page. First the GetParentGrid method that you just implemented is used to gain access to the DataGrid control that is hosting the CheckBox that initiated this event. From there the code loops through all the rows of the DataGrid by iterating through the ItemsSource property. Lastly the IsChecked state is toggled depending on the IsChecked state of the CheckBox control that initiated the event.

Available for download on Wrox.com

```
private void CheckAll_Checked(object sender, RoutedEventArgs e)
{
     DataGrid grid = DataGridHelper.GetParentGrid(sender as CheckBox);

     foreach (ExerciseLogEntry entry in grid.ItemsSource)
     {
          grid.SelectedItem = entry;
          CheckBox selectItem = grid.Columns[grid.Columns.Count -
1].GetCellContent(grid.SelectedItem) as CheckBox;

          if (selectItem != null)
               selectItem.IsChecked = (sender as CheckBox).IsChecked;
     }
}
```

Code snippet ExerciseLog.xaml.cs

Deleting Exercise Log Entries

Now that the Select/Deselect All logic is complete, it's time to turn your attention to the actual code to delete the selected exercise log entries. To make this happen, you need to add a Click event handler for the Delete Button control. Because you have three separate DataGrid controls to worry about, one way to approach the delete code is to write code that iterates through all the `DataGrid` rows to determine which rows are selected and then to delete the records accordingly. Of course, if you go this way, you need to duplicate this same code for all three `DataGrid` controls. A better solution is to make use of the `ExerciseContext` object and iterate through all of the `ExerciseLogEntry` objects that have been loaded regardless of which `DataGrid` control they have been bound to. In the following code, each `ExerciseLogEntry` object determines which `DataGrid` control to work with based on the exercise type. Then the specific `CheckBox` control for each row is extracted by using the `GetCellContent` method on the last available column in the row. From there, you can determine if the `CheckBox` has been checked by the user and delete the entry from the database.

Available for download on Wrox.com

```
private void DeleteSelected_Click(object sender, RoutedEventArgs e)
{
     List<ExerciseLogEntry> entries = new List<ExerciseLogEntry>();

     // First check the cardio grid, then weight training and activities

     foreach (ExerciseLogEntry entry in context.ExerciseLogEntries)
     {
          CheckBox selectItem = null;

          if (entry.Exercise.ExerciseType.type_name == "Cardio")
          {
               CardioLogGrid.SelectedItem = entry;
               selectItem =
CardioLogGrid.Columns[CardioLogGrid.Columns.Count -
1].GetCellContent(CardioLogGrid.SelectedItem) as CheckBox;
          }
          else if (entry.Exercise.ExerciseType.type_name == "Weight Training")
          {
               WeightTrainingLogGrid.SelectedItem = entry;
               selectItem =
WeightTrainingLogGrid.Columns[WeightTrainingLogGrid.Columns.Count -
1].GetCellContent(WeightTrainingLogGrid.SelectedItem) as CheckBox;
          }
          else
          {
               ActivityLogGrid.SelectedItem = entry;
               selectItem = ActivityLogGrid.Columns[ActivityLogGrid.Columns.Count -
1].GetCellContent(ActivityLogGrid.SelectedItem) as CheckBox;
          }

          if (selectItem != null)
               if (selectItem.IsChecked == true)
                    entries.Add(entry);
     }

     foreach (ExerciseLogEntry entry in entries)
          context.ExerciseLogEntries.Remove(entry);

     context.SubmitChanges((EntriesRemoved) =>
          { ProgressBar.Visibility = Visibility.Collapsed; }, null);
}
```

Code snippet ExerciseLog.xaml.cs

In the previous code, the actual delete operation is accomplished by simply removing the selected entry from the ExerciseLogEntries EntityList object of the ExerciseContext object.

Accessing Previous Entries

The final aspect of the code behind to be aware of is the GlobalCalendar. Earlier, you saw how to make the GlobalCalendar work as a ControlParameter to each of the DomainDataSource controls. This means that as the user selects various dates on the calendar, the DomainDataSource controls will automatically refresh and load the exercise log entries associated with the selected date. However, you still need to make sure that the Globals.SelectedDate is updated during this event as well so that if the user changes to the food or measurement log pages the correct entries will be loaded when those pages are displayed. The logic for this is the same as in the previous chapter — just add an event handler for the SelectedDatesChanged event on the GlobalCalendar control and set the Globals.SelectedDate property to the date selected.

Available for download on Wrox.com

```
Calendar.SelectedDatesChanged += (se, ev) =>
{
    if (Calendar.SelectedDate.HasValue)
    Globals.SelectedDate = Calendar.SelectedDate.Value;
};
```

Code snippet ExerciseLog.xaml.cs

SUMMARY

We have come to the conclusion of yet another chapter. You now have two-thirds of the data entry work complete in the form of fully functional food and exercise log pages. Users can select from default foods and exercises or even create their own custom entries. You have also seen how to make use of new powerful new controls such as the DomainDataSource, TimePicker, GlobalCalendar, and DataForm to name a few. You have also been introduced to several control events that, when implemented, can give you access to controls that have been defined in DataTemplate declarations and would normally be difficult to gain access to. An alternate way of displaying the ProgressBar control was proposed in this chapter and should give you the basis for creative ways to make use of the new element-to-element binding feature of Silverlight. Knowing that you can now bind properties such as a control's Visibility to values from their controls can make for some powerful user interface enhancements. Perhaps most important, by creating the cascading ComboBox controls, you have provided users with the most efficient way to perform data entry of exercise log entries.

Now it's time to move on to the final piece of the data entry puzzle — the measurement log page. By creating this page, you will be giving users the ability to record various measurements as well as images of themselves so that they can easily see if they are achieving their desired results. The next chapter covers not only more Silverlight data entry techniques but also how to provide users with the ability to upload and store images from the Silverlight client.

7

Am I Working Hard Enough?

Creating the Measurement Log Page

In this chapter, you will be working on the third and final major data entry screen for the application. The measurement log page is an important aspect of the application in that it will provide users with the ability to keep track of their overall measurements. By keeping track of their measurements over the long-term, users will be able to see if all of their hard work invested in their diet and exercise program is finally paying off.

In the previous chapters, you saw how to make use of powerful new controls in Silverlight and the Silverlight Toolkit such as the `DataGrid`, `GlobalCalendar`, `AutoCompleteBox`, and `DataForm`. By combining all the controls, you were able to provide a rich user interface for quick and easy data entry. Just as you have done in the previous two chapters, you will be providing users with a quick and easy way to perform the required data entry task, which in this case is logging current measurements. You will also be providing users with the ability to create and easily track their own custom measurements. In addition to these features, you will be providing a way for users to upload images of themselves so that on any given day they will be able to easily get a visual representation of the measurements being tracked. You will soon see that even though you are really adding only one new user interface aspect to the data entry screen, you still have some significant design problems to solve such as where to store the uploaded images, and what image types and dimensions should be supported. The main intent of this chapter is to provide you with a Silverlight-based image-uploading solution that you can use in your own Silverlight applications as you will no doubt encounter many of the same design issues that will be worked on here.

PROBLEM

Users of FitnessTrackerPlus can now come to the site and easily keep track of foods and exercises on a daily basis. As with many things in life, however, if you don't have a set goal and a good way to measure the progress of that goal, then all you really have is a bunch of related events and actions with no set purpose. Presumably, users have signed up for this site because they have a specific fitness goal in mind such as losing ten pounds or gaining a couple of inches in arm size. Perhaps they might even want to track progress toward a health-related goal such as lowering their blood pressure or decreasing their overall body fat.

Keeping track of foods and exercises is only one aspect of making sure those goals are achieved. The next important aspect of the fitness plan is to measure the progress being made toward those goals. It is for this reason that users of the site will be expecting the third data entry screen for keeping track of various measurements so users can easily see the progress they have made toward their goals. Similar to how users entered foods and exercises, they will be expecting to select from some standard measurements that apply across all users of the site. Of course, users will also be expecting to track custom measurements as well.

The final problem that needs to be addressed on this page is that although text-based measurements are useful and can give the user a great way to measure progress, nothing is more convincing than a photo. There is perhaps no better way for users to see if they are making progress than to compare photos of themselves from the start of the fitness program to recently uploaded photos. The measurement log page will need to provide users with a way to upload their own photos and tie those images to specific days in their log. This way, with just one click of the `GlobalCalendar` control, they will be able to easily see the physical changes that are occurring as they continue to make use of the site.

DESIGN

To begin the design process for this page, I will once again make use of the user story design tool introduced in the previous two chapters.

User Stories

The problem statement contains several clearly defined requirements for this page, but to ensure nothing is missed, let's take a look at a user story that simulates what a typical user might try to accomplish when arriving at this page to log his or her current measurements.

USER STORY Logging User Measurements

Bill has been working out for many years now and he feels that all his training and hard work has not really paid off as much as he would like. Although he feels he's in better shape than years ago, he really doesn't have much in the way of proof. He decides it's time to track things such as his measurements. Ideally, he would like to keep a photo journal showing how his appearance changes over the next few months as he prepares to go on an even more rigid diet and exercise routine. After finding an advertisement for the FitnessTrackerPlus website at his local gym, he decides to create a new account and see what the site has to offer. He is pleasantly surprised by how easy it is to enter his foods and exercises, so he checks out the measurement log page to see if he will be able to keep track of all his measurements. This page offers him the ability to keep track of all the major measurements that interest him as well as create custom measurements. This is great because he had been planning on keeping a journal of other important measurements such as cholesterol and blood pressure. After adding all of the measurements, he goes back to the table to enter the appropriate values. One of Bill's biggest goals is to lower his overall BMI measurement. He attempts to remember the correct way to calculate BMI but then notices the BMI entry in the table has a hyperlink. After clicking the link, he is presented with a great BMI calculator utility and can enter some basic information. When he hits Enter, the newly calculated *Body Mass Index (BMI)* is reflected in his measurement log. In addition to these great features, he also notices that for every day on the calendar he can upload an image of himself and just by clicking various days on the calendar, he can quickly get a visual representation of the changes in his appearance. The program seems to have everything he is looking for.

After taking a close look at the previous user story, it appears that there may be an additional requirement that was not part of the original problem statement. Bill is attempting to log a measurement that involves a calculation relying on some additional data. Rather than force Bill to leave the site and figure out the correct way to calculate BMI, FitnessTrackerPlus presents him with a modal window containing a BMI calculator control. Bill found this easily because the measurement log entry for BMI showed up as a hyperlink control. As you can see in this particular case writing, Bill's story pointed out an additional feature that might be needed but was not part of the original design requirements. Now let's look at the complete list of requirements for this page including both the requirements from the initial problem statement as well as the new requirement extracted from the user story.

Requirements

The following lists detail the requirements for this chapter. These requirements were extracted from the original problem statement with the exception of the BMI calculator requirement, which were taken from the user story. Users should be able to:

- View a list of measurements recorded in a tabular format.
- Update their current measurements by selecting from a default list of measurements or by creating their own custom measurements.
- Update the values and units of each entry after adding measurement entries.
- Upload images of their progress and tie those images to a given log date.
- Enter past, present, and future log entries.
- Create, read, update, and delete any measurement log entries.

In addition, the interface should include or support:

- Default measurements, including Weight, BMI, Waist, Arms, and Legs.
- Both Metric- and Standard-based units.
- A hyperlink that, when clicked, will display a modal BMI calculator.

Measurement Log

The measurement log page is where users go to see how they are progressing toward their individual fitness goals. After taking the steps to keep track of foods and exercises on a daily basis, it only seems natural to see if anything positive is coming from all the hard work. The measurement log will need to provide the users with a way to keep track of common measurements on a daily basis. Now it may be more common for some users to keep track of information weekly or even monthly, but because you can't be sure, you might as well provide daily access as you did for foods and exercises. In addition to the basic management of measurement log entries, this page will need to display an image of the user that has been associated with the currently selected date. This image, combined with the measurement values, will give users an easy way to determine if they are making solid progress toward their fitness goals.

User Interface

The user interface for the measurement log page will be somewhat different from the previous log page designs. You still need a `GlobalCalendar` control so that users can access past and future entries. You will have only a handful of default measurements for users to choose from so providing an `AutoCompleteBox` control for searching would probably be overkill on this page. Instead, you should provide a `ComboBox` containing both default measurements and any custom measurements that may have been created by the user. In order to display the measurement log entries, you can use a single `DataGrid` control that will display the measurement name, current value, and unit of measure. Should the user add an entry for BMI, that entry should appear as a hyperlink that, when clicked, displays a modal `ChildWindow` control hosting the calculator control for the measurement.

In addition to providing the capability to add entries to the measurement log, you are also required to allow users to upload their current image and tie that image to the currently selected date. The user interface will need to include an area to display any image that has been uploaded for the selected date, and you will also need to add a button to the interface that allows users to select a new image to upload. There really isn't much else required for the user interface so given all of the items mentioned, Figure 7-1 shows what the potential user interface for the measurement log page will look like.

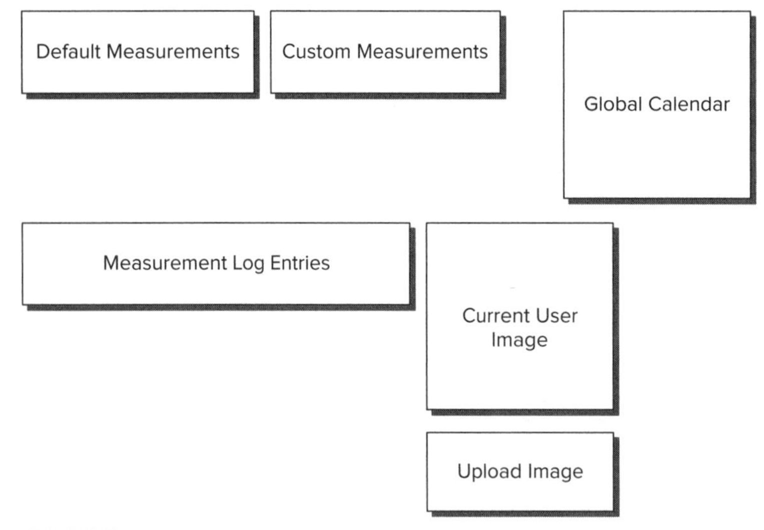

FIGURE 7-1

Database

You will need only a couple of additional database tables for the measurement log page. First, you will need a table to hold the measurement definitions themselves. This measurements table (see Table 7-1) will also be where any custom measurements created by the users will be stored.

TABLE 7-1: measurements

COLUMN NAME	TYPE	DESCRIPTION
id	int	Unique identity field for measurements
measurement_name	varchar(100)	Name of measurement
user_id	int	ID of associated user

Next, you will need a table (see Table 7-2) to store all of the possible units of measure; this table should include both Metric and Standard units of measure that can be used for the default measurements in the measurements table.

TABLE 7-2: measurement_units

COLUMN NAME	TYPE	DESCRIPTION
id	int	Unique identity field for measurement units
unit	varchar(25)	Name of measurement unit

The next table required (see Table 7-3) will be a join table that links measurements to their associated units of measure. The measurements_units table should, by default, contain entries that link the default measurements to their appropriate unit of measure in both Metric and Standard form.

TABLE 7-3: measurements_units

COLUMN NAME	TYPE	DESCRIPTION
id	int	Unique identity field for join record
measurement_id	int	ID of associated measurement
unit_id	int	ID of associated unit

You now need a place to store the actual measurement log entries. The measurement_logs table (see Table 7-4) will contain the current value of the measurement being recorded along with the associated user and measurement.

TABLE 7-4: measurement_logs

COLUMN NAME	TYPE	DESCRIPTION
id	int	Unique identity field for entry
measurement_id	int	ID of associated measurement
user_id	int	ID of associated user
entry_date	datetime	Date of measurement log entry
value	float	Current value of measurement
unit_id	int	ID of associated unit of measure

Before the final database table is created, you must first think about how you are going to solve one of the main issues that came up during the original problem statement. You want to provide a way for users to upload their images, but you never did decide on how you were going to store that image. In this case you have a couple of options. First, you could store the binary image data right in the database table, but of course this would take up quite a bit of additional database space. If you are running the site from a shared hosting provider and manage to get thousands of users, you could fill up your database space quota relatively easily. As I stated earlier, increasing the database storage in a shared hosting plan can get quite expensive once you start talking about support for tens of thousands of users, and that is just using basic data types in your database schema; never mind adding actual raw image data as well.

The second choice is to store the uploaded images in the file system on the web server. Most shared hosting plans actually have no problem giving you large amounts of physical disk space to store files so this would be the most cost-effective route to take until you have a site that is popular enough to justify a dedicated hosting solution. That being said, for FitnessTrackerPlus you will simply store the path to the uploaded image on the file system in the database table, which results in a much smaller column size and makes full use of the generous disk space that is usually offered in shared hosting plans. Now, with that important design decision complete, you can finish the design of the measurement_images table (see Table 7-5). This table will store the full path to the image along with an entry_date field that is used to lookup any images that have been uploaded for the selected date.

TABLE 7-5: measurement_images

COLUMN NAME	TYPE	DESCRIPTION
id	int	Unique identity field for image
file_name	varchar(255)	Full path to the uploaded image on the web server
entry_date	datetime	Measurement log entry date to be associated with the image
user_id	int	ID of associated user

Data Access

For the design of the data access layer, you will once again count on LINQ to SQL to generate the required entity classes. This should be done by dragging and dropping the newly created tables onto the designer and renaming the entity class definitions using the naming convention that was used in the previous chapters.

Business Logic

The business logic required for the measurement log page consists of yet another `DomainService` added to the project. This `MeasurementService` class will need to include all of the methods required for managing custom measurements, measurement log entries, and of course the uploaded user images. The image upload feature will require some custom logic that is not automatically generated by the `DomainService` wizard. Although you should have no problem using the generated code to update the image attributes in the measurement_images table, you will still need some custom code to perform the actual storing of the binary image data somewhere on the server.

While working on the image-uploading code in the service, you need to think about what the business rules will be for this feature. You need to come up with a scheme that ensures users can't overwrite each other's image files if they have the same name. You also need to ensure that only one image is tied to a particular entry date. Finally, you have to think about the characteristics of the image itself. This includes determining which image formats will be supported, as well as what dimensions should be allowed. Before moving on, let's work through these issues in detail.

The first issue essentially requires that you come up with a solid naming convention that will guarantee each uploaded image has a unique file name in the system. One way to solve this is to completely ignore the actual file name being uploaded and instead create a new file name that is relevant to the application. Because each logged-in user has a unique ID in the system, let's start there. If you take the currently logged-in user ID and append the text "measurement_image," that would solve half of our overall naming problem. For example, say a user with an ID of 125 is logged in and attempts to upload an image named jim_loses_weight.jpg. The measurement service would convert that name to 125_measurement_image.jpg. At this point you, can even kill two birds with one stone and tie the image to the selected entry date by including the entry date right in the file name, which would take care of the requirement that only one image can be uploaded and tied to any given entry date.

In this example, assume the user was attempting to tie the image to the entry date of 12/20/09. Now you would have the following file name: 125_12_20_09_measurement_image. Should the same user try to upload another image on the currently selected date, the new image would overwrite the existing one because the file name created would be the same. Doing this ensures that the last uploaded image is always the one being displayed for the selected entry date.

That takes care of the naming convention issue, but what about the image details such as dimensions and size? Although you probably have a good amount of disk space available, you don't want to let users go too crazy here. It would be a huge mistake to put no restrictions at all on the file size, as it would mean users could potentially upload high-resolution images that take up gigabytes of space. Because the actual space that the image will be taking up on this page is relatively small, you might as well restrict images to about 500KB to be safe. Now, when it comes to dimensions, you can give the user a recommendation of 100x200, but if the user uploads something larger you should be able to scale it easily enough using the Silverlight `Image` control.

Another image-uploading issue you need to consider is what file types you should support for the upload operation. The Silverlight `Image` control supports a wide range of image types but does not support .gif files. This being the case, you should probably allow for any type of image other than .gif. Because .gif files are still used quite frequently, you should let the user know that this image type is not supported before prompting to search their hard drive for images to upload only to find out that FitnessTrackerPlus doesn't support this image type.

Finally, after coming to those decisions, you need to consider one more thing — where should the uploaded images actually reside on the web server? The easiest thing to do here is just plan on creating a directory on the server called `UserImages` and place all images in that directory. Because the directory will need to have write access enabled, you should place the `UserImages` directory under the `App_Data` directory in the ASP.NET project. That should take care of the business logic related to the uploading and storage of user images. Of course, there are about a million and one variations on this and any one of them would be valid. When developing your own sites, you will no doubt need to come up with a variation on this scheme that best suits your own design goals. For FitnessTrackerPlus, however, the proposed scheme will work just right.

User Interface Code Behind

In the code behind for the measurement log page, you can count on several event handlers to be required. First, when the page is finished loading, you should get a list of valid measurement log entry dates and update the `GlobalCalendar` day styles to reflect valid entry dates just as you did in the previous two log pages. Next, in the page load event, all measurement log entries for the selected date should be retrieved from the `MeasurementService` and displayed in the `DataGrid` control. Remember, however, that you shouldn't use the current date when retrieving these entries. Instead, you should make use of the `Globals.SelectedDate` variable. Users could have already made a date selection on one of the other two log pages and when they switch between the various log pages, they will most likely still expect to see entries related to the last date that was selected. Once you have the measurement log entries loaded, you then need to retrieve all of the available measurements that can be recorded. You should have a `ComboBox` control to hold the list of measurements and the `ComboBox` should be bound to the list of retrieved measurements. The `MeasurementService` should already have a `Query` method that not only retrieves the default measurements but also any custom measurements that may have been created by the user.

Once the page is loaded, it's time to plan the necessary event handlers that will be required for users to create new log entries. You should have a `SelectionChanged` event handler for the measurements `ComboBox` that creates a new log entry in the database. The `DataGrid` should have the appropriate data binding set up so that newly created entries automatically appear in the list.

Next up is supporting the creation of new custom measurements. By now you should be pretty familiar with how custom entries are handled in FitnessTrackerPlus. You will need a new custom measurement control that allows the user to create a new custom measurement. This control should also let the user either select from one of the existing units of measure already in the database, or just enter the name of a new custom unit of measure to be created along with the measurement. Once the user is finished entering the details of the custom measurement, the code should create a new entry in the measurements table, create a new entry in the measurement_units table if needed, and finally, add a record to the measurements_units join table. After all of this is complete, the control should fire a custom event that the measurement log page can use to create a new log entry using the newly created custom measurement. This mechanism seemed to work well for both the food and exercise log pages so there is no compelling reason to change this custom entry mechanism now.

Updating existing log entries should be as simple as making use of the edit functionality of the `DataGrid` control as you have done before. Users should be able to change the value as well as the unit of measure when the selected row is in edit mode. The unit of measure editing template should make use of a `ComboBox` control containing all of the units of measure that have been associated with the selected measurement in the measurements_units join table. This will require the use of another custom `LoadOptions` object being set in the `DataContext` of the `MeasurementService`.

The next area of the code behind that needs to be designed is the handling of the required calculator control. If a user selects the BMI measurement, you will need to override the appearance of the `TextBlock` control in the measurement name column of the `DataGrid`. By default, the entry will appear as a `TextBlock` control, but you should handle the `LoadingRow` event of the `DataGrid` and swap it for a `HyperlinkButton`, which, when clicked, will display the appropriate calculator control.

Finally, you should expect to have all of the same `DataGrid` event handlers that were required by the food and exercise log pages as well. This means that you should have handlers for selecting all rows in the `DataGrid` using a custom `CheckBox` column header style. You should also have logic that will delete all of the selected entries from the database.

Calculator Controls

Certain measurements that users need to log require more than just a simple trip to the scale or pulling out the old measuring tape. A measurement such as BMI is a result of some basic calculations using a few simple parameters. For the most part, this calculation is easily found on the Web, but it would be nice if users didn't have to leave FitnessTrackerPlus in order to figure out how to calculate this value. Remember that anytime your users need to leave your site to find functionality that you could have easily provided yourself, you run the risk of them finding you competitor's web site and staying there permanently. If users add this measurement type to their measurement log, you need to provide them with an easy-to-use calculator control so they can enter the required parameters and calculate the necessary values. This control should also have a mechanism in place to automatically update the selected measurement value to reflect the calculation result. Because this first release of FitnessTrackerPlus has only one default measurement that requires this functionality, you could easily have handled this scenario with a special case using an if statement like the following:

```
if ( selection == "BMI" )
     ShowCalculatorBMI();
```

This solution, however, is not very robust and you would have to continue adding cases to the previous if statement should you decide to provide additional calculator controls in a future release. A better solution is to implement a plug-in type system where new calculator implementations can easily be added to the application. This first requires that you add a new table to the database to hold records for each potential calculator control that you will be implementing. This table will be called measurement_calculators, as shown in Table 7-6.

TABLE 7-6: measurement_calculators

COLUMN NAME	TYPE	DESCRIPTION
id	int	Unique identity field for calculator
type_name	varchar(100)	Name of calculator class to instantiate
measurement_id	int	ID of associated measurement

In order to support dynamic creation of the calculator controls as opposed to hard coding entries in the if statement, you would need to have a calculator entry in this table tied to a specific measurement. For example, the BMI measurement might have the following row in the table:

```
id = 1, type_name = BodyMassIndexCalculator, measurement_id = 8
```

The type_name in this case refers to the `UserControl` type that you need to dynamically create. By setting up the appropriate `LoadOptions` when retrieving measurement log entries, you can ensure that if a given measurement has an associated calculator entry, then the calculator entity information will be loaded and available in the code behind for the measurement log page. Basically, what this means is that in the `LoadingRow` event handler for the `DataGrid` control, you could make use of the `Activator` class in Silverlight to dynamically create an instance of the calculator with the following line of code:

```
UserControl calc = Activator.CreateInstance(type_name) as UserControl;
```

You now have an instance of the calculator object that you can throw into a modal `ChildWindow` and display to the user. There is, however, one problem — you need to update the selected measurement log entry with the results of the calculator. This was the whole reason for providing the calculator in the first place. The previous line of code was simply casting the result of the `CreateInstance` method to a generic `UserControl`. You could just as easily cast the result to a `BodyMassIndexCalculator` object instead and have full access to the methods of the `BodyMassIndexCalculator` object like this:

```
BodyMassIndexCalculator calc = Activator.CreateInstance(type_name) as
BodyMassIndexCalculator;
```

Assuming the `BodyMassIndexCalculator` object exposed some kind of `GetValue` method, you would then be able to easily update the measurement log entry in the `DataGrid`. There is, however, a problem with this type of solution as well. While you can easily cast the result of `CreateInstance` to a `BodyMassIndexCalculator` object, you would still need a custom if else statement in order to decide between the `BodyMassIndexCalculator` and an alternate calculator control. You are really no better off at this point; it's back to the drawing board for a better solution. There is nothing inherently wrong with casting to the actual object type that is stored in the database, but it doesn't remove the if else logic. To do this, you need to take this solution one step further, which requires interface-based programming. If, rather than casting directly to the class type specified in the database table, you cast to an interface, say `IMeasurementCalculator`, you don't have to worry about special if else logic to determine which object type to create. Every calculator control would really just need a public `CalculationComplete` event and custom event handler that the measurement log page can hook into in order to retrieve the calculated value. So for FitnessTrackerPlus, you use an interface-based approach to dynamically create the required calculator controls.

Now that you have a solid design in place for the calculator control interface logic, you need to design the actual user interface for the specific calculator controls themselves. For the `BodyMassIndexCalculator`, you create a data entry screen that allows the user to enter values that satisfy the equation for calculating BMI, which is weight(kg)/height^2 (m^2). This means adding some `TextBox` controls for the height and weight that are used in the calculation. You should also add a Button control to perform the actual calculation and fire the `CalculationComplete` event to the measurement log page.

SOLUTION

At this point, you have all of the specified design details complete and it's once again time to look at the solution for the chapter. In this section, you will create an image-uploading mechanism that makes use of a custom HTTP handler in the ASP.NET project. You will also see how to modify the `DataGrid` control as it's being loaded in order to support the display of the calculator controls for measurements that require their use. What I won't be covering in this solution is some of the `DataGrid` logic that has already been covered in the previous two chapters. You have already seen how to implement the Select/Deselect all `DataGrid` items logic, and you have also seen how to delete existing entries both using the `DomainContext` as well as the new `DomainDataSource` control. Instead of covering very similar code here for the measurement log page, I will be concentrating more on image-uploading, creating new entries, custom measurements, and of course, the calculator control. If you happen to need a refresher on how entries are deleted from either the `DomainDataSource` or `DomainContext`, you can always feel free to jump back to Chapters 5 and 6 or just fire up Visual Studio and take a quick look at the source code for the measurement log page.

Measurement Log Page

The solution section for the measurement log will consist of a brief overview of the user interface components required on the page followed by the usual format of database, data access, business logic, and user interface code behind. Again, the emphasis for the solution will be on the image-uploading implementation and the calculator plug-in system.

User Interface

The user interface for the measurement log consists of the usual `DockPanel` container along with the `ComboBox` control to hold all available measurements; a `Button` control so users can create new custom measurements; `GlobalCalendar`, which enables users to view past, present, and future measurements should they ever find a valid reason to do so; and a `DataGrid` to hold all of the entries being logged. The XAML code required to display the user interfaces is probably the easiest of the three log pages. You've seen the `DockPanel` container setup that has been used for the previous log pages, so there is no need to cover that area again. Instead, let's start with the main data entry area containing the `ComboBox` control and the custom measurements button. Here is the XAML for the data entry area:

Available for download on Wrox.com

```
<StackPanel Style="{StaticResource MeasurementEntryStackPanelStyle}">
     <ComboBox x:Name="Measurements"
Style="{StaticResource MeasurementEntryComboBoxStyle}"
DisplayMemberPath="measurement_name" />
```

```
    <Button x:Name="CustomMeasurement" Style="{StaticResource
CustomMeasurementButtonStyle}" />
</StackPanel>
```

Code snippet MeasurementLog.xaml

The XAML is pretty straightforward, as it should be. You want users to just quickly select from the measurements that are available in the `ComboBox` in order to create the actual entries in the measurement log. Then they will go back and update the values and units of measure for the various entries just as they do for foods and exercises.

Next up is the XAML for the `DataGrid`. This `DataGrid` will be bound using the `DomainDataSource` control that was used in the previous chapter. In the following XAML code, notice how the measurement name template is currently just a `TextBlock` control. This will change to a `HyperlinkButton` if the measurement has an associated calculator plug-in that needs to be made available to assist in entering the measurement value. You'll see how that functionality works in the coverage of the code behind page.

Available for download on Wrox.com

```
<data:DataGrid x:Name="MeasurementLogGrid" Style="{StaticResource DataGrid}"
ItemsSource="{Binding Path=Data, ElementName=MeasurementData}" >
    <data:DataGrid.Columns>
        <data:DataGridTemplateColumn Header="Measurements"
HeaderStyle="{StaticResource DataGridColumnHeaderCentered}">
            <data:DataGridTemplateColumn.CellTemplate>
                <DataTemplate>
                    <TextBlock Text="{Binding Path=Measurement.
measurement_name}" Style="{StaticResource DataGridTextBlockCentered}" />
                </DataTemplate>
            </data:DataGridTemplateColumn.CellTemplate>
        </data:DataGridTemplateColumn>
        <data:DataGridTemplateColumn Header="Value" HeaderStyle="{StaticResource
DataGridColumnHeaderCentered}">
            <data:DataGridTemplateColumn.CellTemplate>
                <DataTemplate>
                    <TextBlock Text="{Binding Path=value}"
Style="{StaticResource DataGridTextBlockCentered}" />
                </DataTemplate>
            </data:DataGridTemplateColumn.CellTemplate>
            <data:DataGridTemplateColumn.CellEditingTemplate>
                <DataTemplate>
                    <TextBox Text="{Binding Path=value, Mode=TwoWay}" />
                </DataTemplate>
            </data:DataGridTemplateColumn.CellEditingTemplate>
        </data:DataGridTemplateColumn>
        <data:DataGridTemplateColumn Header="Unit" HeaderStyle="{StaticResource
DataGridColumnHeaderCentered}">
            <data:DataGridTemplateColumn.CellTemplate>
                <DataTemplate>
                    <TextBlock Text="{Binding Path=MeasurementUnit.unit}"
Style="{StaticResource DataGridTextBlock}" />
                </DataTemplate>
            </data:DataGridTemplateColumn.CellTemplate>
```

```
                <data:DataGridTemplateColumn.CellEditingTemplate>
                    <DataTemplate>
                        <ComboBox x:Name="Units"
DisplayMemberPath="MeasurementUnit.unit" ItemsSource="{Binding
Path=Measurement.MeasurementsUnits}" SelectedItem="{Binding Path=MeasurementUnit,
Mode=TwoWay, Converter={StaticResource MeasurementUnitConverter}}" />
                    </DataTemplate>
                </data:DataGridTemplateColumn.CellEditingTemplate>
            </data:DataGridTemplateColumn>
            <data:DataGridTemplateColumn HeaderStyle="{StaticResource
DataGridColumnHeaderCheckBox}">
                <data:DataGridTemplateColumn.CellTemplate>
                    <DataTemplate>
                        <CheckBox x:Name="DeleteEntry"
Style="{StaticResource DataGridCheckBox}" />
                    </DataTemplate>
                </data:DataGridTemplateColumn.CellTemplate>
            </data:DataGridTemplateColumn>
        </data:DataGrid.Columns>
    </data:DataGrid>
    <ria_controls:DomainDataSource x:Name="MeasurementData"
        DomainContext="{StaticResource MeasurementContext}"
        QueryName="GetMeasurementLogEntries" AutoLoad="True">
        <ria_controls:DomainDataSource.QueryParameters>
            <ria_controls:ControlParameter ParameterName="entry_date"
                ControlName="Calendar" PropertyName="SelectedDate"
                RefreshEventName="SelectedDatesChanged" />
        </ria_controls:DomainDataSource.QueryParameters>
    </ria_controls:DomainDataSource>
```

Code snippet MeasurementLog.xaml

The only other area of interest in the `DataGrid` is the `CellEditingTemplate` column for the unit of measure. You will be displaying a `ComboBox` containing all units of measure that are associated with the measurement. You must be sure to bind the `SelectedItem` property to the unit of measure assigned to the actual measurement log entry object, not to the collection of measurement units itself or the two-way data binding will fail.

The XAML code for the `GlobalCalendar` uses the exact same technique used in the previous pages in order to make sure that dates that have valid log entries associated with them are styled differently. Here is the XAML for the `GlobalCalendar` declaration.

Available for download on Wrox.com

```
    <StackPanel Style="{StaticResource CalendarPanelStyle}">
        <toolkit:GlobalCalendar x:Name="Calendar"
Style="{StaticResource CalendarStyle}">
            <toolkit:GlobalCalendar.CalendarDayButtonStyleSelector>
                <fitnesstrackerplus_calendar:ValidMeasurementLogDateSelector>
                    <fitnesstrackerplus_calendar:ValidMeasurementLogDateSelector.
ValidLogDateStyle>
                        <Style BasedOn="{StaticResource BasicDayButtonStyle}"
TargetType="toolkit_primitives:GlobalCalendarDayButton">
                            <Setter Property="Background" Value="#FF999999" />
                        </Style>
```

```
                    </fitnesstrackerplus_calendar:ValidMeasurementLogDateSelector.
ValidLogDateStyle>
                    <fitnesstrackerplus_calendar:ValidMeasurementLogDateSelector.
InvalidLogDateStyle>
                         <Style BasedOn="{StaticResource BasicDayButtonStyle}"
TargetType="toolkit_primitives:GlobalCalendarDayButton">
                              <Setter Property="Background" Value="#FFFFFFFF" />
                         </Style>
                    </fitnesstrackerplus_calendar:ValidMeasurementLogDateSelector.
InvalidLogDateStyle>
               </fitnesstrackerplus_calendar:ValidMeasurementLogDateSelector>
          </toolkit:GlobalCalendar.CalendarDayButtonStyleSelector>
     </toolkit:GlobalCalendar>
</StackPanel>
```

Code snippet MeasurementLog.xaml

Finally, you are left with the current image of the user that needs to be displayed. There is no guarantee that any image will actually exist for the currently selected date, so you should plan on displaying a blank "Image not available" image for that particular scenario. This image should be part of the Silverlight project and can be added as a resource to a new Images folder in the project. You can easily create this default image in your favorite image editing software, or you can just use the image_unavailable.png file that I have made available in the source code under the Image directory of the Silverlight project. In order to display this image, you should add a new Image control to the right of the `DataGrid` and set dimensions to 150 × 200 and the Source property to /Images/image_unavailable.png, as shown in the following XAML code.

Available for download on Wrox.com

```
<Style x:Key="CurrentImageStyle" TargetType="Image">
     <Setter Property="Margin" Value="10,0,0,0" />
     <Setter Property="Width" Value="150" />
     <Setter Property="Height" Value="200" />
     <Setter Property="Stretch" Value="Fill" />
     <Setter Property="HorizontalAlignment" Value="Right" />
     <Setter Property="Source" Value="/Images/image_unavailable.png" />
</Style>
<Style x:Key="CurrentImageBorderStyle" TargetType="Border">
     <Setter Property="BorderThickness" Value="2" />
     <Setter Property="BorderBrush" Value="#FF000000" />
     <Setter Property="Width" Value="150" />
     <Setter Property="Height" Value="200" />
     <Setter Property="HorizontalAlignment" Value="Right" />
</Style>
<Border Style="{StaticResource CurrentImageBorderStyle}">
     <Image x:Name="CurrentImage" Style="{StaticResource CurrentImageStyle}" />
</Border>
```

Code snippet MeasurementLog.xaml

This image size should be sufficient for most users, and if there is an image associated with the currently selected date, then the unavailable image will be replaced with the stored image in the code behind logic. Once all of this is complete, you should be left with a user interface like the one shown in Figure 7-2.

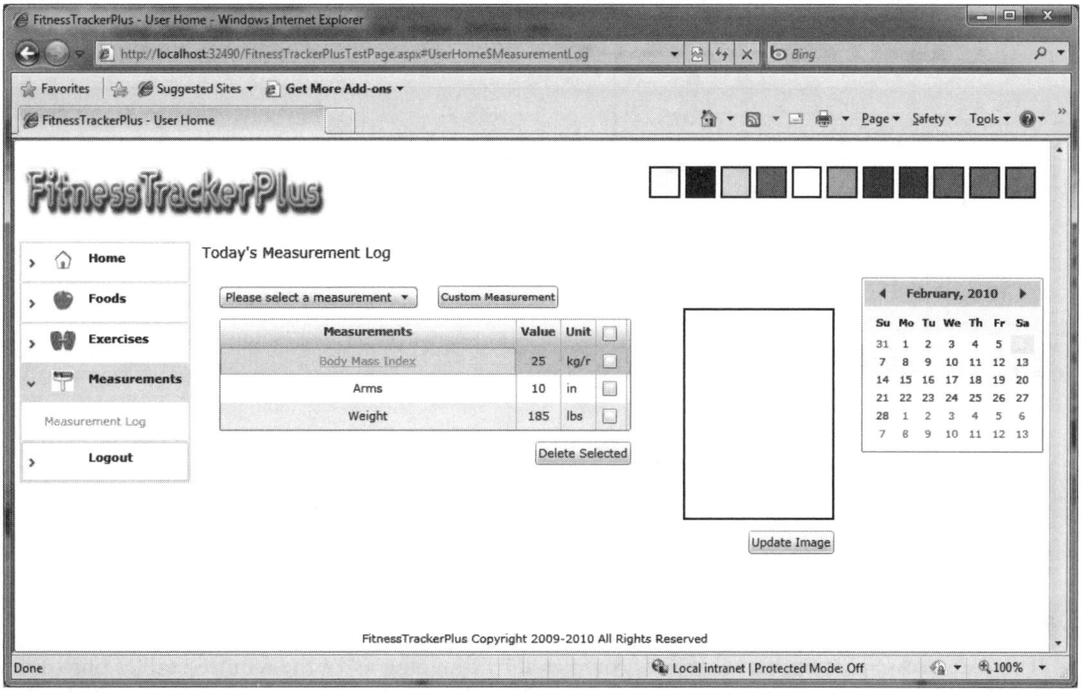

FIGURE 7-2

Database

For the database solution, you will need to create all of the required tables outlined in the design. Figure 7-3 shows the complete database schema for the measurement log page.

In addition to creating the tables and relationships, you also need to add a unique index to the measurement_images table. This will ensure that for any given entry date, users will have only one associated image. You should add a new index called UIX_measurement_images and select both the file_name and user_id columns. The combination of both should take care of the unique image requirement because the entry date is embedded in the file_name column as part of the custom naming convention that was designed.

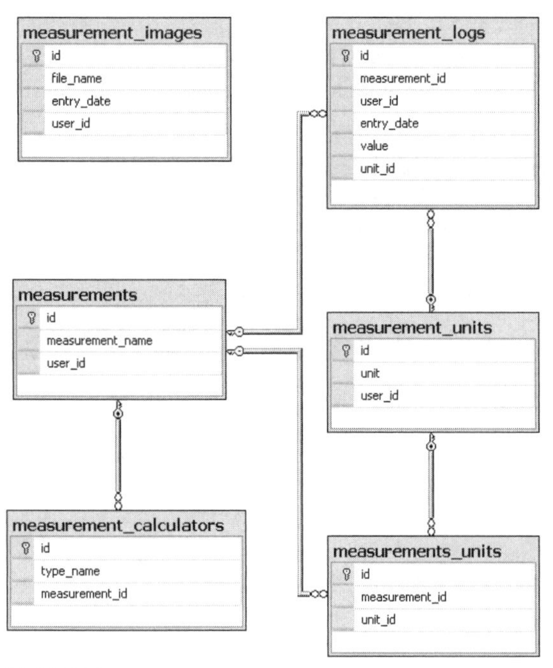

FIGURE 7-3

Data Access

The data access part of this solution is completed by dragging all of the required tables onto a new LINQ to SQL class called Measurements.dbml. You should also rename any entities according to the LINQ to SQL entity naming convention that has been used throughout the project. Figure 7-4 shows the designer window with the final entity definitions.

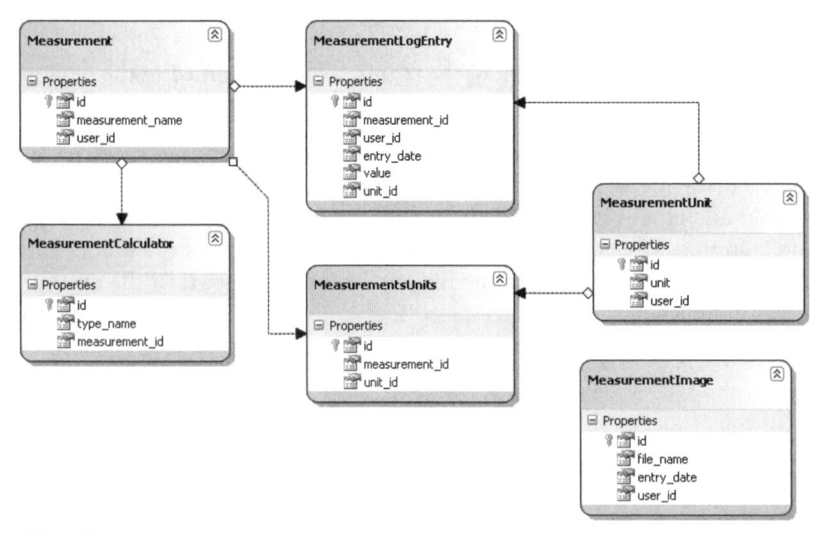

FIGURE 7-4

Business Logic

For the business logic solution, you will need to add a new `DomainService` called `MeasurementsService` to the `Services` folder in the ASP.NET project. When creating the service, you want to point the wizard to the `MeasurementDataContext` and be sure to select all of the entities in the list. You should also go ahead and enable editing for all entities as well as check the "create metadata" option. Once the service is created, you need to make some modifications to some of the generated methods and metadata classes. The first area to concentrate on is the `GetMeasurements` method. You want to ensure that both default and custom measurements are retrieved here, so you will need to add the current user ID as a parameter to the method and modify the LINQ statement to include the user ID when retrieving the measurements. Here is the updated `GetMeasurements` code:

Available for download on Wrox.com

```
public IQueryable<Measurement> GetMeasurements(int user_id)
{
     DataLoadOptions options = new DataLoadOptions();

     options.LoadWith<Measurement>(e => e.MeasurementsUnits);
     options.LoadWith<MeasurementsUnits>(e => e.MeasurementUnit);
     this.DataContext.LoadOptions = options;

     List<Measurement> measurements = (from c in this.DataContext.Measurements
                                       where (c.user_id == 1 || c.user_id ==
                                       user_id)
                                       orderby c.measurement_name ascending
                                       select c).ToList<Measurement>();

     measurements.Insert(0, new Measurement
     {
          id = -1,
          measurement_name = "Please select a measurement"
     });

     return measurements.AsQueryable<Measurement>();
}
```

Code snippet MeasurementService.cs

Notice how a custom `DataLoadOptions` is also used here. You need to ensure that all associated units of measure are also retrieved so that when a measurement is selected in the `ComboBox` control, you can create a new measurement log entry using a default unit of measure. Because you essentially have a many-to-many relationship between measurements and measurement units, LINQ to SQL requires the use of the measurements_measurement_units join table entity so the `DataLoadOptions` ensures that, for all entries in the join table relationship, all units of measure are also loaded.

Next is the measurement log retrieval; now you need a parameter for the entry date and user ID. You also need to retrieve any units of measure that are associated with the measurement being logged. Again, this requires the use of a custom `DataLoadOptions` object.

Available for download on Wrox.com

```
public IQueryable<MeasurementLogEntry> GetMeasurementLogEntries(int user_id,
DateTime entry_date)
{
     DataLoadOptions options = new DataLoadOptions();

     options.LoadWith<Measurement>(e => e.MeasurementsUnits);
     options.LoadWith<Measurement>(e => e.Calculator);
     options.LoadWith<MeasurementsUnits>(e => e.MeasurementUnit);
     options.LoadWith<MeasurementLogEntry>(e => e.Measurement);
     options.LoadWith<MeasurementLogEntry>(e => e.MeasurementUnit);

     this.DataContext.LoadOptions = options;

     return this.DataContext.MeasurementLogEntries.Where(e => e.user_id ==
                                                         user_id &&
                                                         e.entry_date.Date ==
                                                         entry_date.Date);
}
```

Code snippet MeasurementService.cs

Don't forget that in addition to the `DataLoadOptions`, you still need to add the `[Include]` attribute on the entities you are trying to return. The following code highlights which areas of the metadata need to be modified to ensure that both the `GetMeasurements` and `GetMeasurementLogEntries` methods retrieve the required data correctly.

Available for download on Wrox.com

```
[MetadataTypeAttribute(typeof(MeasurementLogEntry.MeasurementLogEntryMetadata))]
public partial class MeasurementLogEntry
{
     internal sealed class MeasurementLogEntryMetadata
     {
          private MeasurementLogEntryMetadata()
          {
          }

          public DateTime entry_date;

          public int id;

          [Include]
          public Measurement Measurement;

          public int measurement_id;

          public MeasurementUnit MeasurementUnit;

          public int unit_id;

          public int user_id;

          public Nullable<double> value;
     }
}

[MetadataTypeAttribute(typeof(Measurement.MeasurementMetadata))]
public partial class Measurement
```

```
{
    internal sealed class MeasurementMetadata
    {
        private MeasurementMetadata()
        {
        }

        public int id;

        [Required]
        [Display(Name = "Measurement Name:")]
        public string measurement_name;

        public EntitySet<MeasurementLogEntry> MeasurementLogEntries;

        [Include]
        public EntitySet<MeasurementsUnits> MeasurementsUnits;

        [Required]
        public int user_id;

        [Include]
        public MeasurementCalculator Calculator;
    }
}

[MetadataTypeAttribute(typeof(MeasurementsUnits.MeasurementsUnitsMetadata))]
public partial class MeasurementsUnits
{
    internal sealed class MeasurementsUnitsMetadata
    {
        private MeasurementsUnitsMetadata()
        {
        }

        public int id;

        public Measurement Measurement;

        public int measurement_id;

        [Include]
        public MeasurementUnit MeasurementUnit;

        public int unit_id;
    }
}
```

Code snippet MeasurementService.metadata.cs

The remaining operations required for management of both measurements and log entries are the same as you have seen in previous chapters, so I won't bother covering the details of these again here. Instead, it's time to shift the focus to the handling of the current image. Image-uploading will require a couple of major areas of code. Users will need to be able to select an image file from their local hard drive and upload the raw bytes to the web server. That piece of code will be covered in the code behind discussion. At the web server level, however, you need to have code running that will save the uploaded image to a predetermined directory. There are several ways to accomplish this task. One way is to design a web service with a specific image-uploading method. This, however, can sometimes lead to a lot of overhead for the web service payload. Another more optimized solution is to create a new generic ASP.NET request handler. For the FitnessTrackerPlus application, you will make use of the custom handler solution. If you are not familiar with custom handlers, you should be sure to check out Wrox *Professional ASP.NET 3.5 in C# and VB.NET* (ISBN: 978-0470187579). For your needs, you will be creating a rather trivial handler, so this shouldn't be terribly difficult. In order to get started building the handler, just right-click on the ASP.NET project and select the "add new item" option. Once the wizard is up, you will want to select a new Generic Handler, as shown in Figure 7-5.

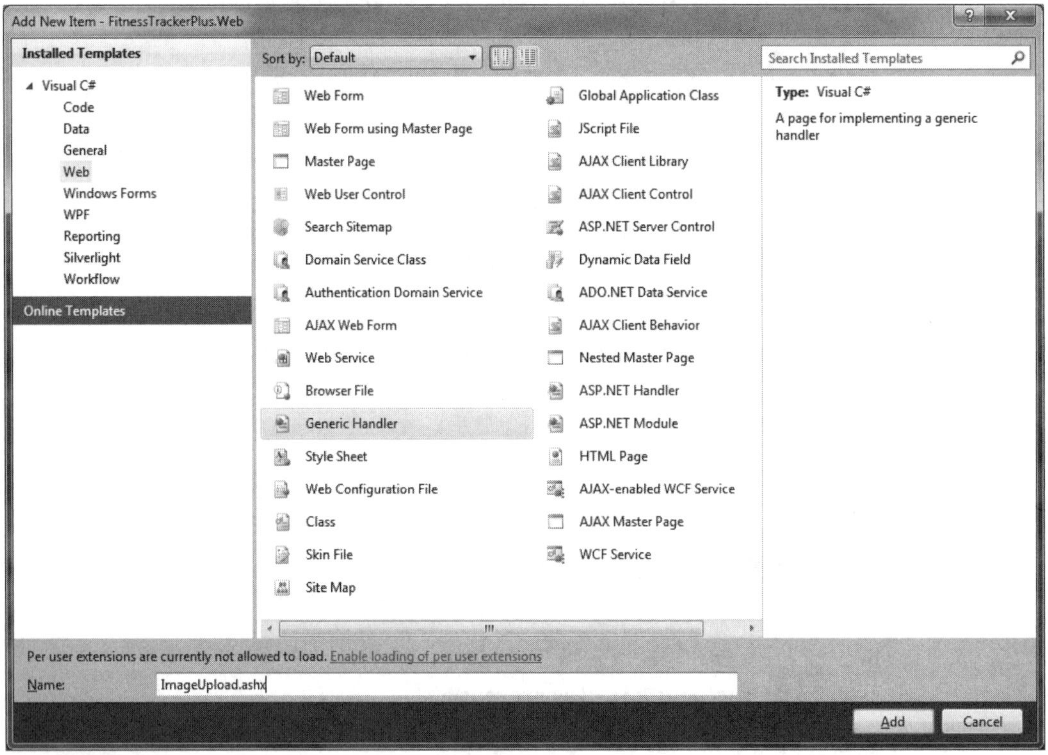

FIGURE 7-5

You can go ahead and call this new handler ImageUpload.ashx. Next you need to implement the `ProcessRequest` method of the `IHttpHandler` interface. In the following code, the file name being uploaded will reside in the query string and I should be using the naming convention outlined in the design earlier. After extracting the file name, you simply create the new file in the `UploadedImages` directory and write the raw image file bytes that exist in the `Request.InputStream` object.

Available for download on Wrox.com

```
 [WebService(Namespace = "http://fitnesstrackerplus.com/")]
[WebServiceBinding(ConformsTo = WsiProfiles.BasicProfile1_1)]
public class ImageUpload: IHttpHandler
{
     public void ProcessRequest(HttpContext context)
     {
          try
          {
               string file_name = context.Request.QueryString["file_name"];

               if (!String.IsNullOrEmpty(file_name))
               {
                    // Check if file exists on server if it does delete it

                    if (File.Exists(context.Server.MapPath(String.Format
("~/UploadedImages/{0}", file_name))))
                         File.Delete(context.Server.MapPath(String.Format
("~/UploadedImages/{0}", file_name)));

                    FileStream file = File.Create(context.Server.MapPath
(String.Format("~/UploadedImages/{0}", file_name)));
                    byte[] image_buffer = new byte[4096];
                    int bytes_read = 0;

                    while ((bytes_read = context.Request.InputStream.Read
(image_buffer, 0, image_buffer.Length)) != 0)
                         file.Write(image_buffer, 0, bytes_read);

                    file.Close();
               }
          }
          catch (Exception ex)
          {
          }
     }

     public bool IsReusable
     {
          get { return false; }
     }
}
```

Code snippet ImageUpload.ashx.cs

There are two things to watch out for here:

- You must not forget to actually create the directory in the ASP.NET project structure.
- You need to ensure that the ASP.NET worker process has been given write access to this new directory. Otherwise, an exception will be thrown on any of the File operations being executed.

If you are using a shared hosting solution, you will need to work with the appropriate technical support personnel to ensure that you can create this directory with the appropriate permissions setup. When the server code to handle saving the uploaded image is complete, you then need to modify the code that returns the current image to the client. After the service code is generated by default, you are left with a `GetMeasurementImages` query method that returns an `IQueryable` object. Users should have only one image tied to any particular entry date, so you should replace this generated method with the one shown in the following code to ensure that only one image is returned for the specified entry date and user.

Available for download on Wrox.com

```
public MeasurementImage GetMeasurementImage(int user_id, DateTime entry_date)
{
    return this.DataContext.MeasurementImages.Where(e => e.user_id == user_id &&
                                                    e.entry_date.Date ==
                                                    entry_date.Date).
                                                    SingleOrDefault();
}
```

Code snippet MeasurementService.cs

That pretty much takes care of the measurement log business logic, so let's move on to implementing the code behind and control event handlers including the Silverlight client code that actually will be responsible for pushing the raw uploaded image data to your newly created handler.

User Interface Code Behind

The first thing to work on in the code behind is the `Loaded` event. First, you need to load all available measurements into the `ComboBox` control, so that users will be able to create new measurement log entries.

Available for download on Wrox.com

```
context.Load<FitnessTrackerPlus.Web.Data.Measurement>(context.GetMeasurementsQuery
(Globals.CurrentUser.id),
LoadBehavior.RefreshCurrent, (MeasurementsLoaded) =>
{
    if (!MeasurementsLoaded.HasError)
    {
        Measurements.ItemsSource = MeasurementsLoaded.Entities;
        Measurements.SelectedIndex = 0;
    }

}, null);
```

Code snippet MeasurementLog.xaml.cs

In addition to loading the control, you need to create a new lambda expression to handle the `SelectionChanged` event. The lambda expression will simply make a call to the `CreateMeasurementLogEntry` method passing in the selected measurement.

Available for download on Wrox.com

```
Measurements.SelectionChanged += (se, ev) =>
{
    FitnessTrackerPlus.Web.Data.Measurement selected = Measurements.SelectedItem
as FitnessTrackerPlus.Web.Data.Measurement;
```

```
        if (selected.id > 0)
            CreateMeasurementLogEntry(selected);
    };
```

Code snippet MeasurementLog.xaml.cs

Once again, the `DomainDataSource` control will be used to bind measurement log entries to the `DataGrid` control. The required `ControlParameter` for handling date selection on the `GlobalCalendar` control was added in the XAML code. The `GetMeasurementLogEntries` method still requires the current user ID as a parameter, so you will also need to manually add the user ID parameter to the `DomainDataSource` `QueryParameters` collection as shown:

Available for download on Wrox.com

```
Parameter user_id = new Parameter();
user_id.ParameterName = "user_id";
user_id.Value = Globals.CurrentUser.id;

// Ensure that the user_id parameter is set for the DomainDataSource control before
// the query is executed

MeasurementData.QueryParameters.Add(user_id);
```

Code snippet MeasurementLog.xaml.cs

Just as you did for the exercise log page, you will also set up a custom binding for the `ProgressBar` control so that it will automatically be made visible whenever the current `DomainContext` is loading data. You've seen this code already, so I won't bother going through it again. Just remember that in order for it to work, you must make use of the `ProgressBarVisibilityConverter` class to convert the `bool` `IsLoading` property to a valid `Visibility` value.

As far as the various event handlers required for handling Delete and Select/Deselect operations on the `DataGrid`, they will all be implemented the same way as they have been in the previous log pages, so there is no need to cover them again here.

Creating new log entries is very similar to what was done for the previous log pages. You've seen that the measurements `ComboBox` control is set up to handle the `SelectionChanged` event and call into the private `CreateMeasurementLogEntry` method, as shown in the following code:

Available for download on Wrox.com

```
private void CreateMeasurementLogEntry(FitnessTrackerPlus.Web.Data.Measurement
measurement)
{
    MeasurementLogEntry entry = new MeasurementLogEntry();

    IEnumerator units = measurement.MeasurementsUnits.GetEnumerator();
    units.MoveNext();

    entry.measurement_id = measurement.id;
    entry.entry_date = Globals.SelectedDate;
    entry.user_id = Globals.CurrentUser.id;
    entry.unit_id = (units.Current as MeasurementsUnits).unit_id;

    context.MeasurementLogEntries.Add(entry);
```

```
        context.SubmitChanges((ChangesSubmitted) =>
        {
            if (!ChangesSubmitted.HasError)
                MeasurementData.Load();

        }, null);
    }
```

Code snippet MeasurementLog.xaml.cs

Of course, this method is shared by both the measurements `ComboBox` control as well as the `Click` event handler of the custom measurement button. As you can see, a default unit of measure is assigned before creating the entry. You can use the first unit of measure in the collection because the `MeasurementsUnits` entity list was retrieved along with the selected measurement through the use of the custom `DataLoadOptions` in the LINQ query.

The final area of concern for the code behind is the image-uploading feature that is invoked when users click the update image `Button` control. The `Click` event handler needs to perform the following actions:

- Display the `OpenFileDialog` control, so that users can choose an image from their hard drive
- Upload the raw image bytes to the custom ASP.NET `ImageUpload` handler
- Add an entry to the measurement_images table
- Refresh the image currently displayed on the page.

First up on the list is the Silverlight `OpenFileDialog` control. Silverlight provides this useful control, so that you can give your users the ability to select and open files from their own hard drive in a Silverlight application. You want users to only be able to select from image types that are supported by Silverlight, so to be safe you should set the Filter property of the control to a filter string that allows for only .png and .jpg file types, as shown in the following code:

Available for download on Wrox.com

```
OpenFileDialog dialog = new OpenFileDialog();

dialog.Multiselect = false;
dialog.Filter = "Supported Images (*.png, *.jpg)|*.png;*.jpg|PNG Images
(*.png)|*.png|JPG Images (*.jpg)|*.jpg";
```

Code snippet MeasurementLog.xaml.cs

After opening the file, you should check the file size because the design calls for a file size restriction of no more than 500KB. The control provides some basic file information, so checking the file size is as simple as checking the `Length` property of the file that was selected.

Available for download on Wrox.com

```
if (dialog.File.Length > 512000)
    MessageBox.Show("Only images up to 500KB are supported");
```

Code snippet MeasurementLog.xaml.cs

The next step is to modify the file name, so that it adheres to the naming conventions outlined in the design step. A simple `String.Format` method call that combines the selected date, user ID, and file extension will do the trick.

Available for download on Wrox.com

```
string finalFileName = "";

finalFileName = String.Format("{0}_{1}_measurement_image{2}",
Globals.CurrentUser.id, Globals.SelectedDate.ToString("MM_dd_yyyy"),
dialog.File.Extension);
```

Code snippet MeasurementLog.xaml.cs

The only piece of the original file name that should remain intact is the file extension itself. After you have the proper name created, it's time to upload the raw bytes of the file to the custom ASP.NET handler created earlier. This involves making use of the `WebClient` class in the `System.Net` namespace. You just need to create a new URI to the handler and be sure to set up the query string variable to the newly created file name. The following code opens up the connection to the handler:

Available for download on Wrox.com

```
WebClient client = new WebClient();
client.OpenWriteAsync(new Uri(String.Format("http://localhost:1154/
ImageUpload.ashx?file_name={0}",
finalFileName), UriKind.Absolute));
```

Code snippet MeasurementLog.xaml.cs

Because opening the connection to the handler is an asynchronous operation, the bulk of the image-uploading code will reside in the `OpenWriteCompleted` event handler. In this handler, the file is opened and the raw bytes are read from the file and written out to the newly created handler connection. After the file is written to the stream, both the file and connection handlers are closed.

Available for download on Wrox.com

```
client.OpenWriteCompleted += (s, ev) =>
{
     if (ev.Error == null)
     {
          FileStream file_stream = dialog.File.OpenRead();
          byte[] image_buffer = new byte[4096];
          int bytes_read = 0;

          if( file_stream != null )
          {
               while ((bytes_read = file_stream.Read(image_buffer, 0,
image_buffer.Length)) != 0)
                    ev.Result.Write(image_buffer, 0, bytes_read);

               file_stream.Close();
               ev.Result.Close();

          }
     }
};
```

Code snippet MeasurementLog.xaml.cs

With the image upload complete, you then need to ensure that the measurement_images table is updated to reflect the new image that has been assigned to the selected entry date. This requires you to make use of the current `DomainContext` that was loaded earlier and submit the changes to the `MeasurementImages` entity list.

Available for download on Wrox.com

```
context.MeasurementImages.Add(new MeasurementImage
{
     entry_date = Globals.SelectedDate,
     user_id = Globals.CurrentUser.id,
     file_name = finalFileName
});

context.SubmitChanges();
```

Code snippet MeasurementLog.xaml.cs

Finally, it's time to actually update the image that is currently being displayed to the user. Because the images will all reside in the `UploadedImages` directory on the web server, you should be able to simply create a new `BitmapImage` object pointing to the correct URI and set the `Source` property of the `Image` control to the new `BitmapImage`. Before creating the URI, you should set up a conditional compiler statement to ensure that during debugging you are setting the URI to the localhost:port address and that when a release mode build is created, the URI will point to the production FitnessTrackerPlus address.

Available for download on Wrox.com

```
BitmapImage updatedImage = null;
#if DEBUG
     updatedImage = new BitmapImage(new
Uri(String.Format("http://localhost:1154/UploadedImages/{0}",
finalFileName), UriKind.Absolute));

#else
     updatedImage = new BitmapImage(new
Uri(String.Format("http://fitnesstrackerplus.com/UploadedImages/{0}",
finalFileName), UriKind.Absolute));
#endif

CurrentImage.Source = updatedImage;
```

Code snippet MeasurementLog.xaml.cs

There is one last problem with the previous code. If a user has selected a given date and uploads the wrong image file by mistake, he or she can easily click the Update Image button to upload another image. Unfortunately, only the previously uploaded image will again be displayed. This occurs because you are not changing the file name when the second image is uploaded. Because the file name has not changed, Silverlight takes it upon itself to cache the previous image. Only a complete browser refresh seems to fix the issue. Luckily, there is something else you can do in the code to help in this situation. The `BitmapImage` object exposes a `CreateOptions` property that actually will let you manipulate the default caching mechanism used for the image. So by adding one more line of code before setting the `Source` property of the `CurrentImage` control, you can be assured that the last uploaded image will always be the one displayed.

Available for download on Wrox.com

```
// This is necessary to ensure that Silverlight refreshes the image even though
// the file name remains the same

updatedImage.CreateOptions = BitmapCreateOptions.IgnoreImageCache;
CurrentImage.Source = updatedImage;
```

Code snippet MeasurementLog.xaml.cs

Another thing to watch out for: although you have a `ControlParameter` set up on the `DomainDataSource` to take care of refreshing the measurement log entries when the user selects a new date from the `GlobalCalendar` control, you don't have a mechanism in place to also refresh the `CurrentImage` control. The following code in the `SelectionChanged` event handler ensures that the latest image is being displayed for the newly selected date.

Available for download on Wrox.com

```
Calendar.SelectedDatesChanged += (se, ev) =>
{
     if (Calendar.SelectedDate.HasValue)
     {
          Globals.SelectedDate = Calendar.SelectedDate.Value;

          LoadCurrentImage();
     }
};

private void LoadCurrentImage()
{
     context.Load<MeasurementImage>(context.GetMeasurementImageQuery
(Globals.CurrentUser.id, Globals.SelectedDate),
MergeOption.OverwriteCurrentValues, (ImageLoaded) =>
     {
          if (!ImageLoaded.HasError)
          {
               IEnumerator<MeasurementImage> enumerator =
ImageLoaded.Entities.GetEnumerator();
               enumerator.MoveNext();

               MeasurementImage image = enumerator.Current;

               if (image != null)
               {
                    BitmapImage updatedImage = null;
#if DEBUG
                    updatedImage = new BitmapImage(new
Uri(String.Format("http://localhost:1154/UploadedImages/{0}",
image.file_name), UriKind.Absolute));
#else
                    updatedImage = new BitmapImage(new
Uri(String.Format("http://fitnesstrackerplus.com/UploadedImages/{0}",
image.file_name), UriKind.Absolute));
#endif

                    updatedImage.CreateOptions =
BitmapCreateOptions.IgnoreImageCache;
```

```
CurrentImage.Source = updatedImage;
                }
                else
                    CurrentImage.Source = new BitmapImage(new
Uri("/Images/image_unavailable.png", UriKind.Relative));
            }
            else
                CurrentImage.Source = new BitmapImage(new Uri("/Images/
image_unavailable.png", UriKind.Relative));

    }, null);
}
```

Code snippet MeasurementLog.xaml.cs

With the image handling code completed, you now just need to add the code that will be responsible for displaying the calculator plug-in when a measurement requiring a calculator is being updated. In order to do this, you will need to find a way to change the `TextBlock` control being used in the measurement name column to a `HyperlinkButton` control that will give users something to click in order to trigger the display of the calculator. The only way that you can make this switch is to create a new event handler for the `LoadingRow` event of the `DataGrid` control. In the following code, the current measurement log entry is checked to see if there are any associated calculator controls. If so, a new `HyperlinkButton` control is created with a `Click` event handler that will display a new modal `ChildWindow` containing the appropriate calculator control.

Available for download on Wrox.com

```
private void MeasurementLogGrid_LoadingRow(object sender, DataGridRowEventArgs e)
{
    MeasurementLogEntry entry = e.Row.DataContext as MeasurementLogEntry;

     // If this entry has a valid calculator associated then change the TextBlock
     // to a HyperlinkButton that when clicked will use the Activator object to
     // dynamically create the appropriate calculator plug-in

     if (entry.Measurement.MeasurementCalculators.Count > 0)
     {
          TextBlock measurementName = MeasurementLogGrid.Columns[0].
GetCellContent(e.Row) as TextBlock;

          if (measurementName != null)
          {
               DataGridCell cell = measurementName.Parent as DataGridCell;
               HyperlinkButton calculatorLink = new HyperlinkButton();

               calculatorLink.Content = entry.Measurement.measurement_name;

               // Repace the TextBlock with the HyperlinkButton control

               cell.Content = calculatorLink;
          }
     }
}
```

Code snippet MeasurementLog.xaml.cs

In order to dynamically create an instance of the calculator plug-in, you will need to make use of the static `Activator` class and its `CreateInstance` method. `CreateInstance` takes a `Type` object as its parameter and currently all you have is a type string. Don't worry — the static `Type` class has a `GetType` method that, wouldn't you know it, takes a string. Remember, however, that you need to create an instance of the `IMeasurementCalculator` interface in order to hook into the `CalculationComplete` event of the control and update the selected measurement log entry value. All of this should take place in the `Click` event handler of the newly created `HyperlinkButton` control. The following code shows this event handler implementation.

Available for download on Wrox.com

```
calculatorLink.Click += (s, ev) =>
{
     ChildWindow modalWindow = new ChildWindow();
     IMeasurementCalculator calc =
Activator.CreateInstance(Type.GetType(String.Format("FitnessTrackerPlus.
Views.Measurement.Calculators.{0}", entry.Measurement.Calculator.type_name)))
as IMeasurementCalculator;

     calc.CalculationCancelled += (se, eve) => { modalWindow.Close(); };
     calc.CalculationComplete += (se, eve) =>
     {
          modalWindow.Close();

          entry.value = calc.CalculatedValue;
          context.SubmitChanges();
     };

     modalWindow.Title = String.Format("{0} Calculator",
entry.Measurement.measurement_name);
     modalWindow.Content = calc;
     modalWindow.Show();
};
```

Code snippet MeasurementLog.xaml.cs

Calculator Controls

This version of FitnessTrackerPlus provides a calculator plug-in control to assist users in calculating BMI. The calculation is well known and can be found in most fitness books or online at Wikipedia or many other fitness sites. Of course, the actual calculation equations, although interesting, are not the main focal point of this topic. Instead, this section will focus on the user interface and `IMeasurementCalculator` implementations that are required in order for the code behind to properly create and make use of the plug-in controls and their calculated values.

Calculating Body Mass Index

In the code behind logic, you used the `Activator` class to create an instance of the appropriate calculator control and all calculator type strings began with `FitnessTrackerPlus.Views.Measurement.Calculators`. Therefore, you should plan on adding a new calculator control to the `Views.Measurement.Calculators` folder, which is of course where the `IMeasurementCalculator` interface class currently resides. For this control, you should add a new `UserControl` to the folder called

BodyMassIndexCalculator. This calculator requires the user to enter both height and weight in either standard or metric units of measure. In the following XAML code, a DataForm control is used to generate the actual user interface. Although you aren't using entities returned from the WCF RIA Services, note that you can still use the DataForm and manually add appropriate form labels to help walk the user through the data entry process. Listing 7-1 shows the XAML code required for the BodyMassIndexCalculator control.

LISTING 7-1: BodyMassIndexCalculator.xaml

Available for download on Wrox.com

```
<UserControl x:Class="FitnessTrackerPlus.Views.Measurement.Calculators.
BodyMassIndexCalculator"
     xmlns="http://schemas.microsoft.com/winfx/2006/xaml/presentation"
     xmlns:x="http://schemas.microsoft.com/winfx/2006/xaml"
     xmlns:data_dataform="clr-
     namespace:System.Windows.Controls;
     assembly=System.Windows.Controls.Data.DataForm.Toolkit">
     <UserControl.Resources>
          <Style x:Key="BodyMassIndexFormStyle"
TargetType="data_dataform:DataForm">
               <Setter Property="AutoEdit" Value="True" />
               <Setter Property="AutoGenerateFields" Value="False" />
               <Setter Property="Foreground" Value="#FF000000" />
          </Style>
          <Style x:Key="SmallTextBoxStyle" TargetType="TextBox">
               <Setter Property="FontSize" Value="10" />
               <Setter Property="TextAlignment" Value="Center" />
               <Setter Property="Width" Value="60" />
          </Style>
     </UserControl.Resources>
     <data_dataform:DataForm x:Name="BodyMassIndexForm" Style="{StaticResource
BodyMassIndexFormStyle}">
          <data_dataform:DataForm.EditTemplate>
               <DataTemplate>
                    <StackPanel>
                         <data_dataform:DataField Label="Unit of Measure">
                              <ComboBox x:Name="Units">
                                   <ComboBoxItem Content="Standard (lbs, in)"
IsSelected="True" />
                                   <ComboBoxItem Content="Metric (kg, cm)" />
                              </ComboBox>
                         </data_dataform:DataField>
                         <data_dataform:DataField Label="Height">
                              <TextBox x:Name="HeightText"
Text="{Binding Path=Height, Mode=TwoWay}" Style="{StaticResource
SmallTextBoxStyle}" />
                         </data_dataform:DataField>
                         <data_dataform:DataField Label="Weight">
                              <TextBox x:Name="WeightText"
Text="{Binding Path=Weight, Mode=TwoWay}" Style="{StaticResource
SmallTextBoxStyle}" />
                         </data_dataform:DataField>
```

```
                    </StackPanel>
                </DataTemplate>
            </data_dataform:DataForm.EditTemplate>
        </data_dataform:DataForm>
    </UserControl>
```

If you are wondering whether or not you can still get the benefits of `DataForm` validation without using the WCF RIA Services entities, you need not worry. As you will soon see, you can easily set the `CurrentItem` property of the `DataForm` to any custom class and still make use of the validation rules and data annotations that are typically made available in the WCF RIA Services metadata files. Because you aren't using any existing entity that is exposed from the WCF RIA Services, you need to first create a new class in the code behind file called `BodyMassIndexParams`. This class will hold the `Height` and `Weight` properties that the controls in the `DataForm` will bind to. By adding a statement for the `System.ComponentModel.DataAnnotations` namespace, you can easily add validation attributes to both of these properties.

```
public class BodyMassIndexParams
{
    [Required]
    [Display(Name="Height")]
    public double? Height { get; set; }

    [Required]
    [Display(Name = "Weight")]
    public double? Weight { get; set; }
}
```

Code snippet BodyMassIndexCalculator.xaml.cs

Now that you have a class to hold the binding values, you can set the `CurrentItem` property of the `DataForm` to a new empty instance of `BodyMassIndexParams` in the `Loaded` event handler.

Available for download on Wrox.com

```
Loaded += (s, e) =>
{
    BodyMassIndexForm.CommandButtonsVisibility =
DataFormCommandButtonsVisibility.Commit |
DataFormCommandButtonsVisibility.Cancel;
    BodyMassIndexForm.EditEnded += new
EventHandler<DataFormEditEndedEventArgs>(BodyMassIndexForm_EditEnded);
    BodyMassIndexForm.CurrentItem = new BodyMassIndexParams
    {
        Height = null,
        Weight = null
    };
};
```

Code snippet BodyMassIndexCalculator.xaml.cs

As you saw earlier, the measurement log page code behind relies on using only `IMeasurementCalculator` objects in order to actually update values in the database. The `BodyMassIndexCalculator` class needs to implement the required property and event in order for the plug-in to work.

Available for download on Wrox.com

```
#region IMeasurementCalculator Members

     public event EventHandler CalculationComplete;
     public event EventHandler CalculationCancelled;

     public double CalculatedValue { get; set; }

#endregion
```

Code snippet BodyMassIndexCalculator.xaml.cs

The final step in this control is to actually calculate the BMI and fire the `CalculationComplete` event, so that the measurement log page can update the selected measurement log entry with the `CalculatedValue` property of the `BodyMassIndexCalculator` control.

Available for download on Wrox.com

```
private void BodyMassIndexForm_EditEnded(object sender,
DataFormEditEndedEventArgs e)
{
     ComboBox units = BodyMassIndexForm.FindNameInContent("Units") as ComboBox;
     TextBox heightText = BodyMassIndexForm.FindNameInContent("HeightText") as
TextBox;
     TextBox weightText = BodyMassIndexForm.FindNameInContent("WeightText") as
TextBox;

     if (e.EditAction == DataFormEditAction.Cancel && CalculationCancelled != null)
          CalculationCancelled(this, null);
     else
     {
          // Calculate the approx body mass index formula is kg / m2
          // convert lbs to kg and ft to m if necessary first

          double weightValue = Convert.ToDouble(weightText.Text);
          double heightValue = Convert.ToDouble(heightText.Text);

          if ((units.SelectedItem as ComboBoxItem).Content.ToString() ==
"Standard (lbs, in)")
          {
               heightValue *= 0.305;
               weightValue *= 0.454;
          }

          // Body Mass Index is usually represented as an integer so
          // cast the result

          CalculatedValue = (int)(weightValue / Math.Pow(heightValue, 2));

          if (CalculationComplete != null)
               CalculationComplete(this, null);
     }
}
```

Code snippet BodyMassIndexCalculator.xaml.cs

When this is complete, you should have a nice and easy way to assist users in calculating their `BodyMassIndex` value without forcing them to actually leave the site. Figure 7-6 shows the `BodyMassIndex` calculator in action.

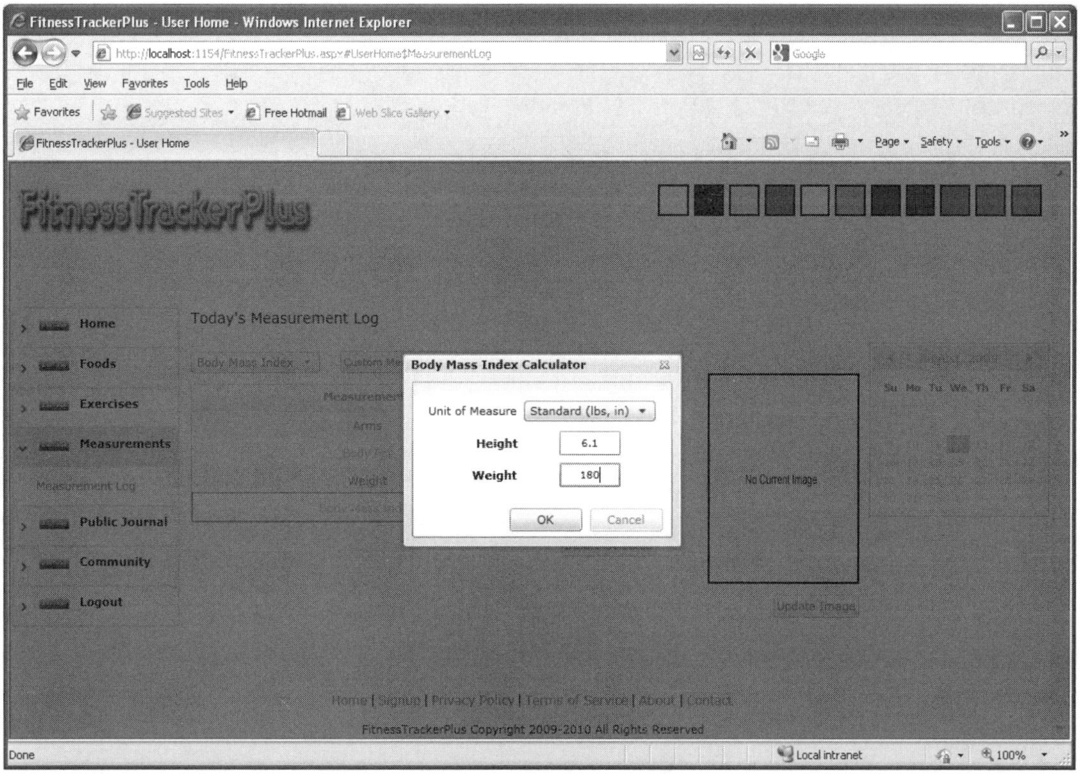

FIGURE 7-6

SUMMARY

Well that's finally it! You now have all three of the major data entry screens complete. FitnessTrackerPlus is finally really starting to feel like a more polished line-of-business application. You've seen how to make use of some newer controls such as the `DomainDataSource`, `GlobalCalendar`, and `DataForm`. You have seen how to make use of the new WCF RIA Services and metadata feature to provide CRUD operations on your generated LINQ to SQL entities complete with client-side validation. You have also seen how to create a basic plug-in system for fitness calculators by using the static `Activator` class and interface-based programming. Now with all of the required data entry screens complete, it's time to go back and finish up that Dashboard screen because you now have some actual data to make use of.

8

Unfinished Business

Finishing up the Dashboard Page

With all of the data entry pages complete, it's time to turn your attention back to the dashboard page that greets users who have logged into the application. At this point, after logging into the application, users are presented with a dashboard page that contains several summary controls that currently have no functionality behind them. Sure, the site announcements are working, but the rest of the page offers nothing to the users.

You could make the argument that these summary pages should have been completed during the original dashboard implementation, but I felt that until you had created pages that actually allowed you to create log entries it would be difficult to actually put any real functionality behind the controls. This chapter walks you through the creation of each of the summary controls and finishes up by taking the screenshot for the main page of the site, which is still blank. In this chapter, you will see how to expose custom types from the WCF RIA Services platform even if they have not been generated with the LINQ to SQL code generator. You will also see coverage of some important additions to Silverlight such as the new charting capabilities that can be found in the Silverlight Toolkit.

Finally, because the title of this chapter is "Unfinished Business" you'll be adding an important line-of-business feature to the log pages — Printing. Since Silverlight's first release, there's been no feature more requested than some kind of printing capability that doesn't rely on the default browser printing functionality. Now, with Silverlight 4 developers finally have an easy interface to perform printing as part of the runtime. In this chapter, you'll see how easy it is to add this new printing functionality to the food, exercise, and measurement log pages in order to allow users to print the data in the various `DataGrid` controls. Since you already have a right-click context menu developed and attached to these `DataGrid` controls, it shouldn't be too difficult to add a print option as well.

PROBLEM

Once users are logged into FitnessTrackerPlus, the first thing they see is the dashboard page. From the dashboard page, users need access to site announcements and summary information of entries that have been logged for the current day. Most sites offer some kind of dashboard functionality that includes basic summary information along with chart controls to enhance the look and feel of the page as well as quickly give users a visual overview of important data points. Earlier, you created placeholder controls for the food, exercise, and `MeasurementSummary` controls. Now that all of the log pages are fully functional, it is time to work out some of the details of the summary controls.

Each of the summary controls on the page should give the user quick insight into the current daily progress being made in each of the three fitness areas. One of the best ways to achieve this is through the use of charts. In previous versions of Silverlight, you would have had to resort to potentially expensive third-party charting libraries and components. Now, with the latest release of the Silverlight Toolkit you have access to a completely free and powerful charting solution. You should find a way to incorporate some of the available charts into the nutrition and `ExerciseSummary` controls. As far as the measurements summary control goes, the most useful information you can probably provide would be the last recorded measurement values for the user along with the most up-to-date image. Because you don't have much room on this control, you can concentrate on displaying the last recorded entries for the standard measurements that apply to all users. The challenge is that you will have to come up with an appropriate LINQ query to retrieve the last recorded measurement for each of the standard measurements. You also will have to accommodate the possibility that there is no recorded value for certain measurements.

An additional problem that you need to resolve in this chapter is probably the easiest one you will face depending on your ability to hit both the Alt and Print Screen keys at the same time. Even the most artistically challenged developers should have no problem taking screenshots. All that is required is entering some data on one of those log pages, and good old Microsoft Paint.

In Chapter 3, you created a placeholder for the screenshot, so that is where you place it once you have one. Remember, this screenshot will be the first thing that users see when they arrive at the main landing page. As unfair as it may sound, most Internet users will judge a book, or in this case a site, by its cover, and if the screenshot does not provide a good representation of the site, the majority of them will immediately leave and find your competitor. Anyone can take a screenshot, but you must make sure it's the right one. As mundane and unimportant as this task may seem, it is absolutely critical to ensuring that your landing page looks professional and well thought out.

Finally, to ensure that the application has features similar to a traditional line-of-business application, you also need to add printing support to all the `DataGrid` controls in the various log pages. Users should be able to right-click any `DataGrid` and select a Print Entries option to get a printed copy of their food, exercise, and measurement log entries.

DESIGN

The "Design" section for this chapter is broken down into three main areas — one for each of the summary controls that need to be created. Once again, I will be using the same design and solution formula, breaking down the components into separate discussions on user interface, database, data access, business logic, and finally the user interface code behind logic. First up is the daily `FoodSummary` control.

Food Summary

Using the list of food log entries that have been created in the food log for the current day, the `FoodSummary` control should show the user a quick visual overview of the major nutrients that have been consumed. You can display many different things here. One of the most obvious choices would be the total number of calories consumed so far. Along with the number of calories, you should probably display some of the individual nutrient totals as well. Because you are attempting to create a dashboard look and feel with each of these summary controls, you need to incorporate some kind of chart control onto each of the summaries. Users will already be able to see the total number of calories consumed for the given day, but they will probably wonder where all of those calories are coming from. By providing a pie chart of the various calorie sources, users will have a good visualization tool to see how many calories each food in their food log is contributing to the overall total calorie count.

User Interface

When designing the user interface for the `FoodSummary`, you need to include both the text-based list of nutrient totals and a chart that shows how the various food sources were added to the food log so far along with the number of calories that each of those foods is responsible for. For this control, you want to display the text-based values and the accompanying chart side by side with the text values, taking up only as much space as is required and the pie chart using up the remainder of the available space. As far as the text-based list, you should plan on displaying the data in a format similar to Table 8-1:

TABLE 8-1: Suggested Text-Based List Display

DATA	VALUE
Total Calories Consumed	1,200
Fat	30
Carbohydrates	100
Protein	40
Sugars	100
Cholesterol	230

For the pie chart, you will need the business logic layer to go through the complete list of food log entries for the given day and return both the food that was logged and the percentage of total calories consumed represented by that food. Although the calculation is pretty simple, you should still make sure that it is done in the business logic layer so that the user interface simply needs to make use of that data in order to draw the pie chart. As stated earlier, each slice of the pie chart will represent one of the foods entered in the food log and the size of the pie slices will depend on the percentage of the total calories consumed that the given food represents.

Database, Data Access

No additional work is needed for these two areas. All you will need to calculate the values is the current list of food log entries, which is already available from the existing database tables and LINQ to SQL classes.

Business Logic

For the business logic layer, you will need to modify the existing `FoodService` class in order to return an object that the user interface can use to display both the nutrient values and calorie percentages for the items in the food log. Everything that is needed for displaying both the text values and pie chart should be encapsulated into a new business object that can be returned by the `FoodService`. Ideally, the user interface should be able to call a new method called `GetDailyFoodSummary`, which returns a `DailyFoodSummary` object that contains the total calories consumed, nutrient value totals, and a list of each food along with the total percentage of calories consumed represented by that entry. Because there is no `DailySummary` table in the database, this class won't be something that is generated automatically with the LINQ to SQL classes code generator. Instead, you will need to create a new entity class and instruct the WCF RIA Services framework to make it available to the client. As you will see in the "Solution" section, just because your `DomainService` extends the `LinqToSqlDomainService` class does not mean that you are necessarily limited to using only those classes that are generated using the existing LINQ to SQL code generation tools.

User Interface Code Behind

In the code behind for the `FoodSummary`, the only real operation that needs to take place is the retrieval of the `DailyFoodSummmary` from the `FoodService` and the display of its information. The first thought might be to just go ahead and place that logic in the `Loaded` event like you have been doing for many of the other control initialization tasks. However, it is entirely possible and in fact quite likely that the user will leave the dashboard, make new entries in the food log, and then return to this dashboard page expecting to see updated information. Unfortunately, if you were to place all of the logic in the `Loaded` event the user would still see old data because the `Loaded` event is triggered only once during this sequence of events. Because this is not a problem that is unique to the `FoodSummary` control, you will need to devise a solution that provides the parent dashboard page a mechanism to trigger a data refresh in all three summary controls. Once again, this seems like a perfect opportunity to make use of interface-based programming because the dashboard page doesn't really need to know any details of the summary control it is trying to initiate the refresh on, just that it is, in fact, a summary control. In the "Solution" section, you will build an `ISummaryControl` interface with one method called `RefreshSummary`. Each of three summary controls will need to implement this interface and refresh their data when the `RefreshSummary` method is called by the dashboard page.

Exercise Summary

The ExerciseSummary control will be responsible for showing the user how many calories they have burned for the current day. At this point, the users are aware of how many calories have been consumed and the sources of those calories. The ExerciseSummary will quickly show the users if they are successfully burning all of those calories and it will also show them which exercises have been the most effective in burning those calories. Like the FoodSummary control, this control will show both a text-based representation of the calorie data as well as a chart control to show which exercises were responsible for burning the calories. For this control, however, instead of making use of a pie chart to provide a visualization of the data, you will be using a horizontal bar chart.

User Interface

The user interface for the ExerciseSummary control will be very similar to the one designed for the FoodSummary control. You should again count on placing some TextBlock controls side by side with a Chart control. When implementing this type of layout, you will no doubt find that the Grid control offers the most flexibility with regards to control layout. The Grid control also offers one of the only ways to ensure that the list of TextBlock controls only takes up the actual space required while at the same time ensuring that the Chart control takes up the remaining available space. The format for the TextBlock control list will also mimic the work done for the FoodSummary control and will need to display the total calories burned, along with the calories burned from cardio, weight training, and other activities. Table 8-2 gives an example of what the TextBlock controls should look like when complete:

TABLE 8-2: TextBlock Controls Example

CONTROL	VALUE
Total Calories Burned	1,200
Cardio	500
Weight Training	200
Other Activities	500

For the horizontal bar chart, you should expect to have a DailyExerciseSummary object available from the ExerciseService that the user interface will make use of in order to create the chart. Each bar on the chart should represent both the exercise that was performed as well as the total number of calories burned.

Database, Data Access

There are no new database tables or LINQ to SQL classes needed to develop the ExerciseSummary control. Just as you did with the FoodSummary, you will make use of the existing database tables and generated LINQ to SQL classes that are available from the ExerciseService you created earlier.

Business Logic

Just as you did for the `FoodSummary` control, you will need to make modifications to the `ExerciseService` that includes adding both a method to return the summary information and a class to hold the various summary data. In this case, you should create a method called `GetDailyExerciseSummary` that will retrieve the current list of exercises that have been added to the exercise journal. Once the list of journal entries has been retrieved, the method needs to both calculate the total number of calories burned as well as populate the `DailyExerciseSummary` object with a list of individual exercises along with the number of calories burned for each exercise.

User Interface Code Behind

The `ExerciseSummary` control will implement the `ISummaryControl` interface and consequently will perform most of its calculation logic in the `RefreshSummary` method. In this method, you will first need to retrieve the summary data from the `ExerciseService` and then use that data to populate both the `TextBlock` controls as well as the horizontal bar chart. You should be able to bind the result of the retrieval method to the `DataContext` property of the control itself and use binding expressions in the `TextBlock` controls in order to display the data.

Measurement Summary

The `MeasurementSummary` control will present users with a quick overview of their latest measurements. This control will only be responsible for displaying a list of the standard measurements that are available to all users along with the latest recorded value for those measurements. In addition to the list of standard measurements, the last recorded user image will also be displayed. There won't be any charts on this control as the main purpose is just to provide a really quick summary of the users' most up-to-date measurements.

User Interface

The user interface for the `MeasurementSummary` control will consist of a list of `TextBlock` controls with binding expressions set up in order to display the measurement values. Once again, this will assume that a `DailyMeasurementSummary` object has been retrieved from the business logic layer and its properties are available for data binding. As in the previous summary controls, the `TextBlock` controls will only take up a portion of the overall user interface. Sitting alongside the `TextBlock` controls will be the most recently updated image of the user. If the user has not uploaded any images, then a default "Image not available" image will be displayed in its place. Because there will be no additional chart controls, this is really going to be a pretty simple user interface.

Database, Data Access

There are no new database tables or LINQ to SQL classes needed to develop the `MeasurementSummary` control. Just as you did with the previous summary controls, you will make use of the existing database tables and generated LINQ to SQL classes that are available from the `MeasurementService` you created earlier in the book.

Business Logic

The business logic layer for the `MeasurementSummary` control follows in the footsteps of the previous summary controls. Once again, you will need to create an additional business object called `DailyMeasurementSummary` and you will also have to add a `ServiceOperation` to the `MeasurementService` class that retrieves this daily summary. The hardest part of this is figuring out the appropriate LINQ statements that are necessary to ensure that only the most recently logged value is returned for each of the standard measurements. As you will see in the solution, the LINQ syntax supports a wide range of options and if it has a statement for the traditional T-SQL, most likely it has a related LINQ option that mimics that behavior.

User Interface Code Behind

The user interface code behind for the `MeasurementSummary` control should be pretty simple. Just like the other summary controls, this one will also implement the `ISummaryControl` interface and all of its logic will be performed in the `RefreshSummary` method. All you will need to do here is call the `GetDailyMeasurementSummary` method of the `MeasurementService` and bind the `DailyMeasurementSummary` object returned to the `DataContext` property of the overall `MeasurementSummary` control. This ensures that all of the standard measurement `TextBlock` controls display the correct information. Finally, you need to extract the latest image URL from the `DailyMeasurementSummary` object and make sure that the `Image` control has its `Source` property set accordingly. Don't forget to include the additional code you saw in the previous chapter to prevent Silverlight from caching the image as it is entirely possible that the user will upload a new image in the measurement journal and then come back to this dashboard expecting to see the new image; without that additional code, the user will only see the previously downloaded image.

Printing Support

The final area of concern in this chapter is going back and updating the right-click context menus to include printing support for the various `DataGrid` controls. The "Solution" section shows you that printing in Silverlight is pretty simple and does not require much code. Basically, the printing programming interface allows you to send just about any `UIElement` or control declared in XAML directly to the printer. As of now, there aren't too many formatting options other than directly sending the desired control to the printer, but you can do some basic things like stretching the content to fit the available space on the paper. In this chapter, you'll see how to specifically add printing support for the food log page. Because the printing requirement spans both the exercise and measurement log pages, you can easily refer to the available sample code to see those implementations that won't really differ much from the food log page anyway.

SOLUTION

In the solution for this chapter, you'll finish up the implementation of the three summary controls for the dashboard page, and you'll add printing support to the existing `DataGrid` controls. Also, you'll finally take that screenshot of the data entry process and place it on the main FitnessTrackerPlus starting page. You will need to have all of these details wrapped up before moving on to the next major feature, which is the public journal. The solution includes details on how to work with the Chart control of the Silverlight Toolkit, as well as how to expose custom entities from your DomainService classes even if they were not generated using the LINQ to SQL code generator. When working with the Chart control, you will see just how easy it is to customize the appearance of the chart using a custom control template. In this case, you'll create a control template that repositions the Legend and Title areas to better fit the available screen area in the individual summary controls.

Food Summary

The first control to work on is the FoodSummary control. The design of the control calls for some TextBlock controls to display the consumed total calories as well as the totals for several important nutrients. Finally, a pie chart will display and show all the individual food entries a user made along with the various calorie counts associated with those foods. Each pie slice will represent a food item added to the current food log; when the user hovers the mouse over a given pie slice, the total calories associated with that food will appear.

User Interface

To provide both the TextBlock fields as well as the pie chart in the space that is available for the summary control, you'll need to have a container that hosts both those components and gives the appropriate amount of space to both visual elements. You could use a StackPanel with its Orientation property set to Horizontal to align the TextBlock controls and pie chart so that they fill up the available space on the control. The downside is that you won't have much control over how much space is allocated to the pie chart versus the TextBlock controls. You would have to resort to a messy combination of setting the Alignment and Margin properties on both elements to get the appearance you're looking for. Instead, you should use a Grid control, which splits the available area in such a way that the column containing the TextBlock controls uses only the required amount of space to properly display itself; and the column containing the Chart control takes up all of the remaining space that is available in the summary control. The Grid control can really come in handy when you need a combination of fixed-width columns and columns that need to take up the remaining available space. The following XAML code shows the FoodSummary control container that will hold the TextBlock and Chart controls.

Available for download on Wrox.com

```
<Border Style="{StaticResource SummaryBorderStyle}">
    <StackPanel Style="{StaticResource SummaryStackPanelStyle}">
        <Border Style="{StaticResource SummaryHeaderBorderStyle}">
            <TextBlock Style="{StaticResource FoodSummaryHeaderTextStyle}" />
        </Border>
        <Grid>
            <Grid.RowDefinitions>
                <RowDefinition />
            </Grid.RowDefinitions>
            <Grid.ColumnDefinitions>
                <ColumnDefinition Width="Auto" />
                <ColumnDefinition Width="*" />
            </Grid.ColumnDefinitions>
            <StackPanel Grid.Column="0" Style="{StaticResource
```

```
SummaryTextStackPanelStyle}">
                    <!-- TextBlock controls will be hosted here -->
               </StackPanel>
          </Grid>
          <!-- Chart control will go here and be assigned to Grid.Column="1" -->
     </StackPanel>
</Border>
```

Code snippet FoodSummary.xaml

As you can see, this container structure does a nice job of allocating the appropriate space for both the `TextBlock` and `Chart` controls, so you can probably count on using the same technique when you start working on the `ExerciseSummary` control as well.

Next, you should take a crack at the fixed `TextBlock` controls. One nice thing about Silverlight data binding is that you can easily set the `DataContext` property of the overall user control and the data will be fully available to any of the child controls being hosted that wish to make use of it. This makes it easy to set up the `Binding` property of the various `TextBlock` controls to values that are available from the `DataContext` property of the parent `UserControl`. In the following code, each `TextBlock` control is bound to the appropriate `DailyFoodSummary` property and a `Converter` formats the string being displayed.

Available for download on Wrox.com

```
<Style x:Key="IndentedSummaryTextStyle" BasedOn="{StaticResource
SummaryTextStyle}" TargetType="TextBlock">
     <Setter Property="TextAlignment" Value="Right" />
     <Setter Property="FontWeight" Value="Normal" />
</Style>

<StackPanel Grid.Column="0" Style="{StaticResource SummaryTextStackPanelStyle}">
     <TextBlock Text="{Binding Path=total_calories, Converter={StaticResource
SummaryConverter}, ConverterParameter='Total Calories Consumed: {0}'}"
Style="{StaticResource SummaryTextStyle}" />
     <TextBlock Text="{Binding Path=total_fat, Converter={StaticResource
SummaryConverter}, ConverterParameter='Fat: {0}g'}" Style="{StaticResource
IndentedSummaryTextStyle}" />
     <TextBlock Text="{Binding Path=total_carbohydrate, Converter={StaticResource
SummaryConverter}, ConverterParameter='Carbohydrate: {0}g'}" Style="{StaticResource
IndentedSummaryTextStyle}" />
     <TextBlock Text="{Binding Path=total_protein, Converter={StaticResource
SummaryConverter}, ConverterParameter='Protein: {0}g'}" Style="{StaticResource
IndentedSummaryTextStyle}" />
</StackPanel>
```

Code snippet FoodSummary.xaml

All the `TextBlock` controls make use of the existing `SummaryConverter` class that you created previously, which handles converting the raw data value into the formatted string assigned to the `ConverterParameter` attribute. With the `TextBlock` controls complete, it's time to dig into the charting component that you'll make use of on both the food and `ExerciseSummary` controls. Before getting into the details of the `FoodSummary` pie chart, it's best to take a quick detour to introduce you to the charting component of the Silverlight Toolkit as well as to give you a simple example of how to get working with the `Chart` control quickly.

Charting with the Silverlight Toolkit

With each revision of the Silverlight Toolkit, many enhancements are made to the available charting feature. It is now really at a point where it successfully blends ease of use with powerful visualization capabilities to form a great and, most important, free charting solution for your application. Once you see how little code it takes to get some charts up and running, I'm sure you'll agree that this sure beats using some of the extremely complex charting solutions available that various third-party control vendors have offered in the past.

To get started with the charting features of the toolkit, first you need to add a reference to the `System.Windows.Controls.DataVisualization` library in the Silverlight project. Creating charts with this toolkit typically involves making use of the included `Chart` control and a corresponding `Series` object. The only exception to this is the new `TreeMap` chart. The `Series` object determines not only the type of chart but also the actual data values that are plotted in the chart. Several different chart types are currently available from the toolkit. Table 8-3 shows all the available chart types along with their associated series and image.

TABLE 8-3: Available Chart Types in Silverlight Toolkit

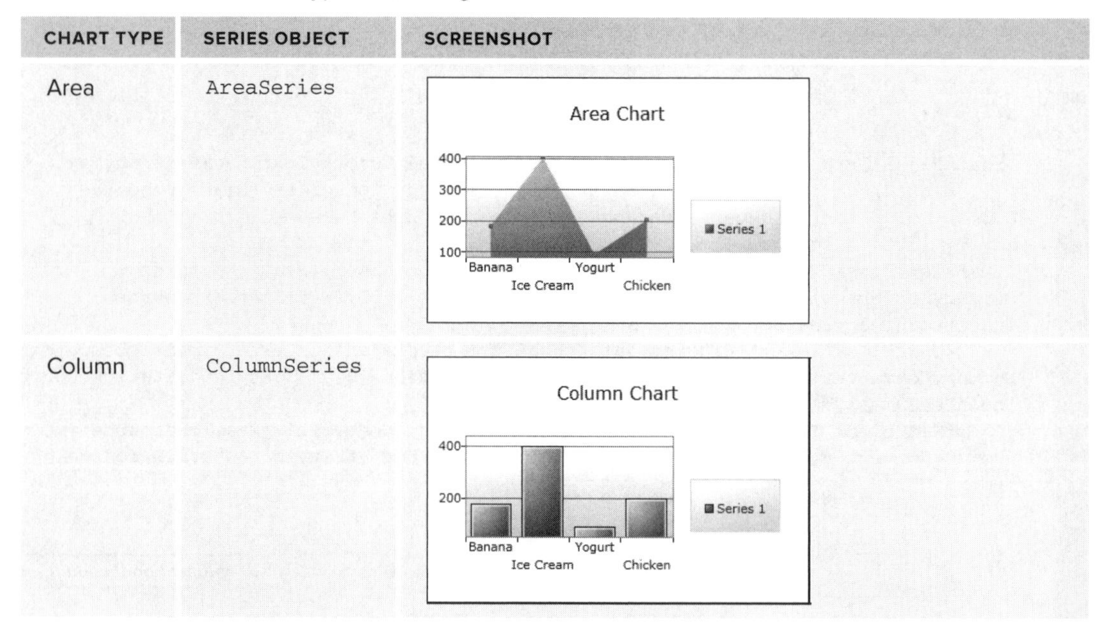

CHART TYPE	SERIES OBJECT	SCREENSHOT
Area	`AreaSeries`	Area Chart
Column	`ColumnSeries`	Column Chart

TABLE 8-3: Available Chart Types in Silverlight Toolkit *(continued)*

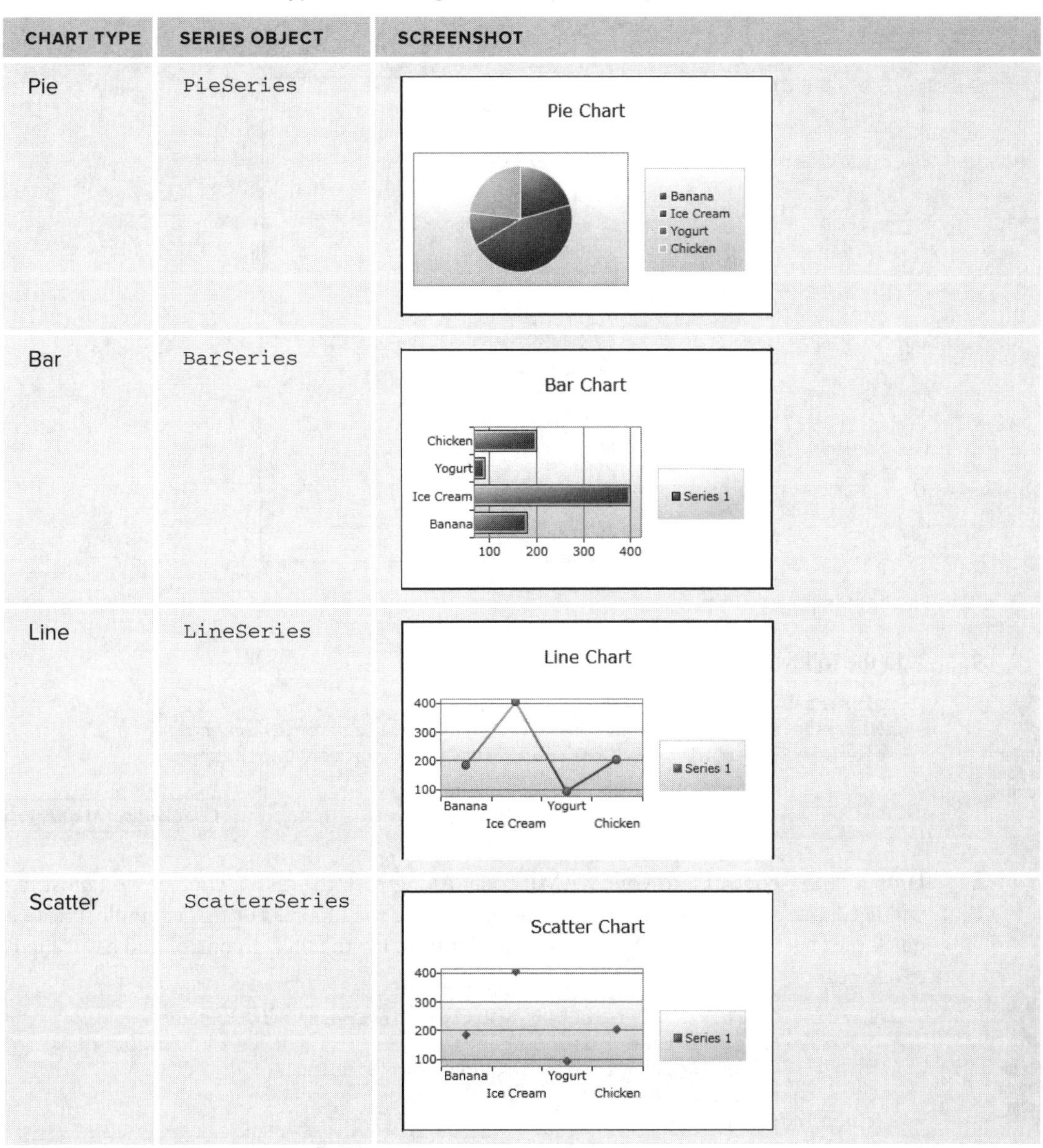

CHART TYPE	SERIES OBJECT	SCREENSHOT
Pie	`PieSeries`	
Bar	`BarSeries`	
Line	`LineSeries`	
Scatter	`ScatterSeries`	

continues

TABLE 8-3: Available Chart Types in Silverlight Toolkit *(continued)*

CHART TYPE	SERIES OBJECT	SCREENSHOT
Bubble	`BubbleSeries`	Bubble Chart 400 200 Series 1 Banana Ice Cream Yogurt Chicken
TreeMap	N/A	Ice Cream Chicken Banana Yogurt

Creating a chart is pretty simple.

1. Add the following namespace declaration:

Available for download on Wrox.com

```
xmlns:charting="clr-
namespace:System.Windows.Controls.DataVisualization.Charting;
assembly=System.Windows.Controls.DataVisualization.Toolkit"
```

Code snippet MainPage.xaml

2. Drop a `Chart` control into your XAML code. Along with the `Chart` control, you most likely will need a `Series` object declared in the XAML for the `Chart`. For this example, create a quick pie chart. Here is the XAML code declaration for the `Chart` control and associated `PieSeries`:

Available for download on Wrox.com

```
<charting:Chart x:Name="PieChart" Title="Pie Chart" Width="350">
     <charting:Chart.Series>
          <charting:PieSeries ItemsSource="{Binding}" />
     </charting:Chart.Series>
</charting:Chart>
```

Code snippet MainPage.xaml located in ChartSample project

3. You can set the data points for your new chart in many different ways, but for this example you'll use a `List<KeyValuePair>` collection. In the code behind, you could have the calorie values of a couple of foods represented as `KeyValuePair` objects.

Available for download on Wrox.com

```
List<KeyValuePair<string, int>> items = new
List<KeyValuePair<string, int>>();

items.Add(new KeyValuePair<string, int>("Banana", 180));
items.Add(new KeyValuePair<string, int>("Ice Cream", 400));
```

```
items.Add(new KeyValuePair<string, int>("Yogurt", 90));
items.Add(new KeyValuePair<string, int>("Chicken", 200));
```

Code snippet MainPage.xaml.cs located in ChartSample project

4. In order for the `Chart` control to actually draw the pie chart, you would simply set the `DataContext` property of the `Chart` control as such:

Available for download on Wrox.com

```
PieChart.DataContext = items;
```

Code snippet MainPage.xaml.cs

5. The last thing required for the pie chart to work is to tell the series which piece of the `KeyValuePair` object will represent the actual data value of the pie slice, and which piece will represent the item being measured. For all Series objects, this is done by setting the `IndependentValuePath` and `DependentValuePath` properties, which you can safely define in the following way.

   - The `IndependentValuePath` represents the item you are measuring. In the current example, this is the food name itself.
   - The `DependentValuePath` is typically the property of the bound object that represents the data points being tracked. Again, using the current example, the `DependentValuePath` is the actual calorie values for each of the foods.
   - More often than not, if you bind to the `Chart` control using a collection of `KeyValuePair` objects, you'll almost always set the `IndependentValuePath` to the `Key` property and the `DependentValuePath` to the `Value` property.

   Here is the XAML code for this example's pie chart with the `IndependentValuePath` and `DependentValuePath` set to the `Key` and `Value` properties, respectively.

Available for download on Wrox.com

```
<charting:Chart x:Name="PieChart" Title="Pie Chart" Width="350">
     <charting:Chart.Series>
          <charting:PieSeries ItemsSource="{Binding}"
               DependentValuePath="Value"
               IndependentValuePath="Key" />
     </charting:Chart.Series>
</charting:Chart>
```

Code snippet MainPage.xaml located in ChartSample project

6. After you complete all this, running this simple example results in the pie chart shown in Figure 8-1.

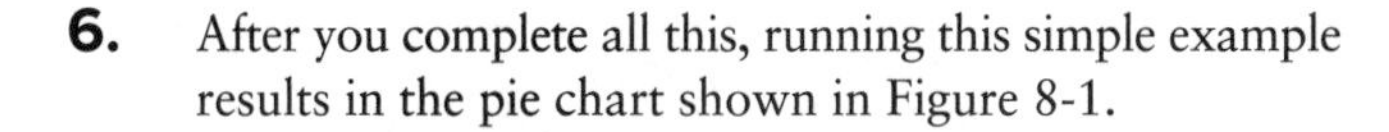

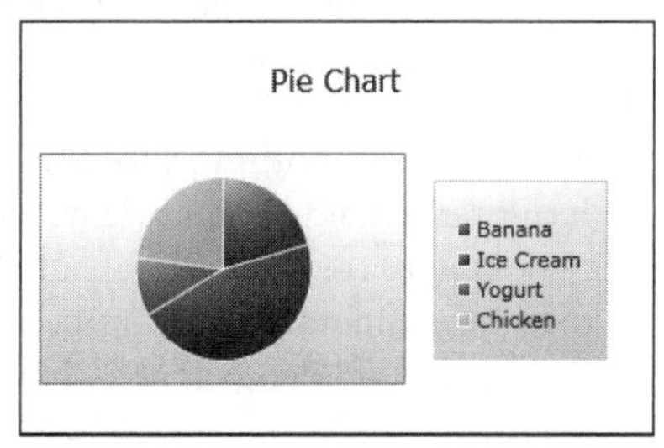

FIGURE 8-1

Just in case the business requirements change and you are given the directive to display a bar chart instead of the pie chart, you can easily make use of the same data, and by just changing the Series object, you can generate a bar chart like the one shown in Figure 8-2. Here is the XAML code required to make the change.

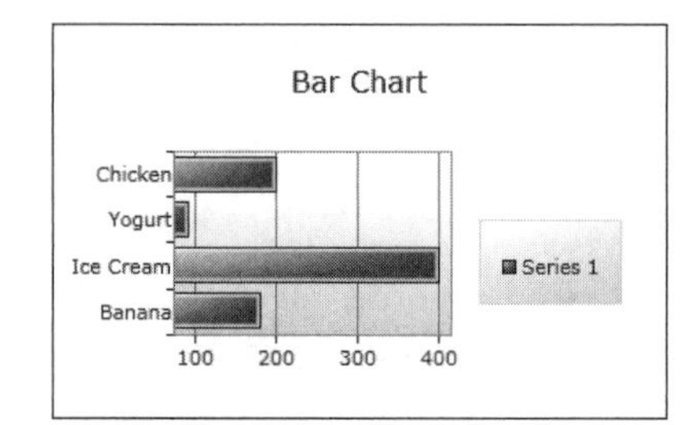

FIGURE 8-2

Available for download on Wrox.com

```
<charting:Chart x:Name="BarChart" Title="Bar Chart" Width="350">
     <charting:Chart.Series>
          <charting:BarSeries ItemsSource="{Binding}"
               DependentValuePath="Value"
               IndependentValuePath="Key" />
          </charting:Chart.Series>
</charting:Chart>
```

Code snippet MainPage.xaml located in ChartSample project

User Interface Continued

After that quick detour, it's time to get back to the user interface for the FoodSummary control. Now that you have seen how easy it is to add charting capabilities to your Silverlight application using the charting component of the toolkit, you'll add a chart to the FoodSummary to display the percentage of calories consumed from fat, carbohydrates, and protein. You have only a limited amount of screen real estate in the summary controls and, as you saw in the previous sample, the Chart control, by default, includes space for the Title and Legend as well as the plot area itself. It would be nice if you could remove the Title area completely from the Chart control because it really isn't needed on the summary control. You really just want to show the pie chart along with the Legend area. To truly make efficient use of the available space, you may even want to move the Legend area from alongside the plot area to below the actual chart drawing. In order to make this happen, you'll basically need to override the default control template of the Chart control.

You can do this a couple of different ways:

- Open the Chart control in Expression Blend and edit a copy of the control template.
- Because it's not assumed that you have Blend available and that you've tried to stick to raw XAML editing in Visual Studio, an alternative and free method involves modifying the control template.

There really is nothing about the Blend solution that you can't do yourself, so open up a new Explorer window and navigate to the installation location of the toolkit; most likely this is C:\Program Files\Microsoft SDKs\Silverlight\v4.0\Toolkit\Nov09. Then go to the Source directory and unzip the Source code.zip file. After the file extraction is complete, you should have a Source code folder available. Now navigate to the Controls.DataVisualization.Toolkit\Themes directory. In this folder you will find the `generic.xaml` file containing the default control template for the `Chart` control. Because you have a ton of XAML code in this file, you may have to search for it, but eventually you will find the default template for the `Chart`. Once you find it, you only need the XAML code for the `Template` property and it looks like this:

```
<Setter Property="Template">
     <Setter.Value>
          <ControlTemplate TargetType="charting:Chart">
               <Border Background="{TemplateBinding Background}"
BorderBrush="{TemplateBinding BorderBrush}" BorderThickness="{TemplateBinding
BorderThickness}" Padding="10">
                    <Grid>
                         <Grid.RowDefinitions>
                              <RowDefinition Height="Auto" />
                              <RowDefinition Height="*" />
                         </Grid.RowDefinitions>

                         <datavis:Title Content="{TemplateBinding Title}"
Style="{TemplateBinding TitleStyle}" />

                         <!-- Use a nested Grid to avoid possible clipping behavior
resulting from ColumnSpan+Width=Auto -->
                         <Grid Grid.Row="1" Margin="0,15,0,15">
                              <Grid.ColumnDefinitions>
                                   <ColumnDefinition Width="*" />
                                   <ColumnDefinition Width="Auto" />
                              </Grid.ColumnDefinitions>

                              <datavis:Legend x:Name="Legend"
Title="{TemplateBinding LegendTitle}" Style="{TemplateBinding LegendStyle}"
Grid.Column="1" />
                              <chartingprimitives:EdgePanel x:Name="ChartArea"
Style="{TemplateBinding ChartAreaStyle}">
                                   <Grid Canvas.ZIndex="-1" Style="{TemplateBinding
PlotAreaStyle}" />
                                   <Border Canvas.ZIndex="10"
BorderBrush="#FF919191"BorderThickness="1" />
                              </chartingprimitives:EdgePanel>
                         </Grid>
                    </Grid>
               </Border>
          </ControlTemplate>
     </Setter.Value>
</Setter>
```

As you can see from the previous code, there isn't too much involved in the creation of the `Chart` control. The current goal is to redisplay the `Legend` below the actual chart. The chart itself is contained in the `Grid` with the custom style called `PlotAreaStyle`. In turn, this plot area and the `Legend` are contained in a `Grid` control that assigns the `PlotAreaStyle` to the left and the `Legend` to the right. To get the effect you are looking for, you just need to alter the `Grid` control container and change it so that you have three rows. The first row will contain the `Title`, the second row the `PlotAreaStyle`, and the third row the `Legend`. The following XAML code shows the custom `Chart` template that you will use for both the `FoodSummary` control and the `ExerciseSummary` control charts.

Available for download on Wrox.com

```
xmlns:charting_visuals="clr-
namespace:System.Windows.Controls.DataVisualization;
assembly=System.Windows.Controls.DataVisualization.Toolkit"

xmlns:charting_primitives="clr-
namespace:System.Windows.Controls.DataVisualization.Charting.Primitives;
assembly=System.Windows.Controls.DataVisualization.Toolkit"

<Style x:Key="FoodSummaryChartStyle" TargetType="charting:Chart">
     <Setter Property="BorderThickness" Value="0" />
     <Setter Property="Width" Value="150" />
     <Setter Property="VerticalAlignment" Value="Top" />
     <Setter Property="HorizontalAlignment" Value="Right" />
     <Setter Property="Template">
          <Setter.Value>
               <ControlTemplate TargetType="charting:Chart">
                    <Border Background="{TemplateBinding Background}"
BorderBrush="{TemplateBinding BorderBrush}" BorderThickness="{TemplateBinding
BorderThickness}" Padding="10">
                         <Grid>
                              <Grid.RowDefinitions>
                                   <RowDefinition Height="Auto" />
                                   <RowDefinition Height="*" />
                                   <RowDefinition Height="Auto" />
                              </Grid.RowDefinitions>
                              <charting_primitives:EdgePanel x:Name="ChartArea"
Style="{TemplateBinding ChartAreaStyle}">
                                   <Grid Style="{TemplateBinding PlotAreaStyle}" />
                              </charting_primitives:EdgePanel>
                              <charting_visuals:Legend x:Name="Legend"
Title="{TemplateBinding LegendTitle}" Style="{StaticResource
SummaryChartLegendStyle}" Margin="0,5,0,0" Grid.Row="2" />
                         </Grid>
                    </Border>
               </ControlTemplate>
          </Setter.Value>
     </Setter>
</Style>
```

Code snippet FoodSummary.xaml

With the custom template for the chart control and the `TextBlock` controls defined, you are pretty much done with the user interface.

Database, Data Access

As stated in the design, no further work is necessary for the database and data access layers. Instead, you simply will be making modifications to the existing `FoodService` and the LINQ to SQL entities you created previously.

Business Logic

For the `FoodSummary` control, the discussion of the business logic layer starts with the existing `FoodService` that was created earlier. You will need to make several modifications to the service in order to give the user interface the necessary data. The user interface requires a new custom business object that contains the total calories consumed along with several nutrient totals. In this summary object, it would also be nice to include the list of foods and associated calorie counts from the pie chart but, unfortunately, WCF .NET RIA Services do not support the return of embedded complex type lists. Therefore, you need to incorporate an additional step to get all of this working.

Follow these steps:

1. Create the required `DailyFoodSummary` class that will hold the total calories consumed as well as the nutrient totals.

2. Because there isn't any direct correlation to any database tables, you can't make use of LINQ to SQL. Because this class still needs to be exposed by the WCF RIA Services engine, you must add the `[EnableClientAccess]` attribute above the class definition. The following code shows the `DailyFoodSummary` class, which you simply add below the `FoodService` class definition.

```
[EnableClientAccess()]
public class DailyFoodSummary
{
    public DailyFoodSummary() { }

    [Key]
    public DateTime entry_date { get; set; }

    public double? total_calories { get; set; }
    public double? total_carbohydrate { get; set; }
    public double? total_fat { get; set; }
    public double? total_protein { get; set; }
}
```

Code snippet FoodService.cs

3. The `[EnableClientAccess]` attribute is not the only requirement for exposing custom classes to the client using WCF RIA Services. In order for the WCF RIA Services framework to expose an entity or a custom business object, you are required to designate at least one property with the `[Key]` attribute. This designation tells the framework that the property can be considered unique for each instance of the object. In this case, each `DailyFoodSummary` object will have a unique `entry_date` property, so that will make a good candidate for the key. All you have to do is add the `[Key]` attribute directly above the property declaration and you are good to go.

4. Once you have created the `DailyFoodSummary` class, you can then create a new service operation that will populate and return a new `DailyFoodSummary` object to the user interface. You will want to create a new method in the `FoodService` called `GetDailyFoodSummary`.

> *The* `GetDailyFoodSummary` *method collects all the existing food log entries and makes use of the* `Sum` *method of LINQ to calculate the total number of calories consumed for the given day.*

5. Additionally, you will tally nutrient totals for protein, carbohydrates, and fat using the same LINQ `Sum` operation. The following code shows the implementation of the `GetDailyFoodSummary` method.

Available for download on Wrox.com

```
public DailyFoodSummary GetDailyFoodSummary(int user_id, DateTime entry_date)
{
     List<FoodLogEntry> entries = GetFoodLogEntries(user_id, entry_date,
false).ToList();
     DailyFoodSummary summary = new DailyFoodSummary
     {
          total_calories = 0,
          total_carbohydrate = 0,
          total_fat = 0,
          total_protein = 0
     };

     if (entries.Count() > 0)
     {
          summary.total_calories = entries.Sum(e => e.Food.calories);
          summary.total_carbohydrate = entries.Sum(e => e.Food.carbohydrate);
          summary.total_fat = entries.Sum(e => e.Food.fat);
          summary.total_protein = entries.Sum(e => e.Food.protein);
     }

     summary.entry_date = entry_date;
     return summary;
}
```

Code snippet FoodService.cs

6. As I said earlier, in a perfect world and most likely in a future release of WCF RIA Services, you would be able to include a list of `FoodSummaryData` objects in the `DailyFoodSummary` so that the user interface has only one method to call. However, because the current version of WCF RIA Services does not support embedding `List<T>` objects of complex types you need to add an additional method. Before doing that, you need to create the `FoodSummaryData` class. In theory, you could just return the `FoodLogEntry` objects themselves but there is a lot of additional information that would be passed over the wire related to food log entries that you really don't need here. The following code shows the `FoodSummaryData` class and its two properties. Again, in order for the WCF RIA Services to be able to work with this, you need both the `[EnableClientAccess()]` and `[Key]` attributes.

Available for download on Wrox.com

```
[EnableClientAccess()]
public class FoodSummaryData
{
     [Key]
```

```
        public string food_name { get; set; }
        public double calories { get; set; }
    }
```

Code snippet FoodService.cs

7. Finally, you need to add the method that will return a list of `FoodSummaryData` objects to the user interface. Because this is a list, you can just create a method that follows the `Query` naming convention in order for the WCF RIA Services runtime to expose it. The following code shows the `GetDailyFoodSummaryData` method, which returns an `IEnumerable<FoodSummaryData>`.

Available for download on Wrox.com

```
public IEnumerable<FoodSummaryData> GetDailyFoodSummaryData(int user_id,
DateTime entry_date)
{
    List<FoodLogEntry> entries = GetFoodLogEntries(user_id, entry_date,
true).ToList();
    List<FoodSummaryData> foods = new List<FoodSummaryData>();

    foreach (FoodLogEntry entry in entries)
        foods.Add(new FoodSummaryData { food_name = entry.Food.food_name,
calories = entry.ServingSize.calories.Value });

    return foods;
}
```

Code snippet FoodService.cs

As you can see, there isn't much to this method other than creating the list of `FoodSummaryData` objects using the food name and calorie values of each `FoodLogEntry` retrieved for the current user. Now the user interface will be able to make use of this list in order to successfully create the pie chart.

User Interface Code Behind

As discussed in the "Design" section, even though you don't have a lot of work to do in the code behind, you can't just place it all in the Loaded event handler because it is possible that the data will need to be refreshed. Instead, the `FoodSummary` class will be implementing the `IDailySummary` interface as shown in Listing 8-1.

Available for download on Wrox.com

LISTING 8-1: IDailySummary.cs

```
using System;

public interface IDailySummary
{
    void LoadSummary(int user_id, DateTime summary_date);
}
```

By implementing the interface, you really only have to worry about adding the `LoadSummary` method. Now, because of the limitations discussed earlier regarding complex types and the current version of WCF RIA Services, you will need to perform two steps. In Listing 8-2, you will see that after retrieving the `DailyFoodSummary` object, you will then need to call the `Load` method of the `DomainContext` using the `GetDailyFoodSummaryDataQuery`.

LISTING 8-2: FoodSummary.xaml.cs

Available for download on Wrox.com

```
using System;
using System.Collections;
using System.Collections.Generic;
using System.Windows.Controls;
using FitnessTrackerPlus.Web.Services;
using System.Windows.Ria;

namespace FitnessTrackerPlus.Views.Dashboard
{
     public partial class FoodSummary : UserControl, IDailySummary
     {
          public FoodContext context = new FoodContext();

          public FoodSummary()
          {
               InitializeComponent();
          }

#region IDailySummary Members

          public void LoadSummary(int user_id, DateTime summary_date)
          {
               context.Load<DailyFoodSummary>(context.
GetDailyFoodSummaryQuery(user_id, summary_date),
               (SummaryLoaded) =>
               {
                    if (!SummaryLoaded.HasError)
                    {
                         IEnumerator<DailyFoodSummary> enumerator =
SummaryLoaded.Entities.GetEnumerator();
                         enumerator.MoveNext();

                         this.DataContext = enumerator.Current;

                         // Load the food summary data for the pie chart

                         context.Load<FoodSummaryData>(context.
GetDailyFoodSummaryDataQuery(Globals.CurrentUser.id, Globals.SelectedDate),
LoadBehavior.RefreshCurrent, (FoodSummaryLoaded) =>
{
     if (!FoodSummaryLoaded.HasError)
     {
```

```
            // Create a new KeyValuePair list with the data for the Pie chart

            List<KeyValuePair<string, double?>> data = new
List<KeyValuePair<string, double?>>();

            foreach (FoodSummaryData food in FoodSummaryLoaded.Entities)
                data.Add(new KeyValuePair<string, double?>(food.food_name,
food.calories));

            FoodSummaryChart.DataContext = data;
        }

}, null);
                        }

                    }, null);
            }

#endregion
    }
}
```

As you can see in Listing 8-2, creating the pie chart is as simple as creating a list of `KeyValuePair` objects where the `Key` is equal to the food name and the Value is equal to the actual number of calories associated with that food. Finally, you just set the `DataContext` property of the `Chart` control and the Silverlight Toolkit does the rest.

This pretty much finishes up the `FoodSummary` control. If you were to now add entries to the food log and come back to the dashboard page you would be presented with a `FoodSummary` that looks like Figure 8-3.

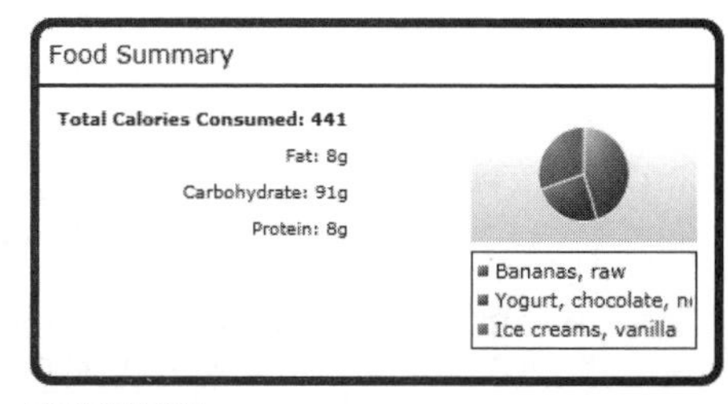

Food Summary
Total Calories Consumed: 441
Fat: 8g
Carbohydrate: 91g
Protein: 8g
Bananas, raw
Yogurt, chocolate,
Ice creams, vanilla

FIGURE 8-3

Exercise Summary

The `ExerciseSummary` control is very similar to the `FoodSummary` in that you are both showing a text-based representation of data along with a chart. It's a little bit simpler, however, in that you only need to display the total calories burned for the current day and a chart that shows how those calories were burned. Although another pie chart could be used here, you'll instead use a column chart just to mix up the visualizations available to the user.

User Interface

The user interface for the `ExerciseSummary` is very similar to the `FoodSummary` in that you use a `Grid` control as the container for both the `TextBlock` control and accompanying `Chart`. As you can see in Listing 8-3, the only major differences are that when you declare the `Chart` you make use of the `ColumnSeries` instead of the `PieSeries`, and the custom `Chart` template consists of only the `PlotAreaStyle`, with no `Title` or `Legend`.

LISTING 8-3: ExerciseSummary.xaml

Available for download on Wrox.com

```
<UserControl x:Class="FitnessTrackerPlus.Views.Dashboard.ExerciseSummary"
     xmlns="http://schemas.microsoft.com/winfx/2006/xaml/presentation"
     xmlns:x="http://schemas.microsoft.com/winfx/2006/xaml"
     xmlns:converters="clr-namespace:FitnessTrackerPlus.Converters"
     xmlns:charting="clr-
namespace:System.Windows.Controls.DataVisualization.Charting;
assembly=System.Windows.Controls.DataVisualization.Toolkit"
     xmlns:charting_visuals="clr-
namespace:System.Windows.Controls.DataVisualization;
assembly=System.Windows.Controls.DataVisualization.Toolkit"
     xmlns:charting_primitives="clr-
namespace:System.Windows.Controls.DataVisualization.Charting.Primitives;
assembly=System.Windows.Controls.DataVisualization.Toolkit">
     <UserControl.Resources>
          <converters:StringFormatConverter x:Key="SummaryConverter" />
          <Style x:Key="ExerciseSummaryHeaderTextStyle"
BasedOn="{StaticResource SummaryHeaderTextStyle}" TargetType="TextBlock">
               <Setter Property="Text" Value="Exercise Summary" />
          </Style>
          <Style x:Key="ExerciseSummaryChartStyle"
TargetType="charting:Chart">
               <Setter Property="BorderThickness" Value="0" />
               <Setter Property="Width" Value="250" />
               <Setter Property="VerticalAlignment" Value="Top" />
               <Setter Property="HorizontalAlignment" Value="Right" />
               <Setter Property="Template">
                    <Setter.Value>
                         <ControlTemplate TargetType="charting:Chart">
                              <Border Background="{TemplateBinding
Background}" BorderBrush="{TemplateBinding BorderBrush}"
BorderThickness="{TemplateBinding BorderThickness}" Padding="10">
                                   <Grid>
                                        <charting_primitives:EdgePanel
x:Name="ChartArea" Style="{TemplateBinding ChartAreaStyle}">
                                             <Grid Style="{TemplateBinding
PlotAreaStyle}" />
                                        </charting_primitives:EdgePanel>
                                   </Grid>
                              </Border>
                         </ControlTemplate>
                    </Setter.Value>
               </Setter>
          </Style>
     </UserControl.Resources>
     <Border Style="{StaticResource SummaryBorderStyle}">
          <StackPanel Style="{StaticResource SummaryStackPanelStyle}">
               <Border Style="{StaticResource SummaryHeaderBorderStyle}">
                    <TextBlock Style="{StaticResource
ExerciseSummaryHeaderTextStyle}" />
               </Border>
```

```
                <Grid>
                     <Grid.RowDefinitions>
                          <RowDefinition Height="Auto" />
                          <RowDefinition Height="*" />
                     </Grid.RowDefinitions>
                     <StackPanel Grid.Row="0" Style="{StaticResource
SummaryTextStackPanelStyle}">
                          <TextBlock Text="{Binding Path=total_calories,
Converter={StaticResource SummaryConverter}, ConverterParameter='Total
Calories Burned: {0}'}" Style="{StaticResource SummaryTextStyle}" />
                     </StackPanel>
                     <charting:Chart x:Name="ExerciseSummaryChart" Grid.Row="1"
Style="{StaticResource ExerciseSummaryChartStyle}">
                          <charting:Chart.Series>
                               <charting:BarSeries ItemsSource="{Binding}"
DependentValuePath="Value"
IndependentValuePath="Key" />
                          </charting:Chart.Series>
                     </charting:Chart>
                </Grid>
           </StackPanel>
      </Border>
</UserControl>
```

Database, Data Access

Once again, no work is necessary in the database or data access layers.

Business Logic

The business logic for the `ExerciseSummary` control will follow the same basic technique used for the `FoodSummary` control. Here you modify the existing `ExerciseService`, adding both a `DailyExerciseSummary` class and a `GetDailyExerciseSummary` method that has been marked with the `[Invoke]` attribute. The following code shows both the `DailyExerciseSummary` class along with the implementation behind the required `GetDailyExerciseSummary` method.

Available for download on Wrox.com

```
[EnableClientAccess()]
public class DailyExerciseSummary
{
     public DailyExerciseSummary() {}

     [Key]
     public DateTime entry_date { get; set; }

     public double? total_calories { get; set; }
     public double? calories_from_cardio { get; set; }
     public double? calories_from_weight_training { get; set; }
     public double? calories_from_activities { get; set; }
}

public DailyExerciseSummary GetDailyExerciseSummary(int user_id,
DateTime entry_date)
{
```

```
        List<ExerciseLogEntry> entries = GetExerciseLogEntries(entry_date,
user_id).ToList();
        DailyExerciseSummary summary = new DailyExerciseSummary
        {
            total_calories = 0,
            calories_from_cardio = 0,
            calories_from_activities = 0,
            calories_from_weight_training = 0
        };

        if (entries.Count() > 0)
        {
            summary.total_calories = entries.Sum(e => e.calories);

            if (summary.total_calories > 0)
            {
                summary.calories_from_cardio += entries.Where(e =>
e.Exercise.ExerciseType.type_name == "Cardio").Sum(e => e.calories);
                summary.calories_from_weight_training += entries.Where(e =>
e.Exercise.ExerciseType.type_name == "Weight Training").Sum(e => e.calories);
                summary.calories_from_activities += entries.Where(e =>
e.Exercise.ExerciseType.type_name == "Activities").Sum(e => e.calories);
            }
        }

        summary.entry_date = entry_date;
        return summary;
    }
```

Code snippet ExerciseService.cs

As you can see, there isn't much to the implementation other than getting the sum of the total calories burned from all of the exercise log entries. In addition, you are also totaling up all of the calories burned based on the type of exercise that was entered in the log. The user interface will use this to create the column chart and each exercise type will be represented by its own column.

User Interface Code Behind

The `ExerciseSummary` control also implements the `IDailySummary` interface and that is where you will be placing all of the code. The `ExerciseSummary` doesn't require the extra workaround step that the `FoodSummary` control needed, so the implementation shown here in Listing 8-4 for the `LoadSummary` method uses less code.

LISTING 8-4: ExerciseSummary.xaml.cs

Available for download on Wrox.com

```
using System;
using System.Collections;
using System.Collections.Generic;
using System.Windows.Controls;
```

```
using System.Windows.Controls.DataVisualization.Charting;
using FitnessTrackerPlus.Web.Services;

namespace FitnessTrackerPlus.Views.Dashboard
{
     public partial class ExerciseSummary : UserControl, IDailySummary
     {
          private ExerciseContext context = new ExerciseContext();

          public ExerciseSummary()
          {
               InitializeComponent();
          }

#region IDailySummary Members

          public void LoadSummary(int user_id, DateTime summary_date)
          {
               context.Load<DailyExerciseSummary>(context.
GetDailyExerciseSummaryQuery(user_id, summary_date),
               (SummaryLoaded) =>
               {
                    if (!SummaryLoaded.HasError)
                    {
                         IEnumerator<DailyExerciseSummary> enumerator =
SummaryLoaded.Entities.GetEnumerator();
                         enumerator.MoveNext();

                         this.DataContext = enumerator.Current;

                         // Create a new KeyValuePair list with the
                         // data for the Pie chart

                         List<KeyValuePair<string, double?>> data = new
List<KeyValuePair<string, double?>>();

                         data.Add(new KeyValuePair<string, double?>("Cardio",
enumerator.Current.calories_from_cardio));
                         data.Add(new KeyValuePair<string, double?>("Weight
Training", enumerator.Current.calories_from_weight_training));
                         data.Add(new KeyValuePair<string, double?>("Activities",
enumerator.Current.calories_from_activities));

                         ExerciseSummaryChart.DataContext = data;
                    }

               }, null);
          }

#endregion
     }
}
```

Once you are complete with the code behind page you can run the application at this point and add some entries to the current exercise log. Once completed, if you navigate back to the dashboard page, you should see an ExerciseSummary similar to the one in Figure 8-4.

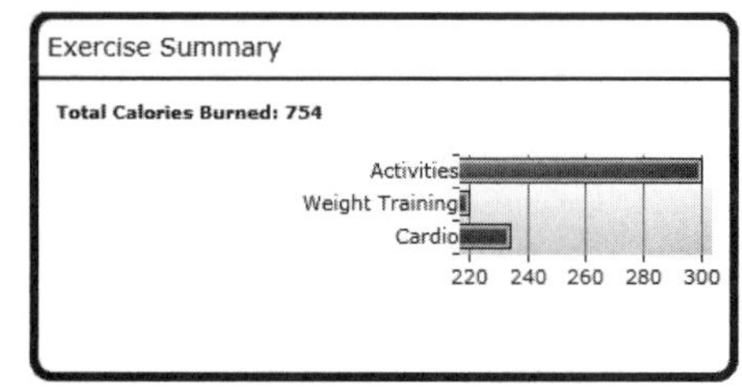

FIGURE 8-4

Measurement Summary

The MeasurementSummary is intended to give users a quick insight into how they are progressing toward their fitness goals. The design calls for the display of the most recently logged values for all of the standard measurements as well as the most up-to-date image that has been uploaded to the site if one has been made available. Many of the same techniques that were used for the food and ExerciseSummary controls will be used here as well with the exception of the Chart control. Because you only really have room for the text-based measurement values and the accompanying image, you won't be able to add any kind of Chart control to the user interface for this control.

User Interface

Just as you did with the previous summary controls, you need to make use of the Grid control to provide a container for the text-based values as well as the Image control that will make up the MeasurementSummary. I've already covered that code in the previous summary controls, so I won't be duplicating that here. Because the design calls for a text-based representation of the standard measurement values, you need to make a decision between declaring XAML for a bunch of TextBlock controls or coming up with an alternate solution. I'm not a big fan of writing tons of TextBlock XAML code in this situation, however, because you can easily achieve the same thing with a simple customized ListBox control. This results in much less XAML code and a cleaner look. You have already seen the creation of a custom ListBox in the previous dashboard chapter when you created the site announcements feature. In that instance, you added HyperlinkButton controls to the ItemContainerStyle. This time you will simply create an ItemContainerStyle that incorporates a single TextBlock control. The following code shows the declaration of the custom ListBox that will hold the standard measurements.

Available for download on Wrox.com

```
<Style x:Key="MeasurementListStyle" TargetType="ListBox">
     <Setter Property="BorderThickness" Value="0" />
     <Setter Property="Background" Value="Transparent" />
     <Setter Property="Margin" Value="10,10,0,0" />
     <Setter Property="MinHeight" Value="150" />
     <Setter Property="ScrollViewer.HorizontalScrollBarVisibility"
Value="Hidden" />
</Style>
<Style x:Key="MeasurementListItemStyle" TargetType="TextBlock">
     <Setter Property="Margin" Value="0,5,0,0" />
</Style>

<ListBox x:Name="MeasurementList" Grid.Column="0" Style="{StaticResource
MeasurementListStyle}" ItemsSource="{Binding Path=values}">
     <ListBox.ItemsPanel>
          <ItemsPanelTemplate>
               <StackPanel />
```

```
            </ItemsPanelTemplate>
        </ListBox.ItemsPanel>
        <ListBox.ItemContainerStyle>
            <Style TargetType="ListBoxItem">
                <Setter Property="Template">
                    <Setter.Value>
                        <ControlTemplate TargetType="ListBoxItem">
                            <TextBlock Text="{Binding Path=.}"
Style="{StaticResource MeasurementListItemStyle}" />
                        </ControlTemplate>
                    </Setter.Value>
                </Setter>
            </Style>
        </ListBox.ItemContainerStyle>
    </ListBox>
```

Code snippet MeasurementSummary.xaml

The custom `ListBox` takes care of displaying all of the standard measurement values. In case you are wondering how the `ListBox` will actually display the standard measurements, notice how the `ItemsSource` property of the `ListBox` is set to `values`. Just as you did for the previous summary controls, you'll create a custom business object to hold the measurement values along with the URL to the most recently uploaded image called `DailyMeasurementSummary`. In this object, you'll have a list of `string` values that will contain a formatted string containing the measurement name and the current value. The only thing left for the user interface is the `Image` control that will display the most recently uploaded image of the user. The XAML code required for this is also pretty simple and only requires a `StackPanel` along with the `Border`, `Image`, and a `TextBlock`, as shown in the following code. As far as the `Source` property of the `Image` control, that will be taken care of soon enough in the code behind. With this XAML completed, you are pretty much finished with the user interface.

Available for download on Wrox.com

```
    <Style x:Key="MeasurementSummaryStackPanelStyle" TargetType="StackPanel">
        <Setter Property="HorizontalAlignment" Value="Right" />
        <Setter Property="Margin" Value="0,0,10,5" />
    </Style>
    <Style x:Key="MeasurementSummaryImageBorderStyle" TargetType="Border">
        <Setter Property="BorderBrush" Value="#FF000000" />
        <Setter Property="Background" Value="#FFFFFFFF" />
        <Setter Property="BorderThickness" Value="1" />
        <Setter Property="Width" Value="175" />
        <Setter Property="Height" Value="200" />
        <Setter Property="Margin" Value="0,10,0,0" />
    </Style>
    <Style x:Key="MeasurementSummaryImageStyle" TargetType="Image">
        <Setter Property="Stretch" Value="Fill" />
    </Style>
    <Style x:Key="MeasurementSummaryImageTextStyle" TargetType="TextBlock">
        <Setter Property="Margin" Value="0,10,0,0" />
        <Setter Property="HorizontalAlignment" Value="Center" />
    </Style>

    <StackPanel Grid.Column="1" Style="{StaticResource
```

```
MeasurementSummaryStackPanelStyle}">
     <Border Style="{StaticResource
MeasurementSummaryImageBorderStyle}">
          <Image x:Name="CurrentImage" Style="{StaticResource
MeasurementSummaryImageStyle}" />
     </Border>
     <TextBlock Text="Current Image" Style="{StaticResource
MeasurementSummaryImageTextStyle}" />
</StackPanel>
```

Code snippet MeasurementSummary.xaml

Database, Data Access

Once again, no additional work is required for the database or data access layers.

Business Logic

For the business logic, you'll again create a custom business object to hold the summary information called `DailyMeasurementSummary`. You'll also need to add a new service operation to the `MeasurementService` class called `GetDailyMeasurementSummary`. Earlier, I discussed the current limitation of not being able to return a list of complex objects embedded in the `DailyMeasurementSummary` class with WCF RIA Services. One way around that limitation is to use the method I showed earlier, which requires two method calls from the user interface layer.

Another potential option is to return a list of string objects. Although you can't embed a list of complex types, you can embed a list of string objects. Because you are only worried about displaying what amounts to a formatted string containing the measurement name, current value, and unit, you can create a `MeasurementValue` class and override the `ToString` method to return a string that can be returned in the collection embedded in the `DailyMeasurementSummary` object. To make more sense out of this, let's go through it step by step:

1. Add a new class called `MeasurementValue` to the `MeasurementService` code file. It needs only three properties: the name, unit, and current value. Because you can't return a list of these `MeasurementValue` objects, you'll return a list of string objects instead where each string is formatted the way it would be in the `ListBox`. In order to do this, you simply override the `ToString` method. The following code shows the `MeasurementValue` class.

Available for download on Wrox.com

```
[EnableClientAccess]
public class MeasurementValue
{
     public MeasurementValue() { }

     [Key]
     public string measurement_name { get; set; }

     public string measurement_unit { get; set; }
     public double? measurement_value { get; set; }

     public override string ToString()
     {
```

```
            return String.Format("{0} {1} {2}", measurement_name,
measurement_value, measurement_unit);
        }
    }
```

Code snippet MeasurementService.cs

2. Create the `DailyMeasurementSummary` class that will contain the measurement values as well as the URL to the most recently uploaded image. Don't forget that in order for this class to be exposed to the client from WCF RIA Services, you need the `[EnableClientAccess()]` attribute and a public property marked with the `[Key]` attribute. In this case, you'll simply use the `entry_date` property as the key. The following code shows the `DailyMeasurementSummary` class.

```
[EnableClientAccess()]
public class DailyMeasurementSummary
{
    public DailyMeasurementSummary() { values = new List<string>(); }

    [Key]
    public DateTime entry_date { get; set; }

    public List<string> values { get; set; }
    public string latest_image { get; set; }
}
```

Code snippet MeasurementService.cs

3. Add the `GetDailyMeasurementSummary` method to the `MeasurementService` class. This method needs to populate and return a `DailyMeasurementSummary` instance with the list of most recent measurement values and the URL to the most recently uploaded image if one is available. If the user has not provided an image, you will simply return the default image. The following code shows the implementation for the `GetDailyMeasurementSummary` method.

```
[Invoke]
public DailyMeasurementSummary GetDailyMeasurementSummary(int user_id,
DateTime entry_date)
{
    DailyMeasurementSummary summary = new DailyMeasurementSummary();
    DataLoadOptions options = new DataLoadOptions();

    options.LoadWith<MeasurementLogEntry>(e => e.Measurement);
    options.LoadWith<MeasurementLogEntry>(e => e.MeasurementUnit);

    this.DataContext.LoadOptions = options;

    // Use the grouping feature of LINQ to SQL in order
    // to get the latest measurement
    // log entries for each available measurement

    var latestEntries = (from c in this.DataContext.MeasurementLogEntries
```

```
            where c.entry_date.Date <= entry_date.Date
            && c.Measurement.user_id == 1
            orderby c.entry_date descending
            group c by c.Measurement.measurement_name into latestMeasurements
            select new
            {
                Measurement = latestMeasurements.Key,
                LatestEntry = latestMeasurements.Take(1).SingleOrDefault()
            }).ToList();

        foreach (var entry in latestEntries)
        {
            summary.values.Add(new MeasurementValue
            {
                measurement_name =
    entry.LatestEntry.Measurement.
    measurement_name,
                measurement_unit = entry.LatestEntry.MeasurementUnit.unit,
                measurement_value = entry.LatestEntry.value
            }.ToString());
        }

        // Now retrieve the most recent user image

        var image = (from i in this.DataContext.MeasurementImages
            where i.user_id == user_id && i.entry_date.Date <= entry_date.Date
            orderby i.entry_date descending
            select i.file_name).Take(1).SingleOrDefault();

        summary.latest_image = image;
        summary.entry_date = entry_date;

        return summary;
    }
```

Code snippet MeasurementService.cs

Before moving on to the code behind I wanted to break down a little bit of the complex LINQ statement in the previous snippet. In order to get the most recent value for each of the standard measurements from the measurements table in the database, you typically use a combination of the ORDER BY and GROUP BY clause in a T-SQL statement. Just because you are using LINQ doesn't mean you can't do something similar. Let's start with the beginning of the statement:

```
var latestEntries = (from c in this.DataContext.MeasurementLogEntries
        where c.entry_date.Date <= entry_date.Date
        && c.Measurement.user_id == 1
        orderby c.entry_date descending
```

This statement will grab all of the measurement log entries for the given day and user and place them in descending order according to their entry date. Although the Where clause specifies to retrieve only those entries that match the given entry date, you still want to order them just in case there are multiple entries for the same date but different times. Next you add the LINQ equivalent of the GROUP BY statement:

```
group c by c.Measurement.measurement_name into latestMeasurements
```

This creates a collection behind the scenes of key value pairs where the key is the `measurement_name` field and the value is, of course, the actual value that was recorded. It is important to know that a key value pair collection is being created because you only want one measurement log entry per standard measurement so you still can't use the result just yet. The next part of the query will create a list of key value pairs but ensure that only one measurement value is added to the list for each of the standard measurements:

```
select new
{
     Measurement = latestMeasurements.Key,
     LatestEntry = latestMeasurements.Take(1).SingleOrDefault()
}).ToList();
```

> *This type of LINQ query can be confusing and I'll be the first to tell you that I am not an expert in creating complex LINQ queries. Any further help on this topic is pretty much out of scope for this book; however, if you refer to* Professional LINQ *(Wrox Press, ISBN: 978-0-470-04181-9) by Scott Klein, I'm sure you will come away with a much better understanding of how the previous query actually works and what goes on behind the scenes.*

User Interface Code Behind

The code behind for the `MeasurementSummary` control is pretty straightforward. As you might have guessed, this control also implements the `IDailySummary` interface and, as you can see, in Listing 8-5, the `LoadSummary` method simply retrieves the `DailyMeasurementSummary` object and sets the `DataContext` property of the summary control. Once complete, the only thing left is to set the `Source` property of the most recent user image and for that you just use the exact same technique that was used for the measurement journal. This includes making use of the `image_unavailable.png` file if the user has not yet uploaded any image files.

LISTING 8-5: MeasurementSummary.xaml.cs

Available for download on Wrox.com

```
using System;
using System.Collections;
using System.Collections.Generic;
using System.Windows.Controls;
using System.Windows.Media.Imaging;
using FitnessTrackerPlus.Web.Services;

namespace FitnessTrackerPlus.Views.Dashboard
{
     public partial class MeasurementSummary : UserControl, IDailySummary
```

continues

LISTING 8-5 *(continued)*

```
    {
        private MeasurementContext context = new MeasurementContext();

        public MeasurementSummary()
        {
            InitializeComponent();
        }

#region IDailySummary Members

        public void LoadSummary(int user_id, DateTime summary_date)
        {
            context.Load<DailyMeasurementSummary>(context.
GetDailyMeasurementSummaryQuery(user_id, summary_date),
            (SummaryLoaded) =>
            {
                if (!SummaryLoaded.HasError)
                {
                    IEnumerator<DailyMeasurementSummary> enumerator =
SummaryLoaded.Entities.GetEnumerator();
                    enumerator.MoveNext();

                    this.DataContext = enumerator.Current;

                    if (enumerator.Current.latest_image != null)
                    {
                        BitmapImage updatedImage = null;
#if DEBUG
                        updatedImage = new BitmapImage(new
Uri(String.Format("http://localhost:1154/UploadedImages/{0}",
enumerator.Current.latest_image), UriKind.Absolute));
#else
                        updatedImage = new BitmapImage(new
Uri(String.Format("http://fitnesstrackerplus.com/UploadedImages/{0}",
SummaryLoaded.Value.latest_image), UriKind.Absolute));
#endif

                        updatedImage.CreateOptions =
BitmapCreateOptions.IgnoreImageCache;
                        CurrentImage.Source = updatedImage;
                    }
                    else
                        CurrentImage.Source = new BitmapImage(new
Uri("/Images/image_unavailable.png", UriKind.Relative));
                }

            }, null);
        }

#endregion
    }
}
```

Now that the code behind is complete, you should be able to run the project and enter some of your current measurements into the measurement log page. Once you finish, you can come back to the dashboard and you should be presented with a `MeasurementSummary` control similar to the one shown in Figure 8-5.

Adding Printing Support

Now that all the summary controls are complete and the dashboard is pretty much finished, it's time to turn your attention to adding printing support for the various `DataGrid` controls on the food, exercise, and measurement log pages. It seems like a reasonable assumption that some users might be interested in printing a hard copy of their entries. Now, of course, those users always have the option of using the basic browser printing functionality. However, printing functionality does not always work out well for a Silverlight application. At best, it leaves the user with a full-blown screenshot of the application including the banner, navigation menu, data input controls and other elements, none of which are interesting to the user making the hard copy.

FIGURE 8-5

As you probably know, one glaring omission from previous versions of Silverlight was interacting with the printer directly from code. Because of this limitation, it became difficult to nearly impossible for users to print reports or other areas of the screen of interest. Luckily, Microsoft heard users' requests and added a great new feature to Silverlight 4 — Printer support.

To use this feature, you first need to add a new item to the right-click context menu on the food log page. The following code shows the updated XAML code for the context menu:

Available for download on Wrox.com

```
<Canvas x:Name="RightClickMenu" Style="{StaticResource RightClickMenuStyle}">
     <Border x:Name="RightClickBorder" Style="{StaticResource
RightClickMenuBorderStyle}">
          <StackPanel>
               <TextBlock x:Name="DeleteEntryMenu"
Text="Delete Selected Entries" Style="{StaticResource
RightClickMenuItemStyle}" />
               <TextBlock x:Name="PrintEntryMenu" Text="Print Entries"
Style="{StaticResource RightClickMenuItemStyle}" />
               <TextBlock x:Name="CancelEntryMenu" Text="Cancel"
Style="{StaticResource RightClickMenuItemStyle}" />
          </StackPanel>
     </Border>
</Canvas>
```

Code snippet FoodLog.xaml

In the code behind, you also need to add a `MouseLeftButtonDown` event handler, which is responsible for the actual printing of the `DataGrid` control.

Available for download on Wrox.com

```
PrintEntryMenu.MouseLeftButtonDown += new
MouseButtonEventHandler(PrintEntryMenu_MouseLeftButtonDown);
```

Code snippet FoodLog.xaml.cs

In the following code, in order to print the contents of the `FoodLogGrid`, you first must create a new `PrintDocument` object. Next, you assign a name for the document, which in this case is just Food Log Entries. Most of the action takes place in the `PrintPage` event handler, which simply uses the `PrintableArea` object to stretch the `FoodLogGrid` to take up all available space. Then the `PageVisual` object is set to the actual `FoodLogGrid`. Finally, the `Print` method is called and this brings up the printer dialog and begins the printing operation.

Available for download on Wrox.com

```
protected void PrintEntryMenu_MouseLeftButtonDown(object sender,
MouseButtonEventArgs e)
{
     PrintDocument entries = new PrintDocument();

     entries.DocumentName = "Food Log Entries";
     entries.PrintPage += (se, ev) =>
     {
          FoodLogGrid.Width = ev.PrintableArea.Width;
          FoodLogGrid.Height = ev.PrintableArea.Height;

          ev.PageVisual = FoodLogGrid;
          ev.HasMorePages = false;
     };

     entries.Print();

     RightClickMenu.Visibility = Visibility.Collapsed;
}
```

Code snippet FoodLog.xaml.cs

Basically, the `PrintPage` event handler is hit just before the page actually prints. This is where you actually need to tell Silverlight what you're printing. Stretching the content is an optional step, so the most important thing to do is make sure the `PageVisual` object is set to the content you want printed. As mentioned earlier, this can be any object derived from `UIElement`.

In this particular example, you are only concerned about printing the `FoodLogGrid`, so there's only one formatted page to be concerned about. This is why the `HasMorePages` variable is set to `false`. If you needed to print a large amount of content and wanted to control exactly what appeared on each page, you could set `HasMorePages` to `true` and the `PrintPage` event handler code would hit again, so that you could format the next available page and set the `PageVisual`.

Again, this is a pretty simple interface and lacks some advanced formatting control — but it is a start. Don't be surprised if upcoming versions of Silverlight tweak the way this all works, adding more formatting options and controlling the printing process, in general.

Home Page Screenshot

There is one final item on the agenda for this chapter and that is to take a screenshot for the main FitnessTrackerPlus home page. Now that all three journal pages are available, you should add some entries to one and take a screenshot using the simple Alt-PrtScrn combination and Paint. You already set up the `Source` property for the main page `Image` control, so all you have to do is make sure that the screenshot is saved in the `Images` folder of the Silverlight project with the filename `screenshot.png`. Once you complete this task, you should see something similar to Figure 8-6 when you fire up the project and navigate to the home page.

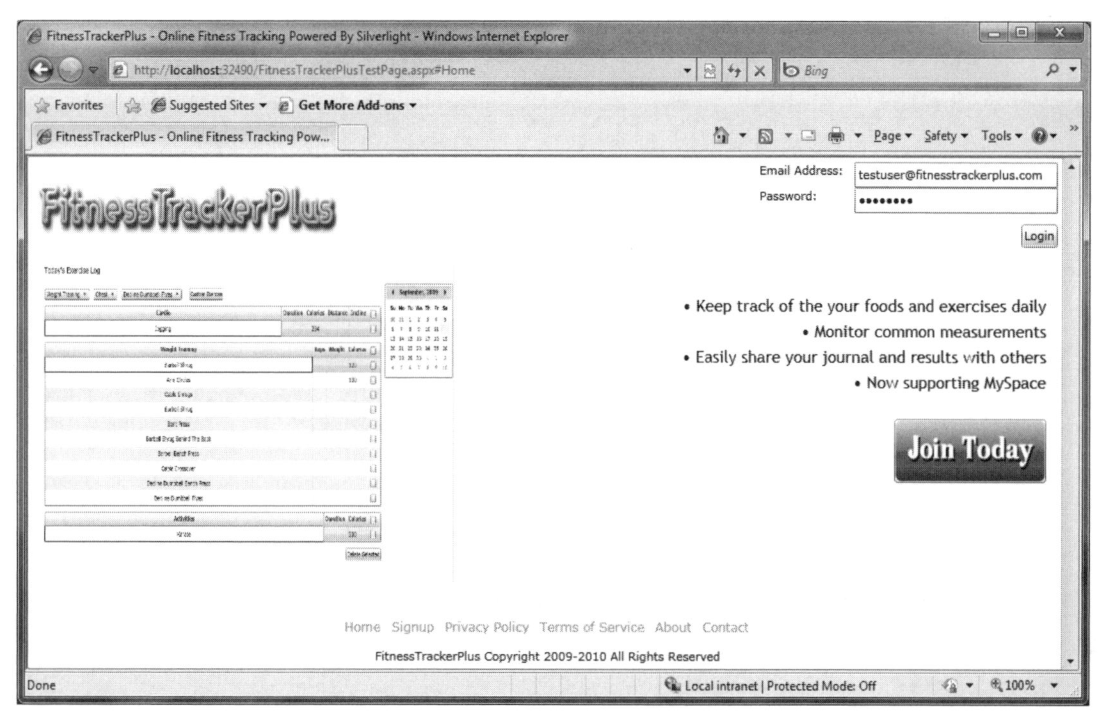

FIGURE 8-6

SUMMARY

Another chapter down and only four more to go! Although this chapter didn't cover any major new features for the site, it was still important because you needed to finish a number of cleanup items before moving on. In this chapter, you finally got back to the non-functional dashboard page and created three summary controls that show the user daily summaries of their food, exercise, and measurement logs. You also became familiar with the new charting features of the Silverlight Toolkit. Finally, you saw how simple it is to add important printing support using the new functionality available in Silverlight 4 — you can basically print any object derived from `UIElement`. By now you should be a master at creating any of the available chart types. Just in case you don't particularly like the default look and feel of a given chart, you have also seen how to create a custom control template for the `Chart` control. With a custom control template, you can rearrange the `Legend` or `Title` properties, and even eliminate them altogether.

At this point, you are on track to add another important feature to the FitnessTrackerPlus site. Next on the agenda is the creation of a public journal feature that will let your users easily share their fitness journals with friends, family, or anyone else on the Internet. Of course, some users may object to the idea of sharing their information so you will have to take that into account when creating the feature and provide users with the ability to customize the data being shared.

9

Sharing Your Success

Creating the Public Fitness Journal

Now that you've finished the main data entry features of the site, it's time to consider adding an additional feature that will make the site feel more like some of the other Web 2.0–style sites on the Internet. This chapter focuses on adding some very basic social networking components to FitnessTrackerPlus. You'll enable users of the site to share their fitness journal information with others. By using the Silverlight Navigation Framework, you'll see how you can provide your users with a URL that will lead visitors directly to their public journal and even allow the page to be bookmarked.

Additionally, visitors that arrive at this public facing version of the user's fitness journal will be able to post HTML-based comments in order to provide motivation and support in helping your users achieve their fitness goals. Yes, you heard me right—I did say HTML-based comments. I know this is a Silverlight application and, as you may have learned the hard way in your own applications, Silverlight has no native support for displaying HTML based content unless you use the new `WebBrowser` control available in Silverlight 4. Unfortunately, this new control only works in out-of-browser scenarios so this doesn't really help much in the FitnessTrackerPlus application.

To provide the comment system you'll make use of an old friend of mine from the ASP.NET world called the Ajax Control Toolkit. This powerful, freely available Toolkit provides you with many Ajax-based controls that integrate nicely in ASP.NET pages. Most important, they also offer a client-side programming model, which will become extremely important when it comes to integrating with a Silverlight-based application. FitnessTrackerPlus may not yet be the next MySpace or Facebook, but still—in order to be relevant on the Web in today's world you must acknowledge the power of social networking and at least learn to incorporate some aspects of this trend in your own Silverlight applications.

PROBLEM

Social networking sites such as MySpace and Facebook work on the premise that users love to share information. Sometimes they can share a little bit too much information but nonetheless the basic principle is that, if given the opportunity, most users will at least take the time to interact with other users on the site by creating a profile page. Typically, this profile page has some basic "about me" text as well as some interests such as favorite movies, bands, and so on. Of course, there is no point to any of this if you can't share this profile with other users online in order to get feedback. Even though you're developing FitnessTrackerPlus in Silverlight, it should not stop you from adding some basic social networking components to the site. Now, you already know that competing with the likes of MySpace and Facebook is a loser's game, but you do have sort of a niche product here. In theory, if you allow users to share their fitness journal information with others you should be able to foster a pretty decent community of fitness-minded users and generate even more traffic to the site.

There are a couple of unique problems you need to solve for your users to share their fitness journals with others:

- You need to decide what information you want users to share on their public profile page. Because users can keep track of their daily foods, exercises, and measurements, that seems like as good a place as any to start.
- Users may also wish to share any images they have uploaded so that visitors can quickly track progress by cycling through the various images of the user over time.
- Not all of your users will be interested in sharing this data. In fact, there is still a select group of people online that really value their privacy and will no doubt balk at any attempt from outside visitors to view their fitness journal. You could ignore this type of user and tell them to go find a time machine and put the setting to 1995 when nobody shared data online and "social network" wasn't the latest buzzword. Doing that, however, would be a huge mistake. In order to have even a moderately successful site, you need to cater to all of your users. Remember that when you are running a site, any user that signs up and makes use of the site is now a customer, and as cliché as it sounds, when trying to generate a buzz for your site the customer really is always right. That being said, it's important to ensure that the public journal feature for FitnessTrackerPlus offers some kind of settings page that allows each individual user to decide on what, if anything, will be made available to outside visitors.
- You should create the public journal page in such a way that visitors can directly access the page with its own URL. You will most likely want to create a URL that makes use of a query string that can be used by the public journal page to determine which user's information to bring up. Before the availability of the navigation framework, something like this was not really possible. The navigation framework not only provides you with a mechanism to achieve this but also the ability to make use of Query Strings, Deep Linking, and more.
- You want to tackle the commenting system. You'll provide visitors of the public journal page with a system that supports HTML-based comments similar to those on MySpace and Facebook. Right out of the gate, you have the difficult issue that Silverlight has no native support for displaying HTML. There are some tricks to overlaying HTML elements over the Silverlight plug-in and you'll need to make use of these to properly display the comments on the public journal page.

- Of course you have to worry not only about displaying the comments but also creating them. This requires some sort of HTML-based editor that visitors can use to post the comments with. This is where the Ajax Control Toolkit comes in. This freely available toolkit from Microsoft provides a ton of cool AJAX-based controls including an HTML Editor. Although it's not a native Silverlight control, you can still make use of it by resorting to the same HTML overlaying tricks being used to display the HTML comments.

DESIGN

This section is broken into a couple of areas. You need to create a page that allows users to customize various aspects of their public journal page as well as the actual public journal page itself. This section also covers how you provide users with a unique URL that can be shared with friends and family so they have direct access to the user's public journal page. In addition, you still have to worry about the HTML-based commenting system. This is going to require design work on both the comments themselves as well as the HTML editor that visitors will use to post their comments. Now just to make sure you catch everything in the design, let's start by creating a detailed list of the requirements.

Requirements

The problem statements gave you a pretty good idea of the work required so it shouldn't be too difficult to come up with a list of requirements for the public journal feature. The following is a detailed list of requirements extracted from the initial problem statement. The site should:

- Provide a public facing version of the user's fitness journal.
- Display a brief "About Me" section of text.
- Display food, exercise, and measurement log entries.
- Display any uploaded measurement images for the selected date.
- Provide a calendar control so visitors can view previous log entries.
- Provide visitors with the ability to post HTML-based comments on the public journal page.
- Have options for users to enable/disable the sharing of food, exercise, or measurement log entries.
- Allow users to modify "About Me" text.
- Allow users to enable/disable comment entry.
- Allow users to enable/disable sharing of any uploaded measurement images.
- Provide a public journal page that's accessible using a direct URL with a query string in a format similar to the following: `http://www.fitnesstrackerplus.com/Journals/username`.
- Ensure that any HTML-based comments are safely encoded using HTML encoding.
- For security purposes, prevent any HTML editor from saving any JavaScript along with the comment.

That just about covers everything that you'll need for the design and implementation of the public journal page. With the requirements set, let's move on to the design of the public journal settings page and see how to best lay out the various settings that will be available to the user.

Public Journal Settings

The first page that you need to design is the public journal settings page. It's a pretty simple page that has the main responsibility of providing a place for users to modify the various settings for their public journal. From here, users can update their "About Me" text, and enable or disable a host of sharing options.

User Interface

The user interface required for this page is really not all that complicated. You basically will require a data entry form that has a `TextBox` control for the "About Me" text along with a list of `CheckBox` controls that will be data bound to the various options. Other than this basic data entry form, the only other control required will be a `Button` control that users can click to save changes to the options.

Database

The database requires a couple of changes to the public journal page options. Because you are already making use of the user profile to store and retrieve the preferred theme for the user, you should plan on just extending the profile to include the public journal options. Rather than create an entirely new database table, you can extend the profile table to include the required columns and then add these new fields to the custom profile provider you created earlier. The WCF RIA Services `AuthenticationService` will automatically pick up these new fields, therefore much less work is required than if you were to add a new table and a separate mechanism for storing and retrieving the public journal options. Table 9-1 shows the updated proposed profiles table that includes all the public journal options along with the original fields:

TABLE 9-1: profiles

COLUMN NAME	TYPE	DESCRIPTION
id	int	Unique identity field for profile.
current_theme	varchar(100)	Preferred site theme.
about_text	varchar(max)	User description text to be displayed on public journal page.
share_journal	bit	Enable/disable sharing of any information on public journal page. Also enable/disable the ability to reach the page with custom URL.
share_foods	bit	Enable/Disable sharing of food log entries.
share_exercises	bit	Enable/Disable sharing of exercise log entries.

COLUMN NAME	TYPE	DESCRIPTION
share_measurements	bit	Enable/Disable sharing of measurement log entries.
share_images	bit	Enable/Disable sharing of measurement images.
enable_comments	bit	Enable/Disable posting and display of HTML comments.
user_id	int	ID of associated user.

Data Access

Because you are saving the new public journal options directly in the user profile object there should be no additional LINQ to SQL classes required for this feature. Everything you need should have already been created earlier on when you were implementing the user registration, login, and theme code.

Business Logic

By deciding to store the public journal options in the existing profile table, you have considerably cut down the amount of required work in the business logic layer. The full user profile is already exposed to the client through the `AuthenticationService`. Just as when you added support for the `CurrentTheme` property, you'll need to update the custom profile provider to reflect the new properties, and add them to the `web.config` file so that the ASP.NET profile engine recognizes the additions. Saving changes to these new properties should be as simple as using the existing `SaveUser` method of the `WebContext.Current.Authentication` class.

User Interface Code Behind

In the code behind for the options page there are two areas of work to be concerned with:

- Retrieving the current values for all of the public journal options and binding these values to the user interface controls. You won't need to invoke any domain service in order to do this because all the options should now be available right from the user's profile object. This means that you can bind the parent of all the data entry controls to the `WebContext.Current.User` instance.
- Handling the `Click` event of the Save button. Because two-way data binding is in use here, the only required code is a call to the `SaveUser` method. Once the method completes, you should probably let the user know that all the changes were saved without error by displaying a `MessageBox` control with a brief success message.

Public Journal

The public journal page will give users the ability to share their fitness progress with friends, family, or any other visitor from the Internet. By providing this feature, you are adding a type of social networking feature that should make the site stand out against some of its other competitors. This page should be directly accessible to visitors using a unique URL that is specific to the FitnessTrackerPlus user. Upon arriving at the page, visitors will be able to potentially access food, exercise, and measurement log entries as well as any uploaded images. In addition to these features, users will also have the ability to leave HTML-based comments providing feedback to other users.

User Interface

The user interface for this page needs to include areas for the "About Me" text, food, exercise, and measurement log entries, uploaded user images, and visitor comments. Before taking a look at what possible controls should make up the user interface you should try sketching out a few possible layouts to see how best to organize the displayed information. Figure 9-1 shows one potential layout for the public journal user interface. This layout gives plenty of space to the log entries, about text, and comment area while still allowing room for a potential `Calendar` control that can be used to view previous log entries.

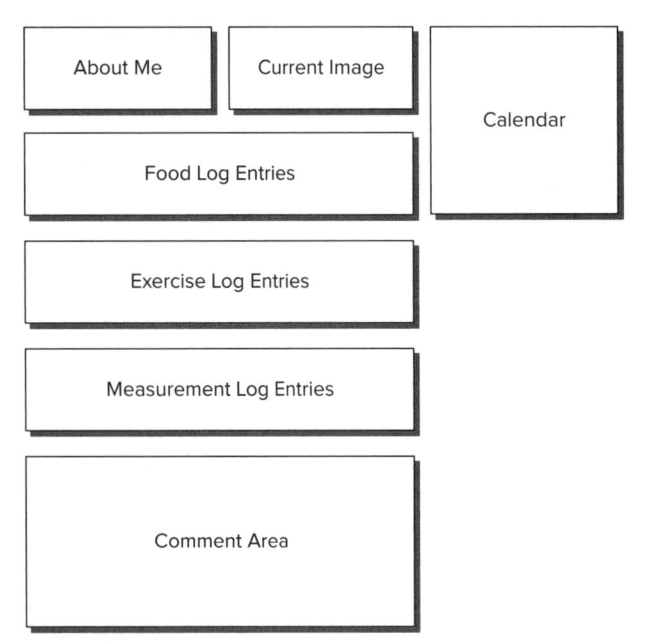

FIGURE 9-1

Once you have decided on the layout, figuring out the required controls is not too difficult. For the "About Me" text area, you just use a basic `TextBlock`. To the right of this text you will display the current image using the same `Image` control you created on the measurement log page. Below this header information are `DataGrid` controls for the food, exercise, and measurement log entries. Unlike the `DataGrid` controls on the various log pages, however, these `DataGrid` controls need to be read-only so you won't have any `CellEditingTemplate` declarations. You should also plan on defaulting these to `Collapsed` until you have retrieved the public journal settings. Once you have the settings, you can see which data the user has opted to make available and display the appropriate `DataGrid`.

The comment area requires you to provide a mechanism for visitors to leave HTML-based comments. As I am sure you are well aware, there is no native support in Silverlight for displaying HTML elements outside of using the new `WebBrowser` control in an out-of-browser scenario. This being the case, you must make use of a trick called *overlays* to achieve the desired effect. Getting this to work requires you to create a couple of DIV elements on the main FitnessTrackerPlus.aspx page that are absolutely positioned and remain hidden until the user navigates to the public journal page. Once the public journal page appears, the code needs to make the DIV elements visible and dynamically create new DIV elements containing the HTML comment text. This sounds like a pretty daunting task but as you'll see in the "Solution," it's not really as complicated as it seems at first.

One additional thing to consider is how you want to structure the displayed comments. Most comment areas on websites display the name of the original poster in a hyperlink form that, when clicked, opens a new browser window to the poster's own website. Below this is the actual HTML comment text followed by a footer element that contains the date that the post was created. In all, you'll add three separate DIV elements for every comment associated with the page.

The final element to the user interface is the comment form itself. You should plan on creating a basic data entry form that collects a name, optional website, and of course the comment itself. Because you want visitors to post HTML and there is no support for it directly in Silverlight, you need to look at an alternative solution. Many HTML editing controls are available for standard ASP.NET websites and several of them are even free. Because you will already be overlaying a DIV to hold the HTML comments themselves, you should be able to use the same tactic to display an HTML editing control over the Silverlight data entry form as well.

In terms of which HTML editor to use, I suggest looking at the `Editor` control, which is available from the ASP.NET Ajax Control Toolkit. Microsoft has provided this toolkit on its CodePlex site for some time now and it has several powerful controls that work great on traditional ASP.NET websites. The controls also provide an excellent client-side programming model, so accessing them through JavaScript is a snap. In the "Solution" section you'll see why this is so important and how easy it is to interact with the `Editor` control directly from the code behind page. In any case, you'll be overlaying the `Editor` control on the data entry form and collecting the raw HTML from this control to support the posting of HTML comments.

> *You can download the Toolkit along with all of the controls by visiting* `http://ajaxcontroltoolkit.codeplex.com`*. This site offers both the binary DLL file as well as all the source code, if you are interested.*

Database

The commenting feature of the public journal page will require the creation of a new database table. Table 9-2 shows journal_comments, which provide a place to store all the comments along with any information relevant to the poster.

TABLE 9-2: journal_comments

COLUMN NAME	TYPE	DESCRIPTION
id	integer	Unique identity of comment
name	varchar(255)	Name of commenter
website	varchar(255)	Optional website of commenter
comment	varchar(max)	Actual HTML-encoded comment text
entry_date	datetime	Date/time that comment was created
user_id	int	ID of associated user

Data Access

As soon as you created the table to hold the comments, you probably realized that that meant that another LINQ to SQL classes file would be generated. Nothing new to discuss here—just plan on adding the new .DBML file to the project and dragging the newly created table over to the designer. Finally, rebuild the ASP.NET project and you should be done.

Business Logic

The business logic layer for the public journal page poses some interesting challenges. The first thing you need is a mechanism that provides users with a unique URL for their public journal page. You can make use of the URI routing features of the navigation framework in order to provide such a URL. The desire is to create something that can be easily bookmarked and potentially distributed to friends and family. In traditional ASP.NET sites you could accomplish something like this without difficulty if you used a query string. For example, in an ASP.NET site you could easily have one .ASPX page for public journals and display the correct information for the user by extracting a query string variable called `user`. Once you had the username you could do a database lookup and dynamically populate the page accordingly. In previous versions of Silverlight, you really couldn't do this. Now, however, with the navigation framework you have full support for query strings. In the Silverlight project, you could have users distribute a URL such as `http://www.fitnesstrackerplus.com/FitnessTrackerPlus.aspx/Journals/PublicJournal.xaml?user=username`. A URL like this works perfectly fine with the navigation framework and if you combine it with the URI routing feature, you can hide the .XAML page from the URL and let visitors simply go to `Journals/username`. An additional entry in the `UriMapper` is required to route users to the public journal page from there.

Having this unique URL to the public journal page poses an additional problem, however, in that when visitors arrive at the public journal page using this direct link there won't be a currently logged in user so the public journal settings won't be available in the code behind. You still need these options to determine what data if any should be displayed on the page. You can't really use the existing `AuthenticationService` class to retrieve the user profile because that would require logging into the site, which you don't want to do in this case. Instead, you need to add a new `DomainService` that retrieves a custom public journal settings class using only the username that is available from the query string variable.

Along with the settings, you'll need some additional methods in this new service that handle both the creation and retrieval of any comments associated with the public journal.

User Interface Code Behind

In the code behind for the public journal page, you need to handle a few things, including:

- Extracting the username from the query string in order to look up the correct public journal settings from the database.
- Determining if the user has enabled sharing the public journal. If not, use the navigation service to redirect the user back to the main FitnessTrackerPlus home page. If sharing is enabled, you need to determine what data is shared and load the necessary items from the various domain services you have already created. For example, if the user has opted to enable sharing food log entries, use the `FoodService` to retrieve all the entries for the currently selected date and bind the data to the read-only food log `DataGrid` control. You must repeat the same operation for the exercise and measurement log entries.
- If comments are enabled, loading all available comments using the `JournalService` and creating individual DIV elements for each of the comments. You'll then need to add all these DIV elements to the `innerHTML` property of the comment area DIV located on the FitnessTrackerPlus.aspx page.
- Making the hidden DIV visible and positioning it in the correct location on the Silverlight control.
- Using the HTML DOM Bridge feature of Silverlight to collect the HTML comment text from the `Editor` control and saving new comment items in the database when the visitor clicks the Submit button.

Again, don't worry yet about the details of this HTML integration; at this point you are just making technology and design decisions. The next section covers how you put all these things together so that they work.

SOLUTION

There is a ton of work to do here in this chapter's "Solution" section. You first need to create the public journal settings page, which involves making some modifications to the existing custom profile created way back in the second chapter. You'll also create a new `DomainService` to handle all the public journal operations. Once you have completed the settings page, it's time to move on to the public journal page itself, which is where the bulk of the work will be. Here, you'll see how to use the HTML `Editor` control of the ASP.NET Ajax Control Toolkit to allow visitors of this page to leave HTML-based comments. You'll also see how to display these comments by overlaying HTML elements over the existing Silverlight plug-in. Finally, you'll make use of the navigation framework in order to provide a unique URL to the public journal page that users can share with others.

Public Journal Settings

Before creating the actual public journal page, your first mission is to create a settings page that allows users to configure what information, if any, should be shared in the public journal. The design dictates that users have the option to share their food, exercise, and measurement log entries as well as any uploaded measurement images. Users can also enable/disable comments, and, of course, can enable/disable sharing of the public journal altogether.

User Interface

The user interface for the settings page is not terribly complicated. You will, however, have to first make some modifications to the `NavigationMenu` control and the App.xaml file before getting started. There is not currently an entry in the menu for the public journal so you should start by adding that to the existing `NavigationMenu` control using the following XAML code:

```
<toolkit:AccordionItem Tag="#JournalSettings">
     <toolkit:AccordionItem.Header>
          <StackPanel Style="{StaticResource NavigationMenuItemHeaderPanelStyle}">
               <Image Style="{StaticResource NavigationMenuItemImageStyle}" />
               <TextBlock Text="Public Journal" Style="{StaticResource
NavigationMenuItemTextStyle}" />
          </StackPanel>
     </toolkit:AccordionItem.Header>
     <toolkit:AccordionItem.Content>
          <StackPanel Style="{StaticResource NavigationMenuItemContentPanelStyle}">
               <HyperlinkButton x:Name="JournalSettingsLink"
Content="Journal Settings" Tag="#JournalSettings" Style="{StaticResource
NavigationMenuItemLinkStyle}" />
               <HyperlinkButton x:Name="ViewJournalLink" Content="View Journal"
Tag="#ViewJournal" Style="{StaticResource NavigationMenuItemLinkStyle}" />
          </StackPanel>
     </toolkit:AccordionItem.Content>
</toolkit:AccordionItem>
```

Code snippet NavigationMenu.xaml

You already have several `AccordionItem` entries in the existing `Accordion` control so you can add the new entry anywhere in the list. Once you've done that, you need to add the following entry to the `UriMapper` defined in App.xaml so that when the `#JournalSettings AccordionItem` is clicked, the navigation framework navigates to the proper URL:

Available for download on Wrox.com

```
<uri:UriMapping Uri="JournalSettings"
MappedUri="/Views/Journal/JournalSettings.xaml" />
```

Code snippet App.xaml

With that out of the way, you can now create the Settings page itself. To get started, you should create a new directory under the current `Views` directory in the Silverlight project called `Journal`. Next, just right-click and add a new `Page` control called JournalSettings.xaml to the newly created Journal folder. Once the control is created, you need to create a user interface that displays all the public journal settings. As shown in the "Design" section, you'll add all the settings to the existing `Profile` object. With this being the case, you can easily create several `TextBox` controls and bind them to the new public journal `Profile` properties. Listing 9-1 shows the XAML required for the public journal settings user interface:

LISTING 9-1: Journal Settings.xaml

Available for download on Wrox.com

```
<navigation:Page x:Class="FitnessTrackerPlus.Views.Journal.JournalSettings"
     xmlns="http://schemas.microsoft.com/winfx/2006/xaml/presentation"
     xmlns:x="http://schemas.microsoft.com/winfx/2006/xaml"
     xmlns:navigation="clr-
namespace:System.Windows.Controls;assembly=System.Windows.Controls.Navigation"
     Title="FitnessTrackerPlus - Public Journal Settings">
     <navigation:Page.Resources>
          <Style x:Key="JournalSettingsHeaderStyle" BasedOn="{StaticResource
HeaderTextStyle}" TargetType="TextBlock">
               <Setter Property="Text" Value="Public Journal Settings" />
          </Style>
          <Style x:Key="JournalSettingsPanelStyle" TargetType="StackPanel">
               <Setter Property="Margin" Value="10,10" />
               <Setter Property="HorizontalAlignment" Value="Center" />
               <Setter Property="MaxWidth" Value="600" />
          </Style>
          <Style x:Key="AboutTextStackPanelStyle" TargetType="StackPanel">
               <Setter Property="Orientation" Value="Horizontal" />
          </Style>
          <Style x:Key="JournalSettingsTextStyle" TargetType="TextBlock">
               <Setter Property="HorizontalAlignment" Value="Right" />
               <Setter Property="Margin" Value="0,10,0,0" />
               <Setter Property="Width" Value="120" />
          </Style>
          <Style x:Key="AboutTextBoxStyle" TargetType="TextBox">
               <Setter Property="HorizontalAlignment" Value="Right" />
               <Setter Property="Margin" Value="10,10,0,0" />
               <Setter Property="Width" Value="400" />
               <Setter Property="Height" Value="200" />
          </Style>
          <Style x:Key="JournalCheckBoxStyle" TargetType="CheckBox">
               <Setter Property="Margin" Value="0,10" />
          </Style>
          <Style x:Key="JournalSettingsButtonStyle" TargetType="Button">
               <Setter Property="HorizontalAlignment" Value="Right" />
               <Setter Property="Margin" Value="0,10" />
          </Style>
     </navigation:Page.Resources>
     <StackPanel>
          <TextBlock Style="{StaticResource JournalSettingsHeaderStyle}" />
          <StackPanel x:Name="JournalSettingsPanel" Style="{StaticResource
JournalSettingsPanelStyle}">
               <StackPanel Style="{StaticResource AboutTextStackPanelStyle}">
                    <TextBlock Text="About Me Text:" Style="{StaticResource
JournalSettingsTextStyle}" />
                    <TextBox x:Name="AboutText" Text="{Binding
Path=AboutText}" Style="{StaticResource AboutTextBoxStyle}" />
               </StackPanel>
               <CheckBox x:Name="ShareJournal" Content="Share Journal:"
IsChecked="{Binding Path=ShareJournal}" Style="{StaticResource
```

continues

LISTING 9-1 *(continued)*

```
JournalCheckBoxStyle}"  />
                <CheckBox x:Name="ShareFoods" Content="Share Foods:"
IsChecked="{Binding Path=ShareFoods}" Style="{StaticResource
JournalCheckBoxStyle}" />
                <CheckBox x:Name="ShareExercises" Content="Share Exercises:"
IsChecked="{Binding Path=ShareExercises}" Style="{StaticResource
JournalCheckBoxStyle}" />
                <CheckBox x:Name="ShareMeasurements" Content="Share
Measurements:" IsChecked="{Binding Path=ShareMeasurements}"
Style="{StaticResource JournalCheckBoxStyle}" />
                <CheckBox x:Name="ShareImages" Content="Share Images:"
IsChecked="{Binding Path=ShareImages}" Style="{StaticResource
JournalCheckBoxStyle}" />
                <CheckBox x:Name="EnableComments" Content="Enable Comments:"
IsChecked="{Binding Path=EnableComments}" Style="{StaticResource
JournalCheckBoxStyle}" />
                <Button x:Name="SaveChanges" Content="Save Changes"
Style="{StaticResource JournalSettingsButtonStyle}" />
            </StackPanel>
        </StackPanel>
</navigation:Page>
```

This code listing is pretty straightforward and, in fact, is very similar to the `AccountSettings` control you created earlier in the book. Each control is just bound to the appropriate property from the user's profile. The intent is that the code behind file takes care of setting the `DataContext` property on the `JournalSettingsPanel` itself and all the `TextBox` and `CheckBox` controls simply inherit the data. Once you have this completed, you are left with a simple and user-friendly interface like the one shown in Figure 9-2.

FIGURE 9-2

Database

Although you created the profile table earlier in the book, you currently have only one profile property column called `current_theme`. To extend the existing `Profile` object to handle the public journal settings, you need to add the additional columns, as shown in the database diagram depicted in Figure 9-3.

You also want to be sure to add a foreign key relationship between the `user_id` field and the users table. This will link any inserted comments with the correct user's public journal.

profiles
id
current_theme
about_text
share_journal
share_foods
share_exercises
share_measurements
share_images
enable_comments
user_id

FIGURE 9-3

Data Access

You'll need to make changes to the data access layer to match the changes you just made to the profile table in the database. You have already built the LINQ to SQL classes required for the `Profile` object, but they do not currently have the additional required properties to handle the public journal settings. One area where LINQ to SQL is a little bit lacking is in refreshing your existing .DBML files to reflect changes to the database. There is no built-in mechanism to synch up with the database. You do have the option of manually adding properties to the table in the diagram but I usually prefer just deleting the item from the designer entirely and adding a new copy containing the updated fields from the database just to be safe. If you do this for the Users.dbml file you created previously, you will now be left with the LINQ to SQL classes, as shown in Figure 9-4.

Profile
Properties
id
current_theme
about_text
share_journal
share_foods
share_exercises
share_measurements
share_images
enable_comments
user_id

FIGURE 9-4

Once you complete this task, just rebuild the ASP.NET project and the LINQ to SQL code generator will now create a `Profile` entity class with the required public journal properties.

Business Logic

To support storage and retrieval of the public journal settings you need to perform a couple of tasks in the business logic layer. The "Design" section called for you to add the required properties to the existing `Profile` class. You have already taken care of the database side, but the custom `Profile` provider you created way back in the beginning of the book currently has no support for these additional properties. To add that support, you start by modifying the custom `Profile` provider in the ASP.NET project to handle them. This requires altering both the `GetPropertyValues` and `SetPropertyValues` methods. The following code shows the updated version of the `GetPropertyValues` method with added support in the `switch` statement for all of the new public journal settings properties.

Available for download on Wrox.com

```
public override SettingsPropertyValueCollection
GetPropertyValues(SettingsContext context, SettingsPropertyCollection
collection)
{
     SettingsPropertyValueCollection valueCollection = new
SettingsPropertyValueCollection();

     try
     {
```

```
            Profile profile = GetProfile(context["UserName"] as string);

            // If a profile was found then loop through all profile properties and
            // assign appropriate values

            if (profile != null)
            {
                foreach (SettingsProperty property in collection)
                {
                    SettingsPropertyValue propertyValue = new
SettingsPropertyValue(property);

                    switch (property.Name)
                    {
                        case "CurrentTheme":
                        {
                            propertyValue.PropertyValue =
profile.current_theme;
                            break;
                        }
                        case "AboutText":
                        {
                            propertyValue.PropertyValue =
profile.about_text;
                            break;
                        }
                        case "ShareJournal":
                        {
                            propertyValue.PropertyValue =
profile.share_journal;
                            break;
                        }
                        case "ShareFoods":
                        {
                            propertyValue.PropertyValue =
profile.share_foods;
                            break;
                        }
                        case "ShareExercises":
                        {
                            propertyValue.PropertyValue =
profile.share_exercises;
                            break;
                        }
                        case "ShareMeasurements":
                        {
                            propertyValue.PropertyValue =
profile.share_measurements;
                            break;
                        }
                        case "ShareImages":
                        {
                            propertyValue.PropertyValue =
profile.share_images;
```

```
                          break;
                     }
                     case "EnableComments":
                     {
                          propertyValue.PropertyValue =
profile.enable_comments;
                          break;
                     }
                }

                valueCollection.Add(propertyValue);
           }
      }
 }
 catch (Exception)
 {
 }

 return valueCollection;
}
```

Code snippet ProfileProvider.cs

The code required for the `SetPropertyValues` method is almost identical so I won't bother duplicating it here. It simply involves adding, once again, additional case statements for each of the new properties.

Once you modify the custom `Profile` provider, you still have one more place to worry about and that is the `web.config` file. Earlier on, you defined the `CustomTheme` property there, but you can't forget to add these new properties as well. The following code shows the required update to the `web.config` file.

Available for download on Wrox.com

```
<profile enabled="true" automaticSaveEnabled="false"
defaultProvider="FitnessTrackerPlusProfileProvider">
     <providers>
          <clear/>
          <add name="FitnessTrackerPlusProfileProvider"
type="FitnessTrackerPlus.Web.Providers.ProfileProvider"/>
     </providers>
     <properties>
          <add name="CurrentTheme" type="String"
customProviderData="current_theme;varchar;100"/>
          <add name="AboutText" type="String"
customProviderData="about_text;varchar;max"/>
          <add name="ShareJournal" type="Bool"
customProviderData="share_journal;bit"/>
          <add name="ShareFoods" type="Bool" customProviderData="share_foods;bit"/>
          <add name="ShareExercises" type="Bool"
customProviderData="share_exercises;bit"/>
          <add name="ShareMeasurements" type="Bool"
customProviderData="share_measurements;bit"/>
          <add name="ShareImages" type="Bool"
customProviderData="share_images;bit"/>
```

```
            <add name="EnableComments" type="Bool"
customProviderData="enable_comments;bit"/>
        </properties>
</profile>
```

Code snippet web.config

Again, you already did similar work when you implemented the theme selection feature so you should be somewhat familiar with the process of extending the existing `Profile` class. With these tasks complete, you can now move on to the code behind logic.

User Interface Code Behind

You need to take care of several items in the code behind file for the public journal settings page. First, there is some additional `CheckBox` logic that should be in place. If a user has opted to not share his or her journal information then that option trumps all others and any other `CheckBox` controls should automatically be unchecked. Consequently, if a user selects one of the options to share information, the `ShareJournal CheckBox` must also be checked. You can put this logic right in the `Loaded` event handler, as shown in the following code:

Available for download on Wrox.com

```
Loaded += (s, e) =>
{
    ShareJournal.Unchecked += (se, ev) =>
    {
        ShareFoods.IsChecked = false;
        ShareExercises.IsChecked = false;
        ShareMeasurements.IsChecked = false;
        ShareImages.IsChecked = false;
        EnableComments.IsChecked = false;
    };

    ShareFoods.Checked += (se, ev) => { ShareJournal.IsChecked = true; };
    ShareExercises.Checked += (se, ev) => { ShareJournal.IsChecked = true; };
    ShareMeasurements.Checked += (se, ev) => { ShareJournal.IsChecked = true; };
    ShareImages.Checked += (se, ev) => { ShareJournal.IsChecked = true; };
    EnableComments.Checked += (se, ev) => { ShareJournal.IsChecked = true; };

    SaveChanges.Click += new RoutedEventHandler(SaveChanges_Click);
};
```

Code snippet JournalSettings.xaml.cs

When the user navigates to this settings page, you need to load the user's `Profile` object and set up the data binding for the `TextBox` controls. This is as simple as overriding the `OnNavigatedTo` event handler and setting the `DataContext` property on the `StackPanel` that is hosting the `TextBox` controls. The following code shows the updated `OnNavigatedTo` method:

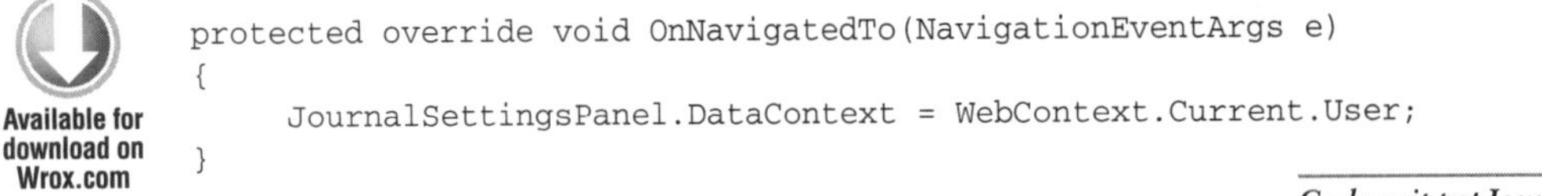

Available for download on Wrox.com

```
protected override void OnNavigatedTo(NavigationEventArgs e)
{
    JournalSettingsPanel.DataContext = WebContext.Current.User;
}
```

Code snippet JournalSettings.xaml.cs

Accessing the current profile for the user can be done easily enough by using the `WebContext.Current.User` object. The WCF RIA Services `AuthenticationService` you created earlier automatically works with the ASP.NET Profile service behind the scenes to ensure that all the new `Profile` properties are available from this `User` object.

The only other item left is adding a handler for the `SaveChanges` button that will use the `AuthenticationService` to persist any changes to the public journal settings. In the following code snippet, notice how you make use of the `SaveUser` method of the `AuthenticationService` once again to persist changes to the user's `Profile` data. Once complete, you just display a short `MessageBox` so that the user knows everything was saved correctly.

Available for download on Wrox.com

```
private void SaveChanges_Click(object sender, RoutedEventArgs e)
{
     WebContext.Current.User.AboutText = AboutText.Text;
     WebContext.Current.User.ShareJournal = ShareJournal.IsChecked.Value;
     WebContext.Current.User.ShareFoods = ShareFoods.IsChecked.Value;
     WebContext.Current.User.ShareExercises = ShareExercises.IsChecked.Value;
     WebContext.Current.User.ShareMeasurements = ShareMeasurements.IsChecked.Value;
     WebContext.Current.User.ShareImages = ShareImages.IsChecked.Value;
     WebContext.Current.User.EnableComments = EnableComments.IsChecked.Value;

     WebContext.Current.Authentication.SaveUser((SettingsSaved) =>
     {
          if( !SettingsSaved.HasError )
               MessageBox.Show("Your public journal settings have been successfully
updated");

     }, null);
}
```

Code snippet JournalSettings.xaml.cs

That takes care of the public journal settings page. Now users can log in and set up the sharing of the public journal however they would like. They can share some data, all of their data, or nothing at all. Now comes the difficult part—creating the actual public journal page. There is no sugarcoating the amount of work involved in creating the public journal page. It's going to take some serious effort, so brew a fresh pot of coffee—you are going to need it!

Public Journal

With the public journal settings page complete you can turn your attention toward creating the actual public journal page. As the "Design" section stated, this page will provide an area for some basic "About Me" text along with any food, exercise, and measurement log entries being shared. In addition to displaying shared fitness journal information, this page also needs to provide visitors the option of leaving HTML-based comments. Although it requires more work than if you just provided basic text comments, Silverlight does give you several classes to make interacting with the DOM relatively painless and, as you will see, the HTML Editor in the Ajax Control Toolkit does the bulk of the heavy lifting anyway.

User Interface

When starting the user interface for the public journal page, you first want to create the page itself by adding a new `Page` control to the Silverlight project in the Views\Journal directory called PublicJournal.xaml. The design suggests that the user interface should consist of a right-aligned `Calendar` control along with the "About Me" text, current image, and shared log entries on the left of the `Calendar` control, making use of all the remaining space. The easiest way to set this up is to use the `DockPanel` control from the Silverlight toolkit and set the `Calendar` control to `Dock` on the right side of the panel. You can then add a `StackPanel` control to the `DockPanel` that takes up all remaining available space. The following XAML shows this initial setup:

Available for download on Wrox.com

```
<Style x:Key="PublicJournalCalendarStyle" TargetType="controls:Calendar">
     <Setter Property="SelectionMode" Value="SingleDate" />
     <Setter Property="toolkit:DockPanel.Dock" Value="Right" />
</Style>
<Style x:Key="ProfileStackPanelStyle" TargetType="StackPanel">
     <Setter Property="toolkit:DockPanel.Dock" Value="Left" />
     <Setter Property="Margin" Value="0,0,10,0" />
</Style>
<toolkit:DockPanel LastChildFill="True">
     <controls:Calendar x:Name="Calendar" Style="{StaticResource
PublicJournalCalendarStyle}"  />
     <StackPanel x:Name="MainStackPanel" Style="{StaticResource
ProfileStackPanelStyle}" >
     </StackPanel>
</toolkit:DockPanel>
```

Code snippet PublicJournal.xaml

With that done, you can start adding controls to the `StackPanel` beginning with a `Grid` control that will house both the "About Me" text and the current image, if one exists, for the currently selected date.

Available for download on Wrox.com

```
<Style x:Key="ImageBorderStyle" TargetType="Border">
     <Setter Property="BorderBrush" Value="#FF000000" />
     <Setter Property="Background" Value="#FFFFFFFF" />
     <Setter Property="BorderThickness" Value="1" />
     <Setter Property="Width" Value="175" />
     <Setter Property="Height" Value="200" />
</Style>
<Style x:Key="ImageStyle" TargetType="Image">
     <Setter Property="Stretch" Value="Fill" />
</Style>
<Style x:Key="ImageTextStyle" TargetType="TextBlock">
     <Setter Property="Margin" Value="0,10,0,0" />
     <Setter Property="HorizontalAlignment" Value="Center" />
</Style>

<Grid>
     <Grid.ColumnDefinitions>
          <ColumnDefinition Width="*" />
          <ColumnDefinition Width="Auto" />
     </Grid.ColumnDefinitions>
     <TextBlock x:Name="AboutText" Grid.Column="0" />
```

```
        <StackPanel Grid.Column="1">
            <Border Style="{StaticResource ImageBorderStyle}">
                <Image x:Name="CurrentImage"
    Style="{StaticResource ImageStyle}" />
            </Border>
            <TextBlock Text="Current Image"
    Style="{StaticResource ImageTextStyle}" />
        </StackPanel>
    </Grid>
```

Code snippet PublicJournal.xaml

If users decide to share their food, exercise, and measurement log entries, you need to have `DataGrid` controls available to display those entries. For obvious reasons visitors should not be allowed to make changes to the data in those `DataGrid` controls, so you will need to alter the existing `DataGrid` controls by removing any `CellEditingTemplate` columns and setting the `DataGrid` controls to be `ReadOnly`. In the following code, you can see the XAML declaration required for the read-only version of the food log `DataGrid`. Because the other `DataGrid` control declarations are very similar they aren't included in this snippet.

Available for download on Wrox.com

```
<Style x:Key="ReadOnlyDataGrid" TargetType="data:DataGrid">
    <Setter Property="AutoGenerateColumns" Value="False" />
    <Setter Property="IsReadOnly" Value="True" />
    <Setter Property="Margin" Value="0,10,0,0" />
    <Setter Property="HorizontalScrollBarVisibility" Value="Auto" />
    <Setter Property="CanUserResizeColumns" Value="True" />
    <Setter Property="SelectionMode" Value="Single" />
    <Setter Property="Visibility" Value="Collapsed" />
    <Setter Property="ColumnWidth" Value="SizeToHeader" />
</Style>

<data:DataGrid x:Name="FoodLogGrid" Style="{StaticResource ReadOnlyDataGrid}">
    <data:DataGrid.Columns>
        <data:DataGridTemplateColumn Header="Foods"
HeaderStyle="{StaticResource DataGridColumnHeaderCentered}">
            <data:DataGridTemplateColumn.CellTemplate>
                <DataTemplate>
                    <TextBlock Text="{Binding Path=Food.name}" />
                </DataTemplate>
            </data:DataGridTemplateColumn.CellTemplate>
        </data:DataGridTemplateColumn>
        <data:DataGridTemplateColumn Header="Servings"
HeaderStyle="{StaticResource DataGridColumnHeaderCentered}">
            <data:DataGridTemplateColumn.CellTemplate>
                <DataTemplate>
                    <TextBlock Text="{Binding Path=servings}"
Style="{StaticResource DataGridTextBlockCentered}" />
                </DataTemplate>
            </data:DataGridTemplateColumn.CellTemplate>
        </data:DataGridTemplateColumn>
        <data:DataGridTemplateColumn Header="Serving Size"
HeaderStyle="{StaticResource DataGridColumnHeaderCentered}">
            <data:DataGridTemplateColumn.CellTemplate>
                <DataTemplate>
```

```
                        <TextBlock Text="{Binding Path=Food.serving_size}"
Style="{StaticResource DataGridTextBlock}" />
                    </DataTemplate>
                </data:DataGridTemplateColumn.CellTemplate>
            </data:DataGridTemplateColumn>
            <data:DataGridTemplateColumn Header="Fat" HeaderStyle="{StaticResource
DataGridColumnHeaderCentered}">
                <data:DataGridTemplateColumn.CellTemplate>
                    <DataTemplate>
                        <TextBlock Text="{Binding Path=Food.fat}"
Style="{StaticResource DataGridTextBlockCentered}" />
                    </DataTemplate>
                </data:DataGridTemplateColumn.CellTemplate>
            </data:DataGridTemplateColumn>
            <data:DataGridTemplateColumn Header="Carb" HeaderStyle="{StaticResource
DataGridColumnHeaderCentered}">
                <data:DataGridTemplateColumn.CellTemplate>
                    <DataTemplate>
                        <TextBlock Text="{Binding Path=Food.carbohydrate}"
Style="{StaticResource DataGridTextBlockCentered}" />
                    </DataTemplate>
                </data:DataGridTemplateColumn.CellTemplate>
            </data:DataGridTemplateColumn>
            <data:DataGridTemplateColumn Header="Pro" HeaderStyle="{StaticResource
DataGridColumnHeaderCentered}">
                <data:DataGridTemplateColumn.CellTemplate>
                    <DataTemplate>
                        <TextBlock Text="{Binding Path=Food.protein}"
Style="{StaticResource DataGridTextBlockCentered}" />
                    </DataTemplate>
                </data:DataGridTemplateColumn.CellTemplate>
            </data:DataGridTemplateColumn>
        </data:DataGrid.Columns>
</data:DataGrid>
```

Code snippet PublicJournal.xaml

Once you have all that set up, you need to start creating the commenting areas. Two things to consider for the comments:

- You need an area to display the HTML comments. As I said earlier, even though it's not directly supported in Silverlight, you can still display HTML in your Silverlight application. The trick is to overlay HTML elements directly over the plug-in. To support this, you make a small change to the Silverlight plug-in declaration in the main FitnessTrackerPlus.aspx page. To display the overlays, you set the `Windowless` property to `true`, as shown in following code:

Available for download on Wrox.com

```
<object data="data:application/x-silverlight-2,"
type="application/x-silverlight-2" width="100%" height="100%">
    <param name="source" value="ClientBin/FitnessTrackerPlus.xap"/>
    <param name="minRuntimeVersion" value="3.0.40624.0" />
    <param name="autoUpgrade" value="true" />
    <param name="Windowless" value="true" />
```

Code snippet FitnessTrackerPlus.aspx

- You need a DIV element somewhere on the page that is responsible for displaying the HTML comments. The basic principle here is that you will retrieve the comments from the database and then in the code behind create individual DIV elements for each comment. You will then add each of these as child elements to the main DIV on the FitnessTrackerPlus.aspx page. The following code is the declaration of the placeholder DIV element that will be used to display all of the public journal comments:

Available for download on Wrox.com

```
<div id="comment_area"
style="position:absolute;top:0px;left:0px;width:600px;display:none;"></div>
```

Code snippet FitnessTrackerPlus.aspx

You'll notice from this snippet that the DIV is absolutely positioned at 0, 0 and is not being displayed. By default, you don't want this placeholder visible until you are sure that the user has enabled comments on his or her public journal page. As far as the location of the DIV, you dynamically size and position it in the code behind using the HTML DOM Bridge feature of Silverlight to make sure the comments appear in the correct place on the page. To correctly position this DIV on the page, you need some kind of reference point. Basically, a Silverlight element should act as a placeholder for this DIV. A `Grid` control will work quite nicely for this purpose, so you can add one directly below the last `DataGrid` control. The following code shows the declaration of the placeholder `Grid`:

Available for download on Wrox.com

```
<Style x:Key="CommentAreaStyle" TargetType="Grid">
     <Setter Property="HorizontalAlignment" Value="Center" />
</Style>

<Grid x:Name="CommentArea" Style="{StaticResource CommentAreaStyle}" />
```

Code snippet PublicJournal.xaml

For now, this is all you need to worry about regarding the comment area. The remainder of the work takes place in the code behind. The last item needed on the user interface is the actual comment form. This isn't terribly difficult and can be implemented using a `Grid` and some `TextBox` controls. The following XAML declaration shows the comment entry form for the page added just below the comment `Grid` placeholder control:

Available for download on Wrox.com

```
<Style x:Key="CommentHeaderStyle" TargetType="TextBlock">
     <Setter Property="FontSize" Value="16" />
     <Setter Property="FontWeight" Value="Bold" />
     <Setter Property="Margin" Value="0,20,0,10" />
</Style>
<Style x:Key="CommentFormStyle" TargetType="Grid">
     <Setter Property="Margin" Value="0,10,0,0" />
     <Setter Property="HorizontalAlignment" Value="Center" />
</Style>
<Style x:Key="CommentEntryDataStyle" TargetType="TextBox">
     <Setter Property="Height" Value="300" />
     <Setter Property="Width" Value="500" />
     <Setter Property="HorizontalAlignment" Value="Left" />
     <Setter Property="Margin" Value="10,0,0,5" />
</Style>
<Style x:Key="CommentEntryTextBoxStyle" TargetType="TextBox">
```

```
            <Setter Property="Height" Value="25" />
            <Setter Property="Width" Value="250" />
            <Setter Property="HorizontalAlignment" Value="Left" />
            <Setter Property="Margin" Value="10,0,0,5" />
        </Style>
        <Style x:Key="CommentSubmitStyle" TargetType="Button">
            <Setter Property="HorizontalAlignment" Value="Right" />
            <Setter Property="Margin" Value="10,10,0,0" />
        </Style>

        <Grid x:Name="CommentForm" Style="{StaticResource CommentFormStyle}">
            <Grid.RowDefinitions>
                <RowDefinition Height="Auto" />
                <RowDefinition Height="Auto" />
                <RowDefinition Height="Auto" />
                <RowDefinition Height="Auto" />
                <RowDefinition Height="Auto" />
            </Grid.RowDefinitions>
            <Grid.ColumnDefinitions>
                <ColumnDefinition Width="Auto" />
                <ColumnDefinition />
            </Grid.ColumnDefinitions>
            <TextBlock Grid.Row="0" Grid.Column="0" Grid.ColumnSpan="2" Text="Leave Your
        Comments" Style="{StaticResource CommentHeaderStyle}" />
            <TextBlock Grid.Row="1" Grid.Column="0" Text="Name:" />
            <TextBlock Grid.Row="2" Grid.Column="0" Text="Website (Optional):" />
            <TextBlock Grid.Row="3" Grid.Column="0" Text="Comment:" />
            <TextBox x:Name="Name" Grid.Row="1" Grid.Column="1" Style="{StaticResource
        CommentEntryTextBoxStyle}" />
            <TextBox x:Name="Website" Grid.Row="2" Grid.Column="1" Style="{StaticResource
        CommentEntryTextBoxStyle}" />
            <TextBox x:Name="Comment" Grid.Row="3" Grid.Column="1" Style="{StaticResource
        CommentEntryDataStyle}" />
            <Button x:Name="Submit" Grid.Row="4" Grid.Column="1" Content="Submit"
        Style="{StaticResource CommentSubmitStyle}" />
        </Grid>
```

Code snippet PublicJournal.xaml

The controls declared in the comment entry form are self explanatory. There is a `TextBox` for each of the properties related to a `JournalComment` object. There is one exception to this, however, and that is the Comment `TextBox` itself. The design makes use of the `Editor` control from the AJAX Control Toolkit to provide comment entry. Because this is yet another HTML-based control, you need a corresponding Silverlight control to use as a placeholder for the `Editor` control. You won't actually use either the `CommentArea Grid` control or the `Comment TextBox` control directly in your code behind. The role of these two controls is strictly to provide a reference point for their HTML counterparts. The code behind logic takes care of moving the HTML-based DIV elements directly over these Silverlight controls so the user will see the HTML-based DIV as opposed to the `TextBox` or `Grid` controls.

The last element of the user interface is the `Editor` control from the AJAX Control Toolkit. For this, you need to first add the assembly to your ASP.NET project by following these steps:

1. Open the FitnessTrackerPlus.aspx file and right-click the Toolbox area.
2. When the menu choices appear, select Add Tab and call the new tab Ajax Control Toolkit.

3. Right-click in the newly created tab and select the Choose Items menu option. This brings up a window that will let you browse for the AjaxControlToolkit.dll file. After selecting the DLL, the toolbox tab will be filled with all of the available toolkit controls.

4. You only need the `Editor` control so you can go ahead and drag it over to a new DIV called `comment_editor` on the main FitnessTrackerPlus.aspx page. At this point, you should have a new DIV with the `Editor` control, as the following code shows:

```
<%@ Register Assembly="AjaxControlToolkit"
Namespace="AjaxControlToolkit.HTMLEditor" TagPrefix="asp" %>

<div id="comment_editor" style="position:absolute;
top:0px;left:0px;display:none;">
     <asp:Editor runat="server" ID="CommentEditor" NoScript="true"  />
</div>
```

Code snippet FitnessTrackerPlus.aspx

The `Editor` control provides a great property called `NoScript` that automatically removes any JavaScript that may have been added to the control. Because the requirements and design state that JavaScript will not be allowed, you will set the `NoScript` property to `true`.

At this point, you have all the required HTML and XAML declarations for the public journal page. The Silverlight plug-in is set up correctly to support the HTML overlay trick that you'll use. The required placeholder controls have been added to both the FitnessTrackerPlus.aspx and PublicJournal.xaml pages. When you run the application and navigate to the public journal page, you should see the HTML comments appear as they do in Figure 9-5, and the data entry form should include the HTML `Editor` control appearing directly over the form, as shown in Figure 9-6.

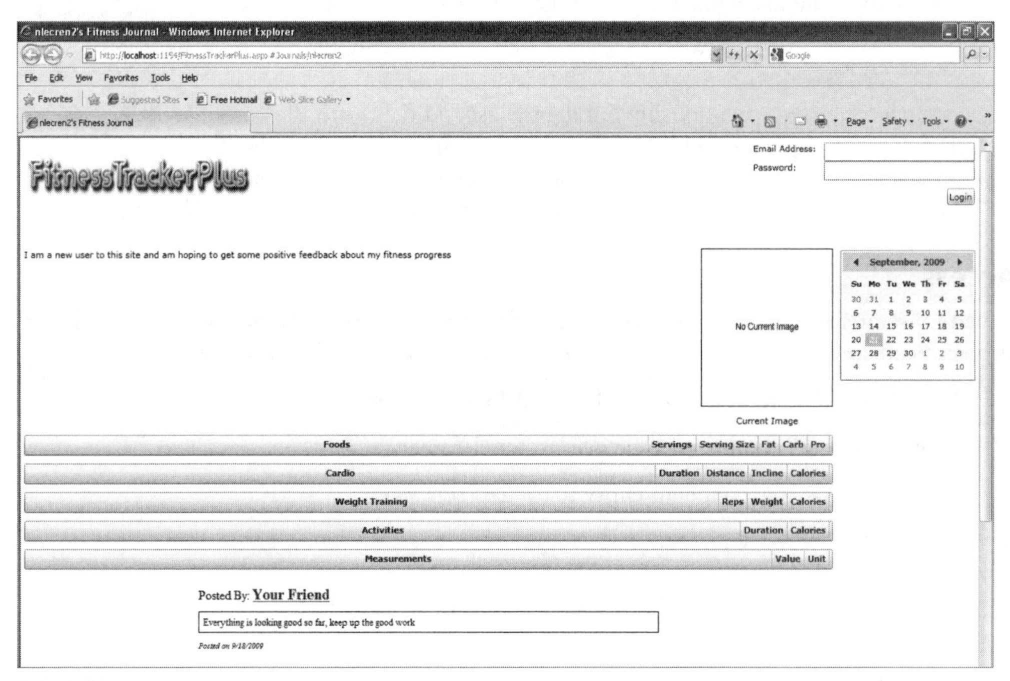

FIGURE 9-5

FIGURE 9-6

Database

For the database layer implementation you need to create the journal_comments table as outlined in the "Design" section. Once again, to do this, follow these steps:

1. Right-click the FitnessTrackerPlus database and add a new table called journal_comments.
2. Add all the columns defined in the design and make sure to set the ID field as an auto-incrementing identity field as well as the primary key for the table.
3. Set up a foreign key relationship linking the user_id field with the ID field from the users table. This makes it possible to load all of the comments for each user's public journal page. Figure 9-7 shows the database diagram you should be left with once the table is created.

FIGURE 9-7

Data Access

Once you finish creating the required database table, you'll need to add a new LINQ to SQL file to the project to create the required entities. In this case, you should follow these steps:

1. Add a new LINQ to SQL classes file called Journal.dbml.
2. Drag the journal_comments table over to the designer.
3. Rename the journal_comment entity to `JournalComment`.
4. Rebuild the ASP.NET project.

At this point, you'll have the required `JournalComment` entity defined and the `DomainService` you are about to create will use this entity. Figure 9-8 shows the updated LINQ to SQL file that you should be left with when you are finished with this step.

FIGURE 9-8

Business Logic

With the database table and data access layer complete, it's time to move on to the business logic once again. The bulk of the work in the remaining part of this chapter is spent in the business logic layer and the code behind. The user interface requires a new DomainService class in order to support both the display and creation of public journal comments by following these steps:

1. Add a new `DomainService` to the ASP.NET project.
2. Call this one `JournalService`.
3. Select the newly created `JournalDataContext` and the `JournalComment` entity.
4. You also need to check the Enable editing and Generate associated classes for metadata options.

When visitors arrive at a particular public journal page, note that certain information will not be available at the user interface layer. For example, even though all the public journal settings are easily retrieved using the `WebContext.Current.User` object under normal circumstances, they are not available to anonymous users that have not logged into FitnessTrackerPlus. The public journal page needs to access these settings in order to determine what data, if any, to make available to the visitor. For security purposes, you don't really want to simply return the `UserInformation` object containing the full users `Profile` because it also includes things such as e-mail address, password, and other user-specific settings. The public journal page does not need any of this information, so rather than return the entire `UserInformation` object, you need an alternate solution.

In most cases, when you use WCF RIA Services you will return a collection of `Entity` classes that are defined using the Entity Framework or LINQ to SQL, but in this case, you want to return just a custom object that contains only a handful of fields and that was not generated using the LINQ to SQL code generator. As you saw in the previous chapter, when using WCF RIA Services, you are not strictly limited to returning predefined entities; you can also return simple POCO objects with just a few additional lines of code. In this case, you just want an object that contains the `user_id` and the public journal settings; so in the JournalService.cs file you should create a new class called `PublicJournalSettings`. Once you add the required properties, you should do the following to ensure that the custom class is exposed:

- Add the `[EnableClientAccess()]` attribute directly above the class declaration.
- Select one of the properties as the unique key for the entity. In this case, that is the `user_name` property.

The following code shows the `PublicJournalSettings` class that you need to create:

Available for download on Wrox.com

```
[EnableClientAccess()]
public class PublicJournalSettings
{
     [Key]
     public string user_name { get; set; }
     public string about_text { get; set; }
     public int user_id { get; set; }

     public bool share_foods { get; set; }
     public bool share_exercises { get; set; }
     public bool share_measurements { get; set; }
     public bool share_images { get; set; }
     public bool enable_comments { get; set; }
}
```

Code snippet JournalService.cs

Once you have a simple class to hold just the public journal properties, you can then add a method to the `JournalService` that returns the public journal settings for the public journal page being queried. In the following code snippet, the custom `MembershipProvider` is used to first retrieve an instance of the `UserInformation` object using just the `user_name` parameter passed in from the client after extracting it from the query string.

```
public PublicJournalSettings GetPublicJournalSettings(string user_name)
{
     // Check the profile for the selected user and see if they have enabled
     // sharing of thier public journal

     FitnessTrackerPlus.Web.Providers.MembershipProvider provider =
Membership.Provider as FitnessTrackerPlus.Web.Providers.MembershipProvider;
     UserInformation user = provider.GetUserByUserName(user_name) as
UserInformation;

     if (user.Profiles[0].share_journal)
          return new PublicJournalSettings
     {
          user_name = user.username,
          user_id = user.id,
          share_foods = user.Profiles[0].share_foods,
          share_exercises = user.Profiles[0].share_exercises,
          share_measurements = user.Profiles[0].share_measurements,
          share_images = user.Profiles[0].share_images,
          enable_comments = user.Profiles[0].enable_comments,
          about_text = user.Profiles[0].about_text
     };

     return null;
}
```

Code snippet JournalService.cs

Notice how once you have a valid `UserInformation` object you can just access the `Profiles` collection. In this case, because you are not supporting multiple profiles for each user, you just make use of the first `Profile` in the collection. If for some reason the user decides not to share his or her journal at all, you will return a `null PublicJournalSettings` object. The code behind for the public journal page can then redirect the user back to the FitnessTrackerPlus home page if no settings are available for the public journal being requested.

The only other operations that are needed in this `DomainService` are support for retrieval and creation of any comments associated with the public journal. The expectation is that the code behind will first call the `GetPublicJournalSettings` method and at that point will have access to not only all of the settings but also the `user_id` for the public journal being queried. For this reason, you can make use of the `user_id` instead of the `user_name` when actually retrieving the comments. The following code shows the `GetJournalComments` method, which retrieves all comments associated with a particular user's public journal, as well as the `InsertJournalComment`, which just simply creates a new comment in the database:

Available for download on Wrox.com

```
public IQueryable<JournalComment> GetJournalComments(int user_id)
{
     return this.Context.JournalComments.Where(e => e.user_id ==
user_id).OrderByDescending(e => e.entry_date);
}

public void InsertJournalComment(JournalComment journalComment)
{
     this.Context.JournalComments.InsertOnSubmit(journalComment);
}
```

Code snippet JournalService.cs

User Interface Code Behind

At this point you should have everything to work on the public journal code behind page. You have a lot of work to do here and this page can quickly become very complex, so before diving into the code let's take a quick look at the various things that you need to accomplish as well as the order you should do them in:

- Provide a unique URL for accessing the public journal page.
- Position the comment DIV elements directly over the associated Silverlight placeholder controls.
- Load the public journal settings when a visitor arrives at the page.
- Determine what data, if any, should display to the visitor.
- Load and display any HTML comments associated with the journal.
- Handle the calendar date selection so visitors can view previously recorded entries.
- Capture and submit any HTML comments being posted by the visitors.

Earlier you created the user interface for the public journal page, but as of now there is no real functionality behind it. You also have no way of actually accessing the page so the first item of work on the list is providing the unique URL where visitors can reach the public journal page. The Silverlight navigation framework gives you the perfect solution for this problem. By combining a simple query string variable with the URI mapping scheme set up in the App.xaml file, you can provide users with a unique URL to their public journal page, which can be bookmarked and visited directly. The goal is to set up a URL in the format `http://www.fitnesstrackerplus.com/#Journals/username`. To do this, you simply add the following line to the `UriMapper` declarations:

Available for download on Wrox.com

```
<uri:UriMapping Uri="Journals/{username}"
MappedUri="/Views/Journal/PublicJournal.xaml?user={username}" />
```

Code snippet App.xaml

As you can see, any URL ending in "Journals/username" is mapped to the PublicJournal.xaml page. The mapped URL also contains a query string variable called `user` that contains the username of the public journal page to be loaded. With this mapping in place, the full URL to any given user's public journal page becomes `http://www.fitnesstrackerplus.com/FitnessTrackerPlus.aspx#Journals/username`. This is still a little bit lengthy, but in Silverlight you are still required to have the # character in the URL. If you are interested in giving your users an easier URL to remember, you could take this concept a step further and add an ASP.NET URL Rewriting feature that takes an even simpler format such as `http://www.fitnesstrackerplus.com/username`. This Rewriting feature is responsible for mapping the simple URL to the one that Silverlight requires. Because the Silverlight version of the URL can be bookmarked and is unique it's sufficient for this first version of FitnessTrackerPlus. If any users start to express a desire for an even shorter URL, you can always add this additional ASP.NET step to accommodate them in a future release.

When creating the user interface, you added a couple of placeholder controls that will be used as a reference point for positioning the comment DIV elements on the .ASPX page. You should have a DIV for the comment area itself as well as a DIV to hold the `Editor` control from the AJAX Control Toolkit. On the public journal page you have a `Grid` control called `CommentArea` that will act as a reference point for the `comment_area` DIV. You also have a `TextBox` control called `Comment` that will be used as a reference point for the `comment_editor` DIV. If you were to simply make both of these DIV elements visible at this point you would see that they both appear overlaid on top of the plug-in at the top-left corner of the screen. Of course, this isn't particularly useful so you need to add a method that's responsible for sizing and positioning these DIV elements directly over their placeholder counterparts.

Before adding this method, consider that the method will need to be called not only when the page is first loaded but also anytime the user makes use of the `ScrollViewer` control. When a user scrolls, the method will move the location of the placeholder controls but the overlaid DIV elements will not automatically stay in synch. Therefore, this method needs to be called whenever the page is scrolled. The best place to do that is in the `LayoutUpdated` event of the `ScrollViewer` control. Earlier you added the `ScrollViewer` control to the static `Globals` class so you should have access to it and its events. Wiring up the event handler to position the comment controls is done with one line of code:

Available for download on Wrox.com

```
Globals.MainScroll.LayoutUpdated += (se, ev) => { PositionCommentControls(); };
```

Code snippet PublicJournal.xaml.cs

That takes care of finding a good place to call the positioning method; now take a look at the full implementation of the `PositionCommentControls` method and break down how it works:

Available for download on Wrox.com

```
private void PositionCommentControls()
{
    UIElement root = Application.Current.RootVisual as UIElement;
    GeneralTransform gt = Comment.TransformToVisual(root);
    Point pos = gt.Transform(new Point(0, 0));

    HtmlElement editor = HtmlPage.Document.GetElementById("comment_editor");
    HtmlElement comments = HtmlPage.Document.GetElementById("comment_area");

    editor.SetStyleAttribute("top", pos.Y.ToString() + "px");
    editor.SetStyleAttribute("left", pos.X.ToString() + "px");
    editor.SetStyleAttribute("width", Comment.ActualWidth.ToString() + "px");
    editor.SetStyleAttribute("height", Comment.ActualHeight.ToString() + "px");

    gt = CommentArea.TransformToVisual(root);
    pos = gt.Transform(new Point(0, 0));

    comments.SetStyleAttribute("top", pos.Y.ToString() + "px");
    comments.SetStyleAttribute("left", pos.X.ToString() + "px");
}
```

Code snippet PublicJournal.xaml.cs

Because the `comment_area` and `comment_editor` DIV elements are absolutely positioned you can make use of the `SetStyleAttribute` method of the `HtmlPage` class to position these DIV elements directly over their Silverlight placeholder counterparts. The trick is to know the coordinates of the placeholder controls. This is where the `TransformToVisual` method, shown in the previous code snippet, is useful. To do this, follow these steps:

1. Grab the `RootVisual object`, which is the parent of all the controls in the Silverlight application.
2. Take the `Comment` placeholder control and call `TransformToVisual`, passing in the root object. This gives you the coordinates of the `Comment` control relative to the `RootVisual`.

> *It is important to note that you can do this with any* `UIElement` *control, so you can easily retrieve the coordinates relative to another.*

3. Once you have the coordinates of the `Comment` control, you just set the `comment_editor` DIV element to be positioned using these same coordinates.
4. Make sure that the size of the `comment_editor` DIV is the same as the `Comment` placeholder control. For that you want to use the `ActualWidth` and `ActualHeight` properties of the `Comment` control.

Once you have completely positioned the comment_editor DIV, you need to do the same thing for the comment_area DIV. You have a placeholder Grid control that the comment_area DIV will be overlaid against. You just use the same TransformToVisual method to get the coordinates of the placeholder Grid control relative to the application root and position the comment_area accordingly. In both calls to the TransformToVisual method, you are passing in a Point object that simply tells the TransformToVisual method any offset you wish to use when calculating the coordinates. In both cases, you won't be passing in any offset. Instead, you just retrieve the coordinates starting from the top-left corner of the application root.

Before loading any data on the public journal page from the JournalService you created earlier, you add a Loaded event handler to set up some required control event handlers. In the following code, the Loaded event ensures that the DataGrid display trick that each journal log page uses is also used on this page. This ensures that the first DataGrid column is expanded to fill up any leftover screen space, eliminating the empty space to the right of the last DataGrid column that is usually displayed. The Loaded event also sets up the ItemsSource properties for the various DataGrid controls and adds event handlers for when the visitor changes the selected date or attempts to post a new comment.

Available for download on Wrox.com

```
Loaded += (s, e) =>
{
    Globals.MainScroll.LayoutUpdated += (se, ev) =>
    {
        PositionCommentEntry();

        DataGridHelper.ResizeGrid(0, FoodLogGrid);
        DataGridHelper.ResizeGrid(0, CardioLogGrid);
        DataGridHelper.ResizeGrid(0, WeightTrainingLogGrid);
        DataGridHelper.ResizeGrid(0, ActivityLogGrid);
        DataGridHelper.ResizeGrid(0, MeasurementLogGrid);
    };

    Calendar.SelectedDate = DateTime.Now;
    Calendar.SelectedDatesChanged += (se, ev) => { LoadPublicJournal(); };

    AboutText.Text = "";

    FoodLogGrid.ItemsSource = foodContext.FoodLogEntries;
    MeasurementLogGrid.ItemsSource =
measurementContext.MeasurementLogEntries;

    Submit.Click += new RoutedEventHandler(Submit_Click);
};
```

Code snippet PublicJournal.xaml.cs

The next step in the code behind is to actually load the required data for the public journal page. The main reason behind mapping to a URL with a query string is so that you know which user's data to load on this page. This query string variable is made available in the OnNavigatedTo event handler.

In the following code, the username is extracted from the query string and retrieves the PublicJournalSettings object. If a null object is returned, then this particular user has declined to share their public journal page so the visitor is redirected to the main FitnessTrackerPlus home page. Otherwise, the `LoadPublicJournal` method, which is responsible for actually retrieving any of the data that the user has decided to share, is called.

Available for download on Wrox.com

```
protected override void OnNavigatedTo(NavigationEventArgs e)
{
    try
    {
        string user = NavigationContext.QueryString["user"];

        // Load the public journal settings for the requested user
        // if the public journal settings instance is null than that
        // user has not elected to share thier journal

        if (!String.IsNullOrEmpty(user))
        {
            Title = String.Format("{0}'s Fitness Journal", user);

            journalContext.Load<PublicJournalSettings>(journalContext.
GetPublicJournalSettingsQuery(user),
            (JournalLoaded) =>
            {
                if (!JournalLoaded.HasError)
                {

                    IEnumerator<PublicJournalSettings> enumerator =
JournalLoaded.Entities.GetEnumerator();
                    enumerator.MoveNext();

                    if (enumerator.Current != null)
                    {
                        // At this point we have a valid PublicJournal
                        // object so the user is currently sharing
                        // journal information now we need to look
                        // at what options have been enabled

                        settings = enumerator.Current;
                        LoadPublicJournal();
                    }
                    else
                        NavigationService.Navigate(new Uri("Home",
UriKind.Relative));
                }
                else
                    NavigationService.Navigate(new Uri("Home",
UriKind.Relative));

            }, null);
        }
        else
            NavigationService.Navigate(new Uri("Home", UriKind.Relative));
    }
```

```
        catch (Exception)
        {
            NavigationService.Navigate(new Uri("Home", UriKind.Relative));
        }
    }
```

Code snippet PublicJournal.xaml.cs

The next area to look at is the `LoadPublicJournal` method, which is responsible for actually loading any shared data and comments. In the following code snippet, the various settings are examined to see if they have been enabled. If so, then the appropriate data is loaded into the various `DataGrid` controls. In addition to loading the data, the `Visibility` property of the user interface controls is toggled depending on whether the user decided to share the associated information.

Available for download on Wrox.com

```
private void LoadPublicJournal()
{
    if (settings != null)
    {
        if (settings.share_foods)
        {
            foodContext.Load<FoodLogEntry>(foodContext.
GetFoodLogEntriesQuery(settings.user_id, Calendar.SelectedDate.Value, false));
            FoodLogGrid.Visibility = Visibility.Visible;
        }
        else
            FoodLogGrid.Visibility = Visibility.Collapsed;

        if (settings.share_exercises)
        {
            exerciseContext.Load<ExerciseLogEntry>(exerciseContext.
GetExerciseLogEntriesQuery(Calendar.SelectedDate.Value, settings.user_id),
            LoadBehavior.RefreshCurrent, (EntriesLoaded) =>
            {
                if (!EntriesLoaded.HasError)
                {
                    CardioLogGrid.ItemsSource =
EntriesLoaded.Entities.Where(ev => ev.Exercise.exercise_type == 1);
                    WeightTrainingLogGrid.ItemsSource =
EntriesLoaded.Entities.Where(ev => ev.Exercise.exercise_type == 2);
                    ActivityLogGrid.ItemsSource =
EntriesLoaded.Entities.Where(ev => ev.Exercise.exercise_type == 3);
                }

            }, null);

            CardioLogGrid.Visibility = Visibility.Visible;
            WeightTrainingLogGrid.Visibility = Visibility.Visible;
            ActivityLogGrid.Visibility = Visibility.Visible;
        }
        else
        {
            CardioLogGrid.Visibility = Visibility.Collapsed;
            WeightTrainingLogGrid.Visibility = Visibility.Collapsed;
```

```
            ActivityLogGrid.Visibility = Visibility.Collapsed;
        }

        if (settings.share_measurements)
        {
            measurementContext.Load<MeasurementLogEntry>(measurementContext.
GetMeasurementLogEntriesQuery(settings.user_id, Calendar.SelectedDate.Value));
            MeasurementLogGrid.Visibility = Visibility.Visible;
        }
        else
            MeasurementLogGrid.Visibility = Visibility.Collapsed;

        if (settings.share_images)
        {
            measurementContext.Load<MeasurementImage>(measurementContext.
GetMeasurementImageQuery(settings.user_id, Calendar.SelectedDate.Value),
            LoadBehavior.RefreshCurrent, (ImageLoaded) =>
            {
                if (!ImageLoaded.HasError)
                {
                    BitmapImage updatedImage = null;
                    MeasurementImage currentImage =
ImageLoaded.Entities.FirstOrDefault<MeasurementImage>();

                    if (currentImage != null)
                    {
#if DEBUG
                        updatedImage = new BitmapImage(new
Uri(String.Format("http://localhost:32490/UploadedImages/{0}",
ImageLoaded.Entities.First<MeasurementImage>()), UriKind.Absolute));

#else
                        updatedImage = new BitmapImage(new
Uri(String.Format("http://fitnesstrackerplus.com/UploadedImages/{0}",
finalFileName), UriKind.Absolute));

#endif
                        // This is necessary to ensure that Silverlight
                        // refreshes the image even though the file name
                        // remains the same

                        updatedImage.CreateOptions =
BitmapCreateOptions.IgnoreImageCache;
                        CurrentImage.Source = updatedImage;
                    }
                    else
                        CurrentImage.Source = new BitmapImage(new
Uri("/Images/image_unavailable.png", UriKind.Relative));
                }

            }, null);

            CurrentImage.Visibility = Visibility.Visible;
        }
```

```
            else
                 CurrentImage.Visibility = Visibility.Collapsed;

            if (settings.enable_comments)
            {
                 HtmlPage.Document.GetElementById("comment_area").
SetStyleAttribute("display", "");
                 HtmlPage.Document.GetElementById("comment_editor").
SetStyleAttribute("display", "");

                 LoadComments();

                 CommentForm.Visibility = Visibility.Visible;
            }
            else
            {
                 HtmlPage.Document.GetElementById("comment_area").
SetStyleAttribute("display", "none");
                 HtmlPage.Document.GetElementById("comment_editor").
SetStyleAttribute("display", "none");

                 CommentForm.Visibility = Visibility.Collapsed;
            }

            AboutText.Text = settings.about_text;
      }
}
```

Code snippet PublicJournal.xaml.cs

An additional aspect of this method that requires some special attention is the use of the `HtmlPage` class to toggle the display of the `comment_area`, and `comment_editor` DIV elements. Earlier I said that Silverlight offers easy access to the DOM of the page hosting the plug-in. The classes required to make use of this functionality reside in the `System.Windows.Browser` namespace. The class that offers access to the DOM is the `HtmlPage` class. In this class, you'll find a host of useful methods from the Silverlight code behind page that you can use to directly manipulate the DOM object. In this case, you'll first check that the commenting feature is enabled for this user's public journal page. If enabled, you need to make the DIV elements on the FitnessTrackerPlus.aspx page visible. In the following code snippet, notice how both the `comment_area` and `comment_editor` DIV elements are accessed and made visible using the `GetElementById` and `SetStyleAttribute` methods of the `Document` instance.

After making both of these DIV elements visible, the next task is to load any comments that are associated with this public journal and create individual DIV elements for each comment that is retrieved from the database. In the following code take note that before actually creating any comments, you need to clear the `innerHTML` property of the `comment_area`. This prevents duplicate comments from appearing in the `comment_area` DIV when the comments are reloaded from the database.

Available for download on Wrox.com

```
private void LoadComments()
{
     journalContext.Load<JournalComment>(journalContext.
```

```
GetJournalCommentsQuery(settings.user_id), LoadBehavior.RefreshCurrent,
     (CommentsLoaded) =>
     {
          if (!CommentsLoaded.HasError)
          {
               HtmlPage.Document.GetElementById("comment_area").
SetProperty("innerHTML", "");

               foreach (JournalComment comment in CommentsLoaded.Entities)
                    CreateComment(comment);
          }

     }, null);
}
```

Code snippet PublicJournal.xaml.cs

Creating each individual DIV element for the comments once again requires the `HtmlPage` class. The design calls for each comment to consist of three separate DIV elements—one for the header, one for the comment text, and one for the footer. The header div is basically the name of the visitor who posted the comment in the form of a hyperlink. The hyperlink opens up a new browser window to the website that was posted in the comment form. Because the website field was considered optional, you must provide a non-functional link if the website field is empty. The next DIV element contains the actual HTML that was posted to the database. When the HTML was posted as a security precaution, you made use of the `HttpUtility.Encode` method to encode the raw HTML. You also set the `Editor` control to disable the posting of JavaScript code, so you should be in good shape there. You will, however, have to use the `HttpUtility.Decode` method before setting the content to the `comment_text` DIV. The following code shows the full implementation of the `CreateComment` method that appends each set of comment DIV elements to the main `comment_area`:

Available for download on Wrox.com

```
private void CreateComment(JournalComment comment)
{
     string headerText = "";

     StringBuilder builder = new StringBuilder();

     if (String.IsNullOrEmpty(comment.website))
          headerText = String.Format("Posted By: <a href='#'>{0}</a>",
comment.name);
     else
     {
          if (comment.website.IndexOf("http://") >= 0)
               headerText = String.Format("Posted By: <a href='{0}'
target='_blank'>{1}</a>", comment.website, comment.name);
          else
               headerText = String.Format("Posted By: <a href='http://{0}'
target='_blank'>{1}</a>", comment.website, comment.name);
     }

     HtmlElement headerDiv = HtmlPage.Document.CreateElement("div");
     HtmlElement commentDiv = HtmlPage.Document.CreateElement("div");
```

```
        HtmlElement footerDiv = HtmlPage.Document.CreateElement("div");

        headerDiv.CssClass = "comment_header";
        commentDiv.CssClass = "comment_text";
        footerDiv.CssClass = "comment_footer";

        headerDiv.SetProperty("innerHTML", headerText);
        commentDiv.SetProperty("innerHTML", HttpUtility.HtmlDecode(comment.comment));
        footerDiv.SetProperty("innerHTML", String.Format("Posted on {0}",
    comment.entry_date.ToShortDateString()));

        HtmlElement comment_area = HtmlPage.Document.GetElementById("comment_area");

        comment_area.AppendChild(headerDiv);
        comment_area.AppendChild(commentDiv);
        comment_area.AppendChild(footerDiv);

        CommentArea.Width =
    Convert.ToInt32(HtmlPage.Document.GetElementById("comment_area").
    GetProperty("offsetWidth"));
        CommentArea.Height =
    Convert.ToInt32(HtmlPage.Document.GetElementById("comment_area").
    GetProperty("offsetHeight"));

    }
```

Code snippet PublicJournal.xaml.cs

At the end of the method, notice how the Silverlight `CommentArea Grid` control has its own `width` and `height` properties adjusted to match the total size of the `comment_area` DIV element. This is achieved by retrieving both the `offsetWidth` and `offsetHeight` properties. You adjust the size of the `CommentArea Grid` control because although the `comment_area` DIV element will grow with each child that is appended to it, the Silverlight plug-in size will remain the same. Changes to the size of DIV elements in the DOM do not automatically grow the size of the Silverlight page. This works for a few comments but very quickly the comments flow right off the page and the visitor cannot see them. Don't forget that although the comments appear to be embedded in the Silverlight page, they are really just overlaid on top of the plug-in and will not affect the size of the Silverlight page itself. By growing the size of the `CommentArea Grid` along with the DIV element itself, you ensure that the total size of the Silverlight page continues to grow and the parent `ScrollViewer` control expands to include all of the available comments.

The final task for this chapter involves saving the HTML comments to the database. The comment entry form requires visitors to supply at minimum a name and message. Visitors can also enter an optional website if they wish. By making use of the AJAX-based `Editor` control, visitors can easily create HTML-based comments. When users click the Submit button, you will first create a new `JournalComment` object and set both the name, website, user_id, and entry_date fields. You then need to grab the HTML data from the `Editor` control.

To do this, you invoke some JavaScript on the main FitnessTrackerPlus.aspx page. The nice thing about the `Editor` control is that you can access it through JavaScript using some of the client-side functions available in ASP.NET AJAX. Accessing standard ASP.NET controls from JavaScript was always a chore and usually involved registering client script dynamically in the code behind using the `ClientID` property of the server controls. From the start, the AJAX Control Toolkit controls were developed with client-side programming in mind so rather that resort to server-side script injections you can simply make use of the `$find` method to access any control from the Toolkit from JavaScript. In this case, you need a couple of JavaScript methods on the main page, one that clears the `Editor` control and another that retrieves the HTML that was entered in the control. The following code should reside at the top of the FitnessTrackerPlus.aspx page:

Available for download on Wrox.com

```
<head runat="server">
     <title>FitnessTrackerPlus</title>
     <script language="javascript" type="text/javascript">
          function setEditorContent(content) {
               $find('CommentEditor').set_content(content);
          }
          function getEditorContent() {
               return $find('CommentEditor').get_content();
          }
     </script>
</head>
```

Code snippet FitnessTrackerPlus.aspx

As you can see, the `Editor` control provides client-side methods called `set` and `get_content` that you can use to access the raw HTML content of the control. Calling these methods from Silverlight is as simple as making use of the `HtmlPage.Window.Invoke` method, which allows you to invoke any JavaScript method that exists on the page hosting the Silverlight plug-in. In the following code for the `Submit` handler, the `getEditorContent` method is called and the result is HTML encoded using the `HtmlEncode` helper method before it's sent to the database. Although the `NoScript` option of the `Editor` control is set, the HTML encoding just adds an additional layer of security.

Available for download on Wrox.com

```
private void Submit_Click(object sender, RoutedEventArgs e)
{
     JournalComment comment = new JournalComment();

     comment.name = Name.Text;
     comment.website = Website.Text;

     comment.comment = HttpUtility.HtmlEncode(HtmlPage.Window.
Invoke("getEditorContent", null) as string);
     comment.user_id = settings.user_id;
     comment.entry_date = DateTime.Now;

     journalContext.JournalComments.Add(comment);
     journalContext.SubmitChanges((CommentSubmitted) =>
     {
          if (!CommentSubmitted.HasError)
          {
               LoadComments();

               Name.Text = "";
```

```
                Website.Text = "";
                HtmlPage.Window.Invoke("setEditorContent", "");
            }

        }, null);
    }
```

Code snippet PublicJournal.xaml.cs

SUMMARY

This chapter had a little bit of everything. You learned how to add some basic social networking components to FitnessTrackerPlus by giving users a public version of their fitness journal. Thanks to the navigation framework, users can share their public facing journal with others using a fixed URL that leads directly to the public journal page. You also should have a good idea of how to integrate HTML elements into your own Silverlight applications even though there is currently no native support for HTML. As you have seen, you can easily make use of this HTML overlay trick to utilize some of the existing AJAX server-based controls from ASP.NET or other AJAX libraries. Don't forget that you'll take a performance hit when you set the Windowless mode of the plug-in to `true`. When integrating HTML into your own Silverlight applications, you must weigh the benefits of HTML integration against the potential performance hit from Windowless mode.

Continuing with the social networking theme, the next chapter takes you through integrating with the popular social networking site MySpace. By doing this, you'll give your users an additional choice for sharing fitness information. If they currently don't belong to an existing social network like MySpace, they can make use of the public journal feature you just created. Or if they prefer to share their fitness data on a social networking site that they have already invested their time in, you'll give them the option to do that as well.

10

Social Networking

Developing a MySpace Application with Silverlight

This chapter covers how to integrate data from FitnessTrackerPlus with the popular social networking site MySpace. Users of FitnessTrackerPlus are currently able to share their fitness progress with others through the use of the public journal page that you just completed. In some cases, however, these users will already have made an investment in another social networking site. These users may wish to just share their fitness journals on another existing social networking site rather than sending their friends and family to yet another URL. There are currently many different social networking sites available on the Internet and to try and support every single one of them is not practical for this book. Instead, I will be focusing my coverage on arguably one of the largest social networking sites — MySpace. Although this chapter cannot possibly offer a thorough examination of the entire MySpace developer API and the OpenSocial platform, you will be able to see step by step how to develop a MySpace application in Silverlight, and by the end of the chapter provide users of FitnessTrackerPlus with another option for sharing their fitness progress with their friends, family, and anyone else on the Internet.

PROBLEM

The public journal page created in the previous chapter provides a great tool for users of FitnessTrackerPlus to gain feedback from others on their individual fitness progress. It provides a social networking-like element to the site that really encourages users to share their food, exercise, and measurement logs with others online. Of course, in this day and age, you can't assume that users will necessarily jump at the opportunity to keep yet another social networking page up-to-date. For this subset of users, the public journal page is yet another link that needs to be shared with friends and family if they want to keep up with what that particular user is doing. These users most likely already have accounts and information shared on one or all of the big social networking sites such as MySpace, Facebook, or Twitter. In order to make everyone happy, you should provide some kind of integration with these sites that allows users to post information that would normally be shared on their public journal page to their social networking site of choice. Because MySpace, Facebook, and Twitter have such massive user bases, you will want to concentrate on integrating with at least one of these three sites for the first version of FitnessTrackerPlus.

When making a determination as to which social networking site you will support, you must take into account a couple of things. First, you will need to decide on what your integration goals are. Most of these social networking sites provide some sort of API that allows you as the developer to retrieve member profile information, friend details, and additional items. In the case of FitnessTrackerPlus, you are really just trying to mimic some of the behavior that is available in the public journal page so that users of FitnessTrackerPlus will have an additional option for sharing their information. In this case, you may not actually need information such as friends, videos, status, and so on. You really just want the food, exercise, and measurement logs to be embedded into a profile page. This integration goal should nudge you toward a site such as Facebook or MySpace as opposed to Twitter because you could potentially have quite a bit of information to share and Twitter is limited to a certain number of characters.

Another thing to consider when making a social networking choice for this first version of Silverlight is that, because you are working with Silverlight, the social networking site that you choose ideally should have support for Silverlight as part of their standard API offering. It will be much easier to integrate with a site that supports Silverlight because you won't necessarily have to resort to all sorts of JavaScript and HTML DOM Bridge tricks to get this working. That is not to say that these things should be avoided, just that if you can find an API that wraps these operations into easier-to-use managed code, your job will be infinitely easier.

DESIGN

The "Design" section for this chapter covers from start to finish how to create a Silverlight application that will be fully integrated with the social networking site MySpace. As stated in the "Problem" section, one of the goals for this feature is to choose a social networking site that provides support for Silverlight-based solutions in its standard API offering. MySpace has already announced and made available a Silverlight SDK that makes integration with its OpenSocial platform a breeze. With official Silverlight support in MySpace applications, it makes sense to go with MySpace for the initial release of FitnessTrackerPlus.

MySpace

At one time, MySpace was hands down the largest social networking site on the Web. It exploded onto the scene before Facebook, Twitter, or any of the other major sites. MySpace became incredibly useful for bands, which made use of the site to spread music clips, news, and tour dates. It essentially wiped out the concept of individual band websites. MySpace continued to grow in popularity among the younger Internet crowd, and soon it seemed as though everyone had a MySpace page to share. After a few years at the top, MySpace had some growing pains, but being bought out for over 500 million dollars was not one of them. One of the issues that MySpace had to quickly deal with was competing sites that were popping up fast. Of course, perhaps the largest competitor was Facebook, and over the course of just a few years Facebook overtook MySpace as the leading social networking site.

With the rapid growth in popularity of Facebook, it became clear that MySpace had to reinvent itself in order to win back crucial market share in the social networking space. Perhaps one of the main reasons for Facebook's tremendous growth was that it was one of the first social networking sites to open up its entire platform to third-party developers. This single decision, not unlike one made by Apple when it introduced iPhone application development, was responsible for the prominent display of thousands of custom Facebook applications on members' profile pages. Facebook instantly attracted developers across the Web to join the site and create these custom applications. A developer- and business-friendly terms of service for the API even offered a chance to potentially generate revenue from some wildly popular applications. It did not take long, however, for MySpace to jump on the bandwagon and create its own developer API so that third-party developers could jump over to the "other" big social networking site and start developing custom applications.

MySpace has continued to evolve its developer platform by joining forces with the popular OpenSocial platform that aims to create a standardized API that will work across multiple social networking sites. Most recently, and most important as far as this book is concerned, MySpace has added official support for Silverlight-based applications. These full-blown Silverlight apps can be embedded directly into a member's home page, or profile page. This official support includes an excellent beta version of the MySpace Silverlight SDK. This new SDK wraps all of the required JavaScript calls that are part of the OpenSocial platform and includes several Silverlight controls that you can make use of to integrate data from MySpace with your own Silverlight application.

MySpace Silverlight SDK

Currently, the best solution available for writing a Silverlight-based MySpace application is to make use of the MySpace Silverlight SDK. This SDK is currently in a beta form so you should be aware that any references made to methods or controls in this book, although valid at the time of this writing, may change with each new release. The SDK is available out on the CodePlex site at `http://myspacesilverlight.codeplex.com`. When you visit the site, you will see that the SDK itself provides several controls that can be dropped into your Silverlight XAML pages. Each of these controls wraps existing functionality of the OpenSocial JavaScript platform. Rather than forcing you to mix JavaScript along with your Silverlight code, the SDK controls make use of the HTML DOM Bridge feature of Silverlight to provide asynchronous calls to the OpenSocial API. Table 10-1 lists the controls that are available in the beta version that exists at the time of this writing.

TABLE 10-1: MySpace Silverlight SDK Controls

CONTROL	DESCRIPTION
`MySpacePeopleRequest`	Loads detailed list of friends for either owner or viewer of the application
`MySpacePersonRequest`	Loads detailed profile information for the specified owner or viewer of the application
`MySpaceVideoRequest`	Loads profile videos for the specified owner or viewer of the application

Because this SDK is currently in a very early beta form, I will be focusing only on the control that will be required for the FitnessTrackerPlus application. The control you will make use of is the `MySpacePersonRequest` control, and it will provide you with an easy way to retrieve the MySpace display name associated with the owner of the profile page that is currently hosting the FitnessTrackerPlus application. The `MySpacePersonRequest` control provides access to just about all of the available MySpace profile properties. The control uses an attribute called `RequestFields` in order to give you the option of specifying exactly what data you want returned. These options can easily be set by specifying the OpenSocial string representation of the properties you want returned. If you leave the `RequestFields` attribute blank, then the control will, by default, attempt to load all of the available properties. Table 10-2 shows the list of possible fields that can be returned with the `MySpacePersonRequest` control.

TABLE 10-2: MySpace OpenSocial Profile Properties

PROPERTY	REQUESTFIELDS STRING
AboutMe	opensocial.Person.Field.ABOUT_ME
Age	opensocial.Person.Field.AGE
BodyType	opensocial.Person.Field.BODY_TYPE
Books	opensocial.Person.Field.BOOKS
Children	opensocial.Person.Field.CHILDREN
CurrentLocation	opensocial.Person.Field.CURRENT_LOCATION
DateOfBirth	opensocial.Person.Field.DATE_OF_BIRTH
Drinker	opensocial.Person.Field.DRINKER
Ethnicity	opensocial.Person.Field.ETHNICITY
Gender	opensocial.Person.Field.GENDER
HasApp	opensocial.Person.Field.HAS_APP
Heroes	opensocial.Person.Field.HEROES
ID	opensocial.Person.Field.ID
Interests	opensocial.Person.Field.INTERESTS
Jobs	opensocial.Person.Field.JOBS
LargeImage	opensocial.Person.Field.LARGE_IMAGE
LookingFor	opensocial.Person.Field.LOOKING_FOR
MediumImage	opensocial.Person.Field.MEDIUM_IMAGE
Movies	opensocial.Person.Field.MOVIES

PROPERTY	REQUESTFIELDS STRING
Music	opensocial.Person.Field.MUSIC
Name	opensocial.Person.Field.NAME
NetworkPresence	opensocial.Person.Field.NETWORK_PRESENCE
Nickname	opensocial.Person.Field.NICKNAME
ProfileSong	opensocial.Person.Field.PROFILE_SONG
ProfileUrl	opensocial.Person.Field.PROFILE_URL
ProfileVideo	opensocial.Person.Field.PROFILE_VIDEO
RelationshipStatus	opensocial.Person.Field.RELATIONSHIP_STATUS
Religion	opensocial.Person.Field.RELIGION
SexualOrientation	opensocial.Person.Field.SEXUAL_ORIENTATION
Smoker	opensocial.Person.Field.SMOKER
Status	opensocial.Person.Field.STATUS
ThumbnailImage	opensocial.Person.Field.THUMBNAIL_URL
TVShows	opensocial.Person.Field.TV_SHOWS
Urls	opensocial.Person.Field.URLS

The `MySpacePersonRequest` also has an additional required attribute called `IdSpec` that is used to determine which person's profile data will be retrieved. The possible values for this attribute consist of either the viewer or the owner of the application. I will be covering this concept in more detail shortly, but for now you can take away from this that if you set the `IdSpec` attribute to the Viewer option, then profile information for the person viewing the application will be loaded. Alternatively, if you were to use the Owner value for the attribute, then profile information would be loaded for the Owner of the profile page that is hosting the application. For example, if you were to visit a page hosting the FitnessTrackerPlus MySpace application such as `http://www.myspace.com/fitnesstrackerplus`, you would be considered the Viewer of the application, and the MySpace user FitnessTrackerPlus would be considered the owner.

FitnessTrackerPlus — MySpace Application

The primary goal of adding a social networking component to FitnessTrackerPlus is to allow users to share their food, exercise, and measurement log information. As you have seen, the implementation of the public journal page involves making use of read-only `DataGrid` controls in order to display the information. Because the decision has been made to integrate with MySpace for this first version of FitnessTrackerPlus, the next decision is what integration option you want to make use of. In the previous section, I made reference to the new MySpace Silverlight SDK that is available for

MySpace applications. Because this seems to offer the path of least resistance, you will most likely go this route, but before making a final decision you should first see what other options are available.

By visiting the MySpace developer page at `http://developer.myspace.com` you will see links that can take you to things such as Documentation, Debugging tools, news, and more. At this point, you are interested in seeing what development options are available, so if you visit the Documentation page, you are presented with three options, as shown in Figure 10-1.

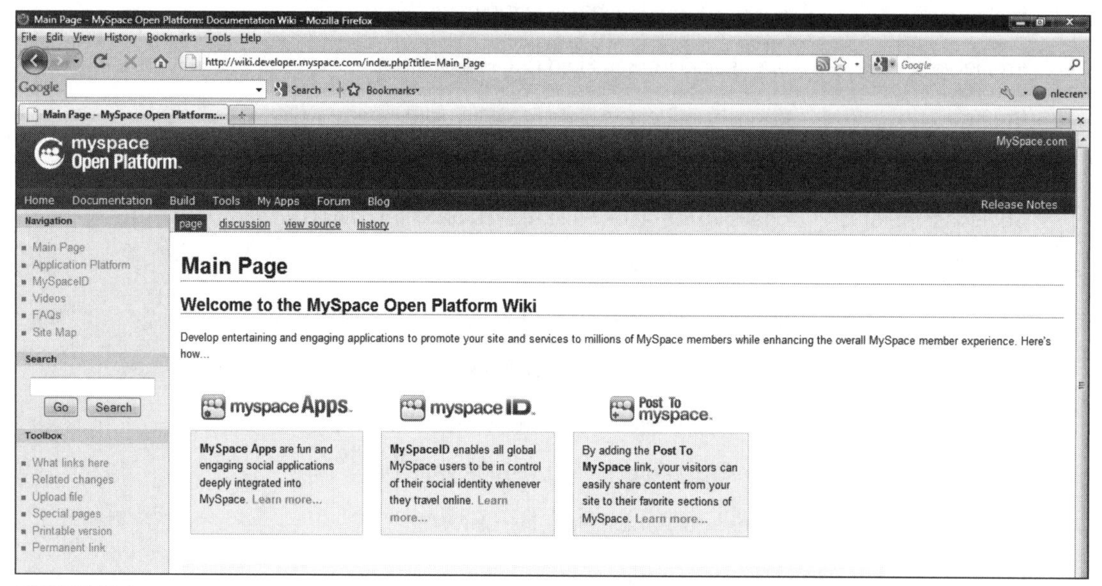

FIGURE 10-1

Your integration options are:

- **MySpaceApps:** This is the solution you will most likely use for FitnessTrackerPlus and it involves the creation of an application that is embedded directly onto a member's home page or profile page. There is also a separate canvas page that hosts only the application itself. Figure 10-2 shows a sample sports application that has been added to the FitnessTrackerPlus profile page. Yes, even FitnessTrackerPlus has its own MySpace page!
- **MySpaceID:** This provides your application with the ability to integrate MySpace data into your own application. This application does not have to be hosted on MySpace and offers you the ability to incorporate things such as Friend Updates, Profile Data, and much more. For FitnessTrackerPlus, this really isn't a good option as you aren't really interested in displaying MySpace data anywhere on the FitnessTrackerPlus site. Perhaps, down the road you could think of some interesting uses for this, but as of now this option may not be what you are looking for.
- **Post to MySpace:** Perhaps the simplest to make use of, Post to MySpace is really nice for quickly posting HTML data to a MySpace profile page. If FitnessTrackerPlus had been written completely in ASP.NET, you would be able to make a very strong case for going with this integration option.

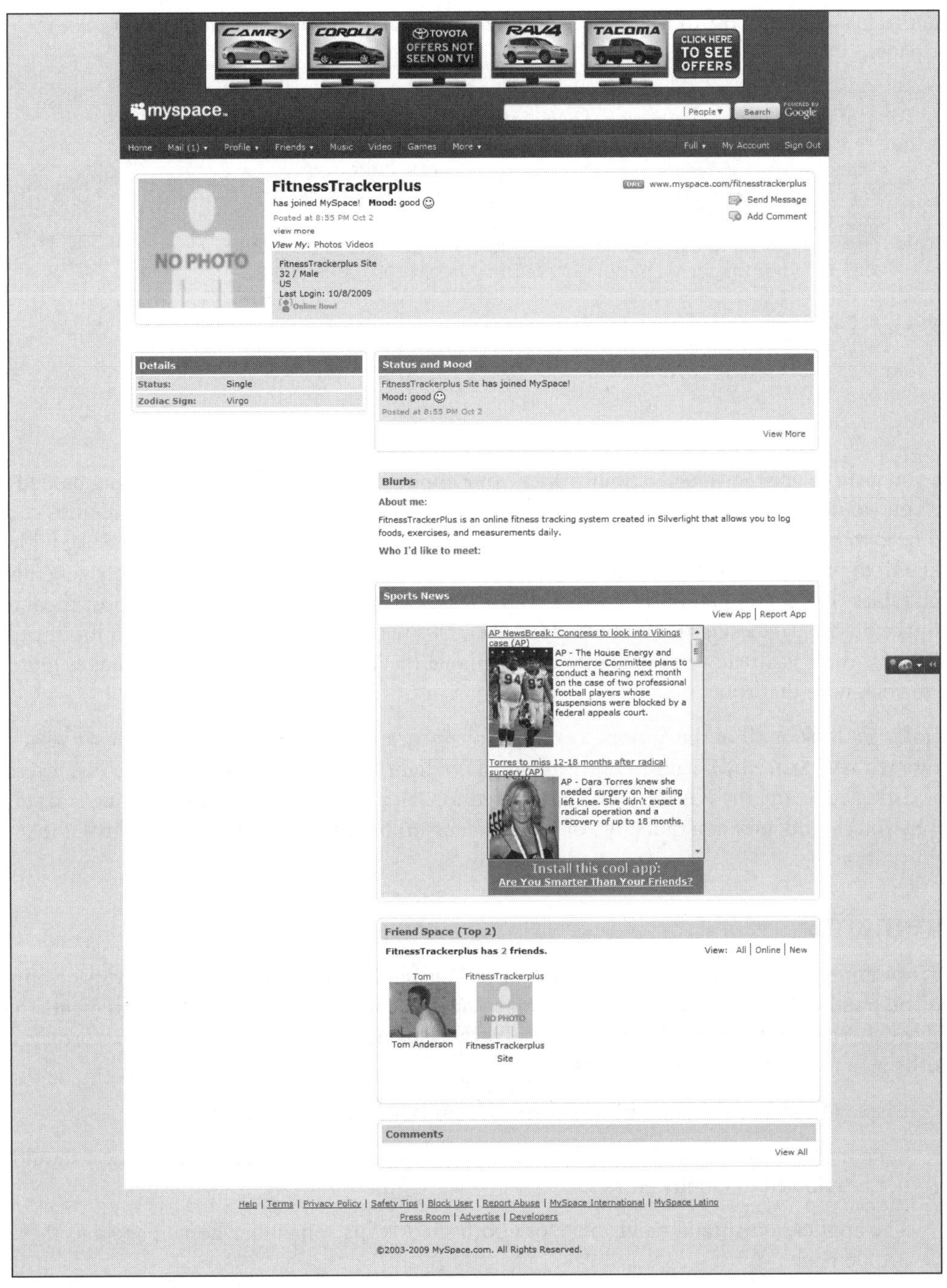
CAMRY
COROLLA
TOYOTA
OFFERS NOT SEEN ON TV!
RAV4
TACOMA
CLICK HERE TO SEE OFFERS
myspace.
People
Search
Google
Home Mail (1) Profile Friends Music Video Games More
Full My Account Sign Out
FitnessTrackerplus
has joined MySpace! Mood: good
Posted at 8:55 PM Oct 2
view more
View My: Photos Videos
www.myspace.com/fitnesstrackerplus
Send Message
Add Comment
NO PHOTO
FitnessTrackerplus Site
32 / Male
US
Last Login: 10/8/2009
Online Now!
Details
Status: Single
Zodiac Sign: Virgo
Status and Mood
FitnessTrackerplus Site has joined MySpace!
Mood: good
Posted at 8:55 PM Oct 2
View More
Blurbs
About me:
FitnessTrackerPlus is an online fitness tracking system created in Silverlight that allows you to log foods, exercises, and measurements daily.
Who I'd like to meet:
Sports News
View App | Report App
AP NewsBreak: Congress to look into Vikings case (AP)
AP - The House Energy and Commerce Committee plans to conduct a hearing next month on the case of two professional football players whose suspensions were blocked by a federal appeals court.
Torres to miss 12-18 months after radical surgery (AP)
AP - Dara Torres knew she needed surgery on her ailing left knee. She didn't expect a radical operation and a recovery of up to 18 months.
Install this cool app:
Are You Smarter Than Your Friends?
Friend Space (Top 2)
FitnessTrackerplus has 2 friends.
View: All | Online | New
Tom
FitnessTrackerplus
Tom Anderson
FitnessTrackerplus Site
Comments
View All
Help | Terms | Privacy Policy | Safety Tips | Block User | Report Abuse | MySpace International | MySpace Latino
Press Room | Advertise | Developers
©2003-2009 MySpace.com. All Rights Reserved.

FIGURE 10-2

In order to make use of Post to MySpace, you first copy the following code and place it on your ASPX page.

```
<form id="myspacepostto" method="post"
action="http://www.myspace.com/index.cfm?fuseaction=postto"
target="_blank">
     <input type="hidden" name="t" value="TITLE_GOES_HERE" />
     <input type="hidden" name="c" value="CONTENT_GOES_HERE" />
     <input type="hidden" name="u" value="URL_GOES_HERE" />
     <input type="hidden" name="r" value="RETURN_URL_GOES_HERE" />
     <input type="hidden" name="l" value="LOCATION_GOES_HERE" />
     <a href="#"
onclick="document.getElementById('myspacepostto').submit();return false;">
    <img src="http://cms.myspacecdn.com/cms/post_myspace_icon.gif"
border="0" alt="Post To MySpace!" /> Share on MySpace!
    </a>
</form>
```

Next, you just replace the value attributes with your application values. The `<input>` tag named `c` is where you would put any HTML content that needs to be posted. In most cases, the previous code would need to be dynamically created so you most likely create this entire code string along with the HTML to post in the code behind file. For FitnessTrackerPlus, you could conceivably generate HTML tables that contain all of the food, exercise, and measurement log entries and post them to a MySpace profile page using this method. However, this method would require quite a bit of code, and, because there is already a Silverlight SDK available for MySpace applications, it makes more sense to stick with that route.

After taking a look at all of the options available for integration, it still makes the most sense to integrate with MySpace by means of a full-blown Silverlight application. This way, you can leverage some existing code and the XAML that you created for the public journal. Before getting started, however, you should look at a quick list of requirements to be sure nothing is missed during the implementation.

Requirements

In order to mimic the behavior of the FitnessTrackerPlus public journal feature, the MySpace application you build will need to accomplish several things. The following is a list of requirements that should satisfy the main goal of allowing FitnessTrackerPlus users to share their fitness information with others on their MySpace profile page.

- Display food, exercise, and measurement log entries in `DataGrid` controls.
- `DataGrid` controls should be read only; visitors who see the embedded application should not be allowed to modify entries.
- The application should be visible from both the MySpace member home page and the profile page.

Before you will be able to populate the required `DataGrid` controls, you will need to solve an additional problem. Because the MySpace application is available to any member of MySpace, you won't necessarily have a link between the MySpace account and the corresponding FitnessTrackerPlus user to retrieve log entries from.

All MySpace members must create a unique display name that MySpace uses as part of the direct URL to the member's profile page. For example, the MySpace page for FitnessTrackerPlus can be found by entering the direct URL of `http://www.myspace.com/FitnessTrackerPlus`. In this particular case, the display name would be FitnessTrackerPlus. In order to display the correct log entries, you are going to need to provide a way for users of FitnessTrackerPlus to link their MySpace display name with their FitnessTrackerPlus account. This way, when the MySpace application is loaded, it should be able to make use of the MySpace API to get the current display name and perform a lookup against the FitnessTrackerPlus database to find out the correct FitnessTrackerPlus user to load entries for.

As an example, let's say there is a FitnessTrackerPlus user named Bill who has a MySpace account, and the URL to his MySpace account is `http://www.myspace.com/Bill`. The MySpace display name in this case would just be Bill. Now he decides to add the FitnessTrackerPlus application to his profile page, but the application at this point has no idea whose profile page it is sitting on. Using methods available in the MySpace API, the FitnessTrackerPlus MySpace application can find out that it is running on Bill's MySpace profile page and link it with his corresponding FitnessTrackerPlus account, providing the application with the ability to load and display his food, exercise, and measurement log entries.

That's about it. There really isn't much more that you need in this application at this point. In the future, you may decide to add a bit more functionality that makes use of things such as Friend lists and Status updates, but for right now these basic features are all you are looking for. With that said, let's get started designing the application itself.

User Interface

The user interface for the FitnessTrackerPlus MySpace application will be pretty simple. All it should consist of is a `StackPanel` control that hosts `DataGrid` controls for the food, exercise, and measurement log entries. Because you don't really have much control over the overall size of the application once it is hosted in a MySpace profile page, you should plan on wrapping all these controls in a `ScrollViewer` just in case the `DataGrid` controls flow off of the main screen.

Database

You will need to make a few modifications to the existing profiles table in the database in order to accommodate the new MySpace application. First, you must add a column that will be used to determine if the user wishes to share his or her information in the MySpace app. Then you need an additional column to hold the MySpace display name. Table 10-3 shows the updated profiles table.

TABLE 10-3: profiles

COLUMN NAME	TYPE	DESCRIPTION
id	int	Unique identity field for profile.
current_theme	varchar(100)	Preferred site theme.
about_text	varchar(max)	User description text to be displayed on public journal page.
share_journal	bit	Enable/Disable sharing of any information on public journal page. Also enable/disable the ability to reach the page with custom URL.
share_foods	bit	Enable/Disable sharing of food log entries.
share_exercises	bit	Enable/Disable sharing of exercise log entries.
share_measurements	bit	Enable/Disable sharing of measurement log entries.
share_images	bit	Enable/Disable sharing of measurement images.
enable_comments	bit	Enable/Disable posting and display of HTML comments.
enable_myspace_sharing	bit	Enable/Disable sharing of fitness log data on MySpace application.
myspace_name	varchar(100)	MySpace display name.
user_id	int	ID of associated user.

Data Access

In the data access layer you will make the necessary modifications to the `Profile` LINQ to SQL classes to reflect the changes made to the profiles table. Typically, the easiest way to achieve this is to simply delete the entity from the designer and then drag and drop a new copy back onto the screen. Building the project at that point will regenerate new versions of the `Profile` entity class.

Business Logic

Several changes are required for the business logic layer. Because the additional fields in the database are being added to the profiles table, you will need to modify the `ProfileProvider`, `AuthenticationService`, and `web.config` in order to make sure that these new properties are exposed through the existing ASP.NET Profile object. After completing those changes, you will need to add a new method to the existing `JournalService` that will return the correct user ID for the associated MySpace display name.

User Interface Code Behind

In the code behind, you must first retrieve the display name of the MySpace member whose profile page is hosting the FitnessTrackerPlus application. Then you need to retrieve the FitnessTrackerPlus

ID that has been linked to the MySpace account in order to then retrieve any food, exercise, or measurement log entries for the current day. Finally, you bind the `DataGrid` controls to any entries that have been loaded.

SOLUTION

The "Solution" section of this chapter guides you through the entire process of creating a MySpace application using the MySpace Silverlight SDK. This application mimics the public journal feature of FitnessTrackerPlus in that it displays food, exercise, and measurement log entries in `DataGrid` controls. This application will be shown on both the member's MySpace home page, as well as his or her profile page.

Getting Started

The first step to creating the FitnessTrackerPlus MySpace application is to get set up with a developer account over at MySpace. Of course, it goes without saying that you will also need a standard MySpace account as well.

Follow these steps:

1. After registering for a developer account, you're sent an e-mail containing a confirmation link that you click to activate your new account. Once all of that is complete, you can get to work. If you click the Build link from the main developer.myspace.com page, you are presented with two choices, as shown in Figure 10-3.

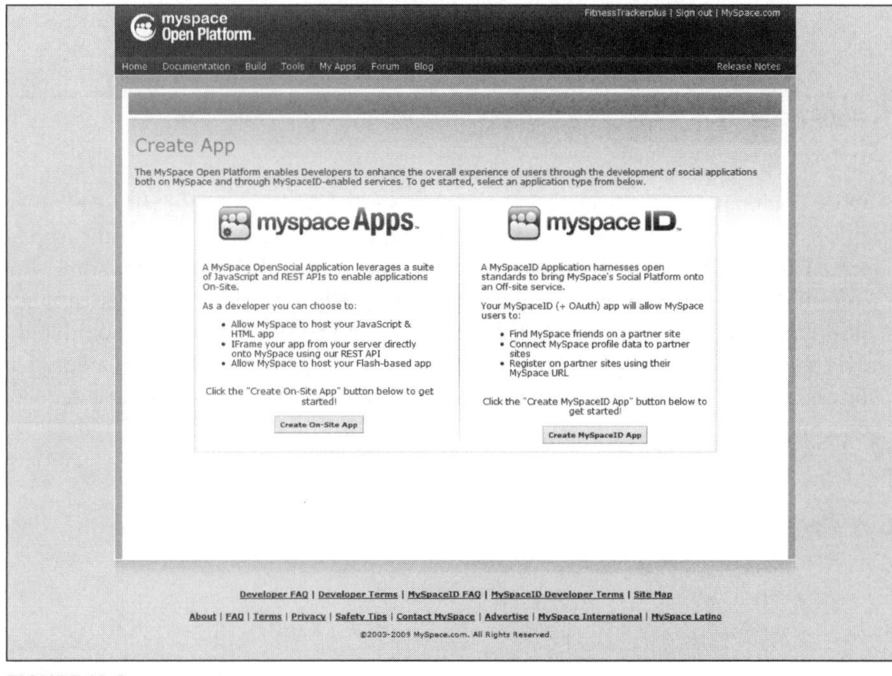

FIGURE 10-3

2. One option is to create a full-blown MySpace application and the other is to create a new application that will make use of the MySpace ID platform. For FitnessTrackerPlus, you choose the MySpace application option. After choosing the MySpace Apps option, you are presented with a Create App page. As shown in Figure 10-4, you must enter some basic information about the application, including a title for the application. You also must agree to the terms of service.

FIGURE 10-4

3. Once you complete this step, you will be presented with the application details page. For this page, you are only concerned with the Edit App information and Edit App Source tabs. Click the Edit App Information tab first, as you still need to enter some more detailed information about your new application. Figure 10-5 shows the complete application information page. At this point, the Common App Settings should be populated from the previous step, so you should start with the App Category and Default Gallery Language; for FitnessTrackerPlus the main language is English, and the best matching category I could find was Sports.

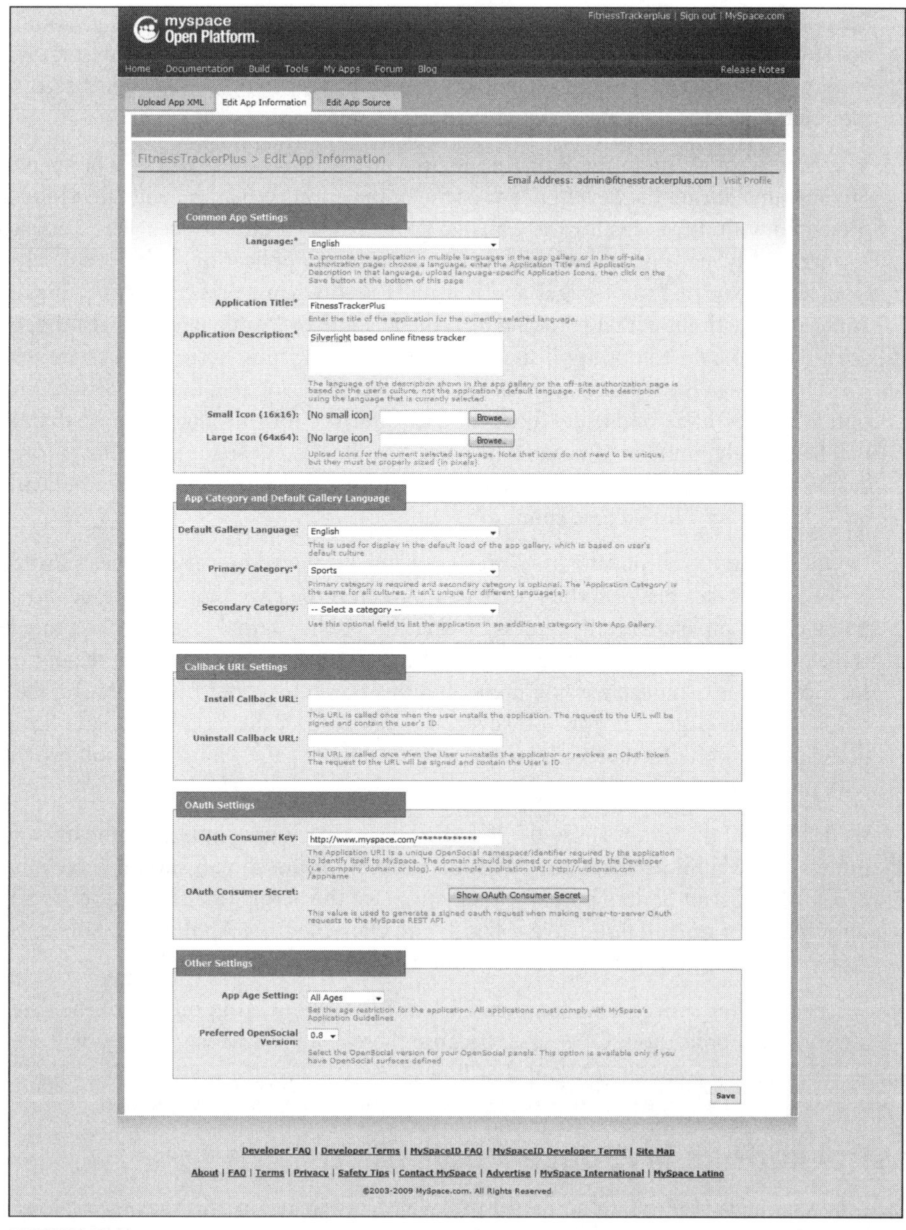

FIGURE 10-5

4. It is important to fill out this page completely, as members of MySpace will use things such as the category to find your application. Of course, there are thousands of applications out there, so you will also have to rely on word of mouth to get people to find yours. In Figure 10-5, there is a section called OAuth Settings and a field called OAuth Consumer Key. This key is used for any calls that your application will make to the OpenSocial platform.

This field is automatically populated when the page is loaded, so your key should already be set by the time you arrive at this page. You also will want to make sure that in the Other Settings section, the Preferred OpenSocial Version is set to 0.8. Silverlight-based solutions require the use of OpenSocial 0.8 at the time of this writing.

5. You need to move on to the Edit App Source tab. This is where you will be spending most of your time during the development of the application. When the page first loads, you are presented with three tabs for the Canvas, Profile, and Home surfaces. The Canvas page is a separate MySpace page that hosts just your custom application. It is completely separate from any Home or Profile pages and is usually used when members want to make use of the application without actually adding it to their Home or Profile pages. It also happens to be a great place to debug your application as it provides the most screen real estate when running. The Home page is the first page that members see after logging into MySpace. You have the option to present a completely different user interface for this page as more than likely you will be severely limited in how much space is available. MySpace now allows for much more customization of the Home page than before, so it's possible users of the application will have designated a little more room for you.

6. On the final tab, you put the user interface to be displayed on the member's Profile page. All of the action takes place on the Profile page, and it is the page that best mimics what you were trying to accomplish with the FitnessTrackerPlus public journal feature. It is a safe bet that this is the tab you will want to concentrate on the most. In fact, you also have the option to disable the Home page completely if you prefer and this prevents users from displaying the application on their Home page. For now, however, let's not restrict the usage of the application. Even though there won't be much screen space on the Home page, you should still provide members with the option.

7. By default, all three tabs show the HTML/JavaScript Source option as the default. For the FitnessTrackerPlus application, this is the correct option so you should leave it as is. The HTML/JavaScript Source box is where you place the actual declaration of the Silverlight object, but for now, if you leave it blank and click the Save Application Source button your custom application is officially built as far as MySpace is concerned.

8. After saving the source, you can then click the Dev App button on any of the three tabs to see a test of the application. Of course, because there is no source yet, all you will see is an empty screen. Let's do something about that now.

FitnessTrackerPlus MySpace Application

At this point you have everything you need to develop applications for MySpace. Now it's time to turn your focus to the FitnessTrackerPlus MySpace application that you will be developing. The requirements are pretty simple as you are just trying to develop an app that will display a user's food, exercise, and measurement log entries. Before getting into any MySpace-specific code, you will first need a working Silverlight application that retrieves these entries and displays them in `DataGrid` controls. To start the development of the FitnessTrackerPlus MySpace application, you will first need to add a new Silverlight application project to the current FitnessTrackerPlus solution. You can call this new Silverlight project FitnessTrackerPlus MySpace. Don't forget to enable WCF RIA Services support when you create the new project. Once the project is available, it's time to start creating the user interface.

User Interface

The user interface is pretty straightforward and you can borrow heavily from the work you did earlier on when creating the public journal page. Because screen real estate is a premium in MySpace applications and you won't have total control over how much space on a profile page the member gives your application, you need to leave the `GlobalCalendar` functionality out of this user interface. Instead, you just declare read-only `DataGrid` controls in a `StackPanel` that will hold all the food, exercise, and measurement log entries. Again, because you can't completely control the space you have on the profile page, your application must support scrolling so that viewers can see all the data; for that reason, the main container for this application must be a `ScrollViewer` control. Listing 10-1 shows the XAML required for the user interface.

LISTING 10-1: MainPage.xaml

Available for download on Wrox.com

```
<UserControl x:Class="FitnessTrackerPlusMySpace.MainPage"
     xmlns="http://schemas.microsoft.com/winfx/2006/xaml/presentation"
     xmlns:x="http://schemas.microsoft.com/winfx/2006/xaml"
     xmlns:data="clr-
namespace:System.Windows.Controls;assembly=System.Windows.Controls.Data">
     <UserControl.Resources>
          <Style x:Key="ReadOnlyDataGrid" TargetType="data:DataGrid">
               <Setter Property="AutoGenerateColumns" Value="False" />
               <Setter Property="IsReadOnly" Value="True" />
               <Setter Property="Margin" Value="0,10,0,0" />
               <Setter Property="HorizontalScrollBarVisibility"
Value="Auto" />
               <Setter Property="CanUserResizeColumns" Value="True" />
               <Setter Property="SelectionMode" Value="Single" />
               <Setter Property="Visibility" Value="Collapsed" />
               <Setter Property="ColumnWidth" Value="SizeToHeader" />
          </Style>
     </UserControl.Resources>
     <ScrollViewer>
          <StackPanel>
               <data:DataGrid x:Name="FoodLogGrid" Style="{StaticResource
ReadOnlyDataGrid}">
                    <data:DataGrid.Columns>
                         <data:DataGridTemplateColumn Header="Foods"
HeaderStyle="{StaticResource DataGridColumnHeaderCentered}">
                              <data:DataGridTemplateColumn.CellTemplate>
                                   <DataTemplate>
                                        <TextBlock Text="{Binding
Path=Food.name}" />
                                   </DataTemplate>
                              </data:DataGridTemplateColumn.CellTemplate>
                         </data:DataGridTemplateColumn>
                         <data:DataGridTemplateColumn Header="Servings"
```

continues

LISTING 10-1 *(continued)*

```
HeaderStyle="{StaticResource DataGridColumnHeaderCentered}">
                            <data:DataGridTemplateColumn.CellTemplate>
                                <DataTemplate>
                                    <TextBlock Text="{Binding
Path=servings}" Style="{StaticResource DataGridTextBlockCentered}" />
                                </DataTemplate>
                            </data:DataGridTemplateColumn.CellTemplate>
                        </data:DataGridTemplateColumn>
                        <data:DataGridTemplateColumn Header="Serving Size"
HeaderStyle="{StaticResource DataGridColumnHeaderCentered}">
                            <data:DataGridTemplateColumn.CellTemplate>
                                <DataTemplate>
                                    <TextBlock Text="{Binding
Path=Food.serving_size}" Style="{StaticResource DataGridTextBlock}" />
                                </DataTemplate>
                            </data:DataGridTemplateColumn.CellTemplate>
                        </data:DataGridTemplateColumn>
                    </data:DataGrid.Columns>
                </data:DataGrid>
                <data:DataGrid x:Name="CardioLogGrid" Style="{StaticResource
ReadOnlyDataGrid}">
                    <data:DataGrid.Columns>
                        <data:DataGridTemplateColumn Header="Cardio"
HeaderStyle="{StaticResource DataGridColumnHeaderCentered}">
                            <data:DataGridTemplateColumn.CellTemplate>
                                <DataTemplate>
                                    <TextBlock Text="{Binding
Path=Exercise.exercise_name}" Style="{StaticResource DataGridTextBlockCentered}" />
                                </DataTemplate>
                            </data:DataGridTemplateColumn.CellTemplate>
                        </data:DataGridTemplateColumn>
                            <data:DataGridTemplateColumn Header="Duration"
HeaderStyle="{StaticResource DataGridColumnHeaderCentered}">
                                <data:DataGridTemplateColumn.CellTemplate>
                                    <DataTemplate>
                                        <TextBlock Text="{Binding
Path=duration, SpringFormat='HH:mm:ss')"
Style="{StaticResource DataGridTextBlockCentered}" />
                                    </DataTemplate>
                                </data:DataGridTemplateColumn.CellTemplate>
                            </data:DataGridTemplateColumn>
                            <data:DataGridTemplateColumn Header="Distance"
HeaderStyle="{StaticResource DataGridColumnHeaderCentered}">
                                <data:DataGridTemplateColumn.CellTemplate>
                                    <DataTemplate>
                                        <TextBlock Text="{Binding
Path=distance}" Style="{StaticResource DataGridTextBlockCentered}" />
                                    </DataTemplate>
                                </data:DataGridTemplateColumn.CellTemplate>
                            </data:DataGridTemplateColumn>
```

```
                    </data:DataGrid.Columns>
                </data:DataGrid>
                <data:DataGrid x:Name="WeightTrainingLogGrid"
Style="{StaticResource ReadOnlyDataGrid}">
                    <data:DataGrid.Columns>
                        <data:DataGridTemplateColumn Header="Weight Training"
HeaderStyle="{StaticResource DataGridColumnHeaderCentered}">
                            <data:DataGridTemplateColumn.CellTemplate>
                                <DataTemplate>
                                    <TextBlock Text="{Binding
Path=Exercise.exercise_name}" Style="{StaticResource DataGridTextBlockCentered}" />
                                </DataTemplate>
                            </data:DataGridTemplateColumn.CellTemplate>
                        </data:DataGridTemplateColumn>
                        <data:DataGridTemplateColumn Header="Reps"
HeaderStyle="{StaticResource DataGridColumnHeaderCentered}">
                            <data:DataGridTemplateColumn.CellTemplate>
                                <DataTemplate>
                                    <TextBlock Text="{Binding Path=reps}"
Style="{StaticResource DataGridTextBlock}" />
                                </DataTemplate>
                            </data:DataGridTemplateColumn.CellTemplate>
                        </data:DataGridTemplateColumn>
                        <data:DataGridTemplateColumn Header="Weight"
HeaderStyle="{StaticResource DataGridColumnHeaderCentered}">
                            <data:DataGridTemplateColumn.CellTemplate>
                                <DataTemplate>
                                    <TextBlock Text="{Binding
Path=weight}" Style="{StaticResource DataGridTextBlockCentered}" />
                                </DataTemplate>
                            </data:DataGridTemplateColumn.CellTemplate>
                        </data:DataGridTemplateColumn>
                    </data:DataGrid.Columns>
                </data:DataGrid>
                <data:DataGrid x:Name="ActivityLogGrid" Style="{StaticResource
ReadOnlyDataGrid}">
                    <data:DataGrid.Columns>
                        <data:DataGridTemplateColumn Header="Activities"
HeaderStyle="{StaticResource DataGridColumnHeaderCentered}">
                            <data:DataGridTemplateColumn.CellTemplate>
                                <DataTemplate>
                                    <TextBlock Text="{Binding
Path=Exercise.exercise_name}" Style="{StaticResource DataGridTextBlockCentered}" />
                                </DataTemplate>
                            </data:DataGridTemplateColumn.CellTemplate>
                        </data:DataGridTemplateColumn>
                        <data:DataGridTemplateColumn Header="Duration"
HeaderStyle="{StaticResource DataGridColumnHeaderCentered}">
                            <data:DataGridTemplateColumn.CellTemplate>
                                <DataTemplate>
                                    <TextBlock Text="{Binding
Path=duration, StringFormat='HH:mm:ss')"
Style="{StaticResource DataGridTextBlockCentered}" />
                                </DataTemplate>
```

continues

LISTING 10-1 *(continued)*

```
                                        </data:DataGridTemplateColumn.CellTemplate>
                                    </data:DataGridTemplateColumn>
                                </data:DataGrid.Columns>
                            </data:DataGrid>
                            <data:DataGrid x:Name="MeasurementLogGrid"
Style="{StaticResource ReadOnlyDataGrid}">
                                <data:DataGrid.Columns>
                                    <data:DataGridTemplateColumn Header="Measurements"
HeaderStyle="{StaticResource DataGridColumnHeaderCentered}">
                                        <data:DataGridTemplateColumn.CellTemplate>
                                            <DataTemplate>
                                                <TextBlock Text="{Binding
Path=Measurement.measurement_name}" Style="{StaticResource
DataGridTextBlockCentered}" />
                                            </DataTemplate>
                                        </data:DataGridTemplateColumn.CellTemplate>
                                    </data:DataGridTemplateColumn>
                                    <data:DataGridTemplateColumn Header="Value"
HeaderStyle="{StaticResource DataGridColumnHeaderCentered}">
                                        <data:DataGridTemplateColumn.CellTemplate>
                                            <DataTemplate>
                                                <TextBlock Text="{Binding Path=value}"
Style="{StaticResource DataGridTextBlockCentered}" />
                                            </DataTemplate>
                                        </data:DataGridTemplateColumn.CellTemplate>
                                    </data:DataGridTemplateColumn>
                                    <data:DataGridTemplateColumn Header="Unit"
HeaderStyle="{StaticResource DataGridColumnHeaderCentered}">
                                        <data:DataGridTemplateColumn.CellTemplate>
                                            <DataTemplate>
                                                <TextBlock Text="{Binding
Path=MeasurementUnit.unit}" Style="{StaticResource
DataGridTextBlock}" />
                                            </DataTemplate>
                                        </data:DataGridTemplateColumn.CellTemplate>
                                    </data:DataGridTemplateColumn>
                                </data:DataGrid.Columns>
                            </data:DataGrid>
                            <TextBlock x:Name="DataNotShared" Text="Data is not being
shared for this member" />
                        </StackPanel>
                    </ScrollViewer>
</UserControl>
```

After creating the user interface for the MySpace application, you then need to make some modifications to the existing public journal settings page. Don't forget that you need to link the MySpace display name with an existing account here at FitnessTrackerPlus in order to populate the `DataGrid` controls with the correct entries. The easiest way to achieve this is to add a field on the journal settings page that lets the users enter their MySpace display name in order to link the two accounts. It is also entirely possible that users won't want any data to be shared on their MySpace account. To account for that possibility, you should add another `CheckBox` control to enable/disable this feature entirely. The MySpace application needs to perform a check first to see if the member has enabled sharing to MySpace. If not, it must display the "Data not being shared" statement. The following code shows the additional section required to support the MySpace sharing settings on the public journal settings page.

Available for download on Wrox.com

```
<CheckBox x:Name="EnableMySpace" Content="Enable MySpace Sharing:"
IsChecked="{Binding Path=EnableComments}" Style="{StaticResource
JournalCheckBoxStyle}" />
<StackPanel Style="{StaticResource AboutTextStackPanelStyle}">
     <TextBlock Text="MySpace Display Name:" Style="{StaticResource
JournalSettingsTextStyle}" />
     <TextBox x:Name="MySpaceName" Text="{Binding Path=MySpaceName}"
Style="{StaticResource MySpaceTextBoxStyle}" />
</StackPanel>
```

Code snippet JournalSettings.xaml

Database

As discussed earlier, you must add two additional columns to the existing profiles table in order to support both the enabling/disabling of the MySpace sharing feature, as well as the MySpace display name that links the two accounts. Once again, you should make use of SQL Server Management Studio to edit the table and add the required columns. Once this is completed, you should be left with the updated profiles table, as shown in the database diagram depicted in Figure 10-6.

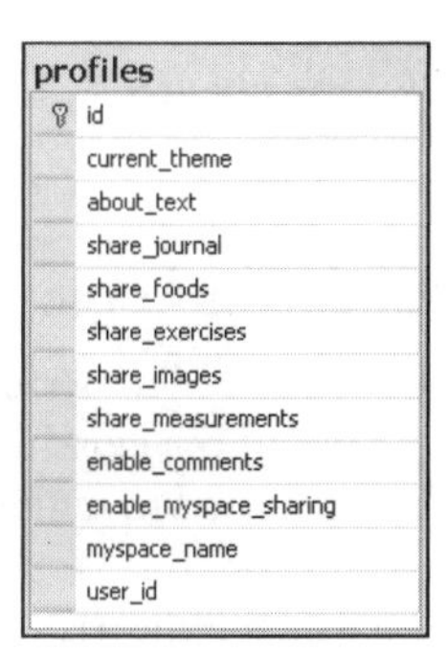

FIGURE 10-6

Data Access

The only work required in the data access layer is to update the `Profile` entity class to reflect the new columns that have been added to the profiles table. The easiest way to do this is to just open up the Users.dbml file and delete the `Profile` entity definition; then drag and drop the profiles table back on to the designer and rebuild. Now the `Profile` entity will update to include the additional properties. Figure 10-7 shows the updated Users.dbml file reflecting the changes.

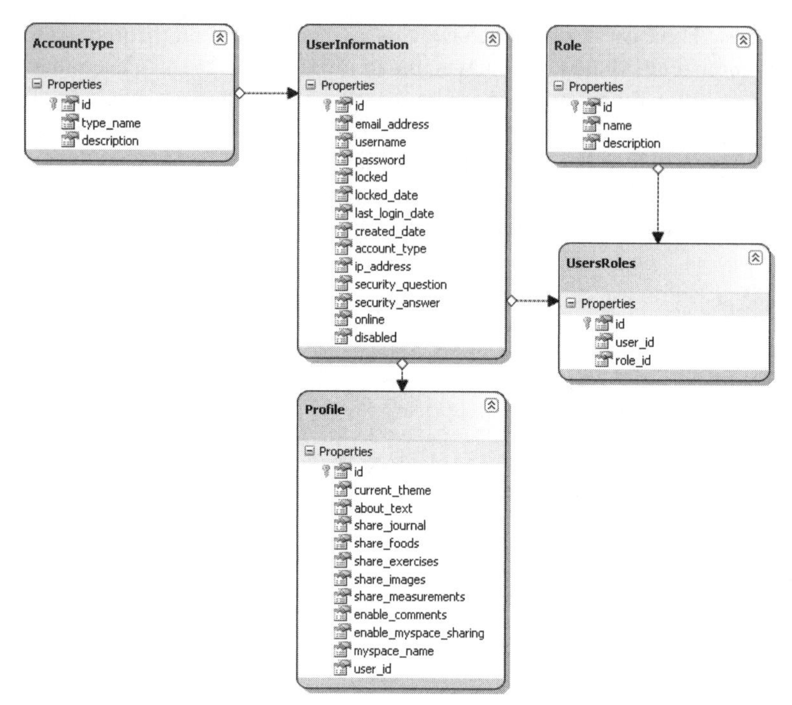

FIGURE 10-7

Business Logic

You need to perform several tasks when you implement the business logic. Although you can make use of the existing `Food`, `Exercise`, and `Measurement` services in order to retrieve log entries, you still need to make some modifications to the `Profile`, `Authentication`, and `Journal` service to retrieve the MySpace application settings and, of course, link the MySpace display name with the user's FitnessTrackerPlus account. The first changes required are to the custom `ProfileProvider` class and these start with the web.config file. Before making any modifications to the provider class, you first need to let ASP.NET know about the additional fields that have been added to the `profiles` table. The following code shows the modified `profile` section of the web.config file that adds support for these new fields.

```
<profile enabled="true" automaticSaveEnabled="false"
defaultProvider="FitnessTrackerPlusProfileProvider">
     <providers>
     <clear/>
          <add name="FitnessTrackerPlusProfileProvider"
type="FitnessTrackerPlus.Web.Providers.ProfileProvider"/>
     </providers>
     <properties>
          <add name="CurrentTheme" type="String"
customProviderData="current_theme;varchar;100"/>
          <add name="AboutText" type="String"
customProviderData="about_text;varchar;max"/>
```

```
            <add name="ShareJournal" type="Bool"
customProviderData="share_journal;bit"/>
            <add name="ShareFoods" type="Bool"
customProviderData="share_foods;bit"/>
            <add name="ShareExercises" type="Bool"
customProviderData="share_exercises;bit"/>
            <add name="ShareMeasurements" type="Bool"
customProviderData="share_measurements;bit"/>
            <add name="ShareImages" type="Bool"
customProviderData="share_images;bit"/>
            <add name="EnableComments" type="Bool"
customProviderData="enable_comments;bit"/>
            <add name="EnableMySpace" type="Bool"
customProviderData="enable_myspace_sharing;bit"/>
            <add name="MySpaceName" type="String"
customProviderData="myspace_name;varchar;100"/>
      </properties>
</profile>
```

Code snippet web.config

After updating the web.config file, you must modify the `GetPropertyValues` and the `SetPropertyValues` methods of the custom `ProfileProvider` class that you worked on earlier. The following code shows the updated `ProfileProvider` methods that should be added to the ProfileProvider.cs file.

Available for download on Wrox.com

```
public override SettingsPropertyValueCollection
GetPropertyValues(SettingsContext context,
SettingsPropertyCollection collection)
{
      SettingsPropertyValueCollection valueCollection = new
SettingsPropertyValueCollection();

      try
      {
            Profile profile = GetProfile(context["UserName"] as string);

            // If a profile was found then loop through all profile properties and
            // assign appropriate values

            if (profile != null)
            {
                  foreach (SettingsProperty property in collection)
                  {
                        SettingsPropertyValue propertyValue = new
SettingsPropertyValue(property);

                        switch (property.Name)
                        {
                              case "CurrentTheme":
                              {
                                    propertyValue.PropertyValue = profile.current_theme;
                                    break;
                              }
```

```
                    case "AboutText":
                    {
                        propertyValue.PropertyValue = profile.about_text;
                        break;
                    }
                    case "ShareJournal":
                    {
                        propertyValue.PropertyValue = profile.share_journal;
                        break;
                    }
                    case "ShareFoods":
                    {
                        propertyValue.PropertyValue = profile.share_foods;
                        break;
                    }
                    case "ShareExercises":
                    {
                        propertyValue.PropertyValue =
profile.share_exercises;
                        break;
                    }
                    case "ShareMeasurements":
                    {
                        propertyValue.PropertyValue =
profile.share_measurements;
                        break;
                    }
                    case "ShareImages":
                    {
                        propertyValue.PropertyValue = profile.share_images;
                        break;
                    }
                    case "EnableComments":
                    {
                        propertyValue.PropertyValue =
profile.enable_comments;
                        break;
                    }
                    case "EnableMySpace":
                    {
                        propertyValue.PropertyValue =
profile.enable_myspace_sharing;
                        break;
                    }
                    case "MySpaceName":
                    {
                        propertyValue.PropertyValue = profile.myspace_name;
                        break;
                    }
                }

                valueCollection.Add(propertyValue);
            }
        }
```

```
        }
        catch (Exception)
        {
        }

        return valueCollection;
    }

    public override void SetPropertyValues(SettingsContext context,
    SettingsPropertyValueCollection collection)
    {
        SettingsPropertyValueCollection valueCollection = new
    SettingsPropertyValueCollection();

        // Extract the username to retrieve property values for

        string userName = context["UserName"] as string;

        // Get the profile for current user

        FitnessTrackerPlus.Web.Data.Profile dataProfile = (from p in
    dataContext.Profiles where p.user_id == (from u in
    dataContext.UserInformations where u.email_address == userName
    select u.id).SingleOrDefault<int>() select p).SingleOrDefault();

        // If a profile was found then loop through all profile properties and
        // assign appropriate values

        if (dataProfile != null)
        {
            foreach (SettingsPropertyValue propertyValue in collection)
            {
                switch (propertyValue.Name)
                {
                    case "CurrentTheme":
                    {
                        dataProfile.current_theme =
    propertyValue.PropertyValue.ToString();
                        break;
                    }
                    case "AboutText":
                    {
                        dataProfile.about_text =
    PropertyValue.PropertyValue.ToString();
                        break;
                    }
                    case "ShareJournal":
                    {
                        dataProfile.share_journal =
    Convert.ToBoolean(propertyValue.PropertyValue);
                        break;
                    }
                    case "ShareFoods":
                    {
```

```
                            dataProfile.share_foods =
Convert.ToBoolean(propertyValue.PropertyValue);
                            break;
                        }
                        case "ShareExercises":
                        {
                            dataProfile.share_exercises =
Convert.ToBoolean(propertyValue.PropertyValue);
                            break;
                        }
                        case "ShareMeasurements":
                        {
                            dataProfile.share_measurements =
Convert.ToBoolean(propertyValue.PropertyValue);
                            break;
                        }
                        case "ShareImages":
                        {
                            dataProfile.share_images =
Convert.ToBoolean(propertyValue.PropertyValue);
                            break;
                        }
                        case "EnableComments":
                        {
                            dataProfile.enable_comments =
Convert.ToBoolean(propertyValue.PropertyValue);
                            break;
                        }
                        case "EnableMySpace":
                        {
                            dataProfile.enable_myspace_sharing =
Convert.ToBoolean(propertyValue.PropertyValue);
                            break;
                        }
                        case "MySpaceName":
                        {
                            dataProfile.myspace_name =
propertyValue.PropertyValue.ToString();
                            break;
                        }
                    }
                }

                dataContext.SubmitChanges();
            }
        }
```

Code snippet ProfileProvider.cs

In addition to the previous step, you must also ensure that these additional properties are exposed to the client through WCF RIA Services. You need to add them as public properties to the `User` class in the `AuthenticationService`. The following code shows the updated `User` class.

Available for download on Wrox.com

```
public class User: UserBase
{
     // Profile properties that should be exposed as part of the User object

     public string CurrentTheme { get; set; }
     public string AboutText { get; set; }
     public string MySpaceName { get; set; }
     public bool ShareJournal { get; set; }
     public bool ShareFoods { get; set; }
     public bool ShareExercises { get; set; }
     public bool ShareMeasurements { get; set; }
     public bool ShareImages { get; set; }
     public bool EnableComments { get; set; }
     public bool EnableMySpace { get; set; }
}
```

Code snippet AuthenticationService.cs

Once you have completed all this, you still have to work out the business logic that will link the MySpace display name with the correct FitnessTrackerPlus user. Now, there are a couple of things to consider here. The client application will need to have a method where it can pass the MySpace display name and be returned a corresponding user ID that can then be used to retrieve the correct food, exercise, and measurement logs. This method should also return a valid ID only if the user has agreed to share FitnessTrackerPlus data on his or her MySpace profile page. The most logical place for such a method at this point is the `JournalService` as it already contains the necessary logic to retrieve a user's profile settings with just a username. Let's add a new method to this service that takes the MySpace display name and returns the corresponding user ID if sharing has been enabled. The following code shows the new `GetUserID` method, which has been added to the `JournalService`.

Available for download on Wrox.com

```
public int GetUserID(string display_name)
{
     UsersDataContext context = new UsersDataContext();
     Profile profile = context.Profiles.Where(e => e.myspace_name ==
                                                display_name).SingleOrDefault();

     if (profile != null)
     {
          if (profile.enable_myspace_sharing)
               return profile.user_id;
     }

     return -1;
}
```

Code snippet JournalService.cs

Now the user interface has a method that can retrieve the correct `user_id` and load the associated food, exercise, and measurement log data.

User Interface Code Behind

The fun really begins in the code behind for the MySpace application. First, however, you need to take care of one preliminary: making a slight modification to the code behind for the public journal settings page. Remember that you added a few fields to the user interface; you want to ensure that you update both the code to load the additional fields as well as the code to save any changes to those settings. Loading the additional fields is already handled through the use of data binding, so there is nothing to add there. Saving the fields, however, requires a couple of additional lines of code. The following code shows the updates required to the `SaveChanges_Click` method, which is responsible for ensuring that changes made to the MySpace display name and the enable/disable sharing of data to MySpace option are persisted to the database.

Available for download on Wrox.com

```
private void SaveChanges_Click(object sender, RoutedEventArgs e)
{
     WebContext.Current.User.AboutText = AboutText.Text;
     WebContext.Current.User.ShareJournal = ShareJournal.IsChecked.Value;
     WebContext.Current.User.ShareFoods = ShareFoods.IsChecked.Value;
     WebContext.Current.User.ShareExercises = ShareExercises.IsChecked.Value;
     WebContext.Current.User.ShareMeasurements = ShareMeasurements.IsChecked.Value;
     WebContext.Current.User.ShareImages = ShareImages.IsChecked.Value;
     WebContext.Current.User.EnableComments = EnableComments.IsChecked.Value;
     WebContext.Current.User.EnableMySpace = EnableMySpace.IsChecked.Value;
     WebContext.Current.User.MySpaceName = MySpaceName.Text;

     WebContext.Current.Authentication.SaveUser((SettingsSaved) =>
     {
          if (!SettingsSaved.HasError)
               MessageBox.Show("Your public journal settings have
been successfully updated");

     }, null);
}
```

Code snippet JournalSettings.xaml.cs

After taking care of the public journal settings page, it's time to move on to the MySpace application code behind page itself. The first step is to grab the MySpace display name of the MySpace profile page that is currently hosting the application. To do this, you make use of the MySpace Silverlight SDK. The SDK wraps most of the required OpenSocial JavaScript functionality into a handful of controls that can be declared in XAML and utilized in the code behind.

As you saw earlier in the "Design" section, there are controls that will assist you in retrieving Friend information as well as information about a single member. When using this SDK, it is important to understand that most of the MySpace OpenSocial calls will refer to either a viewer or an owner. When you supply one of the SDK controls with the `Viewer` parameter, the code loads information that is associated with the MySpace member that is actually viewing the application. When you make use of the `Owner` parameter, you are requesting information that is only associated with the owner of the profile page. This is an important distinction because in this application you are always interested in the owner's display name. You can't be sure about who is visiting the MySpace profile page and you really shouldn't care. The only piece of information that is important here is the display name of the member whose profile page is hosting the FitnessTrackerPlus application. Once you retrieve this, you can do a quick look up in the FitnessTrackerPlus database to figure out which FitnessTrackerPlus user's log data should be retrieved and displayed.

The control you need to add to retrieve the display name is the `MySpacePersonRequest`. In order to make use of this or any of the controls, you first need to add a reference to the MySpaceSilverlightKit .dll. After doing this, you update the namespace declaration in the XAML and add the control to the `UserControl.Resources` section. The following code shows the control declaration along with the required attribute values.

Available for download on Wrox.com

```
xmlns:myspace="clr-namespace:MyOpenSpace;assembly=MySpaceSilverlightKit"

<UserControl.Resources>
        <myspace:MySpacePersonRequest x:Key="PersonRequest"
IdSpec="opensocial.IdSpec.PersonId.OWNER" />
```

Code snippet MainPage.xaml

In the previous code, the `IdSpec` determines which individual's MySpace data to retrieve. Valid values for this are taken directly from the OpenSocial specification and include `opensocial.IdSpec.PersonId.OWNER` and `opensocial.IdSpec.PersonId.VIEWER`. As I said earlier, if you wanted to retrieve MySpace data for the member that is viewing the application, you would use the `opensocial.IdSpec.PersonId.VIEWER` value, but in this case you are only interested in the display name for the owner of the profile page.

When you use the `IdSpec` value of `OWNER`, the `MySpacePersonRequest` will load all the available information for the owner of the profile page using AJAX-based calls behind the scenes. A `Person` property is available from the control and it implements `INotifyPropertyChanged` so that you can easily listen for this event in the code behind to determine when the data has been completely loaded. Now, you must also note that MySpace users always have the option to prevent third-party applications from accessing their data, including the display name, which of course would render the FitnessTrackerPlus application useless. If, for some reason, the user has blocked access to his profile information, the `Person` property will be null and you won't be able to go any further. This is another reason that the "Data is not being shared . . ." message should be the default control that is visible. This way, if the owner has prevented access to their data on MySpace and the `PropertyChanged` event is never fired, you will at least display a message to the visitor that makes sense.

Assuming that the owner has set up MySpace sharing correctly, you should be able to access the `DisplayName` property and call the `GetUserID` method of the `JournalService`. Don't forget that if the user has disabled access to his or her information from the public journal settings page, this call returns a –1, and the "Data is not being shared . . ." message should once again be made visible. The following code shows the `Loaded` event handler where the `PropertyChanged` event of the `MySpacePersonRequest` object is hooked up with its own event handler.

If the Person data is successfully loaded by the MySpace Silverlight SDK, then the `Request_PropertyChanged` event is fired and the `DisplayName` property should then be available. Once you have this, you can successfully populate the `DataGrid` controls with the data loaded from the

GetMySpaceData method. Listing 10-2 shows the complete code behind for the FitnessTrackerPlus MySpace application.

LISTING 10-2: MainPage.xaml.cs

Available for download on Wrox.com

```
using System;
using System.Linq;
using System.Windows;
using System.Windows.Controls;
using System.ComponentModel;
using MyOpenSpace;
using FitnessTrackerPlus.Web.Data;
using FitnessTrackerPlus.Web.Services;
using System.Windows.Ria;

namespace FitnessTrackerPlusMySpace
{
     public partial class MainPage : UserControl
     {
          private MySpacePersonRequest request = null;

          public MainPage()
          {
               InitializeComponent();

               Loaded += (s, e) =>
               {
                    request = this.Resources["PersonRequest"] as
MySpacePersonRequest;
                    request.PropertyChanged += new
PropertyChangedEventHandler(Request_PropertyChanged);
               };
          }

          private void Request_PropertyChanged(object sender,
PropertyChangedEventArgs e)
          {
               string displayName = request.Person.DisplayName;

               JournalContext context = new JournalContext();
               FoodContext foods = new FoodContext();
               ExerciseContext exercises = new ExerciseContext();
               MeasurementContext measurements = new MeasurementContext();

               FoodLogGrid.Visibility = Visibility.Collapsed;
               CardioLogGrid.Visibility = Visibility.Collapsed;
               WeightTrainingLogGrid.Visibility = Visibility.Collapsed;
               ActivityLogGrid.Visibility = Visibility.Collapsed;
               MeasurementLogGrid.Visibility = Visibility.Collapsed;

               DataNotShared.Visibility = Visibility.Visible;

               context.GetUserID(displayName, (Callback) =>
               {
```

```
                    if (!Callback.HasError)
                    {
                        if (Callback.Value > 0)
                        {
                            DataNotShared.Visibility = Visibility.Collapsed;

                            // Retrieve food log entries

                            foods.Load<FoodLogEntry>(foods.
GetFoodLogEntriesQuery(Callback.Value, DateTime.Now, false),
LoadBehavior.RefreshCurrent, (Loaded) =>
                            {
                                if (!Loaded.HasError)
                                {
                                    FoodLogGrid.ItemsSource = Loaded.Entities;
                                    FoodLogGrid.Visibility =
Visibility.Visible;
                                }

                            }, null);

                            // Retrieve exercise log entries

                            exercises.Load<ExerciseLogEntry>(exercises.
GetExerciseLogEntriesQuery(DateTime.Now, Callback.Value),
LoadBehavior.RefreshCurrent, (Loaded) =>
                            {
                                if (!Loaded.HasError)
                                {
                                    CardioLogGrid.ItemsSource =
Loaded.Entities.Where(ev => ev.Exercise.exercise_type == 1);
                                    WeightTrainingLogGrid.ItemsSource =
Loaded.Entities.Where(ev => ev.Exercise.exercise_type == 2);
                                    ActivityLogGrid.ItemsSource =
Loaded.Entities.Where(ev => ev.Exercise.exercise_type == 3);

                                    CardioLogGrid.Visibility =
Visibility.Visible;
                                    WeightTrainingLogGrid.Visibility =
Visibility.Visible;
                                    ActivityLogGrid.Visibility =
Visibility.Visible;
                                }

                            }, null);

                            // Retrieve measurement log entries

measurements.Load<MeasurementLogEntry>(measurements.
GetMeasurementLogEntriesQuery(Callback.Value,
DateTime.Now), (Loaded) =>
                            {
                                if (!Loaded.HasError)
                                {
```

continues

LISTING 10-2 *(continued)*

```
                                                MeasurementLogGrid.ItemsSource =
Loaded.Entities;
                                                MeasurementLogGrid.Visibility =
Visibility.Visible;
                                         }

                                   }, null);
                             }
                       }
                       else
                       {
                             DataNotShared.Visibility = Visibility.Visible;
                             DataNotShared.Text =
String.Format("An error has occurred: {0}", Callback.Error);
                       }

                 }, null);
           }
      }
}
```

Deploying the FitnessTrackerPlus MySpace Application

Once you have completed all the coding tasks, it's time to look at deploying the new application to MySpace and making it available to others. The first thing you do is enable the Silverlight application for cross-domain callers. This allows OpenSocial to communicate correctly with the HTML DOM Bridge wrappers that are part of the MySpace Silverlight SDK library. This requires that you add the `ExternalCallersFromCrossDomain` tag to the current AppManifest.xml file. Listing 10-3 shows the updated file. This is a very important step; without this line your application will not run correctly once it is deployed to MySpace.

Available for download on Wrox.com

LISTING 10-3: AppManifest.xml

```
<Deployment xmlns="http://schemas.microsoft.com/client/2007/deployment"
      xmlns:x="http://schemas.microsoft.com/winfx/2006/xaml"
ExternalCallersFromCrossDomain="ScriptableOnly">
      <Deployment.Parts>
      </Deployment.Parts>
</Deployment>
```

After completing this last step you should rebuild your FitnessTrackerPlusMySpace project, log in to the MySpace developer site, and click the My Apps link in order to configure your new application. Remember earlier that you took the initial steps to create the application and you set up a default canvas and profile page that was empty. For the FitnessTrackerPlus MySpace application, you want to provide a user interface for the main application canvas page as well as the profile page. For this release and because there is not typically much room on the HOME page, you leave the HOME page user interface disabled. Starting with the canvas Surface tab, you simply need to add the Silverlight object tag with the full path to the FitnessTrackerPlusMySpace.xap file as the `Source` property. Now that MySpace has full support for Silverlight-based solutions, you no longer need to resort to `IFrame` tricks to display the plug-in. Instead, you can just place the Silverlight declaration right in the HTML/JavaScript Source area. The following code should be copied to both the Canvas Surface and Profile Surface tabs under the Edit App Source link.

```
<object data="data:application/x-silverlight-2," type="application/x-silverlight-2"
width="100%" height="100%">
     <param name="source"
value="http://www.fitnesstrackerplus.com/ClientBin/FitnessTrackerPlusMySpace.xap"/>
     <param name="minRuntimeVersion" value="4.0.41108.0" />
     <param name="autoUpgrade" value="true" />
     <param name="windowless" value="true" />
     <param name="enablehtmlaccess" value="true" />
     <param name="allowhtmlpopupwindow" value="true"/>
</object>
<iframe id="_sl_historyFrame"
style="visibility:hidden;height:0px;width:0px;border:0px"></iframe>
```

As you can see, there isn't really anything different from any other Silverlight declaration. Don't forget to add the same code to the Profile Surface tab as well. Once this is complete, there are a couple of final steps you need to follow in order for the application to work:

1. Add the application to your account. If you go back to the My Apps link, you will see an entry for the FitnessTrackerPlus application. Click the link for the application and you are presented with the option to add the application to your account, as shown in Figure 10-8. Once you complete this step, you are presented with another dialog.

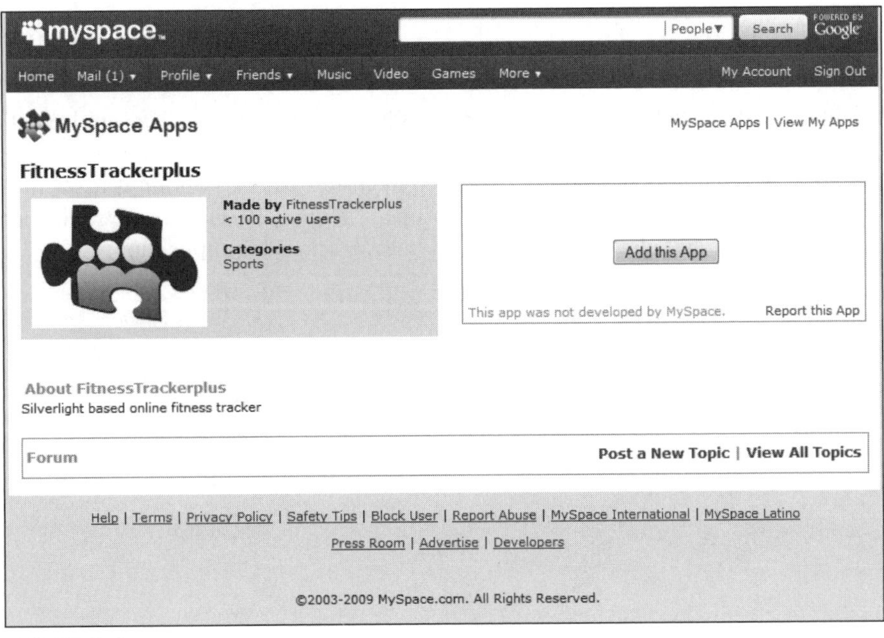

FIGURE 10-8

2. Set some basic settings such as where to place the application. Because you don't have home page support enabled, you can leave that option alone and instead make sure the "Add this app to my profile" option is checked, as it is in Figure 10-9. You are taken to the canvas page for the application.

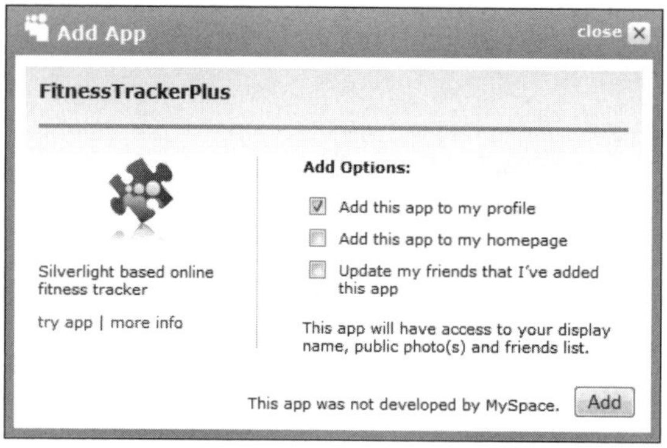

FIGURE 10-9

3. Instead of seeing a working application, you are presented with a blank canvas. The reason for this is that the FitnessTrackerPlus application still does not have permission to read the display name field. Go back to the home page and click the manage apps link shown in Figure 10-10. This link brings up another screen where you can load the permission settings for the various applications installed.

FIGURE 10-10

4. Find the Settings link for the FitnessTrackerPlus application and click it to load the permissions dialog. As you can see in Figure 10-11, by default the application does not have access to your personal info and details. You need to ensure that this option is checked so that the application can access the display name property. Figure 10-11 also shows the permission options that should ideally be set for the FitnessTrackerPlus application.

FIGURE 10-11

Once you save these new settings and return to the canvas area of the app, you should see that the food, exercise, and measurement logs are now being loaded. Figure 10-12 shows the application fully enabled and working in the canvas area.

FIGURE 10-12

The application should also now show up on the profile page as well. Figure 10-13 shows the updated profile page with the FitnessTrackerPlus application running.

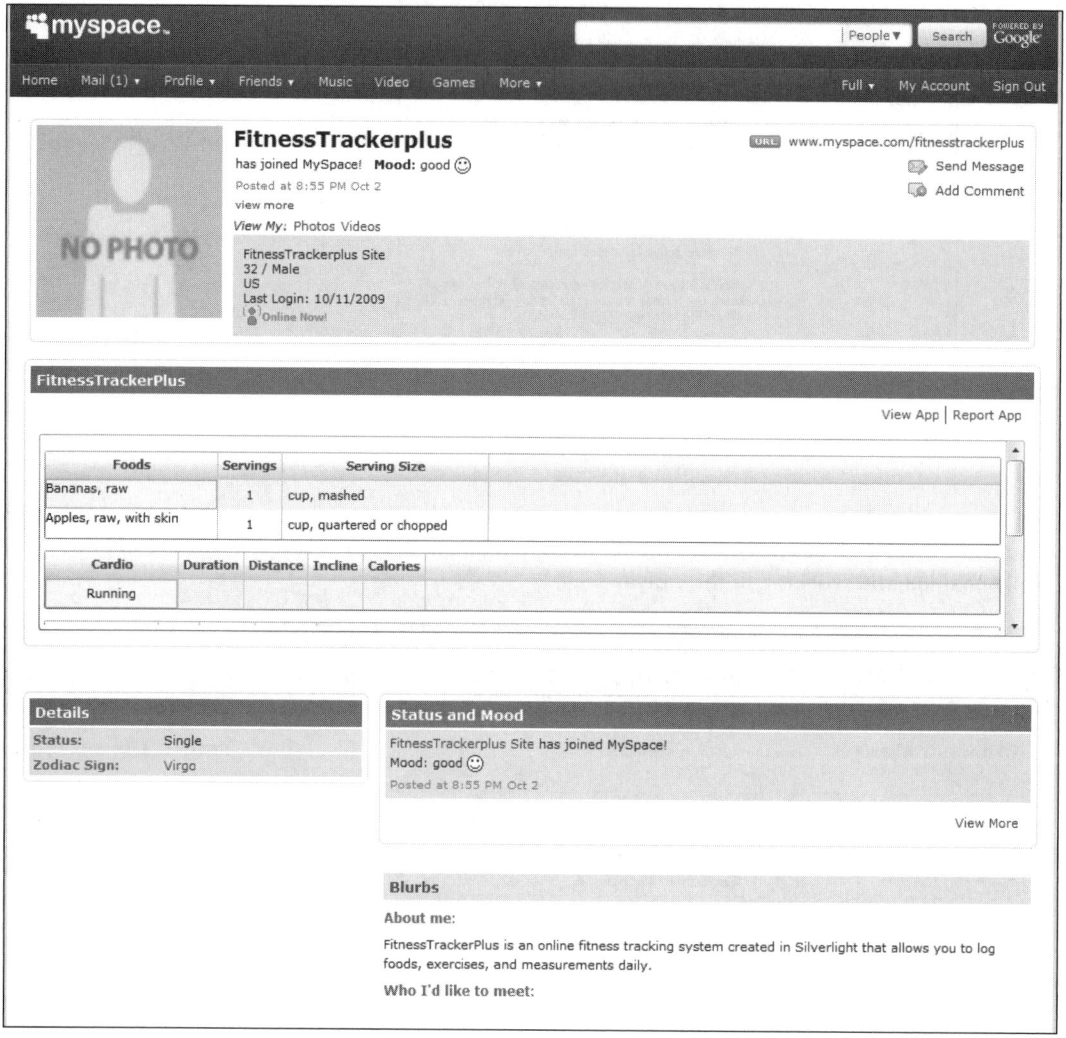

FIGURE 10-13

At this point, you have a working MySpace application. Obviously, there is room for improvement, but at least now FitnessTrackerPlus users have the option of sharing their information on the public journal page, their MySpace profile page, or even both. The official support for Silverlight applications on MySpace along with the MySpace Silverlight SDK really makes it easy for you to add a social networking component into your own Silverlight application.

SUMMARY

Even though this chapter showed you a step-by-step process for creating a Silverlight-based MySpace application, I can't stress enough that this doesn't even begin to scratch the surface of what is available through the combination of the MySpace Silverlight SDK and the OpenSocial API. You will, no doubt, be able to come up with even more compelling features for both the FitnessTrackerPlus MySpace application as well as your own Silverlight applications that can be used in conjunction with MySpace. It is my expectation that, over time, the MySpace Silverlight SDK will make its way out of beta and continue to add great new features.

At this point in the book, the FitnessTrackerPlus application can be considered complete. You have provided users with the ability to keep track of foods, exercises, and measurements. You have also added additional features such as the public journal and MySpace application. Before you package everything up and release it to the world, it's time to see if you can figure out a way to make some money with this application. After all, hosting costs are not free, so even if you can find a way to break even, you will be further ahead of the game than most startups.

11

This Site Doesn't Run Itself

GENERATING REVENUE FOR FITNESSTRACKERPLUS

No doubt, some users will find the features included with FitnessTrackerPlus useful and engaging. At this point in the project, you've put an awful lot of hard work into developing the site and so far you have been paid nothing. Of course, as the site grows in popularity it would be nice if you had some money left over to purchase that new LED TV you have been eyeballing at the local Best Buy store. This chapter takes a look at some possible ways you can potentially generate revenue — from both advertisements and monthly user subscriptions — to help offset the hosting costs of the site.

PROBLEM

You have just spent a considerable amount of time working on FitnessTrackerPlus and getting it ready for its official public release. As much as you love coding, you can't help but realize that after you release the site you'll still have costs and future time investments to keep the site running. You may not love coding enough to keep doing it for free. As the owner and lead developer of the site, you don't really have anyone that you can just invoice for the cost of your development time. Also, as the site grows in popularity, the costs of running and enhancing the site are only going to increase. In fact, to continue enhancing the site with compelling features, you may even find it necessary to bring on additional help. Rest assured, it's tough to find another developer who can jump at the opportunity to work for free. That's not to say you couldn't jump into the world of open source software and receive plenty of help, but your original goal was to eventually generate some revenue from the site and potentially grow it into a business.

In order for any of this to happen, however, you must come up with a way to generate revenue from the site. After initial research you'll conclude that there are really only a couple of viable revenue models for websites and they include advertisements and recurring paid subscriptions. Your first priority is to consider the pros and cons of both these models and decide which of these to use. Because there are many benefits to both these models, you may even want to consider ways of incorporating both schemes to maximize your profits. Either way, it's an important decision that will no doubt affect the user base of FitnessTrackerPlus no matter which of the two options you choose.

DESIGN

In the "Design" and the following "Solution" sections, you will see how to incorporate pay-per-click ads directly into the FitnessTrackerPlus Silverlight application. You'll also see how to alternatively charge a recurring monthly fee in order for users to join and continue making use of the site's features. After this is complete, you will then design and implement an alternative solution that involves charging users a recurring monthly subscription fee.

Advertising-Based Solutions

Currently, one of the most popular ways of generating revenue for a website is to add advertisements to content pages. More often than not, these advertisements are of the pay-per-click variety, which means that you are paid every time a user clicks one of the displayed advertisements. Pay-per-click ads have been the primary revenue model for most major sites through the last few years. They are usually pretty simple to incorporate into a site and often become a lucrative revenue stream. These types of advertisements have become popular over the years because they are usually targeted specifically to the content displayed on the page. By targeting the ads to the content, the advertising provider greatly increases the chance that the visitor will actually click the ad because advertisements are most likely for a product that is relevant to the site or page. Although it is not impossible to come up with your own system of pay-per-click advertisements for FitnessTrackerPlus, you'd be better served by incorporating ads from one of the large pay-per-click ad providers already in existence. These providers specialize in targeted ads and their algorithms are sophisticated enough to do a better job of displaying relevant ads than anything you'll come up with in a short time frame. After all, your business is to provide users with an online fitness tracking application and ideally generate revenue from it — not to become a pay-per-click ad broker.

Google AdSense

Although there are other competitors, the largest provider of pay-per-click ads is a little company called Google whose AdSense advertising system can be used to display targeted pay-per-click advertisements on FitnessTrackerPlus. An advantage that Google has over its competitors is a very low barrier to entry — there are no minimum traffic requirements for a site to join. Some Google competitors specifically target sites with extraordinarily high amounts of traffic and do not usually allow a startup site to register for their advertising program.

The lack of a traffic requirement makes the AdSense program a great fit for a site like FitnessTrackerPlus, especially when you're starting out because you won't have very high traffic until your site's popularity grows. Of course, the low barrier to entry does not change the fact that in order to truly make any decent revenue from a pay-per-click, you must increase traffic to the site. Although the overall click-through rate depends on how relevant the ads are, no matter how relevant they are, some users just simply won't click them. The pay-per-click ad system really becomes a numbers game in that if you have only two percent of your users clicking ads, the only way to increase the revenue is to increase the total number of users so that the two percent quickly translates into a much larger number of clicks.

One thing that you must watch for with a pay-per-click advertising system — especially Google — is resisting the temptation to influence the number of times your advertisements are clicked. The terms of service make it obvious that you are not allowed to click your own ads — doing so almost always results in a suspension of your account. After all, clicking your own ads will be effectively cheating the advertisers who paid Google to display the ads. What may not be so obvious is that you aren't technically even able to suggest to users that they should click the ads to help fund their continued use of the site. For example, on FitnessTrackerPlus you can't say things like "Please click the ads to help pay for new features." Any violation of the Google AdSense terms of service will more often than not result in a permanent suspension of your account, which would immediately terminate your source of revenue and force you to use another advertising broker that may not be as well equipped to serve targeted ads on FitnessTrackerPlus. These things are taken very seriously at Google and if you make the mistake of violating the terms, it can be next to impossible to recover your account.

It would seem that if you are going with an advertising-based solution to generate revenue, Google AdSense is probably the way to go at this point. The question now is where are you going to place the ads? This is always tricky because you want to place the ads in an area where users can see them without annoying users who will ignore advertisements no matter what. In the very early design stages of the FitnessTrackerPlus food, exercise, and measurement log pages, you used the `DockPanel` control of the Silverlight Toolkit to place the `GlobalCalendar` control on the right-hand side of the page in its own column. You may have noticed at this point that there was nothing underneath that control. You can now use this area to place any advertising because the ad won't interfere with the operation of the site and it will still be very noticeable to those users who may be interested in the displayed products. Figure 11-1 shows a sketch of an updated food log page that contains an advertising area just below the `GlobalCalendar` control.

Because you want to maximize the potential revenue that can be generated from the displayed ads, it's wise to include the ads on pages other than just the food log as well. In fact, because the `GlobalCalendar` is used on the food, exercise, and measurement log pages, you should count on including advertisements on those pages in the same space that is available below the `GlobalCalendar` control. By placing these pay-per-click ads in a prominent but unobtrusive location, the hope is that you can generate a sufficient amount of revenue. If you should find, however, that this solution is not working out, you can potentially use another option. This solution involves charging your users a nominal monthly fee to access the site.

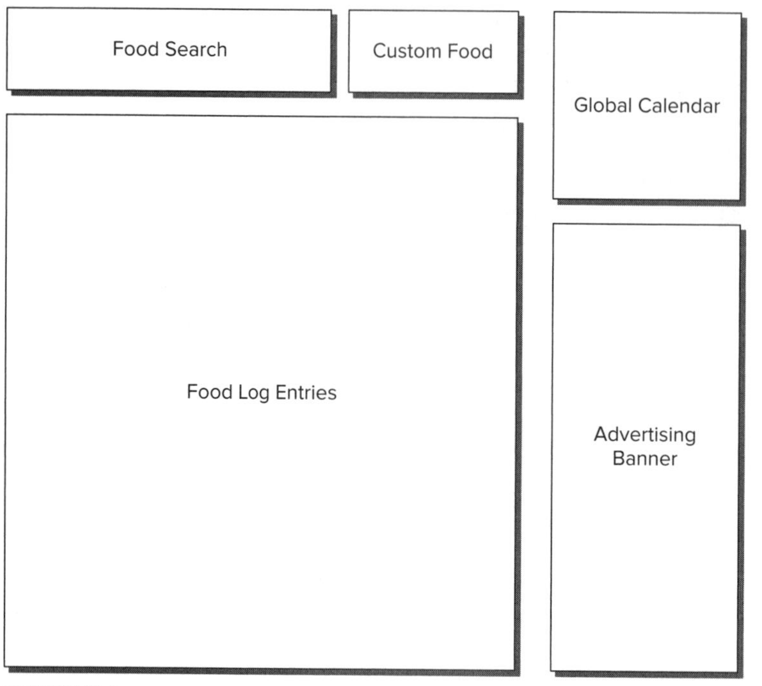

FIGURE 11-1

Recurring Monthly Fees

It is never an easy call to charge users for online content in this day and age, but sometimes it can be an appropriate alternative to displaying advertisements. For the most part, people have become accustomed to getting everything online for free and the only way users will be willing to pay is if the perceived value of the site is far greater than any alternative free solution. When would it make sense to charge money for FitnessTrackerPlus given that you have other free alternatives out there? For starters, because this site is just starting out, you may quickly find that you have a very low volume of traffic initially and that the pay-per-click system isn't generating even enough revenue to pay for the hosting costs of the site. That's not to say that in the future the site won't explode in popularity and that the problem won't correct itself. If it does not, however, this is where the recurring monthly payment solution may come into play and offer an alternative to relying on pay-per-click advertisements as your only source of revenue.

There are a couple of important questions that you need to answer before you choose to collect monthly fees for access to FitnessTrackerPlus:

- How much you will be charging?
- How will you go about collecting the money?

The first question is actually the most difficult one and entire books have been written on answering this particular question. The correct answer, of course, is you should charge the largest amount of money your users are willing to pay. That sounds easy enough, right? On second thought, it's a Catch-22. How can you come up with a definitive answer to this? You probably can't poll your users for an answer as the majority will inevitably tell you that they would prefer to pay nothing. An alternative solution is to take a look at what your competitors are doing. For example, are any of them charging for access to their sites? If so, you should be able to get a pretty good baseline. If none of your competitors are charging for access to their sites then you're on your own — but you should be warned that your competitors may not be charging because users simply won't pay any price for access to this type of site. Nonetheless, it probably won't hurt to try charging — the worst-case scenario is that nobody joins at the price you select and you'll need to continue to lower the price until you see registration rates rise. If you get to a point where the ideal price is zero dollars, it may be time to abandon the recurring monthly fee plan altogether and stick with the pay-per-click route. For now, let's plan on charging a recurring monthly fee of $5 per month and see what happens.

The answer to the second question is a little bit easier. When deciding on how you will be charging your users and how you will be collecting the recurring monthly fee, you have several options. These include collection and processing credit card information directly on the site or making use of a third-party online payment broker.

In-House Credit Card Processing

One option that you have for collecting payments is to collect and store credit card information right from the registration page of FitnessTrackerPlus. With all the recent news about stolen credit card numbers and hackers finding their way into various databases, this solution is not for the faint of heart. When you decide to process credit card transactions directly, you're also making the decision to store this valuable personal information in your own database and opening yourself to all sorts of legal liabilities. If you go this route, you'd better make sure that you have taken all the necessary precautions to properly encrypt credit card data using SSL and ensure that your database is properly locked down from potential intruders. Although you can collect this information directly on your site, you still need to make use of a third-party payment gateway service to actually complete the transaction. These services usually provide their own programming API and will handle actually charging the users' credit card and depositing the funds into your merchant account — for a small fee, of course.

Despite some very large potential drawbacks, one big advantage to processing the credit card information directly on the site is that the user registration process can stay fluid. Users can enter their information right from your signup page and at all times stay connected to the FitnessTrackerPlus site. As long as you are taking the necessary security precautions, this solution can add a more professional feel to the site.

PayPal Subscriptions

Another potential solution for processing monthly subscription charges is to make use of PayPal's subscription feature. If you haven't heard, PayPal is one of the largest online payment brokers in the business. After being purchased by eBay, it became eBay's preferred payment option and a household name. Using PayPal usually involves registering for an account and linking the account with a personal or business bank account or credit card. As the seller, you use the PayPal site to generate custom payment buttons that, when clicked, redirect users to an official PayPal site where they can safely enter their credit card information or login to their own PayPal account in order to complete the transaction.

In recent years PayPal has expanded its service to include:

- **Processing monthly recurring subscription charges:** This means that you can set up a monthly subscription price and PayPal will automatically collect payments from your users every month. When processing credit cards directly on your site, you not only have to take care of the initial purchase but also must handle charging the credit card accounts on a monthly basis. With the PayPal subscription feature, all this is taken care of for you.
- **Service cancellation:** When utilizing PayPal, you won't have to worry about providing users with the ability to cancel their membership as they will have full access to this function right from their own PayPal account page. If for some reason a user decides that FitnessTrackerPlus just isn't what they were looking for, they can easily cancel the membership from PayPal's main site and the PayPal developer API will inform you programmatically of the cancellation.
- **Security:** Security is a large benefit of PayPal. PayPal becomes responsible for all security-related aspects of credit card processing. They are on the hook for providing an SSL connection, storing encrypted card numbers, and taking on the legal liabilities.
- **Product familiarity:** PayPal has become somewhat of a household name and users who have made online purchases in the past will most likely have used the service and feel safe continuing to do so for your monthly subscription. This peace of mind may help you convince some additional users to go ahead and make the purchase.

Which Revenue Solution is the Right One?

Making a decision as to which revenue-generating solution is correct for FitnessTrackerPlus is a difficult one. Using the advertising-based system, you are opening the site up to anyone who is interested in a free online fitness tracker program. As long as this results in large volumes of traffic and high click-through rates, you should be able to generate more than enough revenue to sustain the site. However, if ads are not being clicked or you find that the target market for the site is smaller than you originally expected, you could quickly find yourself in a situation where it costs more to run the site than what you are receiving in AdSense payments.

The alternative to advertisements, charging a recurring monthly fee, also has its pros and cons. For starters, a solution that includes a recurring monthly fee would mean that your business could survive or thrive with only a limited number of users who think highly enough of the site to pay you 5 dollars every month. You would not have to worry about click-through rates, or even necessarily a high volume of traffic. You would, however, run the risk of limiting the popularity of the site as it can be extremely difficult convincing visitors who are not used to paying for websites to pony up the money every month just to use yours. There is also the issue of competing websites that can easily offer their own free advertising-supported version of an online fitness tracker.

For the purposes of this book and the sample application you'll develop both an advertising-based solution using Google AdSense as well as a paid monthly subscription version using PayPal. The main reason for this is so that you can see how to incorporate both possible solutions into the FitnessTrackerPlus sample application. In your own applications, it may very well make more sense to choose one or the other. Alternatively, you can make use of a hybrid approach where you start off the site free to all users, generating revenue through advertisements and then, after the site gains in popularity, add some premium features for which some users may feel it is acceptable to pay. This results in a site that combines advertisements and monthly subscription fees.

SOLUTION

This "Solution" section covers the development of two separate revenue-generating solutions for FitnessTrackerPlus. First, you will see how to modify the application to display advertisements from the Google AdSense program. Following this discussion, you will also see how to set up a recurring monthly subscription system through PayPal. This alternate version of FitnessTrackerPlus will rely on members paying a 5 dollar monthly fee in order to use the site.

Google AdSense

The first revenue-generating solution that you should concentrate on is the pay-per-click advertising system. In the "Design" section, the decision was made to make use of the Google AdSense program to display ads on the food, exercise, and measurement log pages of FitnessTrackerPlus. Let's take a quick look at how to get enrolled in the AdSense program and then look at what code modifications are required in order to incorporate the targeted ads into FitnessTrackerPlus.

Getting Started with AdSense

Getting started with Ad-Sense is a fairly painless process. First you visit the main Google AdSense page at `http://www.google.com/adsense`. From there, you visit the link to the sign-up page. The registration shown in Figure 11-2 is pretty straightforward and consists of the usual fields you would expect to see a name, an address, such as N, A, and so on.

At this point, you enter the name of the site that will link to this AdSense account. As you can see from Figure 11-2, FitnessTrackerPlus.com is linked to the account. An interesting feature of AdSense is that during the initial registration step, you link an existing site with this particular AdSense account. However, there is no limit to how many additional sites you can link to this account. This means that if you choose to develop multiple sites, or even if you have an existing blog, you can add those sites during a later step and have targeted ads displayed on those sites as well. Google will pay you for ads clicked on any of your sites that have been linked with this AdSense account.

Google AdSense

Help

Search AdSense Help

Welcome to AdSense What is AdSense? | Already have an account?
Please complete the application form below.

Website Information

Website URL: http://www.FitnessTrackerPlus.com
• Please list your primary URL only.
• Example: www.example.com

Website language: Select a language:
• Tell us your website's primary language to help our review process.
I will not place ads on sites that include incentives to click on ads.
I will not place ads on sites that include pornographic content.

Contact Information

Account type: Select an account type:
Country or territory: Select a country or territory:

Important - Your payment will be sent to the address below. Please complete all fields that apply to your address, such as a full name, full street name and house or apartment number, and accurate country, ZIP code, and city. Example.

Payee name (full name):
• Your Payee name needs to match the name on your bank account.
• Payee must be at least 18 years of age to participate in AdSense.

Street Address:

City/Town:

State: Select state

ZIP: [?]

UNITED STATES
• To change your country or territory, please change your selection at the top of this form.

I agree that I can receive checks made out to the payee name I have listed above.

Telephone Numbers

Phone:

Email preference: We'll send you service announcements that relate to your agreement with Google.
In addition, send me periodic newsletters with tips and best practices and occasional surveys to help Google improve AdSense.

How did you find out about Google AdSense? Choose an option...

Policies

AdSense applicants must agree to adhere to AdSense program policies (details)
I agree that I will not click on the Google ads I'm serving through AdSense.
I certify that I have read the AdSense Program Policies.
I do not already have an approved AdSense account. (Click here if you do.)

Submit Information

© 2009 Google - AdSense Blog - AdSense Forum - Privacy Policy - Terms & Conditions - Program Policies

FIGURE 11-2

After you have successfully registered for a new AdSense account, the next step is to create the JavaScript responsible for displaying the targeted ads:

1. Click the AdSense Setup tab and select the AdSense for Content selection to view advertising layouts for websites.

2. You are presented with the choice to follow the AdSense for Content wizard or view all possible advertisement selections in a single page. I usually prefer the single-page route so that is what I will be covering here. Set this option.

3. Decide whether you want to display Ad units or Link units. *Ad units* are usually advertisements in the form of a banner and have a variety of sizes available. These advertisements are displayed either as text only or as image-based ads. *Link units* are simply a vertical list of hyperlinks that, when clicked, lead the user to the website of the product being advertised. Link units can offer a nice unobtrusive way to display advertisements on the site. Because you have a pretty large banner area available on the FitnessTrackerPlus log pages, you might as well go with the Ad units.

4. Ad units come in a variety of shapes and sizes. Figures 11-3 and 11-4 show some of the various text-based available ad formats. Figure 11-5 shows some of the similar image-based formats.

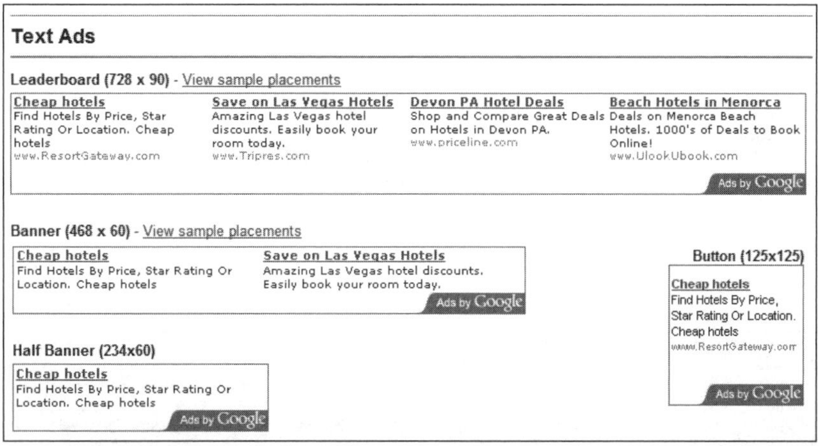

FIGURE 11-3

After looking at the various options, the best fit for FitnessTrackerPlus is probably the 160x600-wide skyscraper format. An advertisement this size will fit nicely in the area that has been reserved under the `GlobalCalendar` control. Although most people go with the text-based ads for FitnessTrackerPlus, you will be using image-based advertisements only. The hope is that any advertisements that appear on FitnessTrackerPlus will be fitness-related and because fitness is an image-based industry, showing image-based advertisements may help increase the overall click-through rate.

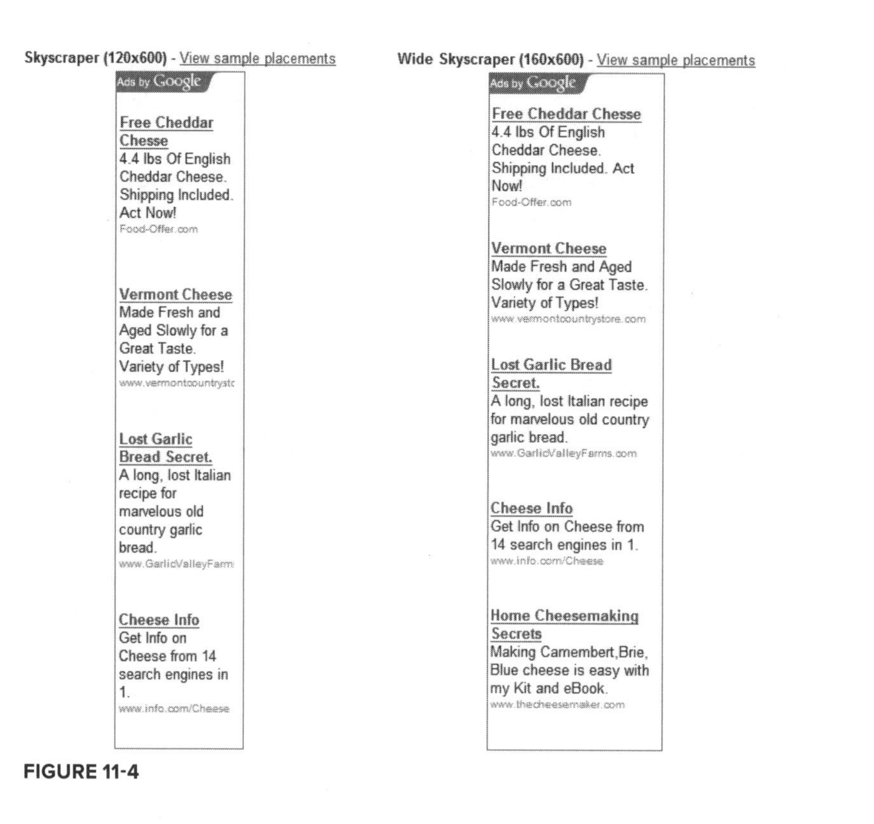

FIGURE 11-4

Image Ads

Leaderboard (728 x 90)

Be Fit. 30dayfitness.com Natural Health for Better Living.
www.30dayfitness.com Feedback - Ads by Google

Banner (468 x 60)

Traveling Dog.net Travel gear and accessories for your dog.
www.travelingdog.net Feedback - Ads by Google

FIGURE 11-5

5. Once you have selected the appropriate ad format, you can then click the Submit and Get Code button. This takes you to another screen that contains the JavaScript code required to generate and display the advertisements. The following code shows the JavaScript generated for the 160x600-wide skyscraper ad that will display on the log pages.

```
<script type="text/javascript">
    <!--
        google_ad_client = "YOUR ADSENSE ID GOES HERE";
```

```
                /* 160x600, created 10/10/09 */
                google_ad_slot = "THIS WILL BE DEPENDENT ON YOUR GOOGLE AD CLIENT ID";
                google_ad_width = 160;
                google_ad_height = 600;
        //-->
</script>
<script type="text/javascript"
src="http://pagead2.googlesyndication.com/pagead/show_ads.js">
</script>
```

One element of the generated code that differs for you is the `google_ad_client` field. This field is specific and unique to every AdSense account, so yours will be different. Now that you have the code required to display the ads, it's time to figure out a way to incorporate them in the FitnessTrackerPlus application. Let's fire up Visual Studio and get started.

Displaying Advertisements in FitnessTrackerPlus

Getting the ads to display in FitnessTrackerPlus requires modifications in a few areas. If you recall from the public journal feature, the trick for getting HTML comments to display on the public journal page is to add an absolutely positioned DIV element to the FitnessTrackerPlus.aspx page and then to manipulate the position and visibility of it from the Silverlight code behind. You'll make use of the same technique to display the Google ads:

1. Add a new DIV element called google_ads to the FitnessTrackerPlus.aspx page, as shown in the following code.

Available for download on Wrox.com

```
<div id="google_ads" style="position:absolute;top:0px;left:0px;
display:none;">
        <script type="text/javascript"><!--
                google_ad_client = "YOUR GOOGLE AD CLIENT ID GOES HERE";
                /* 160x600, created 10/10/09 */
                google_ad_slot = "THIS WILL BE DEPENDENT ON YOUR
GOOGLE AD CLIENT ID";
                google_ad_width = 160;
                google_ad_height = 600;
                //-->
        </script>
        <script type="text/javascript"
                src="http://pagead2.googlesyndication.com/pagead/show_ads.js">
        </script>
</div>
```

Code snippet FitnessTrackerPlus.aspx located in the FitnessTrackerPlus_AdSense project

2. As discussed in the "Design" section, you want these advertisements to display on the food, exercise, and measurement log pages. Let's start with the food log page. In the following code, a placeholder `Grid` control called `AdArea` is added just below the `GlobalCalendar` declaration. The code behind makes sure that the `google_ads DIV` has its position updated so that it overlays this placeholder `Grid` control.

Available for download on Wrox.com

```
<StackPanel Style="{StaticResource CalendarPanelStyle}">
     <toolkit:GlobalCalendar x:Name="Calendar" Style="{StaticResource
CalendarStyle}">
          <toolkit:GlobalCalendar.CalendarDayButtonStyleSelector>
               <fitnesstrackerplus_calendar:ValidFoodLogDateSelector>
<fitnesstrackerplus_calendar:ValidFoodLogDateSelector.
ValidLogDateStyle>
                         <Style BasedOn="{StaticResource
BasicDayButtonStyle}"
TargetType="toolkit_primitives:GlobalCalendarDayButton">
                              <Setter Property="Background"
Value="#FF999999" />
                         </Style>
                    </fitnesstrackerplus_calendar:ValidFoodLogDateSelector.
ValidLogDateStyle>
               <fitnesstrackerplus_calendar:ValidFoodLogDateSelector.
InvalidLogDateStyle>
                    <Style BasedOn="{StaticResource BasicDayButtonStyle}"
TargetType="toolkit_primitives:GlobalCalendarDayButton">
                         <Setter Property="Background" Value="#FFFFFFFF" />
                    </Style>
               </fitnesstrackerplus_calendar:ValidFoodLogDateSelector.
InvalidLogDateStyle>
               </fitnesstrackerplus_calendar:ValidFoodLogDateSelector>
          </toolkit:GlobalCalendar.CalendarDayButtonStyleSelector>
     </toolkit:GlobalCalendar>
     <Grid x:Name="AdArea" Style="{StaticResource AdAreaStyle}" />
</StackPanel>
```

Code snippet FoodLog.xaml located in the FitnessTrackerPlus_AdSense project

3. You need to make sure that the `google_ads` `DIV` element is visible when the user navigates to the page and hidden again when the user leaves the page. The following code overrides the `OnNavigatedTo` and `OnNavigatedFrom` methods making use of the `HtmlPage` object to access the `DIV` element. Just like the public journal page implementation, the display style property is toggled using the `SetStyleAttribute` method.

```
protected override void OnNavigatedTo(NavigationEventArgs e)
{
     LoadFoodLog();

     // Display any advertisements

     HtmlElement ads = HtmlPage.Document.GetElementById("google_ads");
     ads.SetStyleAttribute("display", "");
}

protected override void OnNavigatedFrom(NavigationEventArgs e)
{
     base.OnNavigatedFrom(e);
```

```
            // Hide any advertisements

            HtmlElement ads = HtmlPage.Document.GetElementById("google_ads");
            ads.SetStyleAttribute("display", "none");
        }
```

Code snippet FoodLog.xaml.cs located in the FitnessTrackerPlus_AdSense project

4. Add a method that will take care of positioning the advertisement so that it overlays the placeholder `Grid` control. The following code shows the `PositionAds` method that uses the same technique you used previously to ensure that the HTML comments are positioned in the correct location.

Available for download on Wrox.com

```
private void PositionAds()
{
     if (ActualHeight > 0 && ActualWidth > 0)
     {
          UIElement root = Application.Current.RootVisual as UIElement;
          GeneralTransform gt = AdArea.TransformToVisual(root);
          Point pos = gt.Transform(new Point(0, 0));

          HtmlElement ads = HtmlPage.Document.GetElementById("google_ads");

          ads.SetStyleAttribute("top", pos.Y.ToString() + "px");
          ads.SetStyleAttribute("left", pos.X.ToString() + "px");
          ads.SetStyleAttribute("width",
AdArea.ActualWidth.ToString() + "px");
          ads.SetStyleAttribute("height",
AdArea.ActualHeight.ToString() + "px");
     }
}
```

Code snippet FoodLog.xaml.cs located in the FitnessTrackerPlus_AdSense project

5. Ensure that the advertisement is positioned correctly anytime the `ScrollViewer` control is used. You do this by calling the `PositionAds` method anytime the `LayoutUpdated` event is fired from the `ScrollViewer`. You can do this with the following line of code in the `Loaded` event for the page.

Available for download on Wrox.com

```
Globals.MainScroll.LayoutUpdated += (se, ev) => { PositionAds(); };
```

Code snippet FoodLog.xaml.cs located in the FitnessTrackerPlus_AdSense project

6. Because you are displaying a pretty long advertisement banner, you may want to make sure that the `DockPanel` control has its `MinHeight` property set to something large enough to guarantee that the entire advertisement is visible on the page; if the user has not added any foods to the log yet, the advertisement will cut off the screen because it is an HTML `DIV` element and not actually part of the Silverlight plug-in.

After completing all of these steps, you should be able to easily apply similar code to the exercise and measurement log pages to ensure that the Google ads display when the user navigates to those pages as well. At this point, running the application and navigating to the food log should show a screen similar to Figure 11-6, although the advertisement you see will no doubt be different than the one shown here.

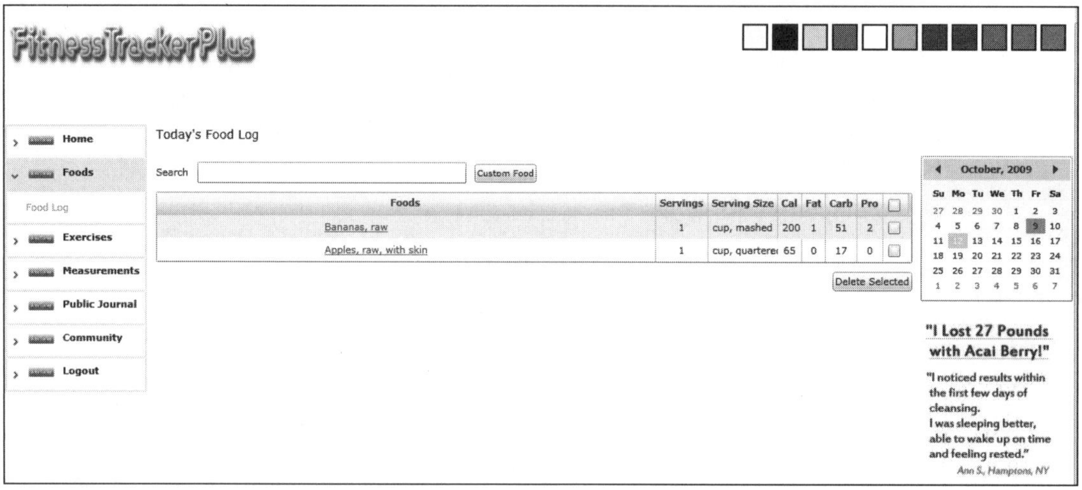

FIGURE 11-6

PayPal

Rather than trying to generate revenue through the use of pay-per-click advertisements, you may decide that you would be better served simply charging a recurring monthly fee for users to gain access to the site. As discussed in the design section, you do have the option of attempting to take care of the credit-card processing completely on your own, but for FitnessTrackerPlus you'll make use of the developer API available from PayPal.

Currently, PayPal offers several different solutions for your site. The two most prominent are Website Payments Standard and Website Payments Pro:

- **Website Payments Standard:** The basic offering from PayPal, this is the most simple to use in your own solutions. The Standard offering typically involves logging into your PayPal account and creating custom payment buttons depending on the product you are trying to sell. Once the button is generated, you simply paste the code onto you web page — similar to AdSense where you are making use of generated code. Once you're finished, users will see the PayPal payment logo and when they click the button they are redirected to a payment processing page.
- **The Website Payments Pro:** This is much more sophisticated in that it provides a complete SDK that you can use to directly integrate payment functionality into your site. This means that your users never leave your site and are redirected to PayPal in order to process the payment.

For FitnessTrackerPlus, you'll make use of the Standard offering for a couple of reasons.

Standard version of the SDK has a much better cost associated with it. PayPal charges a monthly fee for the Pro version and at the time of this writing, if you have less than $3,000 in sales per month you must pay 30 dollars per month to access the Pro version of the SDK. When you start out, it is highly unlikely that you'll have more than 600 paying users joining the site. The Standard version has no monthly fee. You do, however, pay a transaction fee, which varies depending on your volume of sales. The fee is usually in the range of three percent or so and three percent of 5 dollars isn't bad considering PayPal takes on all the additional risk in storing and processing the credit card information.

Getting Started with Website Payments Standard

To get started with PayPal, make sure that you have a verified account with PayPal already set up. You may have already done so if you have spent any time on eBay in the last few years. If not, just hop over to `http://www.paypal.com` and sign up for a new account.

When you create your account, consider changing it to a business account. There are no additional costs associated with a PayPal business account, but if you'll be selling monthly subscriptions, you do gain some nice features that can help you manage the subscriptions better. Registering a business account also helps give your site's membership a professional feel. An added step is required if you do make the decision to create a business account; you'll need to perform account verification by linking the account with a major credit card. Most personal PayPal accounts are linked to a checking account, but when you switch to a business account you must provide a major credit card that PayPal can use if it needs to issue refunds to your customers. Once you have successfully registered for a business account, you can begin collecting payments and create a subscription button to display on your page.

Before doing that, however, make sure that your integration actually works without having to use real money. Both Website Payments Standard and Website Payments Pro users can register for a developer account as well as their primary account. The developer account gives you access to one of the best features that PayPal offers — *the Sandbox*, which is a great tool for testing your site's integration with PayPal. The Sandbox is essentially a complete replication of the real PayPal site with every transaction done with test data. No real money changes hands, but the functionality is identical to the real PayPal site. This allows you to test out a variety of scenarios to see what works and what doesn't without requiring you to test the code with real money or real credit card information. For the most part, if your solution is working in the Sandbox, you can count on it working with the real site; the only change you have to make is to point your PayPal code from the Sandbox URL to the real live URL.

To get started with the Sandbox, you should do the following:

1. Visit the main Sandbox site at `http://developer.paypal.com`.
2. Click the Signup button and fill out the required fields on the registration form.
3. Check your e-mail for a verification link.
4. Click the link to activate your new developer account.
5. Log in to the Sandbox site where you are presented with the screen shown in Figure 11-7. From here, you have access to several links to various testing tools, test accounts, and test e-mail.

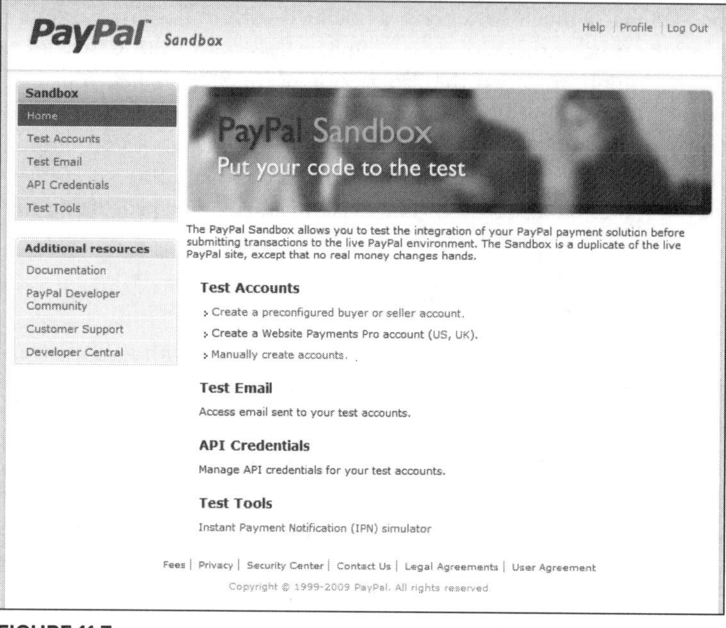

FIGURE 11-7

6. Set up a couple of test accounts. The Sandbox allows you to create both a fictitious buyer and seller account. Click on the Test Accounts link and you are presented with the page shown in Figure 11-8.

7. Click the Preconfigured link. The preconfigured option provides you with a quick and easy way to create both the buyer and seller accounts that you will need.

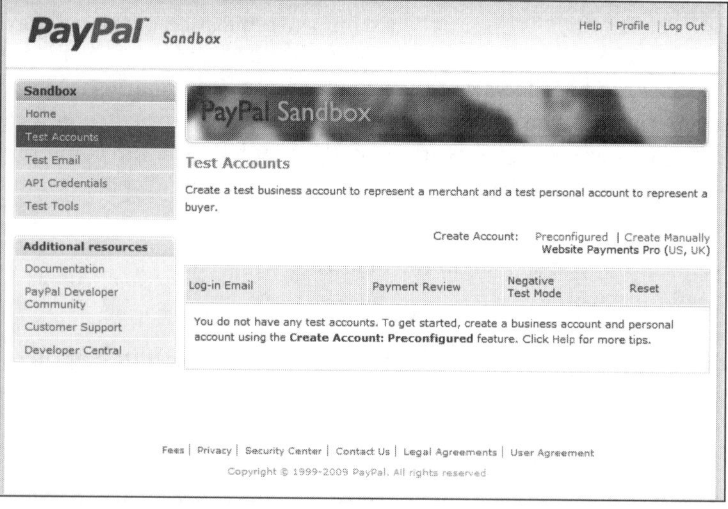

FIGURE 11-8

8. Fill out the appropriate account information. Figure 11-9 shows the completed form for the test buyer account. Remember these are just test accounts, so the only fields you should be concerned with are the Login Email and the Password fields. You will need to use both of these in order to log in to the Sandbox with the newly created test accounts.

FIGURE 11-9

9. Repeat steps 6-8 to create a test account for the seller.

10. Once you have successfully created both test accounts, you need to log in with the seller account and create the FitnessTrackerPlus subscription button that you'll use. You can access the seller test account by selecting it on the Test Accounts screen and clicking the Enter Sandbox Test Site button. You're presented with a popup window containing what looks like a real version

of the PayPal site. As you can see in Figure 11-10, however, the site is clearly labeled with the Sandbox version of the logo and the words Test Site should make it clear that this is not the real PayPal site, although once you log in everything will work the same as the live version.

FIGURE 11-10

11. Log in using the password you generated when you created your test seller account. The e-mail address field should already be filled in for you. You are presented with the typical PayPal home page with all the dashboard information that you would see on the live site.
12. To create the FitnessTrackerPlus subscription button, head on over to the Merchant Services page. As you can see in Figure 11-11, there are many options to choose from on this page.
13. To move forward, you should click the Subscribe link located under the Create Buttons menu.

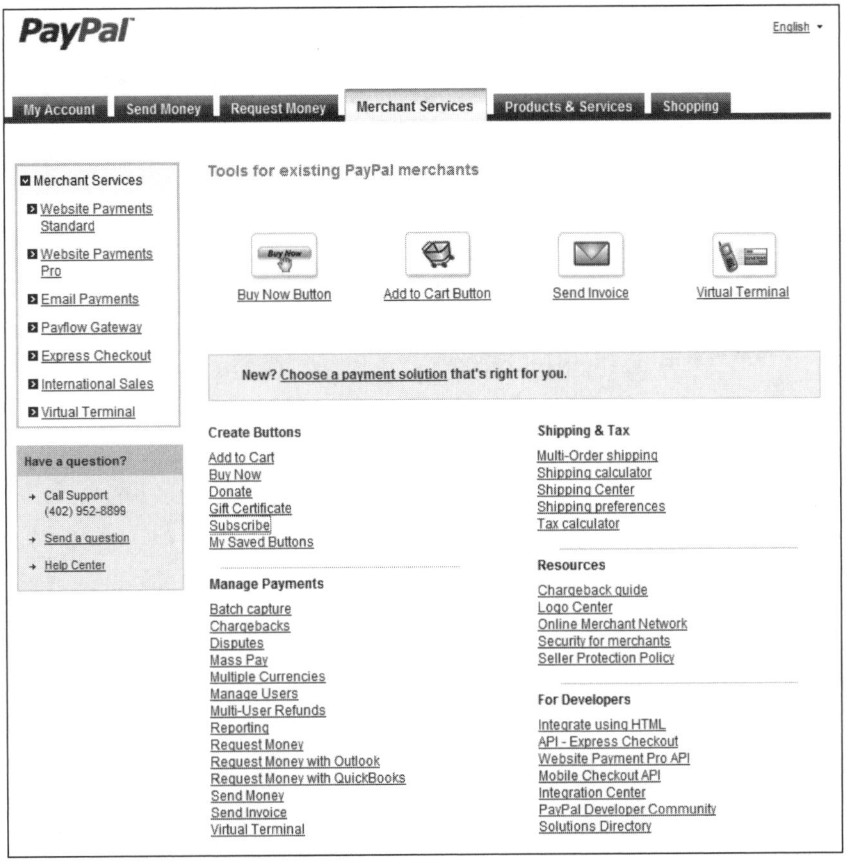

FIGURE 11-11

The next page is divided into several categories. The first one deals with the actual subscription button information. As you can see in Figure 11-12, you will need to enter a name for the subscription as well as the price. As discussed previously, users who wish to join FitnessTrackerPlus will need to pay 5 dollars per month

Step 1: Choose button type and enter payment details

Accept payments for

Subscriptions and recurring billing

View example button

Note: Go to My saved buttons to create a new button similar to an existing one

Item name

FitnessTrackerPlus Subscription

Subscription ID (optional) What's this?

Customize button

Add drop-down menu without prices Example

Add text field Example

Customize appearance

Buyer's View

Subscribe

Have PayPal create user names and passwords for customers What's this?

Notes: IPN and server modifications required.

Auto Return is not compatible with this feature.

Currency

USD

Recurring amount to be billed

5.00

Billing cycle

1 month(s)

After how many cycles should billing stop?

Never

Try to bill a customer again after a failed attempt?

Yes

No

Offer a trial to your subscribers

Merchant ID for purchase transactions: What's this?

Secure merchant account ID Why is this secure?

Plain text e-mail address: seller_1255667141_biz@fitnesstrackerplus.com

Step 2: Track inventory, profit & loss (optional)

Step 3: Customize advanced features (optional)

FIGURE 11-12

14. Save the changes to the newly configured button. In this case, you don't have to worry about any of the additional options so you can skip that step. PayPal stores a copy of the button settings so you can easily retrieve them at a later time without going through the process of recreating the button from scratch. Although not particularly useful for the simple button you just created, these settings can come in handy if you were to set many of the optional button settings and parameters. PayPal now presents you with the HTML code shown in Figure 11-13.

15. Copy and paste this code into the FitnessTrackerPlus application to display the PayPal subscription button. Because you have already integrated HTML-based comments in the public journal feature, you shouldn't have too much trouble introducing some additional HTML elements into the solution.

FIGURE 11-13

So, now that you have the code for the PayPal button, it's time to take a look at how to properly integrate it into the FitnessTrackerPlus application. As you will soon see, these test accounts and the Sandbox environment are invaluable tools for debugging or testing the monthly subscription payments process.

Integrating PayPal Subscriptions with FitnessTrackerPlus

You currently have the PayPal subscription code that needs to be displayed — but in HTML format only. Just as you did for the public journal page, you add a new `DIV` element onto the main FitnessTrackerPlus.aspx page that is responsible for hosting the subscription button. One thing to watch for is closing the existing ASP.NET `form` tag before placing the `DIV` element. The code generated for the PayPal button includes its own `<form>` tag and if you were to simply drop it right below the `DIV` element reserved for the comments, the PayPal code would not function correctly. Instead of redirecting the user to a PayPal payment page, clicking the button just generates a standard ASP.NET post back event, which is not what you want to happen here. By closing the existing `<form>` tag before dropping in the button code, you can be sure that the PayPal code will work correctly.

Don't forget that like the comment area, this new `DIV` element needs to have its `display` style property set to none so that it won't appear when the main page is first visible. Like the comment area, you need to toggle the visibility of this button based on whether or not the `Signup` page is visible. The following code shows a new `DIV` element called `paypal_area` being dropped onto the FitnessTrackerPlus.aspx page after the main `<form>` tag is closed.

Available for download on Wrox.com

```
<div id="comment_area"
style="position:absolute;top:0px;left:0px;width:600px;display:none;">
</div>
<div id="comment_editor" style="position:absolute;top:0px;left:0px;display:none;">
     <asp:Editor runat="server" ID="CommentEditor" NoScript="true"  />
</div>
</form>
<div id="paypal_area" style="position:absolute;top:0px;left:0px;display:none">
     <form name="paypal_form"
action="https://www.sandbox.paypal.com/cgi-bin/webscr" method="post">
          <input type="hidden" name="cmd" value="_s-xclick" />
          <input type="hidden" name="hosted_button_id"
value="YOUR BUTTON ID GOES HERE" />
          <input type='hidden' name='custom' value="" />
          <input type="image"
src="https://www.sandbox.paypal.com/en_US/i/btn/btn_subscribeCC_LG.gif" border="0"
name="submit" alt="PayPal - The safer, easier way to pay online!" />
          <img alt="" border="0"
src="https://www.sandbox.paypal.com/en_US/i/scr/pixel.gif" width="1" height="1" />
     </form>
</div>
```

Code snippet FitnessTrackerPlus.aspx located in the FitnessTrackerPlus_PayPal project

Integrating PayPal with User Registration

With the button in place, it's time to revisit the initial registration page and make some necessary modifications to it in order to display the PayPal subscription button. Follow these steps:

1. Add a placeholder `Grid` control that will be responsible for hosting the PayPal `DIV` element. You can erase the existing button and replace it with the placeholder `Grid`.
2. Change the text to let the visitors know that using the site now costs five dollars per month. You don't want them to be surprised when they click the subscribe button. Listing 11-1 shows the updated `Signup` page with the new placeholder `Grid`.

LISTING 11-1: Signup.xaml

Available for download on Wrox.com

```
<navigation:Page x:Class="FitnessTrackerPlus.Views.Signup"
     xmlns="http://schemas.microsoft.com/winfx/2006/xaml/presentation"
     xmlns:x="http://schemas.microsoft.com/winfx/2006/xaml"
     xmlns:navigation="clr-
namespace:System.Windows.Controls;assembly=System.Windows.Controls.Navigation"
     xmlns:controls="clr-namespace:FitnessTrackerPlus.Controls"
     xmlns:data="clr-
```

```
namespace:System.Windows.Controls;
assembly=System.Windows.Controls.Data.DataForm.Toolkit"
     Title="FitnessTrackerPlus - Signup">
     <navigation:Page.Resources>
          <Style x:Key="SignupGridStyle" TargetType="Grid">
               <Setter Property="HorizontalAlignment" Value="Center" />
          </Style>
          <Style x:Key="UserRegistrationFormStyle" TargetType="data:DataForm">
               <Setter Property="AutoGenerateFields" Value="False" />
               <Setter Property="AutoEdit" Value="True" />
               <Setter Property="CommandButtonsVisibility" Value="None" />
               <Setter Property="Header" Value="Your just seconds
away from starting your journal, membership is only 5 dollars per month,
just fill out the form below to get started" />
          </Style>
          <Style x:Key="RegisterButtonStyle" TargetType="Grid">
               <Setter Property="HorizontalAlignment" Value="Center" />
               <Setter Property="Margin" Value="-10,20,0,0" />
          </Style>
     </navigation:Page.Resources>
     <Grid Style="{StaticResource SignupGridStyle}">
          <Grid.RowDefinitions>
               <RowDefinition />
               <RowDefinition />
          </Grid.RowDefinitions>
          <data:DataForm x:Name="UserRegistration"
Style="{StaticResource UserRegistrationFormStyle}" Grid.Row="0">
               <data:DataForm.EditTemplate>
                    <DataTemplate>
                         <StackPanel>
                              <data:DataField>
                                   <TextBox Text="{Binding email_address,
Mode=TwoWay}" />
                              </data:DataField>
                              <data:DataField>
                                   <controls:PasswordControl
PasswordText="{Binding password, Mode=TwoWay}"/>
                              </data:DataField>
                              <data:DataField>
                                   <TextBox Text="{Binding security_question,
Mode=TwoWay}" />
                              </data:DataField>
                              <data:DataField>
                                   <TextBox Text="{Binding security_answer,
Mode=TwoWay}" />
                              </data:DataField>
                         </StackPanel>
                    </DataTemplate>
               </data:DataForm.EditTemplate>
          </data:DataForm>
          <Grid x:Name="PayPalArea" Grid.Row="1"
Style="{StaticResource RegisterButtonStyle}" />
     </Grid>
</navigation:Page>
```

3. Ensure that the HTML DIV element holding the image is visible when visitors arrive at the signup page, and make sure that it is hidden when users navigate away from the page. In the following code, the `HtmlPage` object again enables you to access the `display` property of the DIV element and toggle it in the `OnNavigatedTo` and `OnNavigatedFrom` event handlers.

Available for download on Wrox.com

```
protected override void OnNavigatedTo(NavigationEventArgs e)
{
     HtmlPage.Document.GetElementById("paypal_area").SetStyleAttribute
("display", "");
}

protected override void OnNavigatedFrom(NavigationEventArgs e)
{
     base.OnNavigatedFrom(e);
     HtmlPage.Document.GetElementById("paypal_area").SetStyleAttribute
("display", "none");
}
```

Code snippet Signup.xaml.cs located in the FitnessTrackerPlus_PayPal project

4. Although the event handlers take care of displaying the new PayPal button on the signup page, you still need to worry about the placement of the DIV. If you remember, when you displayed the comment area on the public journal page, you still had to make sure that it was positioned correctly. Once again, you need a method that ensures the PayPal DIV element displays in the same location as the placeholder `Grid` control. You also need this method to be called any time the page is scrolled. The following code shows a `PositionButton` method that makes use of the same technique you used before by getting the relative location of the `Grid` control and converting it into coordinates that can be used to absolutely position the HTML DIV element.

Available for download on Wrox.com

```
private void PositionButton()
{
     if (ActualHeight > 0 && ActualWidth > 0)
     {
          UIElement root = Application.Current.RootVisual as UIElement;
          GeneralTransform gt = PayPalArea.TransformToVisual(root);
          Point pos = gt.Transform(new Point(0, 0));

          HtmlElement paypal =
HtmlPage.Document.GetElementById("paypal_area");

          paypal.SetStyleAttribute("top", pos.Y.ToString() + "px");
          paypal.SetStyleAttribute("left", pos.X.ToString() + "px");
     }
}
```

Code snippet Signup.xaml.cs located in the FitnessTrackerPlus_PayPal project

5. To make sure that the `DIV` position is updated any time the user scrolls the page, you simply make sure that the `PositionButton` method is called any time the main `ScrollViewer` control's `LayoutUpdated` event is fired.

Available for download on Wrox.com

```
Globals.MainScroll.LayoutUpdated += (se, ev) => { PositionButton(); };
```

Code snippet Signup.xaml.cs located in the FitnessTrackerPlus_PayPal project

This is looking good! So far the button will display and when clicked the visitor is redirected to the PayPal payment site. Because the visitor will actually be leaving this site, this brings up an interesting question. How do you send the user to PayPal and still collect the necessary registration fields in order to create the new user account? Because the PayPal subscription button is an HTML-based input element, there is no Silverlight-based event handler. Consequently, you aren't even notified when the visitor actually clicks the button and leaves the FitnessTrackerPlus site. Even if you were notified, you don't want to actually create the new account until you are sure you have been paid for the membership. Let's try and tackle these problems one at a time.

Validating Fields Before Processing Payment

First things first — you need to be notified somehow that the visitor is leaving the site in order to make the payment. This is necessary because you must ensure that all the registration fields are validated before allowing the visitor to proceed to the payment page. If the validation fails, the visitor must remain on the signup page so that they can see the displayed validation error messages.

To get this working, you make use of the HTML DOM Bridge feature available in Silverlight. You have already seen how to access HTML elements from Silverlight code, but what you do now is essentially the reverse of this process. Follow these steps:

1. Call a method in the `Signup` page that performs the `DataForm` validation and lets the caller know if it is okay to continue on with the form submission. To allow access to the `Signup` page from JavaScript, you register the page object with the HTML DOM Bridge by calling the `RegisterScriptableObject` method of the `HtmlPage` object. This should be done in the constructor for the `Signup` page, as shown in the following code.

```
public Signup()
{
    InitializeComponent();

    UserRegistration.CurrentItem = newUser;
    Globals.MainScroll.LayoutUpdated += (se, ev) => { PositionButton(); };

    HtmlPage.RegisterScriptableObject("Signup", this);
}
```

Code snippet Signup.xaml.cs located in the FitnessTrackerPlus_PayPal project

2. Add a method decorated with the ScriptableMember attribute. This method will be responsible for performing the DataForm validation routine and will be called when the visitor clicks the PayPal subscription button. For now, the following code will just return the result of the ValidateItem method of the DataForm object.

Available for download on Wrox.com

```
[ScriptableMember]
public bool ValidateForm()
{
     return UserRegistration.ValidateItem();
}
```

Code snippet Signup.xaml.cs located in the FitnessTrackerPlus_PayPal project

3. Modify the PayPal button code to add an onclick handler that will call the ValidateForm method. In the following code, the Silverlight plug-in is accessible by calling getElementById with the ID that was assigned to the plug-in. After that, any objects in the Silverlight client that have been registered become available in the Content property. In this case, you access the page with the name that you used in the RegisterScriptableObject call, which is Signup. This gives you an instance of the page to work with and, of course, you can then call the ValidateForm method. The HTML DOM Bridge takes care of the behind-the-scenes work necessary to make all of this work.

Available for download on Wrox.com

```
<script language="javascript" type="text/javascript">

     function validateSignup() {
          var silverlight = document.getElementById("SilverlightControl");

          if (silverlight.Content.Signup.ValidateForm())
               document.paypal_form.submit();
          else
               return false;
          }
</script>

<div id="paypal_area" style="position:absolute;top:0px;left:0px;
display:none">
     <form name="paypal_form"
action="https://www.sandbox.paypal.com/cgi-bin/webscr" method="post">
          <input type="hidden" name="cmd" value="_s-xclick" />
          <input type="hidden" name="hosted_button_id"
value="YOUR BUTTON ID GOES HERE" />
          <input type='hidden' name='custom' value="" />
          <input onclick="return validateSignup();" type="image"
src="https://www.sandbox.paypal.com/en_US/i/btn/btn_subscribeCC_LG.gif"
border="0" name="submit" alt="PayPal - The safer,
easier way to pay online!" />
          <img alt="" border="0"
src="https://www.sandbox.paypal.com/en_US/i/scr/pixel.gif"
```

```
width="1" height="1" />
     </form>
</div>
```

Code snippet FitnessTrackerPlus.aspx located in the FitnessTrackerPlus_PayPal project

Now you can be sure that the validation will occur before the visitor is redirected to the PayPal payment page but what about creating the new user account? You could create the account after performing the validation but you would not be assured that the visitor actually completed the payment process. In this case, the visitor would be redirected to PayPal, but before completing the payment his or her FitnessTrackerPlus account would have already been created and the visitor could just go back and log in rather than actually pay you. Obviously, this is not really a viable solution. Luckily, PayPal offers a couple of features that you can use in order to be sure that have a user has actually completed the payment process before you create a new account.

Auto Return

When you create a new PayPal account, you have the option to enable several features that come in handy when you need to be notified of a completed payment. One of these features, called Auto Return, allows you to provide a URL that PayPal will redirect users to upon completing their payment. In your case, this would send users back to FitnessTrackerPlus so that they can log in to the site rather than being forced to find their way back to the main page.

By harnessing the power of the navigation framework, you can easily provide PayPal with a URL that takes the user to a custom payment complete page embedded in the Silverlight application itself rather than another ASP.NET page. This seems like a good place to potentially put the user account creation code as well because you can be assured that the payment processing pages have been completed by the time they reach this Auto Return URL. To enable Auto Return, follow these steps:

1. Log in to your PayPal Sandbox account and enter the seller test account site.
2. Click the Profile link under the My Account tab. When the profile page loads, you are presented with another batch of links, as shown in Figure 11-14.
3. Click the Website Payment Preferences link under the Selling Preferences column. The very first option that you are presented with is the Auto Return feature.
4. You need to both enable the feature and supply a return URL. In this case, plan on adding a `SignupComplete` page to the project that will be accessible at `http://www.FitnessTrackerPlus.com/FitnessTrackerPlus.aspx#SignupComplete`. Figure 11-15 shows the Auto Return setup for FitnessTrackerPlus.
5. There are some requirements that the Auto Return page has to meet. Basically, this involves letting the user know that the payment process is complete and details of the transaction will be e-mailed to the user. As you can see from Figure 11-15, PayPal gives an example of the required text that is appropriate for the Auto Return page. For FitnessTrackerPlus, you will use similar wording on the `SignupComplete` page.

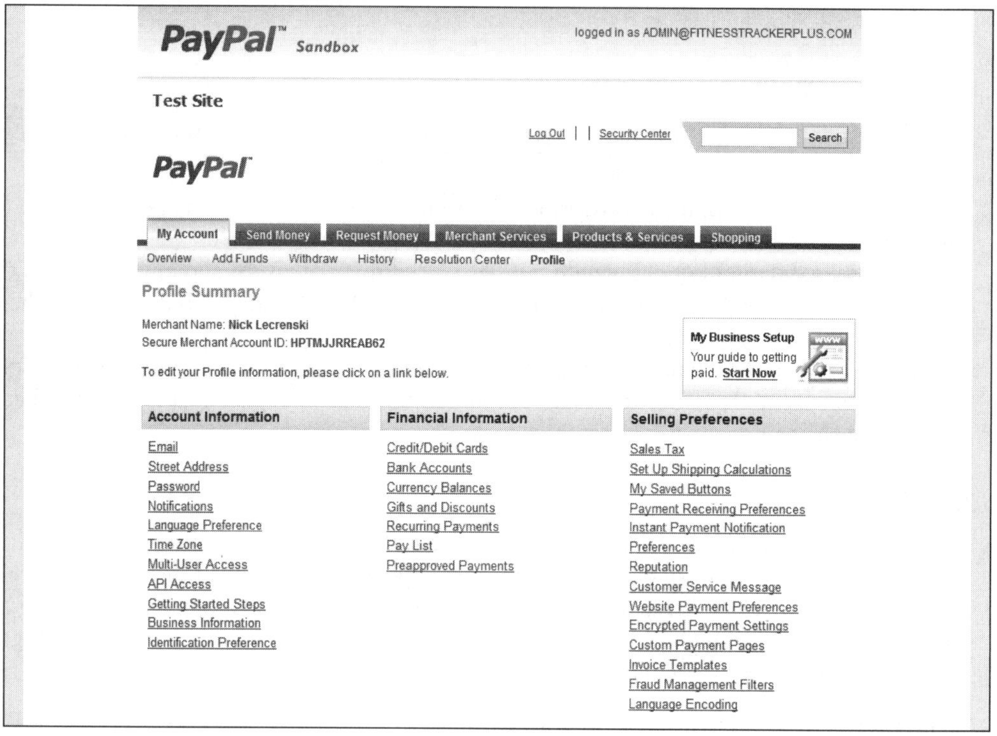

FIGURE 11-14

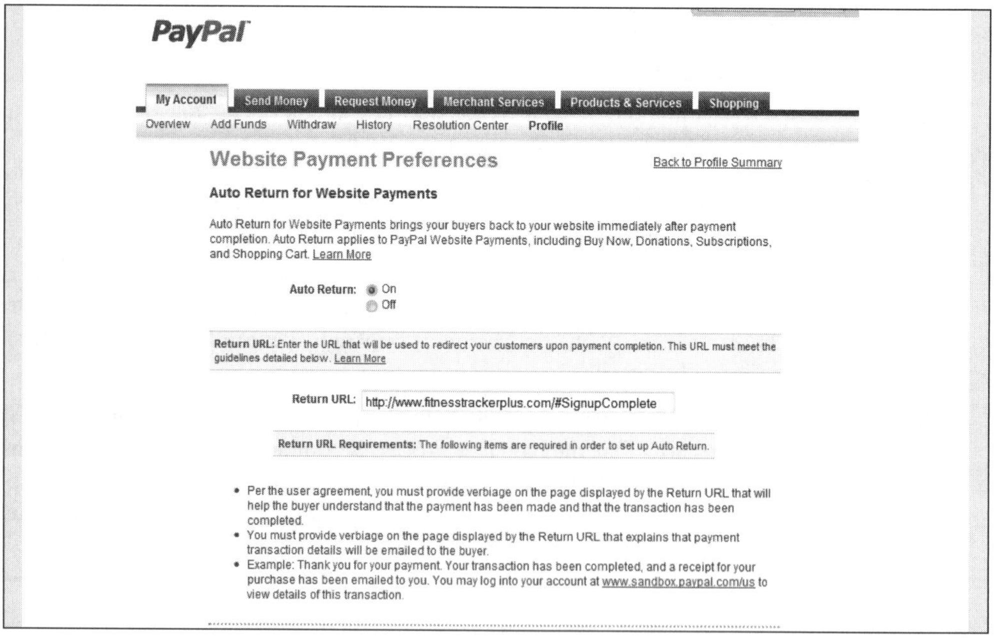

FIGURE 11-15

Payment Data Transfer

At this point, you have PayPal configured to return the user to a custom return page so you'll know when the payment process is completed. You should be able to create the user account when this page is accessed, but there is just one small problem. You no longer have access to any of the user registration field values from the signup page. How are you supposed to create a new account without any of that information? Well, when PayPal redirects users back to the Auto Return page, it does so with a query string that includes all the transaction details. This feature is called Payment Data Transfer and can easily be enabled on the same Website Payment Preferences page. Figure 11-16 shows this option has been enabled for the Sandbox seller account.

Payment Data Transfer (optional)
Payment Data Transfer allows you to receive notification of successful payments as they are made. The use of Payment Data Transfer depends on your system configuration and your Return URL. Please note that in order to use Payment Data Transfer, you must turn on Auto Return.
Payment Data Transfer: On
Off
Identity Token: z7dJ4C-rCbvWQ9cJnjFCqGMmJ9nkclwWpHS3tgD_FgNTXR41uWLikF0Ds6S

FIGURE 11-16

Included in these transaction details are any values that were placed in the hidden `<input>` tag named `custom` on the original payment button. This means that if you can inject the values of the user registration fields into the `<input>` tag before the form is submitted, these same values will be accessible from the query string on the `SignupComplete` page. To access the `<input>` tag, you add an `id` property. The following code shows the updated PayPal payment button code with the custom `<input>` tag modified to include an `id` property of `custom_paypal_field`.

Available for download on Wrox.com

```
<div id="paypal_area" style="position:absolute;top:0px;left:0px;display:none">
     <form name="paypal_form"
action="https://www.sandbox.paypal.com/cgi-bin/webscr" method="post">
          <input type="hidden" name="cmd" value="_s-xclick" />
          <input type="hidden" name="hosted_button_id"
value="YOUR BUTTON ID GOES HERE"/>
          <input id="custom_paypal_field" type='hidden' name='custom' value="" />
          <input onclick="return validateSignup();" type="image"
src="https://www.sandbox.paypal.com/en_US/i/btn/btn_subscribeCC_LG.gif" border="0"
name="submit" alt="PayPal - The safer, easier way to pay online!" />
          <img alt="" border="0"
src="https://www.sandbox.paypal.com/en_US/i/scr/pixel.gif" width="1" height="1" />
     </form>
</div>
```

Code snippet FitnessTrackerPlus.aspx located in the FitnessTrackerPlus_PayPal project

To make sure that you receive the user registration values, you need to make sure they are injected into this hidden `<input>` tag. Because the `ValidateForm` method is called when the button is clicked, this makes for a great place to modify the value of the `<input>` tag. The following code shows the updated version of the `ValidateForm` method modified to inject a comma-delimited string of user registration values into the `custom_paypal_field` tag.

Available for download on Wrox.com

```
[ScriptableMember]
public bool ValidateForm()
{
     if (UserRegistration.ValidateItem())
     {
          HtmlElement custom_input =
HtmlPage.Document.GetElementById("custom_paypal_field");
custom_input.SetProperty("value", String.Format("{0},{1},{2},{3}",
newUser.email_address, newUser.password, newUser.security_question,
newUser.security_answer));

          return true;
     }
     else
     {
          MessageBox.Show("Please ensure that you have filled
out all of the required fields correctly",
"FitnessTrackerPlus Signup", MessageBoxButton.OK);

          return false;
     }
}
```

Code snippet Signup.xaml.cs located in the FitnessTrackerPlus_PayPal project

After making this change, all the user registration variables are now accessible from the query string when the user is redirected to the `SignupComplete` page. Speaking of which — now would be a good time to create this page. You can go ahead and add a new `Page` to the Views folder called `SignupComplete`. As discussed previously, the only requirement for this page is that you let the user know that the payment has been completed and details of the payment will be e-mailed to his or her account. Unfortunately, because of this requirement you will not be able to just automatically log the user in and take her to the dashboard page as you had been doing. The user needs to be able to read the required information before moving on. What you can do, however, is present users with a login button that takes them to the dashboard. You won't need for them to enter their e-mail address and password information again because that information can be easily extracted from the query string. Listing 11-2 shows the XAML code for the `SignupComplete` page.

LISTING 11-2: SignupComplete.xaml

Available for download on Wrox.com

```
<navigation:Page x:Class="FitnessTrackerPlus.Views.SignupComplete"
     xmlns="http://schemas.microsoft.com/winfx/2006/xaml/presentation"
     xmlns:x="http://schemas.microsoft.com/winfx/2006/xaml"
     xmlns:mc="http://schemas.openxmlformats.org/markup-compatibility/2006"
```

```
    xmlns:navigation="clr-
namespace:System.Windows.Controls;assembly=System.Windows.Controls.Navigation">
    <navigation:Page.Resources>
        <Style x:Key="RegistrationCompleteStyle" TargetType="TextBlock">
            <Setter Property="FontSize" Value="16" />
            <Setter Property="Margin" Value="0,0,0,5" />
            <Setter Property="TextAlignment" Value="Center" />
            <Setter Property="Visibility" Value="Collapsed"  />
        </Style>
        <Style x:Key="LoginButtonStyle" TargetType="Button">
            <Setter Property="Margin" Value="0,0,0,5" />
            <Setter Property="Visibility" Value="Collapsed"  />
        </Style>
    </navigation:Page.Resources>
    <StackPanel>
        <TextBlock Text="Congratulations you have successfully joined
FitnessTrackerPlus, please click the Login button below to proceed to your
journal" Style="{StaticResource RegistrationCompleteStyle}" />
        <TextBlock Text="Your payment has been processed and details
will be sent to your email account shortly" Style="{StaticResource
RegistrationCompleteStyle}" />
        <Button x:Name="Login" Content="Login Now" Style="{StaticResource
LoginButtonStyle}" />
        <TextBlock x:Name="FailureText" Text="An error occurred while
creating your account, please contact support for further help."
Style="{StaticResource RegistrationCompleteStyle}" />
    </StackPanel>
</navigation:Page>
```

You may have noticed in Listing 11-2 that both the `Login` button and the `FailureText TextBlock` controls have their `Visibility` property set to `Collapsed`. You only want the `Login` button to be visible if the account creation operation completes without error; otherwise, you need to let the user know that the account has not been created so the `FailureText` will be made visible instead. Either way, you still need to display the text required by PayPal.

In the code behind for this page, before you create a new user account using the information in the query string, you need to take a step back and ask yourself the following questions. How do I know that this page request and the accompanying query string information actually came from PayPal? And how do I know it came as a result of the user filling out the user registration form? You can't just trust that this is the case because nothing prevents hackers from discovering the URL to the `SignupPage` and potentially creating new accounts using query string variables. As part of the Payment Data Transfer mechanism, PayPal also requires you to validate the information it includes in the query string. This involves posting the transaction ID and an additional field called an identity token back to PayPal so it can check to see if it is a valid transaction. The transaction ID is available as one of the query string parameters, but the identity token is actually a hardcoded value that PayPal generates for you when you enable the Payment Data Transfer feature, as shown previously in Figure 11-16.

You need to copy this value and store it as a private variable in the `SignupComplete` page, as shown in the following code. Remember that your identity token will be different from the sample code so you should always replace the PayPal values in the sample code with ones that you generate.

Available for download on Wrox.com

```
private readonly string identityToken =
"z7dJ4C-rCbvWQ9cJnjFCqGMmJ9nkclwWpHS3tgD_FgNTXR41uWLikF0Ds6S";
```

Code snippet SignupComplete.xaml.cs located in the FitnessTrackerPlus_PayPal project

Validating the transaction with PayPal involves a simple HTTP POST operation, but even though it might be tempting to just do this from the Silverlight client it won't work. In fact, any attempt to do so will just result in a `SecurityException`. This is due to the fact that PayPal does not implement a cross-domain policy file, and Silverlight clients can only make calls outside of the main domain if such a policy exists on the destination server. This doesn't mean that the validation can't be done; it just means that you need to make the POST call from a web service hosted at FitnessTrackerPlus.com. In this case, because this operation is related to creating a new user account, you can just add a new method marked with the `[Invoke]` attribute in the `UserInformationService` class. Let's call this method `ValidatePayPal`, and the implementation of this method will simply make use of the `HttpWebRequest` object to post the required validation string to PayPal. PayPal validates the request by checking the string that is posted and if a valid transaction ID and identity token are specified, PayPal sends back a "SUCCESS" message. The following code shows the `ValidatePayPal` method, which has been added to the `UserInformationService` class.

Available for download on Wrox.com

```
[Invoke]
public bool ValidatePayPal(string validationString)
{
     HttpWebRequest request = HttpWebRequest.Create(validationString) as
HttpWebRequest;
     HttpWebResponse response = request.GetResponse() as HttpWebResponse;

     if (response.StatusCode == HttpStatusCode.OK)
     {
          Stream stream = response.GetResponseStream();

          StreamReader reader = new StreamReader(stream,
Encoding.GetEncoding("UTF-8"));
          string result = reader.ReadLine();

          if (result == "SUCCESS")
               return true;
     }

     return false;
}
```

Code snippet UserInformationService.cs located in the FitnessTrackerPlus_PayPal project

The implementation is pretty straightforward and easy to do from the ASP.NET backend. After posting the string, you only need to read the first line of the response. If the message "SUCCESS" is found, then you can be assured that the request is legit and the transaction information is valid.

The only thing left now is to actually parse the query string and validate the request using the transaction ID and identity token. You should do this in the `OnNavigatedTo` event handler of the

`SignupComplete` page. In the following code, the transaction IDs as well as all the user account details are extracted from the query string, and the `ValidatePayPal` method is called using the appropriate information. If the request is successfully validated, the user account is created. When the account creation step is complete, the `CreateUserCallback` method is called and as long as no errors occurred during this step the Log in button is displayed; otherwise, the failure message is made visible.

Available for download on Wrox.com

```
private UserInformationContext context = new UserInformationContext();
private UserInformation newUser = new UserInformation();
private readonly string identityToken = "YOUR IDENTITY TOKEN GOES HERE";

protected override void OnNavigatedTo(NavigationEventArgs e)
{
     if (NavigationContext.QueryString.Count > 0)
     {
          // Custom user registration fields are in the cm query string variable

          string userData = NavigationContext.QueryString["cm"];
          string[] values = userData.Split(',');

          // Save the user information values

          newUser.email_address = values[0];
          newUser.password = values[1];
          newUser.security_question = values[2];
          newUser.security_answer = values[3];

          // Validate that the request came from PayPal and is valid
          // Transaction id is in the tx query string variable

          string validatePayPal =
String.Format("https://www.sandbox.paypal.com/cgi-bin/webscr?tx={0}&
at={1}&cmd=_notify-synch", NavigationContext.QueryString["tx"], identityToken);

          context.ValidatePayPal(validatePayPal, (ValidateComplete) =>
          {
               if (!ValidateComplete.HasError)
               {
                    if (ValidateComplete.Value)
                    {
                         context.CreateUser(newUser.email_address,
newUser.password, newUser.email_address, newUser.security_question,
newUser.security_answer, CreateUserCallback, newUser);
                    }
                    else
                    {
                         FailureText.Visibility = Visibility.Visible;
                         Login.Visibility = Visibility.Collapsed;
                    }
               }
               else
               {
                    FailureText.Visibility = Visibility.Visible;
                    Login.Visibility = Visibility.Collapsed;
```

```
                }

            }, null);
        }
    }

    private void CreateUserCallback(InvokeOperation<UserInformation> result)
    {
        if (!result.HasError)
        {
            FailureText.Visibility = Visibility.Collapsed;
            Login.Visibility = Visibility.Visible;
        }
        else
        {
            FailureText.Visibility = Visibility.Visible;
            Login.Visibility = Visibility.Collapsed;
        }
    }
```

Code snippet SignupComplete.xaml.cs located in the FitnessTrackerPlus_PayPal project

The final step required in this process is to handle the Login `Click` event and automatically log the user into the site. Remember earlier on you made modifications to the `MainPage` code behind to listen for a `SignupComplete` event. You now need to move the `SignupComplete` event code from the original Signup page into the `SignupComplete` page. After doing this, you will need to fire the event when the Log in button is clicked. In the following code, this is handled in the `Loaded` event of the `SignupComplete` class.

Available for download on Wrox.com

```
    public SignupComplete()
    {
        InitializeComponent();

        Loaded += (s, e) =>
        {
            Login.Click += (se, ev) =>
            {
                if (SignupCompleted != null)
                    SignupCompleted(this, new SignupEventArgs(newUser));
            };
        };
    }
```

Code snippet SignupComplete.xaml.cs located in the FitnessTrackerPlus_PayPal project

Finally, you need to modify the `MainSiteFrame_Navigated` event handler to cast the `NavigationEventArgs` variable to an instance of the `SignupComplete` class as opposed to the `Signup` page class. The following code shows this final modification.

Available for download on Wrox.com

```
    private void MainSiteFrame_Navigated(object sender, NavigationEventArgs e)
    {
        if (e.Uri.OriginalString.Contains("SignupComplete"))
        {
            FitnessTrackerPlus.Views.SignupComplete signupComplete = e.Content as
```

```
FitnessTrackerPlus.Views.SignupComplete;

            signupComplete.SignupCompleted += (s, ev) =>
            {
                WebContext.Current.Authentication.Login(new
LoginParameters(ev.NewUser.email_address, ev.NewUser.password),
                    (LoginCompleteCallback) =>
                    {
                        GetUserInformation();

                    }, null);
            };
        }
}
```

Code snippet MainPage.xaml.cs located in the FitnessTrackerPlus_PayPal project

Once you have put all this together, you should be able to run the application and create a new user using the PayPal Sandbox accounts. To really test this, you have to deploy the solution to a live server because the PayPal Auto Return and Payment Data Transfer features will not work against the local Visual Studio web server. Although coverage of the FitnessTrackerPlus deployment is reserved for the next chapter, let's pretend you have already deployed it and walk through the user registration process.

1. Navigate to the new Signup page displayed in Figure 11-17. Notice the new PayPal subscription button is being displayed.
2. Test the validation by skipping a couple of the required fields and clicking the Subscribe button. Instead of being redirected to the PayPal payment page, the submission is cancelled and you are instead left with validation errors like the ones shown in Figure 11-18.

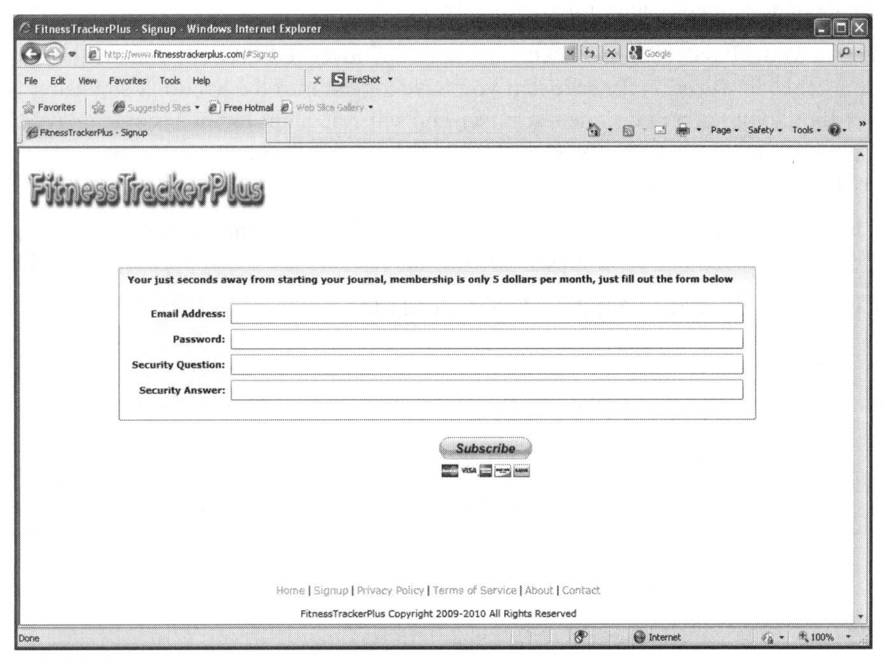

FIGURE 11-17

FIGURE 11-18

3. Enter information into all required fields and click the PayPal button. You are redirected to the PayPal payment page shown in Figure 11-19.

4. Log in to the PayPal Sandbox account using the buyer test account you created earlier. Before doing this, however, make sure that you have logged into the Sandbox site using your main Sandbox login; otherwise, the test buyer and seller account logins become unavailable. These logins are only active when you have already logged into the Sandbox site using your main credentials. You are then presented with the payment review page shown in Figure 11-20.

5. Click the Pay button. You are then redirected back to the FitnessTrackerPlus `SignupComplete` page and presented with the `SignupComplete` page shown in Figure 11-21.

6. Click the Login button. You're taken to the dashboard page.

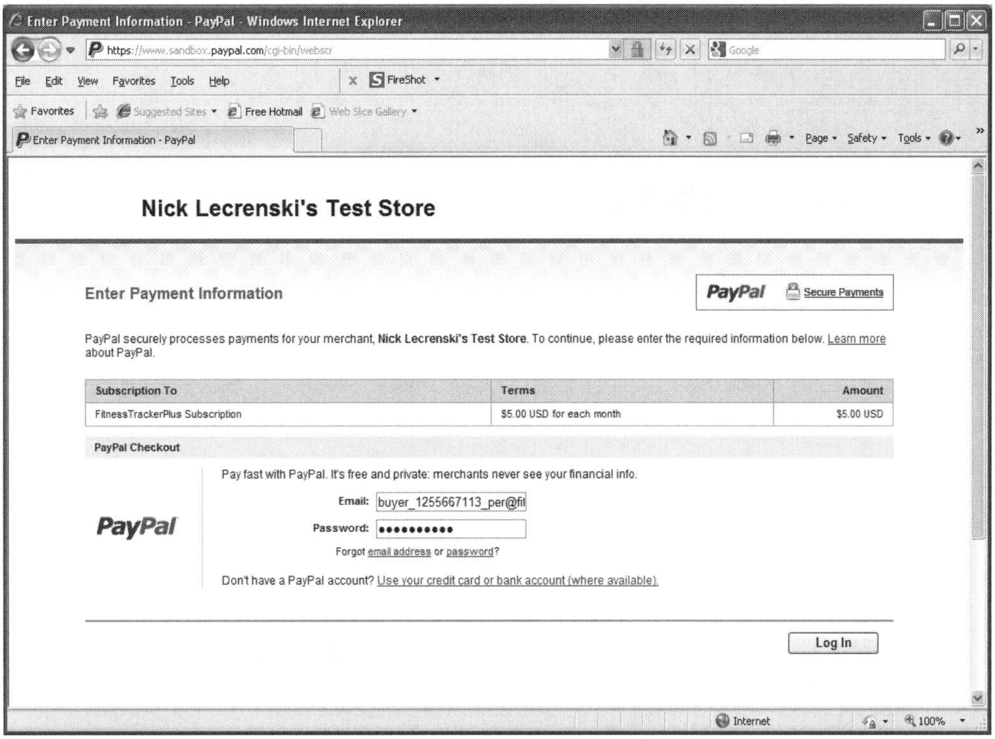

Enter Payment Information - PayPal - Windows Internet Explorer

https://www.sandbox.paypal.com/cgi-bin/webscr

File Edit View Favorites Tools Help

FireShot

Favorites | Suggested Sites | Free Hotmail | Web Slice Gallery

Enter Payment Information - PayPal

Page | Safety | Tools

Nick Lecrenski's Test Store

Enter Payment Information

PayPal Secure Payments

PayPal securely processes payments for your merchant, **Nick Lecrenski's Test Store**. To continue, please enter the required information below. Learn more about PayPal.

Subscription To	Terms	Amount
FitnessTrackerPlus Subscription	$5.00 USD for each month	$5.00 USD

PayPal Checkout

PayPal

Pay fast with PayPal. It's free and private: merchants never see your financial info.

Email: buyer_1255667113_per@fit

Password: ●●●●●●●●●●

Forgot email address or password?

Don't have a PayPal account? Use your credit card or bank account (where available).

Log In

Internet | 100%

FIGURE 11-19

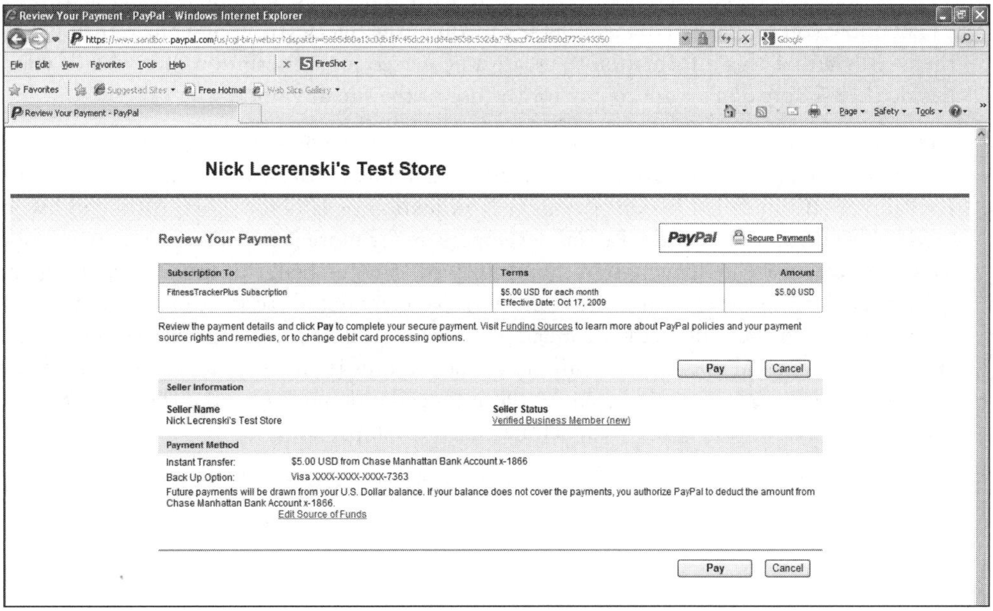

Review Your Payment - PayPal - Windows Internet Explorer

https://www.sandbox.paypal.com/us/cgi-bin/webscr?dispatch=...

File Edit View Favorites Tools Help

FireShot

Favorites | Suggested Sites | Free Hotmail | Web Slice Gallery

Review Your Payment - PayPal

Page | Safety | Tools

Nick Lecrenski's Test Store

Review Your Payment

PayPal Secure Payments

Subscription To	Terms	Amount
FitnessTrackerPlus Subscription	$5.00 USD for each month Effective Date: Oct 17, 2009	$5.00 USD

Review the payment details and click **Pay** to complete your secure payment. Visit Funding Sources to learn more about PayPal policies and your payment source rights and remedies, or to change debit card processing options.

Pay | Cancel

Seller Information

Seller Name
Nick Lecrenski's Test Store

Seller Status
Verified Business Member (new)

Payment Method

Instant Transfer: $5.00 USD from Chase Manhattan Bank Account x-1866

Back Up Option: Visa XXXX-XXXX-XXXX-7363

Future payments will be drawn from your U.S. Dollar balance. If your balance does not cover the payments, you authorize PayPal to deduct the amount from Chase Manhattan Bank Account x-1866.

Edit Source of Funds

Pay | Cancel

FIGURE 11-20

FIGURE 11-21

Canceling Subscriptions

The previous section covered both the Auto Return and Payment Data Transfer features of PayPal. These allow you to collect payment details through the query string on your return page. You can then easily utilize this information to create a new account subscription. But what if your users decide they simply don't want to pay for the use of the site anymore?

PayPal does provide subscription cancellation notifications; however, these notifications are not available through Auto Return and Payment Data Transfer. Instead, you must make use of another PayPal mechanism called *Instant Payment Notification* or *IPN* for short. Although I won't be covering IPN here, you can visit the PayPal developer site for more information on how it works as well as how to create an implementation that utilizes it. In a nutshell, this involves creating another ASP.NET page that PayPal can call at anytime with payment details or cancellation notices. The code is very similar to the code in the `SignupComplete` page, and you still have to send a validation string back to PayPal to check the validity of the request. If you were to handle cancellations for FitnessTrackerPlus, you would listen for these cancellation messages and then simply make the user account inactive whenever users cancel their memberships.

SUMMARY

This chapter has provided you with a couple of potential revenue-generating solutions for not only FitnessTrackerPlus but hopefully your own Silverlight applications. You have seen how easy it can be to take advantage of a pay-per-click advertising solution such as Google AdSense in order to quickly and easily generate revenue. Alternatively, you have seen how to integrate with PayPal in order to charge users a recurring monthly subscription fee. You may very well decide in your own applications that a hybrid of these two systems is the best way to go. You could potentially offer a free version of the site that is supported by pay-per-click advertisements as well as a premium version with additional features and enhancements that require users to pay a monthly premium membership fee. Either way, I think you will find that just because you are developing a Silverlight application, it is not terribly difficult to incorporate either Google AdSense or PayPal subscriptions into your solution.

At this point in the book, you have a fully functioning fitness tracking application, a public journal feature that helps your users share their progress, social networking integration with MySpace, and a couple of potential revenue-generating solutions using Google AdSense and PayPal recurring subscriptions. All that is left is some cleanup work and to find a place to host this thing. The final chapter focuses on tidying up the application for the real world, choosing a hosting provider, and deploying the finished application to the web.

12

Let's Go Live

Finishing and Deploying FitnessTrackerPlus

In this final chapter, you will see that although the application has been fully developed there is still some work left to do before declaring to the world that FitnessTrackerPlus is available and ready to go. This chapter begins with finalizing the application by adding content to the supplemental pages. Next you will see the importance of creating terms of service and privacy policy pages before you actually deploy the site. Finally, I will cover in detail how to build and deploy the site to the popular shared hosting provider Discount ASP.NET. It's been a long journey to get to this point and as tempting as it may be to just upload the site as is and start signing up users, you really need to take a small step back and tie up all the loose ends and get any potential legal issues out of the way before opening up the site to the rest of the world.

PROBLEM

You've completed all the required features for the site. You have working food, exercise, and measurement log pages. You have a public journal feature that allows users to share their success with others. You have successfully integrated with the popular social networking site MySpace, and you have even come up with a pretty good scheme to generate revenue once your site becomes popular. What else could possibly hold up the public launch of FitnessTrackerPlus? Well for starters you still have a bunch of empty supplemental pages. Way back when the project was started, you created some basic placeholder controls for things such as Contact, Terms of Service, Privacy Policy, and About pages. Now it's time to really take a look at adding some content and functionality to these pages so that the site looks polished, professional, and most important, completed.

In a perfect world, people would sign up for a FitnessTrackerPlus account and make use of the site without ever having problems. In the real world, that simply will never happen and you are going to need to provide a means for users to send you feedback. Every major site has a contact page that enables users to quickly send any questions or concerns to the site administrator, which of course in this case is you. A working contact page will be one major requirement for the site before any deployment begins.

Another commonly overlooked problem that you will need to solve as a developer, unfortunately, is never very exciting—legality. In the early days of the Web, it was common for developers to launch websites for others to enjoy without worrying about any legal repercussions. There was no real worry about getting sued because a site did not work correctly, or someone was offended by a comment on your message board. Now, however, there is simply no chance that you can put a website out there without the minimum protection of a terms of service agreement and privacy policy. As developers, this is something that is easily overlooked because there is no real coding and the legal writing involved is usually out of the realm of our expertise. Because you will be charging real money for premium features of the site, it is essential to have terms of service that define what users can expect for the money they are spending. Although you won't be storing any sensitive information about users in the database it's still necessary to have a privacy policy that lets the users know exactly what information is being collected and how it's used to enhance their experience with the site. Again, one of the biggest problems with site legality is that you most likely aren't moonlighting as a lawyer so you probably can't just write something up quickly yourself and expect to be protected.

After you have solved all these outstanding problems, you still have to figure out how to deploy all the application pieces and make them available to the public. For most new sites, it's more than sufficient to make use of a shared hosting provider. As I said way back in Chapter 2, once you start to have millions of users and find yourself needing complete control over the various server settings, you'll then need to look at a dedicated hosting solution, but for now a shared hosting provider is more than adequate. Once you pick a hosting provider, you then need to perform all the necessary steps to upload and configure the Silverlight application as well as the ASP.NET application containing the main FitnessTrackerPlus home page and the WCF RIA Services that have been created. As you can see, there is still quite a bit of work left to do so let's get started.

DESIGN

In this section, you'll look at what steps are required to complete all the supplemental pages for the site. This involves creating a working Contact page, Terms of Service, Privacy Policy, and About page. Once these steps are complete, you can move on to picking a shared hosting provider for the site.

Supplemental Pages

When you first started working on FitnessTrackerPlus, you created several placeholder Page controls that you would design and implement later on. These include the About, Contact, Terms of Service, and Privacy Policy pages. Before deploying FitnessTrackerPlus, you must make sure that users can send you feedback through the contact page, and that the other pages have been completed with the necessary content.

About FitnessTrackerPlus

Most websites now have some kind of About page that covers the origins of the site, including some basic biographical information about the site's owner and founder. Even though the main page has a few bullet points about the main features, most visitors will want to know a little bit more about the site such as:

- Who is running it?
- Why was it developed?
- What is the company behind the site?

Because this is just a sample site, you don't really have much of a company history to talk about. You can, however, provide visitors of this page with a clear mission statement that leaves them with a feeling that you genuinely care about the site and about helping site users achieve their fitness goals. A good mission statement for FitnessTrackerPlus could be the following:

> FitnessTrackerPlus strives to provide the most powerful fitness tracking capabilities on the Web. It is our goal to provide quick and easy tracking of foods, exercises, and measurements as well as to enable you to easily share your success with others.

As the site grows in popularity, this page will most likely start to include things such as customer testimonials, as well as the history of FitnessTrackerPlus. You could even take a look at how other sites use this page to get some ideas. For example, many sites use this page to provide a blog that tells visitors and users what is going on with the site, as well as what features may be in development for future use. No matter what you ultimately decide for this page, you should consider it to be an important piece of any public facing site.

Contact

There are many things that can happen when you open up your site to the rest of the world—some positive, some negative. If your site is running great and users are experiencing fast response times, then most likely you will hear nothing from your users. If, however, the site response gets slow, or users are starting to see cryptic error messages instead of normal page content, you can safely expect to hear from almost every last one of them. It takes a lot of hard work and time to successfully grow a large community of users, and you don't want to lose any of them due to technical issues with the site. You never want things to go wrong with a web application but sometimes they do.

As an owner of a website, it is never easy to hear negative feedback from your users. After all, you put a lot of blood, sweat, and tears into your site and you probably would like to think it is perfect. The truth of the matter is that negative users are really your best friend. If something is wrong with the site that has annoyed a user to such a degree that she has taken time out of a busy day to let you know about the problem, chances are there may be others who are having the very same problem and are just not telling you about it. Unless you have a 24/7 support staff, or you are really into using your own site, you have no way of knowing when things are going wrong except for when users complain directly to you, the site administrator.

Right now, there is no real way for users to give you any kind of feedback—be it positive or negative—and you will need to change that. When you first started creating the site, you added a placeholder for the Contact page, and now you will need to flesh out some requirements for that page so that users can send you feedback. The first and most important requirement is the need for a `TextBox` control where users can type in a message. As the site gets more popular and you are able to bring on support staff you may even want to filter the messages based on an appropriate topic. One way to do this is to add a `ComboBox` control to the page with a list of topics such as the following:

- Technical problems
- Abuse/complaints
- General feedback
- Sales and marketing

One additional thing to consider when providing a means for your users to contact you is the ability to distinguish between real users and automated form submission bots. Several different methods for solving this issue have been developed over the years. Perhaps the most popular solution and one that you have no doubt encountered while visiting sites is the use of a CAPTCHA image. CAPTCHA solutions involve creating an image dynamically on the page, usually a set of numbers or a common phrase, and forcing real users to type the numbers or phrase into a `TextBox` control before submitting the message. The server code will then compare the user-entered phrase with the one that was generated, and if they match, then the message is sent to the appropriate place. If there is not a match then an error message is displayed on the page telling the user, or in this case most likely an automated bot, that the phrase did not match and that the user will need to try again. Automated bots have a difficult time circumventing a system like this, and it can really cut down on the amount of spam e-mails that reach you as the administrator. CAPTCHA isn't fool-proof. However, it does provide a decent solution for cutting down spam while still providing your real users with a way to contact you about issues or concerns. Because this seems like a sufficient way to cut down on the number of spam e-mails that are sent from the site, you should also include a Silverlight-based implementation of the CAPTCHA system for the FitnessTrackerPlus contact page.

Password Reset

After initially registering for the site, users will most likely visit the site on a daily basis to at least enter their foods and exercises. It is entirely possible, however, that at some point the user decides to take an extended hiatus from his diet and exercise routine. When he does decide to come back to the site, he may very well have forgotten his password information. FitnessTrackerPlus needs to provide some easy means of resetting a forgotten password. There are several ways to provide this kind of functionality on the site. Many sites allow you to recover a lost or forgotten password by simply e-mailing you the password information after you have successfully answered your security question. This will not work for FitnessTrackerPlus, however, because the passwords are not stored in the database using a bi-directional encryption system. Remember back in the third chapter during the user registration discussion, the decision was made to make use of a one-way SHA-1 hash value for passwords. This means that you have no way to actually recover the original password value. The alternative solution and the one you'll use for FitnessTrackerPlus is to auto-generate a new password of random characters and send that to a user's primary e-mail account after she has successfully answered her security question.

To provide this feature, you make a small modification to the main FitnessTrackerPlus home page, and you also need to add an additional page to the project that presents the user with her security question. The first modification required is to add a `HyperlinkButton` control with the text "Forgot Password" as part of the existing login control. When this link is clicked, users are taken to a new page that asks for the e-mail address submitted during registration. Once the user enters a valid e-mail address, the security question created during registration displays and the user must successfully answer the question in order to proceed. If the user is able to answer the question, a message displays telling the user that a new password has been generated and is being sent to the e-mail address that the user has provided. Once the user enters this new password, he can log in to the site and change it to something easier to remember in the account settings page.

Privacy Policy

I already discussed in Chapter 3 how vital it is to gain the trust of your users by not collecting more than the minimum amount of personal information you need for users to work with the site. By making use of the site features, users are agreeing to both a terms of service agreement and a privacy policy. The privacy policy will need to outline exactly how you utilize the information you are collecting from the user. It is important to also inform the user that you are collecting the IP address when they visit your site and that this IP address can potentially be used to locate the computer of origin that is accessing the site.

Unless you happen to be lucky enough to have finished law school while learning how to program, it is usually a good idea to use existing resources when you draw up a useful privacy policy. Millions of these policies are on the Internet today so rather than try and do this on your own, you should either hire a professional or look into downloading a privacy policy from a legal website such as `http://www.allbusiness.com` or `http://www.freeprivacypolicy.com`. These sites provide you with a template that you can easily customize to reflect your own site. For any site you create that you have plans to turn into a revenue-generating business, it is always best to consult a lawyer just to ensure that everything that is legally required in a privacy policy is included and worded correctly in your own policy.

Terms of Service

Now that you have outlined for users how their information will be collected and stored in the form of a privacy policy, you need to let users know the rules of your site. No website is complete without both the privacy policy and terms of service document. There is simply no chance that you can put a website out there without the protection of a terms of service agreement.

Your site will include social networking features and you should define rules for those features because you cannot be expected to police your site 24 hours a day, 7 days a week. Therefore, at a minimum, the terms of service agreement should outline what is considered acceptable behavior when a user logs in to the site. Be sure to let users know that breaking the terms could result in the loss of their account. There are many other legal areas of the terms of service that are standard across all websites, and the template sites mentioned in the previous section provide a great starting point in developing your own document. Again, as is the case with the privacy policy, there is no substitute for hiring a lawyer to review your terms of service in order to get the maximum legal protection for your site.

Shared Hosting Providers

When you have completed all of the necessary work required to implement the supplemental pages, you will finally be in a position to deploy the site to the Web and start registering new users. When looking for potential hosting providers for FitnessTrackerPlus, you will no doubt find many viable options. However, you should remember that whatever your choice, it must satisfy your site requirements. In this case, you need a hosting provider that supports ASP.NET, Silverlight 4, WCF RIA Services, and of course SQL Server 2008. I don't think I need to mention that the hosting provider also needs to be running a recent version of IIS as well.

Although there are many possible choices for hosting providers, the one that stands out, at least in my personal experience, is Discount ASP.NET. I have been using Discount ASP.NET for several years to host my own ASP.NET and Silverlight solutions and have had nothing but a positive experience. For FitnessTrackerPlus, the decision to use Discount ASP.NET was an easy one, not only because of my personal experience with it, but also because Discount ASP.NET has a habit of always supporting the latest and greatest .NET technology on their servers. You won't always find hosting providers that are willing to install beta technology on their shared servers, but more often than not you will be able to run just about any new Microsoft-based technology on Discount ASP.NET provided there is at least a Go-Live license available. Personal experience aside, Discount ASP.NET is one of the few hosting providers that currently supports all the FitnessTrackerPlus requirements such as Silverlight 4, SQL 2008, and WCF RIA Services. I understand that in many cases these requirements do not involve a specific installation to be performed on a server but some hosting providers will actually prevent you from using these technologies until the absolute final releases are available.

As you will see, Discount ASP.NET provides many tools that come in handy not only during the deployment of the FitnessTrackerPlus application but also when you're performing any ongoing site maintenance. It is also one of the few hosting providers that offer a full developer API. The API provides programmatic access to many of the tools, settings, and utilities available from the main Control Panel page.

SOLUTION

This section covers the implementation of the contact page. After this is complete, you will see how to implement a simple password reset system that helps users who may have forgotten the password that they created during the initial registration process. Finally, you will see step by step how to build a release version of the application and deploy it to a Microsoft-certified shared hosting provider, making it available to everyone on the Web.

Creating the Contact Page

The first step in creating the contact page is to implement a user interface that contains a `ComboBox` with a list of reasons for contact, a `TextBox` to hold the name of the person leaving the message, another `TextBox` to hold the message, and finally a CAPTCHA image and `TextBox` control that will cut the amount of generated automated spam entries. In Listing 12-1, an Image control named `Captcha` acts as a placeholder for the dynamically generated CAPTCHA image.

Available for download on Wrox.com

LISTING 12-1: Contact.xaml

```
<navigation:Page x:Class="FitnessTrackerPlus.Views.Contact"
     xmlns="http://schemas.microsoft.com/winfx/2006/xaml/presentation"
     xmlns:x="http://schemas.microsoft.com/winfx/2006/xaml"
     xmlns:navigation="clr-
namespace:System.Windows.Controls;assembly=System.Windows.Controls.Navigation"
     Title="FitnessTrackerPlus - Contact">
     <navigation:Page.Resources>
          <Style x:Key="BorderStyle" TargetType="Border">
               <Setter Property="BorderBrush" Value="#FF000000" />
               <Setter Property="BorderThickness" Value="3" />
               <Setter Property="Width" Value="600" />
          </Style>
          <Style x:Key="MainStackPanelStyle" TargetType="StackPanel">
               <Setter Property="HorizontalAlignment" Value="Center" />
          </Style>
          <Style x:Key="ReasonStackPanelStyle" TargetType="StackPanel">
               <Setter Property="Orientation" Value="Horizontal" />
          </Style>
          <Style x:Key="ReasonsStyle" TargetType="ComboBox">
               <Setter Property="Margin" Value="10,0,0,0" />
          </Style>
          <Style x:Key="MessageStackPanelStyle" TargetType="StackPanel">
               <Setter Property="Orientation" Value="Horizontal" />
               <Setter Property="Margin" Value="0,20,0,0" />
          </Style>
          <Style x:Key="NameTextBoxStyle" TargetType="TextBox">
               <Setter Property="Width" Value="200" />
               <Setter Property="Height" Value="25" />
               <Setter Property="Margin" Value="10,0,0,0" />
          </Style>
          <Style x:Key="MessageTextBoxStyle" TargetType="TextBox">
               <Setter Property="AcceptsReturn" Value="True" />
               <Setter Property="Width" Value="400" />
               <Setter Property="Height" Value="200" />
               <Setter Property="Margin" Value="10,0,0,0" />
          </Style>
          <Style x:Key="SubmissionTextStyle" TargetType="TextBlock">
               <Setter Property="Margin" Value="0,20,0,0" />
          </Style>
          <Style x:Key="SubmissionStackPanelStyle" TargetType="StackPanel">
               <Setter Property="Orientation" Value="Horizontal" />
               <Setter Property="HorizontalAlignment" Value="Center" />
               <Setter Property="Margin" Value="0,10,0,0" />
          </Style>
          <Style x:Key="CaptchaTextBoxStyle" TargetType="TextBox">
               <Setter Property="Margin" Value="10,0,0,0" />
               <Setter Property="Width" Value="100" />
               <Setter Property="Height" Value="25" />
               <Setter Property="HorizontalContentAlignment" Value="Center" />
          </Style>
          <Style x:Key="SubmitButtonStyle" TargetType="Button">
               <Setter Property="HorizontalAlignment" Value="Center" />
```

continues

LISTING 12-1 *(continued)*

```
                <Setter Property="Margin" Value="0,10,0,20" />
                <Setter Property="Content" Value="Submit Message" />
            </Style>
        </navigation:Page.Resources>
        <Border Style="{StaticResource BorderStyle}">
            <StackPanel Style="{StaticResource MainStackPanelStyle}">
                <StackPanel Style="{StaticResource ReasonStackPanelStyle}">
                    <TextBlock Text="Please select the reason for contacting us" />
                    <ComboBox x:Name="Reasons" Style="{StaticResource ReasonsStyle}">
                        <ComboBox.Items>
                            <ComboBoxItem Content="General Feedback"
Tag="0" IsSelected="True" />
                            <ComboBoxItem Content="Technical Problems" Tag="1" />
                            <ComboBoxItem Content="Abuse/Complaints" Tag="2" />
                            <ComboBoxItem Content="Sales and Marketing" Tag="3" />
                        </ComboBox.Items>
                    </ComboBox>
                </StackPanel>
                <StackPanel Style="{StaticResource MessageStackPanelStyle}">
                    <TextBlock Text="Name:" />
                    <TextBox x:Name="Name" Style="{StaticResource
NameTextBoxStyle}" />
                </StackPanel>
                <StackPanel Style="{StaticResource MessageStackPanelStyle}">
                    <TextBlock Text="Message:" />
                    <TextBox x:Name="Message" Style="{StaticResource
MessageTextBoxStyle}" />
                </StackPanel>
                <TextBlock Text="To prevent automated submissions please enter
the text displayed in the image below" Style="{StaticResource
SubmissionTextStyle}" />
                <StackPanel Style="{StaticResource SubmissionStackPanelStyle}">
                    <Image x:Name="Captcha" />
                    <TextBox x:Name="CaptchaText" Style="{StaticResource
CaptchaTextBoxStyle}" />
                </StackPanel>
                <Button x:Name="SubmitMessage" Style="{StaticResource
SubmitButtonStyle}" />
            </StackPanel>
        </Border>
</navigation:Page>
```

Because you ultimately want this contact page to provide a way for visitors to send you feedback, you need a mechanism to send an e-mail message to an administrator account. Later on, as the site grows, you may find that messages should be routed to different mailboxes depending on the reason selected from the `ComboBox` control. For now, let's just assume that all messages are sent to the administrator e-mail account. As you may have guessed, you can't send an e-mail message directly from Silverlight, but you can add the functionality to one of the WCF RIA Services you have created and make use of that method from the Silverlight client. You can, however, send email messages easily enough from a web service so the best place to add the new method is probably the `UserInformationService` class. The new method does not return anything to the client and it doesn't make use of any LINQ to SQL entities, so it should be marked with the `[Invoke]` attribute in order for it to be exposed by the WCF RIA Services Framework. The following code snippet shows a `SendEmail` method that uses the ASP.NET `SmtpClient` class to actually send the message.

Available for download on Wrox.com

```
[Invoke]
public void SendEmail(string subject, string text, string toAddress,
string fromAddress)
{
     MailMessage message = new MailMessage();
     SmtpClient server = new SmtpClient("localhost");

     message.From = new MailAddress(fromAddress);
     message.Subject = subject;
     message.Body = text;
     message.IsBodyHtml = true;
     message.To.Add(new MailAddress(toAddress));

     server.Timeout = 10000;
     server.Send(message);
}
```

Code snippet UserInformationService.cs

In the preceding code, the specified mail server is set to `localhost`. You need to modify this to reflect a valid SMTP mail server to which you have access when you add this functionality to your own applications. In this case, it just so happens that for Discount ASP.NET hosted sites `localhost` is a valid SMTP mail server, so if you end up using this hosting provider for your own applications this code will be directly portable.

Once you have a method that you can use to send an e-mail to the administrator, it's time to work on the code behind for the contact page. To prevent automated submissions, you want to display a CAPTCHA image and force the visitor to enter the displayed text in order to send any message. So, you need to create some random text and convert that text into an image for display. The best place to do this is in the `OnNavigatedTo` event handler. In the following code, seven random numbers are converted into a string and inserted into a `TextBlock` control. This dynamically created string is then stored so that it can be compared to what the user enters in the `TextBox`. Next, the `TextBlock` is converted into an image using the new `WriteableBitmap` class that is now available in Silverlight 4. Finally, the newly created image is copied to the placeholder Image control so that it will be displayed when the page is loaded.

Available for download on Wrox.com

```
private string captchaKey = "";

protected override void OnNavigatedTo(NavigationEventArgs e)
{
     TextBlock captchaText = new TextBlock();

     captchaText.FontSize = 22;
```

```
        captchaText.FontWeight = FontWeights.Bold;

        StringBuilder builder = new StringBuilder();
        Random random = new Random();

        // Generate random text

        for (int i = 0; i < 7; i++)
            builder.Append(random.Next().ToString()[0]);

        captchaText.Text = builder.ToString();

        // Store the random text for comparison later

        captchaKey = captchaText.Text;

        // Now draw the captcha image

        WriteableBitmap bitmap = new WriteableBitmap((int)captchaText.ActualWidth,
    (int)captchaText.ActualHeight);

        bitmap.Render(captchaText, null);
        bitmap.Invalidate();

        Captcha.Source = bitmap;
    }
```

Code snippet Contact.xaml.cs

Now the only thing left to make this page work is to implement a `Click` handler for the `SubmitMessage` button. In the following code, a `Click` event handler is created in the `Loaded` event of the page. In that handler, the text the user enters is compared against the CAPTCHA text that was created when the page was loaded to ensure that they match. If the user has entered the information correctly, a new e-mail message is sent using the selected reason, name, and message information.

Available for download on Wrox.com

```
    public Contact()
    {
        InitializeComponent();

        Loaded += (s, e) =>
        {
            SubmitMessage.Click += (se, ev) =>
            {
                // First make sure that the captcha text is correct

                if (CaptchaText.Text == captchaKey)
                {
                    UserInformationContext context = new UserInformationContext();

                    context.SendEmail((Reasons.SelectedItem as
    ListBoxItem).Content.ToString(),
    String.Format("Message From: {0}, Message Text: {1}",
    Name.Text, Message.Text), "admin@fitnesstrackerplus.com",
    "admin@fitnesstrackerplus.com");

                    MessageBox.Show("Your message has been sent,
```

```
you will receive a reply as soon as possible");

                        // Clear the contact form

                        Message.Text = "";
                        Name.Text = "";
                        CaptchaText.Text = "";
                    }
                    else
                        MessageBox.Show("The text you have entered does not match
the image being displayed");

            };
        };
}
```

Code snippet Contact.xaml.cs

I'm not going to pretend that this is any kind of award-winning CAPTCHA solution, but it should sufficiently prevent most automated submissions. The intent of this solution is not only to show you how to write a very basic numerical version of a CAPTCHA solution but also to show you how easy it is to do so using the new `WriteableBitmap` class that is available in Silverlight 4. If you find that you need something more sophisticated there are many other CAPTCHA implementations out on the Web.

With all of this complete, you are left with a functional contact page like the one shown in Figure 12-1. For better or worse, visitors of FitnessTrackerPlus will now be able to leave you feedback about the site.

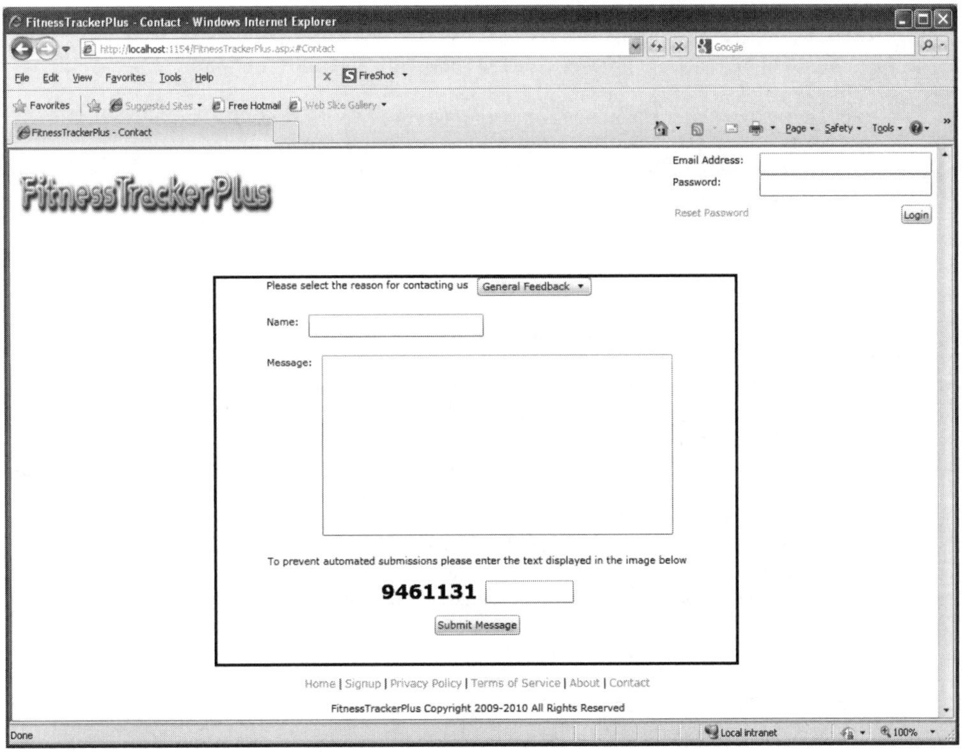

FIGURE 12-1

Enabling Password Resets

One of the final items on the list for FitnessTrackerPlus now that the contact page is ready to go is to allow users to reset their password if they have forgotten it. As mentioned earlier, although ideally users will use the site on a daily basis, some may take an extended break, and then decide to come back having completely forgotten their passwords. In the "Design" section earlier in this chapter, you saw why you really can't provide password recovery; because passwords are stored using a one-way hashing algorithm, you must provide users with a page enabling them to reset their password and send the password to the e-mail address that they gave during the registration process.

The first step in getting this last feature working is to modify the `Login` control so that the Reset Password link is available. Clicking this link simply redirects users to a new page where they must enter the e-mail address that they provided when they registered for the site. Listing 12-2 shows the XAML code for the updated `Login` control. Notice how the only item that was needed was a new `HyperlinkButton` control added to the `Grid`.

LISTING 12-2: Login.xaml

Available for download on Wrox.com

```
<UserControl x:Class="FitnessTrackerPlus.Controls.Login"
     xmlns="http://schemas.microsoft.com/winfx/2006/xaml/presentation"
     xmlns:x="http://schemas.microsoft.com/winfx/2006/xaml">
     <UserControl.Resources>
          <Style x:Key="LoginBoxBorderStyle" TargetType="Border">
               <Setter Property="BorderThickness" Value="2" />
          </Style>
          <Style x:Key="LoginBoxGridStyle" TargetType="Grid">
               <Setter Property="VerticalAlignment" Value="Top" />
          </Style>
          <Style x:Key="LoginTextStyle" TargetType="TextBlock">
          </Style>
          <Style x:Key="LoginTextBoxStyle" TargetType="TextBox">
               <Setter Property="Width" Value="200" />
               <Setter Property="Margin" Value="10,0,0,0"/>
          </Style>
          <Style x:Key="LoginPasswordBoxStyle" TargetType="PasswordBox">
               <Setter Property="Width" Value="200" />
               <Setter Property="Margin" Value="10,0,0,0"/>
          </Style>
          <Style x:Key="LoginErrorStyle" TargetType="TextBlock">
               <Setter Property="Foreground" Value="#FFFF0000" />
               <Setter Property="Margin" Value="0,5,0,0" />
               <Setter Property="HorizontalAlignment" Value="Center" />
          </Style>
          <Style x:Key="LoginButtonStyle" TargetType="Button">
               <Setter Property="HorizontalAlignment" Value="Right" />
               <Setter Property="Margin" Value="0,10,0,0" />
               <Setter Property="Content" Value="Login" />
          </Style>
          <Style x:Key="ResetPasswordStyle" TargetType="HyperlinkButton">
            <Setter Property="Margin" Value="0,10,0,0" />
            <Setter Property="Content" Value="Reset Password" />
```

```
                <Setter Property="NavigateUri" Value="ResetPassword" />
            </Style>
        </UserControl.Resources>
        <Border Style="{StaticResource LoginBoxBorderStyle}">
            <Grid Style="{StaticResource LoginBoxGridStyle}">
                <Grid.ColumnDefinitions>
                    <ColumnDefinition />
                    <ColumnDefinition />
                </Grid.ColumnDefinitions>
                <Grid.RowDefinitions>
                    <RowDefinition />
                    <RowDefinition />
                    <RowDefinition />
                    <RowDefinition />
                </Grid.RowDefinitions>
                <TextBlock Text="Email Address:" Grid.Row="0" Grid.Column="0"
    Style="{StaticResource LoginTextStyle}" />
                <TextBox x:Name="EmailAddress" Grid.Row="0" Grid.Column="1"
    Style="{StaticResource LoginTextBoxStyle}" />
                <TextBlock Text="Password:" Grid.Row="1" Grid.Column="0"
    Style="{StaticResource LoginTextStyle}" />
                <PasswordBox x:Name="Password" Grid.Row="1" Grid.Column="1"
    Style="{StaticResource LoginPasswordBoxStyle}" />
                <HyperlinkButton Style="{StaticResource ResetPasswordStyle}"
    Grid.Column="0" Grid.Row="2" />
                <Button x:Name="LoginUser" Style="{StaticResource
    LoginButtonStyle}" Grid.Column="1" Grid.Row="2" />
                <TextBlock x:Name="LoginError" Style="{StaticResource
    LoginErrorStyle}" Grid.Column="0" Grid.ColumnSpan="2" Grid.Row="3" />
            </Grid>
        </Border>
    </UserControl>
```

After the Login control has been modified, you also need to update the `UriMapper` declaration in the App.xaml file so that the navigation will work correctly. The following code shows the updated `UriMapper` section:

Available for download on Wrox.com

```
    <uri:UriMapper x:Key="UriMap">
        <uri:UriMapping Uri="Home" MappedUri="/Views/Home.xaml" />
        <uri:UriMapping Uri="About" MappedUri="/Views/About.xaml" />
        <uri:UriMapping Uri="Contact" MappedUri="/Views/Contact.xaml" />
        <uri:UriMapping Uri="Privacy" MappedUri="/Views/Privacy.xaml" />
        <uri:UriMapping Uri="Signup" MappedUri="/Views/Signup.xaml" />
        <uri:UriMapping Uri="Terms" MappedUri="/Views/Terms.xaml" />
        <uri:UriMapping Uri="ResetPassword" MappedUri="/Views/ResetPassword.xaml" />
        <uri:UriMapping Uri="UserHome" MappedUri="/Views/UserHome.xaml" />
        <uri:UriMapping Uri="Dashboard" MappedUri="/Views/Dashboard/Dashboard.xaml" />
        <uri:UriMapping Uri="AccountSettings"
    MappedUri="/Views/Dashboard/AccountSettings.xaml" />
        <uri:UriMapping Uri="FoodLog" MappedUri="/Views/Food/FoodLog.xaml" />
        <uri:UriMapping Uri="ExerciseLog"
    MappedUri="/Views/Exercise/ExerciseLog.xaml" />
        <uri:UriMapping Uri="MeasurementLog"
    MappedUri="/Views/Measurement/MeasurementLog.xaml" />
```

```
<uri:UriMapping Uri="JournalSettings"
MappedUri="/Views/Journal/JournalSettings.xaml" />
     <uri:UriMapping Uri="Journals/{username}"
MappedUri="/Views/Journal/PublicJournal.xaml?user={username}" />
</uri:UriMapper>
```

Code snippet App.xaml

A quick look at the preceding code should tip you off that you will also need to add a new `Page` control to the Silverlight project in the `Views` folder called `ResetPassword`.

There are a couple of requirements for the user interface of this new page:

- When users arrive at this page, they should be expected to enter the e-mail address that they used during registration. A `TextBox` control is required to hold this value.
- Once the user enters this value, he or she clicks a Submit button and a `UserInformation` object for the supplied e-mail address is retrieved.
- Assuming that the e-mail address is valid, the user is then presented with the security question and a `TextBox` control to hold the security answer.
- If the security question is answered correctly, a `MessageBox` control is displayed letting the user know that a new password has been sent to them.

Listing 12-3 shows the XAML code required for the `ResetPassword` user interface. Notice how the only items that are visible by default are the e-mail address collection `StackPanel` and the `Submit` button. The security question and answer `StackPanel` are hidden until valid user information has been retrieved.

LISTING 12-3: ResetPassword.xaml

Available for download on Wrox.com

```
<navigation:Page x:Class="FitnessTrackerPlus.Views.ResetPassword"
     xmlns="http://schemas.microsoft.com/winfx/2006/xaml/presentation"
     xmlns:x="http://schemas.microsoft.com/winfx/2006/xaml"
     xmlns:navigation="clr-
namespace:System.Windows.Controls;assembly=System.Windows.Controls.Navigation"
     Title="FitnessTrackerPlus - Reset Password">
     <navigation:Page.Resources>
          <Style x:Key="BorderStyle" TargetType="Border">
               <Setter Property="BorderBrush" Value="#FF000000" />
               <Setter Property="BorderThickness" Value="3" />
               <Setter Property="Width" Value="600" />
          </Style>
          <Style x:Key="MainStackPanelStyle" TargetType="StackPanel">
               <Setter Property="HorizontalAlignment" Value="Center" />
          </Style>
          <Style x:Key="EmailStackPanelStyle" TargetType="StackPanel">
               <Setter Property="Orientation" Value="Horizontal" />
               <Setter Property="Margin" Value="0,10,0,0" />
          </Style>
          <Style x:Key="MessageStackPanelStyle" TargetType="StackPanel">
               <Setter Property="Orientation" Value="Horizontal" />
```

```
                <Setter Property="HorizontalAlignment" Value="Center" />
                <Setter Property="Margin" Value="0,10,0,0" />
            </Style>
            <Style x:Key="SecurityStackPanelStyle" TargetType="StackPanel">
                <Setter Property="HorizontalAlignment" Value="Center" />
                <Setter Property="Margin" Value="0,10,0,0" />
                <Setter Property="Visibility" Value="Collapsed" />
            </Style>
            <Style x:Key="SecurityAnswerStackPanelStyle"
TargetType="StackPanel">
              <Setter Property="Orientation" Value="Horizontal" />
              <Setter Property="HorizontalAlignment" Value="Center" />
              <Setter Property="Margin" Value="0,10,0,0" />
            </Style>
            <Style x:Key="TextBoxStyle" TargetType="TextBox">
                <Setter Property="Margin" Value="10,0,0,0" />
                <Setter Property="Width" Value="200" />
                <Setter Property="Height" Value="25" />
            </Style>
            <Style x:Key="SubmitButtonStyle" TargetType="Button">
                <Setter Property="HorizontalAlignment" Value="Center" />
                <Setter Property="Margin" Value="0,10,0,20" />
                <Setter Property="Content" Value="Submit" />
            </Style>
        </navigation:Page.Resources>
        <Border Style="{StaticResource BorderStyle}">
            <StackPanel Style="{StaticResource MainStackPanelStyle}">
                <StackPanel Style="{StaticResource EmailStackPanelStyle}">
                    <TextBlock Text="Please enter the email address you used
when you registered:" />
                    <TextBox x:Name="Email" Style="{StaticResource
TextBoxStyle}" />
                </StackPanel>
                <StackPanel x:Name="SecurityPanel" Style="{StaticResource
SecurityStackPanelStyle}">
                    <TextBlock Text="Please answer your security question:" />
                    <StackPanel Style="{StaticResource
SecurityAnswerStackPanelStyle}">
                        <TextBlock x:Name="SecurityQuestion" />
                        <TextBox x:Name="SecurityAnswer"
Style="{StaticResource TextBoxStyle}" />
                    </StackPanel>
                </StackPanel>
                <Button x:Name="Submit" Style="{StaticResource
SubmitButtonStyle}" />
            </StackPanel>
        </Border>
</navigation:Page>
```

Before getting into the code behind for the page, you first need to make a modification to the custom `MembershipProvider` class. The `MembershipProvider` class includes an abstract method called `ResetPassword` that you will need to override. In the following code, the implementation of the `ResetPassword` method first retrieves the `UserInformation` object for the user associated with the supplied e-mail address. Next, the user supplied security answer is compared with the one stored in the database. If the two answers match, a random password is generated and encrypted using the SHA1 one-way hash algorithm. Otherwise, the method simply returns `null` indicating that the user failed to answer the security question correctly. After storing the new password in the database, the unencrypted version of the temporary password is then returned to the caller so that it can be sent to the user.

Available for download on Wrox.com

```
public override string ResetPassword(string username, string answer)
{
     try
     {
          // Ensure that the security answer is correct

          UserInformation currentUser = context.UserInformations.Where(e =>
                                            e.email_address == username &&
                                            e.security_answer ==
FormsAuthentication.HashPasswordForStoringInConfigFile(answer,
"SHA1")).SingleOrDefault();

          string tempPassword = CreateRandomPassword();

          if (currentUser != null)
          {
               currentUser.password =
FormsAuthentication.HashPasswordForStoringInConfigFile(tempPassword,
"SHA1");

               context.SubmitChanges();
               return tempPassword;
          }
     }
     catch (Exception)
     {
     }

     return null;
}

public string CreateRandomPassword()
{
     StringBuilder builder = new StringBuilder();
     Random random = new Random();
     char ch;

     for (int i = 0; i < 5; i++)
     {
          ch = Convert.ToChar(Convert.ToInt32(Math.Floor(26 *
random.NextDouble() + 65)));
          builder.Append(ch);
          builder.Append(random.Next().ToString()[0]);
     }

     return builder.ToString();
}
```

Code snippet MembershipProvider.cs

Now, because the Silverlight client won't interact with the MembershipProvider directly, you also need an additional method in the UserInformationService that not only acts as a proxy to the ResetPassword method but also makes use of the SendEmail method created earlier to actually send the new password to the user and return true to the caller. If the user failed to answer the security question correctly, this method does not send the e-mail and instead returns false to the caller. The following code shows the ResetPassword proxy method required by the Silverlight client.

Available for download on Wrox.com

```
[Invoke]
public bool ResetPassword(string email, string answer)
{
     string tempPassword = provider.ResetPassword(email, answer);

     if (!String.IsNullOrEmpty(tempPassword))
     {
          SendEmail("FitnessTrackerPlus Important Information",
String.Format("Here is your new temporary password: {0}", tempPassword),
email, "admin@fitnesstrackerplus.com");

          return true;
     }

     return false;
}
```

Code snippet UserInformationService.cs

At this point, you have service methods that can retrieve the UserInformation instance based on the supplied e-mail, and you can also reset the password for the user assuming that they have answered the security question correctly. Now all you need to do is implement the code behind logic, which really only involves implementing the Click event of the Submit button. In the following code, the behavior of the Click event varies depending on which StackPanel is currently visible. For example, if the StackPanel that collects the e-mail address is currently visible, the UserInformationService is used to collect the UserInformation object containing the security question for the user. Otherwise, if the StackPanel containing the security question is currently being displayed, the ResetPassword method will be called and, assuming the user supplied the correct answer to the security question, a new temporary password will be sent to the e-mail address that was provided.

Available for download on Wrox.com

```
private void Submit_Click(object sender, RoutedEventArgs e)
{
     UserInformationContext context = new UserInformationContext();

     if (EmailPanel.Visibility == Visibility.Visible)
     {
          if (!String.IsNullOrEmpty(Email.Text))
          {
               context.Load<UserInformation>(context.
GetUserQuery(Email.Text),
               (Completed) =>
               {
```

```
                    if (!Completed.HasError)
                    {
                        UserInformation user =
Completed.Entities.FirstOrDefault();

                        if (user == null)
                            MessageBox.Show("No user was found with the
supplied email address");
                        else
                        {
                            SecurityQuestion.Text = user.security_question;

                            SecurityPanel.Visibility = Visibility.Visible;
                            EmailPanel.Visibility = Visibility.Collapsed;
                        }
                    }
                    else
                        MessageBox.Show("No user was found with the
supplied email address");

                }, null);
            }
        }
        else if (SecurityPanel.Visibility == Visibility.Visible)
        {
            context.ResetPassword(Email.Text, SecurityAnswer.Text,
            (Completed) =>
            {
                if (!Completed.HasError)
                {
                    if (Completed.Value)
                        MessageBox.Show("A new temporary password has
been sent to your email address");
                    else
                        MessageBox.Show("You have provided an incorrect
answer to your security question");
                }

            }, null);
        }
    }
```

Code snippet ResetPassword.xaml.cs

Discount ASP.NET

In the "Design" section, the decision was made to deploy FitnessTrackerPlus to a shared hosting provider. The hosting provider is Discount ASP.NET because it provides great support for .NET, Silverlight 4, WCF RIA Services, and so on. In addition to this support, Discount ASP.NET also provides many utilities that make management and deployment of your Silverlight application and SQL Server database a breeze. You can get started by creating and configuring an account over at Discount ASP.NET by following these steps:

1. When you create your new account at Discount ASP.NET, you want to be sure to include the basic SQL Server 2008 Add-On feature to your account so that you can use the FitnessTrackerPlus database.

2. Log into the site. You're presented with a dashboard page, which gives you access to your account information, billing management, e-mail accounts, various web server tools and utilities, database management and more. Figure 12-2 shows the control panel page for FitnessTrackerPlus.

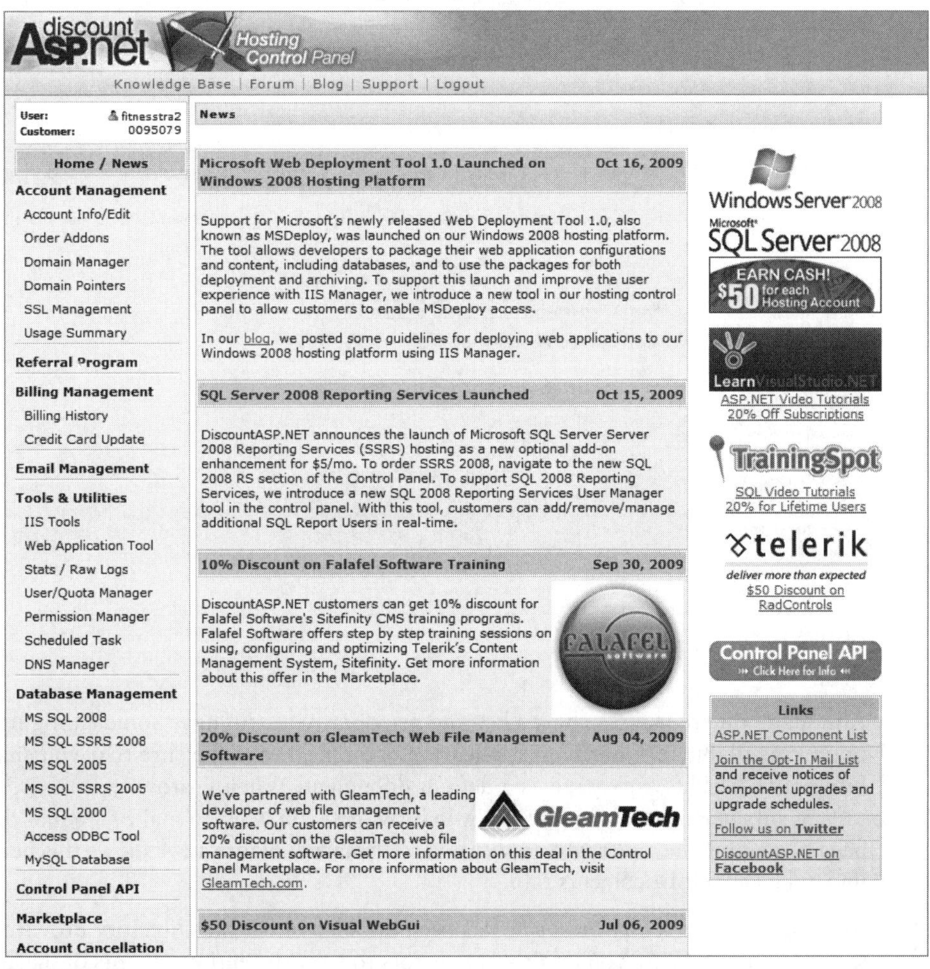

FIGURE 12-2

3. Click the Account Info/Edit link and take note of the FTP Information section. You'll need these details when you are ready to actually deploy the FitnessTrackerPlus application files.

4. For FitnessTrackerPlus you'll deploy everything via FTP, so grab a copy of a good FTP Client program such as Filezilla, which is highly recommended.

5. After you have the FTP Information, it's time to get familiar with a utility that you'll use anytime you want to make changes to the IIS configuration. Click Tools & Utilities ➪ IIS Tools. This loads the page shown in Figure 12-3. As you can see, from here you have access to many important IIS settings.

FIGURE 12-3

6. Although you are using a shared hosting provider, you still have some configuration options available for your web application. You need to make sure that you enable the FitnessTrackerPlus.aspx page as a default document. When visitors type `http://www.fitnesstrackerplus.com` in their web browsers, you want to make sure that the main page containing the Silverlight application is displayed. Figure 12-4 shows this being added under the Default Documents tab.

7. Make sure that directory browsing has been disabled under the Directory Browsing tab shown in Figure 12-5. You don't want visitors to view the entire contents of the application directory because this could compromise the site's security.

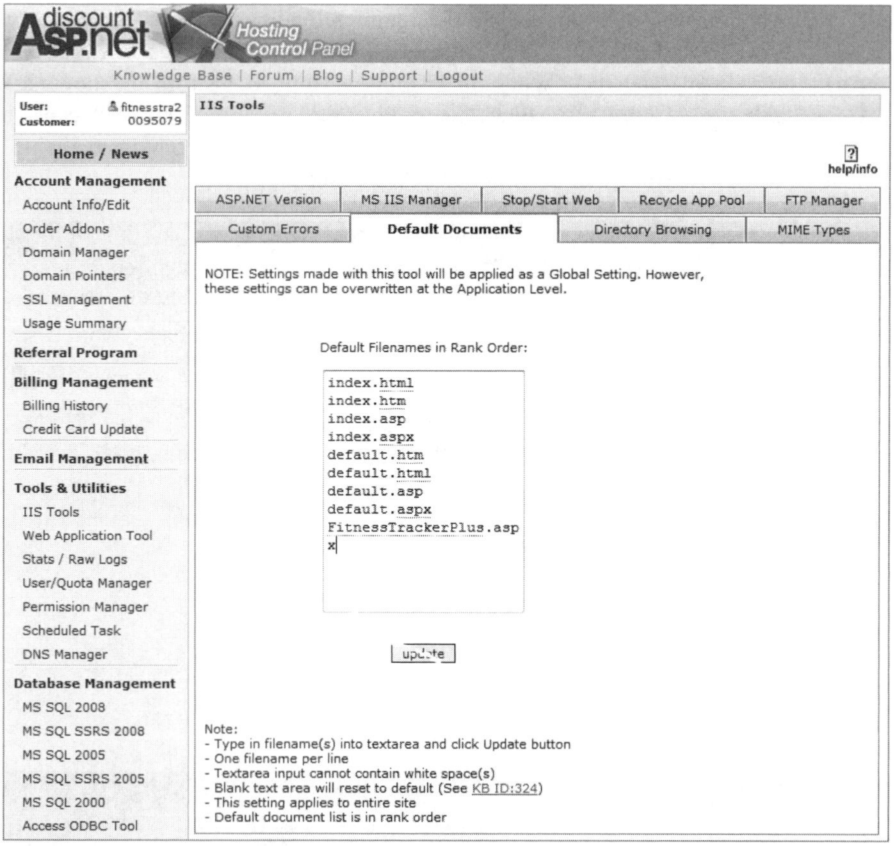

discount ASP.net Hosting Control Panel

Knowledge Base | Forum | Blog | Support | Logout

User: fitnesstra2
Customer: 0095079

Home / News

Account Management
Account Info/Edit
Order Addons
Domain Manager
Domain Pointers
SSL Management
Usage Summary

Referral Program

Billing Management
Billing History
Credit Card Update

Email Management

Tools & Utilities
IIS Tools
Web Application Tool
Stats / Raw Logs
User/Quota Manager
Permission Manager
Scheduled Task
DNS Manager

Database Management
MS SQL 2008
MS SQL SSRS 2008
MS SQL 2005
MS SQL SSRS 2005
MS SQL 2000
Access ODBC Tool

IIS Tools

help/info

ASP.NET Version | MS IIS Manager | Stop/Start Web | Recycle App Pool | FTP Manager

Custom Errors | **Default Documents** | Directory Browsing | MIME Types

NOTE: Settings made with this tool will be applied as a Global Setting. However, these settings can be overwritten at the Application Level.

Default Filenames in Rank Order:

```
index.html
index.htm
index.asp
index.aspx
default.htm
default.html
default.asp
default.aspx
FitnessTrackerPlus.asp
x
```

update

Note:
- Type in filename(s) into textarea and click Update button
- One filename per line
- Textarea input cannot contain white space(s)
- Blank text area will reset to default (See KB ID:324)
- This setting applies to entire site
- Default document list is in rank order

FIGURE 12-4

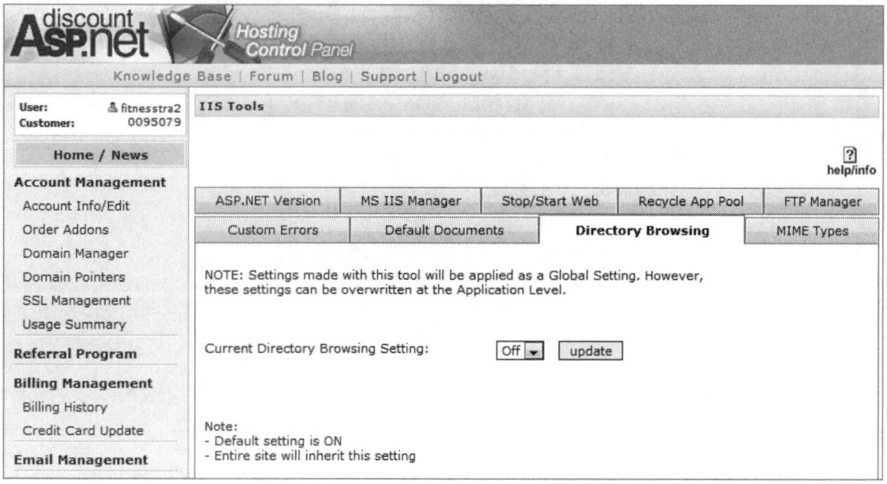

discount ASP.net Hosting Control Panel

Knowledge Base | Forum | Blog | Support | Logout

User: fitnesstra2
Customer: 0095079

Home / News

Account Management
Account Info/Edit
Order Addons
Domain Manager
Domain Pointers
SSL Management
Usage Summary

Referral Program

Billing Management
Billing History
Credit Card Update

Email Management

IIS Tools

help/info

ASP.NET Version | MS IIS Manager | Stop/Start Web | Recycle App Pool | FTP Manager

Custom Errors | Default Documents | **Directory Browsing** | MIME Types

NOTE: Settings made with this tool will be applied as a Global Setting. However, these settings can be overwritten at the Application Level.

Current Directory Browsing Setting: Off update

Note:
- Default setting is ON
- Entire site will inherit this setting

FIGURE 12-5

8. Shut down your website instance before actually uploading any files. Under the Start/Stop Web tab you have the ability to stop and start your website instance whenever you are performing site maintenance. When the instance is stopped, visitors are shown a Web Page Unavailable page. Figure 12-6 shows that the instance of FitnessTrackerPlus has been shut down and is ready for maintenance while Figure 12-7 shows the Site Unavailable page that visitors will see as you work on deploying the site files.

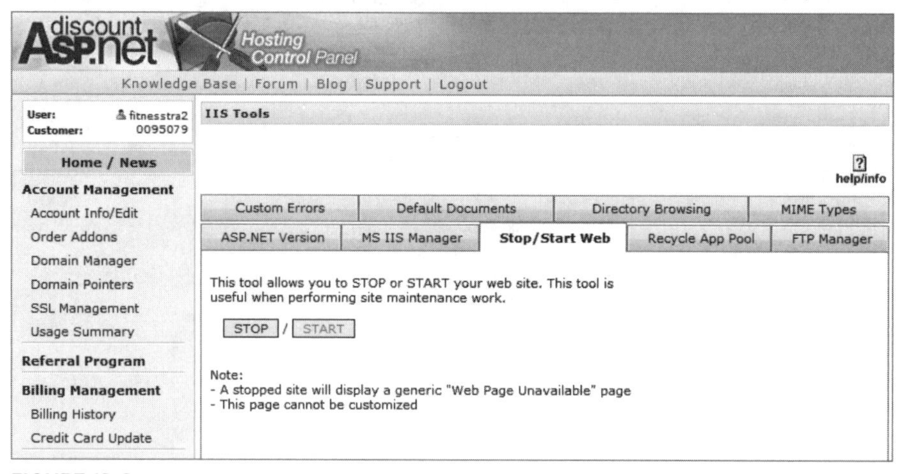

FIGURE 12-6

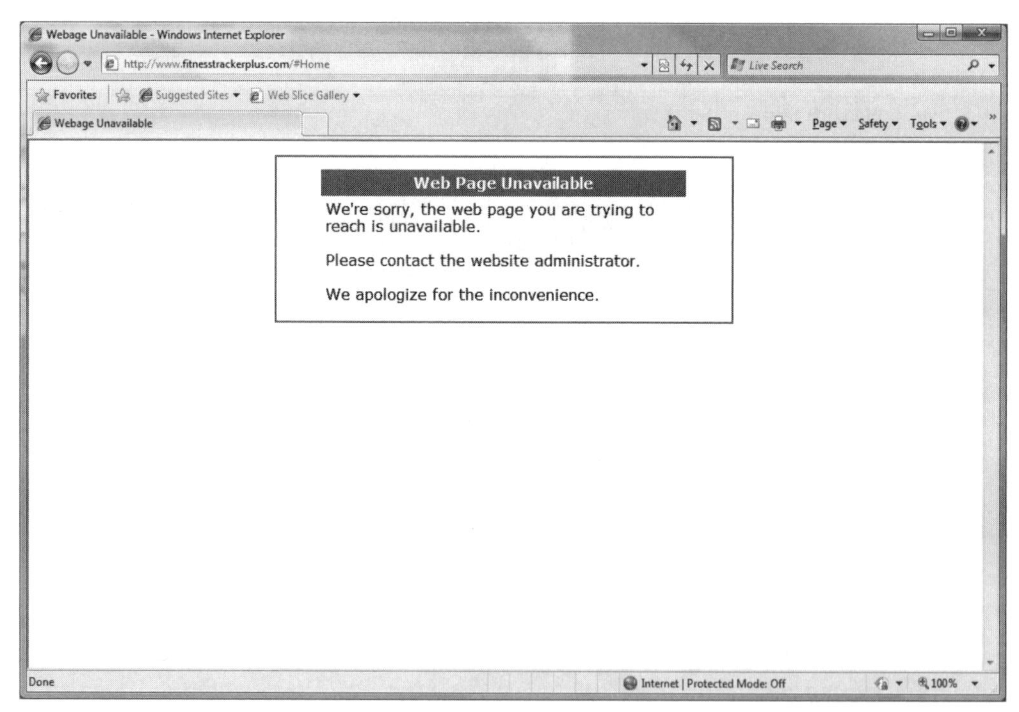

FIGURE 12-7

At this point you are ready to build FitnessTrackerPlus and deploy the necessary files to Discount ASP.NET. To do so, follow these steps:

1. Make sure that you are building a Release version of the application, so in Visual Studio look for the active configuration in the toolbar and change it from Debug to Release.
2. Right-click the ASP.NET project and select Rebuild.
3. Once the build is complete, fire up your FTP client and log in to the appropriate Discount ASP.NET FTP Server using the credentials you were provided on the Account Info page. You may find that some folders have already been created in your root.
4. For FitnessTrackerPlus, these folders aren't needed so they can be safely deleted.
5. Upload the FitnessTrackerPlus files.
6. Navigate to the Release folder that was generated under the ASP.NET Project folder. From this folder, you need to upload all the files/folders in the directory with the exception of the obj directory, if there is one.
7. Once the FTP transfer is completed, you can go back to the Discount ASP.NET Control Panel page and turn the IIS site instance back on. If everything was completed correctly, navigating to the site should bring up the main FitnessTrackerPlus.aspx page.

There is one more crucial step that needs to be followed before declaring FitnessTrackerPlus available to the world and that is to set up the SQL Server database.

Currently, the database resides in a file called FitnessTrackerPlus.mdf. This file was uploaded to the `App_Data` directory. Now the current connection string is set up in a way that allows your local instance of SQL Server Express 2008 to attach the file and run. This won't work for your deployed solution. Instead of attaching the MDF file in the connection string, you will need to make use of the SQL Server instance that has been provided to you as part of your Discount ASP.NET account. Follow these steps:

1. You can find your SQL Server account information along with several other great database tools under the Database Management link on the Control Panel page. Because you added the SQL Server 2008 Add-On to your account, you can find the database connection information by then clicking the MS SQL 2008 link. After the page is loaded, you will be presented with a few tabs; the main display should show you the SQL Server Name, Database Name, Database Space, Database Login, SQL Usage Meter, and even the appropriate Connection String to use in the web.config file.
2. Copy this connection string and replace the following connection string line in the web.config file with the one from your Discount ASP.NET account:

```
<connectionStrings>
     <add name="FitnessTrackerPlusConnectionString"
connectionString="Data
Source=.\SQLEXPRESS;AttachDbFilename=|DataDirectory
|\FitnessTrackerPlus.mdf;Integrated
Security=True;User Instance=True"
providerName="System.Data.SqlClient" />
</connectionStrings>
```

Code snippet web.config

3. After making this change, don't forget to rebuild and upload the new version of the web.config file to the FTP site.

4. Once the web.config file is updated with the correct connection string information, attach the FitnessTrackerPlus.mdf file to the Discount ASP.NET SQL Server instance. This task is made trivial thanks to the database management tools that Discount ASP.NET provides. On the same page that contained the connection string information you'll find a tab called SQL Tool Suite, if you navigate to this tab, you'll see a whole suite of SQL Server database tools. Figures 12-8 and 12-9 show the full list of tools including a backup utility, database restoration tool, attach data file, and a shrink database tool.

5. You'll make use of the Attach Data File tool in order to get the FitnessTrackerPlus database working. Click the Browse Web Server for MDF button and navigate to the `App_Data` folder where the FitnessTrackerPlus.mdf file is located. Select the file and then click the Attach MDF File button. Once the operation is complete the database will be available and your FitnessTrackerPlus application deployment is complete.

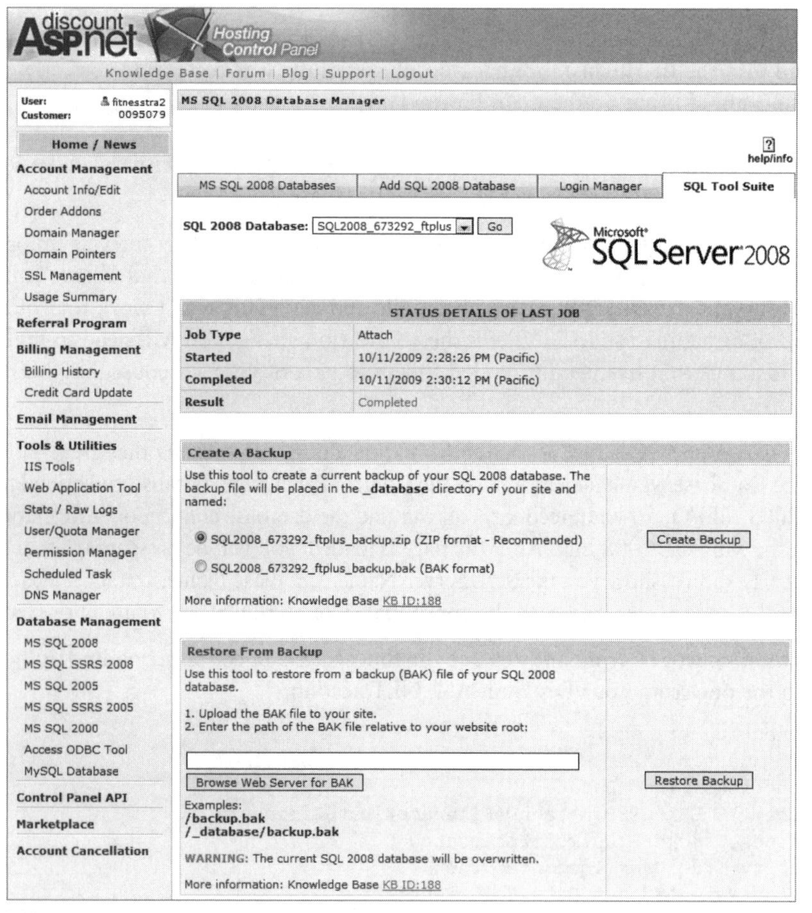

FIGURE 12-8

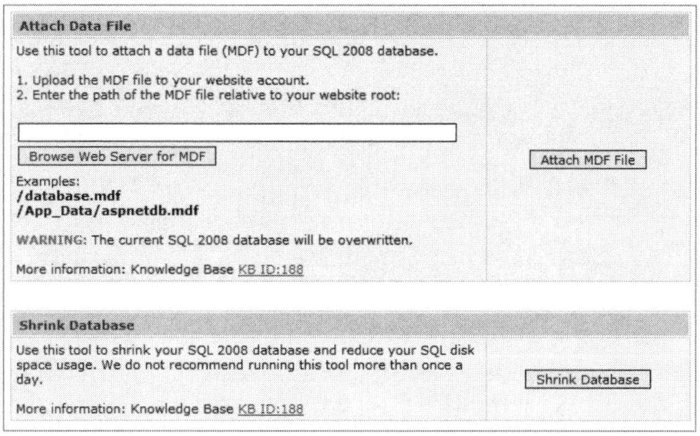

FIGURE 12-9

That's all there is to getting the database working. You'll find that many of the other database tools offered at Discount ASP.NET are invaluable as you work on maintaining the site, especially the SQL Backup utility.

Well, that's it—FitnessTrackerPlus is deployed and ready to go. The only thing missing now is users, so the next step that you need to work on is getting the word out to start attracting new users to the site.

SUMMARY

That's it! FitnessTrackerPlus is complete and deployed. In this chapter, you have completed work on the supplemental pages, implemented a password reset mechanism, created a working contact page, and selected a shared hosting provider for deployment of the application. It's been a long journey but I hope you feel more comfortable about making use of Silverlight 4 and WCF RIA Services in your own applications. As with any application, there is always room for improvement and FitnessTrackerPlus is no exception. There is no doubt that there are other areas of the application that could definitely be improved upon in the next release—reporting, offline availability, and localization to name a few. The development of FitnessTrackerPlus version 2 will no doubt be exciting and filled with new challenges.

I hope you have been made fully aware of the benefits of Silverlight technology in Web-based applications and you will make use of some of the techniques shown in this book to further enhance your own applications. Who knows? With any luck, your Silverlight application will become the next MySpace, Facebook, or Twitter.

INDEX

A

D

E

F

G

H

I

J

K

L

M

P

T

U

V

W

X